Dictionary of Literary Biography

Dictionary of Literary Biography Documentary Series

8 *The Black Aesthetic Movement,* edited by Jeffrey Louis Decker (1991)

9 *American Writers of the Vietnam War: W. D. Ehrhart, Larry Heinemann, Tim O'Brien, Walter McDonald, John M. Del Vecchio,* edited by Ronald Baughman (1991)

10 *The Bloomsbury Group,* edited by Edward L. Bishop (1992)

11 *American Proletarian Culture: The Twenties and The Thirties,* edited by Jon Christian Suggs (1993)

12 *Southern Women Writers: Flannery O'Connor, Katherine Anne Porter, Eudora Welty,* edited by Mary Ann Wimsatt and Karen L. Rood (1994)

13 *The House of Scribner, 1846–1904,* edited by John Delaney (1996)

14 *Four Women Writers for Children, 1868–1918,* edited by Caroline C. Hunt (1996)

15 *American Expatriate Writers: Paris in the Twenties,* edited by Matthew J. Bruccoli and Robert W. Trogdon (1997)

16 *The House of Scribner, 1905–1930,* edited by John Delaney (1997)

17 *The House of Scribner, 1931–1984,* edited by John Delaney (1998)

18 *British Poets of The Great War: Sassoon, Graves, Owen,* edited by Patrick Quinn (1999)

19 *James Dickey,* edited by Judith S. Baughman (1999)

See also DLB 210, 216, 219, 222, 224, 229, 237, 247, 253, 254, 263, 269, 273, 274, 280, 284, 288, 291, 294, 298, 301, 304, 308, 309, 315, 316, 320, 324, 338, 340, 343

Dictionary of Literary Biography Yearbooks

1980 edited by Karen L. Rood, Jean W. Ross, and Richard Ziegfeld (1981)

1981 edited by Karen L. Rood, Jean W. Ross, and Richard Ziegfeld (1982)

1982 edited by Richard Ziegfeld; associate editors: Jean W. Ross and Lynne C. Zeigler (1983)

1983 edited by Mary Bruccoli and Jean W. Ross; associate editor Richard Ziegfeld (1984)

1984 edited by Jean W. Ross (1985)

1985 edited by Jean W. Ross (1986)

1986 edited by J. M. Brook (1987)

1987 edited by J. M. Brook (1988)

1988 edited by J. M. Brook (1989)

1989 edited by J. M. Brook (1990)

1990 edited by James W. Hipp (1991)

1991 edited by James W. Hipp (1992)

1992 edited by James W. Hipp (1993)

1993 edited by James W. Hipp, contributing editor George Garrett (1994)

1994 edited by James W. Hipp, contributing editor George Garrett (1995)

1995 edited by James W. Hipp, contributing editor George Garrett (1996)

1996 edited by Samuel W. Bruce and L. Kay Webster, contributing editor George Garrett (1997)

1997 edited by Matthew J. Bruccoli and George Garrett, with the assistance of L. Kay Webster (1998)

1998 edited by Matthew J. Bruccoli, contributing editor George Garrett, with the assistance of D. W. Thomas (1999)

1999 edited by Matthew J. Bruccoli, contributing editor George Garrett, with the assistance of D. W. Thomas (2000)

2000 edited by Matthew J. Bruccoli, contributing editor George Garrett, with the assistance of George Parker Anderson (2001)

2001 edited by Matthew J. Bruccoli, contributing editor George Garrett, with the assistance of George Parker Anderson (2002)

2002 edited by Matthew J. Bruccoli and George Garrett; George Parker Anderson, Assistant Editor (2003)

Concise Series

Concise Dictionary of American Literary Biography, 7 volumes (1988–1999): *The New Consciousness, 1941–1968; Colonization to the American Renaissance, 1640–1865; Realism, Naturalism, and Local Color, 1865–1917; The Twenties, 1917–1929; The Age of Maturity, 1929–1941; Broadening Views, 1968–1988; Supplement: Modern Writers, 1900–1998.*

Concise Dictionary of British Literary Biography, 8 volumes (1991–1992): *Writers of the Middle Ages and Renaissance Before 1660; Writers of the Restoration and Eighteenth Century, 1660–1789; Writers of the Romantic Period, 1789–1832; Victorian Writers, 1832–1890; Late-Victorian and Edwardian Writers, 1890–1914; Modern Writers, 1914–1945; Writers After World War II, 1945–1960; Contemporary Writers, 1960 to Present.*

Concise Dictionary of World Literary Biography, 4 volumes (1999–2000): *Ancient Greek and Roman Writers; German Writers; African, Caribbean, and Latin American Writers; South Slavic and Eastern European Writers.*

Mark Twain's
Adventures of Huckleberry Finn:
A Documentary Volume

Dictionary of Literary Biography® • Volume Three Hundred Forty-Three

Mark Twain's
Adventures of Huckleberry Finn:
A Documentary Volume

Edited by

Tom Quirk
University of Missouri–Columbia

A Bruccoli Clark Layman Book

GALE
CENGAGE Learning·

Detroit • New York • San Francisco • New Haven, Conn • Waterville, Maine • London

**Dictionary of Literary Biography,
Volume 343: Mark Twain's
Adventures of Huckleberry Finn:
A Documentary Volume**
Tom Quirk

Advisory Board: John Baker,
    William Cagle, Patrick O'Connor,
    Trudier Harris, Alvin Kernan

Editorial Directors: Matthew J. Bruccoli and
    Richard Layman

For product information and technology assistance, contact us at
Gale Customer Support, 1-800-877-4253.

For permission to use material from this text or product,
submit all requests online at **www.cengage.com/permissions**
Further permissions questions can be emailed to
permissionrequest@cengage.com

While every effort has been made to ensure the reliability of the information presented in this publication, Gale, a part of Cengage Learning, does not guarantee the accuracy of the data contained herein. Gale accepts no payment for listing; and inclusion in the publication of any organization, agency, institution, publication, service, or individual does not imply endorsement of the editors or publisher. Errors brought to the attention of the publisher and verified to the satisfaction of the publisher will be corrected in future editions.

EDITORIAL DATA PRIVACY POLICY. Does this publication contain information about you as an individual? If so, for more information about our editorial date privacy policies, please see our Privacy Statement at www.gale.cengage.com

LIBRARY OF CONGRESS CATALOGING-IN-PUBLICATION DATA

Mark Twain's adventures of Huckleberry Finn : a documentary volume / edited by Tom Quirk.
    p. cm. — (Dictionary of literary biography ; v. 343)
"A Bruccoli Clark Layman book."
Includes bibliographical references and index.
ISBN 978-0-7876-8161-6
    1. Twain, Mark, 1835–1910. Adventures of Huckleberry Finn. 2. Twain, Mark, 1835–1910—Characters—Huckleberry Finn. 3. Finn, Huckleberry (Fictitious character). I. Quirk, Tom, 1946–

PS1305.H84 2009
813'.4—dc22

2008024129

ISBN-13: 978-0-7876-8161-6   ISBN-10: 0-7876-8161-X

Gale
27500 Drake Rd.
Farmington Hills, MI 48331-3535

Printed in the United States of America
1 2 3 4 5 6 7 12 11 10 09 08

For James Barbour, Robert Sattelmeyer, and Gary Scharnhorst

Contents

Plan of the Series

. . . Almost the most prodigious asset of a country, and perhaps its most precious possession, is its native literary product—when that product is fine and noble and enduring.

Mark Twain*

The advisory board, the editors, and the publisher of the *Dictionary of Literary Biography* are joined in endorsing Mark Twain's declaration. The literature of a nation provides an inexhaustible resource of permanent worth. Our purpose is to make literature and its creators better understood and more accessible to students and the reading public, while satisfying the needs of teachers and researchers.

To meet these requirements, *literary biography* has been construed in terms of the author's achievement. The most important thing about a writer is his writing. Accordingly, the entries in *DLB* are career biographies, tracing the development of the author's canon and the evolution of his reputation.

The purpose of *DLB* is not only to provide reliable information in a usable format but also to place the figures in the larger perspective of literary history and to offer appraisals of their accomplishments by qualified scholars.

The publication plan for *DLB* resulted from two years of preparation. The project was proposed to Bruccoli Clark by Frederick G. Ruffner, president of the Gale Research Company, in November 1975. After specimen entries were prepared and typeset, an advisory board was formed to refine the entry format and develop the series rationale. In meetings held during 1976, the publisher, series editors, and advisory board approved the scheme for a comprehensive biographical dictionary of persons who contributed to literature. Editorial work on the first volume began in January 1977, and it was published in 1978. In order to make *DLB* more than a dictionary and to compile volumes that individually have claim to status as literary history, it was decided to organize volumes by topic, period, or genre. Each of these freestanding volumes provides a

From an unpublished section of Mark Twain's autobiography, copyright by the Mark Twain Company

biographical-bibliographical guide and overview for a particular area of literature. We are convinced that this organization—as opposed to a single alphabet method—constitutes a valuable innovation in the presentation of reference material. The volume plan necessarily requires many decisions for the placement and treatment of authors. Certain figures will be included in separate volumes, but with different entries emphasizing the aspect of his career appropriate to each volume. Ernest Hemingway, for example, is represented in *American Writers in Paris, 1920–1939* by an entry focusing on his expatriate apprenticeship; he is also in *American Novelists, 1910–1945* with an entry surveying his entire career, as well as in *American Short-Story Writers, 1910–1945, Second Series* with an entry concentrating on his short fiction. Each volume includes a cumulative index of the subject authors and articles.

Between 1981 and 2002 the series was augmented and updated by the *DLB Yearbooks*. There have also been nineteen *DLB Documentary Series* volumes, which provide illustrations, facsimiles, and biographical and critical source materials for figures, works, or groups judged to have particular interest for students. In 1999 the *Documentary Series* was incorporated into the *DLB* volume numbering system beginning with *DLB 210: Ernest Hemingway*.

We define literature as the *intellectual commerce of a nation:* not merely as belles lettres but as that ample and complex process by which ideas are generated, shaped, and transmitted. *DLB* entries are not limited to "creative writers" but extend to other figures who in their time and in their way influenced the mind of a people. Thus the series encompasses historians, journalists, publishers, book collectors, and screenwriters. By this means readers of *DLB* may be aided to perceive literature not as cult scripture in the keeping of intellectual high priests but firmly positioned at the center of a nation's life.

DLB includes the major writers appropriate to each volume and those standing in the ranks behind them. Scholarly and critical counsel has been sought in deciding which minor figures to include and how full their entries should be. Wherever possible, useful references are made to figures who do not warrant separate entries.

Each *DLB* volume has an expert volume editor responsible for planning the volume, selecting the figures for inclusion, and assigning the entries. Volume editors are also responsible for preparing, where appropriate, appendices surveying the major periodicals and literary and intellectual movements for their volumes, as well as lists of further readings. Work on the series as a whole is coordinated at the Bruccoli Clark Layman editorial center in Columbia, South Carolina, where the editorial staff is responsible for accuracy and utility of the published volumes.

One feature that distinguishes *DLB* is the illustration policy—its concern with the iconography of literature. Just as an author is influenced by his surroundings, so is the reader's understanding of the author enhanced by a knowledge of his environment. Therefore *DLB*

volumes include not only drawings, paintings, and photographs of authors, often depicting them at various stages in their careers, but also illustrations of their families and places where they lived. Title pages are regularly reproduced in facsimile along with dust jackets for modern authors. The dust jackets are a special feature of *DLB* because they often document better than anything else the way in which an author's work was perceived in its own time. Specimens of the writers' manuscripts and letters are included when feasible.

Samuel Johnson rightly decreed that "The chief glory of every people arises from its authors." The purpose of the *Dictionary of Literary Biography* is to compile literary history in the surest way available to us—by accurate and comprehensive treatment of the lives and work of those who contributed to it.

The *DLB* Advisory Board

Introduction

In a sense *Adventures of Huckleberry Finn* (first American edition, 1885) was an historical document when it was first published, for the writer famous as Mark Twain had retrieved from "recollection's vaults" the world he had known as Samuel Langhorne Clemens—the dialects, the social mores, and the atmospheric quality of life along the Mississippi River in the 1850s. While some readers recognized that the author had dramatized a way of life that had largely ceased to exist, others refused to believe such occurrences as those depicted in the feud chapters were anything other than pure fancy. Even Twain's contemporary readers might have benefited from a documented history of the novel's origins and sources showing it to be securely anchored in the facts of a vibrant culture. For readers in the twenty-first century, there is a double liability: on the one hand, to confuse fact and fiction and thereby mistake the objects of Twain's satire, and on the other, to fail to appreciate the experimental and artistic daring that resulted in this vernacular tour de force. And if the novel has become one of the most influential and popular of all American books, it is well to remember that it was not always considered so.

Adventures of Huckleberry Finn is an unlikely literary classic. But classic it is, nonetheless. In large part, the background, origins, and initial reception of the novel in no way predict the worldwide popularity, the continuing artistic and social influence, and the critical admiration (sometimes bordering on idolatry) or the critical depreciation (sometimes bordering on verbal assault) that it has both enjoyed and endured for more than a hundred years. Indeed, Clemens himself was curiously slow in acknowledging this novel as his favorite creation, much less his one indisputable masterpiece. He confessed to his special liking for the novel late in his life but before that had several times nominated *Personal Recollections of Joan of Arc* (1896) or *The Prince and the Pauper* (1881) for the honor.

The first recorded mention of *Adventures of Huckleberry Finn* occurred in August 1876, in a letter Twain wrote to his friend William Dean Howells, and there it appeared almost as an afterthought. He had begun "Huck Finn's Autobiography," Twain casually reported, and liked it only "tolerably well." He thought he might "pigeonhole" or burn the manuscript when it

was done. Some seven years later, when he was making final revisions of the book, he was more defiantly proud of the result, confessing to Howells that "I shall *like* it, whether anybody else does or not." When his own publishing company was readying the novel for the market, Mark Twain seemed to regard the novel more as a valuable commodity than as an artistic achievement. After publication, when some readers objected to the vulgarity and coarseness of its title character, Twain took a protective, almost a paternal, interest in Huck as the abused child of his imagination. His attitudes toward *Adventures of Huckleberry Finn* were subject to vacillation and uncertainty, and it is by no means clear that he ever fully understood how extraordinary a book it is.

Sometime during the composition of *The Adventures of Tom Sawyer* (1876), Twain decided to introduce Huckleberry Finn as a comrade for his title character. Eventually, he recognized that this barely literate social outcast, whose experience and expectations were so different from Tom's, had his own story to tell. After a few false starts in trying to dramatize Huck's uncomfortable residence with the Widow Douglas, the author realized that Huck must tell his own story, and in his own distinctive way. Twain himself could identify with, even envy, Huck's casual freedom from social constraint, but he was likely motivated by curiosity, too—curiosity about the boy's more or less agreeable resistance to "sivilisation," to be sure, but also about the technical, which is to say the vernacular, means necessary to render the fictive world he inhabited. Over the next few years, he put the manuscript aside and turned to other projects, only to be drawn back to it again and again. In the process, his interest in the narrative transcended the simple desire to retrieve, if only in the imagination, the world of his own childhood in Hannibal, Missouri. In his identification *with* Huck, Twain could find tonic relief from the cares of a world that seemed to be hemming him in and cramping his style. However, he soon discovered that, *through* Huck, conceived less as a character than as a comic device, he could address that world in biting satiric terms that the boy might utter but whose moral and social significance Huck himself could not understand.

In this sense, acquaintance with the background and sources for and the influences upon *Adventures of Huckleberry Finn* is essential for a proper appreciation of the novel. Clemens's friend John Hay especially responded to the "documentary" quality of the novel; and Clemens's admirer, George Bernard Shaw, thought Twain, by virtue of his historical and satirical chronicle of the times, would one day be reckoned the Voltaire of his country. In any event, Huck's "adventures" are, in large part, an amalgam of Twain's recollected experiences of his youth, of people he knew and events he had witnessed or had heard about. But these various sources and influences were transformed in at least two ways. They were enriched by Twain's own mature reflections on human nature and social institutions, gleaned in large part from his reading during the 1870s and 1880s. They were also made vivid by casting them in the voice of a boy who cannot fully comprehend the things he witnesses (from the violence of the feud or the Boggs's shooting to the peculiarity of waxed fruit or Miss Emmeline's sentimental verse). At the same time, Huck does not doubt the wisdom and rightness of a social world that excludes him, either through its casual indifference to his life or through its exacting intention to "reform" him.

More often than not, Huck's desire to understand, even appreciate, the approved and respected social world of his so-called betters actually registers the degree of Twain's contempt for the manners and prepossessions of those who lived along the Mississippi River valley in the 1850s. The arrogance of Colonel Sherburn, the drunken bluster of Boggs, the timidity of a lynch mob, the cruel stupidity of the feud, the coarse venality of the king and duke and the gullibility of their prey, the shiftlessness of Pap as well as the sloth of the Bricksville loafers, the vaunted privilege of aristocracy—all these and more are the objects of Twain's satire. And looming over it all is the sad fact of chattel slavery. But the institution of slavery itself is not an object of satire, since that question had been rendered moot well before Twain began to write the novel. In some measure *Huckleberry Finn* is a satire of the racial prejudice, formalized and made more brutal after Reconstruction, but it is also a satire of the moral complacency that permitted slavery to exist in antebellum America. Long after the Civil War that bland acceptance of the unacceptable seemed to persist as an ineradicable part of human nature.

In his 1899 essay "My First Lie and How I Got Out of It" Mark Twain reflected upon what he called the "lie of silent assertion"—the unspoken acquiescence in a great wrong: "In the magnitude of its territorial spread it is one of the most majestic lies that the civilizations make it their sacred and anxious care to guard

and watch and propagate," he announced. And he instanced slavery as a telling example:

> It would not be possible for a humane and intelligent person to invent a rational excuse for slavery; yet you will remember that in the early days of the emancipation agitation in the North the agitators got but small help or countenance from any one. . . . they could not break the universal stillness that reigned, from pulpit and press all the way down to the bottom of society—the clammy stillness created and maintained by the lie of silent assertion—the silent assertion that there wasn't anything going on in which humane and intelligent people were interested.

Twain once described Huck and Jim as constituting a "community of misfortune," but, ironically, in their standing together apart from a corrupt civilization they seem fortune's favorites. For Huck's membership in a society that perpetuates this lie, at best, is as an obligation of charity; and Jim's value to the social order is precisely measurable—on the auction block, he would bring $800. They are exempt from Twain's blanket condemnation of a great and inexcusable wrong because they have chosen to escape from a society that is culpable. *Adventures of Huckleberry Finn* is, among many other things, the story of a man and a boy on the run and of a world on the prowl.

Understood in these terms, it is hardly surprising that this novel should prove controversial. From the very beginning, *Adventures of Huckleberry Finn* was subject to complaint. The book was banned from the Concord Public Library in 1885 and from other libraries some years later. On occasion throughout the twentieth century and into the twenty-first century it has been banned from some public schools as well. The earliest objections had to do with the poor moral example Huck set for America's youth. For the last half century, the criticism has been more substantive and serious. Many concerned parents and some teachers and critics have challenged the moral authority of a book that at least on its surface seems to reinforce rather than overthrow racist attitudes. Both of those controversies are documented in *DLB 343: Mark Twain's* Adventures of Huckleberry Finn. What is documented as well is the contemporary reception and persistent influence of the novel.

On balance, and contrary to longstanding opinion, *Adventures of Huckleberry Finn* was widely and usually favorably reviewed in the United States and England. In addition to reviewers, artists and writers recognized the originality and artistic achievement of the novel. Ernest Hemingway observed that "All modern American literature comes from one book by Mark Twain called *Huckleberry Finn*. . . . it's the best book we've had.

All American writing comes from that. There was nothing before. There has been nothing as good since." The remark is probably too grand to be convincing; what is more certain is that a multitude of modern writers, not all of them American, have weighed in on the value of *Adventures of Huckleberry Finn*. Hemingway was hardly unique in celebrating the book; a lengthy but only partial inventory of established writers' reactions to Twain and his novel, from 1885 to 1996, is included in the final section of this volume.

Quite apart from the controversies surrounding the book or the continuing critical appreciation of it, there exists a longstanding appropriation of *Adventures of Huckleberry Finn* as an icon of popular culture. Even before Mark Twain's death in 1910, cartoonists had employed the image of Huck as a satiric device or an emblem of some quintessentially "American" quality, a quality perhaps neglected or unrealized but real nevertheless. The image of Huck has served as a means to debunk everything from political self-righteousness to the pollution of the Mississippi River. And his story has been retold again and again. There have been seven motion pictures depicting the narrative, and many more television adaptations. There have been plays and musicals, songs and even a "cake walk" named after Huck. There are Huckleberry Finn country bluegrass jubilees, and fishing and rafting companies named after him. There is (inappropriately, since the fence-painting episode is Tom Sawyer's feat) a Huckleberry Finn fence-building company, and there is a "Huck Finn" nightclub in Japan, specializing in the punk scene. Finally, there are translations of this seemingly untranslatable book–hundreds of editions in at least thirty-three languages, published in forty-three countries. Willa Cather was astonished to learn from a Russian violinist she knew that he had a longstanding and deep appreciation for the novel: "It seemed to me that the most delightful things in 'Huckleberry Finn' must disappear in a translation. One could easily translate Parkman or Emerson, certainly: but how translate Mark Twain? The only answer seems to be that if a book has vitality enough, it can live through even the brutalities of translators." For whatever reason, *Adventures of Huckleberry Finn* has had from the beginning, and continues to have, sufficient vitality to withstand public disapproval and critical controversy, censorship and bowdlerization, mishap and malice, even the brutalities of translators.

– Tom Quirk

Acknowledgments

This book was produced by Bruccoli Clark Layman, Inc. George Parker Anderson was the in-house editor.

Production manager is Philip B. Dematteis.

Administrative support was provided by Carol A. Cheschi.

Accountant is Ann-Marie Holland.

Copyediting supervisor is Sally R. Evans. The copyediting staff includes Phyllis A. Avant and Rebecca Mayo. Freelance copyeditors are Brenda L. Cabra, David C. King, and James Small.

Pipeline manager is James F. Tidd Jr.

Editorial associate is Dickson Monk.

Permissions editor is Kourtnay King.

Office manager is Kathy Lawler Merlette.

Photography editor is Kourtnay King.

Digital photographic copy work was performed by Kourtnay King.

Systems manager is James Sellers.

Typesetting supervisor is Kathleen M. Flanagan. The typesetting staff includes Patricia M. Flanagan.

Library research was facilitated by the following librarians at the Thomas Cooper Library of the University of South Carolina: Elizabeth Sudduth and the rare-book department; circulation department head Tucker Taylor; reference department head Virginia W. Weathers; reference department staff Marilee Birchfield, Karen Brown, Mary Bull, Gerri Corson, Joshua Garris, Beki Gettys, Laura Ladwig, Tom Marcil, Anthony Diana McKissick, Bob Skinder, and Sharon Verba; interlibrary loan department head Marna Hostetler; and interlibrary loan staff Robert Amerson and Timothy Simmons.

Tom Quirk acknowledges the help and example of Louis J. Budd. I am also grateful for the assistance of the scholars at the Mark Twain Project, Bancroft Library, particularly Victor Fischer.

Permissions

American Literary Realism. Excerpts from Anthony J. Berret, "The Influence of *Hamlet* on *Huckleberry Finn,*" *American Literary Realism,* volume 18, Spring-Autumn 1985. Excerpts from Victor Fischer, "*Huck Finn* Reviewed: The Reception of *Huckleberry Finn* in the United States, 1885–1897," *American Literary Realism,* volume 16, Spring 1983.

Howard Baetzhold. Excerpt from Howard Baetzhold, *Mark Twain and John Bull: The British Connection.* Bloomington: Indiana University Press, 1970.

Walter Blair. Excerpts from Walter Blair, *"The French Revolution and 'Huckleberry Finn,'"* *Modern Philology,* 55 (August 1957): 29–34.

Buffalo and Erie County Public Library. Illustrations on pages 76, 77, 118, 119, 122, 123, 124, 130, 131, 133, 136, 137, 142, 161, 162, 163, 164, 165, 166, 167, 272, 281, 285, and 297.

Duke University Press. David Carkeet, "The Dialects in *Huckleberry Finn,*" in *American Literature,* 51, no. 3 (1979): 315–332. Copyright, 1979, Duke University Press. All rights reserved. Used by permission of the publisher. James Ellis, "The Bawdy Humor of The King's Camelopard or the Royal Nonesuch, in *American Literature,* 63, no. 4 (1991): 729–735. Copyright, 1991, Duke University Press. All rights reserved. Arthur Scott, "The *Century Magazine* Edits *Huckleberry Finn,* 1884–1885," in *American Literature,* 27 (1955): 356–362. Copyright, 1955, Duke University Press. All rights reserved. John H. Wallace, "The Case Against Huck Finn," in *Satire or Evasion? Black Perspectives on Huckleberry Finn,* edited by James S. Leonard, Thomas A. Tenney, and Thadious M. Davis, pp. 16–24. David L. Smith, "Huck, Jim and American Racial Discourse," in *Satire or Evasion? Black Perspectives on Huckleberry Finn,* pp. 103–120. Copyright, 1992, Duke University Press. All rights reserved. Used by permission of the publisher.

Alan Gribben. Alan Gribben, "Manipulating a Genre: *Huckleberry Finn* as Boy Book," *South Central Review,* 5 (Winter 1988): 15–21.

Michael Patrick Hearn. Michael Patrick Hearn, "Mark Twain, E.W. Kemble, and *Huckleberry Finn,*" *American Book Collector,* new series 2.6 (November-December 1981): 14–19.

Houghton Mifflin. Excerpts from Dixon Wecter, *Sam Clemens of Hannibal* (Boston: Houghton Mifflin, 1952), pp. 56–63, 146–151. Copyright © 1952, and renewed 1980 by Elizabeth Farrar Wecter Pike. Reprinted by permission of Houghton Mifflin Company. All rights reserved.

Lucinda H. Mackethan. Lucinda H. Mackethan, "Huck Finn and the Slave Narratives: Lighting Out as Design," *The Southern Review,* 20 (April 1984): 247–264.

Mark Twain Estate. Illustration on page 9.

Mark Twain Home Foundation. Illustration on page 14.

Mark Twain Papers, The Bancroft Library, University of California, Berkeley. Excerpts from Edgar M. Branch and Robert H. Hirst, *The Grangerford-Shepherdson Feud by Mark Twain: Facsimile of That Episode's First Publication Prior to Adventures of Huckleberry Finn, With an Account of Mark Twain's Literary Use of the Bloody Encounters at Compromise, Kentucky* (The Friends of The Bancroft Library, University of California, 1985), pp. 7–11, 33–34, 38–46, 61–64, 67–71. Letters to Clemens from William Dean Howells, E. C. Stedman, James Whitcomb Riley, William L. Alden, Oliver Wendell Holmes, John Hay, Thomas Nash, Joel C. Harris, Orion Clemens, and J. C. Fuller. Illustrations on pages 28, 37, 44, 47, 58, 63, 82, 83, 127, 128, 140, 193, 223, 231, 234, and 242.

The Missouri Review. Louis J. Budd, "The Recomposition of *Adventures of Huckleberry Finn,*" *The Missouri Review,* 10, no. 1 (1987): 113–129.

National Portrait Galley. Illustration on page 215.

New York Public Library. Illustrations on pages 199 and 254.

Mark Twain's
Adventures of Huckleberry Finn:
A Documentary Volume

Dictionary of Literary Biography

A Brief Life of Mark Twain

This brief overview of Mark Twain's life is adapted from the entry on Clemens in Missouri Biographical Dictionary, *edited by Lawrence Christensen and others (Columbia: University of Missouri Press, 1999).*

Mark Twain was born as Samuel Langhorne Clemens, the sixth child of John Marshall and Jane Lampton Clemens, in Florida, Missouri, on 30 November 1835. His father, believing that nearby Hannibal would prove a more prosperous place to conduct his dry goods business and practice law, moved the family some thirty miles to the port village in 1839, and it is with Hannibal and the Mississippi River that runs beside it that Clemens's youth is most closely associated. Sam Clemens was frail and often sick as a child, and he was subjected to home remedies, some of which he recalled in *The Adventures of Tom Sawyer* (1876) and elsewhere. At the age of four he first walked in his sleep; he sleepwalked intermittently for the next several years. By the time he was nine or ten years old, Sam Clemens's health had sufficiently improved for him to enjoy swimming, fishing, and playing pirates with his friends, and he spent two or three months each year with his cousins on the farm of John Quarles.

Clemens's childhood experiences were a mixture of simple and often mischievous pleasure combined with exposure to disturbing local violence and tragedy: he witnessed a shooting in the streets, stumbled upon a corpse in his father's office, and saw one of his friends drown. He was also probably made anxious and confused by the family's reversal of fortunes. In the 1820s and 1830s his father had purchased 75,000 acres of Tennessee land for $500, believing that it would one day make them all wealthy, but the speculation never realized a profit. By 1846 his mother was cooking meals for guests, and they sold their furniture to pay debts. The next year John Clemens died of pneumonia. Although he continued his schooling, Sam took on odd jobs in town, including that of a printer's devil for the *Missouri Courier.* In 1851 he became a typesetter and editorial assistant for his brother Orion's newspaper, the *Western Union;* it was in this paper that he published his first known sketch, "A Gallant Fireman." The next year he signed a sketch "W. Epaminondas Adrastus Perkins," the first of several pen names he adopted until in 1863 he settled on the name "Mark Twain."

By 1853 Clemens's childhood was effectively over, though all his life he retained a boyish exuberance and fondness for mischief that amused and exasperated his friends and family. In June 1853 he left Hannibal for St. Louis to work as a typesetter, and later that summer he traveled to New York where he worked in a large print shop. By the end of the year he was employed in Philadelphia. During the next few years he traveled about working as a typesetter in St. Louis, Keokuk, and Cincinnati. At the age of twenty-two he boarded a steamboat with the intention of traveling to South America; instead, he became a cub riverboat pilot, apprenticing himself to Horace Bixby for $500.

By April 1859 Clemens had received his piloting license and was making good money as a riverboat pilot, but the Civil War brought a halt to the prosperous river traffic, and Clemens joined the Marion Rangers, a group of Confederate volunteers. His stint as a soldier lasted only two weeks, and many years later he recalled his antic military adventures in "A Private History of the Campaign that Failed" (*The Century Magazine,* December 1885). Ill suited for life as a soldier, Clemens traveled to Nevada with Orion, ten years his senior, who recently had been appointed territorial secretary. In the West, Clemens worked for his brother for a time and also did some mining and speculating in silver- and gold-mining stocks, but he found that work as a local reporter for the *Virginia City Territorial Enterprise* was steadier and more profitable.

In February 1863 Clemens sent three articles to the *Enterprise* from Carson City and signed them "Mark Twain," which was the first time he used this pseudonym, a phrase that signifies safe water depth for a riverboat. Forever after, Clemens and Mark Twain became virtually indistinguishable; many of Clemens's closest friends sometimes called him Mark, and he frequently signed his letters with that name. The literary persona he adopted during these years proved the most valuable property he took with him when he left the Nevada Territory. Already he had acquired something of a reputation as a literary comedian, often publishing articles and sketches in New York newspapers, and he profited by his association with other humorists such as Artemus Ward and Bret Harte. The publication of "Jim Smiley and His Jumping Frog" in 1865 marked the beginning of Mark Twain's national reputation as a humorist. Intended for a collection of humorous sketches Ward was preparing, the tale arrived too late to be included. Instead, it was published in the *Saturday Press,* a New York periodical, and was subsequently reprinted all over the country.

After serving as a traveling correspondent for the *Sacramento Union,* writing a series of letters about his experiences in the Hawaiian Islands, Mark Twain gave his first public lecture in October 1866 and shortly thereafter embarked on a lecture tour throughout California and Nevada. Although he disliked lecturing, he had a natural aptitude for tale-telling and speech-making and soon realized that the lecture circuit put money in his pocket and promoted his public reputation. Not long after that first lecture tour, he became a traveling correspondent for the *San Francisco Alta California* and on 8 June 1867 sailed on the *Quaker City,* bound for Europe and the Holy Land. On board he met Mary Mason Fairbanks, who became one of his closest friends and advisers, and a young man named Charles Jervis Langdon, who in a few years became his brother-in-law.

Clemens fell in love with Olivia Langdon, so the story goes, the moment Charles Langdon showed him a photograph of her. The Langdons were a wealthy and well-respected family in New York State, socially far above the station of young Samuel Clemens. Undaunted by their differences and offering his own good moral character as his only collateral, Clemens proposed to the young woman known familiarly as "Livy." His courtship of Olivia was an ardent one. He divided most of his time in 1868–1869 between lecturing and preparing a book on his travels in Europe and the Holy Land to be called *The Innocents Abroad,* but he still found time to write hundreds of love letters to Olivia, expressing his admiration for her and pledging to give up smoking and drinking and to attend church

regularly. All three ventures were successful: His lecture tour was profitable; *The Innocents Abroad* (1869) was well reviewed and sold well; and Clemens and Olivia were married on 2 February 1870. His efforts to reform himself resulted in only a temporary transformation, however.

Olivia's father, Jervis Langdon, generously supplied the capital for Clemens to buy one-third interest in the *Buffalo Express* and, to Clemens's surprise, also bought the newlywed couple a furnished house in Buffalo. Their first child was born in November 1870 and named after his grandfather, but Langdon Clemens died of diphtheria eighteen months later. The Clemenses did not like living in Buffalo. They moved to Hartford, Connecticut, in 1871, and two years later bought a lot in the Nook Farm area of the city. They contracted to have a house built there and moved in on 19 September 1874. For the next seventeen years, their Hartford house was home for the family, though the Clemenses often made extended visits to Quarry Farm, the home of Livy's adopted sister, Susan Crane, in Elmira, New York. In fact, the Clemens's three daughters were born in Elmira: Olivia Susan (Susy) on 19 March 1872, Clara Langdon on 8 June 1874, and Jane Lampton (Jean) on 26 July 1880.

The years from 1872 to 1888 proved to be the most productive and in many ways the happiest of Mark Twain's career. In 1872 he published *Roughing It,* an account of his experiences in Nevada, California, and the Sandwich Islands. That same year he began writing with his Hartford neighbor Charles Dudley Warner his first novel, *The Gilded Age* (1873). Mark Twain's most original contribution to that novel was the character of Colonel Sellers, whom he modeled after his mother's cousin James Lampton; in 1874, he wrote a play titled *Colonel Sellers* that became a long-standing commercial success. That same year he returned to the manuscript of *The Adventures of Tom Sawyer,* which he had begun about two years earlier, and began writing a series of articles about his experiences as a cub pilot for the *Atlantic Monthly,* "Old Times on the Mississippi," which appeared in seven installments beginning in January 1875 and was later incorporated into his book *Life on the Mississippi* (1883). A few months after he had seen *The Adventures of Tom Sawyer* through the press in 1876, Mark Twain began writing what in a letter to his friend William Dean Howells he called "Huck Finn's Autobiography." Clearly, during these years Mark Twain was drawing upon his memories of Missouri and the Mississippi River for inspiration, and the result was some of his most original and memorable work.

Adventures of Huckleberry Finn was Mark Twain's masterpiece, but several times he put the manuscript away, unsure whether he would ever return to it.

Between the time he began *Huck Finn* and its eventual publication in London in 1884 (American publication, 1885), Mark Twain involved himself in other projects. He collaborated with Bret Harte on the play *Ah, Sin* (produced 7 May 1877) and published another travel book, *A Tramp Abroad,* in 1880 and the novel *The Prince and the Pauper* in 1881. The next year he traveled to St. Louis and Hannibal to gather material for *Life on the Mississippi.* After that book was published he returned to the story of Huck Finn with a will and a purpose. Dissatisfied with his publisher, Mark Twain decided to found his own publishing company, Charles L. Webster and Company—named after his business manager and nephew by marriage—and *Adventures of Huckleberry Finn* was the first volume the company published.

During the next few years Mark Twain did relatively little writing, though he did attempt to continue the adventures of Huck Finn and Tom Sawyer in "Huck Finn and Tom Sawyer among the Indians" but was unable to finish it. He became more and more absorbed in business projects and investments. In addition to his involvement with his publishing company, Clemens took a business interest in a perpetual calendar, a history game, and other inventions, but his largest and worst investment was in the Paige typesetter. For forty-four consecutive months, Clemens contributed $3,000 per month to the development of a working prototype of an automatic typesetting machine.

The investment was a disaster, but as late as August 1889 Clemens was confident enough in the financial success of the Paige typesetter to write Howells that he would soon retire from literature and live off its profits. He had long been a believer in progress and technological advancement—some of that faith is evident in his novel *A Connecticut Yankee in King Arthur's Court* (1889)—but his optimism was severely tested by a series of failures. As the decade of the 1890s began, his publishing house was in debt and having cash-flow problems and investors for the Paige machine were difficult to find. In 1891 he closed his Hartford house and moved his family to Europe, partly in the hope that the baths there would improve Livy's health and partly to live more cheaply. Even though rheumatism in his arm made writing difficult, Mark Twain continued to contribute stories and articles to magazines and to work on two novels, *Pudd'nhead Wilson* (1894) and *Personal Recollections of Joan of Arc* (1895).

The financial panic of 1893 made Clemens's prospects even bleaker, and stories published during this period (such as "The Million Pound Bank-Note," "The Esquimau Maiden's Romance," and "Is He Living or Is He Dead?") express both his cynicism and his desperate hopes for a windfall. The windfall came, not in the form of actual cash, but in the person of Henry

Huttleston Rogers, vice president of the Standard Oil Company. Rogers took an immediate and practical interest in Clemens's financial difficulties, and over the next several years advised the author about ways to relieve his indebtedness. In 1894, after assigning his property, including his copyrights, to his wife, Clemens declared his publishing company bankrupt. In an effort to repay his creditors, the next year he embarked on a round-the-world lecture tour, traveling first across the United States and then sailing from Vancouver to Australia, New Zealand, India, South Africa, and eventually arriving in England in July 1896. The lecture tour provided Clemens with much-needed capital and the basis for another travel book, *Following the Equator* (1897). By early 1898 Clemens had repaid all his outstanding debts.

Only a month after arriving in England, the Clemenses learned that their daughter Susy was ill. On 18 August 1896, Clemens received a telegram that Susy had died; Livy and Clara were already on a ship bound for the United States. The death of their daughter caused a lingering sadness in the Clemens household: they did not celebrate birthdays or holidays for several years afterward.

Mark Twain threw himself into his work. Much of what he wrote during this period was, in the author's mind at least, too cynical and scandalous for the reading public. However, most of his unpublished (and often unfinished) manuscripts were no more toxic than his brilliant satire "The Man that Corrupted Hadleyburg," published in *Harper's Magazine* in 1899, or his venomous denunciation of imperialism in "To the Person Sitting in the Darkness," published in the *North American Review* in 1901.

In 1900, after living several years in Europe, Clemens returned to live in the United States and was greeted warmly by an adoring public. The family was glad to be home but found that the sad memories associated with Nook Farm made it impossible for them to live there, so they rented a house in Riverdale, New York. Perhaps Clemens's sadness was somewhat relieved by the appreciative recognition he was receiving. In October 1901 he received an honorary doctor of letters from Yale University, and the next year he received an honorary doctor of laws degree from the University of Missouri–Columbia. He traveled to Columbia to receive the degree in June 1902. It was the last time Clemens visited his native state, and he probably knew it, for he visited St. Louis and Hannibal and took a short trip on the Mississippi River with his old friend and teacher Horace Bixby.

Later that summer Livy became violently ill. For the next several months Clemens was allowed to see his wife for only five minutes on days that she was feeling well, and the whole family worried that she was dying. For the sake of her health, they moved to Florence, Italy, in 1903, and though she did improve for a time, Olivia Clemens died there on 5 June 1904. Something of the quality of love Mark Twain felt for Livy is conveyed in his moving story "Eve's Diary," published the following year, but a sadder and more cynical side of the man is revealed in the three versions of *The Mysterious Stranger* manuscripts (unpublished at the time of his death) and the philosophical dialogue *What Is Man?* (published anonymously in 1906).

Mark Twain had received worldwide acclaim (he received a third honorary degree, from Oxford University, in 1907), but he was often bitter and lonely. He spent much of his time dictating his autobiography; feeling the absence of grandchildren in his life, he also

established a club for young girls he called his "angelfish" and corresponded with them often. In 1908 Clemens moved into his new house in Redding, Connecticut. He wanted to call the house "Innocents at Home" but his daughter Clara persuaded him to name it "Stormfield" after his fictional sea captain who sailed for heaven but entered at the wrong port.

Stormfield was an eighteen-room Italianate villa, a dramatic contrast to the two-room house Sam Clemens had been born in seventy-three years earlier. His daughter Clara was married in the house in July 1909, and his daughter Jean died of an epileptic seizure there on the day before Christmas the same year. Mark Twain himself died at Stormfield on 21 April 1910. He was buried in the family plot in Elmira, New York.

—*Tom Quirk*

Adventures of Huckleberry Finn Chronology

1874

Fall   Mark Twain and his family move into their still-uncompleted house in Hartford, Connecticut.

November   Publication of "A True Story" in the *Atlantic Monthly*. Twain's first attempt to tell a serious story in African American dialect.

Late Fall   Begins writing articles about his years as a Mississippi riverboat apprentice.

1875

January   Publication of the first of the installments called "Old Times on the Mississippi" in the *Atlantic Monthly*.

September   Publication of *Mark Twain's Sketches New and Old*.

1876

June   Publication of "The Facts Concerning the Recent Carnival of Crime in Connecticut" in the *Atlantic Monthly*.

                Publication of *The Adventures of Tom Sawyer* in England; the novel is published in the United States in December.

July   Begins writing "Huck Finn's Autobiography" at Quarry Farm, near Elmira, New York. By September Twain writes 446 manuscript pages, which will become chapters 1–12½, 15–18½ of the published novel.

1877

December   Delivers the "Whittier Birthday Speech" in Boston. Many, including Twain's friend William Dean Howells, are shocked by the burlesque that features tramps impersonating Henry Wadsworth Longfellow, Oliver Wendell Holmes, and Ralph Waldo Emerson.

1878

April   The Clemens family leave on a trip to Germany and throughout Europe, returning home to Hartford in September 1879.

1880

March   Publication of *A Tramp Abroad*.

March   Returns to the manuscript of "Huck Finn." By mid June he writes more than 200 manuscript pages, chapters 18½–21 of the novel.

26 July   Birth of daughter Jane Lampton (Jean) Clemens.

1881

December   Publication of *The Prince and the Pauper*.

1882	In preparation for expanding the "Old Times on the Mississippi" articles into a book, Twain travels to St. Louis and takes a riverboat down to New Orleans and then back north, stopping off at his hometown, Hannibal.
1883	
May	Publication of *Life on the Mississippi,* which includes the raft episode–a section prepared from more than 50 pages of the "Huck Finn" manuscript.
June	Returns to and completes the "Huck Finn" manuscript. By the beginning of September he writes more than 680 manuscript pages, chapters 12½–14 and 22–43 of the novel.
1884	
May	Clemens, with Charles L. Webster, start their own publishing company.
July	Begins writing "Huck Finn and Tom Sawyer Among the Indians."
November	Begins a four-month lecture tour with George Washington Cable, in which he performs passages adapted from his new, soon-to-be-published novel, *Adventures of Huckleberry Finn.*
December	Publication in London of *The Adventures of Huckleberry Finn;* the American edition is published two months later without the definite article in the title.
	Publication of the first of three installments of *Adventures of Huckleberry Finn* in *The Century.*
1885	
18 February	Publication of the American edition of *Adventures of Huckleberry Finn* by Twain's own publishing house, "Charles L. Webster & Company."

Backgrounds and Sources

Adventures of Huckleberry Finn *is in part a rich compound of Mark Twain's recollections of his boyhood in Hannibal, Missouri—of events witnessed or people that he knew and that his elders often found unsavory; of weather and landscape; of customs and superstitions; of institutions, most notably slavery, that he accepted, as children are apt to do, as the absolute condition of things and therefore approved without question; and of an amalgam of dialects and slang and homey metaphor. The novel also benefits from the knowledge of the Mississippi River and the folk who lived along its shores that Sam Clemens acquired as an apprentice and, later, as a licensed riverboat pilot from 1857 to 1861. John Hay was astute when he wrote Clemens that his new work had a "documentary" value because it had recalled and preserved a way of life and a way of speaking that had all but disappeared by the 1880s. Similarly, George Bernard Shaw wrote Twain in 1897 to say that, his* satire notwithstanding, *"the future historian of America will find your works as indispensable to him as a French historian finds the political tracts of Voltaire." Clemens's earlier experience was supplemented by his return to the river in 1882 when he was working on* Life on the Mississippi *(1883), and it is clear, particularly with the feud chapters, that* Adventures of Huckleberry Finn *was in his thoughts as well. Clemens's reading also contributed to the creation of the book. He was an omnivorous reader with catholic tastes, and* Adventures of Huckleberry Finn *shows not only his acquaintance with newspapers and popular literature—from sentimental verse and Southwest humor to boy books and adventurous romances—but also with such established literary worthies as William Shakespeare, Thomas Carlyle, and Charles Dickens. Finally, the novel dramatizes Clemens's ambivalence about human nature and moral responsibility.*

Samuel Langhorne Clemens as a fifteen-year-old printer's devil and a twenty-three-year-old steamboat pilot, occupations that were formative in Mark Twain's career as a writer (left, Mark Twain Estate; right, State Historical Society of Missouri)

In Adventures of Huckleberry Finn, *all of these backgrounds and sources are filtered through the consciousness of a barely literate boy, and rendered in Huck's inimitable vernacular voice. For that reason, even when Mark Twain is borrowing from known sources, there remains an artistic originality and distinctiveness that makes it nearly impossible to think of the book as in any way derivative. Nevertheless, an awareness of the backgrounds of the novel is valuable to any reader who wishes to feel the full force of Mark Twain's satiric bite, the range of his artistic achievement, and the depth of his involvement with his created characters.*

Places and People

In this excerpt from his biography covering Sam Clemens's early years, Dixon Wecter describes Hannibal, Missouri, the model for St. Petersburg in Adventures of Huckleberry Finn. *Clemens was about to turn four years old when his father, John Marshall Clemens, moved his family to Hannibal, where the boy who became Mark Twain was mainly raised.*

In politics, John Clemens was a Whig, the party that opposed the Democrats. In 1842 he ran for and won the office of justice of the peace in Hannibal.

Hannibal, Missouri:
"His Predestined Great Good Place"
Dixon Wecter

Arriving in Hannibal about mid-November 1839, John M. Clemens was promptly drafted for a border war brewing against Iowa over the disputed boundary, but before mid-December the crisis had passed.[1] He settled his family in the Virginia House, the hotel he had acquired along with other frame structures built by Ira Stout in the quarter-block at the northwest corner of Hill and Main—the $7000 purchase which seemingly took most of Clemens' Monroe County holdings and all his cash to achieve.[2] With his careful foresight—doomed, as always, to betray him in the end, despite all his calculated logic—Clemens saw his new holdings as assuring his family a home and an income from rent, as well as a property facing Main Street suitable for opening a general store. On credit he bought probably two thousand dollars' worth of groceries and dry goods from St. Louis merchants and commission houses—Messrs. James Kerr, J. B. Fisher, Woods Christy & Company, Berthold Tesson & Company, and Taylor & Holmes. Late in 1839 and early in 1840 he also borrowed about $950 from James Clemens, Jr., "one of the richest half-dozen citizens of St. Louis," Whig lawyer and merchant of Kentucky origins who accepted the impoverished Clemenses in the northern county as his distant cousins—since he too claimed descent from the regicide judge.[3] John M. Clemens had also borrowed $747.13 from James A. H. Lampton, the erratic young half brother of Jane Clemens,

still a minor, who lived near Florida.[4] With these debts at his back, John M. Clemens opened another in his endless series of general stores—fronting the muddy thoroughfare of Hannibal, with the great river rolling past the wharf one block below. And behind the counter as clerk, "in a new suit of clothes," was Orion, almost fifteen years old, already bookish, absent-minded, inept. The auguries were none too good.

The town of Hannibal, bearing the name of a defeated general—as boosters from the neighboring village of Scipio delighted to point out—had been founded a quarter-century before by "earthquake certificate" granted refugees from the "Big Shakes" of 1811, around New Madrid, Missouri. In its infancy repeatedly harassed by Indians, the town numbered only thirty persons in 1830, but within the next decade had grown to 1034, becoming a miniature porkopolis, cigar manufactory, whisky distillery, and important river port for Northern Missouri and transshipment point to St. Joseph, gateway of the Great West. The rich prairie soil back of Hannibal, from the time it was broken by the plow, began to funnel wheat, hemp, and tobacco into its wharves. "The white town drowsing in the sunshine of a summer morning," which Mark Twain remembered, was bound in economic destiny to "the great Mississippi, the magnificent Mississippi, rolling its mile-wide tide along." When in 1845 the newly-incorporated city chose its seal, it found its fitting emblem in a stern-wheel steamer. The town lies at the mouth of a valley carved through the hills by Bear Creek—from whose waters young Sam Clemens, as he later stated, was rescued six times "in a substantially drown [*sic*] condition. His mother's refrain was, "'People who are born to be hanged are safe in the water.'"[5] Northward of the town lies Holliday's Hill—Cardiff to readers of *Tom Sawyer*—as the nearest bluff of an escarpment that flanks the Mississippi for two miles, cut by a ravine whose "spring branch" supplied the natural roadbed that ran northwest a dozen miles toward Palmyra, the county seat. Above Hannibal in this direction was the old bay mill, with its oak water wheel for grinding corn and wheat, and blacksmith shop beside it—a communal center much used by Hannibal citizens. South of the town looms a steeper cliff above the River, called Lover's Leap, invested with the familiar Indian legend repeated a hundred times over the face of a romantic nation, a spot with "many traditions of love and woful tradegy [*sic*]," as the Hannibal *Gazette* gravely noted in Mark Twain's boyhood.[6]

Past the half-dozen brick houses that Hannibal boasted in 1840 and scores of frame ones with straggling descendants from the log-cabin era, interspersed with vacant lots fragrant with locust trees in spring and choked with Jimson weed during the long dry summers, ran streets laid out by the founder, Abraham Bird. Market Street, later rechristened Broadway,

Mark Twain's boyhood home in Hannibal (from Jack E. Boucher, Historic American Buildings
Survey/Historic American Engineering Record, *Library of Congress)*

bisected the town in a steep climb up the hill from the River. Known as "one of the widest streets in Missouri," it flowed around the market house that stood athwart its course between Third and Fourth. Circuses, minstrels, Fourth of July parades, and torchlight processions—such as the great Log Cabin Campaign rally of July 28 and 29, 1840, which John M. Clemens as a devout Whig surely attended—all converged upon Market Street. But the spine of commercial Hannibal has always been Main or Second Street, intersecting Broadway one block above the riverfront, and running parallel with the wharves. Two blocks above Broadway, in the direction of Holliday's Hill, Main Street crosses Bird at "Wild-Cat Corner," long famous for its store under the sign of the wildcat; just around the corner on Bird still stands the ramshackle clapboard house where John M. Clemens is said for a time to have had his law office, and where Sam was to see the corpse of the stabbed man lying in a pool of moonlight.

A block beyond, Main crosses Hill Street, at the site of the old Virginia House where the Clemenses first lived, and half a block up the steep grade of Hill they later built the house now familiar to thousands of visitors as the Mark Twain home, across the way from the

"Becky Thatcher" place where Laura Hawkins and her family dwelt. Back to back with the old Clemens property but facing upon the less prosperous thoroughfare of North Street stood the big barnlike structure where Tom Blankenship, the original of Huck Finn, lived with his drunken father and slatternly kin, in tempting proximity to young Sam Clemens. These were Hannibal's chief streets, unpaved, deeply rutted by wagon wheels, dusty in summer, cut into ribbons of mud in winter. In late November 1847 the Gazette complained that after a week of snow and rain, "the square between Hill & Bird on Main" was so treacherous as not to be attempted unless—in language familiar on the River—the pedestrian was "prepared in making the 'crossings' to wade in 'scant three feet,' or 'march under mud twain.'"[7]

Hog drovers thronged the streets, bringing some ten thousand swine annually to the two "pork houses" in operation by 1840 near the mouth of Bear Creek. A few years later the first city council would find their location a menace to public health, and recommend that all slaughtering of hogs and beeves be done beyond the creek. But the by-products, in that prodigal generation, supplied meat for even the poorest. "Pork-house—free spareribs, livers, hearts, &c.," wrote

Map of Hannibal, Missouri, where Sam Clemens grew up and that served as the model for Huckleberry Finn's hometown (drawn by A. Ruger, 1869; Library of Congress Panoramic Maps)

Mark Twain in an autobiographical jotting."[8] And as another windfall, it will be remembered that Tom Sawyer and his gang in lieu of balloons played with bladders procured from the slaughterhouse.

In addition to its two pork houses, Hannibal by 1844 took pride in four general stores, three sawmills, two planing mills, three blacksmith shops, two hotels, three saloons, two churches, two schools, a tobacco factory, a hemp factory, and a tanyard, as well as a flourishing distillery up at the stillhouse branch. West of the village lay "Stringtown," so called because its cabins and stock pens were strung out along the road. Here in the forties stood the landmark of Coleman's tavern, where farmers' teams bound to and from market congregated from all over Marion County. Small industry was the life of Hannibal. "Our people have a horrid aversion to the jury box and the witnesses' stand," wrote Orion Clemens in 1851, in words equally true for the previous decade. "They greatly prefer the study of pork and flour barrels, tape, cordwood and the steamboat's whistle."[9]

In a late sketch, Mark recalled the winding country road leading out of his Missouri village, the woods

on one side and a rail fence on the other, "with blackberry vines and hazel bushes crowding its angles," a bluebird and a fox squirrel on the topmost rail.[10] Beyond the scraggly town and its smudge of trade beckoned the real, the irresistible charm of that time and place. South of Broadway lay Draper's Meadow, named for the County Judge, "our oldest citizen" who led the list of "Villagers of 1840-3." Here ran a small stream bordered by elder bushes, where the boys used to fire popguns in their endless Indian games. On higher ground grew the dim woods with their "solemn twilight"–the sugar maple and rock maple, scarlet in the autumn when the sumac flamed crimson, and dogwood and redbud turned to blood, and the hickory to burnished gold, while the red oaks deepened into purple and the very shadows changed from brown to blue, presaging winter. Red haws and persimmons and hickory nuts and walnuts were the season's plunder, but for pecans the boys had to cross over into the Illinois bottoms. Southward winged geese, brant, ducks, and cranes. Clouds of wild pigeons rose from the woods by day, and at night could be knocked from the trees after the lighting of fires to dazzle them. "Game is very abundant in this vicinity," remarked the local newspaper. "Every day we hear of some one having killed a deer." Christmas fare always included venison steaks, ducks, wild turkey, grouse, and quail.

Mark's cherished memories of winter—beyond the adventure of skating across the black ice of the Mississippi when it froze—were apt to be those of nights indoors, whether in Hannibal or sometimes at the Quarles farm, with the house creaking against the howling wind, the warmth of blankets, and the snow sifting in around the sashes. Spring brought new delight to the woods and upland pastures, with the blue or purple shooting star on the hills, and underfoot as summer advanced a wealth of wild strawberries, blackberries, raspberries, and gooseberries.

In Hannibal young Sam Clemens had reached his predestined great good place. Here during most of each year, and back on the Quarles's farm during certain summer weeks, he grew stronger in body and more aware of the world about him. These streets and the people that walked in them, each carrying with him some unforgettable mannerism of speech or dress, some vestige of comedy or pathos, the waters, the woods, the hills, the birds and animals, left the boy with a mortal nostalgia all his life. The peaceful clinking of a blacksmith's hammers or the plaintive wail of a spinning wheel, "the most lonesome sound in nature," like old familiar names or the handwriting on an envelope, always had the effect of powerful evocation upon boyhood memories as benign as those of Wordsworth in *The Prelude,* attuned to a sensibility as keen as that of Proust in the remembrance of things past. A quarter-century afterward at Hilo, Hawaii, he spent several tropical nights talking eagerly until dawn with a chance acquaintance named Cony who by coincidence "knew everybody that ever I knew in Hannibal and Palmyra," and on his honeymoon six years later the arrival of a letter from his Hannibal chum Will Bowen caused "the fountains of my great deep" to be broken up, "and I have rained reminiscences for four and twenty hours."[11] In other moods, revolting against Will Bowen's sentimental infatuation with old days in which "there is nothing. . . worth pickling for present or future use," and cruelly rebuking his friend's "mental and moral masturbation [which] belongs eminently to the period usually devoted to *physical* masturbation, and should be left there and outgrown," Sam Clemens was simply turning upon himself and the artist's ultimate inability to escape from this prison house of memory.[12] The prevailing mood reasserted itself when he wrote Will a dozen years later that "I would have liked to bring up every creature we knew in those days—even the dumb animals—it would be bathing in the fabled Fountain of Youth."[13] This fountain of course was the wellspring from which he drew his clearest inspirations—whether for the sketches of Jimmy Finn the town

drunkard and the Cadets of Temperance which Mark wrote from New York early in 1867 for the *Alta California;* *Tom Sawyer,* "simply a hymn, put into prose to give it a worldly air"; the riper masterpiece of *Huckleberry Finn,* and *Life on the Mississippi,* their lifeblood of reminiscence fortified by his return to Hannibal and the River in 1882; or the inescapable background of *Pudd'nhead Wilson* and of *The Mysterious Stranger* with Tom and Huck clothed in medieval dress.

—*Sam Clemens of Hannibal* (Boston: Houghton Mifflin, 1952), pp. 56–63

1. Return I. Holcombe, *History of Marion County, Missouri* [HMC], pp. 220–23, and 915.
2. HMC, pp. 897 and 914, buttressed by local tradition, gives the name of this hostelry as the Virginia House, although Albert Bigelow Paine, *Mark Twain, a Biography,* p. 27, asserts that the Clemenses first lived in "Pavey's old Tavern" on Hill Street. Pavey's, however, was one block south of Hill near "Wild-Cat Corner," at Main and Bird, where T. R. Selmes later opened his locally-famous store at the sign of the wildcat (Hannibal *Journal,* Jan. 7 and Oct. 14, 1847). Later the name "Virginia House" seems to have been lost to an inn operated on Front Street by J. G. Toncray (Hannibal *Journal,* June 1, 1848).
3. William Hyde and H. L. Conard, eds., *Encyclopedia of the History of St. Louis,* I, 407–8, give the origins and career of James Clemens, Jr. His eminence among the magnates of St. Louis is described in the phrase quoted above from Orion Clemens' Hannibal *Journal and Western Union,* Sept. 25, 1851.
4. All of these debts are listed in Marion County Deed Records, H–375, after transfer of Oct. 13, 1841. For James A. H. Lampton see *Mark Twain Business Man,* pp. 17–18.
5. Autobiographical sketch, Berg Collection, New York Public Library: typescript in the Mark Twain Papers, University of California Library [MTP].
6. In a brief description of the city, Hannibal *Gazette,* Feb. 25, 1847, from which the above summary has been drawn.
7. Hannibal *Gazette,* Nov. 25, 1847.
8. Typescript in MTP, DV 243, from original in Buffalo Public Library. For early disapproval of the packing industry in the heart of town, Hannibal Municipal Records, I, 97, Oct. 1845.
9. Hannibal *Journal and Western Union,* June 12, 1851.
10. Clemens, "My Platonic Sweetheart," *The Mysterious Stranger,* p. 288.
11. Mark Twain to his family, June 21, 1866, text in MTP, Letter File, from original in Webster Collection; to Will Bowen, Feb. 6, 1870, in *Mark Twain's Letters to Will Bowen,* ed. Theodore Hornberger, p. 18.
12. August 31, 1876, *Mark Twain's Letters to Will Bowen,* pp. 23–24. The original letter, which Clemens went to the "unheard of trouble of re-writing and saying the same harsh things softly so as to sugarcoat the anguish" before sending to Bowen, is the only text that survives.
13. Nov. 4, 1888, in *Letters,* p. 502.

* * *

In this excerpt Wecter describes the poor whites Sam Clemens knew in Hannibal who later influenced his characterization of Huck and his father.

Huck and Pap
Dixon Wecter

Poor whites in Hannibal stirred scant interest or sympathy from their adult neighbors of the middle class. Their squalor and shiftlessness branded them as akin to those chill-racked, tobacco-chewing, yellow-faced squatters found in the malaria and ague bottoms of Missouri, or those dirt eaters, pineywoods people, and tattered migrants who haunted all the river towns of the South—often dwelling in shacks or shanty boats or floating down the current on wood-flats. They were the dispossessed wanted by nobody. The Hannibal *Western Union* for May 8, 1851, with Orion as editor, described such a family, a man and wife with four or five children found living in and about a hogshead near the foundry: "A blanket constituted the bedding, a coffee pot and skillet made up the cooking utensils; and a few stones piled up formed a fire place . . . the dirty-faced little cherubs appeared to be as happy as young princes." Later when Dr. Morton presented the town fathers with a bill for medical attendance upon such a family, the council promptly disallowed it, declaring that the "propensity of the man for loafing" exempted the municipality from any responsibility for his luckless brood; nor was there a poorhouse where indoor relief could be sought.[1] Besides, the down-and-outers, being Americans of that day and generation, were by no means servile or disposed to accept patronizing charity. In *Life on the Mississippi* Mark observes that if, in one of his penitential moods he had dared to carry a basket of victuals to the poor, "I knew we had none so poor but they would smash the basket over my head for my pains."

One such family, whose invincible cheerfulness seemed no less a communal scandal than its indolence, is thus sketched in Mark's reminiscent notes: "*Blankenships.* The parents paupers and drunkards; the girls charged with prostitution—not proven. Tom, a kindly young heathen. Bence, a fisherman. These children were never sent to school or church. Played out and dis-

The Blankenship house, long since demolished, which stood back-to-back with the Clemens home. Tom Blankenship and his drunken father were models for Huck and his father (Mark Twain Home Foundation).

14

Huckleberry Finn as drawn by True Williams (1839–1897) for The Adventures of Tom Sawyer, 1876. *Williams illustrated Mark Twain's early books with the American Publishing Company. In an 1876 letter to his friend William Dean Howells, Mark Twain praised Williams's "rattling pictures": "He takes a book of mine, & without suggestion from anybody builds no end of pictures just from his reading of it"*
(from The Adventures of Tom Sawyer, *Mark Twain House, Hartford, Connecticut).*

The First Appearance of Huck Finn

Mark Twain first described Huckleberry Finn in The Adventures of Tom Sawyer.

Shortly Tom came upon the juvenile pariah of the village, Huckleberry Finn, son of the town drunkard. Huckleberry was cordially hated and dreaded by all the mothers of the town, because he was idle, and lawless, and vulgar and bad—and because all their children admired him so, and delighted in his forbidden society, and wished they dared to be like him. Tom was like the rest of the respectable boys, in that he envied Huckleberry his gaudy outcast condition, and was under strict orders not to play with him. So he played with him every time he got a chance. Huckleberry was always dressed in the cast-off clothes of full-grown men, and they were in perennial bloom and fluttering with rags. His hat was a vast ruin with a wide crescent lopped out of its brim; his coat, when he wore one, hung nearly to his heels and had the rearward buttons far down the back; but one suspender supported his trousers; the seat of the trousers bagged low and contained nothing; the fringed legs dragged in the dirt when not rolled up.

Huckleberry came and went, at his own free will. He slept on door-steps in fine weather and in empty hogsheads in wet; he did not have to go to school or to church or call any being master or obey anybody; he could go fishing or swimming when and where he chose, and stay as long as it suited him; nobody forbade him to fight; he could sit up as late as he pleased; he was always the first boy that went barefoot in the spring and the last to resume leather in the fall; he never had to wash, nor put on clean clothes; he could swear wonderfully. In a word, everything that goes to make life precious, that boy had. So thought every harassed, hampered, respectable boy in St. Petersburgh.

—The Adventures of Tom Sawyer (Hartford, Conn.: American Publishing, 1876), pp. 63–64

" PAP. "

Huck Finn's father, as drawn for the 1885 first American edition of
Adventures of Huckleberry Finn *by E. W. Kemble
(Mark Twain House, Hartford, Connecticut)*

"Fish-Belly White"

The illustrator followed Twain's detailed description of Pap carefully.

He was most fifty, and he looked it. His hair was long and tangled and greasy, and hung down, and you could see his eyes shining through like he was behind vines. It was all black, no gray; so was his long, mixed-up whiskers. There warn't no color in his face, not like another man's white, but a white to make a body sick, a white to make a body's flesh crawl—a tree-toad white, a fish-belly white. As for his clothes—just rags, that was all. He had one ankle resting on 'tother knee; the boot on that foot was busted, and two of his toes stuck through, and he worked them now and then. His hat was laying on the floor; an old black slouch with the top caved in, like a lid.

*—*Adventures of Huckleberry Finn *(New York: Charles L. Webster, 1885), p. 39*

appeared." They lived in a ramshackle old barn of a house on Hill Street—a distance quickly covered by Sam when summoned with stealthy catcalls from Tom. The site is now cherished by the Chamber of Commerce as that of "Huck Finn's home," although the house no longer stands, following several generations of habitation by Negro families whose petty thefts, cutting scrapes, and the didos of a one-time denizen called Cocaine Nell Smith lent it a repute still more dubious than it enjoyed in the Blankenships' day.[2]

Head of the family was Woodson Blankenship, a n'er-do-well from South Carolina, who fitfully worked at the old sawmill but drank whenever possessed of cash to jingle in his jeans. In 1845 he appears on the roll of tax delinquents as owing twenty-nine cents. His eldest boy Benson, called Bence, did odd jobs but preferred to angle for catfish and tease the playmates of Sam Clemens by knotting their clothes when they went swimming, or clodding them when they came ashore. But he had a kind streak too—probably furnishing the original for Tom and Huck's friend Muff Potter, who loafed and drank, but shared his catch if they were hungry, and mended their kites. In the summer of 1847 Bence befriended secretly a runaway Negro whom he found hiding among the swampy thickets of Sny Island, a part of Illinois's Pike County that hugged the opposite bank of the river from Hannibal. Ignoring the reward posted for the black man, Bence carried food to him week after week and kept mum about his hiding place—thus inspiring that rare tribute to loyalty in *Huckleberry Finn,* in which the homeless river rat rejects all temptations of gain and even elects to "go to Hell" rather than betray his friend Nigger Jim. But one day woodchoppers flushed the fugitive and chased him into a morass called Bird Slough, where he disappeared. Some days later, Sam Clemens, John Briggs, and the Bowen boys were fishing and roaming about the island as they often did—for the sake of its berries, and a fine grove of Illinois pecans such as the woods behind Hannibal did not bear—and made a discovery thus reported in the Hannibal *Journal* of August 19: "While some of our citizens were fishing a few days since on the Sny Island, they discovered in what is called Bird Slough the body of a negro man. On examination of the body, they found it to answer the description of a negro recently advertised in handbills as a runaway from Neriam Todd, of Howard County. He had on a brown jeans frock coat, home-made linen pants, and a new pair of lined and bound shoes. The body when discovered was much mutilated." One account says that the gruesome thing, released from a snag by their poling about in the drift, rose headfirst like an apparition before their eyes.[3] Endless seem the variations upon terror in the boyhood of Sam Clemens.

Among the Blankenships, whose society was a forbidden pleasure and therefore sought as often as possible, Sam's special joy was the younger brother Tom.[4] Like Huck Finn, whose image Mark Twain repeatedly identified with, Tom was ill-fed, an outrageous wreck of rags, dirty, ignorant, cheerful, carefree, and altogether enviable, being "the only really independent person—boy or man—in the community."[5] Tom went barefoot all the time, both from freedom and necessity, whereas boys from "quality" families were forbidden by parents to "come out barefoot" until warm weather—meanwhile often mocked as "Miss Nancys" by the more emancipated.[6] The woods and the waters around Hannibal were his education. Living by his wits, suspicious of every attempt to civilize him, "to comb him all to hell," he had none of the unimportant virtues and all the essential ones. The school of hard knocks had given him a tenacious grasp on reality, despite his faith in dreams, omens, and superstitions. But it had not toughened him into cynicism or crime, and "he had as good a heart as ever any boy had." The testimony of another witness is interesting, a lad named Ayres, grandson of a pioneer Hannibal settler named Richmond. Younger than Sam Clemens, he knew him slightly and was his fellow member in the Cadets of Temperance, but Tom he knew well and admiringly:

> My grandmother told us that Tom Blankenship was a bad boy and we were forbidden to play with him, but when we went on a rabbit chase he joined us. . . . Black John (a half-grown negro belonging to my grandmother) and Tom Blankenship were naturally leading spirits and they led us younger "weaker" ones through all our sports. Both were "talented," bold, kind, and just, and we all liked them both and were easily led by them. We also played down around the old Robards mill and the school house in the city park.[7]

Long years after, in 1902, Mark heard that his old crony Tom had become justice of the peace and a respected citizen "in a remote village in Montana."

Objects of equal juvenile interest with the Blankenship boys, but naturally less comradeship, were those ultimate dregs of Hannibal society, the village drunkards. Besides old Blankenship himself, the list began with "General" Gaines—an ancient and disreputable relic of the Indian wars, who when full of rotgut used to fancy himself one of the half-man, half-alligator breed, and roar, "Whoop! bow your neck and spread!" like one of the raftsmen whose mixture of cockalorum with cowardice Mark hit off in the third chapter of *Life on the Mississippi*. From him the title of town drunkard, "an exceedingly well-defined and unofficial office of those days," descended to Jimmy Finn, who furnished the name and most of the attributes for Huck's pappy.

"He was a monument of rags and dirt; he was the profanest man in town; he had bleary eyes, and a nose like a mildewed cauliflower; he slept with the hogs in an abandoned tanyard." Judge Clemens once tried without success to reform him; the Judge's son merely enjoyed him. To Will Bowen in later years Sam recalled how "we stole his dinner while he slept in the vat and fed it to the hogs in order to keep them still till we could mount them and have a ride."[8] It was probably with Jimmy Finn in mind that a town ordinance passed in the spring of 1845 made it a misdemeanor to be "found drunk or intoxicated in any streat, alley, avinue, market place, or public square . . . or found a sleep in an such place not his own." But Finn was not long destined to plague the good citizens of Hannibal. On November 6 of that year, among the county records we find the sum of $8.25 allowed "for making a coffin, furnishing a shroud and burying James Finn a pauper." Mark insisted that he died a natural death in a tan vat, from delirium tremens combined with spontaneous combustion—"I mean it was a natural death for Jimmy Finn to die."[9]

                                                                                —Sam Clemens of Hannibal, pp. 146–151

1. Hannibal *Tri-Weekly Messenger*, Feb. 12, 1853.
2. Clemens, *Life on the Mississippi*, p. 401; Mark Twain Papers, University of California Library [MTP], DV 47, "Villagers." Fate of the Blankenship house as reported by a Hannibal newspaper in Sept. 1900 (Morris Anderson scrapbook in the Mark Twain Museum, Hannibal).
3. Albert Bigelow Paine, *Mark Twain, a Biography*, p. 64, probably from the joint recollections of Clemens and Briggs; he errs in calling the young man "Ben," as both "Villagers" and the 1850 census show. The full name of the island was Sny Carta, corruption of the French "Chenal Ecarte," or lost channel, so known because the Mississippi had silted up between the island and the Illinois shore.
4. The 1850 census lists the names and ages of the Blankenship progeny thus: Benson, 21, laborer; Martha, 19; Nancy, 16; Sarah, 14; Elizabeth, 12; Thomas, 19, no occupation; Mary, 6; Catherine, 5. Apparently Tom had a twin sister, and was four to five years older than Sam Clemens.
5. *Mark Twain's Autobiography*, edited by Paine, II, 174.
6. From an obviously autobiographical reminiscence of village custom in "Which Was the Dream?," MTP, DV 301.
7. J. W. Ayres, "Recollections of Hannibal," dated Harriman, Tenn., Aug. 22, 1917, and published in the Palmyra (Mo.) *Spectator* (Morris Anderson scrapbook, Mark Twain Museum). Ayres became superintendent of schools in Marion County in 1866.
8. MTP, DV 310; *Mark Twain's Autobiography*, II, 174–75; and *Mark Twain's Letters to Will Bowen*, p. 18.
9. Hannibal Municipal Records, I, 21; Marion County Court Records, Book C, p. 400; Clemens, *Life on the Mississippi*, p. 414. Probably wholly imaginary is a yarn in MTP, DV 30, about "the time poor old Jimmy Finn fell off Lover's Leap" and Ira Stout clocked his descent.

* * *

Mark Twain sometimes boasted to his New England neighbors and to his in-laws in Elmira, New York, that he had grown up with black people and was thoroughly acquainted with their nature and desires. It is all the more remarkable, then, given his background and his own confidence in his rather narrow and bigoted perspective, that he should have created in Jim a character that is at once representative and individual. Part of Jim's individuality came from the actual people who served in some measure as his prototype, as Arthur G. Pettit describes in this seventh chapter of his study of the influence of the South on Twain, originally titled "Heroes or Puppets? Clemens, John Lewis, & George Griffin."

Jim as a Composite Portrait
Arthur G. Pettit

Unconsciously we all have a standard by which we measure other men . . . we admire them, we envy them, for great qualities which we ourselves lack. Hero worship consists in just that. Our heroes are the men who do things which we recognize, with . . . a secret shame, that we cannot do.

—Autobiography (1909)

Out of love, they [the Clemens family] did not twit [George Griffin] . . . but out of love, I did—and rubbed it in, sometimes.

—"Wapping Alice" (1907)[1]

Nigger Jim is a composite portrait of three black men Clemens knew intimately or casually during his lifetime. One was Uncle Daniel, the Missouri slave whom Clemens vaguely remembered as a boy.[2] Another was John Lewis, a handyman on the farm where the Clemenses spent their summers. By far the most important source of inspiration for Nigger Jim was George Griffin, the Hartford butler who served the Clemenses during the eighteen years in which Nigger Jim appeared in three books.

Uncle Daniel's importance as a source of literary inspiration after *The Gilded Age* has been greatly exaggerated.[3] John Lewis, on the other hand, contributed three traits to Nigger Jim's makeup: physical strength, a bucolic air which was not a part of George Griffin's character, and perhaps a complacent simplemindedness which crops up in Nigger Jim's behavior in the last part of *Huckleberry Finn*, in *Tom Sawyer Abroad,* and in "Tom Sawyer's Conspiracy." Aside from these three traits of Lewis's, which were transplanted to Nigger Jim, the most intriguing part of the story of John Lewis is not Lewis himself, but Clemens's reaction to Lewis.

On August 25, 1877, while the Clemenses were summering at Quarry Farm, John Lewis looked up from the manure he was shoveling and saw a runaway horse careening down the road carrying a cartload of Livy Clemens's relatives to what Clemens, panting desperately after them, considered certain disaster. Lewis planted himself squarely in the path of death and jerked the horse to a stop.[4]

Clemens at once added Lewis to his list of demigods. Although probably the most popular figure of his era, he seemed to feel the need to compare and to pit himself against a number of men less great than himself.[5] The Lewis incident is important not because Clemens found yet another hero, but because this time be gave the wreath to a black man. Before the runaway episode Lewis's greatness had completely escaped Clemens: indeed he had regarded this black man as a mere buffoon, a rustic boor who watched a magnificent sunset with Clemens at Quarry Farm and then remarked that the sight was "dam *[sic]* funny" But after he fetched that horse "up standing," this bowed and bent black scarecrow in "fluttering work-day rags" suddenly became Lewis the Prodigious, a man of superhuman strength and sterling character. Still slouching on the same manure wagon he had always slouched on, Lewis, once crude and boorish, was now beautiful. Overnight be became Clemens's first black Adam.[6]

Chagrined that Lewis's greatness had eluded him before, Clemens set about making up for lost time. When Livy's relatives asked him if a gold watch would be an appropriate medal of honor for Lewis, Clemens at once set himself up as authority-at-large on how to reward deserving members of the colored race.[7] Warning that any scoffer who dared to question the propriety of giving a black man a watch would have to answer to Clemens personally, he declared that Lewis would actually appreciate this fine toy far more than the more valuable rewards, totaling nineteen hundred dollars, that the Langdons and Cranes showered on him. Bright shiny playthings appealed to black people more than expensive gifts. Four years later Clemens congratulated Joel Chandler Harris for shedding light on the black man's faulty "estimate of values by his willingness to risk his soul and his mighty peace forever for the sake of a silver sev'm-punce."[8]

The most astounding part of Lewis's behavior was that he remained modest in the midst of his new fame, humbly giving all the credit to "divine providence" for saving those "presshious" Langdon lives. The man seemed blissfully unaware of his greatness, thereby standing even taller in Clemens's eye. Like Ulysses S. Grant, another of Clemens's heroes, Lewis was noble in spite of himself—an unassuming fellow whose simplicity added to his dignity and to his power over Clemens. Surely here was a natural man with great literary possibilities.

Yet when Lewis finally made his fictional debut more than a quarter-century later, he was a disaster. In a sterile tale about Admiral Stormfield's efforts to erect a monument to Adam as founder of the human race (rightly labelled by Paine as "one of M. T.'s mistakes"), he appears as Uncle Rastus Timson. Although Lewis was actually shorter than Clemens, Uncle Rastus Timson is a ragtag giant: "[He] has a pronounced Atlas stoop, from carrying mighty burdens upon his shoulders; wears what is left of a once hat—a soft ruin which slumps to a shapeless rumple like a collapsed toy balloon when he drops it on the floor; the remains of his once clothes hang in fringed rags and rotting shreds from his booms and yard-arms, and give him the sorrowfully picturesque look of a ship that has been through a Cape Horn hurricane—not recently, but in Columbus's time."[9]

For all his titanic strength, Uncle Rastus Timson is a mental pygmy, a feeble black barometer set up to measure superior white intelligence and to respond to white jokes with such expressions as "Bless yo' soul, honey," "Well, dat do beat me!" and "Sure as you bawn." The problem with Uncle Rastus is that he was modeled after an ordinary handyman who turned out to be even less than ordinary: a timid and foolish darky who "hain't ever struck" anyone so intelligent as Admiral Stormfield, who is even more insane than Colonel Sellers in *The American Claimant*. Only late in the story, when Mark Twain trots him out into the dusty summer road to pull down the horse and rescue the white folks, does Rastus regain part of his dignity. Growing melodramatic, Mark Twain declared that after that episode white people eagerly took Rastus "by his horny black hand and gave it a good grip, and many said, 'I'm proud to do it!'"[10]

But it was too late and too forced. Despite his tardy heroism, Uncle Rastus Timson is not credible because neither Lewis himself nor his heroism was as striking as Clemens made them out to be. The most unusual event that occurred that summer day at Quarry Farm in 1877 was not Lewis's act of courage but Clemens's emotional response. Though he unquestionably admired Lewis's courage, Clemens seemed to admire even more his own capacity to admire Lewis. He could get away with such theatrics in his private relationship with Lewis. But when Mark Twain tried to stitch together a gullible darky and a courageous black hero into a single composite character, the two traits cancelled each other out. We may prefer to remember Lewis's influence on Nigger Jim as the natural shaman of woods and river in the middle portion of *Huckleberry Finn*. But the fact of the matter is that Lewis's more lasting contribution to the character of Nigger Jim was as the powerful but timid giant with the mentality of a

JIM.

The first illustration of Jim in the novel (by E. W. Kemble, from Adventures of Huckleberry Finn, *Mark Twain House, Hartford, Connecticut)*

child who appears in the last quarter of *Huckleberry Finn*, in most of *Tom Sawyer Abroad*, and in all of "Tom Sawyer's Conspiracy." Fortunately in most of *Huckleberry Finn* Lewis is eclipsed by another very different black man.[11]

Sometime in 1875 a large man with a "clear black and very handsome" complexion came to the Clemens home in Hartford to wash windows for one day and, as Clemens put it, accidentally stayed for eighteen years.[12] His name was George Griffin.

In a family sketch that he wrote in the 1890s Clemens noted that Griffin had been a slave in Maryland and a Union general's bodyservant during the war. He described Griffin as "handsome," "faultlessly dressed," "well built, shrewd, wise, polite, always good-natured, cheerful to gaiety, honest, religious, a cautious truthspeaker, devoted friend to the family, champion of its interests," and the children's idol. Griffin was also a confidant for Clemens, a successful gambler, an astute debater, a money-lender in the Hartford black community, and a "strenuously religious" deacon of the African Methodist Episcopal Church.

The Fugitive Slave Act of 1850

In 1850 Congress acted to strengthen the rights of slaveholders through the Fugitive Slave Act. As these sections of the act show, the slaveholder needed only an affidavit to establish his claim to ownership and the person named as a slave had no legal right to contest the claim.

Section 6

And be it further enacted, That when a person held to service or labor in any State or Territory of the United States, has heretofore or shall hereafter escape into another State or Territory of the United States, the person or persons to whom such service or labor may be due, or his, her, or their agent or attorney, duly authorized, by power of attorney, in writing, acknowledged and certified under the seal of some legal officer or court of the State or Territory in which the same may be executed, may pursue and reclaim such fugitive person, either by procuring a warrant from some one of the courts, judges, or commissioners aforesaid, of the proper circuit, district, or county, for the apprehension of such fugitive from service or labor, or by seizing and arresting such fugitive, where the same can be done without process, and by taking, or causing such person to be taken, forthwith before such court, judge, or commissioner, whose duty it shall be to hear and determine the case of such claimant in a summary manner; and upon satisfactory proof being made, by deposition or affidavit, in writing, to be taken and certified by such court, judge, or commissioner, or by other satisfactory testimony, duly taken and certified by some court, magistrate, justice of the peace, or other legal officer authorized to administer an oath and take depositions under the laws of the State or Territory from which such person owing service or labor may have escaped, with a certificate of such magistracy or other authority, as aforesaid, with the seal of the proper court or officer thereto attached, which seal shall be sufficient to establish the competency of the proof, and with proof, also by affidavit, of the identity of the person whose service or labor is claimed to be due as aforesaid, that the person so arrested does in fact owe service or labor to the person or persons claiming him or her, in the State or Territory from which such fugitive may have escaped as aforesaid, and that said person escaped, to make out and deliver to such claimant, his or her agent or attorney, a certificate setting forth the substantial facts as to the service or labor due from such fugitive to the claimant, and of his or her escape from the State or Territory in which he or she was arrested, with authority to such claim-ant, or his or her agent or attorney, to use such reasonable force and restraint as may be necessary, under the circumstances of the case, to take and remove such fugitive person back to the State or Territory whence he or she may have escaped as aforesaid. In no trial or hearing under this act shall the testimony of such alleged fugitive be admitted in evidence; and the certificates in this and the first [fourth] section mentioned, shall be conclusive of the right of the person or persons in whose favor granted, to remove such fugitive to the State or Territory from which he escaped, and shall prevent all molestation of such person or persons by any process issued by any court, judge, magistrate, or other person whomsoever.

Section 7

And be it further enacted, That any person who shall knowingly and willingly obstruct, hinder, or prevent such claimant, his agent or attorney, or any person or persons lawfully assisting him, her, or them, from arresting such a fugitive from service or labor, either with or without process as aforesaid, or shall rescue, or attempt to rescue, such fugitive from service or labor, from the custody of such claimant, his or her agent or attorney, or other person or persons lawfully assisting as aforesaid, when so arrested, pursuant to the authority herein given and declared; or shall aid, abet, or assist such person so owing service or labor as aforesaid, directly or indirectly, to escape from such claimant, his agent or attorney, or other person or persons legally authorized as aforesaid; or shall harbor or conceal such fugitive, so as to prevent the discovery and arrest of such person, after notice or knowledge of the fact that such person was a fugitive from service or labor as aforesaid, shall, for either of said offences, be subject to a fine not exceeding one thousand dollars, and imprisonment not exceeding six months, by indictment and conviction before the District Court of the United States for the district in which such offence may have been committed, or before the proper court of criminal jurisdiction, if committed within any one of the organized Territories of the United States; and shall moreover forfeit and pay, by way of civil damages to the party injured by such illegal conduct, the sum of one thousand dollars for each fugitive so lost as aforesaid, to be recovered by action of debt, in any of the District or Territorial Courts aforesaid, within whose jurisdiction the said offence may have been committed.

–The Avalon Project at Yale Law School

When Clemens wrote that there was nothing commonplace about Griffin he might have added that there was nothing commonplace about what Clemens expected of him, either. Griffin answered the door ("it takes George all of two minutes to answer the door-bell when he is in a hurry, and I have never seen him in a hurry"), and sorted the mail while the Clemenses were summering at Quarry Farm. He acted in family theatricals, served as court jester at the dinner table, and played horse, camel, or elephant for the Clemens children on African safaris. Aside from these regular duties Clemens called on Griffin to use his mollifying tongue in breaking up insurrections in the kitchen, to roar election returns and news reports through a speaking tube up to the billiard room during Clemens's stag parties, and to fire a revolver at three ruffians lurking on the lawn and yelling obscenities at Clemens. Apparently Griffin also served as a scapegoat. When Clemens began swearing on the telephone to a person he presumed was the operator, only to learn that the woman was actually a family friend, he persuaded her that she had just been talking with George and that Clemens would have to upbraid his butler for his indecent language.[13]

To put it mildly, Griffin was a butler in the loosest sense of the word. When he wasn't scapegoat he was, as Howells put it, Clemens's interpreter—that is, Clemens's liar. When Clemens told Griffin he would not come down from the billiard room to see the twelve apostles or the Holy Ghost, much less an unsolicited visitor who was hanging on the door, he expected Griffin to modify the curse to the point that the intruder would leave thinking that Clemens was on his deathbed. Clemens himself expressed satisfaction that he had trained Griffin to be a well-behaved, loyal, and lying sentinel, stationed at the front door to guard his master's privacy.

Yet Clemens also placed an uncommon amount of trust in Griffin, writing that he felt perfectly safe in discharging the police officer he had hired to prowl the premises for imaginary burglars, because he trusted Griffin to perform that task. Clemens also gave his butler, who did not drink, a key to the liquor cabinet and placed him in charge of seeing that the other servants did not raid it—for Clemens a remarkable sign of trust. Griffin, for his part, sometimes showed embarrassment over his employer's crudities of behavior. When Clemens gleefully treated several distinguished dinner guests to some cheap cigars that brought the evening to an abrupt close, Griffin reported with shame that the driveway was strewn with half-smoked "long-nines."[14]

If Clemens expected and received unusual service and loyalty from Griffin, he also credited him with unusual intelligence, especially in matters of finance

where Clemens, with good reason, was uncertain of his own prowess. In the election of 1884, when Clemens bolted the party (much to Griffin's disgust) and voted for Grover Cleveland, Griffin laid his usual heavy bets on the Republican candidate, James G. Blaine. When Blaine committed political suicide with his "Rum, Romanism, and Rebellion" speech, Griffin seemed headed for financial ruin. Instead he won handsomely by covering his bets three-to-one a few hours before the news of Blaine's disastrous speech reached the rest of Hartford. In addition to taking care of his own pocket, Griffin apparently "settled" several criminal cases involving blacks out of court; Clemens did not say how. He also conducted a thriving banking business in the black community at what Paine (who usually played back what Clemens told him) called ruinous interest. And when several of Hartford's elite citizens gathered at the Clemens home on Friday evenings to play billiards, Griffin detained them in deep and mysterious financial discussions in the front hall, which amused Clemens because as a Southerner be recognized that high-class Northerners enjoyed being milked by a black butler.[15]

Of all Griffin's endowments, the most aggravating for Clemens was his "disposition to gallantry" with black cooks in the kitchen. Griffin's unwillingness to adopt a hands-off policy led Clemens to screen his prospective cooks carefully. The principal requirement in a black cook (other than that she be "*tidy*–because when a colored cook *is* untidy she is likely to be intemperate in it") was that she be "old enough, or grave enough,– or above all, strong enough & wise enough, to resist George's fascinations." When Griffin threatened to live with his wife for a change if Clemens did not provide a cook to his taste, Clemens urged him to do just that. Finally things got to the point where Clemens had to issue a household ultimatum: there would be no more black cooks until Griffin experienced what Clemens tactfully called a change of heart.[16]

If Griffin occasionally taxed Clemens's patience, surely it was Griffin whose patience was usually more heavily taxed—and not only by the master of the house. Clemens's daughter Clara recruited Griffin to rattle and bang his "huge black paws" over the piano keys, because "he was the only person in the whole wide world I could hound into the misery of becoming my pupil." Susy Clemens, the oldest daughter, scolded Griffin for his gambling, and Livy sometimes did not "approve of George." According to Clara, the only time Griffin ever looked after anyone's needs was in the presence of guests, when he "could rise to great heights of professional service and throb with feverish excitement." Otherwise Griffin "explained that the intellec-

ANOTHER LITTLE JOB.

The duke with the poster he printed to deflect curiosity about Jim. "The reading was all about Jim," Huck writes, "and just described him to a dot" (drawing by E. W. Kemble; from Adventures of Huckleberry Finn, Mark Twain House, Hartford, Connecticut).

tual inspiration he received in the dining-room saved him from the bad effects of life in the inferior atmosphere of the kitchen." Closing her commentary on Griffin's dinnertime behavior, Clara added: "Often did we hear a prompt laugh filling the room from a dark figure at ease against the wall, before the rest of us at table had expressed our amusement at one of Father's remarks. George was a great addition to the family and afforded Father almost as much amusement as Father did George."[17]

Clemens amused Griffin in a variety of ways, but primarily by acting out the role of father-protector to an erring child. (He once told Howells that he kept a black butler because he could not bear to give orders to a white man.) When Griffin charged into Clemens's billiard study one day in a "high state of excitement" and demanded his employer's revolver to kill a black man with whom he was at odds, Clemens perceived at once that what Griffin needed was not a gun but a man of wisdom, stability, and high authority to talk him out of such a move. Accordingly Clemens slipped into the role

of august adviser, first feigning support for Griffin's violent plan to throw him offguard, then countering with "wise & righteous counsel" for a black man who had shown a "bad streak in him." Griffin went away convinced and converted.

Shortly after this episode Clemens was forced to discharge Griffin for financial reasons. By 1891 his household expenses had gotten so out of hand that he decided to cancel his subscription to *Harper's Magazine* and find a cheaper brand of toilet paper. When these two reductions proved insufficient, he decided to take his family into voluntary exile in Europe to cut down on domestic expenditures. Before he left he secured a position for Griffin as a waiter at the Union League Club in New York. On one of his numerous business trips back to the states during the family's nine-year stay abroad, Clemens sought Griffin out in New York, took him by the arm, and led him into the *Century* publishing house. Describing the episode later, he poked fun at the clerks who looked aghast at this unprecedented breach of etiquette. Glorying in the fact that everyone "took a sight of George & me," Clemens sought out the top editors and introduced them to Mr. Griffin; everyone but Clemens was embarrassed, and everyone but Clemens stopped talking. When the chief editor finally recovered, he asked Clemens to pass judgment on the quality of a certain manuscript they had just received ("You are just the man!"). Instead Clemens collared Griffin, who was decamping toward the door, and read a paragraph of the manuscript to him, asking him how the "literary quality of it struck him." Griffin gave his opinion and Clemens handed the manuscript back unread, stating that that was his opinion too.

Pleased with his performance, Clemens next led Griffin into the *St. Nicholas Magazine*'s editorial room down the street for an encore, this time asking Griffin for his opinion on a new cover design. Griffin complied and Clemens again endorsed his view. Again the ensuing conversation with the editors was not fluent, but Clemens left happy. Still later, on what proved to be a long day for Griffin, Clemens took him on a stroll through the streets for refreshments with a Mr. Carey of *St. Nicholas Magazine*. When Griffin dropped behind the two white men on the sidewalk, Clemens brought him forward and placed him between Carey and himself. When Griffin admitted that he had won six hundred dollars on a prize fight between a white man and a black by betting on the white man, and was challenged by Carey whether it was patriotic to bet against his color, Clemens credited Griffin with the proper reply for a New York businessman in 1893: "Betting is business, sir, patriotism is sentiment. They don't belong together. In politics I'm colored; in a bet I put up on *the best man,* I ain't particular about his paint. That white

"A Slaveholding Community"

Under the terms of the Missouri Compromise, Missouri was admitted to the Union in 1821 as a slave state to counterbalance Maine, which was admitted as a free state. As his recollections in his autobiographical writings make clear, young Samuel Clemens took the institution of slavery for granted and seldom questioned it. His uncle John Quarles owned several slaves and his own family from time to time owned a slave. The sight of cruelty to slaves engendered confusion and sadness in the boy, but not the fierce moral outrage he came to feel many years later. Even so, the fact of slavery and the complacency with which his friends and family accepted it left him with an enduring sense of shame and guilt. He later called the blithe acceptance of the unacceptable the "lie of silent assertion."

In this excerpt from a sketch of his mother, Jean Langhorne Clemens, Mark Twain examines the attitudes toward slavery in the Hannibal of his youth.

As I have said, we lived in a slaveholding community; indeed, when slavery perished, my mother had been in daily touch with it for sixty years. Yet, kind-hearted and compassionate as she was, I think she was not conscious that slavery was a bald, grotesque and unwarrantable usurpation. She had never heard it assailed in any pulpit but had heard it defended and sanctified in a thousand; her ears were familiar with Bible texts that approved it but if there were any that disapproved it they had not been quoted by her pastors; as far as her experience went, the wise and the good and the holy were unanimous in the conviction that slavery was right, righteous, sacred, the peculiar pet of the Deity and a condition which the slave himself ought to be daily and nightly thankful for. Manifestly, training and association can accomplish strange miracles. As a rule our slaves were convinced and content. So doubtless are the far more intelligent slaves of a monarchy; they revere and approve their masters, the monarch and the noble, and recognize no degradation in the fact that they are slaves—slaves with the name blinked, and less respectworthy than were our black ones, if to be a slave by meek consent is baser than to be a slave by compulsion—and doubtless it is.

However, there was nothing about the slavery of the Hannibal region to rouse one's dozing humane instincts to activity. It was the mild domestic slavery, not the bru-

tal plantation article. Cruelties were very rare and exceedingly and wholesomely unpopular. To separate and sell the members of a slave family to different masters was a thing not well liked by the people and so it was not often done, except in the settling of estates. I have no recollection of ever seeing a slave auction in that town; but I am suspicious that that is because the thing was a common and commonplace spectacle, not an uncommon and impressive one. I vividly remember seeing a dozen black men and women chained to one another, once, and lying in a group on the pavement, awaiting shipment to the southern slave market. Those were the saddest faces I have ever seen. Chained slaves could not have been a common sight or this picture would not have made so strong and lasting an impression upon me.

The "nigger trader" was loathed by everybody. He was regarded as a sort of human devil who bought and conveyed poor helpless creatures to hell—for to our whites and blacks alike the southern plantation was simply hell; no milder name could describe it. If the threat to sell an incorrigible "down the river" would not reform him, nothing would—his case was past cure. Yet I remember that once when a white man killed a Negro man for a trifling little offence everybody seemed indifferent about it—as regarded the slave—though considerable sympathy was felt for the slave's owner, who had been bereft of valuable property by a worthless person who was not able to pay for it.

It is commonly believed that an infallible effect of slavery was to make such as lived in its midst hard-hearted. I think it had no such effect—speaking in general terms. I think it stupefied everybody's humanity as regarded the slave, but stopped here. There were no hardhearted people in our town—I mean there were no more than would be found in any other town of the same size in any other country; and in my experience hardhearted people are very rare everywhere.

—The Autobiography of Mark Twain, edited by
Charles Neider (New York:
Harper, 1959), pp. 32–33

man had a record; so had the coon, but 'twas watered." At the end of the day's entertainment, Carey and Clemens agreed that Griffin was, indeed, "no commonplace coon."

The publishing house episode takes up most of the nonfiction sketch Clemens wrote about Griffin. But this black man also appears in two highly dissimilar pieces of fiction. The last and most revealing is a nightmare tale called "The Great Dark" written in 1898. The other is a story called "Wapping Alice," supposedly

about a female servant who turns out to be a man ("why he unsexed himself was his own affair") but actually starring Griffin in the lead role as a black servant named George, who is employed by an author named Mark.

In "Wapping Alice" Mark Twain played upon two contradictory qualities in George's character—one commendable, the other deplorable. The commendable quality was George's lively interest in family affairs, which Mark Twain took pains to explain: Griffin was "an institution—he was a *part* of us, not an excrescence—we had a great affection for him, and he for us; when he said to people 'my family' he meant *my* family, not his."[18] Yet in striking contrast to everything Clemens ever said about the nonfictional Griffin, the most conspicuous trait of the fictional George is not his loyalty but his vanity and selfishness. In "Wapping Alice" George is a master of deceit. When the family leaves town, relying on George to take care of the house and grounds, he leads the entire brigade of servants off on a week-long excursion to the Northampton horse races and manages to keep the news about his negligence as a caretaker from leaking out. But when "Mark" returns and puts George on the spot, the black man tries to lie his way out, first insisting that he always sets the burglar alarm before departing on excursions, then gradually crumbling under Mark's relentless interrogation until he admits that he rarely, if ever, sets the alarm. The longer Mark plays the role of cunning detective the more George resorts to desperate rationalization: the mere *presence* of a burglar alarm, he assures his employer, is enough to discourage burglars. There is no need to turn it on.[19]

In "Wapping Alice" George is not only irresponsible; he is greedy. When Mark reminds him that the house could have been burglarized while George was off on an excursion, the black man pales "to the hue of old amber" (in the "Family Sketch" he bleaches "to the tint of new leather")[20] and bounds upstairs to make sure his private cache of fifteen hundred dollars is still hidden between his "mattrasses." Mark, a bit put out over his butler's lack of concern for the safety of his master's property, accuses George of betting fifteen hundred dollars on the sweeping effects of a "religious epidemic" in the African Methodist Episcopal Church and pocketing the results. The charge pricks the black man's conscience badly, and leads Mark to pour it on: "I could see that that wounded him—poor old George . . . it was a sore spot with [him] . . . but as he never went quite far enough to say it was a lie, and as he was something of a purist in language, this subtle discrimination was noticed by the family, to his damage. Out of love, they did not twit him with it; but out of love, I did—and rubbed it in, sometimes."[21]

Out of love Clemens rubbed a bewildering variety of experiences into Griffin; still there can be no question that butler and boss exchanged a good deal of affection and respect. Griffin's feelings for the family are brought out clearly in a letter he wrote to Clara from New York in 1893, two years after he left Clemens's employ:

Miss Clara I have almost lost sight of Hartford it seems so long since we were there and like yourself I am having such a good time here. . . . Now Miss Clara don't think that I have lost sight of the old family, for that cannot be, for life is too short. . . . One year ago I did miss you all so mutch but today I feel at home in New York and I am glad to say that I am happy. . . . Now Miss Clara I am going to ask one favor of you and this is this, please write me a letter so I can have it to read Christmas morning. I will enjoy it so much and it will be so home like and all I want it to caust you, is the time that it will take to write and a five cent stamp.

You don't know how I enjoy looking at your Pictures Sundays when I am off and it seems as tho I was in Hartford and not in New York.

. . . In spring I think I shall go to work on the rail road if I can get a parlor car that runs out west. I want to see the west very much. . . .

From your old Servant

"George."[22]

On his global lecture tour in 1895 Clemens jotted in his notebook that Australia, "with its specialties of piety & horse-racing, would be heaven for George" and added a reminder to tell all about his butler in a future article. He never got around to it. On June 2, 1897, he scribbled tersely in his London notebook that Griffin was dead.[23]

The most striking part of the story of George Griffin is not Griffin himself, but the similarities between Griffin and Nigger Jim. Both are large, intelligent, argumentative, grand "distorters of the truth," sentimental, polite, usually "cheerful to gaiety," deeply religious, and profoundly loyal to white folks. In the nineteenth-century spectrum of black characters depicted by whites, they stand together somewhere between Harriet Beecher Stowe's complacent Uncle Tom and George Washington Cable's savage Bras Coupé. Both Griffin and Nigger Jim are noble when locked into civilized environment; both are noble when released into a state of nature: Jim on the river, Griffin at sea in his last fictional appearance in "The Great Dark."

Even more striking are the similarities between Huck and Jim on the one hand, and Clemens and Griffin on the other. Early in *Huckleberry Finn* Huck's relationship with Jim is marred by the boy's lack of compassion and sensitivity, which eventually brings him to remorse and apology. Clemens's association with Griffin was sometimes marred by callousness which led to regret and, occasionally, to defending Griffin against criticism by other members of the family.[24] We also recall that Huck tries to explain Jim's goodness by the fact that be must be white inside; Clemens

*Mark Twain in Elmira, New York, with John Lewis, one of the men who influenced the author's
characterization of Jim (Elmira College Library)*

reversed the color scheme by calling Griffin "as good as
he was black." Both Huck and Clemens were fond of
commenting on the unswerving loyalty of their black
companions: Huck is flabbergasted and embarrassed
by Jim's declarations of affection; Clemens was flattered
and awed by Griffin's affirmations of devotion. Above
all both Huck and Clemens were careful to point out
that their black charges were unusual people and not
necessarily to be confused with the rest of their race.
Huck repeatedly calls Jim an uncommon nigger; Clemens insisted that his relationship with Griffin was
wholly proper, because Griffin was by no means a
"commonplace coon."

It is this precarious up-and-down relationship,
alternating between compassion and callousness, companionship and rivalry, that makes George Griffin's last
fictional appearance memorable. Mark Twain's late and
shattering story entitled "The Great Dark" is at once a
fitting end to Griffin's career and the best possible point
of departure for a discussion of Nigger Jim and Huck in
Huckleberry Finn.

Toward the close of the century Mark Twain took
himself on one of the dream voyages that litter his last
manuscripts. While looking through a microscope one
evening at a drop of rainwater (to which he has added
some whiskey to stir up the microbes) a man named
Edwards, alias Clemens, gets bored and falls asleep.
During his nap a dark-clothed Satanic figure disguised
as the Superintendent of Dreams appears from nowhere
awakens Edwards, and offers to take his entire family
on a long pleasure excursion inside the drop of rainwater. Edwards agrees and sails off with his wife Alice
(Livy) and their two daughters, one named Susy and
born on the same day as Susy Clemens, who died six
years before the story. What begins as fantasy turns
into nightmare as the family is cast adrift on a haunted
ship strewn with dead or dying passengers. For ten
years the derelict ship plows through a pitch-dark Ant-
arctic wasteland, dodging icebergs and chasing another
phantom ship that has kidnapped Susy and remains just
beyond reach. To compound the difficulties, whales
with "hairy spidery legs" feed on each other and

threaten to overturn the ship and devour the passengers. Before they die, most of the passengers go mad.

At the outset of the story the Edwardses' servant George[25] (an ex-slave like Griffin) is little more than a chuckling stage darky who bares white fangs in huge grins, says "Bless yo' soul, honey" to Alice, and hardly seems aware that a nightmare is going on. When he reminds Edwards that it is time for their daily boxing exercise on board ship, Edwards responds with the kind of "solid good cussing" that Clara Clemens remembered as the way her father "explained things to George." Edwards finally agrees to box, however. In the sixth round of a lively fight he knocks the big, brawny black man out cold.

It is not likely that Clemens, who once compared his biceps with an oyster wrapped in a rag,[26] ever tested his strength against George Griffin's. But the incident momentarily throws *us* off balance by suggesting that Clemens may have fantasized about such a vicarious physical victory over Griffin. Actually the final message of this story is not hostility but friendship. In striking contrast to his role in "Wapping Alice" George plays the role of hero in "The Great Dark." When an octopus threatens to swallow the ship, he rescues the Edwards children by hiding them in the hold; and we are reminded that John Lewis saved the Langdon children by stopping a runaway horse and that Nigger Jim saves Tom Sawyer from blood poisoning in *Huckleberry Finn* by insisting that Huck go for a doctor after Tom is shot in the "evasion."

After a decade of aimless wandering, the phantom ship comes to a dead stop as the sea begins to boil and to turn into molten brass—dried up by the merciless white light from the microscope lamp. The compasses spin crazily, the surviving crew mutinies, spider-quids attack and consume the surviving passengers, and it becomes George's duty to inform Edwards that his wife and children are dead.[27] In the last scene of this grim story two human beings are left on the planet—Edwards (an adult Huck) and George (a late Jim), sitting and consoling each other in the middle of nothing. The fetching image of Huck and Nigger Jim squatting together in peace and contentment on a sandbar, watching the dawn spread over the river and listening to the sounds of a waking world, has been replaced by two old men imprisoned in a wasteland called the Great White Glare. In the last decade of his life, fifteen years after finishing *Huckleberry Finn*, Mark Twain left one black and one white to share one another's company, briefly, before the snuffing out of the human race.

> *—Mark Twain & the South* (Lexington:
> University Press of Kentucky,
> 1974), pp. 93–106

1. *Autobiography [Mark Twain's Autobiography]* 1: 263; "Wapping Alice," Autobiographical Dictation, April 9, 1907, typescript, DV 344a, p. 1951, Mark Twain Papers [MTP].

2. See chapter 1 and pp. 45–47 above, for remarks about Uncle Daniel. Scholars have customarily regarded Uncle Daniel as the chief, if not the sole, source of Nigger Jim, probably because of Mark Twain's inspired but vague recollections of Uncle Daniel in the *Autobiography*. Orion, ten years older than Sam, thought his brother confused Uncle Daniel of Quarles Farm with one of Marshall Clemens's Hannibal slaves (*Letters*, 2: 403, n. 1).

3. Aside from Lewis's role as Uncle Rastus Timson in "Refuge of the Derelicts," I believe that the character of Dan'l in *The American Claimant* (published in 1892 but largely written in the 1870s) is a composite portrait of Uncle Daniel of *The Gilded Age* and John Lewis, especially in the kitchen squabbling episode between Daniel (Lewis) and Jinny (Aunty Cord).

4. Samuel Langhorne Clemens [SLC] to William Dean Howells [Howells], August 9, 1876; August 25–27, 1877, *Mark Twain-Howells Letters* [MTHL], 1: 144, 194–99. Mrs. Theodore Crane, Livy's foster-sister, owned the farm. Her brother Charles Langdon and his children were in the cart.

5. Off and on, the list included Anson Burlingame (later ambassador to China, whom Clemens met in the Sandwich Islands in 1866), Louis Napoleon III, Cecil Rhodes (for a while), Bret Harte (for a very short while), Ulysses S. Grant, and Henry H. Rogers, the Standard Oil millionaire who rescued Clemens from bankruptcy in the 1890s and the only man whom Clemens consistently called "Mr."

6. SLC to Dr. John Brown, included by Rogers as an appendix to *Simon Wheeler, Detective*, pp. 169–75.

7. Paine thought Clemens's Southern upbringing gave him special understanding of black "humors" and of their "native emotions" (*Biography*, 2: 515).

8. SLC to Joel Chandler Harris, December 12, 1881, *Letters*, 1: 403; Paine, *Biography*, 2: 599–600.

9. Mark Twain, "Refuge of the Derelicts," typescript, p. 156, MTP, published in Tuckey, ed., *Mark Twain's Fables of Man*, but not issued before this study was submitted for publication; hence I cite the typescript pages. In his notes for the story Mark Twain specifically identified Aunty Phyllis as "Cord" who told "the 'True Story,'" and Rastus as the man who "saved the Langdons, 28 yrs ago" (p. 3). There are at least four extant photos of Clemens and Lewis at Quarry Farm . . . but none to my knowledge of George Griffin.

10. "Refuge of the Derelicts," typescript, pp. 109–14, 116–17, 128, 135, 158, 171–76, 178–81, MTP. Mark Twain tried two more times to make the horse-jerking episode work—once in *Simon Wheeler, Detective*, where the hero of the deed is white, and once in a section deleted from *Pudd'nhead Wilson*.

11. Lewis lived until 1906 on a pension provided first by Clemens and then, when Clemens went bankrupt, by Henry H. Rogers (Paine, *Biography*, 2: 600). When Lewis died, Clemens scribbled his usual obituary: "Poor Lewis

is dead, & I am so glad he is set free" (SLC to Clara Clemens, July 27, 1906; MTP, Letter File).

12. *Autobiography,* 1: 296; 2: 60–61; Paine, *Biography,* 2: 573; SLC to Professor Lounsbury, July 21, 1904, MTP, Letter File; *What Is Man?* p. 119. Unless otherwise cited, the information on Griffin in this chapter is taken from Clemens's "Family Sketch," typescript, pp. 7–32, MTP.

13. "Mental Telegraphy," *Harriet Shelley,* p. 136; SLC to Jean Clemens, January 11, 26, 1907, MTP, Letter File; SLC to Karl Gerhardt, May 13, 1891, MTP, Letter File; Paine, *Biography,* 2: 778; 3: 838; Mary Lawton, *A Lifetime with Mark Twain: Memories of Katy Leary* (New York, 1925), pp. 32, 99.

14. *Autobiography,* 1: 298.

15. SLC to "Brer [Frank] Whitmore," August 4, 1889, MTP, Letter File; SLC to Howells, October 11, 1876, MTHL, 1: 158; SLC to Livy Clemens, July 17, n.d., MTP, Letter File; Clara Clemens, *My Father Mark Twain* (New York, 1931), p. 211.

16. Typescript Notebook 15, p. 6, MTP; SLC to Joseph Twichell, October 2, 1879, MTP, Letter File.

17. Clara Clemens, *My Father Mark Twain,* pp. 27–28, 110, 212.

18. "Wapping Alice," Autobiographical Dictation, April 9, 1907, typescript, DV 344a, p. 1948, MTP.

19. Ibid., pp. 1951–52, 1954, MTP.

20. In "Those Extraordinary Twins" a "fool-hearted Negro wench" named Nancy reacts to her first sight of Siamese twins by paling to chocolate, then to off-orange, and finally to amber (*Pudd'nhead Wilson,* p. 279).

21. "Wapping Alice," pp. 1952–53, MTP.

22. Clara Clemens, *My Father Mark Twain,* pp. 110–12.

23. Typescript Notebook 28, p. 30, MTP. "Write Geo Griffin for Forum" and several other comparable entries can be found in Typescript Notebooks 32, p. 12; 32 (I), p. 8; 32a (I), p. 29; 32a (II), pp. 42, 46; and 32b (I), pp. 18, 21, MTP.

24. Paine, *Biography,* 2: 573.

25. Griffin accompanied the Clemenses on an Atlantic voyage to England and the Continent in April 1878 (Kaplan, *Mr. Clemens and Mark Twain,* p. 212).

26. "Taming the Bicycle," *What Is Man?* p. 291.

27. "The Great Dark," Tuckey, *Which Was the Dream?* pp. 102–50.

* * *

Mark Twain prided himself on the variety and accuracy of Mississippi valley dialects in Huckleberry Finn. *His "Working Notes" reveal how meticulously he tried to recall and reproduce authentic speech patterns. Although some critics and readers regard his prefatory claim to dialectical accuracy as exaggerated or as something of a hoax, David Carkeet demonstrates such a suspicion is unfounded.*

Note: Carkeet in part relies on Walter Blair's 1958 essay "When was Huckleberry Finn Written?"—which the most recent scholarship suggests was in error regarding some particulars of the dating of Twain's work on his manuscript. Carkeet's conclusions, however, are not undermined.

The Dialects in *Huckleberry Finn*
David Carkeet

Mark Twain's "Explanatory" preface to *Adventures of Huckleberry Finn* is straightforward enough:

In this book a number of dialects are used, to wit: the Missouri negro dialect; the extremest form of the backwoods South-Western dialect; the ordinary "Pike-County" dialect; and four modified varieties of this last. The shadings have not been done in a hap-hazard fashion, or by guesswork; but pains-takingly, and with the trustworthy guidance and support of personal familiarity with these several forms of speech.

I make this explanation for the reason that without it many readers would suppose that all these characters were trying to talk alike and not succeeding.[1]

Yet an apparent lack of fit between this announcement and the linguistic facts of the novel has long confounded investigators trying to decide just who speaks what dialect. Some have given up the fight and concluded that the preface is a joke. Others have taken the preface seriously but have still failed to decode it.[2] The question of what Clemens meant with the preface is a complex one divisible into several parts: (1) Does a close linguistic analysis of the speech of the characters in the novel show the seven-way dialectal differentiation of which Clemens speaks? (2) What did the preface mean to Clemens? That is, in his lexicon what was the meaning of "dialect," "extremest," "backwoods South-Western," and "ordinary 'Pike County'"? (3) When Clemens wrote the preface, what could he have thought he had done in the way of differentiating dialects? This question is distinct from (1) above, for Clemens's sense of the language of the novel may have been different from the linguistic facts of the novel. (4) Finally, what is the relation between the dialects in the novel and linguistic reality of the Mississippi Valley in the mid-nineteenth century? The first three of these questions will be taken up below. The last question, because it has been dealt with elsewhere and because answering it sheds little light on the meaning of the preface, will not be treated.[3]

It is a characteristic flaw of published research in dialectology to dwell ponderously on methodological preliminaries. Eschewing this practice—which exists, I think, to disguise leanness in the body of many studies of dialects—I will not discuss here the notion of "literary dialect."[4] I will say only that dialects—in literature and out in the field—can differ from each other in their pronunciation (Huck says *get,* Pap says *git*), grammar (Huck says *you want,* Jim says *you wants*), and vocabulary or lexicon (Huck says *smouch* for 'steal,' the King says *hook*).

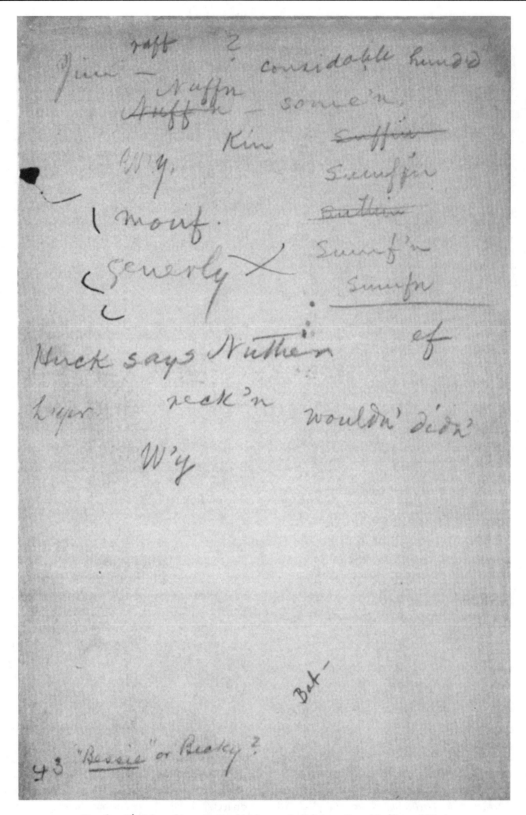

*Page from Twain's working notes in which he records dialect words used by Jim and Huck
(Mark Twain Papers, The Bancroft Library, University of California, Berkeley)*

As to the first question raised above, a detailed examination of *Huckleberry Finn* shows that there are differences in the way people speak that are too systematic to be accidental. For purposes of discussion, Huck's dialect can be taken as the norm from which other dialects, to varying degrees, depart. This approach, besides being convenient, makes sense precisely because our goal is to understand the author's intention. Since Clemens wrote the novel in Huck's dialect, that dialect must have been uppermost in his mind. In a sense it is the "standard" dialect of the novel. Systematic departures from that dialect must, then, reflect conscious choices by the author. Given this approach, it is not necessary to list the hundreds of features distinguishing Huck's dialect from Standard English.[5] Instead, I will focus on the departures from Huck's dialect in the speech of the other characters.

First, there is an obvious difference between the speech of Jim (and the four other black speakers in the novel, whose dialects are identical with Jim's) and that of Huck. Phonologically, Jim shows widespread loss of *r* (*do'* 'door,' *heah* 'here,' *thoo* 'through'), palatalization (i.e., the insertion of a palatal glide–the initial sound of *yes*–in certain environments: *k'yer* 'care,' *dish-yer* 'this here'), (a) *gwyne* as the present participle of *go,* and substitution of voiceless *th* with *f* (*mouf* 'mouth'), of voiced *th* with *d* (*dese* 'these'), and of the negative prefix *un-* with *on-* (*oneasy*). Huck has none of these features. Also, where Huck and Jim share a rule producing nonstandard forms, Jim's use of the rule is much higher in frequency. This holds for final consonant cluster reduction (*ole* 'old'), deletion of initial unstressed syllables (*'crease* 'increase'), and epithetic *t* (*wunst* 'once'). Jim also shows much more eye dialect (nonstandard spellings for standard pronunciations, like *uv* 'of' and *wuz* 'was') than Huck. Grammatically, Huck's and Jim's dialects are very similar. However, Jim's dialect additionally shows the *done*-perfect construction (*she done broke loose),* deletion of the copula, and an *-s* suffix on second-person present-tense verbs. Lexically, Jim's dialect differs from Huck's only in a few exclamations: Jim says *dad-blamedest, dad fetch him,* and *ding-busted,* and Huck does not.

The differences between Huck's dialect and the dialects of the other white characters in the novel are less striking but still significant. As in the treatment of Jim's dialect, these differences will be presented in terms of nonstandard features exhibited in the speech of others (Pap, the King, etc.) that are *not* exhibited in Huck's dialect. This approach rather than the reverse is taken because Huck's corpus is much larger than the corpora of the other characters,

and nonoccurrence of a form in a large body of data is more significant than nonoccurrence in a small body of data. That is, it cannot be maintained that the features below fail to appear in Huck's dialect because there is insufficient occasion for them to appear. Rather, they fail to appear because Clemens more than likely chose not to make them a characteristic of Huck's dialect.

The lists below are arranged as follows. Characters are given in order of appearance in the novel. Under each character's name are given the features of phonology, grammar, and lexicon that distinguish that dialect from Huck's, i.e., features of which there is no evidence in Huck's corpus.[6] The three categories are separated by lines of ellipses; if no grammatical or lexical features distinguish the dialect from Huck's, a dash is entered. In the phonology section of each dialect I have listed the features in descending order of importance (by frequency and salience, the latter being a subjective impression). Items subject to the same phonological rule (e.g., the King's palatalization) are listed across the same line. Items subject to a rule evidenced in Huck's dialect are not given, even though the particular word in question may not appear in the data from Huck; for example, Pap says *'lection* 'election,' showing a rule deleting initial unstressed syllables, and although Huck never says *'lection,* it is clear from spellings like *'low* 'allow' and *'deed* 'indeed' that he has the same rule. Consequently, *'lection* is not given as a distinguishing feature of Pap's dialect.[7] An asterisk means that the form fails to appear in any other white dialect in the novel, that is, that the form is unique to the dialect under whose name it is entered. The number in parentheses indicates the number of instances of a form. The few examples of eye dialect and idioms in these dialects are not given.

Some of the identifying names below need an explanation. Judith Loftus is the Illinois woman whom Huck tries to fool with his girl's disguise; *"Sir Walter Scott"* refers to the dialect spoken by the three thieves on the wreck of that name; "Raftsmen" refers to the dialect of the six speakers in the "Raft Passage," which was first published in *Life on the Mississippi* (chapter 3) and was part of *Huckleberry Finn* (in chapter 16) when Clemens sent the manuscript to his publisher;[8] the Bricksville Loafers are the tobacco-chewing sluggards (nine or ten different speakers) in the town where Colonel Sherburn shoots Boggs; and the Arkansas Gossips are Sister Hotchkiss et al. (five identifiable speakers), who discuss Jim's strange housekeeping on the Phelps plantation.[9]

Pap
**p'fessor (1)
*suthin' (something, 1)
agin (2), git (3)
o' (of, 5)
fitten (fitting, 1)
wust (worst, 1)

. . . .

—

. . . .

*big-bug (big shot, 1)
*hifalutin' (1)
*palaver (talk, 1)
*pungle (pay, 1)

Judith Loftus
*sence (since, 3)
*cheer (chair, 1)
ben (been, 1)

. . . .

—

. . . .

—

Sir Walter Scott[10]
*orter (ought to, 1)
forgit (1), git (2), yit (2)
jest (1), jist (4)
befo' (1), yo' (1)
shore (sure, 1)
't (that: *conj.,* 1)
wrack (wreck, 1)

. . . .

—

. . . .

*pickins (transportables, 1)
*unfavorable to (opposed to, 1)

Raftsmen
*furder (further, 1)
*Sent Louis (1)
*yander (yonder, 1)
bar'l (barrel, 4), thar (there, 2), whar (where, 1)
oncomfortable (1), oneasy (1)
tech (1)

. . . .

ye (1)

. . . .

*jigger (jerk, 1)
*squench (suppress, 1)
*whoo-oop (*exclamation,* 7)

King
*h-yer (here, 2), k'yer (care, 2), these-'yer (these here, 2), thish-yer (this here, 1)
*considable (1), misable (1)
*he'p (2)
*aluz (always, 1)
*drot (drat, 1)
*partickler (1)
agin (2), forgit (1), git (4), yisterday (1), yit (1)
jest (4), jist (2), sech (3), sich (1), shet (1)
oncomfortable (1), oncommon (1), oneasy (1)
thar (1), whar (2)
'at (that: *conj.,* 1; *rel. pro.,* 2)
ben (been, 2)
fitten (fitting, 2)
o' (of, 2)
out'n (out of, 2)
pore (poor, 2)
wisht (wish, 2)
hunderd (1)

. . . .

ye (1)

. . . .

*holt (specialty, 1)
*hook (steal, 1)

Bricksville Loafers
*(a) gwyne (going, 5)
*borry (borrow, 2)
*awready (1)
*cain't (1)
*wunst (once, 1)
thar (2), whar (1)
ben (been, 1)
f'm (from, 1)
jedge (1)
off'n (off of, 1)
waw-path (warpath, 1)
wisht (wish, 1)

. . . .

—

. . . .

—

Aunt Sally and Uncle Silas Phelps
*owdacious (audacious, 2)
*clo'es (clothes, 1)
*Newrleans (1)
*reely (1)
't (that: *conj.,* 3)
childern (1), hunderd (1)
Babtist (1)
shet (1)
shore (sure, 1)

. . . .

ye (3)
. . . .
*bang (surpass, 1)
*beat (that which surpasses, 3)
*Old Harry (devil, 1)
*pass (point, juncture, 1)
Sister, Brother (*forms of address,* 2)

Arkansas Gossips
*s'I (says I, 26), sh-she (says she, 4), s'e (says he, 3)
*that-air (that there, 6)
*Brer (brother, 4)
*amost (almost, 1)
*kiver (cover, 1)
*natcherl (natural, 1)
*sasser (saucer, 1)
jist (2), sich (2)
ben (been, 2)
out'n (out of, 2)
't (that: *conj.,* 1; *rel. pro.,* 1)
fust (first, 1)
git (1)
thar (1)
they (there: *expletive,* 1)
. . . .
hearn (heard: *preterite,* 1)
ye (1)
. . . .
Sister, Brother (*forms of address,* 14)

This list shows real dialectal differences. It is surely no accident that in the entire novel only one group of white speakers (the Bricksville Loafers) uses the typically black *(a) gwyne* participle, or that the King shows palatalization seven times, or that Sister Hotchkiss utters a reduced form of *says* thirty-three times in her brief appearance. In the light of facts like these, Rulon's claim in his dissertation (p. 50) and again in "Geographical Delimitation" (p. 12) that there are only two dialects in the novel, one spoken by blacks and the other by whites, is quite remarkable.

When we add Huck's dialect to the above list, we have nine distinct dialects spoken by white characters, whereas Clemens names only six in the preface. How can we identify the six dialects Clemens had in mind? The degree of divergence from Huck's dialect will certainly play some role, however elusive the principles involved in assessing this may be. One such principle is that asterisked (i.e., unique) forms must weigh heavily in marking a dialect as divergent. A second principle is that phonological features must weigh more heavily than lexical features, because a lexical omission in Huck's dialect is more likely to be accidental than the absence of a phonological feature, and because lexical

choices often reflect a personality more than a dialect— Pap says "hifalutin'" not only because of where he was born but also because of who he is. Third, phonological rules affecting a class weigh more heavily than phonological rules affecting just one word. The sheer number of differences or of words exhibiting a difference is a fourth consideration. Finally, some of these characters speak more than others and thus have greater occasion to exhibit dialectal features different from Huck's; the more a character speaks, the more features distinct from Huck's he must show in order for us to consider his dialect markedly different from Huck's. A precise formula expressing "density" of features could easily be worked out, such rigor would be foolish in the light of the subjective nature of our other considerations.

On the basis of these criteria, then, I would rank the eight dialects roughly in the following order, the dialect of the Arkansas Gossips being least like Huck's, and Judith Loftus's dialect being most like Huck's: Arkansas Gossips, King, Bricksville Loafers, Aunt Sally and Uncle Silas, Raftsmen, *Sir Walter Scott,* Pap, and Judith Loftus. What we have here is the beginning of a conclusion. But our notion "degree of divergence from Huck's dialect" is not sufficiently exact to allow us simply to subtract the last three dialects (or to say they are subspecies of Huck's dialect) and to declare the problem solved. Straight linguistic analysis of the novel takes us only so far. We now must turn our attention to the other questions raised in the opening paragraph.

What could Clemens have meant by "the extremest form of the backwoods South-Western dialect"? The Old Southwest is of course a geographical region into which Huck and Jim move more deeply as the novel progresses. In this respect, characters appearing far down the river are more likely to be speakers of this dialect than, say, Pap or Judith Loftus, residents of St. Petersburg. "Southwestern" also has a literary meaning which is equally important to our question. Clemens was closely familiar with the antebellum literature of Southwestern humorists like George Washington Harris, Johnson J. Hooper, and William Tappan Thompson, both from his general reading and from his editing of *Mark Twain's Library of Humor,* which he worked on for several years before its publication in 1888.[11] Clemens drew from this tradition in his portrayal of the King, a typical Southwestern confidence man whose "conversion" at the camp meeting in chapter 20 recalls that of Hooper's roguish Simon Suggs in "The Captain Attends a Camp-Meeting." The "Raft Passage" shows a similar indebtedness, with its boasting and brawling raftsmen, among them one "from the wilds of Arkansaw," and its spinners of tall tales—characters reminiscent of A. B. Longstreet and Thomas Bangs Thorpe. On these grounds, then, one might be tempted to iden-

FALLING FROM GRACE.

"COME IN."

"HAND OUT THEM LETTERS.

Three of the characters Twain may have had in mind as speakers of "the ordinary 'Pike-County' dialect": Huck's father; Judith Loftus, the Illinois woman who is visited by Huck disguised as a girl; and Tom's aunt Polly, who must "traipse all the way down the river eleven hundred mile" to find out what her nephew is up to "this time" (drawings by E. W. Kemble; from Adventures of Huckleberry Finn, *Mark Twain House, Hartford, Connecticut)*

tify the King or the Raftsmen as speakers of the Southwestern dialect. But the Southwestern humorists also provide us with orthographic criteria with which to make this judgment, for many of them wrote in heavy dialect whose features no doubt impressed Clemens. These criteria point clearly to Sister Hotchkiss and the other Arkansas Gossips as the Southwestern dialect speakers. Sister Hotchkiss's and Mrs. Damrell's unique *that-air* 'that there' appears, spelled *that air, that ere,* or *that ar,* in the sketches of Harris, Hooper, and Thorpe, the last also giving his characters the plural counterpart, *them ar* 'them there.' Brother Marples's *kiver* 'cover' is also used by Simon Suggs, and Sister Hotchkiss's *natcherl,* whatever pronunciation it is meant to indicate, brings to mind the reduced form in Sut Lovingood's recurring epithet, "a nat'ral born durn'd fool." The Arkansas Gossips also show lowering and backing of /ɛr/ to /ɑr/ *(thar),* neutralization of /I/ and /ɛ/ *(git),* and selective loss of /r/ with schwa *(fust* 'first'); all of these features are easily found in Southwestern tales.

Finally, when Sister Hotchkiss says *s'I* 'says I,' *s'e* 'says he,' and *sh-she* 'says she,' she uses a form that has some precedent, particularly in its rhythmic repetition, in stories by some of the writers mentioned above (compare her "s'I, he's crazy, s'I" with "says I, 'Bill,' says I, 'you're an ass,'" from Thorpe's "The Big Bear of Arkansas"). A more direct inspiration, however, appears to be Joel Chandler Harris's "At Teague Poteet's: A Sketch of the Hog Mountain Range," where we find dozens of occurrences of *s'I* 'says I' and *se'she* 'says she,' along with *Sister* as a form of address and *that air* 'that there.'[12] Modern literary historians view the Southwestern school as an antebellum phenomenon, but there is no reason to believe that Clemens did. Linguistically and artistically many of Harris's characters can be seen as "Southwestern." In borrowing these linguistic forms for this scene, as well as the *Brer* of the earlier Uncle Remus stories, Clemens shows his respect for Harris, whom he rightly considered a master of dialect writing. Clemens apparently drew more than dialect from Harris's story. A working note written by him in the summer of 1883 says, "He [Huck] must hear some Arkansas women, over their pipes & knitting (spitting from between teeth), swap reminiscences of Sister this & Brother that . . . " At the end of this note, added later without comment, is "s'I, sh-she, s'ze." A group of gossips very similar to that described here appears in "At Teague Poteet's," and they appear to be the inspiration for Clemens's Arkansas Gossips.[13]

No other speaker or group of speakers in *Huckleberry Finn* shows so many features that also appear in the works of the Southwestern humorists. The Arkansas Gossips reside at the southern extremity of the novel, so they meet the geographical test as well. Their speech is more dense in dialect than that of the other white speakers in the novel, and it is probably for this reason that Clemens calls it the "extremest" form of the Southwestern dialect. In this scene as in no other Clemens has Huck step aside and for eight paragraphs of speech shows us rich local linguistic color.

If this much is correct we are left with eight white dialects in the novel: Huck, Pap, Judith Loftus, *Sir Walter Scott,* Raftsmen, King, Bricksville Loafers, and Aunt Sally and Uncle Silas. However, "the ordinary 'Pike-County' dialect" and "four modified varieties" of it means that three of these dialects must be disregarded or subsumed under another dialect. Which three?

We must first determine what "Pike County" meant to Clemens. In his fiction it is the Missouri county in which St. Petersburg is located, named after a Missouri county to the south of Hannibal. It is also an Illinois county immediately across the river, the home of Judith Loftus in *Huckleberry Finn* and the locale of John Hay's *Pike County Ballads.* If we look hard enough we can find five speakers in the novel, all clearly from Pike County, Missouri, or Pike County, Illinois, and all speaking somewhat differently from each other: Huck, Pap, Judith Loftus, Judge Thatcher, and—stretching it—Aunt Polly or Tom Sawyer. But there are several things wrong with this approach. First, Judge Thatcher speaks a standard variety of English, and Clemens, not being a twentieth-century linguist, probably understood and used the word "dialect" to refer to nonstandard systems only. Second, Aunt Polly and Tom Sawyer both speak dialects identical with Huck's except for a very few features (Aunt Polly says *y'r* once and Tom says *git* once and *per'aps* once; Huck says none of these). Third and more important, if Clemens meant by "Pike County" this small geographic area, then in the preface he perversely called our attention to almost imperceptible dialectal differences (in the case of Aunt Polly or Tom) while ignoring major differences in the speech of characters like the King and the Bricksville Loafers. Such a reading in fact must ignore the speech occurring in three-fourths of the novel.

There is still another reason to look beyond the geographical Pike Counties for the speakers of "Pike County" dialect. Like "Southwestern," "Pike County" is the name of a literary tradition well established by the time Clemens began work on *Huckleberry Finn.* During the 1850's in California there emerged a stock immigrant character known as "the Pike." He figured in early ballads like "Joe Bowers," "California Bank Robbers," and "Sweet Betsey from Pike," and also in plays and sketches of the period. As to his roots, the Pike "was named for Pike County, Missouri, but he came from Illinois, Arkansas, or North Texas quite as frequently."[14] He spoke a dialect variously represented by different writers, part literary artifact and part reflective of actual linguistic features of the Pike County area in Missouri and Illinois. Well before Clemens wrote *Huckleberry Finn*, "Pike County" had come to refer to a literary representation of the speech of Missouri and points south. Clemens, fully aware of this, punctuated the term with quotation marks in his preface.[15] Huck participates actively in this tradition when he tells the King that he is from Pike County, Missouri, and that his family "all died off but me and pa and my brother Ike" (chapter 20); "Ike" is the name of a forever undeveloped character in Pike County balladry, his sole claim to fame being his ability to rhyme with "Pike." Clemens further highlights the geographical indefiniteness of "Pike" by giving the towns along the river names that can be seen as variants: the camp meeting is in Pokeville, the Phelps farm is in Pikesville, and "Bricksville" translates the Greco-Germanic "(St.) Petersburg," the town in the heart of Pike County.

Thus we are free to range down the river in our search for "Pike County" speakers in *Huckleberry Finn*. But what could Clemens have meant by "ordinary" and "modified"? A reasonable guess is that Huck is the speaker of the ordinary Pike County dialect, on the basis of the sheer bulk of his words—that which dominates numerically is "ordinary"—and also considering his geographical roots: Pike County, Missouri. We find some corroboration of this guess if we follow the procedure used above to identify the Southwestern dialect speakers in the novel, that is, if we examine the Pike County literature antedating *Huckleberry Finn* for recurring dialect features. In an early version of "Joe Bowers" we find much that anticipates Huck's dialect—intrusive *r* pronunciations (*orful* 'awful'), deletion of initial unstressed syllables (*'most* 'almost'), preterite *cotched* 'caught,' and infinitival *for to*.[16] We find most of these same features, along with many others shared by Huck, in John Hay's *Pike County Ballads* and Bret Harte's *East and West Poems*, both published in 1871. Huck-like features appear sporadically in some of Clemens's early California newspaper sketches, such as "Those Blasted Children" (1864), but it is in "The Celebrated Jumping Frog of Calaveras County" (1865) that the dialect appears in full bloom. Simon Wheeler and Huck Finn would have little trouble understanding each other. They share nonstandard pronunciations like *jest* 'just,' *terbacker* 'tobacco,' *jint* 'joint,' *fur* 'for,' *'low* 'allow,' and *ca'mly* 'calmly'; they share grammatical forms like preterite *warn't* 'wasn't,' *come* 'came,' *ketched* 'caught,' *see* 'saw,' and *throwed* 'threw,' possessive *his'n*, unmarked plurals (*five pound)*, and unmarked adverbs (*monstrous proud*);

they even share lexical items like *bullyrag* 'abuse' and *snake* 'take.'

Insofar as the "Pike County" dialect in literature can be defined, Huck appears to be a speaker of it. But so do the speakers of the seven other white dialects in *Huckleberry Finn*. In fact some of them show pronunciations (like *thar, git,* and *thish-yer*) that Huck does not show and that can occasionally be found in early Pike County works. This procedure, then, cannot tell us which three dialects to disregard. Let us assume that our earlier guess that Huck speaks the "ordinary" Pike County dialect is correct. We are left with seven dialects competing for four positions. At this point we must take up the third question raised in the opening paragraph: when Clemens wrote the "Explanatory" what could he have *thought* he had done in the way of differentiating the dialects of *Huckleberry Finn?* A glance at the history of the composition of the novel will help us answer this question and also tell us which three of the seven dialects in contention can be eliminated.

According to Walter Blair, *Huckleberry Finn* was written as described below.[17] Dates separated by one dash indicate known limits of a period of concentrated work on the novel; dates separated by three dashes mark limits of a period during which Clemens probably worked on *Huckleberry Finn* in addition to other projects:

July–August, 1876:
chap. 1–middle chap. 12; chaps. 15 and 16 (beginning-raft struck by steamboat; includes "Raft Passage")
October, 1879–June, 1880:
chaps. 17 and 18 (Grangerfords)
June, 1880–June, 1883:
chaps. 19–21 (King and Duke appear; Boggs shot in Bricksville)
June–August, 1883:
middle of chap. 12–chap. 14 (*Sir Walter Scott;* King Solomon discussion); chaps. 22–43 (Colonel Sherburn's speech in Bricksville–end)

When Clemens returned to *Huckleberry Finn* after an interruption he frequently made notes to himself.[18] Some of these are concerned with what he had already written, while others contain suggestions for future scenes. Some are concerned with characters and events: one says, "Widow Douglas—then who is 'Miss Watson?' Ah, she's W D's *sister*" (DeVoto, p. 71). A line crosses out the first sentence, apparently drawn by Clemens when he found (or remembered) the answer. Other notes are concerned with dialect. One apparently written in the summer of 1883 says, "Huck says

"PLEASE DON'T, BILL"

LEAKING.

"GIMME A CHAW."

KEEPING OFF DULL TIMES.

Characters who Twain may have believed represented the "four modified varieties" of "the ordinary 'Pike-County' dialect": the thieves aboard
Walter Scott; *the king, who here is expressing sorrow over the death of Peter Wilks; the loafers of Bricksville who "talked lazy and drawly,
and used considerable many cuss-words"; and Aunt Sally "raising Cain" after discovering "the pick of the flock" of rats Huck
and Tom had captured in their "first haul" (drawings by E. W. Kemble; from* Adventures of
Huckleberry Finn, *Mark Twain House, Hartford, Connecticut)*

Growing Up in Pike County

Mark Twain's friend John Hay (1838–1905) was one of the writers who contributed to making "Pike County" a designation for a literary tradition as well as a recognized dialect with variations. The first poem in Hay's collection Pike County Ballads *is "Little Breeches," which begins with these verses:*

I DON'T go much on religion,
    I never ain't had no show;
But I've got a middlin' tight grip, sir,
    On the handful o' things I know.
I don't pan out on the prophets
    And free-will and that sort of thing,–
But I b'lieve in God and the angels,
    Ever sence one night last spring.

I come into town with some turnips,
    And my little Gabe come along,–
No four-year-old in the county
    Could beat him for pretty and strong,
Peart and chipper and sassy,
    Always ready to swear and fight,–
And I'd larnt him to chaw terbacker
    Jest to keep his milk-teeth white.

When the horses run away with the wagon and the child in a snow storm, the father is "almost froze with skeer" and is close to despair when the search party turns up the "hosses and wagon, / Snowed under a soft white mound, / Upsot, dead beat" but no sign of his son. His prayers are answered, though, when he and a friend go looking for a sheepfold for wood to make torches:

We looked in and seen him huddled thar,
    So warm and sleepy and white;

And THAR sot Little Breeches and chirped,
    As peart as ever you see,
"I want a chaw of terbacker,
    And that's what's the matter of me."

How did he git thar? Angels.
    He could never have walked in that storm.
They jest scooped down and toted him
    To whar it was safe and warm.
And I think that saving a little child,
    And bringing him to his own,
Is a derned sight better business
    Than loafing around The Throne.

*–*Pike County Ballads and Other Pieces *(Boston: J. R. Osgood, 1871), pp. 13–14, 16*

speech. Huck does indeed say "nuther," both early and late in the novel, and Jim shows the pronunciations attributed to him.

But Clemens's recall was imperfect; his attempt at consistency, at least in Huck's dialect, falls short. In the parts of the novel written in the summer of 1883 (the latter half of the novel and the chapters 12–14 interpolation), Huck shows several nonstandard features which do not appear in the parts of the novel written earlier. These features are listed below, again with members of a class listed across the same line and the number of instances of each given in parentheses:

> phonology:
> fur 'for' (9)
> bile 'boil' (5), pison 'poison' (3), pint 'point' (1)
> kinder 'kind of' (9)
>
> grammar:
> possessive ourn (5), his'n (4), hern (1), yourn (1),
>   their'n (1)
> theirselves (2)
> redundant comparative marking (e.g., *more easier;* 4)

Some of these features are quite striking. Except for the summer, 1883, passages, Huck has the standard diphthong, spelled *oi*, in words like *boil, poison,* and *point,* in contrast to Pap's *jint* 'joint' and Jim's *pint* 'point.' Then, writing in 1883, Clemens gives Huck Pap's and Jim's nonstandard /aI/ pronunciation nine times. To take another example, prior to the summer of 1883 Huck has exclusively standard absolute possessives: *ours, yours,* etc. In 1883, however, Huck utters twelve of these with the nonstandard -*n* suffix. Standard versions of all of the forms listed above (*for, kind of, themselves,* etc.) can be found in those parts of the novel written before June, 1883.[19]

This inconsistency in Huck's dialect–along with the working notes on dialect–is strong evidence that in the summer of 1883, when Clemens wrote three-fifths of the novel, he had imperfect recollection of all the details of the dialects he had written in the other two-fifths. In addition, during the months he spent revising the novel before sending it to his publisher (August, 1883–April, 1884), he did not observe and correct these inconsistencies. This is not particularly surprising. After all, in order to make the two parts of *Huckleberry Finn* harmonious–the part written before the summer of 1883 and the part written during that summer–Clemens would have had to make the nonstandard spellings in the second part standard (changed *fur* to *for,* say), or he would have had to make the standard spellings in the first part nonstandard (changed *for* to *fur*); the nonstandard spellings, having just issued from his pen in the preceding months, would not be at all suspect, and the standard spellings in the first part would be very easy

Nuther," and it also contains notes on Jim's dialect–isolated entries like "hund'd," "kin," "Nuffn," "W'y," and so on (DeVoto, p. 74). These notes on dialect are apparently reminders of the features in Huck's and Jim's

Page from Twain's working notes in which he imagines a scene involving women such as "Old Mrs. Hotchkiss"
(Mark Twain Papers, The Bancroft Library, University of California, Berkeley)

OLD MRS. HOTCHKISS.

The woman Huck identifies as "the worst" of the "clack" of Arkansas farmers' wives who marvel over the circumstances of Jim's escape from the Phelpses. Twain may well have seen her as a representative of "the extremest form of the backwoods South-Western dialect" (drawing by E. W. Kemble; from Adventures of Huckleberry Finn, *Mark Twain House, Hartford, Connecticut).*

to overlook: when one reads dialect, one notices what is nonstandard more than what is standard.

There is no evidence as to when Clemens wrote the "Explanatory." He is most likely to have written it shortly before or after completing the novel, since it is improbable that he would write a preface which lists seven distinct dialects before he had actually written the scenes containing those dialects. Now considering what Clemens failed to recall (or notice) in 1883 about Huck's dialect early in the novel, it is reasonable to suspect that he failed to recall other linguistic features long ago written into the novel—features such as Pap's *suthin'* 'something,' Judith Loftus's three pronunciations of *sence* 'since,' or Raftsman Ed's *furder* 'further.' Clemens may once have carefully chosen these features and deliberately used them to distinguish these characters' dialects from Huck's; but he is likely to have forgotten in 1883 a choice made in 1876, and the features are sufficiently subtle to have gone undetected in revision.

When we left the question of the four modified Pike County dialects we were faced with seven dialects from which to choose. Three of these were written in 1876: Pap's, Judith Loftus's, and the Raftsmen's. Three of the four others were constructed in the summer of 1883 (*Sir Walter Scott's*, the King's—some of whose speech was also written earlier—and the Phelpses'), and the fourth (the Bricksville Loafers') was written no earlier than June 1880.

It is reasonable to assume that in reporting on the differences among the dialects in the novel Clemens remembered the distinctions he had drawn most recently at the expense of those he had drawn earlier. Also, the dialects written in 1876 are not greatly different from Huck's—note that they cluster toward the end of our scale ranking the dialects in decreasing order of divergence from Huck's dialect. In addition, Pap and Judith Loftus are both from Pike County, and, with Huck, Tom Sawyer, Aunt Polly, and Ben Rogers, can be seen as speakers of the "ordinary" or Ur-Pike County dialect. Finally, the Raft Passage is suspect not only because it was written in 1876 and shows relatively few distinguishing features but for another reason as well. If Clemens had intended this passage to represent uniquely one of the seven dialects referred to in the preface, then in the letter to his publisher authorizing its deletion he probably would have indicated that the preface needed revising accordingly; but nowhere in this or any other correspondence with his publisher is there a reference to the preface.[20]

Our conclusion, then, is that while it is not the case that there are seven and only seven distinct dialects in *Huckleberry Finn*, it *is* the case that there are seven distinct dialects which Clemens had in mind when he wrote the "Explanatory." These are as follows:

Missouri Negro: Jim (and four other minor characters)

Southwestern: Arkansas Gossips (Sister Hotchkiss et al.)

Ordinary "Pike County": Huck, Tom, Aunt Polly, Ben Rogers, Pap, Judith Loftus

Modified "Pike County": Thieves on the *Sir Walter Scott*

Modified "Pike County": King

Modified "Pike County": Bricksville Loafers

Modified "Pike County": Aunt Sally and Uncle Silas Phelps

The fact that intelligent sense can be made out of the preface falsifies the view that Clemens was joking when he wrote it. This view never had much merit anyway. While the last sentence of the "Explanatory" might raise a smile, there is nothing rib-splitting about a list of dialects. The existence of a separate comical preface (called "Notice" and published on a separate page in the first English and American editions) is irrelevant; it is certainly possible for an author to write two prefaces to a work, one comical and one serious.[21] Clemens's abiding interest in folk speech, his impatience with Harte's use of dialect, and his working notes on the dialects in *Huckleberry Finn* all point to earnestness in the representation of dialects in this novel–as does the evidence of extensive revision of dialect spellings. There are hundreds of corrections of dialect in the manuscript (or discrepancies between a dialect form in the manuscript and the final form in the first edition). A *just* might be corrected to *jest* in the manuscript, for example, and then end up as *jist* in the first edition. Such labored revision makes no sense if the "Explanatory" is frivolous.

Thus Clemens was serious when he wrote the "Explanatory." But he was also partly mistaken about the work he was describing. This makes for a blend of system with chaos which has either confused investigators or discouraged them at the outset. Also, while there is greater differentiation than stated in the "Explanatory" in terms of the number of distinguishable dialects, there is a somewhat smaller degree of differentiation of the dialects than one would expect from such a bold announcement. This is especially true of the varieties of "Pike County" dialect, where the differentiation is so fine that one must wonder what the author hoped the novel could gain from it. In this regard it is worth noting that the speakers of three of the four modified varieties of the "Pike County" dialect–the thieves on the *Sir Walter Scott*, the King, and the Bricksville Loafers–are morally reprehensible, and, in addition, that

their speech differs from Huck's by virtue of features normally found in the speech of the blacks in the novel. The Bricksville Loafers' *gwyne*, for example, occurs elsewhere in the novel only in the speech of slaves. The same can be said for the King's palatalization, which in the manuscript is also given to the thieves on the *Sir Walter Scott* (see note 10). This last group also loses *r* in phonetic environments similar to those where *r* is lost in Jim's speech *(befo', yo')*, whereas Huck very rarely loses *r* and never loses it word-finally (e.g., *stabboard, whippowill*). One's first thought is that it is surprising that Clemens, in a novel concerned with exposing weaknesses in the conventional values of society, calls upon those values in the way he taints these characters' dialects–to "lower" them he draws them with features of black speech. But in doing this Clemens was merely reflecting linguistic reality in his time and, indeed, in the present century: the speech of lower-class rural whites in the South shares a great deal with the speech of blacks.[22] In *Huckleberry Finn*, *gwyne*, palatalization, and *r*-lessness are–for both blacks and whites–physical signals of low social status, and–for whites only–physical signals of "substandard" morals. These white characters may share something of Jim's dialect, but they do not share in his goodness.

Finally, it is important to recognize the showmanship in this ambitious, seven-way dialectal differentiation and in the attention the author calls to it. Clemens composed *Huckleberry Finn* in the heyday of literary dialect in American literature, and no doubt he wanted to show what he too was capable of doing, especially with the "Pike County" dialect that he helped to create.

–*American Literature: A Journal of Literary History, Criticism, and Bibliography*, 51 (November 1979): 315–332

———

1. Mark Twain, *Adventures of Huckleberry Finn*, ed. Henry Nash Smith (Boston, 1958), p. 2. All subsequent references are to this edition. I am grateful to the National Endowment for the Humanities for a Summer Stipend enabling me to investigate Clemens's literary use of dialect.

2. In the first group are William Clark Breckenridge, "Missouri," in *Books Containing American Local Dialects*, ed. Arthur E. Bostwick (St. Louis, 1914), p. 9; Vance Randolph and George P. Wilson, *Down in the Holler: A Gallery of Ozark Folk Speech* (Norman, Okla., 1953), p. 7; and Curt Rulon, "Geographical Delimitation of the Dialect Areas in *The Adventures of Huckleberry Finn*," *Mark Twain Journal*, XIV (Winter 1967); 9–12. In the second group are Katherine Buxbaum, "Mark Twain and American Dialect," *American Speech*, II (Feb., 1927), 233–236, whose sensible (though somewhat casual) analysis suffers because it antedates Walter Blair's determination of the dates of the composition of *Huckleberry Finn* (see note 17) –a determination which, as will be shown below, is essential to an understanding of the preface–and, more recently, Sally Boland, "The Seven Dialects in *Huckleberry Finn*," *North Dakota Quarterly*, XXXVI (Summer 1968), 30–40, a study riddled with errors of observation.

3. For treatments of this question see James Nathan Tidwell, "Mark Twain's Representation of Negro Speech," *American Speech,* XVII (Oct., 3942), 174–176; Curt Rulon, "The Dialects in *Huckleberry Finn,*" (Ph.D. diss., University of Iowa, 1967); and Lee A. Pederson, "Negro Speech in *The Adventures of Huckleberry Finn,*" *Mark Twain Journal,* XIII (Winter, 1965), 1–4. Pederson, in "Mark Twain's Missouri Dialects: Marion County Phonemics," *American Speech,* XLII (Dec., 1967), 261–278, reports on a 1964 dialect survey of northeastern Missouri. Four of his twelve informants were seventy-nine years old or older, and they in turn reported on remembered archaisms; thus there is some raw material here for a comparison of the dialects in *Huckleberry Finn* with actual nineteenth-century speech. Finally, Walt Wolfram and Donna Christian's *Appalachian Speech* (Arlington, Va., 1976) is a linguistic description of two West Virginian counties which lie in the larger South Midland area, whence came the bulk of the antebellum settlement of Missouri; despite the years separating the two, *Appalachian Speech* comes remarkably close to being a grammar of *Huckleberry Finn.*

4. See Sumner Ives's classic article on the subject, "A Theory of Literary Dialect," *Tulane Studies in English,* 11 (1950), 137–182.

5. This has already been done. For a partial list see Buxbaum, and for a nearly complete list see Rulon, "The Dialects in *Huckleberry Finn,*" 59–95. It should be noted here that the nonstandard features characterizing Huck's dialect appear in both his speech and narration, although as Robert J. Lowenherz, "The Beginning of *Huckleberry Finn,*" *American Speech,* XXXVIII (Oct., 1963), 196–201, points out, dialect spellings are somewhat more dense in Huck's speech than in his narration. Below, "Huck's dialect" refers to the language of both.

6. The lexical items are minimally glossed. For fuller treatment see Robert L. Ramsay and Frances Guthrie Emberson, *A Mark Twain Lexicon* (1938; rpt. New York, 1963).

7. I depart from this procedure in two instances. First, I give spellings showing neutralization of the contrast between the vowels of standard English *pit* (/I/) and *pet* (/ɛ/); such neutralization is indicated either with a nonstandard use of the *i* graph for /ɛ/ (*git* 'get') or a nonstandard use of *e* for /I/ (*sence* 'since'). Huck has just one example of this—*resk* 'risk'—and so in some sense has the rule of neutralization, but it is a striking feature of several other dialects and worthy of attention. Second, I give spellings showing /ɛ/ or /I/ for /ʌ/ in *just, such, touch,* etc. Again Huck has just one example (*jest*), whereas other characters have many more.

8. It is highly debatable that Clemens could have been referring to this passage in the preface, and my final conclusion below is that he was not. However, it is listed here for the sake of thoroughness.

9. Excluded from the list are minor characters of various types: speakers of dialects differing very slightly from Huck's (the watchman whom Huck sends to the *Sir Walter Scott,* Buck Grangerford, and the Duke), speakers whose dialects are virtually identical with Huck's (Tom Sawyer, Ben Rogers, Aunt Polly, and the Wilks daughters), and speakers who can be grouped in one of the categories below, e.g., Tim Collins (the "young country jake" from whom the King learns about the Wilkses), who can be grouped with the King by virtue of his two pronunciations of *g'yirls* 'girls,' and the Pikesville boy who tells Huck about Jim's capture, who with his *hunderd* and *Newrleans* belongs with Aunt Sally and Uncle Silas Phelps.

10. Two important dialect spellings in the speech of these characters appear in the partial holograph manuscript but do not appear in the first edition: *weepon* 'weapon' (pp. 81–89 in the manuscript) and *thish-yer* 'this here' (pp. 81–115). The first, which is unique to the thieves, fails to appear in the published version of the novel only because the passage containing it was deleted in revision. Clemens revised the second to *this,* perhaps because the characters are too far north to show palatalization, a feature he associated with the South (see *Life on the Mississippi,* chap. 44). Thus Clemens originally intended to distinguish the speech of these characters from Huck's speech even more than is evident in the published version. I am grateful to the Buffalo and Erie County Public Library for permission to examine this manuscript.

11. See Kenneth S. Lynn, *Mark Twain and Southwestern Humor* (1959; rpt. Westport, Conn., 1972), and Walter Blair, *Mark Twain and Huck Finn* (Berkeley, Calif., 1960), 243–244.

12. *The Century Magazine,* XXVI (May, 1883), 137–150 and XXVI (June, 1883), 185–194. The story also appears in Harris's *Mingo and Other Sketches in Black and White* (Boston, 1884). Clemens wrote the Arkansas Gossips scene in the summer of 1883.

13. Clemens's note appears in Bernard DeVoto, *Mark Twain at Work* (Cambridge, Mass., 1942), p. 76.

14. *Literary History of the United States,* 4th ed., ed. Robert E. Spiller et al. (New York, 1974), 1, 864. "The Pike" is fully described in Fred Lewis Pattee, *A History of American Literature Since 1870* (New York, 1915), 83–98, and in G. R. MacMinn, "'The Gentleman from Pike' in Early California," *American Literature,* VIII (May, 1936), 160–169.

15. The only other reference by Clemens to Pike County dialect that I know of is to be found among his marginalia to Bret Harte's *The Luck of Roaring Camp,* where he also uses quotation marks. Criticizing Harte's dialect, as he often did, Clemens writes of one passage, "This is much more suggestive of Dickens & an English atmosphere than 'Pike County'" (Bradford A. Booth, "Mark Twain's Comments on Bret Harte's Stories," *American Literature,* XXV [Jan., 1954], p. 494).

16. *Johnson's Original Comic Songs* (San Francisco, 1860).

17. "When Was *Huckleberry Finn* Written?," *American Literature,* XXX (March, 1958), 1–25.

18. The notes are given in DeVoto, 63–78, and are discussed there and in Blair, "When Was *Huckleberry Finn* Written?"

19. Tom Sawyer, another character who speaks early and late in the novel, is subject to the same winds of change. In chapter 2 he says *join,* while in chapter 42 he says *spile* 'spoil.'

20. Clemens's letter agreeing to the deletion of the passage, dated April 22, 1884, is in *Mark Twain, Business Man,* ed. Samuel C. Webster (Boston, 1946), 249–250.

21. The "Notice" reads, "Persons attempting to find a motive in this narrative will be prosecuted; persons attempting to find a moral in it will be banished; persons attempting to find a plot in it will be shot. BY ORDER OF THE AUTHOR PER G. G., CHIEF OF ORDNANCE."

22. Walt Wolfram, "The Relationship of White Southern Speech to Vernacular Black English," *Language,* L (Sept., 1974), 498–527.

Sources for Incidents and Episodes

Sam Clemens was familiar with the workings of newspapers from a very early age. In these excerpts from his essay "Mark Twain: Newspaper Reading and the Writer's Creativity," Edgar M. Branch discusses instances that suggest how important contemporary newspapers may have been in supplying the author with a literary "capital" he eventually put to use.

"Narrative Threads"
Newspaper Items as Sources for *Huckleberry Finn*
Edgar M. Branch

Consider the following newspaper items dating from the eight years between the summer of 1853 and the summer of 1861.

> And art thou gone to join that angel band—
> The singing sisters of the spirit-land?
> And will thy voice no more delight the ear—

Julia A. Moore, "The Sweet Singer of Michigan," the poet whose work may have been the specific inspiration for the poetry of Emmeline Grangerford (frontispiece, The Sentimental Song Book *[Grand Rapids, Mich.: C. M. Loomis, [1877]; Library of Congress)*

> Or call from pity's heart the swelling tear?
> And will thy gentle touches no more be
> The gates which lead to realms of harmony?
> Alas! no more! that gentle soul of thine
> Was too expansive—too almost divine.

These lachrymose lines open the poem "Monody" published 30 July 1854 in the *St. Louis Missouri Republican* (p. 2). They were *not* written by Emmeline Grangerford. Nevertheless, as Huck Finn lets us know, the multitalented Emmeline, who collected obituaries, was an inveterate writer of "tributes" to dead persons, and she liked to frame rhetorical questions dripping with a grief-stricken sense of loss. She captioned one of her crayon portraits "And Art Thou Gone Yes Thou Art Gone Alas."[1] The lines *were* written as a "tribute"—the unknown author of "Monody" uses the word—by a friend of the musically talented Lizzie S. Taylor, who died in St. Louis on 23 July 1854 when, like Emmeline, she was in her teens. To the author of "Monody," when Lizzie played the pianoforte and sang "she seemed to . . . luxuriate in an inward world whose light was music and language the melody of song." Drenched in mourners' tears and sentiment, "Monody" belongs to a genre of newspaper poetry that exerted a lifelong fascination on Clemens beginning at least as early as 1853 and 1854.

The *St. Louis Missouri Democrat* for 11 June 1861 (p. 1) published "The Horrors of Delirium Tremens," an item depicting a drunken man

> in a severe attack of delirium tremens . . . raving of devils and snakes, as he expressed it, creeping things innumerable, both small and great; his face flushed, his eyes bloodshot and glistening . . . He was struggling with imaginary demons, and shouting at the top of his voice that he was devil possessed, and that his time was come to go to utter darkness. "Oh, devils of the air, how they glare on me! Messengers of Satan, sent to buffet me, I'll have it out yet! Off, off, I say! Crawl, crawl, creep, creep!" Then would ensue a fearful paroxysm, and he would make snatches at the bed clothes, or cower beneath them, or peep over the edge of the bed, with an expression . . . murderous in its terror. . . . His screams and yells were awful, and when they ceased he gabbled incessantly . . . to the imaginary beings who crowded his chamber, imploring their pity.

To subdue his violent actions, "it required the utmost efforts of four able-bodied men."

The name of this sufferer was Saltoun and not Pap Finn. Yet it was Pap, in his cabin on the Illinois shore, who wakened the sleeping Huck one memorable night with "an awful scream."

Huck's father after he drank "enough whisky . . . for two drunks and one delirium tremens" (drawing by E. W. Kemble; from Adventures of Huckleberry Finn, *Mark Twain House, Hartford, Connecticut)*

ocrat, we read of a man bitten by a rattlesnake. A Good Samaritan then tells how he dosed the victim with "a full quart of strong whisky and ninety drops of hartshorn" given in three portions at intervals of five minutes–a time-honored antidote to rattlesnake poison. Before long, with this "load of raw whisky on his stomach," the patient

commenced to laugh, then to whistle, next to sing, and finally tried to dance. I had him all right then; I knew that the whisky had got ahead of the poison, and had reached his vitals first. In five minutes more he was as drunk as Bacchus, sprawled out on the floor, slept half a day, and next morning was at work as well as ever.[2]

Huck Finn's friend Jim also was bitten by a rattlesnake while he and Huck were hiding out on Jackson's Island. Jim immediately "grabbed pap's whisky jug and began to pour it down." Jim used other folk remedies for counteracting the venom, but mainly he

There was pap, looking wild and skipping around every which way and yelling about snakes. He said they were crawling up his legs; and then he would give a jump and scream, and say one had bit him on the cheek–but I couldn't see no snakes. He started and run round and round the cabin, hollering "take him off! take him off! he's biting me on the neck!" I never see a man look so wild in the eyes. Pretty soon he was all fagged out, and fell down panting; then he rolled over and over, wonderful fast, kicking things every which way, and striking and grabbing at the air with his hands, and screaming, and saying there was devils ahold of him. (*HF,* p. 28)

After a few moments of silence, Pap says: "'Oh, they're here! don't touch me–don't! hands off– they're cold; let go–Oh, let a poor devil alone!' Then he went down on all fours and crawled off begging them to let him alone, and he rolled himself up in his blanket" (*HF,* p. 28). Pap's murderous chase of Huck then follows.

Two columns over from "The Horrors of Delirium Tremens," in the same number of the *Missouri Dem-*

Jim applying a folk remedy for a snake bite (drawing by E. W. Kemble; from Adventures of Huckleberry Finn, *Mark Twain House, Hartford, Connecticut)*

relied on whiskey: "Jim sucked and sucked at the jug, and now and then he got out of his head and pitched around and yelled; but every time he come to himself he went to sucking at the jug again. His foot swelled up pretty big, and so did his leg; but by-and-by the drunk begun to come, and so I judged he was all right" (*HF,* p. 46). Jim was up and around in four days.

On 16 August 1859 the *Missouri Democrat* published "Finding Drowned Persons by Quicksilver" (p. 1). The item tells of a young man drowned in deep lake water: "After a long and almost hopeless search after the body, a very novel idea was suggested. . . . About three ounces of quicksilver were put into a loaf of *brown bread,* well baked, and thrown out into the lake. The loaf was discovered to move directly *against the wind;* soon it stopped, whirled round several times and sunk." At that very spot, rescue workers with grapplers soon removed the body of the young man from "his watery grave" seventy feet down.

This victim, of course, is not Huck Finn, whose body is only thought to be somewhere in the Mississippi River near St. Petersburg. Hiding out on Jackson's Island, well downstream from town, Huck hears a cannon boom and sees "the ferry-boat full of people, floating along down," and he knows they are "trying to make my carcass come to the top":

> Well, then I happened to think how they always put quicksilver in loaves of bread and float them off because they always go right to the drownded carcass and stop there. So says I, I'll keep a lookout, and if any of them's floating around after me, I'll give them a show. (p. 34)

Positioning himself in a sheltered spot on the Illinois edge of the island "where the current set in the closest to the shore," Huck sure enough fishes just such a loaf out of the water as it comes floating by: "I took out the plug and shook out the little dab of quicksilver, and set my teeth in. It was 'baker's bread'— what the quality eat—none of your low-down corn-pone" (*HF,* p. 34).

. . . .

Mark Twain frequently acknowledged a truth about the creation of fiction, including his own: that "the most valuable capital, or culture, or education usable in the building of novels is personal experience."[3] By "personal experience" he seems to have meant not those vicarious realizations gained through reading but rather an individual's vital

WATCHING THE BOAT.

Huck looking out for a loaf of bread plugged with quicksilver (drawing by E. W. Kemble; from Adventures of Huckleberry Finn, *Mark Twain House, Hartford, Connecticut)*

assimilation of ordinary day-by-day events as he lives his life within the natural world and among other people—primarily family, friends, and townspeople. In this sense Clemens's personal experience during his first thirty years has been sorted out and categorized into the matter of Hannibal, the matter of the River, and the matter of the Far West. But at least since the time of Olin H. Moore's 1922 article "Mark Twain and Don Quixote," scholars such as Minnie Brashear, Walter Blair, Howard Baetzhold, and Alan Gribben have explored a secondary "capital, or culture, or education" that Mark Twain used to create his fiction—namely, literary sources.

Less frequently, scholars have noted the indebtedness of Mark Twain's fiction to run-of-the-mill journalism, the ordinary stuff of newspapers, especially the "human interest" items and the informational reports about almost anything at all. My scanning of selected Mississippi Valley newspapers for the years 1853–1861 suggests that here indeed is an important secondary "capital" . . . that Clemens

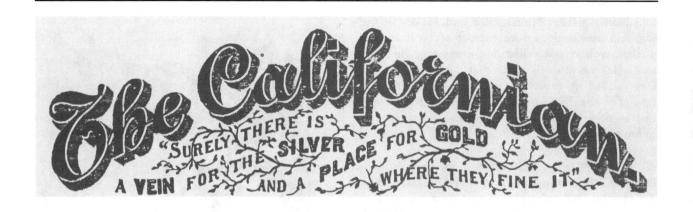

Mastheads for two of the many newspapers on which Sam Clemens worked (Mark Twain Papers, The Bancroft Library, University of California, Berkeley)

drew on. The matters of Hannibal, the River, and the Far West ultimately derive from Clemens's "personal experience," but just as portions of that material show the influence of the literature he read, so portions of it reflect the journalism he knew so intimately. Although the newspaper items quoted . . . may suggest that such material was widely and frequently reported in the newspapers, and hence that the precise sources Clemens read cannot be known, this does not alter the fact that these or similar reports provided material for his fiction. And in these particular cases, with one exception, there is every reason to believe that Clemens was in St. Louis on the days the newspaper items . . . were published there. The exception is "Finding Drowned Persons by Quicksilver," which appeared three days before Clemens arrived at the St. Louis levee on the *Edward J. Gay* from New Orleans. It is possible that Clemens read that number of the *Missouri Democrat* once he was home, or–considering the speed with which St. Louis newspapers were carried down river and distributed– at Cairo, one day out of St. Louis. To be sure, the quicksilver item was making the rounds of other Mississippi Valley newspapers at that very time.

In this connection it is helpful to recall the crucial importance of newspapers in Clemens's early experience. He began his working life in a newspaper

office. Thereafter for several years Orion Clemens's Hannibal newspapers were in large measure a family undertaking in which Sam joined. Having learned typesetting, Clemens left Hannibal in 1853 and worked for four years as a printer, frequently on newspapers, in the East and Midwest. Between 1851 and 1861 he contributed several dozen pieces of varying kinds to newspapers. As a pilot he turned to newspapers for reports of river stages and weather conditions. In the West he became a local editor in Virginia City and San Francisco. For newspapers during the 1860s he wrote "correspondence" from one city to another, legislative reports, feature articles, and travel letters–from Hawaii, from across America, and from Europe and the Near East. To newspapers he also contributed tales and sketches, a surprising number of which took their immediate origin from information and ideas gleaned from newspapers. Early and later he engaged in controversies aired in newspapers. He was an owner, editor, and featured contributor of the Buffalo *Express*. He knew newspapers from the inside out, and during his lifetime he recognized their social value yet vehemently criticized them and the profession of journalism for serious shortcomings. The evidence indicates that during his extended apprenticeship–say from 1851 to 1871–he was a faithful reader of newspapers whenever he could get them. Understandably so, for nineteenth-century American newspapers were the easily available mirrors of American life—its facts, anecdotes and curiosities, its values, beliefs and legends, and its news. They were the popular repositories of contemporary history and biography, and history and biography were two of Mark Twain's favorite areas of reading.

It is likely, then, that a major secondary "capital" of Mark Twain's creative imagination, a significant part of the total flow that filled the "tank"[4] he drew on, was his routine newspaper reading. The content of that reading sometimes overlapped the "capital" or "culture" supplied by his reading of literature—to the extent that newspapers published prominent belletrists and humorists. Resurfacing in his fiction, it supplemented his "capital" of "personal experience" and sometimes substituted for it. It supplied him with raw material selectively used for his imaginative presentation of the matters of Hannibal, the River, and the Far West. Thus the probability is good that Mark Twain drew less from direct "personal experience" and more from newspaper reading in recapturing the stored impressions used to depict Emmeline Grangerford's taste in obituary language and poetry,[5] or in showing Pap Finn racked by delirium tremens, or in granting Jim an effective remedy for rattlesnake venom, or in endowing Huck with the know-how that got him "baker's bread" for lunch. . . . These examples suggest that innumerable other narrative threads, plucked silently and subconsciously by Mark Twain from the mental residue of ancient newspaper reading, are woven into the tapestry of his fiction.

—*Nineteenth-Century Fiction,* 37 (March 1983): 576–579, 582–584

1. *Adventures of Huckleberry Finn: An Annotated Text, Backgrounds and Sources, Essays in Criticism,* ed. Sculley Bradley, Richmond Croom Beatty, and E. Hudson Long, 1st ed. (New York: Norton, 1962), p. 84; hereafter cited parenthetically in the text as *HF.* The Norton edition follows the text of the first American edition, first issue, 1885.
2. "Remarkable Case of a Rattlesnake Bite," *St. Louis Missouri Democrat,* 11 June 1861, p. 1.
3. "To an Unidentified Person," 1890, in *The Portable Mark Twain,* ed. Bernard DeVoto (New York: Viking, 1946), p. 775.
4. *Mark Twain in Eruption,* ed. DeVoto (New York: Harper, 1940), p.197.
5. Walter Blair has demonstrated the probable influence here of Julia A. Moore's poetry. See *Mark Twain and Huck Finn* (Berkeley: Univ. of California Press, 1960), pp. 210–13; hereafter cited parenthetically in the text as *MT&HF.*

* * *

The "feud" chapters are among the most important in Adventures of Huckleberry Finn. *From the manuscript of the first portion of the novel that was recovered in 1990, it has been determined that Mark Twain stopped the first phase of composition of the novel at that point in chapter 18 where Huck asks Buck Grangerford, "What's a feud?" The feud episode as eventually written was more violent and disturbing than earlier events in the novel and indicates that Twain's satire was taking a serious turn.*

In these excerpts from their book-length study, Edgar M. Branch and Robert H. Hirst examine how Twain made use of the Darnell-Watson feud that evolved near the town of Compromise, Kentucky, for his discussion of Southern feuds in Life on the Mississippi *as well as in* Adventures of Huckleberry Finn.

The Grangerford-Shepherdson Feud
Edgar M. Branch and Robert H. Hirst

This excerpt is from the foreword to Branch and Hirst's study.

Early in October 1884 Mark Twain arranged to publish "An Adventure of Huckleberry Finn: with an Account of the Famous Grangerford-Shepherdson Feud" in the *Century Magazine.* This was two months before the first English and nearly five months before the first American edition of *Huckleberry Finn* were published. The "Adventure" appeared in the magazine's December 1884 issue, "taken," as Mark Twain said in a prefatory note, "from an unpublished book called 'The Adventures of Huckleberry Finn, Tom Sawyer's Comrade.'" The excerpt consisted essentially of chapters 17 and 18, slightly abbreviated and lightly edited for the *Century* audience, and typeset from the finally revised page proofs of the first American edition, which along with Edward Windsor Kemble's illustrations had been supplied by the author himself.[1]

The selection was made by Richard Watson Gilder, editor of the *Century,* who had tried (and failed) to persuade Mark Twain to allow him to "print half or three quarters" of the story "before the book comes out." Gilder wanted such an agreement "badly," he admitted, but he was well prepared to settle for less. "If we can only use one installment," he wrote Clemens on October 10, "it may be somewhat awkward to select as the story runs in and out. I am thinking of that part about the feuds—but it would be hard to dovetail it in—can you suggest a way—without making it a mere extract from the book?"[2] Gilder himself easily solved this problem, however, when it became clear that Mark Twain would not agree to full serialization.

The Grangerford-Shepherdson feud was thus, to a degree, singled out and exalted above the novel as a whole. And more than one of Mark Twain's contemporaries heartily agreed with Gilder's judgment in doing so. On 7 January 1885, for instance, the American poet and critic Edmund Clarence Stedman wrote Mark Twain in praise of what he called "your *Vendetta* in the Dec. Century, which, to my mind, is not only the most finished & condensed thing you have done, but as dramatic and powerful an episode as I know in modern literature."[3] Stedman would, in fact, select the feud episode to represent Mark Twain in the multivolume *Library of American Literature* he was then editing.[4] And in 1893, a New York journal reported that at a Lotos Club dinner honoring Mark Twain, Stedman said "He knew nothing more dramatic in any modern book than the final chapter in 'Huckleberry Finn,' and the death of poor little Buck, the last of his race."[5]

In May 1885, the distinguished *Century* critic Thomas Sergeant Perry reviewed *Huckleberry Finn*, singling out the "art" of these two chapters: "The best instance is perhaps to be found in the account of the feud between the Shepherdsons and the Grangerfords, which is described only as it would appear to a semi-civilized boy of fourteen, without the slightest condemnation or surprise,—either of which would be bad art,—and yet nothing more vivid can be imagined." Perry concluded that "the account of the Southern *vendetta* is a masterpiece."[6] Finally, Mark Twain himself appears to have thought highly of these chapters, for in 1894 he marked them up extensively for reading on his around-the-world lecture tour.[7]

Mark Twain had, in fact, published a very similar, but distinct, account of a Mississippi River Valley feud just eighteen months before the *Century* text appeared. Unlike the fictional Grangerfords and Shepherdsons, this account concerned the quite real Darnells and Watsons, whose feud he described in chapter 26 of *Life on the Mississippi* (1883). The design of that book permitted Mark Twain to tell all sorts of yarns, facts, and anecdotes, but its fundamental purpose was to become a "standard work" on the Mississippi River. Still, its factual account was very similar to the fictitious treatment accorded the feud in *Huckleberry Finn*. For example, the climactic scene in each account depicted a young man shielding himself from gunfire by hiding behind a woodpile at a small wooding-station on the Mississippi and then, still pursued by his enemies, plunging into the river where he was soon killed.

A more fundamental similarity, however, was that in *both* accounts Mark Twain tacitly claimed to have grounded his work on historical fact—a claim his English friend Reginald Cholmondeley, for example, was inclined to resist. "I have been reading Huckleberry Finn with delight. You appear to be inexhaustible & evergreen but is it possible that blood-feuds existed in

Arkansas within 50 years?" Mark Twain's reply was explicit and emphatic: "Yes indeed feuds existed in Kentucky, Tennessee, and Arkansas, of the nature described, within my time and memory. [¶] I came very near being an eye-witness of the general engagement detailed in the book. The details are historical and correct."[8]

Some scholars and critics have likewise questioned the author's claim of factuality. One has asserted that "there was no Darnell-Watson Feud" and that Mark Twain based his two versions instead on what he had read about "the Hatfields and the McCoys."[9] Another skeptic, somewhat less sweeping, has suggested that while there was an "actual event" used by Mark Twain, he may well have "allowed himself considerable latitude in his comment about nearly being an eyewitness" to this event, and he "sardonically created the Darnell-Watson title out of his factual information . . . knowing that the readers . . . would be side-tracked into speculating about why he created a mythical feud, or who told him about it, rather than gaining any insight into their society from the facts drawn from actual feuds."[10]

What exactly *were* the "facts" as Mark Twain knew them? How, when, and to what extent could he have learned them? What, for instance, could he have meant in saying that he "came very near being an eye-witness" to them? And if there were feuds in these states "of the nature described" and within his "time and memory," are the "details . . . historical and correct" in *either* account Mark Twain published? We propose to answer these questions insofar as the historical documents in The Bancroft Library and elsewhere give us light to do so, and to account both for the similarities and the differences between chapter 26 of *Life on the Mississippi* and chapters 17 and 18 of *Adventures of Huckleberry Finn*. The answers inevitably yield a better appreciation of what Mark Twain actually achieved in both books, and they can shed light as well on a much misunderstood aspect of his literary art: his use of real persons, places, and events both as the subject of factual narratives and as the basis for fictions.

Simply put, this case helps to demonstrate that Mark Twain consciously abided by a general principle of fiction (and implicitly of nonfiction) that he once formulated for himself in an 1887 notebook entry:

> If you attempt to create & build a wholly imaginary incident, adventure or situation, you will go astray, & the artificiality of the thing will be detectable. But if you found on a *fact* in your personal experience, it is an acorn, a root, & every created adornment that grows up out of it & spreads its foliage & blossoms to the sun will seem realities, not inventions. (*N&J3*, 343)

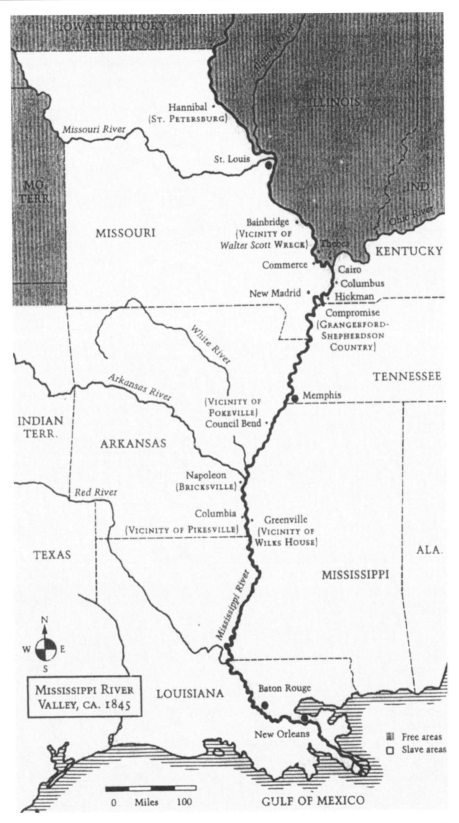

Map showing the location of places in the novel along the Mississippi River (from Adventures of Huckleberry Finn, *edited by
Victor Fischer, Lin Salamo, and Walter Blair [Berkeley: University of California Press, 2003], Collection of Tom Quirk)*

It is this general principle, too, that made him want (in the phrase of Thomas Kennett) "to get hold of true stories to tell them in his own fashion."[11] In fact, Mark Twain held the same opinion about characters in fiction that he held for incidents, adventures, or situations:

> I don't believe an author, good, bad or indifferent, ever lived, who created a character. It was always drawn from his recollection of someone he had known. Sometimes, like a composite photograph, an author's presentation of a character may possibly be from the blending of more than two . . . real characters in his recollection. But, even when he is making no attempt to draw his character from life, when he is striving to create something different, even then, however ideal his drawing, he is yet unconsciously drawing from memory. . . . [A] character one has known some time in life may have become so deeply buried within the recollection that the lens of the first effort will not bring it to view. But by continued application the author will find when he is done, that he has etched a likeness of some one he has known before.
>
> In attempting to represent some character which he cannot recall, which he draws from what he thinks is his imagination, an author may often fall into the error of copying in part a character already drawn by another, a character which impressed itself upon his memory from some book. So he has but made a picture of a picture with all his pains.[12]

One need not subscribe to this skeptical theory of the literary imagination to see that, at least for Mark Twain's conscious understanding of his art, the one essential requirement for avoiding "artificiality" was that the writer shun memories drawn "from some book" in favor of those from his "personal experience." Examining the facts behind the Grangerford-Shepherdson feud and its near nonfiction cousin, the Darnell-Watson feud, should therefore allow us to say how well Mark Twain's practice accorded with his theory.

–pp. 7–11

Abbreviations

N&J3: Mark Twain's Notebooks & Journals, Volume III (1883–1891), The Mark Twain Papers, ed. Robert Pack Browning, Michael B. Frank, and Lin Salamo; Frederick Anderson, General Editor. (Berkeley, Los Angeles, and London: University of California Press, 1979).

1. See the "Textual Introduction," *Adventures of Huckleberry Finn,* ed. Walter Blair and Victor Fischer, The Works of Mark Twain, a publication of The Bancroft Library (University of California Press in cooperation with the University of Iowa, forthcoming). We are grateful to Vic-

tor Fischer for sharing his expertise on this and other matters.

2. Gilder to Clemens, 10 October 1884, Mark Twain Papers, The Bancroft Library.

3. Stedman to Clemens, 7 January 1885, Mark Twain Papers, The Bancroft Library.

4. *A Library of American Literature from the Earliest Settlement to the Present Time,* comp. and ed. Edmund Clarence Stedman and Ellen Mackay Hutchinson, 11 vols. (New York: Charles L. Webster & Company, 1891), 9: 299–305. Also included were the "Jumping Frog" tale and chapter 27 of *The Prince and the Pauper.*

5. "Mark Twain at the Lotos," *The Critic* 23 (18 November 1893): 323. It was not, of course, the "final chapter" in the book.

6. "Mark Twain," *Century Magazine* 30 (May 1885): 171.

7. Our thanks to Harriet Elinor Smith for her expert analysis of when and for what these chapters were revised by Mark Twain. The copy of the book used, published by Tauchnitz, is in the Mark Twain Papers, The Bancroft Library. We reproduce a facsimile of one page later in this keepsake.

8. Cholmondeley to Clemens, 12 March 1885; Clemens to Cholmondeley, 28 March 1885, both in the Mark Twain Papers, The Bancroft Library. Cholmondeley thought the Grangerfords lived in Arkansas only because he mistook a running head ("The Farm in Arkansaw") as a reference to the Grangerford homestead, rather than Huck's explanation of where he had come from (*Century* printing, page 271, left column).

9. Robert H. Sykes, "A Source for Mark Twain's Feud," *West Virginia History* 28 (April 1967): 192. "Now, if there were Darnells and Watsons engaged in a notorious feud of the dimensions the stranger described, some record to substantiate his story should have been preserved. Yet a careful search of newspaper files, chronicles of American feuds, and court records failed to uncover any." Sykes mentions three historians beside himself who were unable to "discover any reference to Darnells and Watsons" (192).

10. Loren K. Davidson, "The Darnell–Watson Feud," *Duquesne Review* 13 (Fall 1968): 76–95; the quotations are from pages 77, 82, and 92. Davidson's pioneering article is the first successful attempt to document, rather than debunk, Mark Twain's various statements and claims about factuality. Yet on very much the same evidence that we discuss in the commentary below, Davidson concludes that whatever feud did exist, it did not "involve altercation between the Darnalls and the Watsons" (78).

11. As paraphrased by Brander Matthews in his review of Albert Bigelow Paine's *Mark Twain: A Biography* (*New York Times,* "Book Review Magazine," 13 October 1912, 597). Kennett is the man from whom Clemens purchased a share of the Buffalo *Express* in 1869.

12. Interview conducted by Lute Pease, "Mark Twain Talks," Portland *Oregonian,* 11 August 1895, 10; reprinted in *A Listing of and Selection from Newspaper and Magazine Interviews with Samuel L. Clemens: 1874-1910,* ed. Louis J. Budd (Arlington, Texas: University of Texas, 1977), 52–53.

* * *

SOUTHERN FEUDS. 285

We struck down through the chute of Island No. 8, and I went below and fell into conversation with a passenger, a handsome man, with easy carriage and an intelligent face. We were approaching Island No. 10, a place so celebrated during the war.

This gentleman's home was on the main shore in its neighborhood. I had some talk with him about the war times; but presently the discourse fell upon "feuds," for in no part of the South has the vendetta flourished more briskly, or held

286   DARNELL AND WATSON.

out longer between warring families, than in this particular region. This gentleman said:—

"There's been more than one feud around here, in old times, but I reckon the worst one was between the Darnells and the Watsons. Nobody don't know now what the first quarrel was about, it's so long ago; the Darnells and the Watsons don't know, if there's any of them living, which I don't think there is. Some says it was about a horse or a cow—anyway, it was a little matter; the money in it was n't of no consequence—none in the world—both families was rich. The thing could have been fixed up, easy enough; but no, that would n't do. Rough words had been passed; and so, nothing but blood could fix it up after that. That horse or cow, whichever it was, cost sixty years of killing and crippling! Every year or so somebody was shot, on one side or the other; and as fast as one generation was laid out, their sons took up the feud and kept it a-going. And it's just as I say; they went on shooting each other, year in and year out—making a kind of a religion of it, you see—till they'd done forgot, long ago, what it was all about. Wherever a Darnell caught a Watson, or a Watson caught a Darnell, one of 'em was going to get hurt—only question was, which of them got the drop on the other. They'd shoot one another down, right in the presence of the family. They did n't *hunt* for each other, but when they happened to meet, they pulled and begun. Men would shoot boys, boys would shoot men. A man shot a boy twelve years old—happened on him in the woods, and did n't give him no chance. If he *had* 'a' given him a chance, the boy 'd 'a' shot *him*. Both families belonged to the same church (everybody around here is religious); through all this fifty or sixty years' fuss, both tribes was there every Sunday, to worship. They lived each side of the line, and the church was at a landing called Compromise. Half the church and half the aisle was in Kentucky, the other half in Tennessee. Sundays you'd see the families drive up, all in their Sunday

DARNELL *vs.* WATSON.

Pages from chapter 26 of Life on the Mississippi, *which was published in May 1883, more than a year and a half before the Grangerford-Sheperdson adventure appeared in* The Century Illustrated Monthly Magazine. *Mark Twain, however, probably wrote this "factual" account of the Darnell-Watson feud after he had written of the Grangerford-Shepherdson feud in the manuscript of* Adventures of Huckleberry Finn *(illustrations by A. B. Shute and E. H. Garrett; Mark Twain House, Hartford, Connecticut).*

288   THE LAST DARNELL.

they galloping and cavorting and yelling and banging away with all their might. Think he wounded a couple of them; but they closed in on him and chased him into the river; and as he swum along down stream, they followed along the bank and kept on shooting at him; and when he struck shore he was dead. Windy Marshall told me about it. He saw it. He was captain of the boat.

"Years ago, the Darnells was so thinned out that the old man and his two sons concluded they'd leave the country. They started to take steamboat just above No. 10; but the Watsons got wind of it; and they arrived just as the two young Darnells was walking up the companion-way with their wives on their arms. The fight begun then, and they never got no further—both of them killed. After that, old Darnell got into trouble with the man that run the ferry, and the ferry-man got the worst of it—and died. But his friends shot old Darnell through and through—filled him full of bullets, and ended him."

The country gentleman who told me these things had been reared in ease and comfort, was a man of good parts, and was college bred. His loose grammar was the fruit of careless habit, not ignorance. This habit among educated men in the West is not universal, but it is prevalent—prevalent in the towns, certainly, if not in the cities; and to a degree which one cannot help noticing, and marvelling at. I heard a Westerner who would be accounted a highly educated man in any country, say "never mind, it *don't make no difference,* anyway." A life-long resident who was present heard it, but it made no impression upon her. She was able to recall the fact afterward, when reminded of it; but she confessed that the words had not grated upon her ear at the time—a confession which suggests that if educated people can hear such blasphemous grammar, from such a source, and be unconscious of the deed, the crime must be tolerably common—so common that the general ear has become dulled by famil-

---

PRAYING AND SHOOTING.   287

clothes, men, women, and children, and file up the aisle, and set down, quiet and orderly, one lot on the Tennessee side of the church and the other on the Kentucky side; and the men and boys would lean their guns up against the wall, handy, and then all hands would join in with the prayer and praise; though they say the man next the aisle didn't kneel down, along with the rest of the family; kind of stood guard. I don't know; never was at that church in my life;

THEY KEPT ON SHOOTING.

but I remember that that's what used to be said.

"Twenty or twenty-five years ago, one of the feud families caught a young man of nineteen out and killed him. Don't remember whether it was the Darnells and Watsons, or one of the other feuds; but anyway, this young man rode up—steamboat laying there at the time—and the first thing he saw was a whole gang of the enemy. He jumped down behind a wood-pile, but they rode around and begun on him, he firing back, and

AN ADVENTURE OF HUCKLEBERRY FINN:

WITH AN ACCOUNT OF THE FAMOUS GRANGERFORD-SHEPHERDSON FEUD.

BY MARK TWAIN.

[THE following episode is taken from an unpublished book called "The Adventures of Huckleberry Finn, Tom Sawyer's Comrade." A word will explain the situation: The negro Jim is escaping from slavery in Missouri, and Huck Finn is running away from a drunken father, who maltreats him. The two fugitives are floating down the Mississippi on a fragment of a lumber-raft, doing their voyaging by night and hiding themselves and the raft in the day-time. When this chapter opens they have already floated four hundred miles — a trip which has occupied ten or twelve adventurous nights. Readers who have met Huck Finn before (in "Tom Sawyer") will not be surprised to note that whenever Huck is caught in a close place and is obliged to explain, the truth gets well crippled before he gets through.— M. T.]

HERE is the way we put in the time. It was a monstrous big river down there—sometimes a mile and a half wide. We run nights, and laid up and hid day-times; soon as night was most gone, we stopped navigating and tied up—nearly always in the dead water under a tow-head; and then cut young cottonwoods and willows and hid the raft with them. Then we set out the lines. Next we slid into the river and had a swim, so as to freshen up and cool off; then we set down on the sandy bottom where the water was about knee-deep, and watched the daylight come. Not a sound anywheres—perfectly still—just like the whole world was asleep, only sometimes the bullfrogs a-cluttering, may be. The first thing to see, looking away over the water, was a kind of dull line—that was the woods on t'other side—you couldn't make nothing else out; then a pale place in the sky; then more paleness, spreading around; then the river softened up, away off, and warn't black any more, but gray; you could see little dark spots drifting along, ever so far away—trading scows, and such things; and long black streaks — rafts; sometimes you could hear a sweep screaking, or jumbled-up voices, it was so still, and sounds come so far; and by and by you could see a streak on the water which you know by the look of the streak that there's a snag there in a swift current which breaks on it and makes that streak look that way; and you see the mist curl up off of the water, and the east reddens up, and the river, and you make out a log cabin in the edge of the woods, away on the bank on t'other side of the river, being a wood-yard, likely, and piled by them cheats so you can throw a dog through it anywheres; then the nice breeze springs up, and comes fanning you from over there, so cool and fresh, and sweet to smell, on account of the woods and the flowers; but sometimes not that way, because they've left dead fish laying around, gars, and such, and they do get pretty rank; and next you've got the full day, and everything smiling in the sun, and the song-birds just going it!

A little smoke couldn't be noticed now, so we would take some fish off of the lines and cook up a hot breakfast. And afterward we would watch the lonesomeness of the river, and kind of lazy along, and by and by lazy off to sleep. Wake up by and by, and look to see what done it, and may be see a steamboat, coughing along up stream, so far off toward the other side you couldn't tell nothing about her only whether she was stern-wheel or side-wheel; then for about an hour there wouldn't be nothing to hear nor nothing to see —just solid lonesomeness. Next you'd see a raft sliding by, away off yonder, and may be a galoot on it chopping, because they're most always doing it on a raft; you'd see the axe flash, and come down—you don't hear nothing; you see that axe go up again, and by the time it's above the man's head, then you hear the *k'chunk!*—it had took all that time to come over the water. So we would put in the day, lazying around, listening to the stillness. Once there was a thick fog, and the rafts and things that went by was beating tin pans so the steam-boats wouldn't run over them. A scow or a raft went by so close we could hear them talking and cussing and laughing — heard them plain; but we couldn't see no sign of them; it made you feel crawly, it was like spirits carrying on that way in the air.

WE shoved out, after dark, on the raft.

Pages from the December 1884 issue of The Century *presenting first of three excerpts from* Adventures of Huckleberry Finn *to appear in the periodical. The text was edited by Richard Watson Gilder, who used a description of the river from chapter 19 as the opening for the selection before proceeding to the account of the Grangerford-Shepherdson feud from chapters 17 and 18. The text is close to that of the published novel, though there are some omissions, such as Emmeline Grangerford's tribute, "Ode to Stephen Dowling Bots, Dec'd"*
(Thomas Cooper Library, University of South Carolina).

AN ADVENTURE OF HUCKLEBERRY FINN.   269

The place to buy canoes is off of rafts laying up at shore. But we didn't see no rafts laying up; so we went along during three hours and more. Well, the night got gray, and ruther thick, which is the next meanest thing to fog. You can't tell the shape of the river, and you can't see no distance. It got to be very late and still, and then along comes a steam-boat up the river. We lit the lantern and judged she would see it. Up-stream boats didn't generly come close to us; they go out and follow the bars and hunt for easy water under the reefs; but nights like this they bull right up the channel against the whole river.

We could hear her pounding along, but we didn't see her good till she was close. She aimed right for us. Often they do that, and try to see how close they can come without touching; sometimes the wheel bites off a sweep, and then the pilot sticks his head out and laughs, and thinks he's mighty smart. Well, here she comes, and we said she was going to try to shave us; but she didn't seem to be sheering off a bit. She was a big one, and she was coming in a hurry, too, looking like a black cloud with rows of glow-worms around it; but all of a sudden she bulged out, big and scary, with a long row of wide-open furnace doors shining like red-hot teeth, and her monstrous bows and guards hanging right over us. There was a yell at us, and a jingling of bells to stop the engines, a pow-wow of cussing, and whistling of steam — and as Jim went overboard on one side and I on the other, she come smashing straight through the raft.

I dived — and I aimed to find the bottom, too, for a thirty-foot wheel had got to go over me, and I wanted it to have plenty of room. I could always stay under water a minute; this time I reckon I staid under water a minute and a half. Then I bounced for the top in a hurry, for I was nearly busting. I popped out to my arm-pits and blowed the water out of my nose, and puffed a bit. Of course there was a booming current; and of course that boat started her engines again ten seconds after she stopped them, for they never cared much for raftsmen; so now she was churning along up the river, out of sight in the thick weather, though I could hear her.

I sung out for Jim about a dozen times, but I didn't get any answer; so I grabbed a plank that touched me while I was treading water, and struck out for shore, shoving it ahead of me. But I made out to see that the drift of the current was toward the left-hand shore, which meant that I was in a crossing; so I changed off and went that way.

It was one of these long, slanting, two-mile crossings; so I was a good long time in getting over. I made a safe landing, and clum up the bank. I couldn't see but a little ways, but I went poking along over rough ground for a quarter of a mile or more, and then I run across a big old-fashioned double log house before I noticed it. I was going to rush by and get away, but a lot of dogs jumped out and went to howling and barking at me, and I knowed better than to move another peg.

"WHO'S THERE?"

In about half a minute somebody spoke out of a window, without putting his head out, and says:

"Be done, boys! Who's there?"

I says:

"It's me."

"Who's me?"

"George Jackson, sir."

"What do you want?"

"I don't want nothing, sir. I only want to go along by, but the dogs wont let me."

"What are you prowling around here this time of night for — hey?"

"I warn't prowling around, sir; I fell overboard off of the steam-boat."

"Oh, you did, did you? Strike a light there, somebody. What did you say your name was?"

"George Jackson, sir. I'm only a boy."

"Look here; if you're telling the truth, you needn't be afraid — nobody'll hurt you. But don't try to budge; stand right where you

270   AN ADVENTURE OF HUCKLEBERRY FINN.

are. Rouse out Bob and Tom, some of you, and fetch the guns. George Jackson, is there anybody with you?"

"No, sir; nobody."

I heard the people stirring around in the house now, and see a light. The man sung out:

"Snatch that light away, Betsy, you old fool — aint you got any sense? Put it on the floor behind the front door. Bob, if you and Tom are ready, take your places."

"All ready."

"Now, George Jackson, do you know the Shepherdsons?"

"No, sir — I never heard of them."

"Well, that may be so, and it mayn't. Now, all ready. Step forward, George Jackson. And mind, don't you hurry — come mighty slow. If there's anybody with you, let him keep back; if he shows himself he'll be shot. Come along, now. Come slow; push the door open yourself — just enough to squeeze in, d'you hear?"

I didn't hurry; I couldn't if I'd 'a' wanted to. I took one slow step at a time, and there warn't a sound, only I thought I could hear my heart. The dogs were as still as the humans, but they followed a little behind me. When I got to the three log door-steps, I heard them unlocking and unbarring and unbolting. I put my hand on the door and pushed it a little and a little more, till some-body said, "There, that's enough — put your head in." I done it, but I judged they would take it off.

The candle was on the floor, and there they all was, looking at me, and me at them, for about a quarter of a minute. Three big men with guns pointed at me, which made me wince, I tell you; the oldest, gray and about sixty, the other two thirty or more — all of them fine and handsome — and the sweetest old gray-headed lady, and back of her two young women, which I couldn't see right well. The old gentleman says:

"There — I reckon it's all right. Come in."

As soon as I was in, the old gentleman he locked the door and barred it and bolted it, and told the young men to come in with their guns, and they all went in a big parlor that had a new rag carpet on the floor, and got together in a corner that was out of range of the front windows — there warn't none on the side. They held the candle, and took a good look at me, and all said, "Why, he aint a Shepherdson — no, there aint any Shepherdson about him." Then the old man said he hoped I wouldn't mind being searched for arms, because he didn't mean no harm by it — it was only to make sure. So he didn't

pry into my pockets, but only felt outside with his hands, and said it was all right. He told me to make myself easy and at home, and tell all about myself; but the old lady says:

"Why, bless you, Saul, the poor thing's as wet as he can be; and don't you reckon it may be he's hungry?"

"True for you, Rachel — I forgot."

So the old lady says:

"Betsy" (this was a nigger woman), "you fly around and get him something to eat, as quick as you can, poor thing; and one of you girls go and wake up Buck and tell him — Oh, here he is himself. Buck, take this little stranger and get the wet clothes off from him, and dress him up in some of yours that's dry."

Buck looked about as old as me — thirteen or fourteen or along there, though he was a little bigger than me. He hadn't on anything but a shirt, and he was very frowsy-headed. He come in gaping, and digging one fist into his eyes, and he was dragging a gun along with the other one. He says:

"Aint they no Shepherdsons around?"

They said, no, 'twas a false alarm.

"Well," he says, "if they'd 'a' b'en some, I reckon I'd 'a' got one."

They all laughed, and Bob says:

"Why, Buck, they might have scalped us all, you've been so slow in coming."

"Well, nobody come after me, and it aint right. I'm always kep' down; I don't get no show."

"Never mind, Buck, my boy," says the old man, "you'll have show enough, all in good time; don't you fret about that. Go long with you now, and do as your mother told you."

When we got upstairs to his room he got me a coarse shirt and a roundabout and pants of his, and I put them on. While I was at it he asked me what my name was, but before I could tell him he started to telling me about a blue jay and a young rabbit he had catched in the woods day before yesterday, and he asked me where Moses was when the candle went out. I said I didn't know; I hadn't heard about it before, noway.

"Well, guess," he says.

"How'm I going to guess?" says I, "when I never heard tell about it before?"

"But you can guess, can't you? It's just as easy."

"Which candle?" I says.

"Why, any candle," he says.

"I don't know where he was," says I; "where was he?"

"Why, he was in the dark! That's where he was!"

"Well, if you knowed where he was, what did you ask me for?"

"Why, blame it, it's a riddle, don't you see? Say, how long are you going to stay here? You got to stay always. We can just have booming times—they don't have no school now. Do you own a dog? I've got a dog—and he'll go in the river and bring out chips that you throw in. Do you like to comb up Sundays, and all that kind of foolishness? You bet I don't, but ma she makes me. Confound these ole britches! I reckon I'd better put 'em on, but I'd ruther not, it's so warm. Are you all ready? All right—come along, old hoss."

Cold corn-pone, cold corn-beef, butter and butter-milk—that is what they had for me down there, and there aint nothing better that ever I've come across yet. Buck and his ma and all of them smoked cob pipes, except the nigger woman, which was gone, and the two young women. They all smoked and talked, and I eat and talked. The young women had quilts around them, and their hair down their backs. They all asked me questions, and I told them how pap and me and all the family was living on a little farm down at the bottom of Arkansaw, and my sister Mary Ann run off and got married and never was heard of no more, and Bill went to hunt them and he warn't heard of no more, and Tom and Mort died, and then there warn't nobody but just me and pap left, and he was just trimmed down to nothing on account of his troubles; so when he died I took what there was left, because the farm didn't belong to us, and started up the river, deck passage, and fell overboard; and that was how I come to be here. So they said I could have a home there as long as I wanted it. Then it was most daylight, and everybody went to bed, and I went to bed with Buck, and when I waked up in the morning, drat it all, I had forgot what my name was. So I laid there about an hour trying to think, and when Buck waked up, I says:

"Can you spell, Buck?"

"Yes," he says.

"I bet you can't spell my name," says I.

"I bet you what you dare I can," says he.

"All right," says I; "go ahead."

"G-o-r-g-e J-a-x-o-n—there now," he says.

"Well," says I, "you done it; but I didn't think you could. It aint no slouch of a name to spell—right off without studying."

I set it down, private, because somebody might want me to spell it next, and so I wanted to be handy with it and rattle it off like I was used to it.

It was a mighty nice family, and a mighty nice house, too. I hadn't seen no house out in the country before that was so nice and had so much style. It didn't have an iron latch on the front door, nor a wooden one with a buckskin string, but a brass knob to turn, the same as houses in a town. There warn't no bed in the parlor, not a sign of a bed; but heaps of parlors in towns has beds in them. There was a big fire-place that was bricked on the bottom, and the bricks was kept clean and red by pouring water on them and scrubbing them with another brick; sometimes they washed them over with red water-paint that they call Spanish-brown, same as they do in town. They had big brass dog-irons that could hold up a saw-log. There was a clock on the middle of the mantel-piece, with a picture of a town painted on the bottom half of the glass front, and a round place in the middle of it for the sun, and you could see the pendulum swing behind it. It was beautiful to hear that clock tick; and sometimes when one of these peddlers had been along and scoured her up and got her in good shape, she would start in and strike a hundred and fifty before she got tuckered out. They wouldn't took any money for her.

Well, there was a big outlandish parrot on each side of the clock, made out of something like chalk, and painted up gaudy. By one of the parrots was a cat made of crockery, and a crockery dog by the other; and when you pressed down on them they squeaked, but didn't open their mouths nor look different nor interested. They squeaked through underneath. There was a couple of big wild-turkey-wing fans spread out behind those things. On a table in the middle of the room was a kind of a lovely crockery basket that had apples and oranges and peaches and grapes piled up in it which was much redder and yellower and prettier than real ones is, but they warn't real, because you could see where pieces had got chipped off and showed the white chalk or whatever it was underneath.

This table had a cover made out of beautiful oil-cloth, with a red and blue spread-eagle painted on it, and a painted border all around. It come all the way from Philadelphia, they said. There was some books too, piled up perfectly exact, on each corner of the table. One was a big family Bible, full of pictures. One was "Pilgrim's Progress," about a man that left his family it didn't say why. I read considerable in it now and then. The statements was interesting, but tough. Another was "Friendship's Offering," full of beautiful stuff and poetry; but I didn't read the poetry. Another was Henry Clay's Speeches, and another was Dr. Gunn's Family Medicine,

which told you all about what to do if a body was sick or dead. There was a Hymn Book, and a lot of other books. And there was nice split-bottom chairs, and perfectly sound, too,—not bagged down in the middle and busted, like an old basket.

They had pictures hung on the walls—mainly Washingtons and Lafayettes, and battles, and Highland Marys, and one called "Signing the Declaration." There was some that they called crayons, which one of the daughters which was dead made her own self when she was only fifteen years old. They was different from any pictures I ever see before—blacker, mostly, than is common. One was a woman in a slim black dress, belted small under the arm-pits, with bulges like a cabbage in the middle of the sleeves, and a large black scoop-shovel bonnet with a black veil, and white slim ankles crossed about with black tape, and very wee black slippers, like a chisel, and she was leaning pensive on a tombstone on her right elbow, under a weeping willow, and her other hand hanging down her side holding a white handkerchief and a reticule; and underneath the picture it said "Shall I Never See Thee More Alas." Another one was a young lady with her hair all combed up straight to the top of her head, and knotted there in front of a comb like a chair-back, and she was crying into a handkerchief, and had a dead bird laying on its back in her other hand with its heels up, and underneath the picture it said "I Shall Never Hear Thy Sweet Chirrup More Alas." There was one where a young lady was at a window looking up at the moon, and tears running down her cheeks; and she had an open letter in one hand, with black sealing-wax showing on one edge of it, and she was mashing a locket with a chain to it against her mouth; and underneath the picture it said "And Art Thou Gone Yes Thou Art Gone Alas." These was all nice pictures, I reckon, but I didn't somehow seem to take to them, because if ever I was down a little, they always give me the fan-tods. Everybody was sorry she died, because she had laid out a lot more of these pictures to do, and a body could see by what she had done what they had lost. But I reckoned that, with her disposition, she was having a better time in the graveyard. She was at work on what they said was her greatest picture when she took sick, and every day and every night it was her prayer to be allowed to live till she got it done, but she never got the chance. It was a picture of a young woman in a long white gown, standing on the rail of a bridge all ready to jump off, with her hair all down her back, and looking up to the moon, with the tears running down her face, and she had two arms folded across her breast, and two arms stretched out in front, and two more reaching up towards the moon—and the idea was to see which pair would look best and then scratch out all the other arms; but, as I was saying, she died before she got her mind made up, and now they kept this picture over the head of the bed in her room, and every time her birthday come they hung flowers on it. Other times it was hid with a little curtain. The young woman in the picture had a kind of a nice sweet face, but there was so many arms it made her look too spidery, seemed to me.

This young girl kept a scrap-book when she was alive, and used to paste obituaries and accidents and cases of patient suffering in it out of the "Presbyterian Observer," and write poetry after them out of her own head. It was very good poetry.

If Emmeline Grangerford could make poetry like that before she was fourteen, there aint no telling what she could 'a' done by and by. Buck said she could rattle off poetry like nothing. She didn't ever have to stop to think. He said she would slap down a line, and if she couldn't find anything to rhyme with it she would just scratch it out and slap down another one, and go ahead. She warn't particular; she could write about anything you choose to give her to write about, just so it was sadful. Every time a man died, or a woman died, or a child died, she would be on hand with her "tribute" before he was cold. The neighbors said it was the doctor first, then Emmeline, then the undertaker. The undertaker never got in ahead of Emmeline but once, and then she hung fire on a rhyme for the dead person's name, which was Whistler. She warn't ever the same after that; she never complained, but she kind of pined away and did not live long. Poor thing! many's the time I made myself go up to the little room that used to be hers, and get out her poor old scrap-book and read in it when her pictures had been aggravating me and I had soured on her a little. I liked all that family, dead ones and all, and warn't going to let anything come between us. Poor Emmeline made poetry about all the dead people when she was alive, and it didn't seem right that there warn't nobody to make some about her, now she was gone; so I tried to sweat out a verse or two myself, but I couldn't seem to make it go, somehow. They kept Emmeline's room trim and nice, and all the things fixed in it just the way she liked to have them when she was alive, and nobody ever slept there. The old lady took care of the room herself, though there

AN ADVENTURE OF HUCKLEBERRY FINN. 273

was plenty of niggers, and she sewed there a good deal and read her Bible there, mostly.

Well, as I was saying about the parlor, there was beautiful curtains on the windows: white, with pictures painted on them, of castles with vines all down the walls, and cattle coming down to drink. There was a little old piano, too, that had tin pans in it, I reckon, and nothing was ever so lovely as to hear the young ladies sing "The Last Link is Broken," and play "The Battle of Prague" on it. The walls of all the rooms was plastered, and most had carpets on the floors, and the whole house was whitewashed on the outside.

It was a double house, and the big open place betwixt them was roofed and floored, and sometimes the table was set there in the middle of the day, and it was a cool, comfortable place. Nothing couldn't be better. And warn't the cooking good, and just bushels of it, too!

Colonel Grangerford was a gentleman, you see. He was a gentleman all over; and so was his family. He was well-born, as the saying is, and that's worth as much in a man as it is in a horse, so the widow Douglass said, and nobody ever denied that she was of the first aristocracy in our town; and pap he always said it, too, though he warn't no more quality than a mud-cat, himself. Colonel Grangerford was very tall and very slim, and had a darkish-paly complexion, not a sign of red in it anywheres; he was clean-shaved every morning, all over his thin face, and he had the

COLONEL GRANGERFORD.

Vol. XXXV.—ₐ

thinnest kind of lips, and the thinnest kind of nostrils, and a high nose, and heavy eyebrows, and the blackest kind of eyes, sunk so deep back that they seemed like they was looking out of caverns at you, as you may say. His forehead was high, and his hair was black and straight, and hung to his shoulders. His hands was long and thin, and every day of his life he put on a clean shirt and a full suit from head to foot, made out of linen so white it hurt your eyes to look at it; and on Sundays he wore a blue tail-coat with brass buttons on it. He carried a mahogany cane with a silver head to it. There warn't no frivolishness about it, not a bit, and he warn't ever loud. He was as kind as he could be—you could feel that, you know, and so you had confidence. Sometimes he smiled, and it was good to see; but when he straightened himself up like a liberty-pole, and the lightning begun to flicker out from under his eyebrows, you wanted to climb a tree first and find out what the matter was afterward. He didn't ever have to tell anybody to mind their manners—everybody was always good-mannered where he was. Everybody loved to have him around, too; he was sunshine most always—I mean he made it seem like good weather. When he turned into a cloud-bank it was awful dark for half a minute, and that was enough; there wouldn't nothing go wrong again for a week.

When him and the old lady come down in the morning, all the family got up out of their chairs and give them good-day, and didn't set down again till they had set down. Then Tom and Bob went to the sideboard where the decanters was, and mixed a glass of bitters and handed it to him, and he held it in his hand and waited till Tom's and Bob's was mixed, and then they bowed and said, "Our duty to you, sir, and madam"; and *they* bowed the least bit in the world and said thank you, and so they drank, all three, and Bob and Tom poured a spoonful of water on the sugar and the mite of whisky or apple brandy in the bottom of their tumblers, and give it to me and Buck, and we drank to the old people, too.

Bob was the oldest, and Tom next—tall, beautiful men, with very broad shoulders and brown faces, and long black hair and black eyes. They dressed in white linen from head to foot, like the old gentleman, and wore broad Panama hats.

Then there was Miss Charlotte; she was twenty-five, and tall and proud and grand, but as good as she could be when she warn't stirred up; but when she was, she had a look that would make you wilt in your tracks, like her father. She was beautiful.

AN ADVENTURE OF HUCKLEBERRY FINN. 274

So was her sister, Miss Sophia, but it was a different kind. She was gentle and sweet, like a dove, and she was only twenty.

Each person had their own nigger to wait on them—Buck, too. My nigger had a monstrous easy time, because I warn't used to having anybody do anything for me, but Buck's was on the jump most of the time.

This is all there was of the family now; but there used to be more—three sons; they got killed; and Emmeline that died.

The old gentleman owned a lot of farms, and over a hundred niggers. Sometimes a stack of people would come there, horseback, from ten or fifteen miles around, and stay five or six days, and have such junketings round about and on the river, and dances and picnics in the woods, daytimes, and balls at the house, nights. These people was mostly kin-folks of the family. The men brought their guns with them. It was a handsome lot of quality, I tell you.

There was another clan of aristocracy around there—five or six families—mostly of the name of Shepherdson. They was as high-toned, and well-born, and rich, and grand, as the tribe of Grangerfords. The Shepherdsons and the Grangerfords used the same steam-boat landing, which was about two mile above our house; so sometimes when I went up there with a lot of our folks, I used to see a lot of the Shepherdsons there, on their fine horses.

HARNEY SHEPHERDSON.

One day Buck and me was away in the woods, hunting, and heard a horse coming. We was crossing the road. Buck says:

"Quick! Jump for the woods!"

We done it, and then peeped down the woods through the leaves. Pretty soon a splendid young man come galloping down the road, setting his horse easy and looking like a soldier. He had his gun across his pommel. I had seen him before. It was young Harney Shepherdson. I heard Buck's gun go off at my ear, and Harney's hat tumbled off from his head. He grabbed his gun, and rode straight to the place where we was hid. But we didn't wait. We started through the woods on a run. The woods warn't thick, so I looked over my shoulder to dodge the bullet, and twice I seen Harney cover Buck with his gun; and then he rode away the way he come—to get his hat, I reckon, but I couldn't see. We never stopped running till we got home. The old gentleman's eyes blazed a minute,—'twas pleasure, mainly, I judged,—then his face sort of smoothed down, and he says, kind of gentle:

"I don't like that shooting from behind a bush. Why didn't you step into the road, my boy?"

"The Shepherdsons don't, father. They always take advantage."

Miss Charlotte she held her head up like a queen while Buck was telling his tale, and her nostrils spread and her eyes snapped. The two young men looked dark, but never said nothing. Miss Sophia she turned pale, but the color come back when she found the man warn't hurt.

Soon as I could get Buck down by the corn-cribs under the trees by ourselves, I says:

"Did you want to kill him, Buck?"

"Well, I bet I did."

"What did he do to you?"

"Him? He never done nothing to me."

"Well, then, what did you want to kill him for?"

"Why, nothing—only it's on account of the feud."

"What's a feud?"

"Why, where was you raised? Don't you know what a feud is?"

"Never heard of it before—tell me about it."

"Well," says Buck, "a feud is this way. A man has a quarrel with another man, and kills him; then that other man's brother kills him; then the other brothers, on both sides, goes for one another; then the *cousins* chip in—and by and by everybody's killed off,

AN ADVENTURE OF HUCKLEBERRY FINN. 275

and there aint no more feud. But it's kind of slow, and takes a long time."

"Has this one been going on long, Buck?"

"Well, I should *reckon!* it started thirty year ago, or son'ers along there. There was trouble 'bout something, and then a lawsuit to settle it; and the suit went ag'in' one of the men, and so he up and shot the man that won the suit—which he would naturally do, of course. Anybody would."

"What was the trouble about, Buck?—land?"

"I reckon, may be—I don't know."

"Well, who done the shooting?—was it a Grangerford or a Shepherdson?"

"Laws, how do *I* know? it was so long ago."

"Don't anybody know?"

"Oh, yes, pa knows, I reckon, and some of the other old folks; but they don't know now what the row was about in the first place."

"Has there been many killed, Buck?"

MISS CHARLOTTE.

"Yes—right smart chance of funerals. But they don't always kill. Pa's got a few buck-shot in him; but he don't mind it, 'cuz he don't weigh much, anyway. Bob's been carved up some with a bowie, and Tom's been hurt once or twice."

"Has anybody been killed this year, Buck?"

"Yes, we got one and they got one. 'Bout three months ago, my cousin Bud, fourteen year old, was riding through the woods on 'tother side of the river, and didn't have no weapon with him, which was blame' foolishness; and in a lonesome place he hears a horse a-coming behind him, and sees old Baldy Shepherdson a-linkin' after him with his gun in his hand, and his white hair a-flying in the wind; and 'stead of jumping off and taking to the brush, Bud 'lowed he could outrun him; so they had it, nip and tuck, for five mile or more, the old man a-gaining all the time. So at last Bud seen it warn't any use, so he stopped and faced around so as to have the bullet-holes in front, you know, and the old man he rode up and shot him down. But he didn't git much chance to enjoy his luck, for inside of a week our folks laid *him* out."

"I reckon that old man was a coward, Buck."

"I reckon he *warn't* a coward—not by a blame' sight. There aint a coward amongst them Shepherdsons—not a one. And there aint no cowards amongst the Grangerfords, either. Why, that old man kep' up his end in a fight one day, for half an hour, against three Grangerfords, and come out winner. They was all a-horseback; he let off his-horse and got behind a little wood-pile, and kep' his horse before him to stop the bullets; but the Grangerfords staid on their horses and capered around the old man, and peppered away at him, and he peppered away at them. Him and his horse both went home pretty leaky and crippled, but the Grangerfords had to be *fetched* home—and one of 'em was dead, and another died the next day. No, sir; if a body's out hunting for cowards, he don't want to fool away any time amongst them Shepherdsons, becuz they don't breed any of that *kind.*"

Next Sunday we all went to church, about three mile, everybody a-horseback. The men took their guns along, so did Buck, and kept them between their knees or stood them handy against the wall. The Shepherdsons done the same. It was pretty ornery preaching—all about brotherly love, and such-like tiresomeness; but everybody said it was a good sermon, and they all talked it over going home, and had such a powerful lot to say about faith, and good works, and free grace, and preforeordestination, and I don't know what all, that it did seem to me to be one of the roughest Sundays I had run across yet.

About an hour after dinner everybody was dozing around, some in their chairs and some in their rooms, and it got to be pretty dull. Buck and a dog was stretched out on the grass in the sun, sound asleep. I went up to our room, and judged I would take a nap

276 *AN ADVENTURE OF HUCKLEBERRY FINN.*

myself. I found that sweet Miss Sophia standing in her door, which was next to ours, and she took me in her room and shut the door very soft, and asked me if I liked her, and I said I did; and she asked me if I would do something for her and not tell anybody, and I said I would. Then she said she'd forgot her Testament, and left it in the seat at church, between two other books, and would I slip out quiet and go there and fetch it to her, and not say nothing to nobody? I said I would. So I slid out and slipped off up the road, and there warn't anybody at the church, except may be a hog or two, for there warn't any lock on the door, and hogs likes a puncheon floor in summer-time, because it's cool. If you notice, most folks don't go to church only when they've got to; but a hog is different.

Says I to myself, something's up—it aint natural for a girl to be in such a sweat about a Testament; so I give it a shake, and out drops a little piece of paper with "*Half-past two*" wrote on it with a pencil. I ransacked it, but couldn't find anything else. I couldn't make anything out of that, so I put the paper in the book again, and when I got home and upstairs, there was Miss Sophia in her door waiting for me. She pulled me in and shut the door; then she looked in the Testament till she found the paper, and as soon as she read it she looked glad; and before a body could think she grabbed me and give me a squeeze, and said I was the best boy in the world, and not to tell anybody. She was mighty red in the face for a minute, and her eyes lighted up, and it made her powerful pretty. I was a good deal astonished, but when I got my breath I asked her what the paper was about, and she asked me if I had read it, and I said no, and she asked me if I could read writing, and I told her "no, only coarse-hand," and then she said the paper warn't anything but a book-mark to keep her place, and I might go and play now.

I went off down to the river, studying over this thing, and pretty soon I noticed that my nigger was following along behind. When we was out of sight of the house, he looked back and around a second, and then comes a-running, and says:

"Mars Jawge, if you'll come down into de swamp, I'll show you a whole stack o' water-moccasins."

Thinks I, that's mighty curious; he said that yesterday. He oughter know a body don't love water-moccasins enough to go around hunting for them. What is he up to, anyway? So I says:

"All right, trot ahead."

I followed a half a mile, then he struck out over the swamp and waded ankle-deep as much as another half-mile. We come to a little flat piece of land, which was dry and very thick with trees and bushes and vines, and he says:

"You shove right in dah, jist a few steps, Mars Jawge, dah's whah dey is. I's seed 'em befo', I don't k'yer to see 'em no mo'."

Then he slopped right along and went away, and pretty soon the trees hid him. I poked into the place a-ways, and come to a little open patch as big as a bedroom, all hung around with vines, and found a man laying there asleep—and by jings it was my old Jim!

I waked him up, and I reckoned it was going to be a grand surprise to him to see me again, but it warn't. He nearly cried, he was so glad, but he warn't surprised. Said he swum along behind me that night, and heard me yell every time, but dasn't answer, because he didn't want nobody to pick *him* up, and take him into slavery again. Says he:

"I got hurt a little, en couldn't swim fas', so I wuz a considable ways behine you toward de las'; when you landed I reck'ned I could ketch up wid you on de lan' 'dout havin' to shout at you, but when I see dat house I begin to go slow. I 'uz off too fur to hear what dey say to you—I wuz afraid o' de dogs—but when it 'uz all quiet ag'in, I knowed you's in de house; so I struck out for de woods to wait for day. Early in de mawnin' some er de niggers come along, gwine to de fields, en dey tuck me en showed me dis place, whah de dogs can't track me on accounts o' de water, en dey brings me truck to eat every night, en tells me how you's a-gitt'n along."

"Why didn't you tell my Jack to fetch me here sooner, Jim?"

"Well, 'twarn't no use to 'sturb you, Huck, tell we could do sumfn—but we's all right now. I b'en a-buyin' pots en pans en vittles, as I got a chanst, en a-patchin' up de raf', nights, when—"

"*What* raft, Jim?"

"Our ole raf'."

"You mean to say our old raft warn't smashed all to flinders?"

"No, she warn't. She was tore up a good deal—one en' of her was—but dey warn't no great harm done, on'y our traps was mos' all los'. Ef we hadn' dive' so deep en swum so fur under water, en de night hadn' b'en so dark, en we warn't so sk'yerd, en be'n sich punkin-heads, as de sayin' is, we'd 'a' seed de raf'. But it's jis' as well we didn't, 'kase now she's all fixed up ag'in mos' as good as new, en we's got a new lot o' stuff, too, in de place o' what 'uz los'."

"Why, how did you get hold of the raft again, Jim—did you catch her?"

AN ADVENTURE OF HUCKLEBERRY FINN. 277

"How I gwine to ketch her, en I out in de woods? No; some er de niggers foun' her ketched on a snag, along heah in de ben', en dey hid her in a crick, 'mongst de willows, en dey wuz so much jawin' 'bout which um 'um she b'long to de mos', dat I come to heah 'bout it pooty soon, so I ups en settles de trouble by tellin' um she don't b'long to none uv um, but to you en me; en I ast um if dey gwine to grab a young white gen'l'man's propaty, en git a hid'n' for it? Den I gin um ten cents apiece, en dey 'uz mighty well satisfied, en wisht some mo' raf's 'ud come along en make um rich ag'in. Dey's mighty good to me, dese niggers is, en whatever I wants um to do fur me, I doan' have to ast 'm twice, honey. Dat Jack's a good nigger, en pooty smart."

"Yes, he is. He aint ever told me you was here; told me to come, and he'd show you a lot of water-moccasins. If anything happens, *he* ain't mixed up in it. He can say he never seen us together, and it'll be the truth."

I don't want to talk much about the next day. I reckon I'll cut it pretty short. I waked up about dawn, and was a-going to turn over and go to sleep again, when I noticed how still it was—didn't seem to be anybody stirring. That warn't usual. Next I noticed that Buck was up and gone. Well, I gets up, a-wondering, and goes downstairs—nobody around; everything as still as a mouse. Just the same outside; thinks I, what does it mean? Down by the wood-pile I comes across my Jack, and says:

"What's it all about?"

Says he:

"Don't you know, Mars Jawge?"

"No," says I, "I don't."

"Well, den, Miss Sophia's run off! 'deed she has. She run off in de night, some time—nobody don't know jis' when—run off to get married to dat young Harney Shepherdson, you know—leastways, so dey 'spec'. De fambly foun' it out 'bout half an hour ago—may be a little mo',—en' I *tell* you dey warn't no time los'. Such another hurryin' up guns en horses you never see! De women folks has gone for to stir up de relations, en old Mars Saul en de boys tuck dey guns en rode up de river road for to try to ketch dat young man en kill him fo' he kin git acrost de river wid Miss Sophia. I reck'n dey's gwine to be mighty rough times."

"Buck went off 'thout waking me up."

"Well, I reck'n he *did!* Dey warn't gwine to mix you up in it. Mars Buck he loaded up his gun en 'lowed he's gwine to fetch home a Shepherdson or bust. Well, dey'll be plenty un 'm dah, I reck'n, en you bet you he'll fetch one ef he gits a chanst."

278 *AN ADVENTURE OF HUCKLEBERRY FINN.*

I took up the river road as hard as I could put. By and by I began to hear guns a good ways off. When I come in sight of the log store and the wood-pile where the steam-boats lands, I worked along under the trees and brush till I got to a good place, and then I clumb up into the forks of a cotton-wood that was out of reach, and watched. There was a wood-rank four foot high, a little ways in front of the tree, and first I was going to hide behind that; but may be it was luckier I didn't.

There was four or five men cavorting around on their horses in the open place before the log store, cussing and yelling, and trying to get at a couple of young chaps that was behind the wood-rank alongside of the steamboat landing—but they couldn't come it. Every time one of them showed himself on the river side of the wood-pile he got shot at. The two boys was squatting back to back behind the pile, so they could watch both ways.

By and by the men stopped cavorting around and yelling. They started riding toward the store; then up gets one of the boys, draws a steady bead over the wood-rank, and drops one of them out of his saddle. All the men jumped off of their horses and grabbed the hurt one and started to carry him to the store; and that minute the two boys started on the run. They got half-way to the tree I was in before the men noticed. Then the men see them, and jumped on their horses and took out after them. They gained on the boys, but it didn't do no good, the boys had too good a start; they got to the wood-pile that was in front of my tree, and slipped in behind it, and so they had the bulge on the men again. One of the boys was Buck, and the other was a slim young chap about nineteen years old.

The men ripped around awhile, and then rode away. As soon as they was out of sight, I sung out to Buck and told him. He didn't know what to make of my voice coming out of the tree at first. He was awful surprised. He told me to watch out sharp and let him know when the men come in sight again; said they was up to some devilment or other—wouldn't be gone long. I wished I was out of that tree, but I dasn't come down. Buck begun to cry and rip, and 'lowed that him and his cousin Joe (that was the other young chap) would make up for this day yet. He said his father and his two brothers was killed, and two or three of the enemy. Said the Shepherdsons laid for them in ambush. Buck said his father and brothers ought to waited for their relations—the Shepherdsons was too strong for them. I asked him what was become of young Harney and Miss Sophia. He said they'd got across the river and was safe. I was glad of that; but the way Buck did take on because he didn't manage to kill Harney that day he shot at him—I haint ever heard anything like it.

All of a sudden, bang! bang! bang! goes three or four guns—the men had slipped around through the woods and come in from behind without their horses! The boys

BEHIND THE WOOD-PILE.

jumped for the river—both of them hurt—and as they swum down the current the men run along the bank shooting at them and singing out, "Kill them, kill them!" It made me so sick I most fell out of the tree. I aint a-going to tell *all* that happened—it would make me sick again if I was to do that. I wished I hadn't ever come ashore that night, to see such things. I aint ever going to get shut of them—lots of times I dream about them. I staid in the tree till it begun to get dark, afraid to come down. Sometimes I heard guns away off in the woods; and twice I seen little gangs of men gallop past the log store with guns; so I reckoned the trouble was still a-going on. I made up my mind I wouldn't ever go anear that house again, because I reckoned I was to blame, somehow. I judged that that piece of paper meant that Miss Sophia was to meet Harney somewhere at half-past two and run off; and I judged I ought to told her father about that paper and the curious way she acted, and then may be he would 'a' locked her up, and this awful mess wouldn't ever happened.

When I got down out of the tree, I crept along down the river bank a piece, and found the two bodies laying in the edge of the water, and tugged at them till I got them ashore; then I covered up their faces, and got away as quick as I could. I cried a little when I was covering up Buck's face, for he was mighty good to me.

It was just dark now. I never went near the house, but struck through the woods and made for the swamp. Jim warn't on his island, so I tramped off in a hurry for the crick, and crowded through the willows, red-hot to jump aboard and get out of that awful country. The raft was gone! My souls, but I was scared! I couldn't get my breath for most a minute. Then I raised a yell. A voice not twenty-five foot from me says:

"Good lan'! is dat you, honey? Doan' make no noise."

It was Jim's voice—nothing ever sounded so good before. I run along the bank a piece and got aboard, and Jim he grabbed me and hugged me, he was so glad to see me. He says:

"Laws bless you, chile, I 'uz right down sho' you's dead ag'in. Jack's ben heah; he say he reck'n you's ben shot, kase you didn' come home no mo'; so I's jes' dis minute a-startin' de raf' down towards de mouf er de crick, so's to be all ready for to shove out en leave soon as Jack comes ag'in en tells me for certain you *is* dead. Lawsy, I's mighty glad to git you back ag'in, honey,"

I says:

"All right—that's mighty good; they wont find me, and they'll think I've been killed, and floated down the river—there's something up there that'll help them to think so; so don't you lose no time, Jim, but just shove off for the big water as fast as ever you can."

I never felt easy till the raft was two mile below there and out in the middle of the Mississippi. Then we hung up our signal lantern, and judged that we was free and safe once more. I hadn't had a bite to eat since yesterday; so Jim he got out some corn-dodgers and buttermilk, and pork and cabbage, and greens—there aint nothing in the world so good, when it's cooked right—and whilst I eat my supper we talked, and had a good time. I was powerful glad to get away from the feuds, and so was Jim to get away from the swamp. We said there warn't no home like a raft, after all. Other places do seem so cramped up and smothery, but a raft don't. You feel mighty free and easy and comfortable on a raft.

In this excerpt Hirst and Branch consider the evidence showing Samuel Clemens's personal experience with the Darnell-Watson feud as well as his research into the subject.

In 1884, when Gilder solicited Mark Twain's permission to serialize *Huckleberry Finn,* he reminded the author that he then commanded "the largest audience of any English writer above ground."[1] Mark Twain was, indeed, at the height of his powers. Behind him lay four years (aged twenty-three to twenty-five) as a pilot on the Mississippi, and six years (aged twenty-six to thirty-one) in Nevada and California as a journalist. This apprenticeship culminated with publication of the *Jumping Frog* book in 1867, and then with a runaway bestseller called *The Innocents Abroad, or the New Pilgrim's Progress* (1869). Thereafter his reputation continued to grow, both here and abroad, with each volume that he issued: *Roughing It* (1872), *The Gilded Age* with Charles Dudley Warner (1873), *The Adventures of Tom Sawyer* (1876*), A Tramp Abroad* (1879), *The Prince and the Pauper* (1881), and most recently, *Life on the Mississippi* (1883). By 1884 he had completed the manuscript of *Adventures of Huckleberry Finn,* a book that he said he had "been working at, by fits and starts, during the past five or six years."[2]

These last two books both profited from his decision to re-visit the Mississippi River, something that he had been planning to do since at least 1866, but that he did not accomplish until April and May of 1882. On April 20 of that year, some seven years after publishing his piloting reminiscences in the *Atlantic Monthly* ("Old Times on the Mississippi"), he left St. Louis aboard the steamboat *Gold Dust,* bound for New Orleans.[3] He had last seen the river in 1868 and had last navigated it as a pilot in 1861, when he was only twenty-five. His purpose was to refresh his memory and to gather materials for a Mississippi book, in which the trip itself would act as a kind of frame. The incomplete manuscript for *Huckleberry Finn* lay in its pigeonhole, drafted at least as far as the end of the Grangerford-Shepherdson feud.[4]

While planning what stops to make on the downriver trip, Mark Twain listed river towns in his notebook, roughly in the order he expected to encounter them:

Stop at Cairo.
Hickman or
Columbus.
New Madrid (1 hour).
Memphis a day.
Napoleon.
Helena
Walnut Bend or
some other wretched place.
Compro

Here he paused a moment, for the phrase "some other wretched place" had reminded him of Compromise, Kentucky, on or very near the Kentucky-Tennessee line, some ninety miles above Memphis—and he had begun to write the name in his list before noticing that it was well out of order. The original notebook page . . . shows that he crossed out the beginning of the name "Compro" and then wrote "Compromise?" just below "Memphis," adding the question mark to signify his uncertainty about its exact location. (It was, in fact, just above Memphis . . .)[5] Compromise *was* a "wretched place" in Mark Twain's memory, a primitive landing with only a wood-yard, a log-cabin store which doubled as the postoffice, a few dwellings, and possibly a schoolhouse. But Compromise also signified something more to Clemens, for he next altered his list in another way. Just below "New Madrid" he squeezed in the words "& ask about the old feuds."

. . . .

As it turned out, Mark Twain was unable to go ashore either at New Madrid or at Compromise, in part because the *Gold Dust* did not make way-stops. But as she passed down through Madrid Bend on April 22, Clemens dictated some memoranda to his secretary Roswell Phelps, who accompanied him, that show just how attentive he was to its peculiar geography:

ISLAND No. 10.

The river passes from Ky. into Tenn., back into Mo. then back into Ky. and thence into Tenn.

That is, a mile or two of Mo. sticks over into Tenn. (*N&J2,* 533)

Mark Twain reproduced these two sentences nearly verbatim in chapter 26 of *Life on the Mississippi* (page 290), which did not finally include a map. Still, it may be worthwhile to remark that the note can hardly be the result of unaided observation, no matter how attentive. The note could not have been *made* without access to a map like Suter's, which clearly labels the states mentioned.

Not until the return trip upriver, however, did Mark Twain get very much opportunity to refresh his memory of "the old feuds." Traveling on *The City of Baton Rouge,* captained by his old friend and mentor Horace Bixby, Clemens reminisced with him about what Bixby called "a long quarrel" between the "Darnell & Watson" families (*N&J2,* 567–568). Phelps recorded the comments of both men. Here is what he set down as Clemens's remarks:

Notebook page showing Mark Twain's list of river towns during his spring 1882 trip down the Mississippi
(Mark Twain Papers, The Bancroft Library, University of California, Berkeley)

One of these families lived on the Kentucky side the other on Missouri side near New Madrid. Once a boy 12 years old connected with the Kentucky family was riding thro the woods on the Mo. side. He was overtaken by a full grown man and he shot that boy dead.

I was on a Memphis packet & at a landing we made on the Kentucky side there was a row. Don't remember as there was anybody hurt then; but shortly afterwards there was another row at that place and a youth of 19 belonging to the Mo. tribe had wandered over there. Half a dozen of that Ky. tribe got after him. He dodged among the wood piles & answered their shots. Presently he jumped into the river & they followed on after & peppered him & he had to make for the shore. By that time he was about dead–did shortly die. (*N&J2*, 568)

Here Clemens recalled two distinct incidents from his personal experience as a pilot (1858–1861). The first he probably heard from the father of the twelve-year-old: "Refugee from a wornout feud in Kentucky or Tenn. Told his story, afraid he might be hunted down. Fictitious name. Saw his boy of 12 riddled but he and his ambushed an open wagon of the enemy driving home from church."[6] It is not known when Clemens heard this story, nor when he recorded it in this cryptic fashion. The second incident, concerning the nineteen-year-old who is murdered, has two parts: the "row" which Clemens says he witnessed while "on a Memphis packet" at a "landing we made on the Kentucky side," and the actual shooting itself, which he says occurred "shortly afterwards."

Mark Twain demonstrably used both incidents in *Huckleberry Finn* and in *Life on the Mississippi*. In the latter, the person telling the story is introduced to us as a "handsome man, with easy carriage and an intelligent face," a "country gentleman," who lived near the Kentucky-Tennessee line "on the main shore" across from Island No. 10 (285). He is a fictional, but clearly a reliable spokesman for the author, and his narrative gives two important details not found in *Huckleberry Finn*: (1) he says that the feuding families lived "each side of the line," rather than on opposite sides of the river, and attended the same church "at a landing called Compromise"; and (2) he says that the murder of the nineteen-year-old took place while there was a "steamboat laying" at the landing, which provided him with an eyewitness account: "Windy Marshall told me about it. He saw it. He was captain of the boat" (286–288).

How well can these complementary but partly conflicting accounts—*Huckleberry Finn,* the 1882 notebook, and *Life on the Mississippi*—be corroborated and their differences explained?

                                        —pp. 33–34, 38–42

This excerpt examines the facts behind Clemens's claim that he "came near being an eye-witness of the general engagement" described in Adventures of Huckleberry Finn. *Through later reports Mark Twain came to understand the larger conflict in which the men named Starr and Beckham were associated with the Watson family of Kentucky, and the man they killed, Shultz, was aligned with the Darnell family of Tennessee.*

In mid-morning on Sunday, 4 September 1859, the twenty-three-year-old Clemens (or his co-pilot) was steering the *Edward J. Gay* upriver, some seventeen hours out of New Orleans, bound for her home port of St. Louis. The *Gay* was a brand new luxury packet, 267 feet long, described as "radiant with beauty,"[7] the most recent addition to the well established St. Louis and

New Orleans Railroad Line. Commanded by Clemens's friend Bart Bowen, she was completing only her second round trip in the St. Louis-New Orleans trade (not the St. Louis-Memphis trade as Clemens recalled).[8]

On that same Sunday morning the *John H. Dickey,* a mailboat in the St. Louis-Memphis Packet Line, was on its way downriver, about to put in at Compromise, Kentucky, near the foot of New Madrid Bend. Clemens was thoroughly familiar with the *Dickey,* having been one of her steersmen for several months in the previous summer (1858). Her master was his good friend Captain John H. Marshall, a veteran steamboat commander, active in the Pittsburgh and Cincinnati Line during the early 1850s and, somewhat later, on the *Forester* in the Cincinnati-St. Louis trade. In July 1858 Marshall had purchased the *Philadelphia,* which became, along with the *Dickey* and the *J. H. Lucas,* a regular packet in the newly formed St. Louis-Memphis Packet Line. Southern in his sympathies, Marshall would join the Confederate side when war came, serving as commander of the *Yazoo.* Because of his loquaciousness, he was known up and down the Ohio and Mississippi rivers as "Windy." He was also known for an overflowing kindness of heart, and for being "a great passenger man . . . morally, and socially and mentally constituted to entertain a crowd."[9] What Captain Marshall and the passengers on the *Dickey* saw that Sunday morning at Compromise was reported, with slight variations, in all four Memphis newspapers. The most detailed of these reports appeared on Tuesday, September 6, in the Memphis *Eagle and Enquirer,* which survives only as reprinted in, for example, the St. Louis *Missouri Democrat* for 8 September (page 2):[10]

HORRIBLE TRAGEDY.
Dreadful Shooting Affray at Compromise.
[From the *Memphis Enquirer,* Sept. 6.]

We are informed by Mr. H. Grove, of Peoria, Ill., a passenger by the J. H. Dickey, which arrived yesterday from St. Louis, that he witnessed a most horrible tragedy on Sunday last, at a place called Compromise. The circumstances of this heart-rending affair, as related to us, are as follows: As the Dickey landed at Compromise to put off the mail, the Postmaster of that place, Mr. Sparr, approached the mail agent, who had not made the two or three last trips, and said to him: "We have had some bloody times here of late, and we have to go prepared," (at the same time throwing back his coat and exhibiting a revolver). "Why?" says the agent. "Because our country is infested by a lot of thieves, such as this man," (pointing to a man close by named Shultz, who was the only one at the levee previous to the landing of the Dickey besides the Postmaster).

Shultz then remarked that he was a most infamous liar, and destitute of every principle of a gentleman.

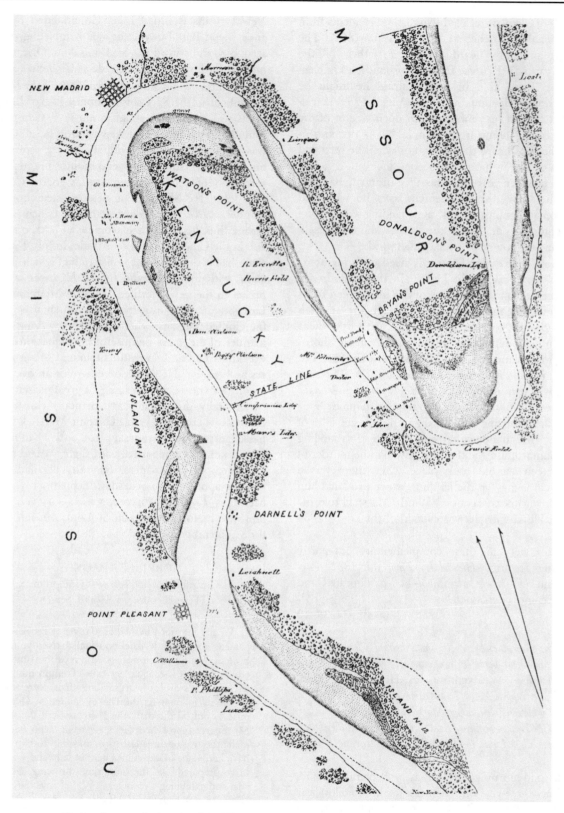

Portion of a reconnaissance map of the Mississippi prepared by Major Charles R. Suter, which Mark Twain
is believed to have consulted (Library of Congress)

Whereupon the Post-master placed his hand on his pistol as if in the act of drawing it, when Shultz shot Mr. Sparr in the left side of his abdomen. Shultz then retreated at a rapid pace about thirty feet, when Sparr fired four shots at him in rapid succession, but without effect. Sparr then took deliberate aim at him across a stump, but his pistol missed. Shultz immediately rushed back at Sparr and shot him twice more through his body. Then they had a hand to hand encounter, Shultz falling under, and Sparr pounding him about the head with his pistol. Presently a third party came up with a double barrel shot-gun to shoot Shultz through the head, but through the advice of the agent and others he did not. Sparr soon became so weak that Shultz threw him off, and on his (Shultz) rising he was struck a powerful blow over the head with the gun, which appeared to craze him, and he instantly run into the river up to his shoulders, and on his looking back and seeing the gun leveled at him, he dodged his head under the water, holding it there as long as he could without strangling, and on his looking up and seeing the gun pointing at him he held it again under water, and this process was repeated till he drowned. The Postmaster was alive when our informant left, but it was thought he could not recover.

By piecing together information from other newspaper accounts of the same event, we learn that "Mr. Sparr" was in fact a "Mr. Starr," identified as "a dry goods merchant,"[11] doubtless filling in for the postmaster, who was his relative Alexander F. Beckham, appointed 26 March 1858.[12] Beckham was the "third party" with the shotgun who kindly offered "to shoot Shultz through the head," being dissuaded by the "agent and others," only to strike him "a powerful blow over the head with the gun" and drive him into the river, where he attempted to swim to a steamboat. Beckham and Starr survived their wounds to stand trial, which "resulted in their honorable acquittal." Shultz's body was recovered from the river on September 11 "and interred in the burying ground at Compromise."[13] Both Starr and Shultz, a schoolteacher, were characterized as "highly respectable citizens of the town of Compromise."[14]

Clemens (or his partner) piloted the *Edward J. Gay* into Memphis, still below Compromise, in the early morning of September 7—three days after the shooting, but only one day after the Memphis papers had reported it. Captain Marshall and the *Dickey* had already left Memphis for St. Louis. James Abbey, the poetizing steward of the *Gay,* recorded her arrival:

We got to Memphis long before nine,

　Making our run in very good time;

Found the people all surprised with a laugh,

　To think we had made it in three days and a half.[15]

The steamer lay at Memphis for only two hours before departing upriver. Still, according to Abbey, there was plenty of time for strolling about town. We may be sure that the Compromise murder (or murders, as some still thought) was common gossip in Memphis streets, and Clemens surely read the newspaper reports, very likely from the sheaf of newspapers routinely taken aboard for delivery to St. Louis's river reporters. As the *Gay* now approached New Madrid Bend and Watson's Point, Clemens would certainly have taken special interest in Darnall's Point and the Compromise landing above it—both "marks" long since lodged in his pilot's memory. On Friday, September 9—the day after the St. Louis newspapers reprinted the Memphis reports—the *Edward J. Gay* docked in St. Louis at about the evening hour the *John H. Dickey* was due to back out for its next Memphis run. Perhaps "Windy" Marshall took that opportunity to speak with Clemens about what he had seen on Sunday; perhaps he supplied the detail of dodging about among the wood-piles, an image prominent in Mark Twain's two accounts and in his 1882 dictation to Phelps, but only vaguely suggested by the newspaper reports that have survived.

The immediate cause of the murder at Compromise did not go unexplained in the newspapers. The Memphis *Appeal* said in part: "The quarrel was general in the neighborhood, and grew out of a dispute between Henry M. Darnell and A. F. Beckham in reference to certain outrages alleged to have been perpetrated by a negro belonging to Mr. Beckham, a detailed account of which we have already published."[16] This "detailed account" consisted of two items published in the *Appeal* on August 11 and 28, the month before. Clemens may very well have read these when they appeared, because at that point he had already been alerted to trouble brewing in the area, as we shall see. But whether or not he read them, they enable us to place the Compromise shootings within the context of an ongoing quarrel that was well known in the area, and they clarify the immediate cause of the shootings, while leaving the origins of the quarrel itself unexplained.[17]

–pp. 42–46

This excerpt shows that particularly violent outbreaks of the feud between the Darnalls and Watsons became national news.

The 1859 incident at Compromise would always be the most important part of Clemens's experience with Southern feuds, and he probably understood it *as* a feud even then. But if he were ever in doubt, surely he would have abandoned all skepticism when he read about another clash between Darnalls and Watsons

ISLAND NUMBER TEN.

Island associated with a feud that became national news in 1869 (from Life on the Mississippi,
Mark Twain House, Hartford, Connecticut)

(and other families) in March 1869. We conjecture that he knew of this incident through the newspapers, and that it provided him with ample evidence for the feud's persisting at least ten years, while also giving him several chilling details that found their way eventually into *Huckleberry Finn*. In 1882, Horace Bixby would give Clemens his own brief, rather garbled version of what occurred in March 1869, but there is some reason to suppose that Clemens learned of the incident much more accurately and fully by reading newspaper reports like the following, the most complete and accurate single report we have found, reprinted in the Buffalo *Express* shortly before Clemens joined the editorial staff of that paper.

ISLAND TEN HORROR.
Further Particulars of the Murderous Feud.
[From the Evansville Journal, 23d.]

The telegraph a few days ago brought us intelligence of a most terrible tragedy, enacted at Island No. 10, in the Mississippi. From Captain John B. Hall we learn further details of the bloody affair, and more correct than the account sent by telegraph.

A difficulty had arisen between a family named Lane and another named Darnell, which created some talk in the neighborhood, and a gentleman named Edwards, a school teacher, had incurred the displeasure of the Darnells by remarks he had made with reference to the difficulty, and they had made threats against him.

The condition of affairs became so unpleasant that Edwards determined to leave the neighborhood. The Darnells, learning of his purpose, swore that he should never leave the neighborhood alive. Ascertaining the time and place of embarkation of Edwards, who had a wife and one child, three of the Darnells, two brothers and a cousin, armed themselves with double-barrel shot guns, revolvers, and knives, and took passage from Darnell's Landing on the Belle Memphis. They told the officers of the boat that parties on the island or opposite the island desired to come on board. As the boat landed two of the Lanes, Edwards, and his wife and child, and a man named Watson were seen on the bank, which there is very high. As the old man Lane, with Mrs. Edwards and her child, were coming on board, one of the Darnells took his position at the head of the stairs, by the side of the clerk, Billy Blanker, who was passing down to escort the lady. As old man Lane started up the steps, Darnell drew up his gun and fired, nineteen buckshot taking effect in Lane's left breast, killing him instantly. At the same moment the other two assassins took aim at young Lane and Edwards, who were coming down the bank, and firing, both fell dead, Edwards rolling down the bank and Lane falling over against the bank. Immediately after shooting old man Lane, the fiend who had committed the deed walked down stairs to Mrs. Edwards and told her she had better go back and see what had become of her husband. After Edwards was dead, one of these inhuman devils went to him, and placing his revolver against the back of his head, fired; then turning him over, he again shot him through the forehead. They also fired at Watson, who had accompanied the Lanes to the boat, but missed him. The bloody work was done so suddenly and so unexpectedly that the officers of the boat were for a moment terror stricken, and before they had fully recovered the assassins had left the boat, and indeed any attempt at interference would doubtless have involved a further loss of life, as the three desperadoes were fully armed to the teeth. After leaving the boat they walked across the neck of land to their horses, mounted and rode away.

As soon as the awful tragedy became known, the whole neighborhood turned out to hunt down the assassins, who, if found, would no doubt receive summary punishment. The Lanes were buried at Island No. 10, and the Norman brought the remains of Edwards to Hickman, together with his widow and child.

This is unquestionably one of the most atrocious, cold-blooded and villainous assassinations that ever transpired in the West. Edwards is represented as a quiet, inoffensive and worthy gentleman, and his wife as a beautiful and accomplished lady. The Darnells were known as desperate characters, who should be hunted from the face of the earth.[18]

As we learn from other sources, the victims of this assault were Captain Robert L. Lane, his younger brother Clinton G. Lane, and Cullen C. Edwards, whose wife and child alone survived. Their assailants were the oldest Darnall boy, Henry M. Darnall, Jr., then about twenty-five; the third son (but second living), Richard M. Darnall, then about nineteen or twenty; and an otherwise unidentified cousin, Mathew Darnall. All three, in addition to General Darnall (who was evidently not present), were indicted for the murder in May 1869. The report of the indictment also makes clear that the "man named Watson" seen on the bank at "Watson's Landing," near the foot of Island No. 10 when the shooting occurred, and who the Darnalls "also fired at . . . but missed," was Daniel Watson's son Randolph, eventually named as a witness for the state.[19] Finally, the Suter map records the dwelling of Mrs. Edwards—presumably the widow—in Watson territory, near Island No. 10, just north of the line.

According to Richard Darnall's rather self-serving account in Goodspeed's *History,* the elder of the Lane brothers was a "graduate of Yale College" who had come "to Lake County in the capacity of teacher."

He met and married a niece of Mr. Darnall's, and the latter generously gave them a nice home, besides lending them several thousand dollars. In spite of this kindness they forged the will of Mr. Darnall, so that she might, at his death, receive $20,000; but as Mr. Darnall was a very robust man, they decided to kill him, selecting Cullen C. Edwards as an accomplice, all three of them being leading Kuklux. One night the youngest Lane went to Mr. Darnall's house and endeavored to insult him; when Mr. Darnall turned to enter the house

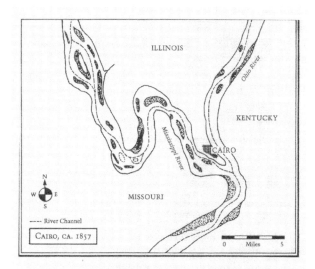

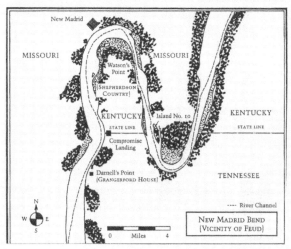

Maps of Cairo and New Madrid (from Adventures of Huckleberry Finn, *edited by Fischer, Salamo, and Blair, 2003, Collection of Tom Quirk)*

Lane drew a navy pistol from the horn of his saddle and attempted to shoot him, but before he could fire, Richard Darnall [the writer of this account] reached him and prevented the shot; he then attempted to shoot him [Richard], but the latter, seeing that it was kill or be killed, drew a pistol from his pocket and shot Lane, inflicting a wound from which he came near dying. After this the two Lanes and Edwards swore vengeance against the Darnalls, and meeting Richard and his oldest brother coming from the steamer Belle of Memphis, they commenced firing upon them; but the Darnall boys succeeded in killing all three of them without receiving any wounds.

Much of what Darnall says here can be corroborated. The 1881 map, for instance, shows two large tracts of land on the river, just south of Darnall's Point, belonging to the "Lane Heirs," presumably part of

General Darnall's original wedding gift to his (unidentified) niece. Richard's shooting Clinton Lane is likewise mentioned in several contemporary reports as the proximate cause of the feud. But no other reports of what occurred in March 1869 support Richard's shifting of blame away from him and his family, who clearly ambushed the two Lanes and the Edwardses.

The incident itself was demonstrably reported in many eastern papers, including the New York *Times*, New York *Tribune*, Buffalo *Express*, Cleveland *Herald*, and Elmira *Advertiser*. . . . The only significant variant among these five separate reports was in the headline, which read as follows: "Three Men Murdered at Island No. 10 in the Mississippi" *(Times)*; "Three Men Shot—A Mysterious Affair" *(Tribune)*; "FEARFUL TRAGEDY. | Murder of Three Brothers at Island No. 10 | Mysterious Details of the Bloody Transaction" *(Express)*; "Bloody Tragedy" *(Herald)*; and "A Triple Murder on the Mississippi" *(Advertiser)*.

All of the newspapers we have seen struggled with early, incomplete reports, and obvious inconsistencies; more than one published a second and presumably more informed account than they had at first. On March 19, for instance, the Memphis *Appeal* devoted one-fourth of the allotted space to headlines: "TERRIBLE AFFRAY | BLOODY TERMINATION OF AN OLD FEUD. | Two Families Engaged, and One Exterminated. | Three Brothers Slain Outright | The Slayers Uninjured." It called the incident "One of the most singular and tragic terminations of an old family feud that we have ever heard of. . . . We await further news with interest, as this is certainly the most cold-blooded affair that we have ever heard of." It identified the assailants as "two brothers named Darnelle" and the victims as "three gentleman, brothers named Lane, [who] came down to accompany their sister-in-law and child on board."[20]

On the same day, the St. Louis *Missouri Republican* trumpeted: "HORRIBLE MURDERS. | Awful Tragedy on the Steamer Belle Memphis. | Three Men Shot Dead | Husband and Father Killed in the Presence of his wife and Children."

. . . .

If Clemens read any of these newspaper reports at the time, he was probably confused about exactly what happened and who was to blame, but it seems inescapable that he would have succumbed to the premise of the headlines, namely that this incident continued an old, family feud—involving the same (or some of the same) warring families he had observed more closely in 1859, ten years before. If he did not recognize that Watsons as well as Darnalls were again embroiled, or that

various reports confused husbands and brothers, fathers and cousins, he could scarcely escape the "fact" of its being a family feud in which a "Husband and Father [Were] Killed in the Presence of His Wife and Children," in which "Two Families [Were] Engaged, and One Exterminated," and of course in which "The Cause of the Feud" was utterly trivial in every sense.

Yet if Clemens were familiar with these 1869 events through the newspapers he read, it may seem odd that he accepted Horace Bixby's summary of the event in 1882 without a demur, even reproducing it nearly verbatim in *Life on the Mississippi*. Bixby evidently said:

> Darnell & Watson were the names of two men whose families had kept up a long quarrel. The old man Darnell & his 2 sons came to the conclusion to leave that part of the country. They started to take steamboat just above "No. 10." The Watsons got wind of it and as the young Darnells were walking up the companion way stairs with their wives on their arms they shot them in the back. (*N&J2*, 567–568)

This summary is hopelessly mistaken: the Darnalls were the assailants, not the victims, who were Lanes, Edwards, and indirectly, Watsons. There was only one wife (Mrs. Edwards), not two. But Bixby's confusion, however massive, is finally irrelevant. What did it matter which side "won"? Even if the facts were not entirely clear, they confirmed Clemens's sense of the family feud at least a decade long, since even if he were unable to sort out the details, the events themselves occurred only two miles from where he had "nearly" witnessed the 1859 shooting.

—pp. 61–65, 67–68

Mark Twain's literary use of his personal experience with feuds is examined in this last excerpt.

Mark Twain had first tried to make literary use of the Southern feud in a burlesque of detective fiction, "Simon Wheeler, Detective," which he abandoned in 1878 before completing it. He subsequently composed the feud chapters for *Huckleberry Finn* (1879–1880), and finally the section on feuds for *Life on the Mississippi* (August 1882), which he then published before he published *Huck*. Between the first and last known accounts he wrote (roughly from 1878 to 1884) Mark Twain kept some features of the feud essentially the same, but in general he moved away from what might be called "literary" models toward an increased reliance on the "factual" model represented by his firsthand experience at Compromise in 1859, modified or embellished by at least what he had read of the 1869 affray, and very likely of other incidents in the Darnalls' lives as well.

In all three efforts there are obvious continuities. Mark Twain portrayed the Southern feud in each of them as unrelenting, all-consuming blood combat, punctuated by bursts of violence separated by years and even by generations. In all three accounts the feud has originated in the distant past, and its cause is trivial both in the sense that it was unimportant to begin with, and in the sense that the present combatants have forgotten or never even knew what it was. In "Simon Wheeler," when asked what the Griswold-Morgan feud was all about, Griswold replies: "I do not remember–that is, I never knew. I think it never occurred to me to ask. But no matter; it is not likely that any of my generation could have told me. Besides, the feud itself was the only thing of consequence; how it originated was a circumstance of no interest. I was only taught that when I should meet a Morgan there was a thing to be done; it was very simple–kill him" (S&B, 318).

Aside from these more or less constant elements in each of the three versions, distinctive elements common to just two of the three are more instructive. For instance, in "Simon Wheeler" and again in *Huckleberry Finn* Mark Twain introduced what may be called the *Romeo and Juliet* gambit, wherein love between members of the younger generation may breach the wall of blind hatred: Hale Dexter and Clara Burnside serve this function in "Simon Wheeler," and Sophia Grangerford and Harney Shepherdson do so in *Huckleberry Finn*. Mark Twain's knowledge of feuds in 1877 certainly embraced such conventional treatments in fiction as John W. DeForest's *Kate Beaumont* (1871), in which a similar bond develops between the warring clans, so that even without directly invoking Shakespeare's play, the *fictional* quality of this device was inescapable. Wary of "copying in part a character already drawn by another," Mark Twain limited the significance of this gambit in *Huckleberry Finn*, where it serves chiefly as the cause of the final violence, and he omitted any hint of it from *Life on the Mississippi*.

More useful to him in dramatizing the conflict between the clans was what appears to be the fiction of two families worshipping in the same church on opposite sides of the state line. Absent from "Simon Wheeler," this device is important in Huckleberry Finn, and especially telling in *Life on the Mississippi*. So far, none of the sources we have found comes close to documenting any such real state of affairs. On the other hand, there is some evidence that the Watsons were Methodists, and that a log church near the line was their normal place of worship, although we have no sign that the Darnalls worshipped there too. This armed worship must be judged, under present evidence, a "created adornment" probably founded on "fact," which may not be recoverable. Even in *Huckle-*

berry Finn, where Mark Twain feels free to include such inventions, there is a small sign that he has some real situation in mind. In contrast to the shared "steamboat landing, which was about two mile above our house," Huck reports that when the Grangerfords went to church, it was "about three mile," a good approximation of the added distance from Darnall's Landing to the Methodist church "just south of the line." Even in *Life on the Mississippi,* where the account of two families worshipping is fullest, the narrator meticulously qualifies his assertions by characterizing his source: "I don't know; never was at that church in my life; but I remember that that's what used to be said" (287). Mark Twain must have heard this rumor, or folklore, independently of what Bixby told him in 1882.

There are, however, two principal points of similarity between *Huckleberry Finn* and *Life on the Mississippi:* (a) what may be called the Lone Encounter with Guns, either in the open or from ambush, between two adversaries, one of whom is manifestly overmatched; and (b) the Young Man Behind a Woodpile, fighting with and losing to a larger force of the enemy, which appears in the climactic position in both accounts. These two points of similarity, of course, correspond exactly with the two incidents Clemens recalled in his 1882 dictation.

–*The Grangerford-Shepherdson Feud by Mark Twain*
(Berkeley: The Friends of The Bancroft
Library, University of California,
1985), pp. 69–71

———

Abbreviations

N&J2: Mark Twain's Notebooks & Journals, Volume II (1877–1883), The Mark Twain Papers, ed. Frederick Anderson, Lin Salamo, Bernard L. Stein. (Berkeley, Los Angeles, and London: University of California Press, 1975).

S&B: Mark Twain's Satires & Burlesques, The Mark Twain Papers, ed. Franklin R. Rogers. (Berkeley and Los Angeles: University of California Press, 1968).

1. Gilder to Clemens, 10 October 1884, Mark Twain Papers, The Bancroft Library.
2. *Life on the Mississippi* (Boston: James R. Osgood and Company, 1883), 42.
3. A useful and reliable chronology of this trip down to New Orleans, then back up to the "upper river," has been published in *N&J2,* 436–37.
4. By his own account, Walter Blair "proves that Mark Twain wrote chapters xvii and xviii between mid-October, 1879, and mid-June, 1880, in Hartford" (*Mark Twain & Huck Finn* [Berkeley and Los Angeles: University of California Press, 1960], 199). But recent work on the edition of *Huckleberry Finn* (see note 1) suggests that in 1876, Mark Twain may well have written as far as the first mention of Harney Shepherdson in chapter 18 (*Century,*

269–74) before abandoning the manuscript for three years, subsequently revising and completing the feud chapters (as Blair has said) in 1879–80. In the absence of the manuscript for this portion of *Huckleberry Finn*, however, it must be acknowledged that revision and addition to these chapters was possible even after Mark Twain acquired three maps of the Mississippi in April 1882.

5. Clemens made several other mistakes in this list: he placed Hickman above Columbus, Helena below Napoleon, and Walnut Bend below Helena, instead of the reverse.

6. From item 193, "The Library and Manuscripts of Samuel L. Clemens," Anderson Auction Company Sale Catalog No. 892, 7 and 8 February 1911; originally cited by Blair, 226, 407 n. 15. The quotation is one of some twenty-nine items or entries listed on a piece of manuscript tipped into a volume from Clemens's library and sold in 1911. We have not seen the manuscript.

7. "River News," St. Louis *Missouri Republican*, 25 July 1859, 3.

8. Clemens's presence on the *Edward J. Gay* at this time has recently been established by the discovery of Virginius C. Dentzel's remark in his river column of 11 August 1859 in the New Orleans *Crescent:* "by the by our friend and correspondent 'Sergeant Fathom' holds forth on the Gay" (Edgar M. Branch, "A New Clemens Footprint: Soleather Steps Forward," *American Literature* 54 [Spring 1982]: 505-6). By contrast, Davidson says that "the *John J. Roe* or the *Crescent City* might have equal claim as the steamboat Twain was then piloting, although 'Memphis packet' still seems to tip the scale for the *City of Memphis*" (82). Clemens was on none of those three boats at this time.

9. "Mail and Passenger Packet Philadelphia for Memphis," St. Louis *Missouri Republican*, 10 September 1858, 3.

10. Independently reprinted from the *Eagle* and *Enquirer* as "Terrible Fight" in the St. Louis *Evening News*, 6 September 1859, 1; and as "Shooting Affray at Compromise" in the Chicago *Press Tribune*, 10 September 1859, 2.

11. "Fatal Difficulty at Compromise, Ky.–One Man Drowned and Another Seriously Wounded," Memphis *Morning Bulletin*, 6 September 1859, 3.

12. Davidson, 93 n. 17.

13. "The Late Tragedy at Compromise," Memphis *Morning Bulletin*, 13 September 1859, 3.

14. Memphis *Morning Bulletin*, 6 September, *ibid.*

15. "River Correspondence," St. Louis *Missouri Republican*, 11 September 1859, 4.

16. "Fatal Affray at Compromise, Ky.," Memphis *Appeal*, 6 September 1859, 3; cited by Davidson.

17. Compare the story in the Memphis *Morning Bulletin*, 6 September, already cited: "The affray arose from a dispute in regard to the possession of a negro." And, from the Memphis *Avalanche*, reprinted in the Louisville *Democrat*, 9 September 1859, 3: "A feud had existed for some time between the parties, and a difficulty has been anticipated for some time past."

18. Buffalo *Express*, 29 March 1869, 1, reprinting the Evansville (Indiana) *Journal* of 23 March 1869.

19. "The 'Coe (boy)' and Randolph Watson were summoned as state witnesses" (Davidson, 85).

20. Memphis *Appeal*, 19 March 1869, 3; cited by Davidson.

* * *

Beginning in the 1840s Sam Clemens read widely in humorists' writing of life in what was then Southwestern frontier—mainly Georgia, Alabama, Mississippi, Arkansas, and Louisiana. Writers such as George Washington Harris, Johnson Jones Hooper, William Tappan Thompson, Augustus Baldwin Longstreet, and Thomas Bangs Thorpe were influences upon Mark Twain's development, particularly his use of dialects and his choice of subjects.

This episode, chapter 10 in Hooper's Some Adventures of Captain Simon Suggs, Late of the Tallapoosa Volunteers *(1845), inspired Mark Twain's treatment of the king at the Pokeville camp meeting in chapter 20 of* Adventures of Huckleberry Finn.

The Captain Attends a Camp-Meeting
Johnson Jones Hooper

CAPTAIN SUGGS found himself as poor at the conclusion of the Creek war, as he had been at its commencement. Although no "arbitrary," "despotic," "corrupt," and "unprincipled" judge had fined him a thousand dollars for his proclamation of martial law at Fort Suggs, or the enforcement of its rules in the case of Mrs. Haycock; yet somehow—the thing is alike inexplicable to him and to us—the money which he had contrived, by various shifts to obtain, melted away and was gone for ever. To a man like the Captain, of intense domestic affections, this state of destitution was most distressing. "He could stand it himself—didn't care a d–n for it, no way," he observed, "but the old woman and the children; *that* bothered him!"

As he sat one day, ruminating upon the unpleasant condition of his "financial concerns," Mrs. Suggs informed him that "the sugar and coffee was nigh about out," and that there were not "a dozen j'ints and middling, *all put together,* in the smoke-house." Suggs bounced up on the instant, exclaiming, "D–n it! *somebody* must suffer!" But whether this remark was intended to convey the idea that he and his family were about to experience the want of the necessaries of life; or that some other, and as yet unknown individual should "suffer" to prevent that prospective exigency, must be left to the commentators, if perchance any of that ingenious class of persons should hereafter see proper to write notes for this history. It is enough for us that we give all the facts in this connection, so that ignorance of the subsequent conduct of Captain Suggs may not lead to an erroneous judgment in respect to his words.

Having uttered the exclamation we have repeated—and perhaps, hurriedly walked once or twice across the room—Captain Suggs drew on his famous old green-blanket overcoat, and ordered his horse, and within five minutes was on his way to a camp-meeting, then in full blast on Sandy creek, twenty miles distant, where he hoped to find amusement, at least. When he arrived there, he found the hollow square of the encampment filled with people, listening to the mid-day sermon and its dozen accompanying "exhortations." A half-dozen preachers were dispensing the word; the one in the pulpit, a meek-faced old man, of great simplicity and benevolence. His voice was weak and cracked, notwithstanding which, however, he contrived to make himself heard occasionally, above the din of the exhorting, the singing, and the shouting which were going on around him. The rest were walking to and fro, (engaged in the other exercises we have indicated,) among the "mourners"—a host of whom occupied the seat set apart for their especial use—or made personal appeals to the mere spectators. The excitement was intense. Men and women rolled about on the ground, or lay sobbing or shouting in promiscuous heaps. More than all, the negroes sang and screamed and prayed. Several, under the influence of what is technically called "the jerks," were plunging and pitching about with convulsive energy. The great object of all seemed to be, to see who could make the greatest noise—

"And each—for madness ruled the hour—
Would try his own expressive power."

"Bless my poor old soul!" screamed the preacher in the pulpit; "ef yonder aint a squad in that corner that we aint got one outen yet! It'll never do"—raising his voice—"you must come outen that! Brother Fant, fetch up that youngster in the blue coat! I see the Lord's a-workin' upon him! Fetch him along—glory—yes!—hold to him!"

"Keep the thing warm!" roared a sensual seeming man, of stout mould and florid countenance, who was exhorting among a bevy of young women, upon whom he was lavishing caresses. "Keep the thing warm, breethring!—come to the Lord, honey!" he added, as he vigorously hugged one of the damsels he sought to save.

"Oh, I've got him!" said another in exulting tones, as he led up a gawky youth among the mourners—"I've got him—he tried to git off, but—ha! Lord!"—shaking his head as much as to say, it took a smart fellow to escape him—"ha! Lord!"—and he wiped the perspiration from his face with one hand, and with the other, patted his neophyte on the shoulder—"he couldn't do it! No! Then he tried to argy wi' me—but bless the Lord!—he couldn't do that nother! Ha! Lord! I tuk him, fust in the Old Testament—bless the Lord!—and I argyed him all thro' Kings—then I threw him into Proverbs,—and from that, here we had it up and down, kleer down to the New Testament, and then I

Johnson J. Hooper, a Southwestern humorist whose character Captain Suggs provided a source for Mark Twain (Alabama Department of Archives and History)

begun to see it work him!—then we got into Matthy, and from Matthy right straight along to Acts; and *thar* I throwed him! Y-e-s L-o-r-d!"—assuming the nasal twang and high pitch which are, in some parts, considered the perfection of rhetorical art—"Y-e-s L-o-r-d! and h-e-r-e he is! Now g-i-t down thar," addressing the subject, "and s-e-e ef the L-o-r-d won't do somethin' f-o-r you!" Having thus deposited his charge among the mourners, he started out, summarily to convert another soul!

"Gl-o-*ree!*" yelled a huge, greasy negro woman, as in a fit of the jerks, she threw herself convulsively from her feet, and fell "like a thousand of brick," across a diminutive old man in a little round hat, who was squeaking consolation to one of the mourners.

"Good Lord, have mercy!" ejaculated the little man earnestly and unaffectedly, as he strove to crawl from under the sable mass which was crushing him.

In another part of the square a dozen old women were singing. They were in a state of absolute extasy, as their shrill pipes gave forth,

"I rode on the sky,
Quite ondestified I,
And the moon it was under my feet!"

Near these last, stood a delicate woman in that hysterical condition in which the nerves are incontrollable, and which is vulgarly—and almost blasphemously—termed the "holy laugh." A hideous grin distorted her mouth, and was accompanied with a maniac's chuckle; while every muscle and nerve of her face twitched and jerked in horrible spasms.*

Amid all this confusion and excitement Suggs stood unmoved. He viewed the whole affair as a grand deception—a sort of "opposition line" running against his own, and looked on with a sort of professional jealousy. Sometimes he would mutter running comments upon what passed before him.

"Well now," said he, as he observed the full-faced brother who was "officiating" among the women, "that ere feller takes *my* eye!—thar he's een this half-hour, a-figurin amongst them galls, and's never said the fust word to nobody else. Wonder what's the reason these here preachers never hugs up the old, ugly women? Never seed one do it in my life—the sperrit never moves 'em that way! It's nater tho'; and the women, *they* never flocks round one o' the old dried-up breethring—bet two to one old splinter-legs thar,"—nodding at one of the ministers—"won't git a chance to say turkey to a good-lookin gall to-day! Well! who blames 'em? Nater will be nater, all the world over; and I judge ef I was a preacher, I should save the purtiest souls fust, myself!"

While the Captain was in the middle of this conversation with himself, he caught the attention of the preacher in the pulpit, who inferring from an indescribable something about his appearance that he was a person of some consequence, immediately determined to add him at once to the church if it could be done; and to that end began a vigorous, direct personal attack.

"Breethring," he exclaimed, "I see yonder a man that's a sinner; I *know* he's a sinner! Thar he stands," pointing at Simon, "a missubble old crittur, with his head a-blossomin for the grave! A few more short years, and d-o-w-n he'll go to perdition, lessen the Lord have mer-cy on him! Come up here, you old hoary-headed sinner, a-n-d git down upon your knees, a-n-d put up your cry for the Lord to snatch you from the bottomless pit! You're ripe for the devil—you're b-o-u-n-d for hell, and the Lord only knows what'll become on you!"

"D—n it," thought Suggs, "*ef* I only had you down in the krick swamp for a minit or so, *I'd* show you who's *old! I'd* alter your tune *mighty* sudden, you sassy, 'saitful old rascal!" But he judiciously held his tongue and gave no utterance to the thought.

The attention of many having been directed to the Captain by the preacher's remarks, he was soon surrounded by numerous well-meaning, and doubt-less very pious persons, each one of whom seemed bent on the application of his own particular recipe for the salvation of souls. For a long time the Captain stood silent, or answered the incessant stream of exhortation only with a sneer; but at length, his countenance began to give token of inward emotion. First his eye-lids twitched—then his upper lip quiv-ered—next a transparent drop formed on one of his eye-lashes, and a similar one on the tip of his nose—and, at last, a sudden bursting of air from nose and mouth, told that Captain Suggs was overpowered by his emotions. At the moment of the explosion, he made a feint as if to rush from the crowd, but he was in experienced hands, who well knew that the battle was more than half won.

"Hold to him!" said one—"it's a-workin in him as strong as a Dick horse!"

"Pour it into him," said another, "it'll all come right directly!"

"That's the way I love to see 'em do," observed a third; "when you begin to draw the water from their eyes, taint gwine to be long afore you'll have 'em on their knees!"

And so they clung to the Captain manfully, and half dragged, half led him to the mourner's bench; by which he threw himself down, altogether unmanned, and bathed in tears. Great was the rejoicing of the brethren, as they sang, shouted, and prayed around him—for by this time it had come to be generally known that the "convicted" old man was Captain Simon Suggs, the very "chief of sinners" in all that region.

The Captain remained grovelling in the dust during the usual time, and gave vent to even more than the requisite number of sobs, and groans, and heart-piercing cries. At length, when the proper time had arrived, he bounced up, and with a face radiant with joy, commenced a series of vaultings and tum-blings, which "laid in the shade" all previous perfor-mances of the sort at that camp-meeting. The brethren were in extasies at this demonstrative evi-dence of completion of the work; and whenever Suggs shouted "Gloree!" at the top of his lungs, every one of them shouted it back, until the woods rang with echoes.

The effervescence having partially subsided, Suggs was put upon his pins to relate his experience, which he did somewhat in this style—first brushing the tear-drops from his eyes, and giving the end of his nose a preparatory wring with his fingers, to free it of the superabundant moisture:

"Friends," he said, "it don't take long to curry a short horse, accordin' to the old sayin', and I'll give you the perticklers of the way I was 'brought to a knowledge'"—here the Captain wiped his eyes, brushed the tip of his nose and snuffled a little—"in less'n no time."

"Praise the Lord!" ejaculated a bystander.

"You see I come here full o' romancin' and devilment, and jist to make game of all the purceedins. Well, sure enough, I done so for some time, and was a-thinkin how I should play some trick—"

"Dear soul alive! *don't* he talk sweet!" cried an old lady in black silk—"Whar's John Dobbs? You Sukey!" screaming at a negro woman on the other side of the square—"ef you don't hunt up your mass John in a minute, and have him here to listen to his 'sperience, I'll tuck you up when I git home and give you a hundred and fifty lashes, madam!—see ef I don't! Blessed Lord!"—referring again to the Captain's relation—"aint it a *precious* 'scource!"

"I was jist a-thinkin' how I should play some trick to turn it all into redecule, when they began to come round me and talk. Long at fust I didn't mind it, but arter a little that brother"—pointing to the reverend gentlemen who had so successfully carried the unbeliever through the Old and New Testaments, and who Simon was convinced was the "big dog of the tanyard"—"that brother spoke a word that struck me kleen to the heart, and run all over me, like fire in dry grass—"

"*I-I-I* can bring 'em!" cried the preacher alluded to, in a tone of exultation—"Lord thou knows ef thy servant can't stir 'em up, nobody else needn't try—but the glory aint mine! I'm a poor worrum of the dust" he added, with ill-managed affectation.

"And so from that I felt somethin' a-pullin' me inside—"

"Grace! grace! nothin' but grace!" exclaimed one; meaning that "grace" had been operating in the Captain's gastric region.

"And then," continued Suggs, "I wanted to git off, but they hilt me, and bimeby I felt so missuble, I had to go yonder"—pointing to the mourners' seat—"and when I lay down thar it got wuss and wuss, and 'peared like somethin' was a-mashin' down on my back—"

"That was his load o' sin," said one of the brethren—"never mind, it'll tumble off presently, see ef it don't!" and he shook his head professionally and knowingly.

"And it kept a-gittin heavier and heavier, ontwell it looked like it might be a four year old steer, or a big pine log, or somethin' of that sort—"

"Glory to my soul," shouted Mrs. Dobbs, "it's the sweetest talk I *ever* hearn! You Sukey! aint you got John yit? never mind, my lady, I'll settle wi' you!" Sukey

SIMON SUGGS.

Captain Suggs, as drawn by E. W. Kemble (from Mark Twain's Library of Humor *[New York: Charles L. Webster, 1888],* Thomas Cooper Library, University of South Carolina)

quailed before the finger which her mistress shook at her.

"And arter awhile," Suggs went on, "'peared like I fell into a trance, like, and I seed–"

"Now we'll git the good on it!" cried one of the sanctified.

"And I seed the biggest, longest, rip-roarenest, blackest, scariest–" Captain Suggs paused, wiped his brow, and ejaculated "Ah, L-o-r-d!" so as to give full time for curiosity to become impatience to know what he saw.

"*Sarpent!* warn't it?" asked one of the preachers.

"No, not a serpent," replied Suggs, blowing his nose.

"Do tell us *what* it war, soul alive!–whar *is* John?" said Mrs. Dobbs.

"Allegator!" said the Captain.

"Alligator!" repeated every woman present, and screamed for very life.

Mrs. Dobb's nerves were so shaken by the announcement, that after repeating the horrible word, she screamed to Sukey, "you Sukey, I say, you Su-u-ke-e-y! ef you let John come a-nigh this way, whar the dreadful alliga–shaw! what am I thinkin 'bout?' 'Twarn't nothin' but a vishin!"

"Well," said the Captain in continuation, "the alligator kept a-comin' and a-comin' to'ards me, with his great long jaws a-gapin' open like a ten-foot pair o' tailors' shears–"

"Oh! oh! oh! Lord! gracious above!" cried the women.

"SATAN!" was the laconic ejaculation of the oldest preacher present, who thus informed the congregation that it was the devil which had attacked Suggs in the shape of an alligator.

"And then I concluded the jig was up, 'thout I could block his game some way; for I seed his idee was to snap off my head–"

The women screamed again.

"So I fixed myself jist like I was purfectly willin' for him to take my head, and rather he'd do it as not"–here the women shuddered perceptibly–"and so I hilt my head straight out"–the Captain illustrated by elongating his neck–"and when he come up and was a gwine to *shet down* on it, I jist pitched in a big rock which choked him to death, and that minit I felt the weight slide off; and I had the best feelins–sorter like you'll have from *good* sperrits–any body ever had!"

"Didn't I *tell* you so? Didn't I *tell* you so?" asked the brother who had predicted the off-tumbling of the load of sin. "Ha, Lord! fool *who!* I've been *all* along thar!–yes, *all along thar!* and I know every inch of the way jist as good as I do the road home!"–and then he

turned round and round, and looked at all, to receive a silent tribute to his superior penetration.

Captain Suggs was now the "lion of the day." Nobody could pray so well, or exhort so movingly, as "brother Suggs." Nor did his natural modesty prevent the proper performance of appropriate exercises. With the reverend Bela Bugg (him to whom, under providence, he ascribed his conversion,) he was a most especial favourite. They walked, sang, and prayed together for hours.

"Come, come up; thar's room for all!" cried brother Bugg, in his evening exhortation. "Come to the 'seat,' and ef you won't pray yourselves, let *me* pray for you!"

"Yes!" said Simon, by way of assisting his friend; "it's a game that all can win at! Ante up! ante up, boys–friends I mean–don't back out!"

"Thar aint a sinner here," said Bugg, "no matter ef his soul's black as a nigger, but what thar's room for him!"

"No matter what sort of a hand you've got," added Simon in the fulness of his benevolence; "take stock! Here am *I,* the wickedest and blindest of sinners–has spent my whole life in the sarvice of the devil–has now come in on *narry pair* and won a *pile!*" and the Captain's face beamed with holy pleasure.

"D-o-n-'t be afeard!" cried the preacher; "come along! the meanest won't be turned away! humble yourselves and come!"

"No!" said Simon, still indulging in his favourite style of metaphor; "the bluff game aint played here! No runnin' of a body off! Every body holds four aces, and when you bet, you win!"

And thus the Captain continued, until the services were concluded, to assist in adding to the number at the mourners' seat; and up to the hour of retiring, he exhibited such enthusiasm in the cause, that he was unanimously voted to be the most efficient addition the church had made during that meeting.

The next morning, when the preacher of the day first entered the pulpit, he announced that "brother Simon Suggs," mourning over his past iniquities, and desirous of going to work in the cause as speedily as possible, would take up a collection to found a church in his own neighbourhood, at which he hoped to make himself useful as soon as he could prepare himself for the ministry, which the preacher didn't doubt, would be in a very few weeks, as brother Suggs was "a man of mighty good judge*ment,* and of *a great discorse.*" The funds were to be collected by "brother Suggs," and held in trust by brother Bela Bugg, who was the financial officer of the circuit, until some arrangement could be made to build a suitable house.

"Yes, breethring," said the Captain, rising to his feet; "I want to start a little 'sociation close to me, and I want you all to help. I'm mighty poor myself, as poor as any of you—don't leave breethring"—observing that several of the well-to-do were about to go off—"don't leave; ef you aint able to afford any thing, jist give us your blessin' and it'll be all the same!"

This insinuation did the business, and the sensitive individuals re-seated themselves.

"It's mighty little of this world's goods I've got," resumed Suggs, pulling off his hat and holding it before him; "but I'll bury *that* in the cause any how," and he deposited his last five-dollar bill in the hat.

There was a murmur of approbation at the Captain's liberality throughout the assembly.

Suggs now commenced collecting, and very prudently attacked first the gentlemen who had shown a disposition to escape. These, to exculpate themselves from any thing like poverty, contributed handsomely.

"Look here, breethring," said the Captain, displaying the bank-notes thus received, "brother Snooks has drapt a five wi' me, and brother Snodgrass a ten! In course 'taint expected that you *that aint as well off as them,* will give *as much;* let every one give *accordin'* to ther means."

This was another chain-shot that raked as it went! "Who so low" as not to be able to contribute as much as Snooks and Snodgrass?

"Here's all the *small* money I've got about me," said a burly old fellow, ostentatiously handing to Suggs, over the heads of a half dozen, a ten dollar bill.

"That's what I call maganimus!" exclaimed the Captain; "that's the way *every* rich man ought to do!"

These examples were followed, more or less closely, by almost all present, for Simon had excited the pride of purse of the congregation, and a very handsome sum was collected in a very short time.

The reverend Mr. Bugg, as soon as he observed that our hero had obtained all that was to be had at that time, went to him and inquired what amount had been collected. The Captain replied that it was still uncounted, but that it couldn't be much under a hundred.

"Well, brother Suggs, you'd better count it and turn it over to me now. I'm goin' to leave presently."

"No!" said Suggs—"can't do it!"

"Why?—what's the matter?" inquired Bugg.

"It's got to be *prayed over,* fust!" said Simon, a heavenly smile illuminating his whole face.

"Well," replied Bugg, "less go one side and do it!"

"No!" said Simon, solemnly.

Mr. Bugg gave a look of inquiry.

"You see that krick swamp?" asked Suggs—"I'm gwine down in *thar,* and I'd gwine to lay this money down *so*"—showing how he would place it on the ground—"and I'm gwine to git on these here knees"—slapping the right one—"and I'm *n-e-v-e-r* gwine to quit the grit ontwell I feel it's got the blessin'! And nobody aint got to be thar but me!"

Mr. Bugg greatly admired the Captain's fervent piety, and bidding him God-speed, turned off.

Captain Suggs "struck for" the swamp sure enough, where his horse was already hitched. "Ef them fellers aint done to a cracklin," he muttered to himself as he mounted, "I'll never bet on two pair agin! They're peart at the snap game, theyselves; but they're badly lewed this hitch! Well! Live and let live is a good old motter, and it's my sentiments adzactly!" And giving the spur to his horse, off he cantered.

—*Adventures of Captain Simon Suggs,* Late of the Tallapoosa Volunteers (Philadelphia: Carey & Hart, 1845)

---

*The reader is requested to bear in mind, that the scenes described in this chapter are not now to be witnessed. Eight or ten years ago, all classes of population of the Creek country were very different from what they now are. Of course, no disrespect is intended to any denomination of Christians. We believe that camp-meetings are not peculiar to any church, though most usual in the Methodist—a denomination whose respectability in Alabama is attested by the fact, that very many of its worthy clergymen and lay members, hold honorable and profitable offices in the gift of the state legislature; of which, indeed, almost a controlling portion are themselves Methodists.

* * *

In this excerpt, Blair discusses an 1845 incident in Hannibal that Mark Twain transposed to the fictional Bricksville of the novel. Blair writes that Bricksville is based on Napoleon, Arkansas—for that town and state are "locales which by repute are appropriate for the violent events Huck witnesses there."

The Boggs Shooting
Walter Blair

I have noticed that the shooting of Boggs by Sherburn, the first of these, closely resembles the footnote in chapter xl of *Life on the Mississippi* about General

THE DEATH OF BOGGS.

The shooting of Boggs by Colonel Sherburn that was based on a murder Clemens may have witnessed as a nine-year-old (drawing by E. W. Kemble; from Adventures of Huckleberry Finn, *Mark Twain House, Hartford, Connecticut)*

Mabry's shooting of Thomas O'Connor in Knoxville. This affair, though, is so much like a shooting in Hannibal during the author's boyhood that I suspect Mark of having based it upon memory rather than upon the "Associated Press Telegram" which he credits. And the author himself testified that the shooting in *Huck* derived from the shooting near the Clemens doorstep in Hannibal of Sam Smarr by William Owsley.[1]

Concerning this murder we have unusually good information: John Marshall Clemens, J.P., who earned a $1.81 fee for administering oaths to twenty-nine witnesses and a $13.50 fee for writing out depositions totaling 13,500 words, left a full account in his own hand. These tell this story:

Early in January, 1845, Smarr traveled from his farm to nearby Hannibal for one of his occasional sprees. Shortly, as was his habit when turbulent with drink, he began cursing wealthy merchant Owsley before audiences of townsfolk. None who knew Smarr well worried much: he was doing this in a neighborly spirit, since he believed the damned pickpocket and son

of a bitch (as he called Owsley) had cheated not him but two friends. Smarr had done this before without any aftermath, and acquaintances agreed that he was not dangerous. When the early winter twilight fell he was reeling along the street, firing his pistol, shouting, "O yes, here's Bill Owsley, has got a stock of goods here, and stole two thousand dollars from Thompson in Palmyra!"

From his store Owsley, a haughty dandified migrant from Kentucky, heard the accusation. "He had a kind of twitching," a customer testified, "and said it was insufferable." But the merchant did nothing that night and Smarr returned home.

SHERBURN STEPS OUT.

Colonel Sherburn confronting a lynch mob (drawing by E. W. Kemble; from Adventures of Huckleberry Finn, *Mark Twain House, Hartford, Connecticut)*

Colonel Sherburn and Mark Twain

In chapter 22 of Adventures of Huckleberry Finn, *Colonel Sherburn faces down a lynch mob after he has murdered the drunken Boggs. A man "born and raised in the South" who has "lived in the North," Sherburn claims to know the true nature of the average man: "The average man's a coward. In the North he lets anybody walk over him that wants to, and goes home and prays for a humble spirit to bear it. In the South one man, all by himself, has stopped a stage full of men, in the day-time, and robbed the lot. Your newspapers call you a brave people so much that you think you are braver than any other people—whereas you're just* as *brave, and no braver. Why don't your juries hang murderers? Because they're afraid the man's friends will shoot them in the back, in the dark—and it's just what they* would do" (p. 190).

Before returning in summer 1883 to his manuscript of Huckleberry Finn *and writing of Sherburn's encounter with the mob, Mark Twain had written a chapter in* Life on the Mississippi—*which he decided not to include—in which he expressed a similar attitude to Sherburn's. This excerpt from the suppressed chapter suggests that Sherburn may be speaking for Twain.*

Now, in every community, North and South, there is one hot-head, or a dozen, or a hundred, according to distribution of populations; the rest of the community are quiet folk. What do these hot-heads amount to, in the North? Nothing. Who fears them? Nobody. Their heads never get so hot but that they retain cold sense enough to remind them that they are among a people who will not allow themselves to be walked over by their sort; a people who, although they will not insanely hang them upon suspicion and without trial, nor try them, convict them, and then let them go, but who will give them a fair and honest chance in the courts, and if conviction follow will punish them with imprisonment or the halter.

In the South the case is very different. The one hot-head defies the hamlet; the half-dozen or dozen defy the village and the town. In the South the expression is common, that such-and-such a ruffian is the "terror of the town."Could he come North and be the terror of a town? Such a thing is impossible. Northern resolution, backing Northern law, was too much for even the "Mollie Maguires," powerful, numerous, and desperate as was that devilish secret organization. But it could have lived a long life in the South; for there it is not the rule for courts to hang murderers.

Why?—seeing that the bulk of the community are murder-hating people. It is hard to tell. Are they torpid, merely?—indifferent?—wanting in public spirit?

Their juries fail to convict, even in the clearest cases. That this is not agreeable to the public, is shown by the fact that very frequently such a miscarriage of justice so rouses the people that they rise, in a passion, and break into the jail, drag out their man and lynch him. This is quite sufficient proof that they

do not approve of murder and murderers. But this hundred or two hundred men usually do this act of public justice with masks on. They go to their grim work with clear consciences, but with their faces disguised. They know that the law will not meddle with them—otherwise, at least, than by empty form—and they know that the community will applaud their act. Still, they disguise themselves.

The other day, in Kentucky, a witness testified against a young man in the court, and got him fined for a violation of a law. The young man went home and got his shotgun and made short work of that witness. He did not invent that method of correcting witnesses; it had been used before, in the South. Perhaps this detail accounts for the reluctance of juries to convict and perhaps, also, for the disposition of lynchers to go to their grewsome labors disguised.

Personal courage is a rare quality. Everywhere in the Christian world,—except, possibly, down South,—the average citizen is not brave, he is timid. Perhaps he is timid down South, too. According to the Times Democrat, "the favorite diversion of New Orleans hoodlums is crowding upon the late street cars, hustling the men passengers and insulting the ladies." They smoke, they use gross language, they successfully defy the conductor when he tries to collect their fare. All this happens, and they do not get hurt. Apparently the average Southern citizen is like the average Northern citizen—does not like to embroil himself with a ruffian.

The other day, in Kentucky, a single highwayman, revolver in hand, stopped a stagecoach and robbed the passengers, some of whom were armed—and he got away unharmed. The unaverage Kentuckian, being plucky, is not afraid to attack half a dozen average Kentuckians; and his bold enterprise succeeds—probably because the average Kentuckian is like the average of the human race, not plucky, but timid.

In one thing the average Northerner seems to be a step in advance of the average Southerner, in that he bands himself with his timid fellows to support the law, (at least in the matter of murder,) protect judges, juries, and witnesses, and also to secure all citizens from personal danger and from obloquy or social ostracism on account of opinion, political or religious; whereas the average Southerners do not band themselves together in these high interests, but leave them to look out for themselves unsupported; the results being unpunished murder, against the popular approval, and the decay and destruction of independent thought and action in politics.

—*Life on the Mississippi,* with previously suppressed passages, edited by Willis Wager (New York: The Limited Editions Club, 1944), pp. 413–415

Two or three weeks later, Smarr was again in Hannibal on the corner of Hill and Main. Owsley came up behind him. At four paces he shouted, "You, Sam Smarr!" The farmer whirled, saw Owsley draw a pistol, and begged him not to shoot. Owsley fired. As Smarr stumbled backward, Owsley without lowering his arm fired again. Bystanders lifted the wounded man and carried him to Dr. Grant's drugstore a few steps away. There Grant and another doctor opened the victim's clothes but left him alone when he showed signs of fainting. About half an hour later he died.

The remarkable accuracy with which Mark Twain duplicated this incident in *Huck* suggests that it made a deep impression upon him as a nine-year-old, a likelihood supported by his recounting it on at least four other occasions[2] and by his stating in his *Autobiography* that it haunted his dreams. Yet a study of invented details which he added is revealing. Some make Boggs, Smarr's fictional counterpart, more sympathetic. The townsfolk, Huck reports, welcome him because they are "used to having fun out of Boggs." Huck's description shows a comic red-faced drunk "a-tearing along on his horse, whooping and yelling like an Injun, . . . singing out . . . weaving about in his saddle." He shouts, "Cler the track, thar. I'm on the waw-path, and the price uv coffins is a gwyne to raise." His exchanges with the loafers are good natured: "Everybody yelled at him, and laughed at him, and sassed him, and he sassed back, and said he'd attend to them and lay them out in their regular turns, but he couldn't wait now, because he'd come to town to kill old Colonel Sherburn, and his motto was 'meat first, and spoon vittles to top off on.'" Like the extravagant boasts in the traditional comic pattern in the raftsmen chapter, this good natured banter and four specific statements by townspeople that Boggs is harmless underline the nonseriousness of his threats.

One detail, though, makes Boggs slightly less sympathetic than Smarr: he is angry because he believes the merchant has swindled not friends but Boggs himself. And some invented details make Sherburn more sympathetic than Owsley. As Boggs abuses this "proud-looking man," not a handful of customers but "the whole street packed with people" is shown "listening and laughing and going on." More important, Sherburn, unlike his counterpart, specifically warns his torturer that he will endure his abuse until one o'clock, thus giving him a chance to escape. (The author based this detail upon another violent scene of his Hannibal youth—Widow Wier's warning that she would shoot a man bent on invading her home and raping her if he did not leave before she counted to ten.[3])

But all the invented details which follow this warning build sympathy for Boggs at Sherburn's expense. Boggs is shown trying desperately to escape, "a-reeling . . . , bare-headed, with a friend on both sides of him aholt of his arms and hurrying him along. He was quiet, and looked uneasy; and he warn't hanging back any, but was doing some of the hurrying himself." Sherburn is completely unmoved by this pitiful spectacle and by Boggs' pleadings—"standing perfectly still," his pistol uplifted, then bringing the gun down "slow and steady to a level—both barrels cocked," shooting twice so efficiently that both shots take effect. Then "Colonel Sherburn he tossed his pistol onto the ground, and turned around on his heels and walked off."

None of the many 1845 witnesses mentions a daughter of the murdered man who is sent for by worried townsfolk and who arrives just as her father is shot; so the likelihood is that she is an imagined character. She too serves to avert sympathy from Sherburn: "That young girl screamed out, and comes rushing, and down she throws herself on her father, crying, and saying, 'Oh, he's killed him, he's killed him!' After Boggs' death the crowd pulls her away from him "screaming and crying." Huck ends the account with other pathetic details: "She was about sixteen, and very sweet and gentle-looking, but awful pale and scared."

—Mark Twain and Huck Finn (Berkeley & Los Angeles: University of California Press, 1960), pp. 306–308

---

1. A full account is in Wecter's *Sam Clemens of Hannibal*, pp. 106–108. Parallels between the Hannibal episode and the novel: the man committing the murder was a leading merchant; he called out his victim's name before shooting; only two shots were fired; only one man was killed; the victim was carried to a nearby store to die; some fool tortured the dying man by placing a big Bible on his chest. None of these details occurs in the "newspaper item." In the typescript of his *Autobiography* Mark annotated his mention of the shooting in Hannibal thus: "See 'Adventures of Huckleberry Finn.'" *Mark Twain Papers.*

2. In a letter to Will Bowen in 1870: "Villagers of 1840-3"; *Autiobiography,* I, 131, and a manuscript notation: "Owsley and Smar *[sic]*—Bible on breast. Gave him spiritual relief, no doubt, but must have crowded him physically"; and six other lines, listed in *Anderson Auction Company Catalogue,* no. 892 (New York, 1911), p. 31, as an insert in a volume from Clemens' library entitled, ironically enough, *God in His World.*

3. Hannibal *Missouri Courier,* May 20, 1850. Wecter suggests that possibly Mark Twain wrote the story. Mark's penciled footnote to the portion of the *Autobiography* dealing with this: "Used in 'Huck Finn,' I think." *MTP.*

* * *

Mark Twain lamented having to tone down the story that was the basis for the episode of the "Thrilling Tragedy of The King's Camelopard or The Royal Nonesuch." In this essay, James Ellis considers the probable contents of the original "unprintable" tale.

The Bawdy Humor of
The King's Camelopard or The Royal Nonesuch
James Ellis

The nature of Mark Twain's "Thrilling Tragedy of The King's Camelopard or The Royal Nonesuch"[1] remains, it seems to me, something of a mystery. We know that the particular tale that Twain had in mind was a story he heard told by Jim Gillis when he was living with Gillis in Jackass Gulch, California.[2] Gillis called the story "The Tragedy of the Burning Shame," and Twain referred to the skit by that title throughout the manuscript of *Huckleberry Finn,* only changing it to "The Royal Nonesuch" just before publication.[3] Twain wrote in his *Autobiography,* "I had to modify [the story] considerably to make it proper for print and this was a great damage. . . . [I]t was one of the most outrageously funny things I have ever listened to. How mild it is in the book *[Huckleberry Finn]* and how pale; how extravagant and how gorgeous in its unprintable form!"[4]

Apparently the earliest attempt to describe what it was that Twain was dramatizing was by Robert Bridges, who in his 1885 review of the novel identified the skit as a "polite version" of the Giascutus hoax. Michael Patrick Hearn cites Bridges and explains the hoax. Two con men would pretend to have for exhibition some terrible creature known as the Giascutus; one would collect money from the curious crowd, who upon entering the theater would be treated to a curtain on stage, behind which would issue terrible roars and sounds, presumably from the Giascutus. After all the money had been collected the seller of tickets would come on stage and begin to "lecture on the beast's ferocity all the while poking it behind the curtain with a stick." Suddenly the beast would give out "a tremendous roar, and the man before the curtain would scream that the Giascutus had escaped and all should run for their lives. The two con men would then exit by the back door and move on to another locale.[5] The only problem with the Giascutus story as the source of Jim Gillis' tale and Twain's skit is that there is nothing bawdy about it, no reason for its advertisement in the novel to have carried the warning LADIES AND CHILDREN NOT ADMITTED, and no reason for Twain to have felt that the material was so scandalous that it would have to be suppressed.

Much more recently Wallace Graves has taken up the question and proposed a new understanding of the skit based on a story told to him by Douglas Haven in the early 1930s. In introducing his remarks, Graves says that "neither the meaning of the title 'The Burning Shame' nor the events in the story are known to Twain scholars" (p. 94). He cites as an example Walter Blair, "who in his book *Mark Twain & Huck Finn* states he has found no 'indecent connotations' in the title 'The Burning Shame,' and who therefore is baffled by the fact that Twain deleted it from *Huckleberry Finn* in a final revision just before publication, calling the performance instead 'The Royal Nonesuch.'" Graves then tells Haven's story, which takes place in Sweden and carries the title of Gillis' story, "The Tragedy of the Burning Shame":

> It was about two destitute traveling actors who decided to raise some money by giving a performance in a small town. Women and children were not admitted; they rigged a stage with a curtain, and made sure that an escape door at the rear of the stage was open for a quick getaway after the show. One man collected money while the audience filed in, then came round and appeared before the curtain announcing that a great dramatic play called "The Burning Shame" was about to be shown. The curtain was then raised, and his partner, naked, came out on his hands and knees. The other said, "And now, gentlemen, you are about to see The Tragedy of the Burning Shame." He inserted a candle in the naked man's posterior, and lit it. When nothing further happened, the audience shouted for something more; the man said the performance was over; the viewers shouted "You mean, that's all?" "Yes," the man said, "have you ever seen a better example of a 'Burning Shame'?" Then the two dashed out of town, the audience in hot pursuit. (P. 98)

Graves writes that the evidence "must remain circumstantial" as to whether this is the version that Twain heard from Jim Gillis, but he says that it has "somewhat more to recommend it" than the story of the Giascutus: "it supplies unquestionably an indecent connotation which Blair found lacking; its title is identical to Twain's, and it is an extremely apt and telling title; in no way is it inconsistent with the details related by Huck, but simply continues where Huck leaves off with 'And–but never mind the rest of his outfit; it was just wild, but it was awful funny.'"[6]

In both Twain's and Graves's versions, the audiences finally feel that they have been "sold." But there are important differences between the two versions. In Graves's version there is no naked and painted man, only a naked man; and there is no fantastic capering so outrageously funny that the audience made the man

183

what they wanted was low
comedy — & maybe something
still worse than low comedy,
he reckoned. He said he
judged he could caper to their
base instincts; 'lowed he
could size their style. So next
morning he got some big
sheets of wrapping paper &
some black paint, & drawed
off some handbills & stuck
them up all over the village.
The bills said:

At the Court House!

For 3 Nights Only!

The manuscript version describing the bill for the king and duke's Bricksville performance
(Buffalo and Erie County Public Library)

184

The World-Renowned Tragedians

David Garrick the Younger !

and

Edmund Kean the Elder !

of the London + Continental
Theatres,

in their Thrilling tragedy of

The Burning Shame !!!

Admission 50 cents.

Then at the bottom was the
biggest line of all — which said:
Ladies + Children not Admitted.

come back and do it over and over again. This discrepancy—no painting, no prancing and capering, and no laughter—leads me to believe that the story told by Graves is not the story that Twain heard from Jim Gillis and that he intended as the basis of his skit. Hearn's conjecture that "the king performed some obscene tricks" (p. 224) is probably closer to the mark of what Twain intended.

As an example of the kind of "obscene tricks" he has in mind, Hearn cites a story told by Daniel P. Mannix in his *Step Right Up!* (1951) having to do with a sideshow "for men only" that he saw performed during the depression:

A man comes out and explains he is going to present a trained dog act. Maybe they aren't interested in trained dogs? Well, they'll be interested in this one. He then calls. Off stage come barks and whines. Finally, the man exits and returns dragging a naked girl who is on all fours. She is generally painted in some way as with spots to represent a Dalmatian. The man tells her to sit up and beg, roll over, play dead, etc. Whenever he stops to address the "tip" (the crowd), the girl goes over and, raising one leg pretends to urinate on him whereupon he indignantly kicks her away. This is used as a running gag throughout the show[.] The girl goes through the motions of defecating, afterwards scratching with her hind legs. The man tells her there's a rat in the corner and she goes after it, wiggling her backside as she scratches in the corner. As a climax, the man calls on another dog which is invisible. He says this one is female. The girl goes through the motions of sniffing the imaginary dog's backside and then gets excited and pretends to mount [the imaginary dog], going through the motions of breeding. The man tells her that that isn't nice and tries to get the invisible dog away from her but the girl holds it. In his efforts, the man falls to his hands and knees whereupon the girl mounts him and starts to breed him. Still crawling, the man exits, yelling for help and carrying the girl with him. (P. 224)

A close examination of Twain's text will lend strong evidence for something akin to the story told by Mannix and cited by Hearn. My argument is based on an examination of not only what Twain describes but also his use of bawdy language. Indeed the language of the passage is bawdy to a remarkable degree, and this so far as I know has never been pointed out.

But before we look at "The Royal Nonesuch," we would do well to question its other title, "The King's Camelopard." Now a camelopard is an archaic name for a giraffe, and Hearn tells us also that even before the term was used for the giraffe it was used to describe "a mythical beast of the size of a camel and spotted like a leopard" (p. 222).

My first assumption in trying to understand what Huck found so "wild" and so "awful funny"

about the king's act has to do with what Huck calls "the rest of his outfit" (p. 223). This "outfit" is not a lighted candle but a gargantuan, artificial phallus attached to the king at its appropriate place. Surely one is justified in assuming, given our familiarity with such a common farm animal as the horse, that the size of the giraffe's phallus might very well be imagined to be of monumental proportions. It is here that Twain means for his readers to look for a definition of the rest of the king's outfit. Though I don't think this in itself accounts for the bawdy fun of the scene, the mere size of the phallus must have evoked some laughter in that all-male audience.

The alternate title, "The Royal Nonesuch," has not been much discussed. Hearn glosses the term "nonesuch" in pretty much the way the word is defined in most dictionaries. He writes that "a 'nonesuch' is something unmatched and unrivaled and then goes on to discuss its source in Jim Gillis' story of "The Burning Shame." But the word "nonesuch" suggests much more than its polite dictionary definition. Eric Partridge tells us that since the eighteenth century "nonesuch" has been used in a vulgar sense to refer to "the female pudend[um]."[7] So it would appear that Twain in his twin titles of "The King's Camelopard or The Royal Nonesuch" brought together terms referring both to the male and the female genitalia. But if "nonesuch" carries this vaginal reference, are we to assume that the original for which "nonesuch" was substituted—"The Burning Shame"—also carries a reference to the female genitalia? The answer, I believe, is yes. Graves in his conjecture notes that scholars have not found an indecent connotation in Twain's working title. But the indecency of "The Burning Shame" has been before us since 1785, only awaiting our discovery. Partridge cites the first edition of Francis Grose's *Dictionary of the Vulgar Tongue*[8] and defines "burning shame" as "a lighted candle stuck into the private parts of a woman" (p. 160).[9]

But notice the distinction between Grose's definition involving the vagina of a woman and the version cited by Graves that involves the anus of a man. A correct understanding of the vaginal reference in "the burning shame" lends credence to my argument that the king is equipped with a gargantuan phallus, perhaps one that could be made to rise and fall in enacting "the thrilling tragedy" of "The King's Camelopard," and that in all likelihood the king's act involved a phallic pantomime that was directed toward an invisible woman's vagina, "The Royal Nonesuch." In this way the two titles taken collectively, "The King's Camelopard or The Royal Nonesuch," suggest the sexual concept that earlier had

TRAGEDY.

The king playing the main part in the story Mark Twain heard from Jim Gillis, originally called "The Tragedy of the Burning Shame"
(drawing by E. W. Kemble; from Adventures of Huckleberry Finn, *Mark Twain House, Hartford, Connecticut)*

been unified under the single title that Twain had used in manuscript, "The Tragedy of the Burning Shame."

That this may be so is supported, I think, by an understanding that etymologically "pudendum" and "shame" are related. The *NED* gives as the source of "pudendum": "L., neuter gerundive of *pudēre* to cause shame, ashame, lit. 'that of which one ought to be ashamed.'"[10]

Thus it would seem in substituting "nonesuch" for "burning shame" Twain wished to make his story less obviously obscene while at the same time preserving the essence of his ribald story. The text, I think, further substantiates this reading of the king's acting out a phallic pantomime, for Twain continues in this passage his use of bawdy language and innuendo: "when the king got done *capering*, and *capered* off behind the scenes, they roared and clapped and stormed and haw-hawed

till he come back and done it over again; and after that, they made him do it another time. Well, it would a made a *cow* laugh, to see the *shines* that old idiot cut" (p. 196, italics mine).

The added bawdiness of this scene derives from Partridge's explanation that from about the 1860s "shines" had the additional meaning of "capers" and that these two words could be used vulgarly to mean "copulation between human beings: from *ca*. 1870" (p. 1051). No wonder that Twain concludes this passage by saying that the antics of the king were so funny that it would have made "a *cow* laugh, to see the *shines* that old idiot cut." An innocent reader might assume only the ridiculous notion of a cow brought to laughter by the king's antics, but a reader made aware of Twain's phallic pantomime can well appreciate even more the idea of a *cow*, not only as the bovine, but also as representative of the female of all species, including Homo sapiens, brought to helpless laughter over the ridiculous attempts of the male of the species to perform that all-so-important-to-him act of sexual intercourse. The *cow's* laughter, of course, ostensibly at the expense of the king and the male, also suggests the sexual knowledge and proclivity of the female, who would—Twain seems to be saying—pretend to the spiritual but whose laughter shows her to be as sexually vulnerable and as interested in the pleasures of sexuality as is the male of the species.

        —*American Literature,* 63 (December 1991): 729–735

1. *Adventures of Huckleberry Finn,* ed. Walter Blair and Victor Fischer (Berkeley: Univ. of California Press, 1988), p. 195. Subsequent references will be incorporated parenthetically in the text.
2. In *Mark Twain: A Biography* (New York: Harper, 1912), Albert Bigelow Paine cites the location as "Jackass Hill." In his *Mark Twain's Autobiography* (New York: Harper, 1924), he makes no mention of the location. Both Bernard DeVoto's *Mark Twain in Eruption* (New York: Harper, 1940) and Charles Neider's *The Autobiography of Mark Twain* (New York: Harper, 1959) cite the location as "Jackass Gulch."
3. Wallace Graves, "Mark Twain's 'Burning Shame,'" *Nineteenth-Century Fiction,* 23 (1968), 94, 96. Subsequent references will be incorporated parenthetically in the text.
4. *The Autobiography of Mark Twain,* pp. 139–40.
5. *The Annotated Huck Finn,* ed. Michael Patrick Hearn (New York: Clarkson N. Potter, 1981), pp. 223–24. Subsequent references will be incorporated parenthetically in the text.
6. John Seelye was apparently convinced by Wallace Graves's argument. In *The True Adventures of Huckleberry Finn* (New York: Simon and Schuster, 1971), Seelye incorporated Graves's explanation into his retelling of the skit and also restored Twain's working title, "The Burning Shame."
7. *A Dictionary of Slang and Unconventional English,* 8th ed., ed. Paul Beale (New York: Macmillan, 1984), p. 801. Subsequent references will be incorporated parenthetically in the text.
8. *A Classical Dictionary of the Vulgar Tongue* (London: S. Hooper, 1785).
9. In *Letters from the Earth* (New York: Harper and Row, 1962), Twain describes the sexual proclivity of men and women in terms of "the candlestick" and "the candle": "During twenty-three days in each month (in the absence of pregnancy) from the time a woman is seven years old till she dies of old age, she is ready for action, and *competent*. As competent as the candlestick is to receive the candle. Competent every day, competent every night. Also, she *wants* that candle—yearns for it, longs for it, hankers after it, as commanded by the law of God in her heart" (p. 40). I am indebted to Pamela Postma, a doctoral candidate in English at UNCG, for pointing out to me Twain's use of the candlestick metaphor.
10. *A New Dictionary on Historical Principles,* ed. Sir James A. H. Murray (Oxford: Clarendon Press, 1909), p. 1567.

Literary Influences

These excerpts are from Berret's essay "The Influence of Hamlet *on* Huckleberry Finn," *which examines Mark Twain's incorporation in his novel of burlesques of the works of William Shakespeare.*

Shakespeare Burlesques in *Huckleberry Finn*
"Ambiguous Responses to
High Culture and Great Literature"
Anthony J. Berret

Besides being a collection of different dialects, as the author explains, *Adventures of Huckleberry Finn* is a collection of literary references, quotations, and allusions which receive mixed ratings from the characters and the reader. The Widow Douglas tries to interest Huck in the story of "Moses and the Bulrushers," but he doesn't "take no stock in dead people." Tom Sawyer appeals to Don Quixote as an authority for his raid on the Sunday-school picnic, and to Sir Walter Scott and Alexandre Dumas for his "evasion" plot, but Huck dismisses Tom's flamboyant style and literary authorities as a pack of lies causing unnecessary trouble. Nevertheless, Huck finds the Shakespearean productions of the king and the duke "grand," "beautiful," and "perfectly lovely," and here the reader has to question Huck's critical judgment. The reader would especially like to know how the author feels about these literary works, and whether he uses them "in a haphazard fashion" or as painstakingly as he claims to have used his dialects.

Mark Twain had mixed feelings about great works of literature. He was often reluctant to admit that he had read them. Yet he wanted his first book to be called "The New Pilgrim's Progress," and he based another book on Malory's *Morte D'Arthur.* He also wrote several literary burlesques, and some of these showed reverence rather than scorn for the works on which they were based. His burlesques of Shakespeare, for instance, would ridicule inferior productions and adaptations of the plays but maintain respect for the originals. This combination of ridicule and reverence makes the Shakespeare burlesques most representative of Mark Twain's general attitude toward literature. A study of them should clarify the value and function he gave to literary references, especially since Shakespeare burlesques are incorporated into the plot of his classic, *Huckleberry Finn.*[1]

There are three pieces in *Huckleberry Finn* that qualify as Shakespeare burlesques. They are part of the motley program staged by the king and the duke. Their many ambiguities draw mixed reactions from the reader. In the first place, they are three tragedies put on in comic fashion. The duke, however, wants them to be serious. Even though the bald and bearded king plays Juliet, the duke instructs him to say his lines "soft and sick and languishy," and not to "bray like a jackass." In practicing the sword-fight from *Richard III,* the duke prances about the raft in grand style, but the king trips and falls overboard.[2] If the duke's efforts at delicacy and prowess do not give the reader much hope for a decent performance, they at least remind the reader that Shakespeare's plays are sublime when they are done with mastery. It is ironic that even the inept performance of the king and the duke seems to go over the heads of the Arkansas audience. Since Shakespeare proves too much for them, the duke must resort to low comedy to fetch the house. Through all this the reader laughs at the pretensions and follies of the two imposters, and at the coarseness and gullibility of the Arkansas villagers, but he is constantly reminded of the excellence of Shakespeare's plays and the skill with which they should be performed. This awareness of possible artistry helps him rise above the buffoonery, and not just by laughter.

The balcony scene from *Romeo and Juliet* is rehearsed by the king and the duke soon after the Grangerford-Shepherdson feud. Since the feud also deals with romance between members of rival families and ends in a bloodbath, the balcony scene may be considered a burlesque of the feud as well as of Shakespeare's play. It mocks the romantic bravado of the feud, but it also expresses the tragedy by evoking memories of Shakespeare's play. These memories set the feud in a broader terrain and help the reader see and accept it as part of a universal tragic theme.[3] The sword-fight scene from *Richard III* has a similar effect on the Boggs-Sherburn "duel." Its rehearsal, advertisement, and performance surround the duel, satirizing the duel's stupidity, but also placing the duel in a larger and more comprehensible tragic context. This interplay of event and artistic expression runs through the whole novel, and the Shakespearean references enrich it because of the diverse reactions they arouse in the reader. The burlesques expose the comic absurdity of the events, but the original plays which they recall and which stay on the reader's mind introduce broader tragic perspectives that help interpret and alleviate the sadness and horror.

One Shakespearean prop which the king and the duke have but do not use in their performance is a King Lear costume. They force Jim to wear it on the raft while they are off claiming the Wilks legacy. Its presence associates the river experiences of Huck and Jim with Lear's ordeal on the heath. Both Huck and Lear prefer storms and nakedness to the cruelties and superficialities of civilization.[4] What is more, the Lear costume connects literary references with the raft and the river. All the Shakespeare rehearsals occur on the raft,

and they have the same effect as the river. They help Huck and the reader escape from the violence and vulgarity of the shore towns, but like the river they also inspire deep thought. Their lyric and tragic passages resemble the stars, sunrises, storms, and floods experienced on the river. They set the temporary and localized events of the shore into more universal patterns.

The only burlesque proper of a Shakespeare text in *Huckleberry Finn* is the rendition of Hamlet's soliloquy. It is a conglomeration of phrases from *Macbeth, Richard III,* and different parts of *Hamlet,* and it resembles in this aspect the collective character of the whole novel. It ridicules the phony grandeur of the duke as he tears a passion to tatters in his efforts to recall the speech and "learn" it to the king, and it excites Huck's admiration. He finds the speech "beautiful" and "noble" enough to remember it and deliver it himself to the reader. Whether the flaws in it are his or the duke's is unclear. In contrast to the other Shakespeare scenes, this speech does not seem to attempt an artistic expression of some specific event in the novel. . . .

In the background of *Huckleberry Finn* lay Mark Twain's intermittent plans and attempts to write a burlesque *Hamlet.* He is supposed to have first considered the idea after seeing Edwin Booth play Hamlet in New York on November 3, 1873. Albert Bigelow Paine says that Twain went backstage and told Booth he would add a comic character to the play. In a letter to William Dean Howells on September 3, 1881, Twain said that he first—nine years before—tried to add a country cousin of Hamlet but that the attempt failed.[5] He tried again in September of 1881. He wrote almost two acts of the play with the addition of Hamlet's foster brother, Basil Stockmar, a subscription book agent. He cut pages out of paperback editions of *Hamlet* and pasted them between the speeches of Stockmar that he added.

Basil Stockmar wears a swallow-tail coat and top hat, carries a satchel and umbrella, smokes a cigar, speaks slang, and parodies the "grandest kind of book-talk" of the other characters. He describes a servant ordering a carriage: "Me lord hath given commandment, sirrah, that the vehicle wherein he doth, of ancient custom, his daily recreation take, shall unto the portal of the palace be straight conveyed. . . ." He is relevant to *Huckleberry Finn* because he was created around the same time as the king and the duke, the years 1880 to 1882.[6] He also resembles those other two con men. He uses Shakespeare to plug his wares, and he combines in his talk the colloquialism of the king and the pseudo-grandeur of the duke. As Hamlet's foster brother, he too is a claimant to nobility. Since he was added to *Hamlet* around the time that the king and the duke were added to *Huckleberry Finn,* and since his hab-

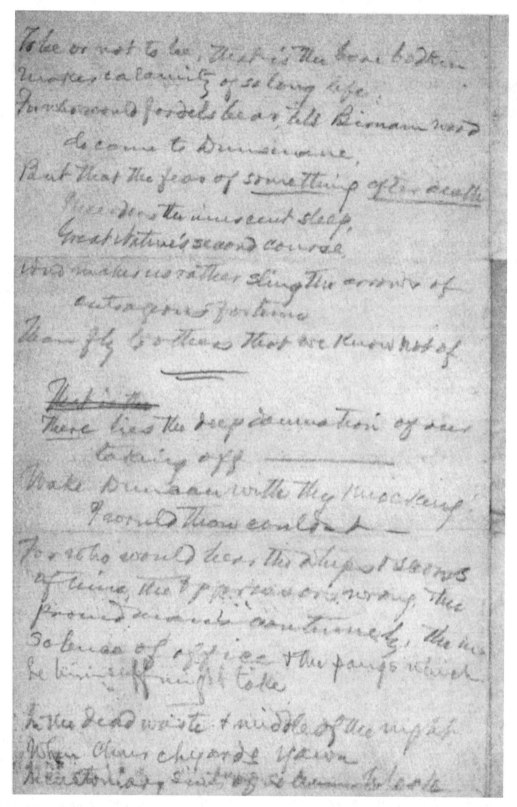

A version of "Hamlet's Immortal Soliloquy" that Twain wrote on the blank pages of a 19 March 1883 letter from Charles Webster to Olivia L. Clemens. Twain had already written the version of the soliloquy that appears in the Adventures of Huckleberry Finn *manuscript, so these pages are thought to represent an abortive attempt to revise the passage (Mark Twain Papers, The Bancroft Library, University of California, Berkeley).*

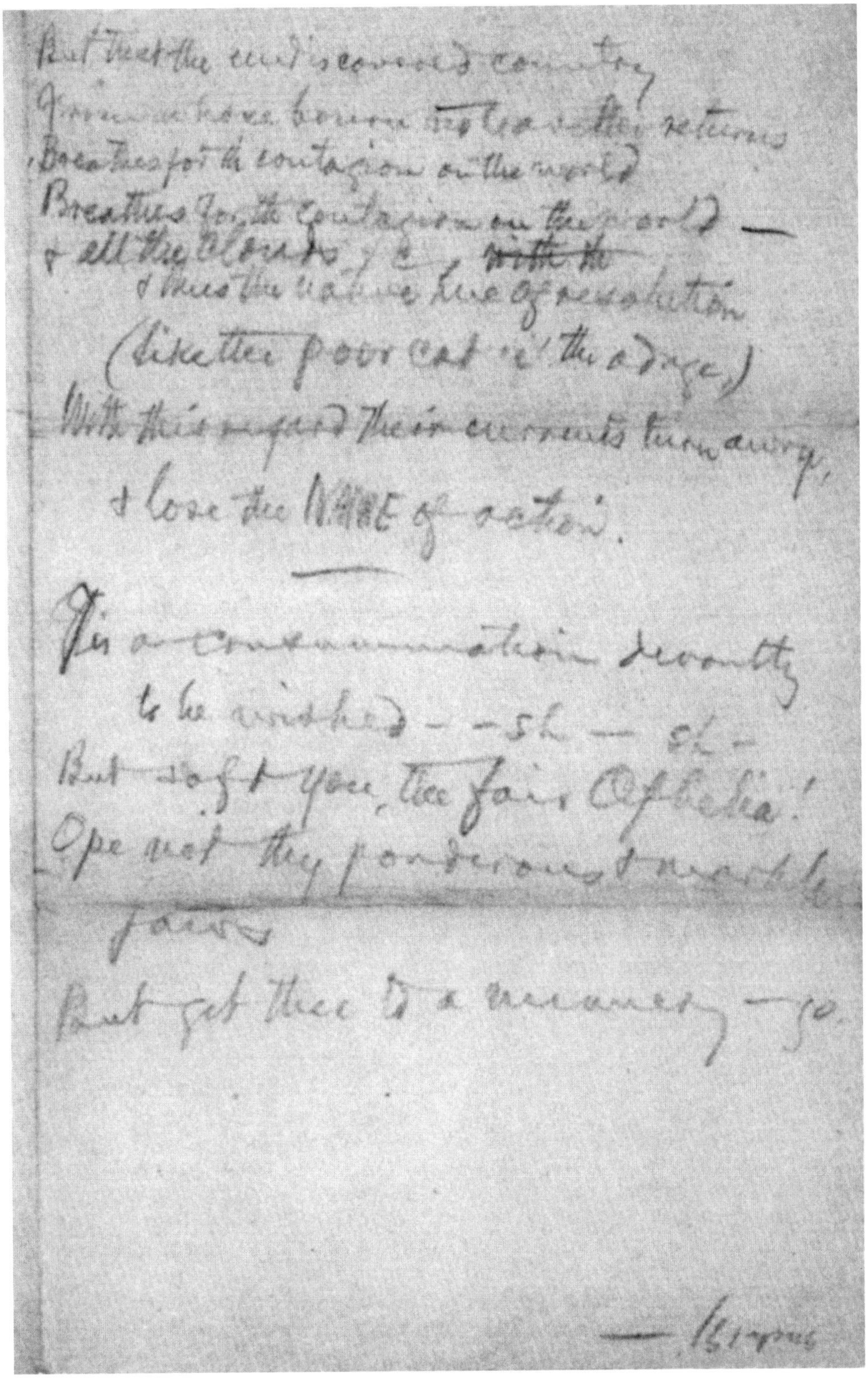

HAMLET'S SOLILOQUY.

The duke performing Hamlet's "sublime" soliloquy, a pastiche made of misremembered lines from Hamlet, Macbeth, *and* Richard III *(drawing by E. W. Kemble; from* Adventures of Huckleberry Finn, *Mark Twain House, Hartford, Connecticut)*

its and pursuits are similar to theirs, it appears that Mark Twain worked on the burlesque and on the middle section of the novel together, using one to help him with the other, and perhaps seeing in the process a resemblance between the two larger stories, *Hamlet* and *Huckleberry Finn.*

Other attempts at a burlesque *Hamlet* appeared in 1883. In March, Twain received from his old editor, Joseph T. Goodman, the rough copy of a play, "Hamlet's Brother," which he was supposed to revise.[7] Like Twain's earlier burlesque, this intersperses clipped sections of *Hamlet* with speeches of an added comic character. Here the character is Bill, Hamlet's brother, who has a sprightly and playful temperament and who tries by several tricks to cure Hamlet of his morbid, dreamy, conceited, and verbose nature. He disguises as the ghost, doctors up the play-within-the-play, has Polonius and Ophelia play dead and endure mock obsequies, and gets Laertes to fake revenge. The play ends with Laertes disarming Hamlet in a duel and the supposed dead showing up alive.[8]

Apparently Twain did some work on this burlesque. He wrote a speech for Bill to give in the ghost disguise. He also claimed to have found a letter stating that Bill received a pair of boxing gloves from a Tom Sayers.[9] Sayers was a famous British prize fighter in the mid-nineteenth century, but the name is close enough to Sawyer for one to see a correspondence between Bill and Tom. Both characters are lively and enjoy doing things with grand style, and they both bring rousing finales to their stories by theatrical games based on literary classics. Twain was working on Goodman's burlesque around the time that he was planning how to end *Huckleberry Finn,* so the one could have inspired the other. It was also in March of 1883 that Twain composed his burlesque of Hamlet's soliloquy and inserted it into Chapter XXI of his novel.[10]

These attempts at a burlesque Hamlet contain the two motifs that Twain used to continue and complete *Huckleberry Finn:* the comic pretensions of traveling con men and the theatrical antics of an energetic boy. They might therefore be called preliminary exercises for the novel. Franklin Rogers has described a process by which Twain moved from burlesque to serious and original fiction. He demonstrates how the early stages and models of *Huckleberry Finn* were burlesques of children's stories, detective stories, and travelogues. Although he does not mention a burlesque *Hamlet,* his theory of progression should allow for one as a forerunner to *Huckleberry Finn.*[11]

Burlesques of Shakespeare's plays filled English and American stages in the nineteenth century. Those of *Hamlet* are stressed here only because they relate more closely to *Huckleberry Finn.* John Poole's *Hamlet Travestie* (1810), one of the first and most famous, was printed and performed in England and America throughout the century, and it inspired many imitators. It is a three-act play with comically rhymed dialogue and soliloquies, songs sung to popular tunes, and numerous colloquialisms and anachronisms. Characters drink punch, smoke pipes, and wind watches. In the final scene, Hamlet and Laertes fight a duel with boxing gloves and Claudius pours arsenic into a mug of ale.[12] Probably the most famous American burlesque was George Edward Rice's *Hamlet, Prince of Denmark: An Old Play in a New Garb* (1852). Much of its humor, as in Poole's play, is based on anachronism. Hamlet and his friends are dandies with swallow-tail coats, top hats, and umbrellas. Hamlet stabs Polonius with a bowie knife, duels Laertes with a bow and arrow, and speaks his soliloquy while holding a revolver under his dressing gown. Since Osric puts Russian Salve instead of poison on the arrows and Ophelia fakes death by chloroform, the play ends happily with the whole cast singing to the tune of "Oh Susannah."[13] Shakespeare burlesques were also popular with minstrel companies. Griffin and Christy produced

PRACTICING.

The king and the duke practicing the sword fight from Richard III (drawing by E. W. Kemble; from Adventures of Huckleberry Finn, *Mark Twain House, Hartford, Connecticut)*

Hamlet the Dainty: An Ethiopian Burlesque, in which Hamlet wears the usual minstrel costume—a swallow-tail coat and a narrow-brimmed top hat. He winds a tin watch when he asks, "What is't o'clock?" and his father's ghost smokes a cigar and reads a newspaper. It ends, like Poole's play, with a boxing match and poison in a beer mug.[14]

These few examples show that Mark Twain was familiar with the tradition of Shakespeare burlesques. His exercises on *Hamlet* have features similar to other plays in the genre. His purpose for writing these burlesques and including them in *Huckleberry Finn* seems to coincide with the reason for their popularity and proliferation in the nineteenth century. Social mobility and social reform caused the century to react ambivalently to aristocracy and gentility. People could aspire to the upper class and at the same time ridicule those who dressed or acted above their station. The grand gestures and exuberant speeches of Shakespeare's plays, especially when they were burlesqued by dandies and minstrels, demonstrated perfectly both the appeal and the pretense of aristocracy. In *Huckle-*

berry Finn the king and the duke claim to be disinherited royalty and renowned tragedians. Their pretensions may not fool Huck, but they do fascinate him. Huck's mixed reaction to high culture echoes that of his fellow Americans and of his creator. The comic Mark Twain was also the serious and upright Mr. Clemens. He posed as dandy and squatter, pilgrim and sinner, prince and pauper. Burlesques of Shakespeare proved to be perfect vehicles for his ambiguous responses to high culture and great literature.

      —American Literary Realism, 1870–1910, 18 (Spring–Autumn 1985): 196–200

1. For Mark Twain's general reading and use of Shakespeare, see Howard G. Baetzhold, *Mark Twain and John Bull* (Bloomington: Indiana Univ. Press, 1970), pp. 255–262, 371–374; and Alan Gribben, *Mark Twain's Library: A Reconstruction* (Boston: G. K. Hall, 1980), II, 623–636; also see my unpublished dissertation, "Mark Twain's Use of Shakespeare," The Johns Hopkins Univ., 1980.
2. *Adventures of Huckleberry Finn* (Berkeley and Los Angeles: Univ. of California Press, 1985), Ch. XXI; further references to chapters will be given in the text.
3. Association of the play with the feud has been made by Baetzhold, p. 258, and by Edward Mendelsohn, "Mark Twain Confronts the Shakespeareans," *Mark Twain Journal,* 17 (Winter 1973–1974), 20.
4. For a study of this *Lear* imagery, see Paul Schacht, "The Lonesomeness of Huckleberry Finn," *American Literature,* 53 (May 1981), 193–196.
5. Albert Bigelow Paine, *Mark Twain, A Biography* (New York: Harper & Bros., 1912), I, 495; *Mark Twain-Howells Letters,* ed. Henry Nash Smith and William Gibson (Cambridge: Harvard Univ. Press, 1960), I, 369–370; *Mark Twain's Satires and Burlesques,* ed. Franklin Rogers (Berkeley, Los Angeles: Univ. of California Press, 1967), pp. 49–50.
6. *Satires and Burlesques,* pp. 69–70; for the time see Walter Blair, "When Was Huckleberry Finn Written?" *American Literature,* 30 (March 1958), 7–10, and *Mark Twain and Huck Finn* (Berkeley: Univ. of California Press, 1960), pp. 199–203.
7. *Satires and Burlesques,* pp. 51–53; see letter dated March 18, 1883, DV 320a, Mark Twain Papers, The Bancroft Library, University of California at Berkeley.
8. "Hamlet's Brother," DV 320a, Mark Twain Papers.
9. See *The Twainian,* 2, No. 9 (Jun. 1943), 4–6.
10. See Blair, *Mark Twain and Huck Finn,* pp. 301–303. Blair found a rough version of the speech on a paper dated 19 March. He believes that the speech was written on or soon after that date.
11. Franklin Rogers, *Mark Twain's Burlesque Patterns* (Dallas: Southern Methodist Univ. Press, 1960), pp. 128, 138.
12. *Nineteenth Century Shakespeare Burlesques,* ed. William Stanley Wells (Wilmington, Del.: Michael Glazier, Inc., 1978), I, 3–53.
13. Wells, V, 1–55.
14. Wells, V, 117–125.

* * *

In this essay Gribben shows that Adventures of Huckleberry Finn *was written and read within and against the evolving conventions of books treating boyhood in America.*

Manipulating a Genre: *Huckleberry Finn* as Boy Book
Alan Gribben

Scholars routinely classify Mark Twain's *The Adventures of Tom Sawyer* (1876) among the designated "Boy Books" of nineteenth-century American literature, that series of works extolling American boyhood which burst forth in emulation of Thomas Bailey Aldrich's *The Story of a Bad Boy* (1869). However, Twain's *Adventures of Huckleberry Finn* (1885) is much less frequently assigned to this category, at least in part because *Huckleberry Finn* seems so manifestly superior to any label. For that matter, it might be observed that the American Boy Book itself is one of the most casually accepted notions in literary history and criticism. The curious assortment of what we loosely define as "Boy Books" (or sometimes "Bad Boy Books") embraces an amazingly heterogeneous collection of writings—sentimental autobiography, juvenile romance, quasi-sociological documentary, comic slapstick, literary burlesque—that mainly have in common a reverence for boyhood, an autobiographical flavor, a setting in the past, and a code of behavior alien to most adults.

Thomas Hughes probably sired this particular type of Victorian nostalgia with his *Tom Brown's School Days* (1857); the shenanigans of Tom Brown in his native Berks county village and his hazing at the hands of Flashman at Rugby set the tone and established many of the incidents of the successful Boy Book. Charles Dickens's novels depicting boyhood deprivations, including *Oliver Twist* (1838), *David Copperfield* (1850), and *Great Expectations* (1861), rehearsed the pangs of childhood disappointments and terrors, but cannot be said to have produced the nearly complete formula that Thomas Hughes offered to Thomas Bailey Aldrich. (In chapter ten of *The Story of a Bad Boy,* Aldrich significantly refers to *Tom Brown's School Days* as "one of the best books ever written for boys.") Since Twain neither began nor ended the Boy Book, it helps to appreciate his achievements if we read forward and backward in the tradition of the Boy Book, especially in Charles Dudley Warner's sentimental recollections of Massachusetts farm-life, *Being a Boy* (1878); William Dean Howells's wistful and occasionally chilling chronicle of small-town life in Ohio, *A Boy's Town* (1890); Hamlin Garland's *Boy Life on the Prairie* (1899), a record of sensory privilege and cultural martyrdom for a boy transported by ox-cart to the Iowa prairie, there to grow into manhood; and Stephen Crane's tales about boy-

hood in a small town in New York state (many of them collected in *Whilomville Stories* [1900]), so evocative of the victories and humiliations of childhood.[1]

What literary critics nowadays dislike most about Twain's greatest fictional work are actually the vestigial parts of the conventions within which it originated. As Edwin Cady has astutely pointed out, *Huckleberry Finn* "consists of a long central narration, picaresque in form and substance and framed on either end by boy-book narratives"; consequently it "returns upon itself to end as it began in boy-life."[2] Our contemporary readers, barely familiar with Aldrich's Tom Bailey or Warner's farmboy John, find fully satisfying only the chapters in which Huck outwits his degenerate father, links up with a fleeing black slave, and surveys the sparsely settled banks of a river from the vantage point of a raft. The rest they dismiss as just an artistic mistake on Twain's part, owing (depending on the critics' point of view) to Twain's absurd affection for Tom Sawyer, his penchant for literary burlesque, his inability to understand his true strengths as an author, the inhibiting effect of his friends and family, or the lamentable tastes of the New England literary and publishing scene.

Very likely the publishing world *was* responsible for the inconsistencies in mood and theme that many readers abhor in *Huckleberry Finn,* but not for the reasons ordinarily given. The probability is that Twain wanted to exploit the increasingly popular Boy Book trend while experimenting with some new artistic possibilities that occurred to him. Those resulting internal shifts are one reason the novel could never possibly be duplicated by imitators, as Aldrich's book repeatedly was; there are built-in defects of structure and mood that incalculably contribute to its qualities of originality and its impression of spontaneity.

Taking the fictional and the purely autobiographical works together, what *did* these diverse books by Aldrich, Warner, Twain, Howells, Garland, and others have in common as a literary tradition? To begin with an obvious feature, one can perceive that in every Boy Book the normal adult sense of scale, of perspective, is tremendously magnified. Since these are books about children, an Ohio or Missouri or New Hampshire village becomes equivalent in dimensions and cultural activity to a metropolis as important as London. Predictably, then, the basic order of the town—its legal, political, and social codes—can never be fundamentally challenged, as Judith Fetterley has pointed out.[3] The wintertime snowball wars recounted in Warner's *Being a Boy* pay tribute to the random raid of American Indians, not the wholesale upheaval of revolutionaries. All the same, the boys in these books often make fools of the townspeople and farmers, causing communities to form into anxious, mindless mobs (as in the cannon-firing

THE STORY OF A BAD BOY.

CHAPTER I.

IN WHICH I INTRODUCE MYSELF.

HIS is the story of a bad boy. Well, not such a very bad, but a pretty bad boy; and I ought to know, for I am, or rather I was, that boy myself.

Lest the title should mislead the reader, I hasten to assure him here that I have no dark confessions to make. I call my story the story of a bad boy, partly to distinguish myself from those faultless young gentlemen who generally figure in narratives of this kind, and partly because I really was *not* a cherub. I may truthfully say I was an amiable, impulsive lad, blessed with fine digestive powers, and no hypocrite. I

First page of Thomas Bailey Aldrich's The Story of a Bad Boy *(1869), a semi-autobiographical novel that began a trend of "Boy Books" in American literature. Along with* The Adventures of Tom Sawyer, Adventures of Huckleberry Finn *was regarded as belonging to this genre (Thomas Cooper Library, University of South Carolina).*

episode of *The Story of a Bad Boy* or the abolitionist-scare conclusion to *Huckleberry Finn*). A preponderance of the Boy Books, including Howells's study of his Ohio childhood, also insist that to their boys the few surviving bands of unregenerate Native American Indians exemplify the ideal state of existence–packs of savages supposedly able to merge at will with a shadowy forest surrounding white villages.⁴

Abandoned savagery, however, is what the boys merely long for during a few hours of the day, when they seek to escape the rigors of school or the discipline of family life. The family unit may be the victim of their

bloody fantasies, but it is simultaneously a solace and refuge for besieged warriors. Stephen Crane's "His New Mittens" and "The Fight" effectively convey this anomaly, as do Howells's sensitive recollections. Indeed, in virtually every Boy Book or short story, well-intentioned parents or guardians resume control of the situation at the end, as in Aldrich's and Twain's narratives, removing the boy from the environment of his adventures (the endings of Aldrich's and Howells's books do this, for example, and Huckleberry Finn himself is about to be returned to St. Petersburg at the end of his narrative).

Of course, there was only so much that could be portrayed by the dedicated chronicler of boyhood; the possible experiences of a nineteenth-century boy, after all, were inherently limited–his education, siblings, church, chores, gangs, games, pranks, and a few other subjects defined the extent of a boy's permitted activities and illicit aspirations. Again, the cue for potential subject matter often came from Thomas Hughes's account of *Tom Brown's School Days*. In Part II of Hughes's novel, Tom's close friend, George Arthur, lies ill at Rugby with a contagious "fever" for many days, until Tom is finally summoned to his bedside. "Tom remembered a German picture of an angel which he knew; often had he thought how transparent and golden and spirit-like it was; and he shuddered to think how like it Arthur looked" (305). Arthur survives, but another lad, Thompson, sickens and dies at Tom's school, and illnesses would thereafter confine and chasten many American boy-outlaws, who must be nursed by solicitous relatives and visited by anxious chums. Mark Twain traced this convention to the Sunday School books for children, but Hughes's book probably had a large influence in making it a fixture of juvenile literature. Certainly Thomas Bailey Aldrich's boy-character Tom Bailey sets a fine example for his Boy Book brethen-to-be, reacting to a playmate's drowning death with an alarming collapse: "I was in a forlorn state, physically and mentally. Captain Nutter put me to bed between hot blankets, and sent Kitty Collins for the doctor. I was wandering in my mind, and fancied myself still on Sandpeep Island . . . and, in my delirium, I laughed aloud and shouted to my comrades. . . . Towards evening a high fever set in, and it was many days before my grandfather deemed it prudent to tell me that the Dolphin had been found, floating keel upwards" (170–171). This is to say, in other words, that Tom Sawyer's feverish swoons which conclude both *The Adventures of Tom Sawyer* and *Adventures of Huckleberry Finn* actually became a staple of Boy Books, usually prolonging the illness of the boy-hero or his good friend to the point of near-death. The modern reader should therefore not be skeptical when encountering that passage in which Tom, being transported on a mattress in chapter forty-two of *Huckleberry Finn,* "turned his head a little, and muttered something or other, which showed he warn't in his right mind" (356).

Other story patterns also indicate the common heritage of American Boy Books.[5] Perhaps Dickens's novels about children were partly responsible for the high mortality rate among boys' parents. Frequently, though not always, the primary character is, or becomes, an orphan. Tom Sawyer suffers this fate, of course, and Huck Finn unknowingly joins him (when Jim discovers Pap Finn's body) midway through Huck's

novel. Tom Bailey loses his father to cholera at the end of *The Story of a Bad Boy,* and Tom's days as a Centipedes gang member are ended by his grieving mother's arrival in town and his own decision to leave school. The death of Doctor Arnold at the conclusion of *Tom Brown's School Days* affects Tom Brown so profoundly that Arnold's role as a father-figure is apparent: "If he could only have seen the Doctor again for one five minutes; have told him all that was in his heart, what he owed to him, how he loved and reverenced him, and would by God's help follow his steps in life and death . . ." (374).

Huck Finn joins a boy-gang at the beginning of his book, another way in which he resembles the typical Boy Book protagonist. Also, Huck's peers do not discriminate against him, in spite of his outcast status in St. Petersburg, and this basic egalitarianism of boy-comrades is a tendency emphasized in virtually every Boy Book. Thomas Hughes writes, "Squire Brown held . . . that it didn't matter a straw whether his son associated with lord's sons, or ploughmen's sons, provided they were brave and honest. He himself had played football and gone birds'-nesting with the farmers whom he met at vestry and the labourers who tilled their fields, and so had his father and grandfather with their progenitors. So he encouraged Tom in his intimacy with the boys of the village" (53). William Dean Howells remembered that in childhood "his closest friend was a boy who was probably never willingly at school in his life. . . . Socially, he was as low as the ground under foot, but morally he was as good as any boy in the Boy's Town, and he had no bad impulses" (191). In *Huckleberry Finn,* as in most Boy Books, there is no rank except what one earns in the neighborhood; adult-assigned economic hierarchies and social distinctions count for next to nothing.

Yet the differences that set *Adventures of Huckleberry Finn* apart from its rivals are the more fascinating aspects of Twain's achievement. For example, the schoolboy "crush" quickly became a standard bit of comedy in the American Boy Book–Tom Bailey moons over the unattainable Miss Nelly Glentworth: "I wonder if girls from fifteen to twenty are aware of the glamour they cast over the straggling awkward boys whom they regard and treat as mere children," sighs the narrator (231). Warner's boy named John stammers out his admiration for Cynthia Rudd and walks her home under the stars from a party. Tom Sawyer's antics for the purpose of catching Becky Thatcher's attention are legendary. However, Huck Finn is truly helpful to Mary Jane Wilks, and his shy affection for her seems practically noble because it gives him the courage to save her from embarrassment and financial ruin; his reward is her gratitude when, "laying her silky hand on min[e] in that kind of a way that I said I would die first," she says, "'You tell me what to do, and whatever you say, I'll do it'"(241).

Huck does not face and vanquish a school bully, as plucky Tom Brown must outwit and outfight the swaggering Flashman and Aldrich's Tom Bailey must thrash Conway, who "never failed to brush against me, or pull my cap over my eyes. . . . I felt it was ordained ages before our birth that we should meet on this planet and fight" (65). Tom Sawyer opens his novel by "licking" a newcomer to St. Petersburg, whereas in Stephen Crane's splendid boy-tale "The Fight" (1900), Johnnie Hedge, forced to win a place for himself in the Whilomville school yard, bloodily defeats both Jimmie Trescott and his leader, Willie Dalzel. Huck Finn, on the contrary, finds a friend rather than an enemy in Buck Grangerford, and Huck's only antagonists are scheming adults.

Then, too, Huck is not the addict of romance-reading that Tom Bailey, Tom Sawyer, and others prove to be; even Warner's farmboy John conceals a worn copy of the *Arabian Nights* in the barn, imagining that he "had but to rub the ring and summon a genius *[sic]*, who would feed the calves and pick up chips and bring in wood in a minute" (70). Aldrich's juvenile hero finds a trunk in the garret of his grandfather's house that contains a "collection of novels and romances, embracing the adventures of Baron Trenck, Jack Sheppard, Don Quixote, Gil Blas, and Charlotte Temple—all of which I fed upon like a bookworm"; he also keeps copies of Robinson Crusoe and the *Arabian Nights* near his bed (40–41). But Huck Finn, less deluded, periodically rejects Tom Sawyer's appeals to published "authorities"—"I couldn't see no profit in it," says Huck, resigning after a month of membership in Tom's robber gang, "we hadn't killed any people, but only just pretended" (30).

In most Boy Books the climactic test of courage involves a large, dangerous body of water, a sudden, thunderous storm, and a boatload of foolhardy boys. The expedition in Hamlin Garland's *Boy Life on the Prairie* occurs on Clear Lake, where a storm almost upends the boys' sailboat. Little Binnie Wallace is not so lucky in Aldrich's *Story of a Bad Boy;* Binnie drowns in a storm after the boys take their small boat, the *Dolphin,* out in the bay to Sandpeep Island. Tom Sawyer, of course, commands a watery expedition midway through his novel: Tom, Huck, and Joe Harper establish a pirate-camp on Jackson's Island that is besieged by a "furious blast," "one blinding flash after another," and "peal on peal of deafening thunder," and then return to town, chastened yet triumphant, to witness their own funeral services.

Adventures of Huckleberry Finn turns this element of the ritual "expedition" across water into a full-scale journey rather than a single episode—a panoramic view of islands, steamboats, small towns, and the South in general. In other words, Twain's second attempt at a Boy Book about Tom and Huck was not limited to one locale, as Aldrich's had been, or even to one point of view (since *Adventures of Huckleberry Finn* presents both Tom's and Huck's in tandem). When Twain forwent the privilege of commenting directly and explicitly on his own childhood, instead delegating the narrative to a boy not even old enough or sophisticated enough to know whether he was writing an epistolary novel, a truthful letter, or an autobiography, this decision ultimately led to the structural feature that chiefly distinguishes *Huckleberry Finn* from its Boy Book companions. After Pap Finn abducts and transports his son outside the St. Petersburg environs, Huck is drawn by circumstances into a slow drift down the massive Mississippi River. The journey format moved the novel closer in the direction of Le Sage's *Histoire de Gil Blas de Santillane* (1735) than toward *The Story of a Bad Boy,* and yet Twain still enjoyed the commercial advantage of having produced a volume that could be marketed as another American Boy Book. And by casting the work in fiction rather than in a purely autobiographical mode, he was able (as he had been previously with *Tom Sawyer*) to put the emphasis on the "Adventures" promised in his book title, making the other entries in the Boy Book field seem tame by comparison. If the first three and the last eleven chapters of *Huckleberry Finn* were to be considered together as an integral unit, the volume would recognizably resemble another humorous (if brief) conventional Bad Boy Book about Tom Sawyer.

At the end of Huck's book, there is no actual departure for college or the business world or another region (and ultimately, for manhood), as in the books by Dickens, Hughes, Aldrich, Garland, and others. Huck Finn ends his novel in the present tense, an immensely daring decision on Twain's part; Huck does not grow up and look back wishfully at his boyhood, like Garland's Lincoln Stewart. In one sense, Huck's narrative, so vastly dissimilar from Garland's idealized, softened adult view of his "days of cattle-herding, berrying, hazel-nutting, and all the other now vanished pleasures of boy life on the prairies" (423), is absolutely the best Boy Book of them all. Huck's "expedition" has mythic dimensions, and his random brushes with death can be taken as the real thing, unlike Tom Sawyer's gleeful, make-believe demises in Twain's earlier book. Huck, presumed dead by his fellow villagers, gloomily views himself as already departed from earthly society, and thus is capable of risking damnation to save a fearful black man. To put it another way, *Huckleberry Finn* manages to overcome most restrictions of the Boy Book.

Certain recognizable features admittedly link *Adventures of Huckleberry Finn* with *The Adventures of Tom Sawyer* and other Boy Books; at its beginning and in its conclusion, the boys fear and defy adult authorities, adulate brave deeds, experiment with various identities, are controlled by parental decisions, plot rebellions against injustice, play cruel pranks. But if Mark Twain initially planned to abide by prevailing conventions of the autobiographical Boy Book, his decision to allow this boy to narrate his own story *without first growing up* blocked those intentions, obliging (or rather enabling) him to ignore, and ultimately elude, the limitations of a predictable form. The principal determinant in this outcome was his protagonist: Huck simply existed too far beyond the pale of family and propriety to be capable of the speech, viewpoint, and action of typical boy characters. It might be said that in *Adventures of Huckleberry Finn*, Mark Twain set out to write another conventional Boy Book but his experiences and reading–and above all, his literary imagination–got the better of him, and the book veered away from generic formulas to become something even more vital and inspiring–a combination of voice and place and event that has moved and challenged writers and readers ever since.

–*South Central Review*, 5 (Winter 1988): 15–21

1. In preparing this study I have consulted the following editions: Thomas Hughes, *Tom Brown's School Days* (New York: Macmillan, 1884); Thomas Bailey Aldrich, *The Story of a Bad Boy* (Boston: Houghton Mifflin, 1914); Mark Twain, *The Adventures of Tom Sawyer, Tom Sawyer Abroad, Tom Sawyer, Detective*, eds. John C. Gerber, Paul Baender, and Terry Firkins, Works of Mark Twain Series (Berkeley: U of California P, 1980); Charles Dudley Warner, *Being a Boy* (Boston: James R. Osgood, 1878); Mark Twain, *Adventures of Huckleberry Finn (Tom Sawyer's Comrade)* (New York: Charles L. Webster, 1885); William Dean Howells, *A Boy's Town, Described for "Harper's Young People"* (New York: Harper & Bros., 1890); Hamlin Garland, *Boy Life on the Prairie*, intro. by B. R. McElderry, Jr. (Lincoln: U of Nebraska P, 1961); Stephen Crane, *The Complete Short Stories & Sketches of Stephen Crane* (Garden City, NY: Doubleday, 1963). All quotations will derive from these volumes. To focus and condense my discussion, I am omitting other examples of this subgenre, including, most notably, William Allen White's *Court of Boyville* (1899) and Booth Tarkington's *Penrod* (1914). For recent treatments of this branch of literary realism, see John W. Crowley, "*Little Women* and the Boy Book," *New England Quarterly* 58 (1985): 384–99; and Crowley, "Polymorphously Perverse? Childhood Sexuality in the American Boy Book," *American Literary Realism*, 19 (Winter 1987): 2–15. I have previously investigated in detail the relationship of Aldrich's *Story of a Bad Boy* to Twain's most esteemed works of juvenile fiction; see "'I Did Wish Tom Sawyer Was There': Boy-Book Elements in *Tom*

Sawyer and Huckleberry Finn," in *One Hundred Years of Huckleberry Finn: The Boy, His Book, and American Culture*, eds. Robert Sattelmeyer and J. Donald Crowley (Columbia: U of Missouri P, 1985) 149–70.
2. Edwin H. Cady, *The Light of Common Day: Realism in American Fiction* (Bloomington: Indiana UP, 1971) 101, 118.
3. Judith Fetterley, "The Sanctioned Rebel," *Studies in the Novel* 3 (1971): 293–304.
4. See especially Alfred Habegger's incisive study of Howells's *A Boy's Town* in *Gender, Fantasy, and Realism in American Literature* (New York: Columbia UP, 1982) 139, 215, though in Howells's book the Indian and his wilderness are portrayed as vanishing sights, lost causes, a doomed order of natural harmony.
5. Like many other scholars, I am indebted to John G. Cawelti's example in studying the impact of a *literary formula*, even though he originally employed that term as an aid in understanding the relationships between American culture and stories about detectives, gangsters, science-fiction, Westerns, and social melodramas. It is tempting to apply Cawelti's general ideas about conventional story patterns to the Boy Book, which was, when Twain wrote his contributions, a nascent formula establishing its traditions very rapidly in the Realist period of American literature, and if the Boy Book did not flourish with the long-term-commercial success of Cawelti's examples of adventure, romance, and mystery, it nevertheless exhibited traits that are suggestive along the same lines. See John G. Cawelti, *Adventure, Mystery, and Romance: Formula Stories as Art and Popular Culture* (Chicago: U of Chicago P, 1976).

* * *

In the first section of his essay "The French Revolution and 'Huckleberry Finn,'" Blair writes, "It was not by chance that a sizable body of Twain's reading during the years 1876–83, when he wrote Adventures of Huckleberry Finn, *was in a period of history"–specifically "the French Revolution and the decades immediately following it." While he read widely, including such authors as S. Bering-Gould, Hippolyte Taine, and Alexandre Dumas, Mark Twain's favorite works on "what he once called 'his subject'" were* Thomas Carlyle's The French Revolution: A History *(1837) and Charles Dickens's novel* A Tale of Two Cities *(1859), both of which he read repeatedly. After treating specific parallels between these and other works and* Adventures of Huckleberry Finn, *Blair in this excerpt considers the broader, thematic influence that Carlyle in particular as well as Dickens may have had upon Twain's novel.*

Thomas Carlyle, Charles Dickens, and *Huckleberry Finn*
Walter Blair

As recent critics have indicated, the themes developed by *Huckleberry Finn* are important elements in its richness. Not surprisingly, therefore, some of the most interesting relationships are between sources involving

"I Cannot Quite Say I Have Read Nothing"

This is an excerpt from Mark Twain's 6 August 1877 letter to his friend Mary Mason Fairbanks in which he describes his recent reading on the French Revolution.

I cannot quite say I have read *nothing*. No, I have read half of Les Miserables, two or three minor works of Victor Hugo, & also that marvelous being's biography by his wife. I have read Carlyle's wonderful History of the French Revolution, which is one of the greatest creations that ever flowed from a pen. I followed that with Mr. Yonge's recent "Life of Marie Antoinette," which is without exception the [worst] blindest & slovenliest piece of literary construction I ever saw, & is astounding in another way; it starts out to make you a pitying & lamenting friend of Marie, but only succeeds in making you loathe her all the way through & swing your hat with unappeasable joy when they finally behead her.

I followed that with "In Exitu Israel," a very able novel by Baring-Gould, the purpose of which is to show the effect of some of the most odious of the privileges of the French nobles under *l'ancien regeme,* & of the dischurching of the Catholic Church by the National Assembly in '92. I *pr*eceded this with one of the Dumas's novels, "The Taking of the Bastille," & another which illustrated the march of the rioters upon Versailles, the massacre upon the Champs de Mars, the frightful scenes of the 10th of August & 2d of September &c.

I followed all these with a small history of France in French & a story by Madame de Genlis, also in French, neither of which cast much light upon my subject or amounted to much. I would have done well to stop with Carlyle & Dumas. The others only confuse one—except some chapters in Taine's "Ancient Regime," a book I forgot to mention.

You may easily suppose I hate all shades & forms of republican government, now—or rather with an intensified hatred, for I always hated them. To make matters worse, I read as much of Motley's Dutch Republic as I could stand, on my way to Bermuda, & would have thrown the book into the sea if I had owned it, it did make me so cordially despise those pitiful Dutchmen & their execrable Republic. Pittsburgh & the riots neither surprised nor greatly disturbed me; for where the government is a sham, one must expect such things.

Mind, I believe this: Republican government, with a sharply restricted suffrage, is just as good as a Constitutional monarchy with a virtuous & powerful aristocracy; but with an unrestricted suffrage it ought to [perish, execrable] perish because it is founded in wrong & is weak & bad & tyrannical.

—Mark Twain to Mrs. Fairbanks, edited by Dixon Wecter (San Marino, Cal.: Huntington Library, 1949), pp. 207–209

not only happenings but also attitudes and their counterparts in the book. Deeply interested in moral issues, despite his dislike for "theology," Twain studied his subject with lessons it might teach in mind. His course of reading gave him new ideas or bolstered old ones about humanity.

"The Reign of Terror," he wrote in a notebook in 1879, "shows that, without distinction or rank, the people were savages. Marquises, dukes, lawyers, blacksmiths, they each figure in due proportion to their crafts."[1] Having thus learned that men of all ranks are beasts, according to their opportunities, Twain in *Huckleberry Finn* manages to condemn the full range of classes, from kings to commoners.

Kings get their comeuppance in chapter xiv. Kings, Huck informs Jim, "don't do nothing! . . . They just set around . . . except, maybe, when there's a war. But other times they just lazy around; or go hawking–just hawking and sp—." The attitude is shared by several of Twain's writers. Carlyle, for instance, twice levels this criticism. "Who is it," he asks, "that the King (Able-man, named also *Roi, Rex,* or *Director*) now guides? His own huntsmen and prickers: when there is no hunt, it is well said, *'Le Roi ne fera rien'* (To-day his Majesty will do *nothing*)" (I, 1, ii). Again: "Were not the king so languid! . . . Unhappy king, *he* has but one resolution: not to have a civil war. For the rest, he still hunts . . . still dozes, and digests; is clay in the hands of the potter" (I, 7, ii). Huck's highly vernacular comment–so different from Carlyle's mannered passages–makes his kings figures in a comic picture. An anticlimactic sentence helps, too, and Carlyle has no perceivable tendency, as the plebeian Huck does, to follow "hawking," mechanically, with two other words.

But Twain felt that he moved beyond Carlyle in his attitude. When he first read Carlyle, he wrote Howells, he had been a moderate revolutionist, "a Girondin"; but after several readings, "changed, little by little, by life and environment (and Taine and Saint-Simon). . . . I am a Sansculotte! And not a pale, characterless Sansculotte, but a Marat. Carlyle teaches no such gospel; so the change is in me–in my vision of the evidence."[2] Though he does not define his terms, his remarks then and later suggest that, for him, a Sansculotte is one who fiercely and recklessly battles to destroy nobility and royalty. With the exception of Yonge's biography [Charles D. Yonge's *Life of Marie Antoinette*], most of the books which Twain read about the French Revolution would have inclined him toward the attitude he mentions. His letter of 1877 characterizes as "a very able novel" Sabine Baring-Gould's *In exitu Israel,* "the purpose of which," he says, "is to show the effect of some of the most odious of the privileges of the French nobles under *l'ancien regeme [sic]* & of the Catholic Church by the Assembly in '92." The chapters in Taine which, in the same letter, he says have been useful were probably among those which Edmund Wilson has called "admirable social-documentary chapters" showing "the intolerable position of the peasants."[3] Dickens, Baring-Gould, Dumas, Carlyle, and Michelet all melodramatically picture the heartless cruelty of nobility and royalty which forced revolt.

In chapter xxiii, "The Orneriness of Kings," when Jim voices astonishment at the low morals of the king and the duke, Huck refuses to be surprised because, says he, "all kings is mostly rapscallions":

> "You read about them once—you'll see. Look at Henry the Eight this'n's a Sunday-school Superintendent to *him*. And look at Charles Second, and Louis Fifteen, and James Second, and Edward Second and Richard Third, and forty more; besides all them Saxon heptarchies that used to rip around so in old times and raise Cain. . . . I don't say that ourn is lambs, because they ain't, when you come down to the cold facts; but they ain't nothing to *that* old ram, anyway. All I say is, kings is kings, and you got to make allowances. Take them all around, they're a mighty ornery lot. It's the way they're raised."
>
> "But" [says Jim], "dis one do *smell* so like de nation, Huck."
>
> "Well, they all do, Jim. We can't help the way a king smells; history don't tell no way."
>
> "Now de duke, he's a tolerable likely man in some ways."
>
> "Yes, a duke's different. But not very different. This one's a middling hard lot for a duke. When he's drunk there ain't no nearsighted man could tell him from a king."

This passage, largely because of its humor, is much more devastating than Clemens' frequent direct attacks upon the hereditary classes.[4] The disgust of Huck and Jim, both lowly—and both relatively tolerant—with the king and the duke and Huck's nonchalant suggestion that these rapscallions are relatively admirable specimens are impressive.

Twain's study of the ways of those below the privileged classes during the Revolution led him to a conclusion quite the opposite of that drawn by Michelet. The French historian found in the period documentation for his mystical belief that "the very people, the whole people," were reasonable for "the humane and benevolent period of our Revolution."[5] In the letter of 1877[6] . . . Clemens reports that his reading, by contrast, has led him to "hate all shades & forms of republican government . . . with an intensified hatred." He cites Carlyle, Dumas, and Taine as his most valuable instructors. Of this trio, Carlyle is the most outspoken in his criticism of republican government; a number of passages in *The French Revolution* point out its weaknesses, for example:

> Is it the nature of National Assemblies generally to do, with endless labour and clangour, Nothing? Are Representative Governments mostly at bottom Tyrannies too? Shall we say, the *Tyrants,* the ambitious contentious Persons, from all corners of the country do, in this manner, get gathered in one place; and there, with motion and counter-motion, with jargon and hubbub, *cancel* one another, like the fabulous Kilkenny Cats; and produce, for net-result, *zero* . . . ? [I, 2, i].

Twain ignores the Transcendental explanation offered by Carlyle for such weakness and advances another. "Mind," he says, "I believe this: Republican government, with a sharply restricted suffrage, is just as good as a Constitutional monarchy with a virtuous & powerful aristocracy, but with an unrestricted suffrage it ought to perish because it is founded in wrong & is weak & bad & tyrannical." The weakness of such a system and its cause, as Twain sees it, are satirically set forth in Pap Finn's longest speech (chap. vi), wherein he comments upon a Negro's voting:

> "They said he was a p'fessor in a college, and could talk all kinds of languages, and knowed everything. And that ain't the wust. They said he could *vote* when he was at home. Well, that let me out. Thinks I, what is the country a-coming to? It was 'lection day, and I was just about to go and vote myself if I warn't too drunk to get there; but when they told me there was a state in this country where they'd let that nigger vote, I drawed out. I says I'll never vote ag'in . . . and the country may rot for all me."

Pap, portrayed from the start as physically, mentally, and morally despicable, is perfect for satirical utterance and pretty certain, therefore, to voice views completely opposed to those of his creator. Here, for the wrong reason, he attacks a man who is qualified to vote and, for another wrong reason, disqualifies himself as a voter.

But Twain's writers naturally had less to say about common men in republican governments than about them in revolutionary mobs. From the records, he told his friend Fisher, he learned "that men in a crowd do not act as they would as individuals . . . they don't think for themselves, but become impregnated by the mass sentiment uppermost in the minds who happen to be en masse."[7] Compare S. Baring-Gould, *In exitu Israel*, II, 156: " . . . the mob swayed and roared, and cheered, like one living body, not as an assemblage of individuals, each with a will and thoughts of its own." Other writers remark the same phenomenon.

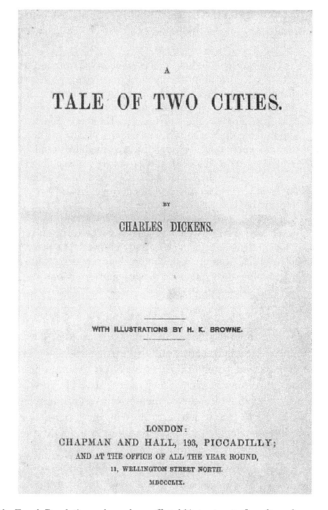

THE

FRENCH REVOLUTION:

A HISTORY.

IN THREE VOLUMES.

By THOMAS CARLYLE.

Μέγα ὁ ἀγὼν ἔστι, θεῖον γὰρ ἔργον· ὑπὲρ βασιλείας· ὑπὲρ ἐλευθερίας·
ὑπὲρ εὔροιας· ὑπὲρ ἀταραξίας.—ARRIANUS.
Δόγμα γὰρ αὐτῶν τίς μεταβάλλει; χωρὶς δὲ δογμάτων μεταβολῆς, τί
ἄλλο ἢ δουλεία στενόντων καὶ πείθεσθαι προσποιουμένων;—ANTONINUS.

VOL. I.—THE BASTILLE.

LONDON:
JAMES FRASER, 215 REGENT STREET.

M.DCCC.XXXVII.

A

TALE OF TWO CITIES.

BY

CHARLES DICKENS.

WITH ILLUSTRATIONS BY H. K. BROWNE.

LONDON:
CHAPMAN AND HALL, 193, PICCADILLY;
AND AT THE OFFICE OF ALL THE YEAR ROUND,
11, WELLINGTON STREET NORTH.
MDCCCLIX.

Title pages for the works that were Mark Twain's favorite reading on the French Revolution and may have affected his treatment of royalty and the mob in Adventures of Huckleberry Finn *(Special Collections, Thomas Cooper Library, University of South Carolina)*

This mass sentiment might be morbid fascination of the sort Carlyle emphasizes as he tells about the execution of Robespierre:

> . . . Never before were the streets of Paris so crowded . . . one dense stirring mass; all windows crammed; the very roofs and ridge-tiles budding forth Curiosity, in strange gladness . . . All eyes are on Robespierre's tumbril. . . . The Gendarmes point their swords at him, to show the people which is he. . . . Samson's work [with the guillotine] done, there bursts forth shout on shout of applause. [III, 6, vii].

After Colonel Sherburn shoots down Boggs on the main street of Bricksville, the crowd becomes a mob, and when Boggs is carried to the drugstore to die, it manifests "strange gladness." Huck writes (chap. xxi):

> Well, pretty soon the whole town was there, squirming and scrouging and pushing and shoving to get at

the window and have a look, but people that had the places wouldn't give them up, and folks behind them was saying all the time, "Say, now, you've looked long enough, you fellows, 'tain't right and 'tain't fair for you to stay thar all the time, and never give nobody a chance; other folks has their rights as well as you."

The impression of a surging, packed crowd which Carlyle creates by telling of the jammed streets, the crammed windows, and the stirring mass, Twain achieves by a series of participles, "squirming and scrouging and pushing and shoving."[8] "Scrouging," since it is a word in the vernacular, introduces a comic note not found in Carlyle. The representation of the insatiable curiosity, the refusal to budge, of those by the window initiates satire. The satire becomes cutting in the quoted pleas of those behind who, ironically, demand in the names of "fairness" and innate human "rights" that they be allowed to sate their inhuman curiosity. The paragraph which follows distils the same commentary into an individual characterization:

> The streets was full, and everybody was excited. Everybody that seen the shooting was telling how it happened, and there was a big crowd around each. . . . One long, lanky man, with long hair and a big white fur stove-pipe hat on the back of his head, and a crooked-handled cane, marked out the places on the ground where Boggs stood and where Sherburn stood, and the people followed him around . . . watching everything he done . . . and then he stood up straight and stiff where Sherburn had stood, frowning and having his hat-brim down over his eyes, and sung out, "Boggs!" and then fetched his cane down slow to a level, and says "Bang!" staggered backwards, says "Bang!" again, and fell down flat on his back. The people that had seen the thing said he done it perfect; said it was just exactly the way it all happened. Then as much as a dozen people got out their bottles and treated him.

This rivertown Bottom, who grabs both leading roles in his little chronicle play, and his gloating audience are individualized embodiments of the "strange joy" derived from witnessing a gory melodrama. He and the audience wallow in morbid memories. And the uptilted bottles at the end, so incongruous with the scene of horror just enacted, climax this bodying-forth of human insensibility.[9]

The crowd next shows the "mob-lawlessness" which Twain equated with "lynch law"—a phenomenon Twain found exemplified in *Le Moniteur,* Carlyle, and Dickens. Dickens' picture in *A Tale of Two Cities* (2, xiv) of a mob following a funeral procession shows as well as others in the reading how a mercurial group acts in an unreasoning fashion as one man when someone starts it. Somehow, the cry "Spies!" starts, and everyone joins in. "Pull 'em out, there!" shouts someone.

> The idea [says Dickens] was so acceptable in the prevalent absence of any idea, that the crowd caught it up with eagerness, and loudly repeating the suggestion . . . mobbed the two vehicles. . . . The dead man disposed of, and the crowd being under the necessity of providing some other entertainment for itself, another bright genius (or perhaps the same) conceived the humour of impeaching casual passersby, as Old Bailey spies, and wreaking vengeance on them. Chase was given to some scores of inoffensive persons. . . . At last . . . a rumour got about that the Guards were coming. Before this rumour, the crowd gradually melted away . . . and this was the usual progress of a mob.

The Bricksville crowd is similar. Says Huck: "Well, by and by somebody said Sherburn ought to be lynched. In about a minute everybody was saying it; so away

they went, mad and yelling, and snatching down every clothes-line they come to to do the hanging with."

What follows resembles many scenes in Twain's reading wherein some forceful figure appears before a raging crowd, speaks to it, and sways or even quells it. Carlyle, as one knowing his theories about heroes might expect, describes several such scenes, picturing, for instance, Mirabeau, (II, 3, ii), Marat and Robespierre (III, 2, i), and Danton (III, 6, ii) as the forceful speakers. Dickens, who acknowledged "Carlyle's wonderful book" as a source in his preface, may have imitated him, as may Baring-Gould in *In exitu Israel,* II, 190, 52–56, and 219–23. Only Carlyle, however, steps into his book to ask, " . . . Is it not miraculous how one man moves hundreds of thousands. . . . Military mobs are mobs with muskets in their hands. . . . To the soldier himself, revolt is frightful, and oftenest perhaps pitiable" (II, 2, ii).

Sherburn addresses the Bricksville crowd (chap. xxii) in circumstances which make his words compel attention. The mob has come to his house "a-whooping and raging" with screaming women and crying children rushing to escape it. It rips and smashes the fence and has "begun to roll in like a wave" when "Sherburn steps out onto his little front porch, with a double-barrel gun in his hand, and takes his stand, perfectly ca'm and deliberate not saying a word." He stares the crowd into silence, then, "slow and scornful," says:

> "The idea of *you* lynching anybody! . . .Your mistake is, that you didn't bring a man with you. . . . You brought *part* of a man—Buck Harkness, there—and if you hadn't had him to start you, you'd 'a' taken it out in blowing. . . . The pitifulest thing out is a mob; and that's what an army is—a mob; they don't fight with the courage that's born in them, but with courage that's borrowed from their mass, and from their officers. But a mob without any man at the head of it is *beneath* pitifulness. . . . Now *leave*—and take your half-a-man with you."

In addition to the dramatic situation, these words in the speech augment its significance: "I know you clear through. I was born and raised in the South, and I've lived in the North; so I know the average all around." Since fictional probability demands only that Sherburn know Bricksville, these words suggest that he is Twain's *raisonneur.*[10] The reaction of the crowd proves Sherburn's claims: "The crowd washed back sudden, and then broke all apart, and went tearing off. . . ." And Huck's sheepish and comic conclusion makes the speech still more memorable: "I could 'a' stayed if I wanted to, but I didn't want to."

Twain and his narrator, despite disillusionments about folk along the river, resemble Carlyle, finally, in being deeply sympathetic toward victims of human cruelty. Whether he admires or despises such victims, Carlyle shows great compassion when he tells of their suffering–writing of the dauphin (III, 6, iii); the queen (III, 4, vii); Marat and his murderess, Charlotte Corday (III, 4, xii); particularly of the king, the Girondins, and Robespierre. On the death of the king (III, 2, viii) he writes: "For Kings and for Beggars, for the justly doomed and the unjustly, it is a hard thing to die. Pity them all: thy utmost pity . . . how far short is it of the thing pitied!" After recounting the executions of the Girondins (III, 4, viii): "Alas, whatever quarrel we had with them, has not their cruel fate abolished it? Pity only survives." And after telling of the death of Robespierre (III, 6, vii) he says: "His poor landlord . . . loved him; his Brother died for him. May God be merciful to him, and to us!"

After his account of Boggs's death, Huck similarly centers attention upon his daughter (chap. xxi): "Then they pulled his daughter away from him, screaming and crying, and took her off. She was about sixteen, and very sweet and gentle looking, but awful pale and scared." Although Huck says little here about his own reactions, the details communicate his pity. When the boy tells about the tarring and feathering of the king and the duke,[11] he combines a description of the mob's cruel action with an expression of sympathy reminiscent of Carlyle:

> Here comes a raging rush of people with torches, and an awful whooping and yelling, and banging tin pans and blowing horns . . . and as they went by I see they had the king and the duke a-straddle of a rail–that is, I knowed it *was* the king and the duke, though they was all over tar and feathers, and didn't look like nothing in the world that was human–just looked like a couple of monstrous big soldier-plumes. Well, it made me sick to see it; and l was sorry for them poor pitiful rascals, it seemed like I couldn't ever feel any hardness against them any more in the world. It was a dreadful thing to see. Human beings *can* be awful cruel to one another. [chap. xxxiii].

This, like several passages by Carlyle, moves from the mob to its victims and then to the writer's generalizations. Carlyle's addresses to the reader are much more obviously literary in tone than Huck's report and brief comment; but, unobtrusive though they are, Huck uses poetic devices which create an effect. The crowd is figuratively represented as "a raging rush" moving noisily through torchlit darkness. Then the king and the duke are shown, first unrecognizable as individuals, then as "nothing in the world that is human," as if they themselves have become embodiments of the inhuman abuse of which they are victims. They look like "mon-

strous big soldier-plumes," the "monstrous" repeating the unhuman note, and the soldier-plumes simile doing the same, but adding a grotesque touch. Huck's report of his reactions, first to the sight of the victims, then to the action of the crowd, is quite literal except for a phrase which echoes an earlier one–"in the world"– here connoting death, which is the utmost result of mob fury. Thus, though it says about the same things Carlyle does, this passage makes its points in terms more typical of a fictional work.

–*Modern Philology*, 55 (August 1957): 29–34

1. Albert Bigelow Paine, *Mark Twain: A Biography* (New York, 1912), p. 644.
2. *Mark Twain's Letters,* ed. Albert Bigelow Paine (New York, 1917), II, 490. This was written in 1887 after *Huckleberry Finn* had been published; but, as has been indicated, he read Taine before 1877, and he may also have read St.-Simon while the book was in progress.
3. Edmund Wilson, *To the Finland Station* (New York, 1940), 53.
4. Typical diatribes written later include *Letters,* pp. 514, 519–20; *Mark Twain's Notebooks,* ed. Paine (New York, 1935), 197–200, 509; Paine, *Biography,* pp. 874, 890.
5. J. Michelet, *Historical View of the French Revolution* (London 1888), p. 10.
6. Letter to Mollie Fairbanks, *Mark Twain to Mrs. Fairbanks,* ed. Dixon Wecter (San Marino, 1949), pp. 207–209. Twain evaluates much of his reading on the French Revolution.
7. Henry W. Fisher, *Abroad with Mark Twain and Eugene Field* (New York, 1922), p. 59.
8. The passage by Twain which is closest to that by Carlyle in detail occurs in the first paragraph of chap. xxii: "every window along the road was full of women's heads, and there was nigger boys in every tree, and bucks and wenches looking over every fence." This is not close enough to suggest specific and conscious influence; its chief value is for purpose of comparison.
9. Dickens also shows a character smacking his lips over his memories of violent deaths–the little wood-sawyer, *Tale of Two Cities* (3, xv), but I doubt that Twain had this scene specifically in mind. However, the contrast in methods is of interest. Dickens' character is ironically humorous in his talk; Twain's lanky ham actor, as well as the crowd watching him, is completely humorless.
10. Several points which Sherburn makes were made by Twain as his own in a chapter discarded from *Life on the Mississippi* (see the Heritage Press edition [New York, 1940], 412–16).
11. The incident recalls Fuller's surprise that the false dauphins were not "dragged to horse-ponds." [Horace W. Fuller's *Imposters and Adventurers: Noted French Trials* (Boston, 1882), signed "S. L. Clemens, June, 1882," was in Mark Twain's library at his death.] Twain's emphasis upon human cruelty is aided by his giving his imposters the exit described.

* * *

In this essay MacKethan examines the inspiration for Adventures of Huckleberry Finn *that Mark Twain may have found in slave narratives.*

Huck Finn and the Slave Narratives: Lighting Out as Design
Lucinda H. MacKethan

When Huck Finn tells us at the end of his Adventures that he has "got to light out for the Territory ahead of the rest," he gives a definitive name to a mythic image of American experience. The dream that consistently provides a rationale for Huck's actions in the novel is fixed in the frontiersman's expression, "lighting out," which Huck appropriates to label his need to escape. Escape, or lighting out, is finally Huck's only theme, and his conception of lighting out is, on the surface level, the traditional one of his time, particularly of his border-state heritage; lighting out means escape to a new country where there are no rules or rulers or restraints, but instead a perfect freedom, a life of endless, unfettered possibility. In Huck's lighting out we seem to see an original yet paradigmatic enactment of the American impulse that Fitzgerald was later to frame for Gatsby: "tomorrow we will run faster, stretch out our arms farther," and someday we will grasp that "orgiastic future that year by year recedes before us."

The value of Huck's lighting out as an expression of an American ideal is emphasized by Bernard DeVoto's comment that "Beyond awareness, a need for freedom, an insatiable hunger for its use, finds in [Huck] a kind of satisfaction."

The movement from escape to freedom and the concept of escape as freedom give form and content to Huck's story, and this design for *The Adventures of Huckleberry Finn* has provided the shape for many subsequent quests for freedom that we find in American literature. Hemingway was most probably thinking of Huck's gift for idiomatic language when he asserted that "All modern American literature came from one book by Mark Twain called *Huckleberry Finn.* It's the best book we've had. . . . There was nothing before." It would be easy to conclude that there was also "nothing before" for Mark Twain to use as a model for Huck's indelible brand of lighting out. However, the very words *escape* and *freedom* uttered in connection with American idealism call up what would seem an almost unavoidable source of stimulation. As a writer from a slave state whose book explores the drama of conscience and whose character Jim is an articulate fugitive slave, Mark Twain would have many reasons to consult the narratives of slaves who had successfully made the escape that was finally beyond Jim's power to complete. The question of influence remains largely speculative,

300 DOLLARS
REWARD!

**RUNAWAY from John S. Doak on the 21st inst., two NEGRO MEN; LOGAN 45 years of age, bald-headed, one or more crooked fingers; DAN 21 years old, six feet high. Both black.
I will pay ONE HUNDRED DOLLARS for the apprehension and delivery of LOGAN, or to have him confined so that I can get him.
I will also pay TWO HUNDRED DOLLARS for the apprehension of DAN, or to have him confined so that I can get him.
                        JOHN S. DOAKE,
Springfield, Mo., April 24th, 1857.**

Poster for runaway slaves (Missouri Historical Society)

but we can certainly establish the point that a consideration of parallels between the American fugitive slave narratives and *The Adventures of Huckleberry Finn* enlivens and deepens our understanding of both. Ralph Ellison's Invisible Man made the link as he alluded both to Frederick Douglass and to Huck Finn as he tried to find a frame for his own predicament as a "free" American. Invisible Man also makes the point that "to be unaware of one's form is to live a death." The story of Huck's discovery of his distinctively American program of escape to the Territory is also the story of American slavery, told in very different (and ironically much more restrained) dialect but in very similar form by fugitive slaves whose "territory" was also very close to Mark Twain's.

The story begins with a young man growing up in the new territory of Missouri. He belongs to a family that can trace ancestors back to landed Kentucky gentry. The boy becomes an apprentice to a master of a great trade on a Mississippi steamboat, and by this means he is launched on an adventurous journey down the haunting and majestic river. Years later, as he sits at a desk in a cold New England city, the scenes of his travels return to him; he will write a novel, an autobiography, and many stirring lectures with which to enthrall audiences with the world he knew as a boy. His themes will be freedom, escape, courage, deceit, honor, hypocrisy, conscience, and truth. The story, of course, is Mark Twain's, but it is also the story of William Wells Brown, a Missourian who grew up, as Mark Twain did, with the great river at his door, but who, unlike Mark Twain, grew up a slave.

William Wells Brown was born near Lexington, Kentucky, but was moved to Missouri along with his owner's other possessions while he was still very young. Eventually, the master settled on a farm near St. Louis. Dr. Young, as Brown's owner was named in his narrative, was actually young William's uncle, and when Brown was old enough, his master-kinsman began hiring him out to different citizens of St. Louis. In one of his first jobs, he ran errands for a newspaper office, a place which introduced him to letters and to literacy. Later, while he worked as a waiter on a steamboat named the *Enterprize,* he marveled at the freedom of the passengers to come and go as they pleased. Once, while his boat was docked in Hannibal, Missouri, Brown took special notice of a drove of slaves being brought aboard. Shortly thereafter, he was hired out to a slave trader who took gangs of slaves from Missouri to the market in New Orleans. After spending one terrifying year as the trader's "assistant," Brown made an attempt with his mother to flee to the free states. In a stolen skiff, the two made their way across the river to the Illinois shore, where they hid in the woods during

the day and traveled by foot at night. Nine days after they began their flight, one hundred and fifty miles away from St. Louis, Brown and his mother were caught and returned to their owners. After this escapade, Brown's mother was sold down the river by her master, and Brown himself was finally sold to a steamboat owner named Enoch Price. Working diligently to prove himself a totally devoted slave, Brown was at last deemed loyal enough to accompany Price and his family on a trip by boat to Ohio. Brown notes that "the first place in which we landed in a free state was Cairo, a small village at the mouth of the Ohio River." When they reached Cincinnati, Brown simply took a trunk from the boat deck and walked ashore with it, and kept on walking. His narrative was published in 1847; his novel, *Clotel,* in 1853; he also published an anthology of anti-slavery songs, a drama, a travel book, and a black American history text, all before the Civil War had ended.

Both William Wells Brown's and Mark Twain's imaginations were stirred by boyhood lives spent on or near the great boats always in motion on the Mississippi River. In *Life on the Mississippi,* Mark Twain tried to explain why he was so obsessed with what he called "the science of piloting": "The reason is plain; a pilot, in those days, was the only unfettered and entirely independent human being that lived in the earth. . . . In truth, every man, and woman, and child has a master, and worries and frets in servitude; but in the day I write of, the Mississippi pilot had none. . . . His movements were entirely free." *Life on the Mississippi* records Mark Twain's dream of achieving the freedom that he associated with the pilot's vocation, but it also records the disappearance of the pilots and the great boats into the "dead and pathetic past." More complex and more complete as an examination of fettered versus unfettered lives would be the other "Mississippi chronicle" that he worked on during the same years that he put together *Life on the Mississippi. The Adventures of Huckleberry Finn,* like Brown's narrative, explored life on the river during slavery times from the viewpoint of an ignorant but acute boy, part picaro, part quester, part moral microscope on humanity. The significant difference between the authors behind the boy protagonists is the one we can glean from a comment Mark Twain made in *Life on the Mississippi* concerning his trip back to Hannibal after a twenty-one year absence: "On my way through town to the hotel," he wrote, "I saw the house which was my home when I was a boy. At present rates, the people who now occupy it are of no more value than I am, but in my time they would have been worth not less than five hundred dollars apiece. They are colored folk." The plan of *Huckleberry Finn,* Mark Twain had advised Howells in 1875, was to "take a boy of twelve and run him on through life (in the first person)." William Wells Brown's plan for his autobiographical narrative might have been framed in much the same way, with emphasis on the word "run." Both plans resulted in works whose theme is enslavement and whose design is lighting out. Granting the premise that one of American literature's most compelling versions of the American dream is the myth of freedom, rooted in the ideal of self-realization and achieved by escape, the theory that I would like to submit is this: that Mark Twain's *Adventures of Huckleberry Finn* erects a paradigm for the American myth of freedom through Huck's recurring motions of lighting out, and that an important source for Mark Twain's design was the slave narratives, to which he turned in large measure because he often identified his own need to escape oppressing circumstances of his life with that of the fugitive slaves.

In *Life on the Mississippi,* Mark Twain recalled that "I first wanted to be a cabin boy, so that I could come out with a white apron on and shake a table-cloth over the side, where all my old comrades could see me." Mark Twain could not have been on the dock on the day that the steamboat *Enterprize* came in at Hannibal and a young cabin boy watched Mr. Walker come on board with his cargo, who "numbered from fifty to sixty consisting of men and women from eighteen to forty years of age." Had Mark Twain been there, would he have noticed the loading of this human cargo? Brown tells us that "no one, not even the passengers, appear to notice it, though they clank their chains at every step." But William the cabin boy noticed it, and evidently Mr. Walker noticed William, because not long afterward he tried to buy William and ended up hiring his time from Dr. Young for one year. Brown's response to this opportunity for an extended river voyage is the opposite of young Sam Clemens' feeling, but perhaps the mature Mark Twain would have understood Brown's explanation: ". . . I found that my opportunity of getting to a land of liberty was gone, at least for the time being." On the *Enterprize,* a vessel that worked only the upper part of the river, Brown had been able to think of escape: ". . .in passing from place to place. . . [I] thought of leaving the boat at some landing place, and trying to make my escape to Canada, which I had heard much about as a place where the slave might live, be free, and be protected." To be hired out to Mr. Walker, however, to step onto a boat "bound" for New Orleans with gangs of chained slaves, was an end to the dream of freedom and the beginning of a nightmare that Brown's narrative records in terse, unemotional tones. His trip with Walker, the "longest year of my life," becomes a catalog of horrors. One example gives the tenor of the whole. The slaves were chained, Brown says, because sometimes, if left loose,

they "made their escape at landing-places." Taking the point of view of the master or slave driver at this point, Brown goes on: "and with all our care we lost one woman who had been taken from her husband and children, and having no desire to live without them, in the agony of her soul jumped overboard, and drown'd herself. She was not chained." After this remark Brown adds, "It was almost impossible to keep that part of the boat clean."

Brown's eyewitness account of the atrocities committed against slaves was a regular feature of slave narratives published in the decades before the Civil War. Before we examine some of Mark Twain's variations on slave narrative themes and forms, summarizing some of the staples of the genre's plots and organization will provide a necessary background. The slave narratives, most of them written in the 1840s and 1850s, were best sellers in their time, often running through several editions in one or two years. Reviewing them as a group in 1849, one writer called them "the most remarkable productions of the age." By 1853, after Harriet Beecher Stowe had acknowledged some of the narratives as sources for *Uncle Tom's Cabin,* a less enthusiastic reviewer wrote, "The shelves of the booksellers groan under the weight of Sambo's woes, done up in covers." For all that these works and their authors received wide attention before the Civil War, their effect on American letters has scarcely been examined at all. Bruce Franklin notes that "In less than a century . . . this literary achievement had been effectively expunged from the study of American literature." Living in New England, slave narrators Frederick Douglass, William Wells Brown, and James Pennington were neighbors of Thoreau, Emerson, and, we might add, Mark Twain's future father-in-law, Jervis Langdon. What students of American literature are just now beginning to acknowledge is that in this region so noted for nurturing America's first literary "Renaissance," Douglass, Brown, and Pennington became masters of a form that has important artistic as well as historical dimensions.

The most serious problem connected with viewing the slave narratives as relevant to the study of American literature has been the argument that was automatically used against them when they were first brought out—they lacked originality and were often of questionable authenticity. As slave narrative historian Charles Nichols says, "almost any victim of slavery could be published." Yet some of their stories were written for them by abolitionist ghost writers who sometimes acknowledged their contributions and sometimes did not, who sometimes checked facts for accuracy and often did not. (Mark Twain's one-time satiric target, John Greenleaf Whittier, was involved in a hoax of this kind, the publication of the supposed narrative of James

William Wells Brown, Frederick Douglass, and James Pennington, authors of slave narratives that may have influenced Mark Twain (top, from William Wells Brown, My Southern Home *[Boston: A. G. Brown, 1880], University of North Carolina; bottom left, The Frederick Douglas National Historic Site, Washington, D.C.; bottom right, courtesy of the Commonwealth of Connecticut)*

Williams.) Even when one feels safe in trusting the subtitle that accompanies many of the narratives—"written by himself"—one might question their claim to originality or literary merit. First, they were written under the auspices of abolition societies which often assumed a right to control material. In addition, the narratives had to be directed to genteel white northern audiences, often addressed as "delicate reader" as if to underscore the slave narrator's awareness that this audience's tastes, scruples, and prejudices had somehow to be accommodated. For many reasons, then, the slave narratives became formulaic.

Some recent studies of the narratives as a genre outline features that are common fare. Darwin Turner, in an essay entitled "Uses of the Antebellum Slave Narratives in Collegiate Courses in Literature," lists four elements that are prevalent in the narratives, calling them "structural modes" of the genre: "1) a description of the conditions of oppression, 2) an account of the manner by which the slave developed a concept of freedom, 3) a report of the method of attempting to secure that freedom and, 4) a statement of the contrast between the actuality of freedom and the ideal of freedom." Turner's list provides a convenient summary of the surface layer of most slave narratives; the basic ingredients were usually the same. Yet Turner shows us something else as well; his list reveals that the slave narrator developed, through his discussion of his life and its meaning, a progressively complex attitude toward the issue of freedom, which both shaped his purposes and defined his identity. The elements of structure that Turner names indicate that individual narratives could be given dynamic, original forms, could be used by an artistic sensibility to explore selfhood as well as cultural values, the ironies as well as the assets implicit in the American dream.

Frederick Douglass, James Pennington, and William Wells Brown were three writers of slave narratives fully capable of taking advantage of the artistic as well as the polemic opportunities that the market for their stories afforded. As paid platform speakers for the Massachusetts Antislavery Society in the 1840s and 1850s, they were widely hailed orators who could use common motifs of their form without sacrificing any of the unique expression of their own formidable personalities. The slave narratives of all three conform to the structural design mentioned by Turner. What concerns us more, however, is the fact that their narratives also fully exploit many of the same elements dominating Huck's quest for freedom. First, in the slave narratives as in *Huckleberry Finn,* escapes lead initially to increasingly intense exposures to oppression. Secondly, for the slave narrators as for Mark Twain, examining the right to freedom compels the writer to confront and to challenge other "rights" and "wrongs": the demands of honesty, the ties of loyalty, the gift of compassion. Finally, the slave narrators were, like Mark Twain in his design for Huck, "unwilling to provide overall closure for the narrative itself even if they could," as Raymond Hedin tells us. Perhaps Huck Finn's conclusion is ambiguous for essentially the same reason that the slave narratives remained unfinished. The slave narrators kept their works open because the issue of slavery was itself unfinished, still to be reckoned with beyond the narrative itself. Hedin remarks that for the slave narrators, "conventional narrative coherence was actually undesirable." In sum, the narratives contain many elements joining them in design to *Adventures of Huckleberry Finn:* structures organized around shifting threats to and implications of freedom; confrontations with established values in conflict with the right to freedom; and at the last, refusals to close the narrative because moral implications go beyond protagonists and into the volatile world of the author.

How familiar was Mark Twain with actual slave narratives? Three different kinds of evidence demonstrate his rather extensive exposure to them: first, his library holdings; second, his mentioning of slave narrators or literature related to them in letters or conversations; third, his direct use of incidents or strategies found prominently in the narratives. Alan Gribben's indispensable two-volume work, *Mark Twain's Library: A Reconstruction,* shows us that Mark Twain did have several narratives in his possession. One of these, the one that has long been acknowledged as an important source of material for *A Connecticut Yankee in King Arthur's Court,* is Charles Ball's extensive 1837 narrative, entitled in part, *Slavery in the United States: A Narrative of the Life and Adventures of Charles Ball.* Mark Twain drew on many of Ball's stories of torture, suicide by slaves, and heartless separations of slave mothers and children for his own portrayal of slaves met by the King and Hank Morgan in *Connecticut Yankee;* Mark Twain wrote to Sue Crane that Ball's narrative contained "terrible things in the Dismal Swamp in slavery times." Another slave narrative found in his library, James Pennington's *The Fugitive Blacksmith,* is a skillfully plotted, eloquently voiced work that Mark Twain could have used as a resource for both incidents and attitudes in *Connecticut Yankee* and *Huckleberry Finn,* a point that I will stress in more detail later. Mark Twain's library contained at least one other slave narrative, that of Amos Dresser, and in addition, held other works dealing with slave life, including Lydia Maria Child's 1836 *Anti-Slavery Catechism,* William Ellery Channing's *Letter on Slavery,* and Harriet Martineau's essay, "Morals of Slavery."

Two close contemporaries of Mark Twain, whose works have direct ties to the slave narratives, were well represented in his library: Harriet Beecher Stowe and Joel Chandler Harris. The relationship between Mark Twain and his Nook Farm neighbor Stowe was a complex one. He once described her as "the authoress who wrote 'Uncle Tom's Cabin,' the Emancipation Proclamation, the Dred Scott Decision, and I believe several other colored works." She knew and promoted Douglass, Pennington, and Brown, and she documented her references to their narratives in *Uncle Tom's Cabin,* a work to which Mark Twain made frequent reference. Mark Twain's friendship with Joel Chandler Harris was less ambivalent. He greatly admired Harris's gifts as a humorist and was especially taken with Harris's Uncle Remus. In 1894 Mark Twain gleefully dressed himself up as Uncle Remus for a costume ball he attended in Paris. Certainly Huck's Jim had Remus for one of his literary models, as critics have noted; however, another aspect of Harris's Remus stories that critics have not considered bears an equally important relationship to *Huckleberry Finn.* Remus is an artful trickster as well as a paternal companion to a little boy, and Remus's Brer Rabbit is *the* trickster of black American folklore. The slave narrators often elaborated on Brer Rabbit tricks and adapted Brer Rabbit's use of deceit to their own situations. For Brer Rabbit, for Harris's Uncle Remus, for the slave narrators, and for Mark Twain's Jim and Huck, tricks, the use of clever deceit, were often the only weapon of the weak against a world of powerful adversaries.

Alan Gribben's list of Mark Twain's library holdings does not include either Frederick Douglass's famous 1845 narrative or Brown's 1847 one. Still, it seems unlikely that the works of these two most famous black fugitive slave writers would have been unknown to Mark Twain in some form. In 1881, Mark Twain wrote a letter to president-elect James Garfield on behalf of Douglass; in pushing for a federal appointment for Douglass, Mark Twain wrote, "He is a personal friend of mine. . . ." Arthur Pettit, who in *Mark Twain and the South* studies Mark Twain's attitudes towards and experiences with blacks, doubts that Douglass and Mark Twain were as close as this letter claims but notes that they were bound to have met socially through Olivia Langdon's family. We can assume that Mark Twain would have had many opportunities to meet or at least to know of Brown and his writings in the same way.

The most important indications of Mark Twain's exposure and response to the slave narratives come from his use of them in his novels—in *Connecticut Yankee,* in *Pudd'nhead Wilson,* and in *Huckleberry Finn.* We know of Mark Twain's use of some of the case-study-styled stories in Ball's *Slavery in the United States* to introduce the King to slavery in *Connecticut Yankee;* in addition, one

incident and one commentary from Pennington's *The Fugitive Blacksmith* are very close to the king's experience in detail and emphasis. After his initial escape, Pennington, like Mark Twain's king, is taken prisoner because he can provide no papers to prove that he is a free man. Unlike the king, Pennington actually is, in point of law, a slave. But like the king, he cannot be made to be a slave, no matter how he is designated by law. Concerning the king's refusal to put on the style of a peasant, Hank Morgan says, "Even that dull clod of a slave-driver was able to see that there can be such a thing as a slave who will remain a man till he dies; whose bones you can break, but whose manhood you can't." At the end of his narrative, Pennington addresses his master in a similar vein: "I called you master when I was with you from the mere force of circumstances; but I never regarded you as my master. The nature which God gave me did not allow me to believe that you had any more right to me than I had to you, and that was just none at all." Freedom and manhood are the opposites of slavehood and are states of being, not of law, an important distinction that is stressed in *Huckleberry Finn* as well as in both *Connecticut Yankee* and *The Fugitive Blacksmith.*

Pudd'nhead Wilson is Mark Twain's most direct treatment of black characters shaped and trapped in a corrupt slaveholders' society, and through its Missouri and Mississippi River settings, the novel brings to mind several scenes from William Wells Brown's narrative. While many correspondences are worth exploring, we might here simply note that, as in Brown's narrative, the refrain "sold down the river" sounds throughout the pages of *Pudd'nhead,* from Roxy's opening banter with a fellow slave to her exposed black-white son's final sentencing in court. It is, of course, the same call which sets *Huckleberry Finn* in motion, as Jim hears of Miss Watson's plan to "sell me down to Orleans" for the too-tempting sum of eight hundred dollars. Brown's world, in the *Narrative,* is bound by the same river that terrorizes Roxy and Jim; the river, the boats, the hiding by day and sneaking by night, the mourning of children sold from parents or parents from children—Brown's narrative is a definitive prototype for Mark Twain's treatment of these issues in both of his Missouri novels.

In one additional respect, Brown's narrative suggests a strategic choice adopted by Mark Twain for *Huckleberry Finn,* and this is in the matter of tone as a function of point of view. Louis D. Rubin, Jr., has said that Huck represents "the views and sensibilities of the *adult* Mark Twain. His role in *Huckleberry Finn* is to search out the moral dimensions of the community of Sam Clemens' rearing." Like Brown's William, Huck is a young picaro-protagonist, a pair of outcast's eyes and an irreverent tongue, free to see and free to talk because orphaned, alone, outside the structure of the community for whom slavery, as Bernard DeVoto said, was "the bloodstream." Yet the judgments in both *Huckleberry Finn* and Brown's *Narrative* are not those of the black boy slave or the white boy runaway but of an adult author who has brought his mind back to the world of slavery with the express purpose of exposing it. Thus the tone in which that world is delivered to us has the modulations of the adult retrospective voice—removed, dry, rather frighteningly controlled for the most part. So it is that, in the scene I have described above, Brown so coolly tells of the slave woman who, in "the agony of her soul," jumped overboard, and then he comments that she was not chained, and then he remarks that "it was impossible to keep that part of the boat clean." So too we have the callousness of Huck's famous reply to Aunt Sally Phelps when she has asked if anyone was hurt in the steamboat accident. In order that Mark Twain's adult perceptions of slavery can be magnified, Huck's "N'm. Killed a Nigger" is shockingly insensitive, shaped that way to match Aunt Sally's typical white southern reply, "Well it's lucky, because sometimes people do get hurt."

I would like to look now at the chapter of *Huckleberry Finn* which makes some direct borrowings of slave narrative incidents and the one which, because of its pivotal place in Mark Twain's development of his novel, reveals perhaps the most important insights into his overall design. William L. Andrews, in a 1981 study entitled "Mark Twain and James W.C. Pennington: Huckleberry Finn's Small-pox Lie," has been the first to note that in Chapter 16, Mark Twain borrowed a trick for Huck Finn that James Pennington had devised to save himself from certain reenslavement when he was captured while trying to make an escape through Maryland countryside. Pennington, taken captive by a large group of whites, was asked to explain why he was on the road with no pass. He concocted on the spot a remarkable ruse: he was, he told them, traveling with a large gang of slaves and a trader, bound for Georgia, when the trader "was taken sick, and died with the small-pox. Several of his gang also died with it, so that the people of the town became alarmed . . . . No one claimed us, or wished to have anything to do with us." The result of Pennington's story was that only one of his captors had enough greed to outweigh his fear of the dread disease. The rest of the crowd dispersed uneasily, and shortly afterwards, Pennington found the means to escape from the one who remained. Andrews notes that Huck uses Pennington's story when he meets with the slave traders who want to check his raft to see if there is a slave aboard. Andrews also notes Pennington's crucial moral evaluation of his lie: "If you ask me

UNCLE REMUS.

Joel Chandler Harris's Uncle Remus, a literary model for Jim, as drawn by E. W. Kemble for Mark Twain's Library of Humor *(Thomas Cooper Library, University of South Carolina)*

if I expected when I left home to gain my liberty by fabrications and untruths? I answer, no! . . . I was arrested, and the demand made upon me, 'Who do you belong to?' Knowing the fatal use these men would make of *my* truth, I at once concluded that they had no more right to it than a highwayman has to a traveller's purse." The event, Pennington goes on, has instilled in him "the most intense horror at a system which can . . . send [a man] in haste to the bar of God with a lie upon his lips." Pennington's words, as Andrews notes, seem to belong to the thematic thrust of *Huckleberry Finn* that is anticipated in Chapter 16; they have a direct bearing, he points out, on Huck's later decision to "go to hell" to "save" Jim. Whatever else Huck's tearing up of his note in Chapter 31 is, we can see it, by the light of Pennington's remarks, as a means for Mark Twain to turn society's truth on its ear. In the manner of a Brer Rabbit trick, Pennington's lie, and Huck's duplication of it in Chapter 16, enable both of them not only to survive but also to indict a whole culture opposed to freedom and truth. As Mark Twain himself put it, *Huckleberry Finn* is a book "where a sound heart and a deformed conscience come into collision and conscience suffers defeat." At least in Chapter 16 and Chapter 31, this seems to be the case, and Mark Twain drew on Pennington's assertion of personal truth in order to dramatize Huck's dilemma.

Mark Twain's appropriation of Pennington's smallpox ruse comes in a portion of Chapter 16 which Mark Twain subtitled "A White Lie." Parts of Chapter 16, Walter Blair determined, represent the last work that Mark Twain did on his novel in 1876 before he somehow became stalled and put this manuscript aside. The chapter is thus crucial in many ways, and the correspondences between its final design and material from the slave narratives help to illuminate its significance for the whole novel. The "white lie" to the slavecatchers does seem dramatically to prepare for Huck's later "All right then, I'll go to hell" decision; it links Huck irreversibly to the slave's confrontation of his enslavement, to the slave's dream of freedom, and to the slave's only weapon against the hypocrisy, self-delusion, and corruption of the slaveholding culture. In Chapter 16, Huck is made to use a black slave narrator's trick to save his black slave friend. By the time he tears up his letter to Miss Watson in the later chapter, he has this precedent, and more importantly, he himself has become symbolically the enslaved one. Still, it is essential to observe that Huck's smallpox lie is set up by an ironic twist that gives other staggering complications for Mark Twain to resolve, and these complications and their resolutions hinge upon strategies that also relate closely to slave narratives.

What Andrews does not pursue in his study of the smallpox lie is the fact that, when Huck meets the slave traders and lies to them to protect Jim, he has just left *Jim* with a different lie upon his lips. He has told Jim that he is going off to see if the lights that Jim has spotted are the lights of Cairo; however, in his mind, he has just decided that the only way to make peace with his conscience, to redeem himself for the sin of helping a runaway slave, is to "paddle ashore at the first light, and tell." That decision made, Huck sits and "waits for light." The ironic variety of meanings for "light" here is emphasized by what Huck says concerning how his decision makes him feel: "I felt easy, and happy, and light as a feather, right off." In *The Fugitive Blacksmith*, Pennington too is well aware of how to pit kinds of light against kinds of darkness. At one point he says, "Whether *my* deed was evil, *you* may judge, but I freely confess that I did *then* prefer darkness rather than light."

Huck's plan to turn Jim in, contrived after much soul-searching, had been stimulated first by his shock at

how Jim begins to behave when lights on the shore seem to indicate that he is close to freedom. Those lights in the distance that Jim keeps seeing all through Chapter 16 are to Jim what the green light at the end of Daisy's dock is to Gatsby–just as deceptive, just as unreachable, just as exhilarating. As they look for Cairo's lights at the very beginning of the chapter, Huck says of Jim, "He said he'd be mighty sure to see it, because he'd be a free man the minute he seen it, but if he missed it he'd be in slave country again and no more show for freedom." Jim, who has had to hide in daylight and move in darkness for so long, can now jump up at every light, whether "Jack-o-lanterns or lightning bugs." Huck reports, "Jim said it made him all over trembly and feverish to be so close to freedom." Huck, on the other hand, who has had the freedom to move in daylight, now has the opposite response to the lights that might mean freedom for Jim. What goes on in his mind is one of the most ironic as well as dramatic sequences of the novel:

> I got to feeling so mean and so miserable I most wished I was dead. I fidgeted up and down the raft, abusing myself to myself, and Jim was fidgeting up and down past me. We neither of us could keep still. Every time he danced around and says, "Dah's Cairo!" it went through me like a shot, and I thought if it *was* Cairo I reckoned I would die of miserableness.
>
> Jim talked out loud all the time while I was talking to myself. He was saying how the first thing he would do when he got to a free State he would go to saving up money and never spend a single cent, and when he got enough he would buy his wife . . . and then they would both work to buy the two children, and if their master wouldn't sell them, they'd get an Ab'litionist to go and steal them.
>
> It most froze me to hear such talk. He wouldn't ever dared to talk such talk in his life before. Just see what a difference it made in him the minute he judged he was about free. It was according to the old saying, "give a nigger an inch and he'll take an ell." . . .
>
> I was sorry to hear Jim say that, it was such a lowering of him. My conscience got to stirring me up hotter than ever, until at last I says to it, "Let up on me–it ain't too late, yet–I'll paddle ashore at the first light and tell."

The key sentences and sentiments in this section have a close correspondence to some ideas and some stylistic features of Frederick Douglass's 1845 *Narrative of the Life of Frederick Douglass, An American Slave*. When Huck says, "Just see what a difference it made in him the minute he judged he was about free. It was according to the old saying, 'Give a nigger an inch and he'll take an ell,'" he is mouthing what must have been a common expression concerning slaves but one which also, in this particular context, relates directly to an important scene in Douglass's *Narrative*. Douglass is

"BOY, THAT'S A LIE."

Huck and the men looking for runaway slaves. Mark Twain may have borrowed Huck's small-pox stratagem from James Pennington's 1849 slave narrative The Fugitive Blacksmith *(drawing by E. W. Kemble; from* Adventures of Huckleberry Finn, *Mark Twain House, Hartford, Connecticut)*

talking of how his mistress in Baltimore had begun to teach him to read until her husband, Mr. Auld, found out and told her, "If you give a nigger an inch, he will take an ell. . . . Now . . . if you teach that nigger how to read, there would be no keeping him. It would forever unfit him to be a slave." Douglass points to this scene as being the exact moment that he began to see his way out of slavery: "From that moment, I understood the pathway from slavery to freedom."

For Jim, the light of Cairo is the dawning realization of what freedom means, and once he sees it, he can never be a slave again, in terms of his self-regard. Douglass, in his famous fight scene with the overseer, Mr. Covey, said that after he defeated Covey, he underwent a crucial mental transformation: "however long I might remain a slave in form, the day had passed when I could be a slave in fact." A scene from Pennington's narrative also bears on our reading of how Jim begins to act when he sees how close freedom is. Pennington, describing his feelings as he realized that he must be near free soil, said that "my spirits were so highly

elated, that I took the whole of the road to myself; I ran, hopped, skipped, jumped, clapped my hands, and talked to myself." Huck tells us that Jim, seeing one last light that looks like Cairo, says, "We's safe, Huck, we's safe! Jump up and crack yo' heels, dat's de good ole Cairo at las', I jis knows it."

We need to note with special care Huck's response to Jim's joy at seeing the symbolic lights that signal for him his successful escape to freedom. Mark Twain sets up Huck's feelings so that even his wording of them dramatizes how directly opposite his reaction to the supposed lights of Cairo is from Jim's. Huck says, "Every time he danced around and says, 'Dah's Cairo!,' it went through me like a shot, and I thought if it *was* Cairo I reckoned I would die of miserableness. Jim talked out loud all the time while I was talking to myself." Huck, even down to the rhetorical balance and evenly shaped syntax of these sentences, contrasts his state of being to Jim's, as if to separate himself even in his language as wholly as he can from this slave, who heretofore has been a man, and his friend. In the passage of Douglass cited above, wherein Douglass notes his master's fear of his learning to read, Douglass shapes the same kind of antithetically balanced sentences that Huck employs in this passage. Such sentences are, in fact, a trademark of Douglass's style, which he designed in order to italicize the opposition between his state of mind and his master's: "What he most dreaded, that I most desired," Douglass tells us. "What he most loved, that I most hated. That which to him was a great evil, to be carefully shunned, was to me a great good, to be diligently sought." The similarities both in strategy and form between Douglass's sentences and Huck's are striking, to say the least.

Mark Twain's Chapter 16, with its black and white lie, its deceiving lights, its double dance and dread of freedom, has close parallels to the slave narratives in both incident and design. As this chapter proceeds, Huck is immediately rewarded for the lie with which he cancels his lie to Jim. He is able to return to his friend with two twenty-dollar gold pieces, given to him by the slavecatchers to ease their consciences while they tell him that "you can make money by runaway slaves." Huck, who had planned to turn Jim in, continues but reverses the irony of his earlier position as he tells the men, "I won't let no runaway niggers get by me if I can help it." When he gets back to the raft, Huck receives Jim's praise for his trickery, "Dat *wuz* de smartes' dodge," and he decides that, as neither satisfying his heart nor appeasing his conscience makes him feel good, he will simply, henceforth, "do whichever come handiest at the time." Yet the scheme of spending the gold pieces to buy steamboat passage up the Ohio River is shortlived; the different colors of the water, the "clear Ohio water in shore, sure enough, and outside . . . the old regular Muddy," tell the runaways that "it was all up with Cairo." And before they have a chance to figure out how to get back upstream, along comes the steamboat, and the rest is history.

Two often debated artistic questions concerning Chapter 16's final form take on new dimensions when we acknowledge the chapter's use of elements found prominently employed in slave narratives. A long raft scene, as it is called, was originally part of Chapter 16; Mark Twain pulled it out for inclusion in *Life on the Mississippi,* returned it to the original manuscript of *Huckleberry Finn,* but finally decided or was persuaded to remove it. If Mark Twain had left the raft scene in Chapter 16, he would have damaged the chapter's unity and obscured its focus. As it now stands, without the raft scene, the chapter begins with Jim's and Huck's search for Cairo's lights and ends with the lights of the steamboat bearing down on the runaways; furthermore, everything in the chapter resembles an incident or strategy that a slave narrator developed, including a

consistent, ironic emphasis on light and darkness. We can also draw on slave narrative strategies in considering the question of why Mark Twain sent his runaways on down the Mississippi River instead of having them romp on to Canada. Canada was not Huck's territory, but more to the point, Douglass's and Brown's first escapes were also not successful. Brown and his mother were caught when they tried simply crossing the river and proceeding through Illinois; Huck's Jim very early in his flight considers this expedient and abandons it. Douglass's and Brown's recaptures and reenslavements helped to define their eventual freedom through stark contrasts which furthered their critical work of protest and exposure. The same seems true for *Huckleberry Finn.*

When Huck went under in Chapter 16, he was a white boy whose introduction to a black slave's quest for freedom evoked an ambivalent response, with no accommodation of conscience and heart available in the world of the river or the world of the shore. The Mississippi had been the regular Muddy all along, but not until Chapter 16 is Huck brought, by Jim's startling assertions of his manhood, face to face with the two sides of his own nature, on the one hand, free white boy enslaved by his slaveholding culture's deformed conscience, and on the other, fugitive black slave, legally unfree but free in mind and spirit because insistent upon his mastery of self, with a potential for saying, as Jim can say, "I's rich now, come to look at it. I owns myself. . . ." As Huck makes his way to the shore after the raft has been hit, in Chapter 16, he watches the current and sees "that I was in a crossing"; when he climbs out in Chapter 17, on the Kentucky shore, ready with a new name and a new story, he has crossed not just the river but also, for the time being, the self enslaved by the dictates of a white conscience.

In Chapter 17 Huck becomes, in relation to the white, southern, slave-owning culture that he meets, a homeless, powerless outcast threatened with return to the oppression he has fled; in other words, he becomes a fugitive slave. Several incidents underscore Huck's new relation to the white world; significantly, they are all incidents bearing close resemblance to events described in slave narratives. When Huck crawls up the bank on the Kentucky side of the river, he is set upon by dogs and threatened by guns before he is taken into the Grangerford house, much in the way that Pennington was attacked when he was caught in Maryland. Another detail in Chapter 17 which puts Huck in a slave narrative scenario is the Grangerfords' generosity to him when they finally do accept him. The scene is reminiscent of Pennington's description of his arrival at a Quaker Pennsylvanian's home, where wet, cold, and hungry, he heard the magical words, "Come in and take thy breakfast, and get warm." Once the Grangerfords adopt Huck, he becomes an observer of this southern slaveholding family in much the same position as Brown was as he observed life in Dr. Young's household. And finally, when Huck tricks Buck Grangerford into helping him to remember the alias he invented when he arrived, he employs a strategy that duplicates one that Frederick Douglass devised. When Douglass was trying to get neighborhood children in Baltimore to teach him the alphabet, he would challenge them to spell certain words, and thus he would learn the shapes of letters. Huck tells us that when he woke up at the Grangerfords, "I had forgot what my name was," a predicament he solves easily by saying to Buck, "I bet you can't spell my name."

The matter of names is an important source of meanings throughout *Huckleberry Finn;* his alias in Chapter 17 is only one of many that he easily assumes during his travels in hostile environs. Changing name and changing identity become key thematic questions for Huck, as they are also a central focus in slave narratives, where naming is equated with the power to control destiny. William Wells Brown, traveling through Ohio towards freedom, asked, "What should be my name?" He decided to take the name *William,* which he had been given at birth. He had been forced as a boy to change this name to *Sandford* so as not to be confused with his master's nephew, also named William (this "white" William was a close blood relative of the "slave" William, a matter of some embarrassment to the master). Brown tells us that, even though he was very young, he objected vehemently to the name change and was frequently beaten for refusing to answer to the name *Sandford.* He explains that he had nothing against the new name, but rebelled because "it had been forced upon me," so that as he traveled through Ohio, "I was not only hunting for my liberty, but also hunting for a name; though I regarded the latter as of little consequence, if I could but gain the former." Soon after Brown relates his rebellion, he shows himself finding refuge at the home of Wells Brown, a Quaker who astonishes William by treating him as an equal. Wells Brown insists that William needs more than just his first name: "Since thee has got out of slavery, thee has become a man, and men always have two names." William gives to Wells Brown the privilege of naming him, though he insists on keeping the name *William,* "taken from me once against my will," and so he becomes *William Wells Brown.*

Huck Finn, like Brown, does not mind changing a name when liberty is to be gained, yet unlike Brown, he also does not mind losing his self-shaped identity. Huck's last alias in the novel, we have to recall, is not one forged by himself, but is one given to him in ironic confusion by the family who takes him in and makes him one of their own. When Aunt Sally says, as Huck

arrives at the Phelps's farm, "It's Tom Sawyer," Huck's reaction is significant: "But if they was joyful, it warn't nothing to what I was; for it was like being born again, I was so glad to find out who I was." Huck will, we know, spend the last portion of the novel living up to or down to his newly prescribed name, as he acquiesces to Tom Sawyer's dehumanizing schemes for Jim's "escape." Mark Twain throughout *Huckleberry Finn* illustrates an understanding similar to Brown's of the power involved in name-giving and name-taking.

William Wells Brown, at last a free man, places himself in the last scene of his narrative in Cleveland, Ohio, working on a lake steamboat and ferrying fugitive slaves to Canada. Yet William Wells Brown the author never settled in Canada. Just before the last vignette, in which he depicts himself as the pilot guiding many slaves on their journeys over the lake to Canada and freedom, Brown gives us our only glimpse of himself as the writer he became. He says, "And while I am seated here in the sight of Bunker Hill Monument, writing this narrative, I am a slave, and no law, not even in Massachusetts, can protect me from the slaveholder!" Brown's narrative position, then, remained precarious and open-ended, freedom as he defined it always a matter of life and death, a dream still ahead, in Massachusetts as in Missouri. He could seize that dream with finality only within the sense of self that was enclosed within his narrative, where he could say, "I wanted to see Captain Price, and let him learn from my own lips that I was no more a chattel, but a man!" Perhaps Mark Twain, like Brown, saw himself at the end of his story both as a young fugitive, asserting a self out of innocence and honesty, and as an embattled author, whose challenges were ahead, who could enlist his own book in a cause yet to be decided and not inevitably lost to post-Civil War corruption and a "dead and pathetic" past. In 1842, the year in which Brown conveyed sixty-nine fugitives over Lake Erie to Canada, Mark Twain's father, Marshall Clemens, took an old slave named Charley to Natchez and sold him for ten barrels of tar worth forty dollars. And about the year 1845, Huck Finn—with Jim free, Pap dead, and Aunt Sally in hot pursuit—decided that he would have to "light out for the Territory ahead of the rest, because Aunt Sally she's going to adopt me and sivilize me and I can't stand it." Like William Wells Brown writing in the shadow of the Bunker Hill Monument, Huck could look up the river and into the future along with Mr. Mark Twain, who told the truth mainly, and say, "I been there before."

–*The Southern Review,* 20 (April 1984): 247–264

* * *

In this excerpt from his study of Mark Twain's relationship with Britain and British authors, Howard Baetzhold examines some of the writers and works, especially W. E. H. [William Edward Hartpole] Lecky's The History of European Morals *(1870), that affected the author's creation of Huck's moral sensibility.*

"The Triumph of Huck's 'Sound Heart'"
Howard Baetzhold

. . . From his first encounter with Lecky's *History of European Morals from Augustus to Charlemagne* (probably during the summer of 1874), he [Clemens] had read, marked, and inwardly digested many of its arguments. Often he noted marginally his agreement or disagreement with what the historian said, or even with how he said it. But at one point, after revising several clumsy constructions in the text, he revealed an abiding affection: "It is so noble a book, & so beautiful a book, that I don't wish it to have even trivial faults in it."[1] And he would continue to borrow ideas and incidents from it for the remainder of his writing career.

In his own works, one may perhaps mark the beginnings of his fascination with the historian's graphic analysis of medieval asceticism in Chapter Thirteen of *Tom Sawyer* (written in 1874), where Huck Finn ridicules the habits of hermits described by Tom. By 1876, as Walter Blair has shown in detail,[2] ideas stimulated by Lecky had permeated the chapters of *Huckleberry Finn* written that summer.

In *The Prince and the Pauper* Lecky's influence seems three-fold, stemming from the historian's examination of the conflicting moral theories of the "intuitionists" and the "utilitarians"; his emphasis on education as a stimulus to the imagination; and his portrait of man's subjection to fear and superstition down through the ages.

The first two of these elements appear in the historian's long opening chapter. Because they were to be important to Clemens' future works . . . they deserve discussion in some detail.

For many years to come Clemens would implicitly carry on what Walter Blair has called his "discussion with Lecky" concerning the relative value of the two systems of moral theory characterized by the historian as "the stoical, the intuitive, the independent or the sentimental" and "the epicurean, the inductive, the utilitarian, or the selfish." The "intuitive" view, which Lecky espoused, argues that moral choices are governed by an innate moral sense, a "power of perceiving" that some qualities (like benevolence, chastity, or veracity) are better than others. A natural accompaniment to this power is a sense of *duty,* an obligation to cultivate the good qualities and suppress their opposites. This

sense, in turn, becomes, "in itself, and apart from all consequences," a sufficient reason for following any particular course of action. The "utilitarian" theory, to which Clemens was increasingly drawn over the years, *denies* that man possesses any such innate perception of virtue. Rather, his standards of right and wrong, his consideration of the "comparative excellence of . . . feelings and actions" depend solely on the degree to which those feelings and actions are conducive to happiness. That which increases happiness and lessens pain is good; that which does the opposite is evil. Hence it is external forces rather than intuitive perceptions of good or evil which determine moral choices.[3]

A number of marginal comments reveal Clemens', attraction to the utilitarian side. On page five of the history, for instance, Lecky summarizes the utilitarian position as follows: "A desire to obtain happiness and to avoid pain is the only possible motive to action. The reason, and the only reason, why we should perform virtuous actions, or in other words, seek the good of others, is that on the whole such a course will bring us the greatest amount of happiness." Besides heavily underscoring the whole statement, Clemens bracketed the "should," underlined the "us" a second time, and wrote in the margin: "Leave the 'should,' out—then it is perfect (& true!)" In several other places he challenged Lecky's agreement with the intuitionists that man's moral perceptions were innate. At one point he contended that "all moral perceptions are acquired by the influences around us," and that since those influences begin in infancy, "we never get a chance to find out whether we have any that are innate or not."[4]

This is not to say that this was the humorist's first encounter with the idea that man's moral choices depend largely on forces outside himself. During his days as a cub-pilot he had absorbed the teachings of Tom Paine's *Age of Reason,* with its emphasis on the immutability of natural law. The notion that man's character and actions were molded primarily from without was doubtless reinforced also by some of Oliver Wendell Holmes' musings on hereditary and environmental influences in *The Autocrat of the Breakfast Table,* which Clemens and Olivia used as a "courting-book" in 1869. Even more important was Clemens' interest in nineteenth-century evolutionary theory.[5]

Because of a fragmentary essay by Clemens that Albert Bigelow Paine included in *Mark Twain's Autobiography,* it has generally been accepted that the author's first instruction in the mysteries of evolution came from a Scotsman named Macfarlane, who preached his own version of the theory in a Cincinnati boarding-house "fourteen or fifteen years before Mr. Darwin's *Descent of Man* startled the world."[6] It now appears, however, that the piece was intended as a magazine or newspaper article and that "Macfarlane" was probably a *persona,* a means of presenting Clemens' own current views of man's pettiness and conceit without publicly committing himself to opinions that might well prove unpopular. It could be that "Macfarlane" owes something to the author's association with J. H. Burrough, his literary-minded St. Louis roommate of 1854–55, who was also at least partially the model for Barrow, the boarding-house philosopher of *The American Claimant* (1892). But until additional evidence becomes available, one must accept the likelihood that Clemens' interest in evolution came primarily from a knowledge of Darwin's writings themselves, or from discussions of those works in contemporary periodicals.

Whether the humorist read *The Origin of Species* (1859) is not certain, but marginal notations in his copy of *The Descent of Man* (1871) show that he may well have been among those whom the book "startled." He thoroughly accepted the theory of evolution, and would later in his own *What is Man?* adapt specific ideas and details from *The Descent of Man.* Yet he apparently was not entirely satisfied with Darwin's attempts to support, on purely evolutionary grounds, the argument that the moral sense was the most important characteristic separating man from the lower animals. He was more impressed, it seems, by Darwin's reference to the notion that the impulse to relieve the sufferings of others stemmed not from altruism but from the desire to alleviate one's own painful feelings which the sight of suffering aroused. For in the margin beside that latter comment he wrote: "Selfishness again—not charity nor generosity (save toward ourselves.)"[7]

These years also marked the beginnings of Clemens' lifelong fascination with Edward FitzGerald's *Rubaiyat of Omar Khayyam.* The haunting quatrains first enchanted him shortly after his return from Europe in 1879, when the Hartford *Courant* quoted a number of them in its front-page review of the new fourth edition of the "translation," published in England that August. From then on, the *Rubaiyat* became his favorite poem, one of the few examples of literary expression that he considered "perfect."[8] Though the effects were to be more obvious later on, particularly during the 1890's, there is little doubt that the deterministic overtones of Omar's discussion of morality and personal responsibility added their elements to Clemens' considerations in the late 'seventies and early 'eighties.

The fact remains, however, that in Lecky he probably first encountered a systematic development of the utilitarian and intuitionist arguments. And for many years his works would show that even though strongly attracted to the utilitarian position, he did not wholly accept it. The "discussion with Lecky" would continue for most of his life.

One of the matters on which Clemens partly agreed with Lecky at this time concerned the nature of the conscience. The historian agreed with the intuitionist view that the conscience was an "original faculty," arising from man's innate perceptions of good and evil. The utilitarians, on the other hand, regarded it simply as an "association of ideas" based on the pleasure-pain theory and society's standards of right and wrong.

To show the inadequacy of the utilitarian concept, Lecky argues that the operation of the conscience does not really fit the view that "self-interest" is the one ultimate reason for virtue. What one "ought or ought not" to do cannot depend merely upon "the prospect of acquiring or losing pleasure." For, if a man had a tendency toward a certain vice, he might well attain happiness by a "moderate and circumspect" indulgence of that vice. But if he sins, his conscience judges his conduct, and "its sting or its approval constitutes a pain or pleasure so intense, as to more than redress the balance." This would happen whether the conscience were an "association of ideas" or "an original faculty."

But (the argument continues) conscience is more often a source of pain than of pleasure, and if happiness is actually the sole end of life, then one should learn to disregard the proddings of conscience. If a man forms an association of ideas that inflicts more pain than it prevents, or prevents more pleasure than it affords, the reasonable course would be to dissolve that association or destroy the habit. "This is what he 'ought' to do according to the only meaning that word can possess in the utilitarian vocabulary." Therefore, a man who possessed such a temperament would be happier if he were to "quench that conscientious feeling, which . . . prevents him from pursuing the course that would be most conducive to his tranquillity."[9]

Clemens had dramatized this very theme in "The Facts Concerning the Recent Carnival of Crime in Connecticut," written in January, 1876, and published in the June issue of the *Atlantic Monthly.* As the story opens, the narrator muses over efforts of friends and relatives to keep him in the paths of virtue. Suddenly, his Conscience appears in the form of a "nauseating" dwarf, resembling the narrator himself but covered with a greenish mold. ("Considered as a source of pain," Lecky says, "conscience bears a striking resemblance to the feeling of disgust.") The two discuss at some length the function of the Conscience as tormentor. Finally, a recitation of his many sins goads the narrator into throttling the dwarf, tearing him to pieces, and throwing the "bleeding rubbish" into the fire. Having thus followed Lecky's advice to obliterate his conscience, the narrator embarks on a career of "unalloyed bliss," committing all sorts of heinous crimes without a moment's remorse.

Huck on Hermits

Scholar Howard Baetzhold suggests that this passage is one of the earliest to show the influence of W. E. H. Lecky's ideas on Mark Twain.

"You see," said Tom, "people don't go much on hermits, now-a-days, like they used to in old times, but a pirate's always respected. And a hermit's got to sleep on the hardest place he can find, and put sack-cloth and ashes on his head, and stand out in the rain, and—"

"What does he put sack-cloth and ashes on his head for?" inquired Huck .

"*I* dono. But they've *got* to do it. Hermits always do. You'd have to do that if you was a hermit."

"Dern'd if I would," said Huck.

"Well, what would you do?"

"I dono. But I wouldn't do that."

"Why Huck, you'd *have* to. How'd you get around it?"

"Why I just wouldn't stand it. I'd run away."

"Run away! Well you *would* be a nice old slouch of a hermit. You'd be a disgrace."

—The Adventures of Tom Sawyer, p. 119

THE PIRATES ASHORE.

Tom Sawyer, Joe Harper, and Huckleberry Finn at their camp on Jackson's Island, where they discuss pirates and hermits (drawing by True Williams; from The Adventures of Tom Sawyer, *Mark Twain House, Hartford, Connecticut)*

Fantastic as the piece is, it nevertheless parallels Lecky's discussion almost exactly. Certainly Clemens' own experiences with a tormenting conscience, which must have been one of the keenest in literary history, had led him here to agree with Lecky's assertion that the reproaches of conscience often prevented a man from following a course that might be "most conducive to his tranquillity." And since the proddings of conscience obviously could not be so easily dismissed, Clemens at least implicitly agreed that Lecky had found a fallacy in the utilitarian reasoning.

Echoes of this idea of "quenching" the conscience occur also in the chapters of *Huckleberry Finn* written in 1876. Furthermore, Huck's struggles with his conscience about turning Jim over to the authorities show Clemens agreeing with the historian in a slightly different way. The climax of that conflict in Chapter Thirty-one, when Huck decides to "go to hell" rather than reveal Jim's whereabouts was not to be written for several years. But the struggle itself was clearly established in 1876, especially in Chapter Sixteen, when Huck decides to paddle ashore "and tell," but then recants and lies to the slave-catchers about the color of the man on the raft. Some years later, in a notebook plan for an elaborate "lay sermon on morals and things of that stately sort," Clemens proposed to use that very chapter from his novel to show how "in a crucial moral emergency a sound heart is a safer guide than an

ill-trained conscience."[10] Though Clemens here was obviously regarding the conscience as an "association of ideas" rather than an "original faculty," both this passage and Huck's later decision not to write to Miss Watson dramatize the triumph of Huck's "sound heart" over his community-trained sense of right and wrong. This "sound heart" is first cousin, if not brother, to the "innate moral perceptions" championed by Lecky and the intuitionists.

—Mark Twain and John Bull: The British Connection (Bloomington: Indiana University Press, 1970), pp. 54–59

1. All references to Clemens' marginalia and underscorings in [*The History of European Morals*] *EurMor* (in both this and later chapters) are from Chester L. Davis, "MT'S Religious Beliefs as Indicated by Notations in His Books," *Twainian* (May–June, July–August, Sept.–Oct., Nov.–Dec., 1956). Davis describes an 1874 edition of Lecky—*EurMor*, was first published in 1869–the flyleaf of which

is inscribed "T. W. Crane, 1874) and "S. L. Clemens, 1906." As Walter Blair points out (*Mark Twain and Huck Finn*, p. 401n.), many of Clemens' notes were obviously made much earlier than 1906. Clemens may also have had another copy. All of my references are to the 1870 ed., (D. Appleton & Co.), which has the same pagination as the 1874 edition.

2. *Mark Twain and Huck Finn*, pp. 132–145 and passim.
3. *EurMor*, I, 3 ff.
4. *EurMor*, II, 20, 21, 22.
5. He would hardly have failed to notice the Autocrat's assertion that both mind and body function "not *by*, but *according to* laws, such as we observe in the larger universe." He was probably struck, too, by Holmes' use of mechanical "imagery to describe the workings of man's mind, as well as by the various arguments that hereditary and environmental influences made free will all but nonexistent (*Autocrat*, Boston, 1892, pp. 71, 85, 86, 89). See Sherwood Cummings' discussion of the influence of Holmes and Darwin, *What is Man?: The Scientific Sources*," in *Essays on Determinism in American Literature* (Kent, Ohio, 1965), pp. 108–116.
6. *Mark Twain's Autobiography*, edited by Albert Bigelow Paine, I, 146. See Paul Baender,' "'Alias Macfarlane': A Revision of MT Biography," *AL*, XXXVIII (May 1966), 187–197.
7. *Descent of Man* (1871), I, 78, in The Mark Twain Papers, quoted by Cummings, op. cit., in n. 5.
8. Notebook entry 19, p. 25; Albert Bigelow Paine, *Mark Twain: A Biography*, II, 614. Clemens had heard of "old Omar-Khéyam" (as he called him in a letter to Howells) as early as 1876 (*Mark Twain-Howells Letters*, I, 164). In 1878 James Osgood had published the first American edition of the *Rubaiyat*, a reprint of the third English edi-

tion of 1872. But the *Courant* article (clipping in The Mark Twain Papers) shows that the stimulus for Clemens' enthusiasm was Bernard Quaritch's fourth English edition, which had gone on sale in England in August, 1879 (A. M. Terhune, *Life of Edward FitzGerald*, New Haven, 1947, pp. 329–330). Besides a number of references to the poem over the years (e.g. Samuel L. Clemens to Charles L. Webster, 5/19/84, *Mark Twain Business Man*, p. 254; Notebook entry 19, p. 11, Apr., 1885, The Mark Twain Papers; Samuel L. Clemens to Clara Spaulding Stanchfield, Sept, 1886, TS, The Mark Twain Papers; *Mark Twain's Letters to Mary*, 8/26/06, p. 54; Samuel L. Clemens to "Mr. Logan," 2/2/07, TS, The Mark Twain Papers; see also notes to Chapter Eleven, *post*),Clemens remarked in an autobiographical dictation of 11/7/07 how strange it seemed to think that there was a time when he had never heard of Omar Khayyam, and then went on to say that the *Rubaiyat* was the only poem he had ever carried about with him–that it had not been "from under [his] hand for twenty-eight years" (TS, pp. 2317–2318, The Mark Twain Papers; last part quoted in slightly different form, *Mark Twain: A Biography*, III, 1295). *Anderson Auction Company catalogue no. 892–11*, pp. 55–56, lists two editions of FitzGerald's *Rubaiyat*: Boston, n.d. (almost certainly the Osgood edition) and Philadelphia, n.d., inscribed "S. L. Clemens, 1900" and another translation by E. F. Thompson, privately printed, 1901, inscribed "S. L. Clemens, 1907," a presentation copy from one James Logan of Worcester, Mass., obviously the "Mr. Logan," above.

9. For Lecky's discussion of the role of the conscience, see *The History of European Morals*, I, 64–67.
10. Quoted in *Mark Twain and Huck Finn*, p. 143.

Composition and Illustration

Mark Twain's process of writing Adventures of Huckleberry Finn has been the subject of critical and scholarly attention for nearly a century. In The Ordeal of Mark Twain (1920) and elsewhere, Van Wyck Brooks argued that Twain's sensibility was formed by the restraining influences of Victorian morality and a crude Western environment and that he was at best indifferent to his craft. Bernard DeVoto challenged this thesis in Mark Twain's America (1932), insisting that it was his experience of the West that made Twain into a vigorous writer. In Mark Twain at Work (1942) DeVoto used the available manuscript evidence to provide an account of how Adventures of Huckleberry Finn was composed and to reaffirm his conviction that Twain was not a thwarted artist, repressed by a puritanical mother. Even before DeVoto's book, J. DeLancey Ferguson in his essay "Huck Finn Aborning" (1938) argued on the basis of his inspection of the surviving manuscript that Twain did not submit to censorship in Adventures of Huckleberry Finn; to the contrary, Ferguson argued—as have later critics—that Twain's revisions reveal a general artistic improvement throughout. Walter Blair continued the inquiry inaugurated by DeVoto, into the gestation and composition of the novel providing penetrating insights into Twain's creative process. In Mark Twain and Huck Finn (1960) Blair gave a thorough account of the genesis and composition of the novel and paid special attention to sources and influences that affected the author. The most exhaustive study of Twain's revisions is to be found in Victor Doyno's Writing Huck Finn (1991) and Beginning to Write Huck Finn (2002). The first book was in press at the time of the discovery of

The gazebo study Susan Crane had built for her brother-in-law, Mark Twain. It was moved to the campus of Elmira College (courtesy of Galen R. Frysinger).

the missing portion of the manuscript; the second book takes into account the newly found first part of the manuscript of Mark Twain's novel.

"The Loveliest Study"

Most summers in the years between 1874 and 1889, Mark Twain and his family made extended visits to the home of Susan and Theodore Crane, Olivia Clemens's sister and brother-in-law. In an 11 June 1874 letter to his friends Joseph and Harmony Twichell, Mark Twain described the study at Quarry Farm where he did most of his summer writing.

Susie Crane has built the loveliest study for me, you ever saw. It is octagonal, with a peaked roof, each octagon filled with a spacious window, & it sits perched in complete isolation on top of an elevation that commands leagues of valley & city & retreating ranges of dis-

tant blue hills. It is a cosy nest, with just room in it for a sofa & a table & three or four chairs—& when the storms sweep down the remote valley & the lightning flashes above the hills beyond, & the rain beats upon the roof over my head, imagine the luxury of it! It stands 500 feet above the valley & 2½ miles from it.

—Mark Twain's Letters, Volume 6: 1874–1875, edited by Michael B. Frank and Harriet Elinor Smith (Berkeley, Los Angeles & London: University of California Press, 2002), p. 58

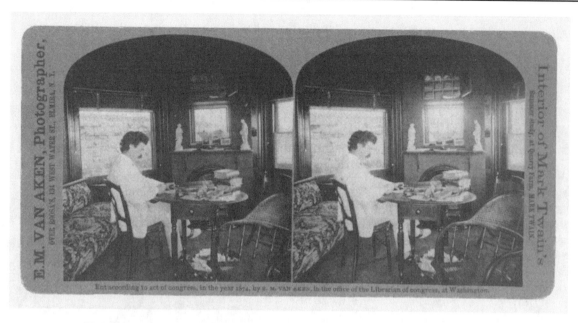

Mark Twain working in his study at Quarry Farm, near Elmira, New York, where he began writing Adventures of Huckleberry Finn *in summer 1876 (Elmira College Library)*

Writing *Huckleberry Finn*

This essay, revised in light of the new evidence provided by the discovery of the first part of the manuscript of Adventures of Huckleberry Finn, *builds especially on the work of Walter Blair. It also benefited enormously from the published work of and conversations with Victor Fischer, who is the editor of the revised edition of the novel published in 2003 by the University of California Press.*

Nobility out of Tatters:
The Writing of *Huckleberry Finn*
Tom Quirk

Willa Cather once wrote, "There is a time in a writer's development when his 'life line' and the line of his personal endeavor meet."[1] For her, the intersection of these two lines occurred when she wrote her first significant novel, *O Pioneers!* (1913). The writing of this novel produced in her the excitement that comes from writing out of one's "deepest experience" and "inner feeling,"[2] and her course was directed by the "thing by which our feet find the road on a dark night, accounting of themselves for roots and stones which we have never noticed by day."[3] These remarks are as true for Mark Twain as they were for Cather herself; and whether he knew it or not, the lines of his familiar experience and his literary ambition converged sometime in July 1876, when he began to write the book he would eventually name *Adventures of Huckleberry Finn*.

Cather's personal endeavor was distinctly artistic, and she had committed herself to the high calling of art at least twenty years before she achieved in *O Pioneers!* the sort of satisfaction that allowed her to say that she had hit the "home pasture" at last. Twain's literary development was more haphazard. He once remarked that his life consisted of a series of apprenticeships and that he was surprised to discover, at the age of thirty-seven, that he had become a "literary person." Only four years after this revelation he embarked on the writing of "Huck Finn's Autobiography" (as he had described it in a letter to W. D. Howells),[4] the book that has secured for him the reputation as something significantly more than a mere "literary person." And part of the mystery of *Huckleberry Finn* is how Twain's achievement in this book outran his qualifications to write it. But Twain too was guided by some "thing" within him, though he seems often to have lost his way. At times, in fact, he wanted to abandon the journey altogether. But he did not, and the result was a book that transmuted fact and experience into memorable fiction.

"No more beautiful or instructive example of the artist's dilemma, of the source of his passions, and how, if ever, he must lovingly resolve them, is available to us than this passion of Mark Twain, resolved in *Huckleberry Finn*."[5] So wrote another Midwestern novelist, Wright Morris. Artistic development and maturity, Morris insisted, demand more than the acquisition of literary technique; they require, as well, the recognition of the contingency of fact and the permanence of fiction. The edges of fact and fiction sometimes blurred for Twain, but in *Huckleberry Finn,* "in one moment of vision, a state of hallowed reminiscence, he seemed to grasp the distinction," and "his genius flowed into it."[6] What we know of the composition of *Huckleberry Finn* suggests not a single moment of vision, however, but several. Nevertheless, a general statement about the relation of fact to fiction Morris once made in an essay has an appropriateness to Mark Twain's relation to his book:

> We are, indeed, cunning and inscrutable creatures, mad for facts that we must turn into fiction to possess. If it's about man, it's about fiction, and the better the fiction, the more it's about. The worse the fiction, the less we have of the facts of life. If we are to be more rather than less human—one of our many stimulating options—we will turn from what we see around us, and attend to the promptings within us. The imagination made us human, but *being* human, becoming more human, is a greater burden than we imagined. We have no choice but to imagine ourselves more human than we are.[7]

The facts of the composition of *Huckleberry Finn* tell us something about the fiction that is the novel. And one of the things they tell us is that Mark Twain, mainly through his identification with Huck, imagined himself more completely human than he probably was himself, and in doing so provided his readers with the same opportunity.

I

In a sense we know both too much and too little about the making of *Huckleberry Finn.* The extant evidence for its composition is of several sorts. The single most important piece of evidence is a holograph manuscript of the novel housed in the Buffalo Public Library. James Gluck, a curator for the library of the Young Men's Association had written Twain asking for any manuscripts he might care for pass on to them. At the time, the author could find only the last half of *Huckleberry Finn,* which he dutifully sent to Buffalo, supposing the remainder had never been returned from the printer. In point of fact the manuscript had never gone to the printer, and a year and a half later Twain discovered the remainder of the manuscript and had it sent along to be placed with the portion the library already housed. The entire holograph was meant to be bound together and placed on display, but that never happened, and for a hundred years and more it was supposed that the first part of the novel had been permanently lost. We will have more to say about the importance of the discovery of the "lost" portion of the manuscript in a moment. For now, it is enough to say that Twain scholars who studied the composition of the

novel prior to the reemergence of the earlier portion of the book were limited by the extant evidence.

Until fairly recently, this manuscript holding represented approximately three-fifths of the novel and consists of most of chapter 12, all of chapters 13 and 14, and chapters 22 through the concluding chapter 43, all written in Twain's beautifully clear hand. Now, however, we have the complete novel, including two excised portions that, for whatever reasons, Twain decided should be removed from the narrative. And, of course, there already existed in print the familiar "raft chapter" extracted from the novel and included in *Life on the Mississippi* (1883), and now, in the California edition of the novel, restored to chapter 16. There are as well letters and other sorts of testimony related to *Huckleberry Finn,* and there are various references to the book in Twain's notebooks. Finally, there are the "Working Notes" for the novel, which Bernard DeVoto divided into three distinct groups and which are particularly significant in reconstructing the composition of the novel. These notes record ideas for future episodes, reminders about what he had already written, and notations about the vernacular speech of his characters. We know as well that as many as three partial typescripts of the novel were made; that Twain made extensive revisions of the first two; that one served as the printer's copy for the first edition and that the illustrator, Edward Kemble, worked from another. No portion of the typescripts has survived.

On the basis of most of this evidence (not all of it was available to him), DeVoto speculated that *Huckleberry Finn* was composed in two distinct stages.[8] Chapters 1 through 16, he argued, (minus the interpolated *Walter Scott* episode and the King Solomon debate) he argued were written in the summer of 1876, for Twain wrote Howells on 9 August that he had written about 400 manuscript pages in a month and was only partly satisfied by the result and had decided to pigeonhole or burn the novel when it was complete. The remainder, claimed DeVoto, was written in an eruptive burst of inspiration in 1883. We do know, at any rate, that on 1 September 1883 Twain wrote his English publisher that he had just finished the book.

DeVoto's account of the composition of *Huckleberry Finn* was based upon a conscientious inspection of available evidence, and it placed special emphasis on the effect that Twain's Mississippi River trip in 1882 had in revitalizing the author's interest in the pigeonholed manuscript of Huck's adventures. Twain made this trip to gather firsthand reacquaintance with life along the river in order to complete *Life on the Mississippi,* a book which had its origin in the simple reminiscence he published as "Old Times on the Mississippi" in 1875. For DeVoto and others, the real beneficiary of this trip

When Was HUCKLEBERRY FINN *Written?**

WALTER BLAIR
University of Chicago

I

ALBERT BIGELOW PAINE, Clemens's first literary executor, believes that Mark Twain composed *Adventures of Huckleberry Finn* in three periods—in 1876, 1880, and 1883. Bernard DeVoto, Paine's successor, holds that he wrote it in two—in 1876 and 1883. Although when DeVoto disagrees with Paine, usually DeVoto is right, in this instance I believe that Paine is nearer the truth. Furthermore, I believe that both, with most other students of Twain, overestimate the influence of Clemens's Mississippi River trip of 1882 on the novel. If my beliefs prove to be well founded, significant revisions of the story of the genesis of the book will be necessary.

Since both Paine's brief account and DeVoto's meticulous and lengthy one of the writing of the book are readily accessible,[1] I shall, for the sake of brevity and clarity, not summarize them, but shall set down my account, presenting whatever evidence for it I can. At appropriate points, I shall offer arguments opposed to those of DeVoto. In conclusion, I shall indicate the implications of my account.

Available evidence includes: (1) letters and recorded conversations relevant to the novel; (2) three groups of Twain's "working notes" —labeled A, B, and C by DeVoto, who first saw their significance;

*For a number of years this topic has been a favorite one for discussion and research in my courses dealing with Mark Twain. I thank collectively the many students who have helped answer this question. In particular, I am grateful to George E. Schindler, Jr., who in 1952 suggested doubts about DeVoto's description of the hypothetical typescript of the novel, and to Dewey Ganzel, who in 1955 first pointed out what I think must be the true functions of pp. 7 and 10 of Group A of the working notes.

[1] Albert Bigelow Paine, *Mark Twain: A Biography* (New York, 1912, hereinafter cited as *Biography*), pp. 578, 683-684, 754; Bernard DeVoto, "Introduction" to *Adventures of Huckleberry Finn* (New York: Limited Editions Club, 1942); "Noon and Dark," in *Mark Twain at Work*, ed. Bernard DeVoto (Cambridge, 1942, herinafter cited as *MTAW*), pp. 45-82.

First page of a seminal essay from the March 1958 issue of American Literature. *Walter Blair's careful conclusions regarding Mark Twain's writing process were only slightly modified by the new evidence provided by the 1991 discovery of the first half of* Adventures of Huckleberry Finn *manuscript (Thomas Cooper Library, University of South Carolina).*

was not his river book, however, but *Huckleberry Finn*. DeVoto had divided the working notes into three distinct groups (A, B, and C), but he assumed that all of these notes for continuing the Huck manuscript were written after that trip and offered evidence that Twain had at last discovered the "true purpose" of the book he had abandoned six years earlier. In the remaining chapters Twain would "exhibit the rich variety of life in the great central valley," a variety that included in its diverse effects the chicanery and venality of the king and duke, the senseless cruelty of the Bricksville loafers, and the stupid and violent attachment to clannish pride of the feuding Grangerfords and Shepherdsons.[9] Such was the prevailing view of the making of *Huckleberry Finn* through most of the 1940s and 1950s, until Walter Blair challenged that view in 1958 with his essay "When Was *Huckleberry Finn* Written?"[10]

The Working Notes for *Huckleberry Finn* were written in a variety of ink colors and on different kinds of paper. Taking his cue from DeVoto that a study of the kinds of paper and ink Twain used between 1876 and 1884 might yield useful information about the dates of composition of these notes, Blair undertook an exhaustive and impressive investigation of Twain's writing materials during that period. He surveyed more than 400 of Twain's letters, 26 of his manuscripts, and all the notebook entries he made during these years. He found that Twain used pencils, typewriters, and at least five kinds of ink; he noted the many kinds and sizes of paper that the author used in letters, notes, and manuscripts. This massive array of evidence of Twain's writing habits is dizzying in its variety and complexity—sometimes Twain used two kinds of paper in a single letter, and a manuscript of any length might contain a half a dozen kinds. But Blair was nevertheless able to discern a pattern in the evidence that he collected, one that enabled him to date the working notes and, in turn, to plot the development of the novel over those seven years.

The violet ink used in Group A of the working notes was particularly significant because Blair discovered that with only a few exceptions Twain used this color ink sporadically between 1876 and 1880 and only when he was at Hartford, and more importantly that he ceased to use it altogether after the fall of 1880. Blair's conclusion, of course, was that these notes were written before the summer of 1880 and, therefore, that DeVoto was wrong in claiming they were written when Twain was "fresh" from his river trip in 1882.[11]

A more precise dating of Twain's working notes enabled Blair to reconsider other available evidence (including the internal evidence provided by the notes themselves) in a new light and to offer the convincing hypothesis that *Huckleberry Finn* was written in at least

four rather than two stages. The first stage occurred in the summer of 1876 and Blair believed that Twain wrote the first sixteen chapters (excluding the *Walter Scott* and King Solomon episodes), or up to that point chapter 16 where the steamboat smashes through the raft. Then, sometime in 1879–80, he resumed the manuscript. Huck had survived the smashup and had climbed ashore to be a witness to the stupidity and needless violence of the Shepherdson-Grangerford feud. Evidently he paused halfway through this episode to write the first set of working notes for the continuation of Huck's adventures, for one of the notes indicates a belated decision to resurrect the raft and to continue the river voyage of Huck and Jim: "Back a little, CHANGE–raft only *crippled* by steamer."[12]

At some period or periods between 1880 and June 1883, Twain wrote chapters 19 and 20 and most of 21, the chapters that introduce the king and the duke and dramatize their various con games. At some time after that, Twain wrote the Group C notes. The following summer he completed the novel in a final explosive burst of creative inspiration or, perhaps, of simple determination to finish a book that had begun so long before. In any event Twain was so productive that he confessed to Howells in a letter dated 22 August 1883 that he himself could not believe how much he had written in so short a time.[13] Blair speculated that Twain wrote two Bricksville chapters, the Wilks chapters, and the *Walter Scott* episode (part of chapter 12 and all of chapter 13) before he carried his narrative to its conclusion. The King Solomon debate may have been written separately (the manuscript shows that he numbered those pages 1–17 and then renumbered them to conform with the pagination of the manuscript).[14] It is possible that this debate represents Twain's final contribution to the novel that had begun seven years earlier.

Blair's account of when *Huckleberry Finn* was written is so thoroughgoing and his conclusions so meticulously intelligent that for thirty-five years it withstood the minute scrutiny of scholars and critics (including those involved in the Mark Twain Project specifically engaged in accumulating new evidence about the book). His conclusions about the stages of composition remained pretty much intact. Even so, there was circumstantial evidence, such as that amassed by Robert Hirst and Edgar M. Branch concerning the feud chapters, that suggested that Twain, during the first stint of composition, might have carried his story beyond that point in chapter 16 where the steamboat runs over the raft.

Still, the work Blair had done in charting the stages of composition of the book was but preliminary to determining its genesis as an imaginative creation.

William Dean Howells, circa 1874, when he was editor in chief of the Atlantic Monthly. *A respected novelist and man of letters, Howells was a longtime friend and adviser to Twain (Howells Memorial, Kittery Point, Maine).*

Having plotted in its essential outlines the genetic history of *Adventures of Huckleberry Finn,* Blair made it possible to give a fuller and more comprehensible story of the making of this American classic. If some of the customary beliefs about the book had to be abandoned, other hypotheses about the novel and its author might be plausibly asserted. Moreover, *Huckleberry Finn* could be more accurately placed within the full range of Twain's interests and activities during the seven-year period of its growth.

Mark Twain was a man of many enthusiasms and as many angers. He was a man so easily diverted, so constantly and busily employed in so many projects, that one is reminded of an acrobat who spins a dozen plates atop as many sticks–rushing back and forth between and among the plates to keep them spinning while starting yet another that will further scatter his attention. Blair's scholarly adventures in tracing the chronology of *Huckleberry Finn* led him to trace as well the several forces that shaped it. This he did in his "biography of a book," *Mark Twain and Huck Finn* (1960). It was a study every bit as complex and as instructive, though in a different way, as sifting through the evidence of composition, but it gave a human and circumstantial coherence to the process he had identified mostly on the basis of physical evidence.

It would be pointless to give a comprehensive survey of Blair's findings in *Mark Twain and Huck Finn.* He offers there a detailed account of Twain's activities between 1874 and 1884–an account of his reading and writings, his business affairs, his political attitudes, and his family situation. Blair chose to give greater empha-

---

"Huck Finn's Autobiography"

These excerpts are from the earliest letters Mark Twain wrote to William Dean Howells concerning the novel that became Adventures of Huckleberry Finn. *In this first excerpt, from a letter dated 5 July 1875, written when he had just finished* The Adventures of Tom Sawyer, *Twain is already considering an autobiographical approach to telling a boy's story.*

. . . I have finished the story and didn't take the chap beyond boyhood. I believe it would be fatal to do it in any shape but autobiographically–like Gil Blas. I perhaps made a mistake in not writing it in the first person. If I went on, now, and took him into manhood, he would just lie like all the one-horse men in literature and the reader would conceive a hearty contempt for him. It is not a boy's book, at all. It will only be read by adults. It is only written for adults. . . .

This excerpt from a 9 August 1876 letter includes Twain's first mention of his work on Adventures of Huckleberry Finn. *It is unclear whether the author thought so little of the book at this time or was instead being self-deprecating.*

. . .[I] began another boys' book–more to be at work than anything else. I have written 400 pages on it–therefore it is very nearly half done. It is Huck Finn's Autobiography. I like it only tolerably well, as far as I have got, and may possibly pigeonhole or burn the MS when it is done. . . .

–*Selected Mark Twain-Howells Letters, 1872–1910,* edited by Frederick Anderson, William M. Gibson, and Henry Nash Smith (Cambridge: Belknap Press of Harvard University Press, 1967), pp. 48, 75

sis to Twain's immediate circumstance than to the remembered experiences of his childhood in Hannibal or his pilot years on the Mississippi, because he considered the ways the author modified youthful recollection and reminiscence according to his present state of mind more important in determining how such a book came to be.

One of the conclusions Blair had drawn in "When Was *Huckleberry Finn* Written?" after determining that the first group of the working notes was written before Twain's river trip in 1882 was that Twain did not need to revisit the places of his youth in order to revitalize his imagination. He was capable in this book, as he had been in others of his writings, of "generating within himself, without external stimuli, the power to summon to his memories vivid recollections of times past and to give them form and meaning."[15] A consideration of Twain's immediate situation and state of mind disclosed as well that such vivid remembrance was spurred by his immediate present, for which the fiction served as satisfactory expression, compensation, or resolution.

One other important study of the novel was published prior to the discovery of the missing portion of the manuscript. In *Writing Huck Finn: Mark Twain's Creative Process* (1991), Victor A. Doyno offered a comprehensive and finely detailed study of Twain's revisions of that part of the manuscript available to him. Doyno was principally interested in Twain's craftsmanship, as opposed to the chronology of the composition or the state of mind of the author during that process. Instead, he showed how, through Twain's conscientious attention to matters of tone, characterization, humor, plot, and theme, the author shaped his narrative into ever new and more subtle patterns of meaning. Doyno also provided fuller social and historical contexts for many of the episodes than anyone had previously done. To a large extent, Doyno's study was not particularly damaged by the new manuscript evidence that surfaced while his book was in production. In fact, in a Preface to this book, Doyno observed that the newly discovered pages "contain absolutely nothing to contradict and much to confirm the findings of this book." He went on to predict that, after the legal problems concerning the ownership of the new materials were settled, he might well write another, similar study called "Beginning to Write *Huck Finn*." And that book is now published in the CD-ROM edition *Huck Finn: The Complete Buffalo Manuscript–Teaching and Research Digital Edition* (2002), and Doyno has extended his previous study in acute and important ways.

In October, 1990, a granddaughter of James Gluck, then living in Hollywood, California, opened a trunk in her attic. There she found a stack of 664 manuscript pages in Twain's hand. It was the "lost" por-

tion of the *Huckleberry Finn* manuscript. Her grandfather had died in 1897, at the age of forty-five, and the manuscript, along with other belongings, were matter-of-factly packed up in trunks. Why this part of the manuscript was in Gluck's home instead of in the library remains a mystery. There followed upon this discovery considerable and considerably complicated legal wrangling over the ownership of the discovery; evidently the disputes were resolved to everyone's satisfaction. In any event, the entire manuscript is now at the Buffalo Public Library and available in digital format as well. This new evidence invalidates many of the speculative conclusions scholars had drawn previously, and I offer here an inventory of the most significant or surprising revelations that have come from the availability of the complete manuscript:

- Victor Fischer in the 2003 California edition of the novel identifies the three principal "stints" of composition of the book. There were three, not four, important phases of composition, though Twain may have intermittently returned to the manuscript throughout the seven year period of composition. Stint one occurred July–September, 1876; Twain wrote chapters 1–12 1/2 and chapters 15–18 1/2. Stint two occurred sometime between mid-March and mid-June 1880; Twain wrote chapters 18 1/2–21. Sometime after June 1880, he also wrote the "Notice" page that appears in the front-matter of the book. Stint three occurred June–September 1883; he wrote the title page, chapters 12 1/2–14, and chapters 22–43.

- It had long been assumed that the first phase of composition in 1876 ended at that part of chapter 16 where the riverboat runs over the raft. This is a very appealing notion because it invites us to imagine an author who didn't quite know how his narrative was developing. Huck and Jim had passed Cairo in the fog, and the author was in the absurd position of having a runaway slave escaping into the deep South. It would have been just like Twain to have gotten frustrated with this turn of events and, rather angrily one supposes, to have busted the raft all to flinders and to have pigeonholed the manuscript. The evidence reveals, however, that Twain's first stint of composition got him well beyond this point, to that part of chapter 18 where Buck Grangerford asks Huck, "Don't you know what a feud is?"

- The most surprising revelation disclosed by the new evidence, perhaps, is that the so-called Hamlet soliloquy the duke teaches the king at the beginning of chapter 21 appears not to have been inserted into the chapter later, as Walter Blair had supposed. Though there may have been some interval between the creation of the dramatic situation for the recitation and the writing of the soliloquy itself, it evidently was planned as an integral part of the incident as it had originally been written, probably in 1880. This discovery is surprising because other evidence had convinced Blair that the parodic soliloquy had been written on a March

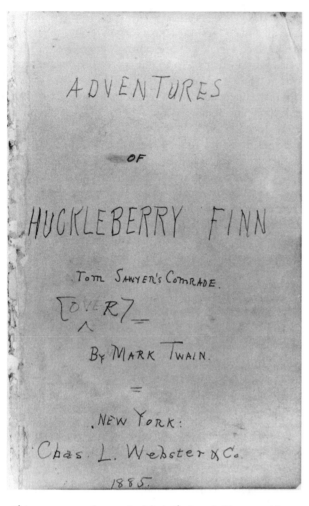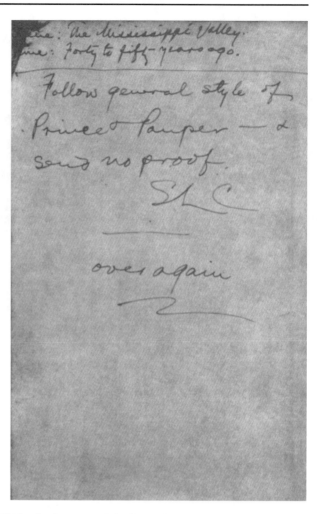

Title page, recto and verso, that Mark Twain probably prepared in summer 1883, when he was completing his novel. He is believed to have added the publication year and the first two lines on the verso in summer 1884. In a 24 July letter to Charles Webster, he wrote "Can you alter the title-page so as to say, 'Time, forty to fifty years ago' instead of 'Time, forty years ago.' . . . If the printing isn't begun, you can make the alteration, of course—so do it; but if it has begun, never mind, let it go" (Buffalo and Erie County Public Library).

1883 night when Clemens had refused to go to the opera with his wife Olivia and Charlie Webster and his wife. Blair's contention conforms so nicely with what we know (or think we know) about Mark Twain that it is easy to picture this amusing mishmash of lines from Shakespeare as a typical act of Twainian mischief and a private triumph over efforts to civilize him.

• Twain significantly revised the camp meeting episode in chapter 20. The scene was substantially shortened and he toned down the religious satire, probably in deference to the sensitivities of his readers. But he probably also wanted to remove the rather obvious echoes of Johnson J. Hooper's similar scene in chapter 10 of *Adventures of Captain Simon Suggs* (1844).

• He also removed from chapter 9 a grotesque episode about Huck and Jim wondering whether or not lightning casts a shadow followed by Jim recalling his adventures in fright while warming a cadaver for a young medical student. This "ghost" story may well have been the one that his daughter Susy remembered her father reading aloud to the family. She and her sister Clara found the story "perfectly fascinating it was so dreadful," and they were both stricken when their mother turned down the corner of the page, indicating that it was to be removed from the story. The girls, at least, thought "the book would be almost ruined without it." If this story was, in fact, the same one that Twain removed from the manuscript, he did not remove it in deference to his wife's disapproval. It was carefully revised and survived at least through the stage of being typed. It is possible, even likely, that the story was still in chapter 9 when Edward Kemble was making illustrations for that portion of the book. The illustration with the caption "In the Cave" shows an engrossed and animated Jim in the process of telling Huck *something* and of Huck's expression registering a certain frightened amazement. Since the only thing Jim

Mark Twain's manuscript version of the warning to the reader that was placed at the beginning of the novel. Because of the type of paper and ink used, it is believed that he wrote the note in late June 1880 or after. The canceled note at the top of the page refers to an early working title for the novel; the uncanceled note above "Notice" is apparently a note Twain made to himself regarding Jim's dialect (Buffalo and Erie County Public Library).

says in the cave in the printed text is that the birds know when it is going to rain, it seems implausible that Kemble's illustration could refer to anything so benign as that remark.

• The manuscript discloses a few other notable surprises, as well. Though he evidently plotted his narrative according to episodes or adventures, Twain's chapter divisions in the first half of the manuscript do not correspond to those in the printed book. Also, there are a few teasing changes in the title page and in the opening statement of the book. As we have known, Twain originally had given his story the working title "Huckleberry Finn/Reported by Mark Twain," thus placing himself in a rather definite relation to his created character. The newly discovered manuscript shows that Huck's famous introduction of himself to the reader had at first been a good deal more proper and grammatical: "You will not know about me," Twain wrote; then he amended the opening statement to read "You do not know me" before he settled on the familiar "You don't know about me without you have read. . . ."

In sum, the additional manuscript evidence has caused scholars to rethink the chronology of composition, to appreciate more fully Twain's meticulous revisions, and to abandon some notions about how the book was developing in his mind, even as he wrote it. Still, the accounts that DeVoto and, later, Blair offered of the genesis and composition of *Huckleberry Finn* should not be entirely discounted. If our picture of this process is now in sharper focus than it was for them, theirs were pioneering efforts that, while in error regarding some particulars, continue to yield provocative insights into Mark Twain's creative process.

II

Walter Blair's *Mark Twain and Huck Finn* made concretely and amply clear what Bernard DeVoto had also noted—namely, that *Huckleberry Finn* had its origins and peculiar motivation in a certain sort of romantic escapism. The world was too much with Twain in the early to mid-1870s. He had tried, since his marriage in 1870, to accommodate what he took to be his wife Olivia's desires for his reform but had eventually rebelled. If he had taken up wickedness again, he did so with the overly tender conscience of a backslider; and he now pretty much confined his smoking to his study and kept his cussing out of earshot. He consumed his three old-fashioneds a day with a punctuality that might support his claim that they were good for his digestion. Twain had, like Huck in *Tom Sawyer,* decided "to smoke private and cuss private, and crowd through or bust."[16]

But other things were troubling him as well. His family and friends had been plagued by illness or death, and financial worries made his recently completed

Hartford mansion seem as much an excess as a comfort. It was at any rate not a citadel, for the Clemenses had constant visitors, some of them invited, and Twain was bothered by the burden of his enormous correspondence. He was overworked by his diversions and diverted from his work in a way that made his literary output seem depleted or inconsequential. Added to this was the fact that he had turned forty in November 1875. His friend John Hay had told him that forty was the "zenith" of a man's life, the time when one was on the "top of the hill," but Twain may have felt he was already over it.[17] He was at least weary and pestered and frustrated, and it was in this state of mind that he allowed himself to dwell on Huck Finn's autobiography.

Mark Twain had resisted Howells's urgings that he carry Tom Sawyer's story into his adulthood, and he observed in a letter on 5 July 1875 that such a book would have to be autobiographical. But he promised that by and by he would "take a boy of twelve & run him on through life (in the first person)."[18] This impulse may have combined with another he had indulged in a final, probably discarded chapter of *Tom Sawyer,* which recorded in some detail Huck's miserable and cramped life at the Widow Douglass's. The opening chapter of *Huckleberry Finn* may in fact be a rewritten version of that discarded chapter from Huck's point of view, and even as he was reading proof for *Tom Sawyer* at Quarry Farm, overlooking Elmira, in the summer of 1876, Twain had begun to fulfill his promise to his readers at the conclusion of that book to "take up the story of the younger ones again and see what sort of men and women they turned out to be."[19] If this is so, he must have realized almost immediately that he could not take Huck into his maturity. That summer he wrote 446 manuscript pages (by his mistaken reckoning he was halfway through the novel), and though it was crowded with incident his hero had aged only a few months. More importantly, he must have recognized at some level that he could better ease his own adult worries and youthful longings and speak his own dissatisfactions in the vernacular idiom of a boy who as yet had had no childhood of his own.

Quarry Farm provided the seclusion he needed to finish reading proof for *Tom Sawyer.* It provided as well the occasion and opportunity for Twain to contemplate Huck's character as he appeared in that book and to develop the suggestiveness he found there in his new novel. Huck resisted the widow's efforts to civilize him in ways that resembled Twain's own rebellion and that could be characterized as simple, boyish mischief. Huck had promised Tom in the earlier book that he would endure the widow's pestering and would stick with her so long as he could join in the high adventures Tom's proposed gang of robbers promised. But in the autobiographical story Huck is as disappointed by Tom's lies about magic and elephants and A-rabs as he had been by the widow's talk about Providence and prayer, and he likens Tom's boasts and deeds to Sunday school.

The appearance of Pap imposed a new and all too real set of circumstances on Huck. He manfully rebelled against his father (including going to school just to spite him), but after his abduction and subsequent confinement in Pap's cabin he found that it "was kind of lazy and jolly, laying off comfortable, all day, smoking and fishing, and no books nor study" (*HF*, 30).[20] However, when Pap got too handy with the hickory, and when he threatened to "stow" Huck in some distant hiding place, Huck plotted his own escape. Jackson's Island was a better retreat, but it was lonesome too, and when Twain introduced the slave Jim as a companion and the raft and the river as their home he had found an ideal image for lightening the load of frustrations that bore down upon him.

But the reintroduction of Jim committed the author to a different kind of narrative. Unlike his persona's companion the "Reverend" in "Some Rambling Notes of an Idle Excursion" (1877), or Harris in *A Tramp Abroad* (1880)—both modeled after Twain's friend, the minister Joseph Twichell—Jim resisted the role of straight man and butt for pranks. Though Jim had appeared as a comic figure in the opening chapters, the seriousness of his situation as a runaway slave forced upon his creator an immediate awareness of the complexity of his circumstance and character that only slowly dawned on Huck, and was sometimes forgotten by Twain himself.

When Huck and Tom played their tricks on the sleeping Jim in chapter 2, their joke had no grave consequences and in fact provided for a certain burlesque treatment. But Huck's prank with the dead rattlesnake in chapter 10 is potentially lethal and makes Huck sorry enough to make sure Jim does not find out that the snakebite is his fault. In chapter 15 Huck plays a second trick on him by convincing Jim that he merely dreamed that they had been separated in the fog. Again the joke backfires, for when he discloses the trick in order to have his laugh, Jim gives him a tongue-lashing that so affects Huck that he "humbles himself to a nigger."

Jim's situation provided a rationale for the two to drift along nights, idle away the time, and stay clear of people. But Jim's escape was fundamentally more serious than Huck's, and more serious than Mark Twain's own desire to escape. For Jim could endure Miss Watson's rough treatment and her constant "pecking" at him; he could even endure, as we later learn, the enforced separation from his family. But the fearful prospect of being sold down the river was something he could not bear.

Mark Twain's identification with his young hero enabled him to vent his feelings of constraint and frustration and to relieve symbolically the pressures that seemed to be hemming him in. But providing Huck with a runaway slave as companion meant that Twain was dragging along with him a portion of his own troubled conscience in a way that had social and personal implications. It forced upon Huck a sense of the "real" that the merely aggravating sham and pretense of the world at large could not, and presented him with a moral dilemma that a boy could not comprehend intellectually but might mysteriously solve emotionally. It also committed Huck to a course of action that was in absolute defiance of everything he took to be moral and correct. This he did when he cleverly deceived the slave traders in chapter 16 and was to do again more dramatically in chapter 31 when he had his crisis of conscience and decided to go to hell rather than turn Jim in.

But the introduction of Jim had other effects upon Twain's fiction as well. If it qualified and corrected the impulse toward a simple romantic escapism, Jim's various protective gestures gave to Huck an innocence and sense of belonging that a place under the widow's roof or in Tom's band of robbers could not. Jim's presence enfolded Huck in what Kenneth Burke would call a "preforensic circle"—an atmosphere of familiar attachment and mutual trust that some may prefer to call family but that is at any rate happily free of the necessity to be on the lookout for double dealing and masquerade.[21] The very qualities—canniness and deviousness—that Huck acquired in fending for himself, and that make him a precocious expert in the ways of the world, are at the same time obstacles to a recognizable childhood. Only by degrees does Huck learn how to respond to Jim's affection and care.

Mark Twain well recognized that the idyllic existence of their life on the raft was a fragile and precarious one, and if he at first indulged in a romantic escapism in fashioning his story and in establishing an image of perfect freedom, it soon became the sort of honorable romanticism and escapism Wallace Stevens identified as the foundation of artistic creation. In "The Noble Rider and the Sound of Words," Stevens remarks that "the pressure of reality is, I think, the determining factor in the artistic character of an era and, as well, the determining factor in the artistic character of an individual. The resistance to this pressure or its evasion in the case of individuals of extraordinary imagination cancels the pressure so far as those individuals are concerned."[22] Such evasiveness is not to be condemned, for the art that issues out of it enriches the world and sets out to express the human soul. And if this is true, Stevens

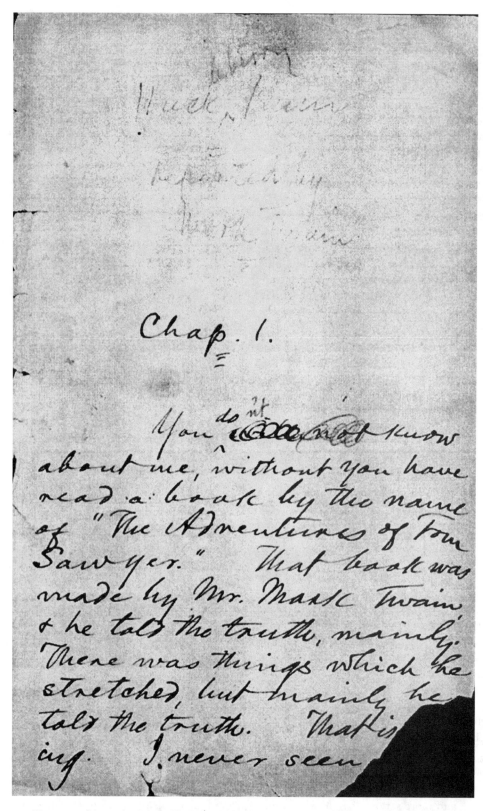

*First pages of the manuscript that Mark Twain began working on in 1876. The working title and attribution—
"Huckleberry Finn/Reported by Mark Twain"—was added at the top of the page in pencil, probably
in 1880, and was later superceded (Buffalo and Erie County Public Library).*

2

body but lied, one time or another, without it was aunt Polly, or the widow, or ~~the~~ or maybe Mary. Aunt Polly, — Tom's aunt Polly, she was — & Mary, & the widow Douglas, is all told about in that book — which is mainly a true book; with some stretchers, as I said before.

Now the way that that book winds up, is this. Tom & me found the money that the robbers hid in the cave, & it made us rich. We got six thousand dollars apiece — all gold. It was an awful sight of money when it was piled up. Well,

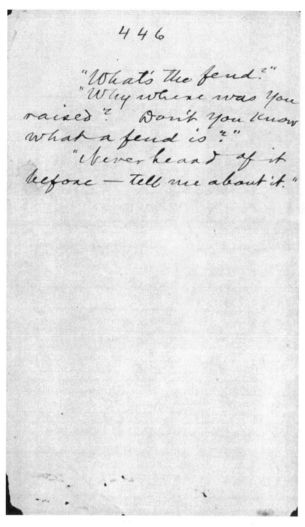

446

"What's the feud?"
"Why where was you raised? Don't you know what a feud is?"
"Never heard of it before — tell me about it."

Last manuscript page of Mark Twain's work on Adventures of Huckleberry Finn *from summer 1876. He stopped work after writing most of what became the first sixteen chapters of the novel and "pigeonholed" the manuscript for three years (Buffalo and Erie County Public Library).*

asks, "how is it possible to condemn escapism?": "The poetic process is psychologically an escapist process. The chatter about escapism is, to my way of thinking, merely common cant. My own remarks about resisting or evading the pressure of reality mean escapism, if analyzed. Escapism has a pejorative sense which it cannot be supposed that I include in the sense in which I use the word. The pejorative sense applies where the poet is not attached to reality, where the imagination does not adhere to reality, which, for my part, I regard as fundamental."[23]

Mark Twain's attachment to reality—not only the reality of his own immediate circumstance and the remembered evocations of his youth, but of the possibilities of his created characters and the cultural and political realities of life in the Mississippi valley "forty or fifty

years ago"—and his attendant resistance to the pressures of that same reality invested his fiction with a form that transcended the narrowly personal and provincial character that impelled it. The humor at the very center of the book and the laughter it provokes, as James M. Cox has observed, is itself a "relief from responsibility,"[24] but it is also Twain's artistic manner and his own peculiar form of resistance to the pressures of reality. It was not flight from fact, but a resistance to, even an evasion of the pressure of fact that prompted Twain's fiction, and this quality makes Morris's observation about the "beautiful example" of the writer's dilemma as it was eventually resolved in *Huckleberry Finn* especially acute. For Huck stands as a palpable fiction whose very existence is determined by the dogged recalcitrance of the world as it is. Or, as Roy Harvey Pearce once noted, Huck forever exists "not as an actuality but as a possibility" in a way that led Pearce to define him as the ideal type expressed in the phrase of Wallace Stevens, an "impossible possible philosopher's man."[25]

It is not likely that Twain's involvement in *Huckleberry Finn* occurred to him in anything like these terms. But his attachment to the reality of the world Huck lived and breathed in, a world Twain knew from his own experience, forced upon him in chapter 16 a decision about the narrative direction his book would take. Twain's personal experience superbly outfitted him to recall in vivid detail life along the Mississippi, all the way to New Orleans if necessary. It constituted a reservoir of memory that might be given fictional form. But his familiarity with the Ohio River (Jim's road to freedom) was insufficient to sustain his story. At any rate he let his heroes slip past Cairo in the fog and was now presented with the narrative difficulty of taking a runaway slave ever deeper into the South.

In evident frustration with this dilemma, Twain had a steamboat run over the raft, and it is at this point that Twain's imagination began to falter, for after the collision Huck scrambles on shore and, though he calls out for Jim a few times, he demonstrates no overwhelming sorrow. Instead, he is soon embarked on a new set of adventures. At the Grangerford plantation, he meets the young Buck Grangerford and Twain may have had in mind yoking these two together in a new round of "adventures" in the way he had entwined the fates of Huck and Tom Sawyer earlier. Placing Huck within the precinct of supposed gentility would afford Twain the opportunity to satirize aristocratic pretensions, cloying sentimentality, and tasteless gestures toward domestic refinement. But this impulse, if it ever existed, was momentary, for in conversation with Buck Grangerford, Huck is informed of the ongoing feud between the Grangerfords and the Shepherdsons. Huck asks Buck "What's a feud?" Clearly Twain was moving beyond such easy satirical targets as chalk fruit, gaudy art, and terrible verse and into the more serious subjects such as senseless violence, false pride, and tribal loyalties. But for some reason Twain stopped at that point in the manuscript. He would not return to it for three years.

Huck and Jim attribute their misfortune in missing the Ohio to the evil effect of the rattlesnake skin. And in a paragraph just previous to the smashup Huck addresses the reader on this point: "Anybody that don't believe, yet, that it's foolishness to handle a snake-skin, after all that that snake-skin done for us, will believe it now, if they read on and see what more it done for us" (*HF*, 130). The paragraph may allay any fears the reader might have that Jim might have died in the accident, for no further mention of Jim is made until Huck is reunited with him in the middle of chapter 18. But wrecking the raft was a gesture symbolic of Twain's own frustration with the way his story was developing, and it is by no means clear that he intended at this time to resurrect either the raft or Jim. Certainly the easiest way out of his dilemma was to get rid of Jim altogether. He could drown him or let him find his freedom or otherwise dispose of a character that was an encumbrance to Huck and his creator alike. Huck could have acquired a new companion and continued his drift downstream in a way that would have allowed Twain, through Huck, to survey Southern manners and customs with greater latitude and freedom. These were some of Twain's options, but he did not choose to exercise them.

As Henry Nash Smith observes, Twain was constantly discovering meanings in his narrative as he went along and inventing the technical methods to explore them. The gestation of *Huckleberry Finn* reveals a "dialectical interplay" in Twain, a process in which "the reach of his imagination imposed a constant strain on his technical resources, and innovations of method in turn opened up new vistas before his imagination."[26] He did not, in any event, follow the path of least resistance in developing his story, and the paradoxical situation of having a runaway slave escape into the deep South stretched his imagination to the end of its tether. Or, as Twain himself would have said, his "tank" had run dry by the end of that summer, and it would be some time before it had sufficiently filled for him to take up his story once again.

III

When Twain did return to Huck's autobiography, sometime in spring 1880, a new set of circumstances defined his state of mind, and evidently he began the boy's new adventures with little thought about reviving the romantic image of a pair of lazy drifters on the Mississippi. Apparently Twain was anxious to involve

---

"When the Tank Runs Dry"

Looking back on his career in 1906, Mark Twain described how he discovered his best approach to writing. By the time of his work on Adventures of Huckleberry Finn, *his habit of following his fancy and switching between the several projects he was working on was well established.*

It was by accident that I found out that a book is pretty sure to get tired, along about the middle, and refuse to go on with its work until its powers and its interest should have been refreshed by a rest and its depleted stock of raw materials reinforced by lapse of time. It was when I had reached the middle of "Tom Sawyer" that I made this invaluable find. At page 400 of my manuscript the story made a sudden and determined halt and refused to proceed another step. Day after day it still refused. I was disappointed, distressed, and immeasurably astonished, for I knew quite well that the tale was not finished, and I could not understand why I was not able to go on with it. The reason was very simple—my tank had run dry; it was empty; the stock of materials in it was exhausted; the story could not go on without materials; it could not be wrought out of nothing. When the manuscript had lain in a pigeon-hole two years I took it out, one day, and read the last chapter I had written. It was then I made the great discovery that when the tank runs dry you've only to leave it alone and it will fill up again, in time, while you are asleep—also while you are at work at other things, and are quite unaware that this unconscious and profitable cerebration is going on. There was plenty of material now, and the book went on and finished itself without any trouble.

Ever since then, when I have been writing a book I have pigeon-holed it without misgivings when its tank ran dry, well knowing that it would fill up again without any of my help within the next two or three years, and that then the work of completing it would be simple and easy.

—*Mark Twain in Eruption,* edited by Bernard DeVoto (New York & London: Harper, 1940), pp. 196–197

Huck in the new dramatic conflicts that had inspired him to return to the novel, and it was not until he was well into the feud episode that he paused to record his first set of working notes and there decided that the raft should only be damaged, not destroyed. In short, Twain had other things on his mind, and he resurrected his adolescent hero to give voice to his own mature convictions.

Some three years intervened between the time Twain dropped the *Huck* manuscript and the time he picked it up again. During those years he had toured

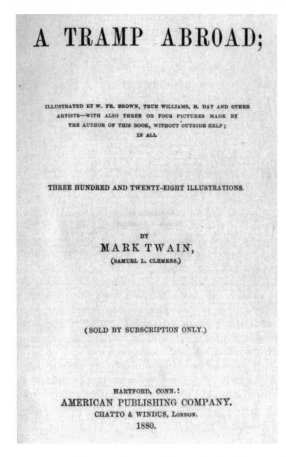

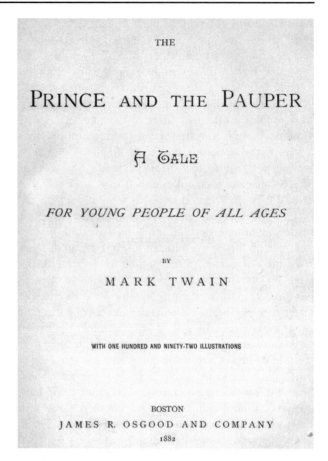

Title pages for two satirical works Mark Twain published during the seven years that passed between his beginning
Adventures of Huckleberry Finn *and its publication (Mark Twain House, Hartford, Connecticut)*

Germany, France, and Italy and had published an imaginative autobiographical account of his travels as *A Tramp Abroad;* and by 1880 he had written a good deal of the novel he would call *The Prince and the Pauper* (1882). In both books he was working out powerful, antagonistic feelings about elitist culture and aristocratic pretense.

Early in 1879 he wrote Howells that he wished he could give the "sharp satires on European life" his friend had mentioned, but he was in no mood for satire: "A man can't write successful satire except he be in a calm, judicial good-humor; whereas I *hate* travel, and I *hate* hotels, and I *hate* the opera, and I *hate* the old masters. In truth I don't ever seem to be in a good enough humor with ANYthing to satirize it; no, I want to stand up before it & *curse* it, and foam at the mouth."[27] Nevertheless he employed in *A Tramp Abroad* a satirical device adequate to his anger and sufficiently muted to preserve his humor. It was a strategy he had already employed in *Huckleberry Finn* when he had Huck attempt to comprehend and admire Emmeline's art. Whenever Huck soured on her or got annoyed with her pictures, he

would steal up to the room she had had when alive and drag out her morbid scrapbook in order to soften his antagonism toward her. By adopting in *A Tramp Abroad* a persona who was rather more apt to question his own feelings of astonishment or revulsion when confronted by senseless or violent European customs (as, for example, the student duels in Germany) than to express his contempt for the customs themselves, Twain could convey the full measure of his contempt by ironically cursing his own lack of sophistication. And in *The Prince and the Pauper* he found that he could satisfy his immediate impulse toward strong satire without risking adverse reaction by making his subject historically remote. As early as 1872 Twain had wanted to write a satire of English institutions, but his subsequent travels to England had softened him toward the British. His reading in English history reawakened his anger however, and the result was a book that expressed his deepest dissatisfactions and at the same time could be advertised as "A Tale for Young People of All Ages."

Both of these fictional strategies entered into *Huckleberry Finn* when he began the Grangerford-Shepherdson

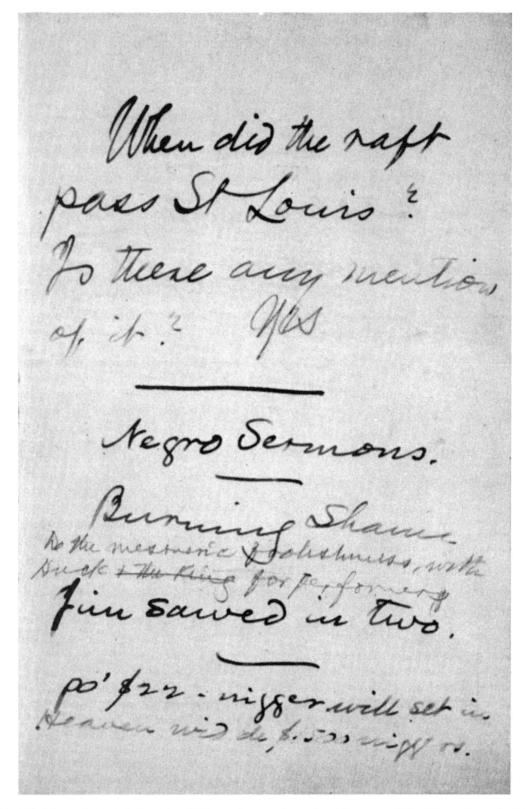

Page from Mark Twain's notes that he probably made in 1880 when he returned to work on Adventures of Huckleberry Finn *after "pigeonholing"*
the manuscript for some three years. He is reminding himself of what he has covered and indicating possible directions for the story
(Mark Twain Papers, The Bancroft Library, University of California, Berkeley)

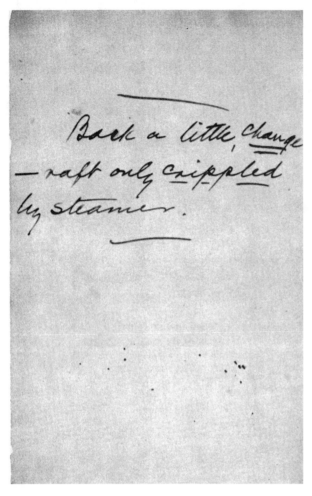

*Page from Mark Twain's working notes, probably written in 1880,
indicating his decision not to let Huck and Jim's raft be
destroyed by the steamship (Mark Twain Papers,
The Bancroft Library, University of
California, Berkeley)*

yet represent, more generally, an American version of the aristocracy that, through his recent reading about the French Revolution, Twain had come to despise to the extent that he might be described (as he in fact did describe himself a few years later) as a "Sansculotte."[28]

As Michael Davitt Bell has observed, Huck Finn exists as both a literary character and a literary device, and to collapse this distinction often results in unnecessary critical confusions because the same character is often made to serve different artistic purposes.[29] Throughout most of the feud chapters Twain used Huck as a satirical device designed to establish his own strong feelings through his narrator's naive reactions. But when Huck, in clipped and defensive understatement, reported on his reaction to Buck Grangerford's killing, Twain was dramatizing the traumatic effects of violence on his created character.

By the end of chapter 18, however, he had reinstalled Huck and Jim on the raft, where things were once again "free and easy and comfortable." He opened the next chapter with his lyrical description of how they put in the time on the river. These evocations of idyllic drift, as Walter Blair points out, could have been written at almost any time during the period from 1880 to 1883. For whenever he was vexed by the pressures of reality, Twain allowed his imagination to dwell on the possibilities of escape and seclusion. But during most of the second phase of composition he had been more aggressively ironic in his treatment of the bugbears of his imagination: aristocratic values, cloying sentimentality, and unnecessary violence.

This sort of control over his material signals a shift in Twain's creative process as it developed alongside the accumulating pages of the manuscript. In the first phase of composition he had found the means to project his own complex feelings of frustration into his created character in a way that required only the simplest explanation of their causes. A whippoorwill's song might convey his loneliness, and a stiff collar or the widow's "pecking," his feelings of repression. But when he returned to the manuscript Twain had bigger fish to fry, and the result was that though he still identified with him, he absorbed Huck into himself rather than the other way round. He made his young vernacular hero serve the mature purposes of his creator. In a word, Twain's manner and motivation had progressed from those of an escapist writer to those of a professionally skillful one, one whose imaginative impulses were the same but whose technical means were more rational and whose artistic effects more calculated.

chapters. Twain's sardonic response toward the sentimental "obituary" verse of the day found an outlet in Huck's undoubting admiration for Emmeline Grangerford's poetic gifts. The same is true of Huck's description of the Grangerford house itself. And Twain's own mordantly satirical purposes were only thinly disguised by Huck's uncomprehending curiosity about the origin and nature of the feud itself. Huck's naiveté adequately conveyed the author's solid contempt for such timid and senseless attachment to prejudice. In Huck's eyes the tribes of Shepherdson and Grangerford are a "handsome lot of quality" (*HF*, 144) whose possessions and sentiments alike participate in an order of cultivation and gentility quite beyond his understanding. In Twain's, they both epitomize the sham and pretense that Twain (now an ardent Republican) had come to localize in the South and

The same imaginative process obtained when he wrote the king and duke chapters, though the motivating circumstances were somewhat different. Twain's finances were always complicated and his extravagant expenditures and investments in the early 1880s bordered on caprice. Twain's financial worries were legitimate enough but he was constitutionally suspicious anyway and had come to believe he was being defrauded by all sorts of cheats and con-men. Something of this suspiciousness went into the creation of his famous rascals, the king and the duke, whose diverse talents as confidence men adequately symbolized the various cheats, from plumbers to publishers, that Twain was convinced were attempting to hoodwink him. And by having these characters adopt titles of royalty Twain could continue his burlesque of aristocratic values.

The king and duke are composite figures, partly inspired by Twain's "recollection's vaults" (*HF*, 178) and partly by present acquaintance. As he had done in the feud chapters, in fashioning his homespun picaros he also drew upon the reading in Southwestern humorists he was doing for the volume that would eventually appear as *Mark Twain's Library of Humor* (1888). The king and duke were so characterized by humbug, chicanery, and pretense that they became objects of contempt and figures of fun. But as fictional devices this pair provided their creator with a double opportunity. He could satirize *in them* such despicable or laughable qualities as false eloquence, venality, backbiting, deception, or invented claims to privilege; and he could satirize *through them* the ignorant, credulous, or sentimental victims who were their prey.

Mark Twain's rogues also solved a narrative problem for the author: for they enabled him to continue to move Huck and Jim further downstream. They effectively commandeered the raft and, by printing up a reward poster for Jim, devised a way to travel daytime and make temporary excursions onshore to ply their trade. This, in turn, provided Huck with the opportunity to describe loathsome backwater behavior and to witness the Boggs shooting. By 1880 Twain had begun to develop a general bitterness that he would succinctly express as a larger contempt for the "damned human race," and by freeing Huck to wander about town and observe the manners and customs of a representative cross section of humanity Twain's scorn could be delivered broadcast.

IV

In his rendering of the Bricksville loafers and the Boggs shooting in chapter 21 Twain had already begun to dramatize his disdain of the common man and woman. When he settled down in Elmira in June 1883

to finish his book, he began with Colonel Sherburn's verbal attack on the mob. Twain had prepared his readers for a lynching and had several times in his working notes made references to such a scene. But he had also conveyed more subtly in chapter 21 his distrust of the mob, and by the time he came to write chapter 22, his contempt for the crowd outstripped his contempt for the Southern aristocrat.[30] Colonel Sherburn, who had lived in the North and had been raised in the South, spoke the author's own convictions about the cowardice of the "average" man in a way that made him as much a hero in chapter 22 as he had been a villain in chapter 21.

Life on the Mississippi and *Huckleberry Finn* had a cross-pollinating effect upon one another. The Huck manuscript provided germs for development of certain portions of *Life on the Mississippi*, and Twain had lifted the raft episode from it and put it in chapter 3 of his "standard" work on the Mississippi. In turn, Twain's return to the river in 1882 and his writing about the modern South had stimulated certain youthful memories that might pay dividends in *Huck*. But nostalgia had combined with outrage, and Twain had excised from *Life on the Mississippi* two chapters of strident social criticism and had generally toned down his more virulent attacks upon the South. The intensity of his anti-Southern feeling remained, however, and in fact may have been exacerbated by this same restraint. In any event the author allowed Sherburn, rather than Huck, to speak his contempt in the scene that began the last phase of composition of the novel.

Mark Twain soon resumed Huck's persona, however, and his methods of satire become more familiar. He concluded the chapter with Huck at the circus, where he worries over the drunken bareback rider. The comedy of this episode was meant to comment upon the seriousness of the Boggs episode in the previous chapter and is one of the more conspicuous examples of satirical pairings of incidents that occur throughout the book. But the development of the circus scene as a counterstatement to the Boggs episode points to the workmanlike attitude Twain brought to his book that summer.

By 1883 *Adventures of Huckleberry Finn* had become a commercial venture, and it is difficult to tell whether inspiration or simple determination supplied the kind of motivation that allowed Twain to produce so many pages of manuscript so quickly and, by his own account, so effortlessly.[31] He had been disappointed by the sales of *The Prince and the Pauper* and *Life on the Mississippi* and, soon after he finished *Huckleberry Finn*, decided to publish the book himself under the imprint of Chas. L. Webster & Co. The last phase of composition betrays something of the practical attitude of a professional nov-

408

447

Chap.

"Well," says Buck, "a feud is this way. A man has a quarrel with another man, & kills him; then that other man's brother kills him; then the other brothers, on both sides, goes for one another. Then the cousins chip in — & by & by everybody's killed off, & there ain't no more

The first and last pages of more than two hundred pages of manuscript, written in purple ink on wove paper, that Mark Twain composed in summer 1880, corresponding to what became the middle of chapter 18 through chapter 21. The penciled note at the bottom of page 663—"No, let them lynch him"—shows that Twain was uncertain as to how to resolve the Sherburn episode (Buffalo and Erie County Public Library).

663

treated him.

Well, by & by somebody
said Sherburne ought
to be lynched. In about a
minute everybody was
saying it; so away they
went, mad & yelling,
& snatching down every
clothes line they come to,
to do the hanging with.
But they was too late. Sherburn's friends had got
him away, long ago.

elist intent on finishing a book in which he had invested considerable time and energy. At any rate Twain pushed toward his conclusion and most days found the going easy.

In the last half of *Huckleberry Finn* the author was able to make the most of his invention. He had recorded in his working notes a few episodes he wanted to develop (the circus rider incident and the obscene Royal Nonesuch were included, but fortunately Twain's desire to have Huck and Jim and Tom explore the countryside on an elephant remained unfulfilled), and he had made elaborate notes for the evasion narrative. But this second half is remarkable for its relative lack of incident. The improvisations of the Wilks funeral and the evasion at least are stretched to the point of artificiality and seem to have less to do with resolving the inner tensions of the author than with delivering broad and popular comedy. These episodes had been prepared for in advance, and the notes show that the evasion had been planned with a good deal of calculation. But the notes also show that Twain carefully reread the portion of the manuscript that he had already completed, and the most interesting and memorable events are those that drew upon the emotional attitudes he had established in the earlier portions and now contemplated and probed for their implications.

The proletarian sympathies Twain had acquired a few years before persisted, despite his distrust of the mob, and they became localized and found a certain focus in his attitude toward Jim. Twain's last group of working notes reveal an interest in developing Jim's character more fully. He twice reminded himself that Jim has a wife and two children and anticipated the moment in chapter 23 where Jim grieves because he believes he will never see his family again and, in turn, recalls his unintended cruelty to his infant daughter, whom he discovered to be deaf and dumb. Jim's mourning makes Huck believe that Jim "cared just as much for his people as white folks does for their'n. It don't seem natural, but I reckon it's so" (*HF*, 201). This incident immediately follows, and therefore comments on, Huck's description of the conduct of "Henry the Eight," who used to marry a new wife every day and "chop her head off" the next morning. And it comments as well on the feigned deaf and dumbness of the king in the next chapter.

Mark Twain also wrote in his working notes: "Back yonder, Huck reads & tells about monarchies & kings &c. So Jim stares when he learns the rank of these 2."[32] Again, Twain was preparing to use Jim's reaction rather than Huck's as the vehicle for his satire, and the "back yonder" became the interpolated

chapter 14, where Huck describes the "style" kings and dukes put on. The only king Jim is familiar with is King Solomon, whom he knows "by de back" (*HF*, 95). Solomon's apparent insensitivity regarding the child he was going to chop in two derives, so Jim believes, from the way he was "raised" and his circumstance. A man, such as Jim, "dat's got on'y one er two chillen" cannot afford to be wasteful of them, but Solomon, who has some "five million," may treat them as expendable items of property.

This debate apparently satisfied the author's intention rather telegraphically recorded in another note—"Solomon with child by de hine laig."[33] And Huck and Jim's debate about why a Frenchman "doan' talk like a man" (which concludes the chapter) probably derived from a stray remark Twain had written at the end of chapter 20: "I found Jim had been trying to get him [the king] to talk French, so he could hear what it was like" (*HF*, 176).

Chapter 14 was written separately, and possibly after Twain had taken his story through "Chapter the Last." In any event it not only prepares the reader for Jim's reaction to the king and duke but gives to a slave a native intelligence, a righteous indignation, and a vernacular eloquence that had not been fully dramatized before. Moreover, Jim can get riled by the example of Solomon as a man who seemingly treats his children and wives as chattels, and who would rather live in the confusion of a "bo'd'n house" than, as Jim believes a truly wise man would, "buil' a biler-factry" (*HF*, 94). Jim's reaction to Solomon is the reaction of a slave to the Southern mentality, which immorally prefers the chaos of a "harem" of kept servants to sensible industrialization.

If chapter 14 was written out of the felt necessity to add to the picture Twain had drawn of Jim, Huck's recollection of Jim's self-sacrifice and affection in chapter 31 offers a consolidated picture of Jim's generosity of spirit:

[I] got to thinking over our trip down the river; and I see Jim before me, all the time, in the day, and in the night-time, sometimes moonlight, sometimes storms, and we a floating along, talking, and singing, and laughing. But somehow I couldn't seem to strike no places to harden me against him, but only the other kind. I'd see him standing my watch on top of his'n, stead of calling me—so I could go on sleeping; and see him how glad he was when I come back out of the fog; and when I come to him again in the swamp, up there where the feud was; and such-like times; and would always call me honey, and pet me, and do everything he could think of for me, and how good he always was; and at last I struck the time I saved him by telling the men we had small-pox aboard, and

160

They swarmed up the street, towards
Sherburn's house, a-whooping
& raging
& yelling, like Injuns, & everything had to clear the way or get
run over & tromped to mush
& it was awful to see. Children
was heeling it ahead of the mob,
screaming & trying to get out
of the way; & every window
along the road was full of
women's heads, & there was
nigger boys in every tree, &
bucks & wenches looking over
every fence; & as soon as the
mob would get nearly to
them they would break & skaddle

First page of the manuscript Mark Twain returned to in summer 1883 after a second three-year hiatus from sustained work on the novel, picking up the story at the mob's attempt to lynch Colonel Sherburn. During the interim, the first 663 pages of the manuscript had been typed, so the new manuscript began with "160" to follow a 159-page typescript (Buffalo and Erie County Public Library).

Out of the Pigeonhole Once More

After completing Life on the Mississippi, *Mark Twain evidently acquired a reinvigorated interest in returning to Huck's "Autobiography." In this excerpt from his 20 July 1883 letter to Howells, he reported on his progress.*

I haven't piled up MS so in years as I have done since we came here to the farm three weeks and a half ago. Why, it's like old times, to step right into the study, damp from the breakfast table, and sail right in and sail right on, the whole day long, without thought of running short of stuff or words. I wrote 4000 words today and I touch 3000 and upwards pretty often, and don't fall below 2600 any working day. And when I get fagged out, I lie abed a couple of days and read and smoke, and then go it again for 6 or 7 days. I have finished one small book, and am away along in a big one that I half-finished two or three years ago. I expect to complete it in a month or six weeks or two months more. And I shall like it, whether anybody else does or not. It's a kind of companion to Tom Sawyer. There's a raft episode from it in second or third chapter of Life on the Mississippi. . . .

—Selected Mark Twain-Howells letters, 1872–1910,
pp. 212–213

The next day he wrote a similarly positive letter to his brother Orion: "I haven't had such booming working-days for many years. I am piling up manuscript in a really astonishing way. I believe I shall complete, in two months, a book which I have been fooling over for 7 years. This summer it is no more trouble to me to write than it is to lie."

In this excerpt from a 22 August 1883 letter to Howells, Twain announced that he had finished the book except for revisions.

How odd it seems, to sit down to write a letter with the feeling that you've got time to do it. But I'm done with work, for this season, and so have got time. I've done two seasons' work in one, and haven't anything left to do, now, but revise. I've written eight or nine hundred MS pages in such a brief space of time that I mustn't name the number of days; *I* shouldn't believe it myself, and of course couldn't expect you to. I used to restrict myself to 4 or 5 hours a day and 5 days in the week, but this time I've wrought from breakfast till 5.15 p.m. six days in the week; and once or twice I smouched a Sunday when the boss wasn't looking. Nothing is half so good as literature hooked on Sunday, on the sly.

—Selected Mark Twain-Howells letters, 1872–1910,
p. 214

The revisions Twain referred to may or may not have entailed the interpolated Walter Scott *and "King Sollermun" episodes (the second half of chapter 12 through chapters 13 and 14 in the published novel). It is clear, at any rate, that those two episodes were written separately.*

---

he was so grateful, and said I was the best friend old Jim ever had in the world, and the *only* one he's got now (*HF*, 269–270).

It is this catalog of recollections that decides Huck on going to hell rather than turning Jim in. One can easily imagine that (as he studied the completed portion of the manuscript, and as the working notes to some extent reveal) Twain similarly recollected the accumulated examples of Jim's humanity and generosity of spirit and discovered in him a fit emblem for the best there is in the common lot, one for whom one might even risk everlasting fire. In this sense Jim plays a role analogous to the peasant Gerasim in Tolstoy's *The Death of Ivan Ilych*—a figure of such warm and authentic sympathies that in the midst of misery and doubt he inspires a mystical faith in human possibility and, by his example, urges a revaluation of conventional political pieties.

In the tangle of contrived narrative improbabilities Huck's decision to go to hell stands out as the most improbable event of all. For it gathers together in a single dramatic moment the implications of the fiction Twain was creating and runs absolutely counter to what he believed to be the incontestable facts of the world. But unlike those improbable details and incidents designed to prolong or resolve dramatic conflicts—such as the broken arm of William Wilks, the mystery of the tattoo, the appearance of Tom Sawyer with his ever proliferating plans for the evasion, or the implausible guilty conscience of the widow that resulted in her freeing Jim before her death—Huck's decision to go to hell is not mere contrivance. Rather it is a fiction that affirms a certain faith in the possibility of human freedom and nobility and runs counter to Twain's announced cynicism.

By the time the author settled down to finish his novel in the summer of 1883, he had formed a set of generalized convictions and had embraced the deterministic philosophic position he had articulated a few months earlier in "What Is Happiness?"—a paper he had delivered at the Monday Evening Club. The conclusions he drew in this lecture, he later recalled, were straightforward and absolute: there is no such thing as personal merit; man is merely a "machine automatically functioning"; "no man ever does a duty for duty's sake"; "there is no such thing as free will and no such thing as self-sacrifice."[34] Some years before Twain had privately recorded similar beliefs in the margins of his copy of W. E. H. Lecky's *History of European Morals,* and his subsequent reading and experience had only fortified those convictions. Twain's philosophic opinions had to some extent always been present in *Huck,* but in this last phase of composition they entered into the novel at some expense to narrative credibility.

In *Life on the Mississippi* Twain had recalled the emotional quality of youth as "a time when the happenings of life were not the natural and logical results of great general laws, but of special orders, and were freighted with very precise and distinct purposes—partly punitive in intent, partly admonitory; and usually local in application."[35] At odd moments Twain had abandoned this quality in the last half of the novel and allowed Huck to speak with a latitude of experience and moral authority beyond his years and beyond his immediate interests. He permitted him to conclude on the cruelty of the "human race" and make comments about the "average" man or woman (something Colonel Sherburn could do more plausibly because he had traveled in the North and lived in the South and had acquired the cynicism of age and experience); and he had had Huck make such observations as "kings is kings" or "Take them all around, they're a mighty ornery lot. It's the way they're raised" (*HF*, 200).

One could not say that Huck had become worldly wise or jaded, but his commentary sometimes tends toward general observation at the expense of local assertion. The qualities of stupefaction and surprise that he had before displayed and that served as satirical strategy are frequently shifted onto Jim, and the particularity of experience is too often reserved for the purely technical virtuosity of the humbug of the duke and dauphin or the childish pranks of the evasion.

Everything Twain rationally thought to be true militated against Jim's recorded self-sacrifice and Huck's dramatic decision to help him to freedom. But these were fictions that mysteriously commanded belief, and they were latent in the emotional attitudes Twain had established in earlier portions of the novel. Twain himself recalled, in 1895, that Huck's first bout with his conscience in chapter 16 represented a contest between a "sound heart" and a "deformed conscience" and that "conscience suffers defeat."[36] Huck's white lie to the slave traders in that

chapter suggested the more affecting decision in chapter 31, and the latter is more powerful because Huck actively chooses what he takes to be an everlasting damnation in the "bad place" Miss Watson had so vividly described to him.

The evasion chapters undoubtedly compromise the purity of Huck's purpose, but they do not entirely overthrow it. And Twain may have anticipated the erosion of Huck's moral dignity in those chapters where Tom Sawyer superintends their high-jinks. In any event he seems to have written the interpolated *Walter Scott* episode just before he began the Phelps chapters. DeVoto suggested that the primary motivation for inserting this episode was to provide Huck with the history books he reads to Jim.[37] This may be so, but it would have been much simpler to have included those books with the "truck" they took off the floating house in chapter 9. Blair argues, more plausibly, that Twain had his eye out for opportunities to repeat "motifs with variations" and that this scene of a real robber gang provided a dramatic parallel to Tom Sawyer's gang of robbers in chapter 3.[38] Certainly the name of the steamboat evokes an image of the romanticism so characteristic of Tom. But the same episode also provides a parallel to the evasion scene, and with a significant variation.

Huck himself invites the comparison when he rebukes Jim's hesitancy to board the wreck and reminds him that Tom would never miss the chance for such an adventure. When they find that they are trapped on the *Walter Scott* with real murderers, however, Huck instantly recognizes that this is no time for "sentimentering" (*HF*, 86). After he and Jim escape in the gang's boat, Huck begins to worry about the men and to hatch a plot that will get them out of their scrape. His resolution and plan are acted out with efficiency and dispatch and are happily free of the romantic impulse. This scene provides a dramatic contrast to the evasion episode. Huck may call the experience an "adventure," but his natural sympathy for the other Jim (the murderer Jim Turner) and his practical attempt to rescue him and the others demonstrate Huck's native decisiveness, uncorrupted by the influence of Tom Sawyer. The evasion in its way is as "mixed-up en splendid" (*HF*, 340) as Jim says it is, but Twain had to some extent preserved the purity of Huck's sound heart by dramatizing his reaction to the moral emergency aboard the *Walter Scott.*

The final two chapters of *Huckleberry Finn* hastily tie up the loose ends of Twain's narrative. Jim learns that he had been set free in Miss Watson's will two months earlier. The mystery of Tom's cooperation in Jim's rescue is explained by the fact that

The last pages of the manuscript of Adventures of Huckleberry Finn, *finished in summer 1883 (Buffalo and Erie County Public Library)*

787

me & sivilize me & I
can't stand it, I been there
before.

The End, yours truly Huck Finn.

he thought it great fun to set a free nigger free. And Huck learns that Pap was the dead man aboard the floating house. The end of *Huckleberry Finn* is inexcusably happy–Jim owns himself, Huck is rid of Pap and free to use his six thousand dollars to sponsor a new adventure in the Indian Territory, and the bullet Tom received in the leg is now proudly worn around his neck for all the world to see. But Twain concluded on the same note of resistance to the pressures of civilization that had been in the book from the beginning, and by having Huck light out for the Territory ahead of his comrades, he promised his readers and committed himself to a continuation of their adventures in another book.

For the next seven months Twain worked on several projects and may have actually begun to write his promised sequel in *Tom and Huck among the Indians;* at least he did some reading for it. But much of his time was spent preparing his manuscript for publication. He made many revisions and did some rewriting, nearly always with an artistic intent rather than out of deference to contemporary literary taste or personal squeamishness, and by mid-April 1884 mailed off the manuscript. He carefully supervised E. W. Kemble's illustrations for the book and Webster's promotional campaign to sell it by subscription, and he embarked on a lecture tour with George Washington Cable, in part as an effort to promote sales of the new novel. He also had to put up with the aggravation of the technical problems of supplying his book with a heliotype of a bust of himself as a frontispiece[39] and the obscene joke of some mischief-maker who had defaced the plate of Kemble's illustration of Huck standing before Aunt Sally and Uncle Silas. But at last the book was complete. It was published in England and Canada in December 1884 and in the United States the following February.

V

The seven years' genesis of *Huckleberry Finn* eventuated in a book that was more hopeful than its happy ending might suggest. For it made potent, and in a thoroughly original and unstarched idiom, a drama of human possibility that transcended its narrowly human origins. "Give us a new work of genius of any kind," wrote Willa Cather in an open letter in defense of "escapism" in literature, "and if it is alive, and fired with some more vital feeling than contempt, you will see how automatically the old and false makes itself air before the new and true."[40] *Huck Finn* is brimming with contempt, or at least feelings of anger and frustration, but it is also alive with the feeling and the fiction of human possibility.

The novel made vivid an original image, or several images really, of nobility in tatters: The absurd image of Jim in a dress forgoing his chance for freedom in order to nurse his wounded tormentor, Tom Sawyer. Of Huck sitting in a wigwam choosing between everlasting and everlasting. Or of Huck and Jim together, forming what Twain once called a "community of misfortune,"[41] floating down the Mississippi River on a hot summer night. And there is some evidence that Twain wanted to highlight those same qualities.

Three of Twain's significant revisions, as Blair pointed out, signal the final emphasis the author wanted to give to his book. He trimmed the excessively rhetorical eloquence from Colonel Sherburn's speech and made it more colloquial and therefore more local and authentic. He supplemented the scene of Jim's homesickness with the passages that disclose the man's sense of regret for the way he had treated his daughter. And he added enough to Huck's struggle with his conscience to rid the scene of any tinge of burlesque and to give it the sort of memorable emphasis it has in the printed book.

The attempt to establish such nobility on so slight and improbable a foundation as the adventures of a barely literate and necessarily suspicious boy provided Twain with (to borrow the language of Henry James) "as interesting and as beautiful a difficulty as you could wish."[42] The difficulties were unsought, however, and the solutions were sometimes improvised or finessed. And there are gaps in the narrative logic of the book big enough to throw a dog through. But the novel is sustained by its rendering of life rather than by a formal narrative coherence, and the manifold impulses that produced it call into question the desire of critics to find a unified intention or an artistic wholeness in works of the imagination. The enduring interest of the book derives from its quiet affirmations rather than its satire, however brilliant.

"There is no element more conspicuously absent from contemporary poetry than nobility," observed Wallace Stevens in a passage that, coincidentally, has a special relevance to *Huckleberry Finn:*

> There is no element that poets have sought after, more curiously and more piously, certain of its obscure existence. Its voice is one of the inarticulate voices which it is their business to overhear and to record. The nobility of rhetoric is, of course, a lifeless nobility. . . . For the sensitive poet, conscious of negations, nothing is more difficult than the affirmations of nobility and yet there is nothing that he requires of himself more persistently, since in them

and in their kind, alone, are to be found those sanctions that are the reasons for his being and for that occasional ecstasy, or ecstatic freedom of the mind, which is his special privilege.[43]

That Twain's cynicism and skepticism made him supremely "conscious of negations" is a familiar truth. That he experienced in the writing of his masterpiece an "occasional ecstasy, or ecstatic freedom of mind," scarcely less so. Something of that ecstasy must have derived from the satisfaction that came from finding, in the tangle of his material and the meanness he knew to be the world, the room to affirm as well as condemn. For Wallace Stevens, and one may suppose for Twain as well, the capacity to affirm nobility as a permanent fiction forever at odds with the contingency of fact has less to do with artistic freedom than it does with the power of the imagination over events. "It is the violence from within that protects us from a violence from without. It is the imagination pressing back against the pressure of reality. It seems, in the last analysis, to have something to do with our self-preservation; and that, no doubt, is why the expression of it, the sound of its words, helps us to live our lives."[44]

In the making of *Huckleberry Finn,* and virtually from the beginning, Twain had resisted the pressures of reality by the efforts of his imagination and in a voice he eventually made his own. Nothing about the book commanded Twain's more minute attention than the sounds of its words. His working notes disclose how exactingly he had overheard and recorded the otherwise inarticulate voices of his created characters, and even if we did not have Twain's "Explanatory" to tell us that the book is a vernacular tour de force, the novel itself shows how absolutely he earned the evident pride he took in its language. But the language of the novel, the angle of its vision, the ample reach of its imagining, did more than retrieve the life of the Mississippi valley, now more than a hundred and fifty years past. In part, the achievement of the *Adventures of Huckleberry Finn* is revealed in its creative vision, for it showed how completely Twain might imagine things as bad as they can be, and better than they are. The book provided its author, as it has its readers, with a means to resist the pressures from without. It is a novel that, finally, may have to do with something as improbable as self-preservation.

—revised from *Writing the American Classics,* edited by
James Barbour and Tom Quirk (Chapel Hill:
University of North Carolina Press,
1990), pp. 79–105

1. Cather, "Preface" to *Alexander's Bridge,* vi.
2. Ibid.
3. Ibid., ix.
4. *Twain-Howells Letters,* 1:144.
5. Morris, *The Territory Ahead,* 88.
6. Ibid., 84.
7. Morris, "If Fiction Is So Smart, Why Are We So Stupid?" 182.
8. See DeVoto, "Noon and the Dark," in *Mark Twain at Work,* 45–82.
9. Ibid., 69.
10. This essay, as any essay having to do with the composition of *Huckleberry Finn* must be, is deeply indebted to the work of Walter Blair. The indebtedness here is extensive enough to omit elaborate documentation; unless otherwise indicated, discussion of the physical evidence of composition, the state of the author's mind at the time of writing, and the several influences on the book derive in some measure from Blair's "When Was *Huckleberry Finn* Written?" or *Mark Twain and Huck Finn.* A more recent and succinct accounting of the composition that takes into account evidence not available to Blair is Victor Fischer's "Note on the Text" in the 2002 California paperback edition of the novel, pp. 549–561. From the substantial body of scholarship and criticism related in some way to the composition of *Huckleberry Finn* the following might be profitably consulted as well: Budd, "Introduction" to the facsimile edition of the manuscript of *Huckleberry Finn;* Ensor, "The Contributions of Charles Webster and Albert Bigelow Paine to *Huckleberry Finn*"; Krause, "Twain's Method and Theory of Composition"; Pauly, "Directed Readings"; and Smith, *Mark Twain,* 113–137.
11. The complete working notes are published in DeVoto, *Mark Twain at Work,* 63–78, passim, and in the 2003 University of California edition of *Huckleberry Finn,* 461–516. Blair made still other refinements on DeVoto's interpretation of the working notes. Group B of the notes consists of only two manuscript pages. Blair concluded, on the basis of the kind of paper used, that B-1 also belongs to the period when Twain wrote Group A. Page B-2 was written separately and probably belonged to a series of notations the author made while he was going through the portion of the manuscript written in 1876. Hence page B-2 probably also belongs to the period when Twain wrote Group A. Blair agreed with DeVoto that Group C was likely written in the summer of 1883. This last group includes reminders about what Twain had already written and suggestions for possible narrative development, only a few of which are realized in the novel.
12. DeVoto, *Mark Twain at Work,* 67.
13. *Twain-Howells Letters,* 1:438.
14. I have given a conjectural account of the significance of this episode in "'Learning a Nigger to Argue.'"
15. Blair, "When Was *Huckleberry Finn* Written?" 24.
16. *Tom Sawyer,* ed. Gerber and Baender, 259.
17. Reported in Blair, *Mark Twain and Huck Finn,* 88.
18. *Twain-Howells Letters,* 1:92.
19. *Tom Sawyer,* ed. Gerber and Baender, 260.
20. *Huckleberry Finn,* ed. Victor Fischer and Lin Salamo, with the late Victor Blair, 30. Cited hereafter as *HF.*
21. Burke uses the term in *Attitudes toward History,* 209, and elsewhere. He discusses the same concept under the label "inner circle" in "The Relation Between Literature and Science." A passage in that essay is coinciden-

tally pertinent to my later discussion of Twain's shift from an escapist writer to one who discovered he could embody more abstract thought in a work of regionalism: "The inner circle is essentially the childhood level of experience. Such a thought makes one realize the special appeal that 'regionalism' may have for the poetic mind. For regionalism tends simply to extend the perspective of intimacy and immediacy that one gets in childhood. In childhood one does not think by concepts. . . . The poet is happiest in handling material of this sort. In his scrupulous childhood, he evolves a structure of meanings, all highly intimate and personalized. And as he confronts 'new matter,' the abstract, impersonal, political, and economic matter of adult experience, his earlier integration is threatened. Some poets, when encountering this threat, tend to 'freeze' at the earlier intimate level. They continue perfecting their personalized perspective, simply ignoring the matter that lies outside its circle. I think that we get in uncritical forms of regionalism an aspect of this tendency. Whatever abstractness in the outer critical-conceptual circle they cannot humanize, they reject" (166–167). The integrations of childhood and adult experience in *Huckleberry Finn* prove that Twain did not "freeze" in the creation of his book, though the same integration may have cost him a certain narrative credibility.

22. Stevens, "The Noble Rider and the Sound of Words," 22–23.

23. Ibid., 30–31.

24. Cox, *Mark Twain: The Fate of Humor,* 44.

25. Pearce, "Yours Truly, Huck Finn," 323.

26. Smith, *Mark Twain,* 113.

27. *Twain-Howells Letters,* 1:248–249.

28. Ibid., 2:595.

29. See Bell, "Mark Twain, 'Realism,' and *Huckleberry Finn,*" 50.

30. For a discussion of the significance of the crowd in *Huckleberry Finn* see Mills, *The Crowd in American Literature,* 66–75.

31. In August 1883 Twain wrote Howells how delicious his productivity was, confessing that "nothing is half so good as literature hooked on a Sunday on the sly" (*Twain-Howells Letters,* 1:438).

32. DeVoto, *Mark Twain at Work,* 75.

33. Ibid.

34. Quoted in Blair, *Mark Twain and Huck Finn,* 337.

35. *Life on the Mississippi,* 337.

36. Quoted in Blair, *Mark Twain and Huck Finn,* 143.

37. DeVoto, *Mark Twain at Work,* 62.

38. Blair, *Mark Twain and Huck Finn,* 347.

39. For an account of Twain's decision to include this heliotype and the possible reasons for it see Budd, "'A Noble Roman Aspect.'"

40. Cather, "Escapism," 26.

41. Quoted in Blair, *Mark Twain and Huck Finn,* 143.

42. James, "Preface" to the New York edition of *Portrait of a Lady,* 51.

43. Stevens, "The Noble Rider and the Sound of Words," 35.

44. Ibid., 36.

This essay was written when only the second half of the manuscript was known to exist.

Adventures of Huckleberry Finn
The Growth from Manuscript to Novel
Victor Doyno

In the Rare Book offices of the Buffalo and Erie County Library, behind two doors of a double safe, the partial manuscript of *Adventures of Huckleberry Finn* rests, compact and well preserved. Over six hundred and eighty-seven pages (circa 21.3 by 13.5 centimeters each), usually with sixteen to eighteen lines per page, survive. The sheets reveal numerous legible cancellations, interlinear insertions, and, occasionally, large block insertions on the reverse sides. Some sheets appear to be early drafts, and some must be copy sheets, presumably transcriptions of Twain's complicated revisions of earlier, simpler versions. Renumbered sheets and inserted sheets indicate reorderings and expansions. Significant changes within the manuscript and between the manuscript and the first edition make this material a complex, fascinating record of Twain's

Mark Twain at his desk, circa 1884 (Mark Twain Project, The Bancroft Library, University of California, Berkeley)

creative process and so allow us to observe closely his artistic practices.

Subsequent generations of scholars and critics have been grateful to James Fraser Gluck for securing this national treasure from Mark Twain, and the manuscript has of course been studied to explore several mysteries.[1] Did Olivia Clemens bowdlerize the artistic achievement of her creative husband? No evidence exists in the manuscript to convict her of censorship. Walter Blair has examined the manuscript in his determination of the dates of composition. DeLancey Ferguson and Sidney Krause, among others, pointed out that Twain revised with artistic rather than "popular" considerations uppermost in mind. The publication of the facsimile edition, edited by Louis J. Budd, now offers the fascinating material to any inquiring mind.

Can any further insight be gained by continued exploration? For the past dozen years, I have studied the manuscript, almost microscopically, with a view toward understanding the genetic process and can now share some examples of how Twain's artful revisions create dynamic, interactive meanings in the novel.

Because Sam Clemens promoted the public persona of Mark Twain as a careless, naive native genius, too casual to do anything so difficult as worry a sentence into shape, the scholar-critic who insists on Twain's deliberate artistry still has an uphill battle. Let a small example serve as an introduction to this problem. One of Huck's comments about Tom Sawyer is surprisingly emblematic of Twain's actual compositional practice. The first manuscript version reads:

In them circumstances he could always throw in an amount of style that was suitable.[2]

"Throw in" creates an impression of casual imprecision, and "an amount of style" phrases style as a measurable quantity. But Twain crossed out "he could always throw" and substituted above the line an insertion that makes the second version read:

In them circumstances it warn't no trouble to him to throw in an amount of style that was suitable. (p. 286)

Huck's double negative, grammatically asserting a positive, helps to characterize his idiom. There is only a slight difference between the versions; the constancy of "always throw" becomes "it warn't no trouble to throw" (making the action less difficult, less burdensome). But, of course, the increased casualness is itself the product of revision; thus the tone of bravado conceals the trouble; *ars celare artem*. The manuscript permits us to examine precisely how much trouble Twain took to throw in

an amount of style and how each change dynamically affected the completed work of art.

Let us observe first how Twain modulated his narrator's voice. The main surviving portion of the manuscript begins in the Sherburn episode (Chapter 22) where Huck is describing the mob's attempt to avenge the shooting of Boggs by lynching Colonel Sherburn. The townspeople have arrived at Sherburn's house and torn down his fence as he appears:

Sherburn never said a word—just stood there, looking down. It seemed to me that the stillness was as awful, now, as the racket was before; and somehow it was more creepy and uncomfortable. Sherburn run his eye slow along the crowd; and wherever his eye struck, the people tried a little to outgaze him, but couldn't; they dropped their eyes and looked [sickish and] sneaky. Then pretty soon Sherburn sort of laughed; not the kind of laugh you hear at the circus, but the kind that's fitten for a funeral—the kind that makes you feel crawly. (MS pp. 162–63)

This is Huck's voice, but with a touch of his author's more sophisticated accent; the syntax is far too measured and balanced, the diction too formal and abstract. By the time we reach the climactic vernacular coinage, "crawly," we have the sense of a word that is truly Huck's but nonetheless fails to objectify the pervasive emotions of the crowd. Twain revised the passage at least twice. He canceled "sickish and," preferring to portray the townspeople as furtive but not ill. (A fair number of changes of this type drop acceptable but unemphatic phrases.)

A more important revision affecting Huck's voice happened when Twain was revising the novel for print. He compressed the one sentence with measured literary balance: "It seemed to me that the stillness was as awful, now, as the racket was before; and somehow it was more creepy and uncomfortable." The revised, shorter form does not declare a concern with Huck's point of view; instead it characterizes the scene with a sense of palpable reality: "The stillness was awful creepy and uncomfortable."

A similar modification of Huck's skill in rendering complex psychological states as vivid sense impressions occurred at this paragraph's conclusion. Twain had originally written, "Not the kind of laugh you hear at the circus, but the kind of laugh that's fitten for a funeral, the kind that makes you feel crawly." But perhaps the author thought the negative comparison would appear as an obvious foreshadowing of the immediately following circus episode with the trick rider and the ringmaster. The purely conceptual funeral-circus polarity was canceled when the grim laughter was re-created as "not the pleasant kind, but

500

~~what~~ lays over the yaller fever,
for interest, when he does come.
Tom was over the stile & starting
for the house; the wagon
was spinning up the road
for the village, & we was
all bunched in the front
door. Tom had his store
clothes on, & an audience — &
that was always nuts for Tom
Sawyer. In them circum-
stances, it warn't no trouble to him to throw ~~he could always them~~
in an amount of style that
was suitable. He warn't a boy
to meeky along up that yard
like a sheep; no, he come
c'am & important, like the ram.

Manuscript page, corresponding to text in chapter 33, in which Tom Sawyer arrives at the Phelpses. The highlighted revision is one of hundreds of alterations Mark Twain made in the manuscript, indicating the attention he paid to matters of craft (Buffalo and Erie County Public Library).

the kind that makes you feel like when you are eating bread that's got sand in it" (p. 190). Twain enabled Huck to speak in the concrete, tactile, ordinary words that express both his verbal ability and his physical experience. The unrealized feeling "crawly" is now dramatized in a vivid image of physical discomfort. The result of revisions such as these is a tone of voice and set of words for Huck that live precisely because any apparent literary polish has been concealed.

Many who love the novel and think of it as a nonliterary book will be surprised to find out how central a role literary topics played in the earliest surviving version. But, of course, these thematic concerns caused difficulties with Huck's voice, because such matters were beyond his experience. In early drafts literary diction and topics push through Huck's voice and burden it with inappropriately bookish language. For example, at one point, Huck originally related, "The king was saying—in the middle of a sentence." But clearly Huck would be unlikely to say "sentence" in this context, as Twain realized when he revised to "in the middle of something he'd started in on—"(p. 217). A similar, angrier authorial voice breaks through Huck's original explanation to Jim about the King's morality while Huck is conflating the Scheherazade demand for stories with Henry VIII's beheading his wives:

> [F e t c h] 'Ring up fair Rosamun,'" Fair Rosamun answers the bell. Next morning, 'Chop off her head'—and next thing you see is the Chief of police with it in [a blanket] a rag. [Ole] And he made every one of them tell him a tale every night; and he kept that up till he had hogged a thousand and one tales that way, and then he got out a copyright, and published them all in a book, and called it Domesday Book—which was a good name, and stated the case. Of course most any publisher would do that, but you wouldn't think a king would. (MS pp. 199–200)

Apparently Clemens's/Twain's own attitude toward some publishers seethes through the boy's voice. But Twain deleted both the bloody description and the "copyright" and "publisher" segments in a deliberate and artistic effort to cancel this appearance of the adult Hartford author behind Huck's voice. Contemporary critics should be aware simultaneously of the extent to which Twain had literary concerns and of the effort he exerted to expunge them from Huck's voice, thereby not only preserving the consistency of his narrative mask but also creating Huck's character by way of his original voice.

The appeal of the novel resides largely in the consistency of this severely restricted point of view and voice: the struggle of that creation arises from the conflict of the adult's knowledge and evaluation with the boy's voice and perception. The creation of the imaginative fusion—almost seamless in the finished novel—can be observed in the manuscript. Huck's remarks about the other characters are, of course, self-characterizations because phrased in his language; they are also descriptions, so that Twain's problem was how to indicate precisely the character of other characters in language that would be appropriate to Huck. Twain lavished much attention in this regard upon Huck's comments about the King, the aging con man. For example, when the King and Duke begin to deceive the Wilks family by posing as distant relatives, they approach a townsperson to inquire where Peter Wilks lives. The local man replies:

> "I'm sorry, sir, but the best we can do is to tell you where he *did* live, yesterday evening."
> The derned old cretur fell up against him; and put his chin on his shoulder, and cried down. (MS p. 233)

The novelist modified, momentarily, the awkward and ineffective up-down, physical gestures of the King. First Twain wrote in "kerflummoxed," a word he tried repeatedly to apply to this character, but then decided to make the action more flamboyant by inserting "went all to smash." And he added a splendid ironic simile that captures the King's duplicity: "Sudden as winking, the derned old cretur went all to smash." The simile combines unexpected speed and deception, for the wink also conveys collusion. Moreover, the revised version is open to at least two interpretations; the King may have planned a performance of this sort, or perhaps the simile implies instead his instinctive, unplanned, spur-of-the-moment genius for con games.

By the time the passage reached print, Twain had again touched up the description, inserting "ornery" for "derned." This minor change makes the segment slightly more polite, because the slang for "damned" is dropped. But the major aesthetic effect is part of a pattern of Twain's revising words that assert to words that dramatize. In this instance, the simple explicit condemnation of "derned" was transformed when Twain substituted a word that justified the attitude.

Once their deception is underway, the King and Duke must not talk in public because of the Duke's pretense about being a deaf semimute. Only in private can the rascals plot their moves. Twain originally has the King explain his plan to the Duke, saying, "after we disappear" (MS p. 290). But when revising, reseeing—and perhaps even refeeling—the novel for print, Twain created a more tactile and perhaps a more ominous turn of phrase, "after we've slid" (p. 228). The elusive deception thus carries relevant connotations of both moral sliminess and the precariousness of the King and the Duke's position.

In his public speech, the King must adopt a different verbal style, one appropriate to his pose as the bereaved English brother, the Reverend Harvey Wilks. The King assumes a higher level of diction—which Twain has him control only imperfectly—and a sanctimonious, condescending tone. He ingratiates himself with the townspeople by making the correct invitations:

> "–they being partickler friends of the diseased. That's why they're invited here this evenin'; but to-morrow we want all to come–everybody; for he respected everybody; he liked everybody, and so it's fitten that his funeral orgies should be public."(MS pp. 256–57)

Many readers have not perceived how cleverly Twain constructed this paragraph, giving the speaker two outrageous malapropisms that characterize him as careless and ignorant. Most readers catch the mistake of "orgies," but the earlier error of "diseased" for "deceased" is seldom observed. Because readers perceive at least one error, but probably do not realize the full extent, their situation resembles Dr. Robinson's, and the similarity of perception may predispose readers to sympathize with the honest doctor in the verbal confrontation.

The King repeats "orgies" and receives a corrective note from the Duke, but nonetheless blathers on pretentiously:

> "I use the word orgies, not because it's the common term, because it ain't–obsequies is the common term–but because it's the right term." (MS p. 258)

This passage Twain revised in an enormously subtle way; the modified manuscript version reads: "obsequies bein, the common term–but because orgies is the right term." The insertion of "bein'" subordinates the correct word, makes it more parenthetical, more under the breath, as if less time and emphasis are needed. In addition, the shift to the more declarative, emphatic "orgies is the right term" boldly asserts the malapropism.

The King's voice seems to be in command of the situation as he explains:

> Obsequies ain't used in England no more, now–it's gone out. We say orgies, now, in England. Orgies is better, because it means the thing you are after, more exact. It's a word that's made up out of the Greek *orgo*, outside, open, abroad; and the Hebrew *jeesum*, to plant, cover up; hence *inter*. So, as you see, funeral orgies is an open or public funeral. (MS pp. 258–59)

Twain's meticulous care for the exact sound led him to revise for the printed version, changing "out of"

to "out'n" and, with equal attention to detail, turning the "open or public funeral" to "open er public funeral." Tiny changes of this sort certainly improve the dialect, but more importantly such fine tuning of the voice gives greater emphasis to the humorous incongruity between the King's pedantic derivations and his nonstandard usage. His pretentious and ignorant arrogance appears in his voice; he is a master of wordy mispronunciation.

A dramatic conflict arises as the King's ignorance alerts Dr. Robinson to the fraud. The surface conflict involves the two characters, but a deeper contrast exists in how Twain–typically–revised the doctor's speech to emphasize his difference from the King. After Dr. Robinson laughs at the King's imitation of an English accent, he turns to the girls and says:

> "I was your father's friend, and I'm your friend; and I warn you *as* a friend, and an honest one, that wants to protect you and keep you out of harm and trouble, to turn your backs on that scoundrel, and have nothing to do with him, the ignorant hog, with his putrid and idiotic Greek and Hebrew as he calls it. He is the thinnest of thin imposters."(MS p. 262)

Because the doctor is an educated person, he can use unusual words–such as "putrid"–accurately. But Twain revised to make the doctor's language more ordinary, less aristocratic in vocabulary and structure. His contempt is moderated slightly, in the printed version, by the removal of "the ignorant hog" and "putrid." The easy, predictable, intensive "thinnest of thin imposters" Twain simplified to "the thinnest kind of an imposter." Such changes create a characterization of a more approachable, less livid doctor.

In the manuscript, Dr. Robinson first has a vocabulary that is polysyllabic and elevated. He states that the rascal

> "has come here with a lot of empty names and facts which he has picked up somewhere, and you weakly take them for *proofs*, and are assisted in deceiving yourselves by these thoughtless unreasoning friends here, who ought to know better." (MS pp. 262–63)

But his diction becomes more ordinary as "assisted in deceiving yourselves" changes to "helped to fool yourselves." Twain also modified the doctor's characterization of the townspeople by revising "thoughtless unreasoning friends" to "foolish friends." The doctor, in obvious contrast to the King, appears unpretentious and blunt. Moreover, Twain refocused the doctor's judgmental ire by suppressing "weakly." The resulting "you take them for *proofs*" recognizes his fellow townspeople's desire for evidence, and the resulting printed passage characterizes the doctor as a forceful, intelligent, but ordinary person who confronts his neighbors forthrightly.

Originally, the doctor's impassioned pleas had been melodramatic in tone:

> "Mary Jane Wilks, you know me for your friend, and your honest and unselfish friend. Now listen to me: cast this paltry villain out–I beg you, I beseech you to do it. Will you?" (MS p. 263)

But Twain had already had the doctor describe himself as "honest" in his earlier speech, and this self-characterization was dropped. The clichéd phrase–"cast this paltry villain out"–sounds so melodramatic that a standard gesture, a pose, and a tableau spring immediately to mind; the printed "turn this pitiful rascal out" seems more contemptuous. "I beseech you" was dropped, but the printed form of the request gains a lifelike emphasis of tone with "beg" in italics. With revisions of this sort, the doctor's voice becomes more genuine, less pedantic, clichéd, or melodramatic, and the contrast between the pretentious King and the correct, blunt, honest country doctor can be heard more clearly in the finished text. Twain's attention to voice, tone, characterization, and dialogue contributes to the sense of realism and guides the reader's precise allocation of sympathy among the characters.

The development of a more significant character, such as Mary Jane Wilks, apparently required additional novelistic skills. Interacting changes in description or imagery usually also affect the tonality of a passage. When Huck explains the fraud to Mary Jane, his tone is fairly serious in the first version:

> and she set there, mighty impatient and excited and beautiful, but looking kinder happy. So I went to studying it out. I says to myself, [so] I reckon [that] a body that tells the truth[,] when he is in a tight place, is taking considerable many risks; though I ain't had no experience, and can't say for certain. (MS p. 329)

A minor change lightened the tone; Twain added the nonstandard verb "ups," which conveys irregular or surprising action as a young boy would express it: "a body that ups and tells the truth." But a more significant change in imagery reinforces the change to a lighter tone. Creating an additional description of Mary Jane, Twain inserted a simile picturing her as "eased-up like a person that's had a tooth pulled out." The brilliant addition conveys exactly relief from pain and anxiety. Moreover, the ordinariness of the description makes Mary Jane more familiar, hence a less threatening person to whom to tell the truth. The informality of

the revised version fits Huck's voice. By the time the passage reached print, it read:

> and she set there, very impatient and excited, and handsome, but looking kind of happy and eased-up, like a person that's had a tooth pulled out. (p. 240)

The change from the manuscript's "beautiful" to "handsome" is in accord with other changes, deemphasizing Mary Jane's physical attractiveness, that keep Huck's point of view appropriate to that of a prepubescent youth. "Handsome" conveys an implication of admiration for a pal. These revisions present an example of the kaleidoscopic interrelationship of speaking voice, characterization, and description. In context they also lighten the tone of the full passage sufficiently to make Huck's moral-philosophical questioning seem spontaneous rather than cunning or conniving.

Similar modifications about sexuality, as well as a change about religion, happen in Huck's emotional farewell scene with Mary Jane, when she offers to pray for him. The first manuscript version reads:

> Pray for me–good land! I reckoned if she'd knowed me she'd tackle a job that was nearer her size. But I bet you she done it, just the same–she was just that kind. She had the grit to pray for Judas Iscarott if she took the notion–there warn't no back-down to her, if I know a girl by the rake of her stern; and I think I do. You may say what you please, but in my opinion that girl had more sand in her than any girl I ever see; in my opinion she was just *full* of sand. And when it comes to beauty–*and* goodness–she lay over them all. I hain't ever seen her since that time I see her go out at that door, turn at the stairs and kinder throw a kiss back at me; no, I hain't ever seen her since; but I reckon I've thought of her a many and a many a million times, and of her saying she would pray for me; and if ever I'd a thought it would do any good for me to pray for *her*, I'm dum'd if I wouldn't a done it or bust. (MS pp. 351–52)

Mary Jane's femme fatale gesture, throwing a kiss from the stair, is excised in the manuscript. Had Twain allowed it to stand, the novel would have had an explicit suggestion of a topic it studiously avoids. Part of Huck's innocence is his presexual condition; however appropriate the gesture may have been for the slightly older Mary Jane, it would have complicated Huck's characterization. Either he must ignore it or respond to it, and either choice would have changed the novel. Instead, Twain wrote in an insertion above the cancellation so the section reads, "I hain't ever seen her since that time that I seen her go out at that door, like light and comfort a-going out of a body's life." This sim-

BJUYT KIOP M LKJHGFDSA;QWERTYUIOP;_?8V#643234 A⁻
                                                          HA
                            HARTFORD, DEC. 9,

DEAR BROTHER:

I AM TRYING T TO GET THE HANG OF THIS NEW F
FANGLED WRITING MACHINE, BUT AM NOT MAKING
A S-INING SUCCESS OF IT. HOWEVER THIS IS THE
FIRST ATTEMPT I EVER HAVE MADE, & YET I PER-
CEIVETHAT I SHALL SOON & EASILY ACQUIRE A FINE
FACILITY IN ITS USE. I SAW THE THING IN BOS-
TON THE OTHER DAY & WAS GREATLY TAKEN WI:TH
IT. SUSIE HAS STRUCK THE KEYS ONCE OR TWICE,
& NO DOUBT HAS PRINTED SOME LETTERS WHICH DO
NOT BELONG WHERE SHE PUT THEM.
THE HAVING BEEN A COMPOSITOR IS LIKELY TO BE
A GREAT HELP TO ME,SINCE O NE CHIEFLY NEEDS
SWIFTNESS IN BANGING THE KEYS.THE MACHINE COSTS
125 DOLLARS.THE MACHINE HAS SEVERAL VIRTUES
I BELIEVE IT WILL PRINT FASTER THAN I CAN WRITE.
ONE MAY LEAN BACK IN HIS CHAIR & WORK IT. IT
PILES AN AWFUL STACK OF WORDS ON ONE PAGE.
IT DONT MUSS THINGS OR SCATTER INK BLOTS AROUND.
OF COURSE IT SAVES PAPER.

                                SUSIE IS GONE,
NOW, & I FANCY I SHALL MAKE BETTER PROGRESS.
WORKING THIS TYPE-WRITER REMINDS ME OF OLD
ROBERT BUCHANAN, WHO, YOU REMEMBER, USED TO
SET UP ARTICLES AT THE CASE WITHOUT PREVIOUS-
LY PUTTING THEM IN THE FORM OF MANUSCRIPT.I
WAS LOST IN ADMIRATION OF SUCH MARVELOUS
INTELLECTUAL CAPACITY.

                                LOVE TO MOLLIE.
                        YOUR BROTHER,
                            SAM.

The model of typewriter Mark Twain is believed to have purchased in 1874 and his first typewritten letter. Although he found the machine too balky and soon gave it away, he later found typewritten text to be a boon to his writing process (from Wilfred A. Beeching, Century of the Typewriter *[London: Heinemann, 1974], Thomas Cooper Library, University of South Carolina).*

ile pays explicit attention only to the emotional impact of separation.

Similar considerations about sexuality–and about tone and characterization–clearly influenced Twain's later revisions for print. Huck's voice first used a slang phrase, and then, perhaps, the author's mind shifted to the girl's figure. The result was a complex tone more appropriate to an experienced Mississippi riverboat pilot than to Huck's presexual naturalness: "there warn't no back-down to her, if I know a girl by the rake of her stern; and I think I do." But Huck's innocent voice is restored in the final version, as he simply praises, "There warn't no back-down to her, I judge" (p. 245).

His innocence is also preserved by a suppression of some intricate satire on religion. The passage opens with Mary Jane's offer to pray for Huck, and he concludes, in the manuscript version, by saying, "if ever I'd a thought it would do any good for me to pray for *her,* I'm dum'd if I wouldn't a done it or bust." The dialect statement, "I'm damned if I wouldn't have prayed for her," carries a witty involution that was lost when Twain shifted the word choice for print to "blamed." Once more Huck seems younger, and the adult author's potential for satiric sharpness is concealed.

The wake and funeral of Peter Wilks provide several opportunities for humor, satire, and social criticism, but much rewriting involved toning down what might have been regarded as too strong or too cruel a satire. One such instance arises after the King and Duke, posing as the relatives, have cried over the coffin:

> every woman, nearly, went up to the girls, without saying a word, and kissed them, solemn, on the forehead, and then put their hand on their head, and looked up towards the throne, with the tears running down, and [then let go] then busted out and went off sobbing and swabbing, and give the next [heifer] woman a show. I never see anything so disgusting. (MS pp. 240–41)

The satire on religion is diffused–even to the point of disappearance–by the revision of the manuscript's "throne," a reference to the seat of God, to the printed text's general "sky." The revised text keeps the satire on the woman striking a melodramatic pose, in the manner of Emmeline Grangerford, but omits the religious component in the mockery. Similarly, Twain's original comparison of the women to heifers pictures them as large, dumb, and easily led, and the cancellation of "heifer" and substitution of "woman" was clearly less offensive. The target of the satire remains ostensibly the King and Duke, and

only by extension and implication the manipulated townspeople.

The funeral itself could, of course, be a dismal part of the novel, but Twain managed to brighten the ceremony in a remarkable way. After the people have filed past the coffin, while the family is sobbing, Huck observes: "There warn't no other sound but the scraping of feet on the floor, and blowing noses." Then Twain inserted, on the back of MS p. 302: "because people always blows them more at a funeral than they do at other places except church" (p. 232). The scene is lightened by Huck's quasi-philosophical comment; the range of human activity is momentarily summoned and compared. There is a deft jab at church behavior, but Huck's innocent observation seems objective, and whatever emotion the scene deserves is placed in a cultural context.

"My Copying Is Always Done on The Type-Writer"

Much of Mark Twain's revising of his original manuscript of Adventures of Huckleberry Finn *was done on typescripts that have not survived. This excerpt from a 24 April 1883 letter of recommendation for one of his typists was typed and revised by the author on an all-capitals machine. His handwritten revision is shown in lowercase letters.*

THIS EXPERIENCE WITH THE TYPE-WRITER HAS BEEN OF SO HIGH A VALUE TO ME THAT NOT EVEN THE TYPE-WRITER ITSELF CAN DESCRIBE IT. IT HAS BANISHED ONE OF THE PRIME SORROWS OF MY LIFE. AFTER ONE HAS READ A CHAPTER OR TWO OF HIS LITERATURE IN THE TYPE-WRITER CHARACTER, THE PAGES OF THE SHEETS BEGIN TO LOOK NATURAL, AND RATIONAL, AND AS VOID OF OFFENSE TO HIS EYE AS DO HIS OWN WRITTEN PAGES, THEREFORE HE CAN ALTER AND AMEND THEM WITH COMFORT AND FACILITY; BUT THIS IS NEVER THE CASE WITH A BOOK COPIED BY PEN. THE PEN PAGES HAVE A FOREIGN AND UNSYMPATHETIC LOOK, AND THIS THEY NEVER LOSE. ONE CANNOT RECOGNIZE HIMSELF IN THEM. THE EMENDING AND REVAMPING OF ONE'S LITERATURE IN THIS FORM IS AS BARREN OF INTEREST, and indeed as repellant, AS IF IT WERE THE LITERATURE OF A STRANGER AND AN ENEMY. MY COPYING IS ALWAYS DONE ON THE TYPE-WRITER, NOW, AND I SHALL NOT BE LIKELY TO EVER USE ANY OTHER SYSTEM.

–Collection of Samuel N. Freedman

Huck's narration of the rest of the ceremony is subtly comic: "They had borrowed a melodeum; and when everything was ready, a young woman set down and pumped up its sufferings, and everybody [joined] jined in and sung"(MS p. 304). Twain inserted, after "a melodeum," "a sick one," a qualification clarifying the idea of the instrument as having "sufferings." However, "sufferings" may have been uncomfortably close to the understandable emotions of the Wilks girls, and the printed version relates that "a young woman set down and worked it, and it was pretty skreeky and colicky, and everybody joined in and sung"(p. 232). The idea of sickness is thus redefined in nonemotional but audible fashion. "Skreeky" is a brilliantly created portmanteau word conveying, one assumes, a discordant combination of "scream" and "shriek," while "colicky" suggests minor sickness in a rasping, irregular cough.

Twain's humor was also frequently spontaneous, subtle, and on occasion intricate. The quickness of his verbal wit is aptly demonstrated by a minor revision in his original composition. After the funeral, the real brothers arrive and the townspeople must then determine which pair of brothers is genuine. The doctor says:

> Come along, Hines; come along, the rest of you. We'll take these fellows to the tavern and [confront] affront 'em with the t'other couple. (MS p 379)

This is an amusing modification; "confront" would be perfectly satisfactory, but "affront" is an apt malapropism, implying insult. Twain had the quickness to seize an ordinary word and spin it in midsentence, converting conventional serviceable language into humor.[3] The doctor's word choice reveals his human imperfections, and the following confrontation will, accordingly, be more interesting.

During the trial scene, Twain originally planned to use the word "kerflummox"; the genuine brother tries to trap the king by asking what Peter Wilks had tattooed on his chest:

> I'm blamed if the king didn't have to brace up mighty quick, or he'd a kerflummuxed, it took him so sudden—and mind you it was a thing that was calculated to make most *anybody* kerflummux, to get fetched such a stunner as that without any notice. (MS pp. 391–92)

However, in print, the unusual "or he'd a kerflummuxed" is canceled and replaced by a different word joined to a simile drawn from the locale: "or he'd a squshed down like a bluff bank that the river has cut under" (p. 256). The coinage—"sqush" for collapse into

liquid—reinforces the striking image of a large, impressive facade sinking.

Twain apparently kept an attentive eye on creative transformations of his settings. When Huck is exploring the Phelps farm, an important location—the area where Jim will be imprisoned—was first described as "three little log nigger-cabins in a row beyond the smoke-house; one little hut by itself, down against the back fence"(MS p. 463). Later, probably after Twain had imagined some details of Jim's imprisonment, he added to the manuscript so that the single cabin is portrayed as "one little hut <u>all</u> by itself, <u>away</u> down against the back fence." With admirable verbal economy, with the magic of words the cabin and the fence are moved and Jim's prison made more isolated; hence the tricks and descriptions become more possible and plausible. One could even speculate that the boys attempting to reach Jim would be able to conceal their approach behind the distant fence.

Deliberately, I've reserved two examples of Twain's re-creative artistry, those involving Jim, for the concluding portion of this survey. Quite late in the novel, after Tom and Huck have engineered Jim's escape, Huck and Jim are talking. Huck's voice was obviously continuously present to Twain, but because Jim had been silent for many pages, Twain did not, at first, "hear" Jim:

> "*Now,* old Jim, you're a free man *again,* and I bet you you won't ever be a slave [any] <u>no</u>more."
> "En a mighty good job it was, too, Huck. It was planned beautiful, en it was *done* beautiful; en [day] dey ain't *nobody* kin git up a plan dat's mo, mixed up [XXXX] den what dat one wuz."(MS p. 707)

The fascinating revision develops when Twain's aural imagination works on Jim's voice. The change of "day" to "dey" was done in the original flow of the composition, and thereafter no dialect changes are needed because Twain was listening to Jim in his mind. But once the voice was "heard" accurately, Twain had to revise, rehearing, to change the earlier "was" to "wuz" or "'uz," capturing precisely Jim's speech.

At an earlier point in the novel, when Jim discusses his daughter's deafness, Twain made the highly unusual change of modifying Jim's speech toward standard. And he inserted a reinforcing phrase in standard English as well. Although the idea might seem surprising, I ask the open-minded critic to read Jim's speech, keeping in mind the conclusion of Shakespeare's *King Lear,* when Lear speaks of Cordelia's death with the overwhelming line of five words, "Never, never, never, never, never." Jim relates that he had punished the child for disobedience and that she did not hear the door slam:

> "–en my lan', de chile [nuvver] never move'! My breff mos' hop outer me; en I feel so–so–I doan know *how* I feel. [XX] I crope out, all a-tremblin', en crope aroun' en open de do, easy en slow, en poke my head in behine de chile, sof' en still, en all of a sudden I says *pow!* jus, as loud as I could yell. She never move'! O, Huck, I bust out a-cryin', en grab her up in my arms en say, 'O de po, little thing! de Lord God Amighty fogive po' ole Jim, kaze he never gwyne to fogive his-seff as long as he live!' O, she was plumb deef en dumb, Huck, plumb deef and dumb–en I'd ben a treat'n her so!"(MS pp. 209–10)

Could the moving passage include an allusion in situation and word choice to *Lear?* There is relevant contextual evidence to support this view. Twain was working at the time on a parodic play in which a bookseller wanders about in the middle of *Hamlet.* Earlier in *Huck* the King had used a garbled soliloquy, and after the Grangerford-Shepherdson elopement and massacre the King and Duke practice *Romeo and Juliet* and *Richard III.* And there is evidence from the manuscript itself–just two paragraphs after Jim's speech–in a passage where the King and the Duke dress Jim up. At first Twain has them costume Jim as King Richard, but that is heavily canceled, and instead Jim assumes the hitherto unmentioned clothing of "King Leer."

The significance of this revision goes far beyond implying that the admirable slave has Shakespearean feelings, as indicated by his speech about his daughter. Once the notion of *King Lear* was echoing in Twain's mind, he had, in his next episode, the King and Duke attempt to rob the inheritance of three orphan daughters. Twain's inverse duplication of *King Lear* has its trial scene, its stormy scene, its revelation of a body. Moreover, when Huck flees and returns to the raft, he jumps into Jim's arms, but is frightened because he has forgotten that Jim is dressed as Lear. It must be emphasized that nonbookish Huck has no idea in the Wilks episode that he may be wandering around in a parodic version of *King Lear.*

Indeed, Twain could "always throw in an amount" of art that is suitable, and far more often than not his efforts at revision and re-creation create a more consistent voice and a more compelling novel. Genetic criticism of this sort remains attentive to the words of the text and the words that were excluded. Exploring the actions of these dynamic, interactive revisions, we can more fully appreciate not only the genius but also the craft of Twain's creative process.

—One Hundred Years of Huckleberry Finn: The Boy, His Book, and American Culture, edited by Robert Sattelmeyer and J. Donald Crowley (Columbia: University of Missouri Press, 1985), pp. 106–116

---

1. For example, DeLancey Ferguson wrote *"Huck Finn* Aborning," *Colophon,* n.s. 3 (1938): 171–180, and then *Mark Twain, Man and Legend* (Indianapolis: Bobbs-Merrill, 1943). Although Ferguson was concerned with the possibility of censorship by Olivia Clemens, he must be credited with realizing the importance of the manuscript for aesthetic study. Bernard DeVoto, in *Mark Twain at Work* (Cambridge: Harvard University Press, 1942) concludes that the evidence reveals Twain was self-censoring, especially about sexuality. Walter Blair's convincing article, "When Was *Huckleberry Finn* Written?" *American Literature* 30 (March 1958): 1–25, draws upon the manuscript, and in *Mark Twain and Huck Finn* (Berkeley: University of California Press, 1962), he discusses the craftsmanship of the revisions. Sidney J. Krause has used the manuscript to survey "Twain's Method and Theory of Composition," *Modern Philology* 56 (February 1959): 167–177. Krause finds Twain "a far more scrupulous craftsman than he is generally given credit for being" and presents to the scholarly world two pages of citations comparing the manuscript and printed text in tabular form.

  I am grateful to the late Miss Jane G. Van Arsdale and Mr. William H. Loos, Curators of the Rare Book Room of the Buffalo and Erie County Public Library.

2. MS p. 500; I present first the earliest surviving version, then describe the growth into the finished text. In the following transcriptions, contractions are silently expanded. Illegible cancellations are represented by [XXX]. Cancellations are presented in square brackets, and insertions are underlined. Thus a word that was immediately corrected in the initial writing would be shown as "The man [said] stopped and muttered," but if the passage was later revised it would be noted as "The man [said] stopped and muttered." The second notation represents cancellation and insertion, above the line, with a caret. MS p. ____ indicates the location in the manuscript; the quotations from the first American edition are noted simply by page number.

3. A similar, midword change occurs when the King is looking for another town to swindle:

> Well, early one morning we hid the raft in a good safe place, about two mile below a little bit of a shabby village, named Pikeville, and the king he went ashore, and told us all to stay hid whilst he went up to town and smelt around to see if anybody had [hear] got any wind of the Burning Shame there yet. (MS p. 428)

> Shortly before completing the word *heard,* Twain self-critically changed his word choice to be consistent with the emphasis on sense of smell. His artistic imagination, then, was rapid enough to censor mixed sense imagery in midword. But then the significance of the olfactory imagery decreased when, in print, the phallic romp became retitled "The Royal Nonesuch."

Excised Episodes

Two substantial episodes were removed from Adventures of Huckleberry Finn *as the manuscript went through the process of becoming the published novel: the well-known account of Huck's encounter with raftsmen, nearly fifty-four manuscript pages, that was first published in* Life on the Mississippi *(1883) and has since often been included in chapter 16 of modern editions of the novel; and Jim's "ghost" story, fifteen and a half manuscript pages, a late deletion from what became chapter 9 of the novel that was first published in 1995 in* The New Yorker *as "Jim and the Dead Man."*

Even after publishing the raft episode in Life on the Mississippi, *Mark Twain intended to restore the episode to its original place in* Adventures of Huckleberry Finn. *In this excerpt he responds to Webster's suggestion that the episode not be restored. The reason for Webster's suggestion had nothing to do with literary merit or judgment; he wanted to market* Adventures of Huckleberry Finn *with* The Adventures of Tom Sawyer *as a set. Since* Adventures of Huckleberry Finn *was much longer than the earlier novel, Webster believed that the two volumes would not look like companion pieces. By leaving out the raft episode the volumes would be nearer in length.*

Mark Twain to Webster, 22 April 1884

Yes I think the raft chapter can be left wholly out, by heaving in a paragraph to say Huck visited the raft to find out how far it might be to Cairo, but got no satisfaction. Even *this* is not necessary unless that raft-visit is referred to later in the book. I think it is, but am not certain.

—*Mark Twain, Business Man,* pp. 249–250

* * *

The American Publishing Company held the copyright for The Adventures of Tom Sawyer *and apparently did not offer to relinquish it for a sum that would make the project of publishing* Huckleberry Finn *and* Tom Sawyer *as a set profitable. This excerpt seems to indicate that Mark Twain may not have played a helpful role in Webster's negotiations.*

Mark Twain to Webster, 1 September 1884

That question appears to answer itself: if the Am. Pub. Co. will not give you terms on Tom Sawyer which will afford you a profit, does not that end the project?

When you send me pirate ads which are calculated to enrage me, I wish you would also send me a form for a letter to the Am. Pub. Co to fit the case. You lay me liable to make trouble under a sudden & frantic impulse when there is no occasion for it. Besides, the episode unfits me for work for a week afterward. I have lost $3,000 worth of time over this pirate business, & I do not see where any good has been done, unless the erection of a quarrel with the Pub. Co can come under that head.

If you would *help* me get along with the Pub. Co. we could doubtless manage them to our advantage; but I have no diplomacy in my own nature, & you don't suggest any to me. Try to remember that I fly off the handle altogether too easily, & that you want to think twice before you send me irritating news.

—*Mark Twain, Business Man,* pp. 272–273

* * *

Although the marketing plan for the two novels was abandoned, the raftsmen episode was not restored to the first edition of Adventures of Huckleberry Finn, *nor did Mark Twain agree to its being included in any subsequent editions of the novel published during his lifetime.*

The impetus behind the deletion of Jim's tale is less certain. It may well be that it was among the passages Clemens read aloud to his family, as recalled by his daughter Susy Clemens in her memoir.

"One Part Pertickularly"
Olivia Susan Clemens

Papa read "Hucleberry Finn" to us in manuscript just before it came out, & then he would leave parts of it with Mamma to expergate, . . . and sometimes Clara & I would be sitting with Mamma while she was looking the manuscript over, & I remember so well, with what pangs of regret we use to see her turn down the leaves of the pages, which meant, that some delightfully dreadful part must be scratched out. And I remember one part pertickularly that Clara & I used to delight in, which was perfectly fascinating it was so dreadful, & oh with what dispair we saw mamma turn down the leaf on which it was written, we thought the book would be almost ruined without it.

—*Papa: An Intimate Biography of Mark Twain,*
edited by Charles Neider (Garden City, N.Y.:
Doubleday, 1985), pp. 188–189

Along with Olivia, Clemens was interested in how "Mark Twain" was publicly represented through his work. Clemens may have agreed with his wife that a grotesque episode about Jim's adventures with a cadaver would have offended readers or he may simply have decided that the episode no longer fit in the novel as it had developed over seven years.

42   MIGHTY RAFTS.

characters whom I have been trying to describe. I remember the annual processions of mighty rafts that used to glide by Hannibal when I was a boy, — an acre or so of white, sweet-smelling boards in each raft, a crew of two dozen men or more, three or four wigwams scattered about the raft's vast level space for storm-quarters, — and I remember the rude ways and the tremendous talk of their big crews, the ex-keelboatmen and their admiringly patterning successors; for we used to swim out a quarter or third of a mile and get on these rafts and have a ride.

A LUMBER RAFT.

By way of illustrating keelboat talk and manners, and that now-departed and hardly-remembered raft-life, I will throw in, in this place, a chapter from a book which I have been working at, by fits and starts, during the past five or six years, and may possibly finish in the course of five or six more. The book is a story which details some passages in the life of an ignorant village boy, Huck Finn, son of the town drunkard of my time out west, there. He has run away from his persecuting father, and from a persecuting good widow who wishes to make a nice, truth-telling, respectable boy of him; and with him a slave of the widow's has

AN UNPUBLISHED CHAPTER.   43

also escaped. They have found a fragment of a lumber raft (it is high water and dead summer time), and are floating down the river by night, and hiding in the willows by day, — bound for Cairo, — whence the negro will seek freedom in the heart of the free States. But in a fog, they pass Cairo without knowing it. By and by they begin to suspect the truth, and Huck Finn is persuaded to end the dismal suspense by swimming down to a huge raft which they have seen in the distance ahead of them, creeping aboard under cover of the darkness, and gathering the needed information by eavesdropping: —

But you know a young person can't wait very well when he is impatient to find a thing out. We talked it over, and by and by Jim said it was such a black night, now, that it would n't be no risk

"I SWUM ALONG THE RAFT."

to swim down to the big raft and crawl aboard and listen, — they would talk about Cairo, because they would be calculating to go ashore there for a spree, maybe, or anyway they would send boats ashore to buy whiskey or fresh meat or something. Jim had a wonderful level head, for a nigger: he could most always start a good plan when you wanted one.

I stood up and shook my rags off and jumped into the river, and struck out for the raft's light. By and by, when I got down nearly

Pages from Life on the Mississippi *that were prepared from the raft episode, originally written in the manuscript of* Adventures of Huckleberry Finn *(Mark Twain House, Hartford, Connecticut)*

44   "GIVE US A REST."

to her, I eased up and went slow and cautious. But everything was all right—nobody at the sweeps. So I swum down along the raft till I was most abreast the camp fire in the middle, then I crawled aboard and inched along and got in amongst some bundles of shingles on the weather side of the fire. There was thirteen men there—they was the watch on deck of course. And a mighty rough-looking lot, too. They had a jug, and tin cups, and they kept the jug moving. One man was singing—roaring, you may say; and it wasn't a nice song—for a parlor anyway. He roared through his nose, and strung out the last word of every line very long. When he was done they all fetched a kind of Injun war-whoop, and then another was sung. It begun:—

"There was a woman in our towdn,
    In our towdn diid dwed'l (dwell,)
She loved her husband dear-i-lee,
    But another man twyste as wed'l.

Singing too, riloo, riloo, riloo,
    Ri-too, riloo, rilay - - e,
She loved her husband dear-i-lee,
    But another man twyste as wed'l."

And so on—fourteen verses. It was kind of poor, and when he was going to start on the next verse one of them said it was the tune the old cow died on; and another one said, "Oh, give us a rest." And another one told him to take a walk. They made fun of him till he got mad and jumped up and begun to cuss the crowd, and said he could lam any thief in the lot.

They was all about to make a break for him, but the biggest man there jumped up and says:—

"Set whar you are, gentlemen. Leave him to me; he's my meat."

Then he jumped up in the air three times and cracked his heels together every time. He flung off a buckskin coat that was all hung with fringes, and says, "You lay thar tell the chawin-up's done;" and flung his hat down, which was all over ribbons, and says, "You lay thar tell his sufferins is over."

Then he jumped up in the air and cracked his heels together again and shouted out:—

"Whoo-oop! I'm the old original iron-jawed, brass-mounted,

THE CORPSE-MAKER CROWS.   45

copper-bellied corpse-maker from the wilds of Arkansaw!—Look at me! I'm the man they call Sudden Death and General Desolation! Sired by a hurricane, dam'd by an earthquake, half-brother to the cholera, nearly related to the small-pox on the mother's side! Look at me! I take nineteen alligators and a bar'l of whiskey for

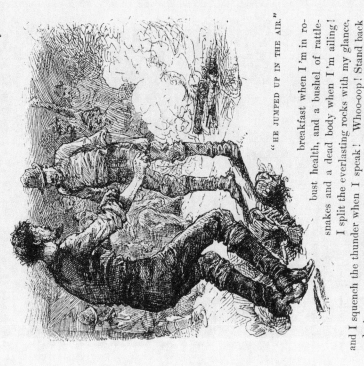

"HE JUMPED UP IN THE AIR."

breakfast when I'm in robust health, and a bushel of rattle-snakes and a dead body when I'm ailing! I split the everlasting rocks with my glance, and I squench the thunder when I speak! Whoo-oop! Stand back and give me room according to my strength! Blood's my natural drink, and the walls of the dying is music to my ear! Cast your eye on me, gentlemen!—and lay low and hold your breath, for I'm bout to turn myself loose!"

All the time he was getting this off, he was shaking his head and looking fierce, and kind of swelling around in a little circle, tucking up his wrist-bands, and now and then straightening up and beating

46   "THE CHILD OF CALAMITY."

his breast with his fist, saying, "Look at me, gentlemen!" When he got through, he jumped up and cracked his heels together three times, and let off a roaring "whoo-oop! I'm the bloodiest son of a wildcat that lives!"

Then the man that had started the row tilted his old slouch hat down over his right eye; then he bent stooping forward, with his back sagged and his south end sticking out far, and his fists a-shoving out and drawing in in front of him, and so went around in a little circle about three times, swelling himself up and breathing hard. Then he straightened, and jumped up and cracked his heels together three times before he lit again (that made them cheer), and he begun to shout like this:—

"Whoo-oop! bow your neck and spread, for the kingdom of sorrow's a-coming! Hold me down to the earth, for I feel my powers a-working! whoo-oop! I'm a child of sin, *don't* let me get a start! Smoked glass, here, for all! Don't attempt to look at me with the naked eye, gentlemen! When I'm playful I use the meridians of longitude and parallels of latitude for a seine, and drag the Atlantic Ocean for whales! I scratch my head with the lightning and purr myself to sleep with the thunder! When I'm cold, I bile the Gulf of Mexico and bathe in it; when I'm hot I fan myself with an equinoctial storm; when I'm thirsty I reach up and suck a cloud dry like a sponge; when I range the earth hungry, famine follows in my tracks! Whoo-

"WENT AROUND IN A CIRCLE."

THEY BOTH WEAKEN.   47

oop! Bow your neck and spread! I put my hand on the sun's face and make it night in the earth; I bite a piece out of the moon and hurry the seasons; I shake myself and crumble the mountains! Contemplate me through leather—*don't* use the naked eye! I'm the man with a petrified heart and biler-iron bowels! The massacre of isolated communities is the pastime of my idle moments, the destruction of nationalities the serious business of my life! The boundless vastness of the great American desert is my enclosed property, and I bury my dead on my own premises!" He jumped up and cracked his heels together three times before he lit (they cheered him again), and as he come down he shouted out: "Whoo-oop! bow your neck and spread, for the pet child of calamity's a-coming!"

Then the other one went to swelling around and blowing again—the first one—the one they called Bob; next, the Child of Calamity clipped in again, bigger than ever; then they both got at it at the same time, swelling round and round each other and punching their fists most into each other's faces, and whooping and jawing like Injuns; then Bob called the Child names, and the Child called him names back again: next, Bob called him a heap rougher names and the Child come back at him with the very worst kind of language; next, Bob knocked the Child's hat off, and the Child picked it up and kicked Bob's ribbony hat about six foot; Bob went and got it and said never mind, this war'n't going to be the last of this thing, because he was a man that never forgot and never forgive, and so the Child better look out, for there was a time a-coming, just as sure as he was a living man, that he would have to answer to him with the best blood in his body. The Child said no man was willinger than he was for that time to come, and he would give Bob fair warning, *now*, never to cross his path again, for he could never rest till he had waded in his blood, for such was his nature, though he was sparing him now on account of his family, if he had one.

Both of them was edging away in different directions, growling and shaking their heads and going on about what they was going to do; but a little black-whiskered chap skipped up and says:—

"Come back here, you couple of chicken-livered cowards, and I'll thrash the two of ye!"

48 LITTLE DAVY STEPS IN.

And he done it, too. He snatched them, he jerked them this way and that, he booted them around, he knocked them sprawling faster than they could get up. Why, it war n't two minutes till they begged like dogs — and how the other lot did yell and laugh and clap their hands all the way through, and shout "Sail in, Corpse-

"HE KNOCKED THEM SPRAWLING."

Maker!" "Hi! at him again, Child ot Calamity!" "Bully for you, little Davy!" Well, it was a perfect pow-wow for a while. Bob and the Child had red noses and black eyes when they got through. Little Davy made them own up that they was sneaks and cowards and not fit to eat with a dog or drink with a nigger; then Bob and the Child shook hands with each other, very solemn, and said they

AFTER THE BATTLE. 49

had always respected each other and was willing to let bygones be bygones. So then they washed their faces in the river; and just then there was a loud order to stand by for a crossing, and some of them went forward to man the sweeps there, and the rest went aft to handle the after-sweeps.

I laid still and waited for fifteen minutes, and had a smoke out of a pipe that one of them left in reach; then the crossing was finished,

AN OLD-FASHIONED BREAK-DOWN.

and they stumped back and had a drink around and went to talking and singing again. Next they got out an old fiddle, and one played, and another patted juba, and the rest turned themselves loose on a regular old-fashioned keel-boat break-down. They couldn't keep that up very long without getting winded, so by and by they settled around the jug again.

They sung "jolly, jolly raftsman's the life for me," with a rousing chorus, and then they got to talking about differences betwixt hogs, and their different kind of habits; and next about women and their

4

different ways; and next about the best ways to put out houses that was afire; and next about what ought to be done with the Injuns; and next about what a king had to do, and how much he got; and next about how to make cats fight; and next about what to do when a man has fits; and next about differences betwixt clear-water rivers and muddy-water ones. The man they called Ed said the muddy Mississippi water was wholesomer to drink than the clear water of the Ohio; he said if you let a pint of this yaller Mississippi water settle, you would have about a half to three quarters of an inch of mud in the bottom, according to the stage of the river, and then it war'n't no better then Ohio water — what you wanted to do was to keep it stirred up — and when the river was low, keep mud on hand to put in and thicken the water up the way it ought to be.

The Child of Calamity said that was so; he said there was nutritiousness in the mud, and a man that drunk Mississippi water could grow corn in his stomach if he wanted to. He says : —

"You look at the graveyards; that tells the tale. Trees won't grow worth shucks in a Cincinnati graveyard, but in a Sent Louis graveyard they grow upwards of eight hundred foot high. It's all on account of the water the people drunk before they laid up. A Cincinnati corpse don't richen a soil any."

And they talked about how Ohio water didn't like to mix with Mississippi water. Ed said if you take the Mississippi on a rise when the Ohio is low, you'll find a wide band of clear water all the way down the east side of the Mississippi for a hundred mile or more, and the minute you get out a quarter of a mile from shore and pass the line, it is all thick and yaller the rest of the way across. Then they talked about how to keep tobacco from getting mouldy, and from that they went into ghosts and told about a lot that other folks had seen; but Ed says : —

"Why don't you tell something that you've seen yourselves? Now let me have a say. Five years ago I was on a raft as big as this, and right along here it was a bright moonshiny night, and I was on watch and boss of the stabboard oar forrard, and one of my pards was a man named Dick Allbright, and he come along to where I was sitting, forrard — gaping and stretching, he was — and stooped down on the edge of the raft and washed his face in the

river, and come and set down by me and got out his pipe, and had just got it filled, when he looks up and says, —

"'Why looky-here,' he says, 'ain't that Buck Miller's place, over yander in the bend?'

"'Yes,' says I, 'it is — why?' He laid his pipe down and leant his head on his hand, and says, —

"'I thought we'd be furder down.' I says, —

"'I thought it too, when I went off watch,' — we was standing six hours on and six off — 'but the boys told me,' I says, 'that the raft didn't seem to hardly move, for the last hour,' — says I, 'though she's a slipping along all right, now,' says I. He give a kind of a groan, and says, —

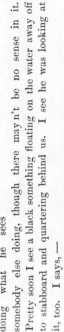

THE MYSTERIOUS BARREL.

"'I've seed a raft act so before, along here,' he says, ''pears to me the current has most quit above the head of this bend durin' the last two years,' he says.

"Well, he raised up two or three times, and looked away off and around on the water. That started me at it, too. A body is always doing what he sees somebody else doing, though there may'n't be no sense in it. Pretty soon I see a black something floating on the water away off to stabboard and quartering behind us. I see he was looking at it, too. I says, —

"'What's that?' He says, sort of pettish, —

"''Tain't nothing but an old empty bar'l.'

"'An empty bar'l!' says I, 'why,' says I, 'a spy-glass is a fool to your eyes. How can you tell it's an empty bar'l?' He says, —

"'I don't know; I reckon it ain't a bar'l, but I thought it might be,' says he.

"'Yes,' I says, 'so it might be, and it might be anything else, too; a body can't tell nothing about it, such a distance as that,' I says.

"We hadn't nothing else to do, so we kept on watching it. By and by I says, —

"'Why looky-here, Dick Allbright, that thing's a-gaining on us, I believe.'

"He never said nothing. The thing gained and gained, and I judged it must be a dog that was about tired out. Well, we swung down into the crossing, and the thing floated across the bright streak of the moonshine, and, by George, it *was* a bar'l. Says I, —

"'Dick Allbright, what made you think that thing was a bar'l, when it was a half a mile off,' says I. Says he, —

"'I don't know.' Says I, —

"'You tell me, Dick Allbright.' He says, —

"'Well, I knowed it was a bar'l; I've seen it before; lots has seen it; they says it's a hanted bar'l.'

"I called the rest of the watch, and they come and stood there, and I told them what Dick said. It floated right along abreast, now, and didn't gain any more. It was about twenty foot off. Some was for having it aboard, but the rest didn't want to. Dick Allbright said rafts that had fooled with it had got bad luck by it. The captain of the watch said he didn't believe in it. He said he reckoned the bar'l gained on us because it was in a little better current than what we was. He said it would leave by and by.

"So then we went to talking about other things, and we had a song, and after that the captain of the watch called for another song; but it was clouding up, now, and the bar'l stuck right thar in the same place, and the song didn't seem to have much warm-up to it, somehow, and so they didn't finish it, and there warn't any cheers, but it sort of dropped flat, and nobody said anything for a minute. Then everybody tried to talk at once, and one chap got off a joke, but it warn't no use, they didn't laugh, and even the chap that made the joke didn't laugh at it, which ain't usual. We all just settled down glum, and watched the bar'l, and was oneasy and oncomfortable. Well, sir, it

shut down black and still, and then the wind begin to moan around, and next the lightning begin to play and the thunder to grumble. And pretty soon there was a regular storm, and in the middle of it a man that was running aft stumbled and fell and sprained his ankle so that he had to lay up. This made the boys shake their heads. And every time the lightning come, there was that bar'l with the blue lights winking around it. We was always on the look-out for it. But by and by, towards dawn, she was gone. When the day come we couldn't see her anywhere, and we warn't sorry, neither.

"But next night about half-past nine, when there was songs and high jinks going on, here she comes again, and took her old roost on the stabboard side. There warn't no more high jinks. Every-body got solemn; nobody talked; you couldn't get anybody to do

"SOON THERE WAS A REGULAR STORM."

anything but set around moody and look at the bar'l. It begun to cloud up again. When the watch changed, the off watch stayed up, 'stead of turning in. The storm ripped and roared around all night, and in the middle of it another man tripped and sprained his ankle, and had to knock off. The bar'l left towards day, and nobody see it go.

"Everybody was sober and down in the mouth all day. I don't mean the kind of sober that comes of leaving liquor alone, — not that. They was quiet, but they all drunk more than usual, — not together, — but each man sidled off and took it private, by himself.

"After dark the off watch didn't turn in; nobody sung, nobody talked; the boys didn't scatter around, neither; they sort of huddled together, forrard; and for two hours they set there, perfectly still, looking steady in the one direction, and heaving a sigh once in a while. And then, here comes the bar'l again. She took up her old place. She staid there all night; nobody turned in. The storm come on again, after midnight. It got awful dark; the rain poured down; hail, too; the thunder boomed and roared and bellowed; the wind blowed a hurricane; and the lightning spread over everything in big sheets of glare, and showed the whole raft as plain as day; and the river lashed up white as milk as far as you could see for miles, and there was that bar'l jiggering along, same as ever. The captain ordered the watch to man the after sweeps for a crossing, and nobody would go, — no more sprained ankles for them, they said. They wouldn't even *walk* aft. Well then, just then the sky split wide open, with a crash, and the lightning killed two men of the after watch, and crippled two more. Crippled them how, says you? Why, *sprained their ankles!*

"The bar'l left in the dark betwixt lightnings, towards dawn. Well, not a body eat a bite at breakfast that morning. After that the men loafed around, in twos and threes, and talked low together. But none of them herded with Dick Allbright. They all give him the cold shake. If he come around where any of the men was, they split up and sidled away. They wouldn't man the sweeps with him. The captain had all the skiffs hauled up on the raft, alongside of his wigwam, and wouldn't let the dead men be took ashore to be planted; he didn't believe a man that got ashore would come back; and he was right.

"THE LIGHTNING KILLED TWO MEN."

"After night come, you could see pretty plain that there was going to be trouble if that bar'l come again; there was such a muttering going on. A good many wanted to kill Dick Allbright, because he'd seen the bar'l on other trips, and that had an ugly look. Some wanted to put him ashore. Some said, let's all go ashore in a pile, if the bar'l comes again.

"This kind of whispers was still going on, the men being bunched together forrard watching for the bar'l, when, lo and behold you, here she comes again. Down she comes, slow and steady, and settles into her old tracks. You could a heard a pin drop. Then up comes the captain, and says: —

"'Boys, don't be a pack of children and fools; I don't want this bar'l to be dogging us all the way to Orleans, and *you* don't; well, then, how's the best way to stop it? Burn it up, — that's the way. I'm going to fetch it aboard,' he says. And before anybody could say a word, in he went.

"He swum to it, and as he come pushing it to the raft, the men spread to one side. But the old man got it aboard and busted in the head, and there was a baby in it! Yes sir, a stark naked baby. It was Dick Allbright's baby; he owned up and said so.

"'Yes,' he says, a-leaning over it, 'yes, it is my own lamented darling, my poor lost Charles William Allbright deceased,' says he, — for he could curl his tongue around the bulliest words in the lan-

56 ALLBRIGHT ATONES.

guage when he was a mind to, and lay them before you without a jint started, anywheres. Yes, he said he used to live up at the head of this bend, and one night he choked his child, which was crying, not intending to kill it,—which was prob'ly a lie,—and then he was scared, and buried it in a bar'l, before his wife got home, and off he went, and struck the northern trail and went to rafting; and this was the third year that the bar'l had chased him. He said the bad luck always begun light, and lasted till four men was killed, and then the bar'l did n't come any more after that. He said if the men would stand it one more night,—and was a-going on like that,—but the men had got enough. They started to get out a boat to take him ashore and lynch him, but he grabbed the little child all of a sudden and jumped overboard with it hugged up to his breast and shed-

"GRABBED THE LITTLE CHILD."

ding tears, and we never see him again in this life, poor old suffering soul, nor Charles William neither."

"*Who* was shedding tears?" says Bob; "was it Allbright or the baby?"

"Why, Allbright, of course; did n't I tell you the baby was dead? Been dead three years—how could it cry?"

"Well, never mind how it could cry—how could it *keep* all that time?" says Davy. "You answer me that."

ED GETS MAD. 57

"I don't know how it done it," says Ed. "It done it though—that's all I know about it."

"Say—what did they do with the bar'l?" says the Child of Calamity.

"Why, they hove it overboard, and it sunk like a chunk of lead."

"Edward, did the child look like it was choked?" says one.

"Did it have its hair parted?" says another.

"What was the brand on that bar'l, Eddy?" says a fellow they called Bill.

"ED GOT UP MAD."

"Have you got the papers for them statistics, Edmund?" says Jimmy.

"Say, Edwin, was you one of the men that was killed by the lightning?" says Davy.

"Him? O, no, he was both of 'em," says Bob. Then they all haw-hawed.

"Say, Edward, don't you reckon you'd better take a pill? You look bad—don't you feel pale?" says the Child of Calamity.

"O, come, now, Eddy, says Jimmy, "show up; you must a kept

58　　SNAKE OR BOY?

part of that bar'l to prove the thing by. Show us the bunghole — do — and we'll all believe you."

"Say, boys," says Bill, "less divide it up. Thar's thirteen of us. I can swaller a thirteenth of the yarn, if you can worry down the rest."

Ed got up mad and said they could all go to some place which he ripped out pretty savage, and then walked off aft cussing to himself, and they yelling

and jeering at him, and roaring and laughing so you could hear them a mile.

"Boys, we'll split a watermelon on that," says the Child of Calamity; and he come rummaging around in the dark amongst the shingle brindles where I was, and put his hand on me. I was warm and soft and naked; so he says "Ouch!" and jumped back.

"Fetch a lantern or a chunk of fire here, boys — there's a snake here as big as a cow!"

So they run there with a lantern and crowded up and looked in on me.

"Come out of that, you beggar!" says one.

"Who are you?" says another.

"What are you after here? Speak up prompt, or overboard you go."

"WHO ARE YOU?"

59　　"SNAKE HIM OUT."

"Snake him out, boys. Snatch him out by the heels."

I began to beg, and crept out amongst them trembling. They looked me over, wondering, and the Child of Calamity says: —

"A cussed thief! Lend a hand and less heave him overboard!"

"No," says Big Bob, "less get out the paint-pot and paint him a sky blue all over from head to heel, and *then* heave him over!"

"Good! that's it. Go for the paint, Jimmy."

When the paint come, and Bob took the brush and was just going to begin, the others laughing and rubbing their hands, I begun to cry, and that sort of worked on Davy, and he says: —

"Vast there! He's nothing but a cub. I'll paint the man that tetches him!"

So I looked around on them, and some of them grumbled and growled, and Bob put down the paint, and the others didn't take it up.

"Come here to the fire, and less see what you're up to here," says Davy. "Now set down there and give an account of yourself. How long have you been aboard here?"

"Not over a quarter of a minute, sir," says I.

"How did you get dry so quick?"

"I don't know, sir. I'm always that way, mostly."

"Oh, you are, are you? What's your name?"

I war'n't going to tell my name. I didn't know what to say, so I just says: —

"Charles William Allbright, sir."

Then they roared — the whole crowd; and I was mighty glad I said that, because maybe laughing would get them in a better humor.

When they got done laughing, Davy says: —

"It won't hardly do, Charles William. You couldn't have growed this much in five year, and you was a baby when you come out of the bar'l, you know, and dead at that. Come, now, tell a straight story, and nobody'll hurt you, if you ain't up to anything wrong. What *is* your name?"

"Aleck Hopkins, sir. Aleck James Hopkins."

"Well, Aleck, where did you come from, here?"

"From a trading scow. She lays up the bend yonder. I was born on her. Pap has traded up and down here all his life; and he

60   SOME LIVELY LYING.

told me to swim off here, because when went by he said he would like to get some of you to speak to a Mr. Jonas Turner, in Cairo, and tell him —"

"Oh, come!"

"Yes, sir, it's as true as the world; Pap he says —"

"Oh, your grandmother!"

They all laughed, and I tried again to talk, but they broke in on me and stopped me.

"CHARLES WILLIAM ALLBRIGHT, SIR."

"Now, looky-here," says Davy; "you're scared, and so you talk wild. Honest, now, do you live in a scow, or is it a lie?"

"Yes, sir, in a trading scow. She lays up at the head of the bend. But I war n't born in her. It's our first trip."

"Now you're talking! What did you come aboard here, for? To steal?"

OFF AND OVERBOARD.   61

"No, sir, I did n't. — It was only to get a ride on the raft. All boys does that."

"Well, I know that. But what did you hide for?"

"Sometimes they drive the boys off."

"So they do. They might steal. Looky-here; if we let you off this time, will you keep out of these kind of scrapes hereafter?"

"'Deed I will, boss. You try me."

"All right, then. You ain't but little ways from shore. Overboard with you, and don't you make a fool of yourself another time this way. — Blast it, boy, some raftsmen would rawhide you till you were black and blue!"

I did n't wait to kiss good-bye, but went overboard and broke for shore. When Jim come along by and by, the big raft was away out of sight around the point. I swum out and got aboard, and was mighty glad to see home again.

The boy did not get the information he was after, but his adventure has furnished the glimpse of the departed raftsman and keelboatman which I desire to offer in this place. I now come to a phase of the Mississippi River life of the flush times of steamboating, which seems to me to warrant full examination — the marvellous science of piloting, as displayed there. I believe there has been nothing like it elsewhere in the world.

198

says: "I wouldn't
want to be nowhere else
than here. Pass me along
another piece of fish &
some ~~hot corn-bread.~~"
"Well, you wouldn't a
been here, if it hadn't been
for Jim. You'd a been
down dah in de woods
widout any dinner, &
gittin' most drownded,
too, dat you would, honey.
Chickens knows when
it's gwyne to rain, an' so
do de birds, child."
"I been in a storm
here once before, with
Tom Sawyer & Jo Har-
per, Jim. It was a storm
like this, too — last summer. We didn't know

Manuscript pages beginning an excised episode that Mark Twain based on the experience of his uncle Jim Lampton, who studied at McDowell Medical College in St. Louis in the latter half of the 1840s. The text above the paragraph beginning "I been in a storm . . ." is included in chapter 9 of the novel (Buffalo and Erie County Public Library).

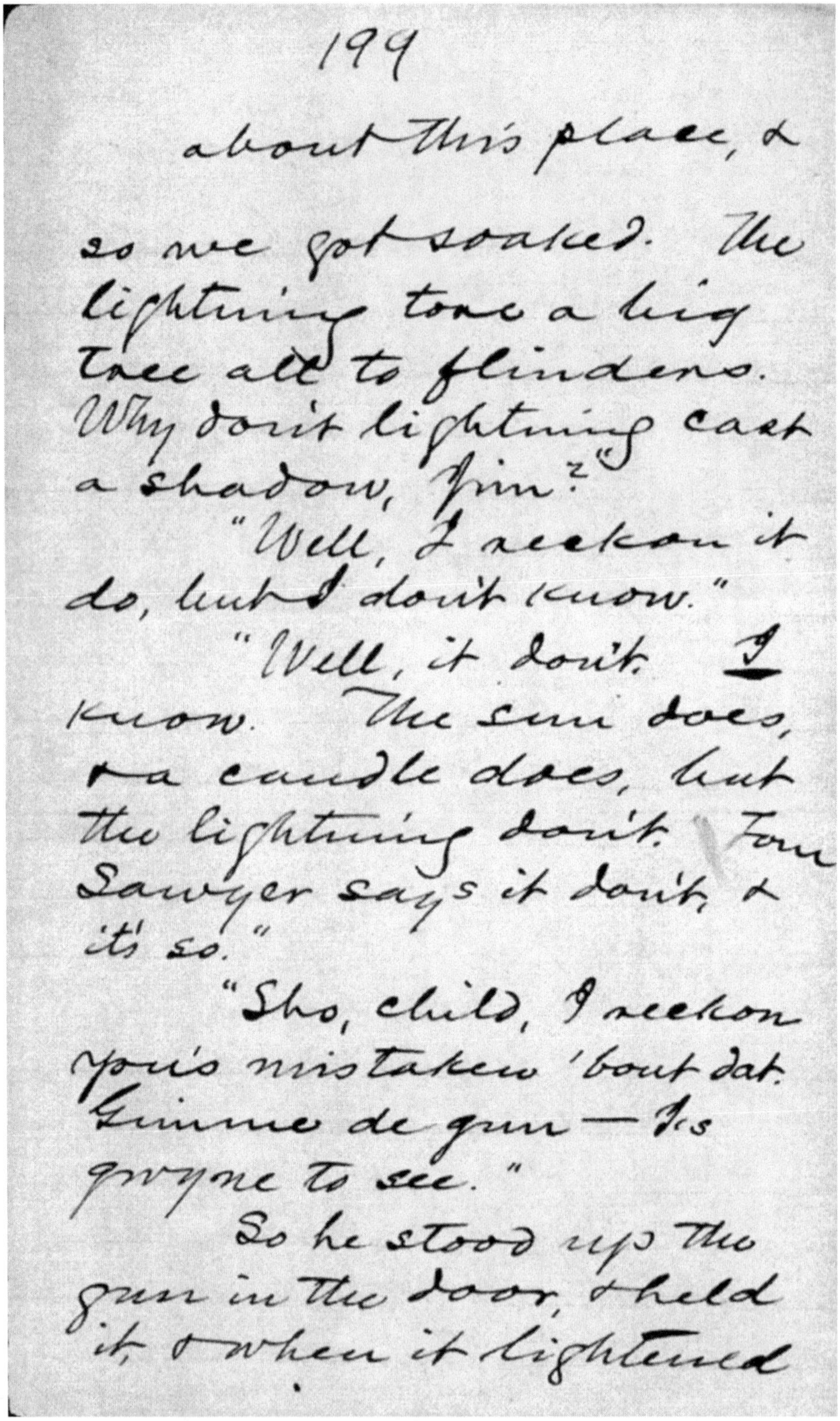

199

about this place, &
so we got soaked. The
lightning tore a big
tree all to flinders.
Why don't lightning cast
a shadow, Jim?

"Well, I reckon it
do, but I don't know."

"Well, it don't. *I*
know. The sun does,
& a candle does, but
the lightning don't. Tom
Sawyer says it don't, &
it's so."

"Sho, child, I reckon
you's mistaken 'bout dat.
Gimme de gun — I's
gwyne to see."

So he stood up the
gun in the door, & held
it, & when it lightened

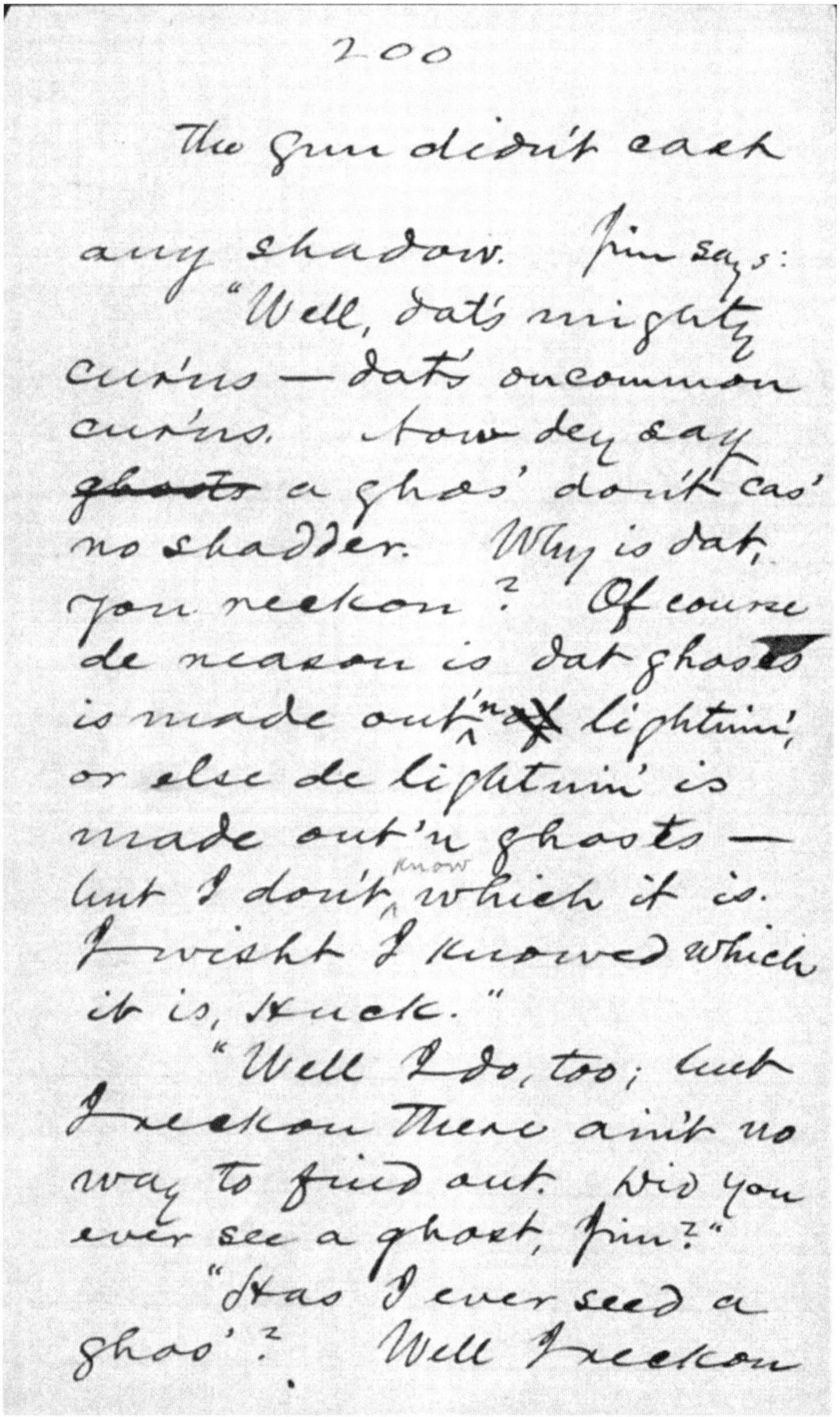

200

the gun didn't cast

any shadow. Jim says:

"Well, dat's mighty
cur'us — dat's oncommon
curn's. Now dey say
~~ghosts~~ a ghos' don't cas'
no shadder. Why is dat,
you reckon? Of course
de reason is dat ghosts
is made out 'n lightnin',
or else de lightnin' is
made out'n ghosts —
but I don't know which it is.
I wisht I knowed which
it is, Huck."

"Well I do, too; but
I reckon there ain't no
way to find out. Did you
ever see a ghost, Jim?"

"Has I ever seed a
ghos'? Well I reckon

201

I has."

"O, tell me about it, Jim — tell me about it."

"De storm's a rippin' an' a tearin', an' a carryin' on so, a body can't hardly talk, but I reckon I'll try. Long time ago, when I was 'bout sixteen year old, my young Mars. William, dat's dead, now, was a stugent in a doctor college in de village whah we lived den. Dat college was a powerful big brick building three stories high, & stood all by herself in a big open place out to de edge of de village. — Well, one night in de mid-

202

dle of winter young
Mars. William he tole
me to go to de college,
an' go up stairs to de
dissectin' room on de
second flo,' & warm
up a dead man dat
was dah on de table,
& git him soft so he
can cut him up—"
"What for, him?"
"I don't *~~do~~* know—
see if can find suffin
in him, maybe. Any-
ways, dat's what he
tole me. An' he tole me
to wait dah tell he
~~come~~. So I takes a
~~candle~~ lantern & starts out
acrost de town. My,
but it was a-blowin' &
an' a-sleetin' an' cold!

213

"What made him
hop on to your neck,
Jim?"

"Well, Mars. William
said I didn't prop him
good wid de rollers. —
But I don't know. It
warn't no way for a
dead man to act any-
way; it might a'scared
some people to death."

"But Jim, he warn't
rightly a ghost — he was
only a dead man. Didn't
you ever see a real
sure-'nough ghost?"

"You bet I has —
lots of 'em."

"Well, tell me about
them, Jim."

"All right, I will,
some time; but

The last manuscript pages of Jim's story about his encounter with a cadaver. The text in the published novel continues with the paragraph that begins, "The river went on raising . . . ," at the top of the manuscript page 214 (Buffalo and Erie County Public Library).

214

storm's a-slackin' up,
now, so we better go
an' tend to de lines an'
bait 'em agin."

       'The river went on
o as raising for ten or twelve days,
raising tell at last it was
over the banks. The water
was three or four feet deep
on the island & on the Illinois bottom. On that side
(the east side)
   it was a good many miles
wide; but on the Missouri
side it was the same old
distance across — half a
mile — because the Mis-
souri shore was just
a wall of high bluffs. —
       Daytimes we paddled all
over the island in the canoe.
It was mighty cool & shady
in the deep woods even if

Illustrating the Novel

Because Sam Clemens's own company published Adventures of Huckleberry Finn, *he had greater authority over the production of the book than do most authors—and he energetically exercised that authority, including choosing and hiring the illustrator for the volume.*

Mark Twain, E. W. Kemble, and *Huckleberry Finn*
Michael Patrick Hearn

Samuel L. Clemens made his national reputation as "Mark Twain" largely through the highly profitable nineteenth-century American business of subscription publishing. Unlike the regular trade volume, the subscription book was offered door-to-door across the country by an army of local independent book agents, primarily "broken-down clergymen, maiden ladies, grass widows, and college students,"[1] and to people who never went into bookstores. Within two years of publication, his first commissioned work, *The Innocents Abroad* (1869), had sold 100,000 copies. Within a decade, works by Mark Twain, "the people's author," were as common to rural parlors as the family Bible and Webster's dictionary. However, convinced that he had been swindled by the American Publishing Co., of Hartford, Connecticut, the most aggressive of the major subscription houses, Twain broke with that firm in 1881 and published his next book, *The Prince and the Pauper,* with a reputable Boston trade publisher. Unfortunately, its sales were disastrous. For Twain, "anything but subscription publishing is printing for private circulation."[2] He then allowed the same Boston house to issue *Life on the Mississippi* (1883) door-to-door, but it did no better than *The Prince and the Pauper.* The only answer for his next effort, *Adventures of Huckleberry Finn,* was to publish that book by subscription himself. So, by May 1884, after setting up his nephew-in-law in a couple of offices in New York City, Twain established Charles L. Webster and Company.

An important feature of a subscription book was that, since they generally cost more than a regular trade book, the salesman had to offer the buyer more for his money. The solution to this problem was to fill the book with pictures. Initially the publishers considered "a *very* cheap man" named Hooper to illustrate *Huckleberry Finn.* However, Twain enjoyed a cartoon of "the applying of electrical protectors to doorknobs, door-mats, etc., and electrical hurriers to messengers, waiters, etc." which had recently appeared in *Life,* the humor weekly; so in late March he wrote Webster that he wanted the artist responsible for that drawing for his new book.[3]

But Edward Windsor Kemble (1861–1933) was not cheap; although he had been illustrating professionally for only two years, Kemble was so in demand as a cartoonist that he charged $1200 for his first book commission, to make 175 pen-and-ink drawings for *Huckleberry Finn.* Born in Sacramento, California,[4] Kemble studied for only a year at the Art Students League in New York. "I don't know what good it did," he later admitted, "for no one ever looked at what I drew."[5] Consequently, Kemble was largely self-taught. Undaunted by this lack of training, he secured a job as staff cartoonist on the New York *Daily Graphic* in 1881 and, when *Life* was founded in 1883, Kemble was one of its early contributors.

Kemble never met with Twain to discuss his drawings for the new novel. "I am not going to tell you what to draw," Twain later told another of his artists. "If a man comes to me and says, 'Mr. Clemens, I want you to write me a story,' I'll write it for him; but if he undertakes to tell me what to write, I'll say, 'Go hire a typewriter.'"[6] But Twain was not above letting an illustrator know what *not* to draw. Kemble communicated directly with Webster, and the publisher kept the author informed of every step of the artist's progress. Then, if anything displeased Twain, Webster reported it back to Kemble.

Because the book had to be ready for the vital Christmas season of 1884, Kemble immediately set to work. Unfortunately, he was soon delayed. "I cannot have many of the illustrations finished until the latter part of next week," he wrote Webster on May 1, "as we all have the moving craze and are experiencing such little delights as eating our meals off the mantle piece, bathing in a coal scuttle behind a screen, etc., etc. I have tried to work but cannot make it go." The artist appended to his note a sketch of "a faint idea of my condition." In spite of the circumstances, Kemble did deliver the first batch of drawings as promised; but evidently he had hurried the work and Twain was not pleased with the results. "Some of the pictures are good," he wrote Webster on May 24, "but none of them are very *very* good. The faces are generally ugly, and wrenched into over-expression amounting sometimes to distortion. As a rule (though not always) the people in the pictures are forbidding and repulsive. Reduction will modify them, no doubt, but it can hardly make them pleasant folk to look at." The cover sketch for the "book-back" was "all right and good, and will answer; although the boy's mouth is a trifle more Irishy than necessary." However, Kemble depicted only what he found in the text; indeed, many of the people in *Huckleberry Finn* are forbidding and repulsive, but letter-perfect accuracy was not what Twain expected from the illustrations. "An artist shouldn't follow a book too literally, perhaps," he explained to Webster, "if this be the necessary result. And mind you, much of the drawing in these pictures is careless and bad."

Kemble worked with several disadvantages. Not only was his home disrupted, he evidently never had the complete manuscript to refer to.[7] He also used the same model for all the novel's many characters. The New York City boy who posed for Huck himself doubled for everyone else, from Mrs. Judith Loftus to the "late Dauphin."[8] Certain problems in the sketches may be traced to Kemble's having to interpret rather than to copy the characterizations. Even for Huck Finn, the young model was not perfect. "He was a bit tall for the ideal boy," Kemble admitted, "but I could jam him down a few pegs in my drawing." Twain found even this characterization wanting. "The frontispiece has the usual blemish–an ugly, ill-drawn face," the author complained to his publisher. "Huck Finn is an exceedingly good-hearted boy, and should carry a good and good-looking face."

Twain was as concerned with Kemble's illustrations as he was with his own text. Certain subjects could not be depicted. Although Huck admits in Chapter 19 that "we was always naked, day and night," Kemble never portrays the boy and the slave nude; and Twain suppressed Kemble's drawing of the "lecherous old rascal kissing the girl at the campmeeting" in Chapter 20, because, Twain told Webster on June 11, "the subject won't *bear* illustrating. It is a disgusting thing, and pictures are sure to tell the truth about it too plainly." Again, suggestion was important, in the illustrations as well as the text. Only reluctantly did Twain say, "the pictures will *do* they will just barely do–and that is the best I can say for them." He approved them apparently because the publisher needed sample drawings for their agents, canvassing books, bound prospectuses made up of representative chapters and their appropriate illustrations with strips of the various available bindings laid in the front and blank ruled pages at the back for orders. These had to be ready no later than midsummer, for Twain demanded a prepublication sale of 40,000 copies before he would issue the book at holiday time. The author did have faith in Kemble's abilities. He warned Webster, "don't dishearten the artist– show him where he has *improved,* rather than where he has failed and punch him up to improve more." Happily, on receipt of more illustrations, Twain proudly wrote Webster on June 11, "I *knew* Kemble had it *in* him, if he would only modify his violences and come down to careful, painstaking work. This batch of pictures is most rattling good. They please me exceedingly."

Because *Huckleberry Finn* was advertised as "a companion to *The Adventures of Tom Sawyer,*" Kemble was expected to follow the general design of True W. Williams' illustrations in the previous novel. At first glance, the two books with their myriads of spot line drawings darting in and out of the type do look alike, but the differences between Williams' and Kemble's art are greater than their similarities. Kemble was clearly the better of the two draftsmen, but the pictures in *Tom Sawyer* are certainly prettier than those in *Huckleberry Finn.* Williams, as much as the author himself, idealized "St. Petersburg" Clemens' boyhood home in Hannibal, Missouri; the artist captured the slightly sentimental view of childhood immortalized in what Twain called "simply a hymn, put into prose form to give it a worldly air."[9] The abrupt change in atmosphere within the same locale is established in the opening illustration of each novel. In the first, Tom Sawyer's humble home looks like a mansion; in the second, the Widow Douglas' mansion looks like any other backwoods dwelling. Kemble was less self-consciously a stylist than was Williams, and his strong, matter-of-fact drawings are free of the sweet fussiness of his predecessor's designs. Even when drawing violences (such as the murder of Dr. Robinson), Williams emphasized the romance, the melodrama of the event; but in the shooting of Old Boggs by Colonel Sherburn, Kemble depicted the crime as coolly, as distantly, as Huck describes it.

But Kemble was by profession a cartoonist, and so humor was essential to his drawings for *Huckleberry Finn.* What is most remarkable about these illustrations is the way the artist extended even the minor comedy that was merely suggested in the text. With tongue firmly in cheek, Kemble literally interpreted some ignorant absurdity, whether it concerned Solomon and his million wives, the king as Juliet, or Hannah with the mumps, mentioned only in passing by some character in the story. And the artist added his own private jokes into the drawings: for example, the tailpieces of Huck's entering and re-entering his window at the Widow Douglas' in Chapters 1 and 2 are exact mirror images of each other, a device employed earlier by John Tenniel in Chapter 1 of *Through the Looking-Glass* (1872). Further levity came from the captions, written, like the running heads, by the publisher. Particularly effective are Webster's sardonic puns, such as "Falling from Grace" in Chapter 5 and "A Dead Head" in Chapter 22. Unnecessarily, some carelessnesses crept into the drawings. For example, in Chapter 14, Kemble gave the king a black hat rather than the white beaver mentioned in the text, and Joanna is shown in Chapter 26 as several years older than Huck rather than the same age as the boy.

Nevertheless, in his illustrations for *Huckleberry Finn,* Kemble proved himself an American master of humorous characterization. He was not strictly a caricaturist; his comedy came from the situation to be illustrated rather than

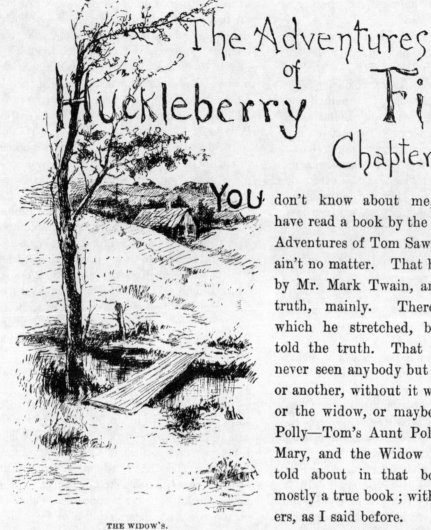

The Adventures of Huckleberry Finn
Chapter I.

YOU don't know about me, without you have read a book by the name of "The Adventures of Tom Sawyer," but that ain't no matter. That book was made by Mr. Mark Twain, and he told the truth, mainly. There was things which he stretched, but mainly he told the truth. That is nothing. I never seen anybody but lied, one time or another, without it was Aunt Polly, or the widow, or maybe Mary. Aunt Polly—Tom's Aunt Polly, she is—and Mary, and the Widow Douglas, is all told about in that book—which is mostly a true book; with some stretchers, as I said before.

THE WIDOW'S.

Now the way that the book winds up, is this : Tom and me found the money that the robbers hid in the cave, and it made us rich. We got six thousand dollars apiece—all gold. It was an awful sight of money when it was piled up. Well, Judge Thatcher, he took it and put it out at interest, and it fetched us a dollar a day apiece, all the year round—more than a body could tell what to do with. The Widow Douglas, she took me for her son, and allowed she would sivilize me ; but it was rough living in the house all the time, considering how dismal regular and decent the widow was in all her ways ; and so when I couldn't stand it no longer, I lit out. I got into my old rags, and my sugar-hogshead again, and was free and satisfied. But

2

The first pages of Mark Twain's novels that show how E. W. Kemble in Adventures of Huckleberry Finn *followed through on the design motifs—including incorporating a drawing at the beginning of a chapter and hand-drawing the first word—that True Williams had established in the earlier novel (Mark Twain House, Hartford, Connecticut)*

THE ADVENTURES OF TOM SAWYER.

CHAPTER I.

"TOM!"

No answer.

"TOM!"

No answer.

"What's gone with that boy, I wonder? You TOM!"

No answer.

The old lady pulled her spectacles down and looked over them about the room; then she put them up and looked out under them. She seldom or never looked *through* them for so small a thing as a boy; they were her state pair, the pride of her heart, and were built for "style," not service— she could have seen through a pair of stove lids just as well. She looked perplexed for a moment, and

TOM AT HOME.

then said, not fiercely, but still loud enough for the furniture to hear:

A cartoon Kemble included in a letter to publisher Charles Webster to show his circumstances while he was working on the illustrations for Adventures of Huckleberry Finn *(from* Mark Twain, Business Man, *Thomas Cooper Library, University of South Carolina)*

from any stylistic trick he might employ. Whatever he may have lacked in technical grace (and some of his pictures are badly drawn), Kemble shared with the greatest illustrators the ability to give even the minor individual in a text his own distinct visual personality; just as Twain in a few sentences could suggest a fully rounded character, so too could Kemble depict with a few strokes of his pen that same whole personage. Kemble may have initially relied somewhat on Williams' depictions in *Tom Sawyer*, but he made the characters his own in his drawings for *Huckleberry Finn*.

Despite Twain's overseeing of the book's production, an unanticipated problem with the printing delayed the book's publication. While Charles L. Webster was in San Francisco on business, one of his salesmen showed him an odd detail in one of the illustrations in the canvassing book. In "Who do you reckon it is?"(prophetically beneath the running head "In a Dilemma") of Chapter 33, something now protruded from Uncle Silas' trousers like an erect penis.

Webster immediately returned to New York and offered a $500 reward for the apprehension and conviction of the person responsible for the obscene alteration of the engraving. He also demanded that each agent now remove the offensive page from every copy of the prospectus or face immediate dismissal; and all released copies of the finished book were recalled for correction of the unsightly error. "The book was examined by W. D. Howells, Mr. Clemens, the proofreader, and myself," Webster told a reporter in the New York *Herald* (November 29, 1884). "Nothing improper was discovered. . . . By the punch of an awl or graver, the illustration became an immoral one. But 250 copies left the office . . . before the mistake was discovered. Had the first edition been run off our loss would have been $250,000. Had the mistake not been discovered, Mr. Clemens' credit for decency and morality would have been destroyed." The only answer was to excise the offending page and tip in a corrected leaf. "This cost me

---

Working on Proof

With Charles Webster following his every order, Mark Twain was essentially his own publisher. He nevertheless found proofreading his novel a frustrating experience, as these excerpts from August 1884 letters to Webster indicate. Twain was then reviewing proofs with illustrations and captions added by Webster.

In this excerpt from a letter written on the seventh, the author complained about characters accidentally turned upside down in the newly added captions.

I miscalculated my fortitude. I *can't* read any more proof. I sent this batch to Howells without glancing at it—except to note that that proof reader had left it to me to mark turned letters under cuts! Howells will maybe return it to *you* to read—in which case you may send it to me again, & I will get my profanity together & tackle it.

—*Mark Twain, Business Man,* p. 271

The author soon resumed reviewing galleys, or slips, writing again to Webster on the eleventh.

Most of this proof was clean & beautiful, & a pleasure to read; but the rest of it was read by that blind idiot whom I have cursed to much, & is a disgraceful mess.

Send me slips from where the frauds arrive & *sit down to supper* in Miss Mary's house, up to slip No. 73.

Send me also slips from No. 75 up to 81.

And insist that the rest of the proofs be *better read.*

—*Mark Twain, Business Man,* p. 272

This excerpt is from a letter written on the fourteenth.

If all the proofs had been as well read as the first 2 or 3 chapters were, I should not have needed to see the revises at all. On the contrary it was the worst & silliest proof-reading I have ever seen. It was never read by copy at all—not a single galley of it.

—*Mark Twain, Business Man,* p. 272

plenty," J. J. Little, the printer, later admitted; but so competently did his firm handle the problem that no known copies of the first edition survive with the obscene plate. The initial investment was saved, but the Christmas market was lost; Webster did not officially release the novel until February 18, 1885. However, although the story of the obscene illustration did somewhat taint the author's reputation for decency, Kemble remained unaffected by the notorious corruption of his drawing.

Even before the book was published, Kemble was recognized for his significant contribution to *Huckleberry Finn*. "We are not only indebted to you for a good chapter for our next number," Richard Watson Gilder of *The Century* told Twain in November, "but are profoundly indebted to you for unearthing a gem of an artist for us. As soon as we saw Kemble's pictures in your proofs, we recognized the fact that that he was a find for us and so we went for him and we've got him. He is going to New Orleans for us to illustrate a long article." *Huckleberry Finn* made Kemble's reputation as one of the most admired of American illustrators of the late nineteenth century; it also determined the course of the rest of his career. Ironically, although he had never been farther south than Sandy Hook when he made the drawings for Twain's novel, through this bestseller Kemble became famous for his depiction of the rural South; and then, whenever an editor such as Gilder needed an artist for a piece about that part of the country, he turned first to Kemble. Kemble was so in demand that, in addition to *Century, Harper's, Collier's, St. Nicholas,* and other major magazines competed for Kemble to illustrate work by such popular Southern writers as Joel Chandler Harris, George W. Cable, and Thomas Nelson Page.[10] Kemble did visit the South and filled his sketchbooks with sensitive studies of Black life; these drawings were particularly helpful for his fine illustrations for *Uncle Tom's Cabin* (1892). However, he earned his widest popularity at the century's end for his unfortunate caricatures "Kemble's Coons" and "Blackberries," and consequently his present reputation has suffered for these dated stereotypes. *Huckleberry Finn* may have made Kemble's career, but he found time to illustrate only one other book prepared by Twain and published by Webster, *Mark Twain's Library of Humor,* and he was not even considered for either *Tom Sawyer Abroad* (1894) or "Tom Sawyer, Detective" (1896).

But Kemble did return to his first success, from time to time, to make new pictures for the famous story. In 1899, he provided four pen-and-wash illustrations for the reprint in the standard "Author's Edition" of Mark Twain's collected works; and for a special Mark Twain number of the Sunday colored comic supplement "The Funny Side" of the New York *World* (December 10, 1899), Kemble contributed three new pen-and-ink sketches of incidents from Twain's greatest novel. One of the artist's last drawings was made for the 1933 Limited Editions Club edition. When George Macy learned that the original illustrator of *Huckleberry Finn* lived nearby, in Ridgefield, Connecticut, he asked Kemble to add something to the new edition, and the artist produced a

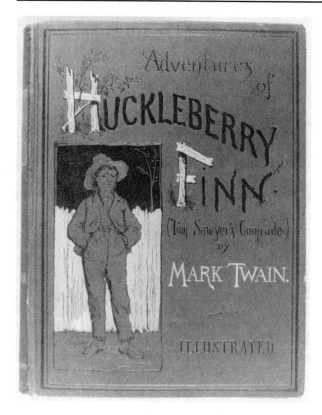

Cover for the first American edition, designed by E. W. Kemble
(Vassar College Library)

fine picture of Huck, Tom, and Jim reading the famous account of their Mississippi adventures.

Many other illustrators (including Norman Rockwell, Thomas Hart Benton, Edward Ardizzone, and Warren Chappell) have attempted *Huckleberry Finn,* but none of their efforts have surpassed the first illustrations. No other artist has depicted pious Miss Watson, drunken Pap Finn, the blubbering king and the bombastic duke, and all the others, so convincingly as did Twain's original illustrator. And Huck Finn himself is remembered as much for Kemble's image of the good-hearted boy as by Twain's description. In Kemble, Twain found an artist of ability in full sympathy with his work. Being a perfect marriage of author and illustrator, *Huckleberry Finn* joins *Oliver Twist* and *Alice's Adventures in Wonderland* as a classic of the nineteenth-century illustrated novel.

–*American Book Collector,* new series 2.6
(November–December 1981): 14–19

----

1. Quoted by Milton Meltzer, *Mark Twain Himself* (New York: Thomas Y. Crowell, 1960), p. 194.
2. In a letter to William Dean Howells, quoted by Justin Kaplan, *Mr. Clemens and Mark Twain* (New York: Simon and Schuster, 1966), p. 62.
3. According to a note in *Mark Twain's Letters to His Publishers,* edited by Hamlin Hill (Berkeley and Los Angeles: University of California Press, 1967), p. 174; in a letter to Charles L.

Webster, March 31, 1884, *Mark Twain, Business Man,* edited by Samuel Charles Webster (Boston: Little Brown and Co., 1946), p. 246. Unless otherwise stated, all further references to correspondence with Webster are from the latter work.
4. Twain may have known the artist's father, Edward Cleveland Kemble, the founder of the *Alta California,* for which Twain was a traveling correspondent and in which first appeared the series of letters which became *The Innocents Abroad.*
5. Quoted in his obituary in the *New York Times,* September 20, 1933.
6. In a letter to Dan Beard, quoted by Albert Bigelow Paine, *Mark Twain: A Biography,* Vol. II (New York and London, Harper & Bros., 1912), p. 888.
7. This situation is suggested by a letter from Kemble to Webster, June 2, 1884, quoted by Beverly R. David in "The Pictorial *Huckleberry Finn*: Mark Twain and His Illustrator, E. W. Kemble" (*American Quarterly,* October 1979, p. 33), in which the artist asked the publisher to "send me the manuscript from XIII Chapter on . . . as these are illustrations here which are described minutely and I'm afraid to touch them without the reading matter to refer to." Kemble also apparently worked from the uncorrected manuscript, rather than from galleys, because there are details in his drawings which are not in the published book; for example, the two Phelps children depicted in the illustration in Chapter 32 are described in the manuscript but not in the book.
8. For the king, the young model "wore an old frock coat and padded his waist with towels until he assumed the proper rotundity. Then he would mimic the sordid old reprobate and twist his boyish face into the most outlandish expressions." "If I could have drawn the grimaces as they were," Kemble continued in "Illustrating *Huckleberry Finn*" (*The Colophon,* February 1930), "I would have had a convulsing collection of comics, but these would not have jibed with the text and I was forced to forgo them."
9. In an unmailed letter, September 8, 1887, *Mark Twain's Letters,* edited by Albert Bigelow Paine, Vol. II (New York and London: Harper & Bros., 1935), p. 477.
10. Not all of Kemble's collaborators cared for his work. "For a man who has no conception whatever of human nature," Harris complained, "Kemble does very well. But he is too dog-goned flip to suit me." Harris disapproved of the dependence upon stock characters, such as those used by Kemble in his cartoons. "Neither fiction nor illustrative art," argued the author of *Uncle Remus,* "has any business with types. It must address itself to life, to the essence of life which is character, which is individuality." See "Visions of the South: Joel Chandler Harris and His Illustrators" by Beverly R. David, *American Literary Realism,* Summer 1976, pp. 198–199. And Twain came to share Harris's disappointment with Kemble as an illustrator. He regretted the "blackboard outlines and charcoal sketches" in *Mark Twain's Library of Humor* (1888): "If Kemble illustrations for my last book were handed me today, I would understand how tiresome to me the sameness would get to be, when distributed through a whole book, and I would put them promptly in the fire" (in a note to *Mark Twain's Letters to His Publishers,* p. 254).

* * *

Clemens was very conscious of his image as "Mark Twain." That image was damaged, he believed, when his speech at the seventieth birthday celebration for John Greenleaf Whittier was not well received. His persona was recuperated, so he thought, when his humorous remarks were applauded at a banquet for Ulysses S. Grant. In this excerpt Louis J. Budd examines the author's decision to include a serious, even austere, image of himself in marble as a frontispiece.

"A Nobler Roman Aspect" of *Adventures of Huckleberry Finn*

Louis J. Budd

By now it takes a Tom Sawyer to dream of finding the master-clue to *Adventures of Huckleberry Finn* that has been overlooked by all the capable scholars and critics who have ransacked the apparently simple text, and not even Poe's Auguste Dupin would dare to sneer that it was in plain sight all along. But an important clue to appreciating *Huckleberry Finn* stands right there up front for anyone who looks at a very early printing. I mean the full-page photograph or, more precisely, the heliotype of a bust of Mark Twain. Only descriptive bibliographers and collectors have looked hard because they find it useful for trying to establish the earliest states of the first edition. That fact is revealing in itself. Because of technical problems, the plate had to be remade about a hundred times for the first printing of thirty thousand.[1] Perhaps because of that, the heliotype was soon dropped.

It was expensive also because of the timing: it held up publication or at the least incurred charges for rush service. On 19 August 1884, from his summer hideout in Elmira, New York, Twain wrote to Charles L. Webster, the nephew running a newly founded publishing firm for him in New York City: "Gerhardt is completing a most excellent bust of me." There was an accident, however, and not until 31 August could Twain inform William Dean Howells that the "finishing touches" would come the next day. Indeed on 9 September he described the bust as "just finished," adding that the sculptor "has just gone" to Philadelphia for the casting into bronze. Then, as early as 20 September, Twain was fuming that the "heliotype Co." in Boston had not sent "that bottle of ink for the autographs."[2] It still had not arrived four days later. These details gain significance from the timetable of publication. Twain had mailed the revised manuscript on 12 April 1884 and had finished with the proofs—galley and page—before the end of August. But long before one of his books issued, he was impatiently counting on the royalties. Also, his letter to Webster on 20 September had called for an unbound copy, probably to use in getting ready for his barnstorming tour with George Washington Cable.

In fact, unbound copies were available by 19 September. Why did Twain take on the problems of inserting that heliotype so late? It surely was not meant to add comedy. Twain, who had been doggedly trying to educate his tastes and had learned deeper respect for fine art than seems likely from *The Innocents Abroad,* assured Howells that the bust was "about as good a one as nearly anybody could make." Serious in expression, it was sternly imposing from the front, and he must have worried that some apprentice Mark Twain might make sparkling fun of it. It came from the hands of his protégé, Karl Gerhardt, fresh back from Paris after more than three years of study paid for by Twain, who ordered his nephew to make sure that the sculptor's name showed on the bust (as it does in only some of the plates). Twain hoped to launch Gerhardt, probably not to recover an investment but to prove an ability to recognize a gifted artist in the rough. Obviously Twain would also enjoy getting credit for generosity, all the more because the envious were starting to gossip about his success at raking in dollars. His "P.S." primed Howells with: "If you run across anybody who wants a bust, be sure & recommend Gerhardt on my say-so."

Another obvious motive was royalties from *Huckleberry Finn.* The short ad for "agents" would dangle a "Fine Heliotype of the Author" as a wedge for their door-to-door battle. As early as 1869 an alert operator in Cleveland had sold photographs of Twain after his lecture. During the 1870s he had to notice that his face evidently helped various lines of business–cigars, "White & Fancy Goods, Sewing Machines, & C," and the services of "Plumbers, Steam and Gas Fitters." A haggler over words could argue that the first separate biography of Twain was packed in Duke's Cigarettes soon after 1886. Of course it put his portrait on the cover, which measures 1 1/2 by 3 inches. Partly to tap such demand, *A Tramp Abroad* (1880) carried a solemn engraving of Twain in coat and tie. Suggestively for my argument to come, it balanced (or was balanced by) a spurious "Titian's Moses," featuring a bawling infant holding a dish with a live frog on it.

The plausible motives fall short of explaining why the heliotype, even with the side view it used, clashes so sharply with the tone of *Huckleberry Finn.* Pseudo-classical in the style that the early nineteenth century had established for our statesmen, it lacks only the folds of a toga gathered at one of the bare shoulders. The *Boston Literary World,* more impressed than quizzical, decided that it "gives the humorist a nobler Roman aspect than that which he wears in real life."[3] The *New York Critic,* a weekly devoted to aesthetic and intellectual affairs, cautiously quoted from a long description by Charles Dudley Warner–Twain's neighbor in Hartford, to be sure, but a genteel prophet honored nationally. He especially admired the bust's "broad masses, full of strength and character–no pettiness, here. . . . It is simple in all its lines, but massive and solid in treatment, and it has a noble dignity and repose." While professing tentativeness, Warner grew positive that it was "more worthy of study than anything of the sort that has appeared here in a long time." The creator of Huck Finn had seemingly modeled for a near-masterpiece himself.

Twain, we know, carefully supervised the illustrations in his books. For *Huckleberry Finn* he came up with a young artist whom he treated like a draftsman or a tailor. Incongruously with the yet unmade bust he picked E. W. Kemble through his centerspread in *Life,* a new comic weekly. Kemble's cartoon had seized on the latest technology to imagine "the applying of electrical protectors to door-knobs, door-mats, &c & electrical hurriers to messengers, waiters &c." He would draw the now familiar frontispiece of Huck holding a dead rabbit and a rifle. But for the second frontispiece Twain did not choose Kemble or the *Life* artist who had him (22 March 1883) studying a skull while an owl and black cat glare from a weird set of props.[4] By 1884 at least twenty other cartoonists, including Twain's famous friend Thomas Nast, had run him through a gamut of exaggeration, but none of them got an offer. Avoiding a humorously stylized portrait of himself was a significant decision at some level of consciousness.

He likewise ignored the models for another engraving like the one in *A Tramp Abroad.* Fascinated by the newfangled camera, he had already posed for it many times. We have to suspect self-ridicule beneath his insistence that it's human nature to center on your own face in a group picture. Furthermore, anybody whose photograph has never appeared more publicly than in a college yearbook may underestimate the trauma when it gets national visibility. In 1887 Twain raged: "leave out that woodcut of me [from *The Library of American Literature* published by his firm]. The more I think of the gratuitous affront of wood where [a] steel [engraving] is lavished upon the unread & the forgotten, the more my bile rises. Don't leave it out, simply–put it in the fire."[5] Some sympathy is due here. How many of his would-be betters had already sat for at least two portraits by established artists?

Besides those oil portraits Twain might have used the one taken recently by Napoleon Sarony,

---

Mark Twain's Frontispiece

This excerpt is from Mark Twain's 8 September letter to Webster.

Here is a photograph from the bust. How would it do to heliotype it (reducing it to half the present size) & make a frontispiece of it for Huck Finn, with

Mark Twain
from the bust by Karl Gerhardt

printed under it.

–Mark Twain, Business Man, p. 275

---

since 1870 or so "the photographer of the country" according to the *New York Times* obituary. "His pictures are as well known in the shops of Paris as they are in Broadway and in the theatres of the United States."[6] As for his head-and-shoulders photograph of Twain, the subject sighed in 1905 that it had "spread about the world" and "turns up every week in some newspaper some where or other." But at first it pleased him so much that soon he went back to Sarony with Cable and then, ten years later, alone. In March 1885 he instructed Webster: "Don't forget that I want a dozen of my photos from Sarony's." Eventually he joked at length that it made him look like a gorilla. It did give him a fierce stare and would have suited almost as well what I think he was after. However, the bronze bust had more "tone" in the ironic sense in which he often used that word.

Given the kaleidoscope of Twain's career, my argument should stick close to 1884. Still, it is relevant that alertness toward his visual image never sagged. In 1905 he drolled for a prearranged, syndicated interview:

Many people think I am a happy man, but I am not; it is because my portraits do me justice. I have a highly organized and sensitive constitution and an educated taste in esthetics, and I cannot abide a portrait which is too particular. I am as I was made–this is a disaster which I cannot help and am in no way responsible for; but is there any fair reason why the artist should notice that? I do him no harm, yet he always exercises this wanton and malicious frankness upon my portraits.

I should like to be drawn once, before I reach 70 again, as I should look if I had been made right instead of carelessly.[7]

Revealing by omission, very few photographs of a smiling Twain survive despite such typical clowning. When asked why his face froze even for snapshots, he explained he did not want to go down to posterity with a foolish grin. The caricatures of Twain as a madcap entertainer must have left him edgy and rueful. However welcome the publicity, he must have brooded about upgrading it. The persons illustrated in his books whom a reader could take for Mark Twain rise in sedateness from *The Innocents Abroad* through *Life on the Mississippi* and of course beyond. So we should ponder that heliotype inserted at the cost of money and vexation to an impatient man. He proposed it to Webster with: "I suppose it would help sell the book." The next day he added, "I thought maybe it would advantage the book." Curiously tentative words from somebody poor in false modesty and increasingly rich in confidence as a promoter.

II

To present all sides of Twain's mind properly would outdo Emmeline Grangerford's spidery drawing. So I may slight his aesthetic impulses by concentrating on his awareness of his public image. Still, the heliotype represents deep anxieties about the novel ready to appear, not just about its sales and those of previous books and any to come but also about his future as a personality conducting a range of enterprises—from authorship to lecturing to hard-sell merchandising. Those anxieties had intensified since 1876, when he decided to start Huck's "Autobiography" yet worked at it only sporadically before the summer of 1883. Comedy that often depended on irreverence ran to the heart of Twain's genius; but practical self-interest, his share of the submissive instinct, and his sense for communicable reality hobbled him. My approach to that bust expands into the still-open questions: Why did he soar to the heights of *Huckleberry Finn* just once; why did its acclaimed solution of a lowly vernacular hero, boyish yet wise, evade him before 1876 and after 1884? Posterity, I add, should put such questions humbly, not accusingly.

Many of Twain's devotees cannot help dismissing his nonliterary activity as a quirky distraction, especially when he was winding up *Huckleberry Finn*. They cannot understand how he could put tense effort into a board game for teaching historical facts, finally patented as Mark Twain's Memory Builder in August 1885. Likewise numb to his considering his books a commodity, they pay little attention to a private letter of 13 December 1876 that, angry over royalty problems, declares: "If I can make a living out of plays, I shall never write another book. For the present I have placed the three books in mind, in the waste basket."[8] They need to size up the first edition of *Huckleberry Finn* as a physical object designed to

catch the eye and sell through a big drive instead of word-of-mouth praise from readers. Twain the publisher, hoping for trailed glory from *The Adventures of Tom Sawyer*, first proposed marketing the old and new novels as a pair; to bring them closer in size, he easily agreed to cut the raftsmen's passage borrowed earlier for *Life on the Mississippi*. Comparing the original *Huckleberry Finn* with its format in the collected editions that began in 1899 leads into the changing faces of Twain's career. The respective readers had significantly different experiences, particularly because of the illustrations.

Both for better and worse, Twain thought of himself as publishing under a brand name, tied first to the Jumping Frog story and then to *The Innocents Abroad*, which, he bragged, kept selling right along like the Bible. As early as 1873 he fought literary pirates by contending in court that Mark Twain was a trademark, not a pseudonym, and he pushed another such case in 1883. An interview in 1891 had him discussing the "trademark" the public stamps on authors where we would say it "types" them. Testifying later in behalf of Rudyard Kipling, he "expressed the view that trade marks ought to be respected, and there is no difference between counterfeiting a label on a book, a box of blacking, or a bottle of whiskey."[9] It was logical to incorporate under his pen name in 1908, creating a legal grayland still with us. That made a triumphant answer to the warning—or threat—from genteelist critics that comic writers better count on a brief run. Some of those critics had even ranked him well down among the pack of funny-men. In 1882 a fellow humorist—long forgotten—who spent a day knocking around St. Louis with Twain commented that he was "too sensible a man not to realize that humor, of all things, is the most ephemeral, and that which will convulse the world today, will appear flat and insipid tomorrow."[10] The prospects for immortality aside, writing a comic novel was a short-term gamble of much effort. In fact, *Huckleberry Finn* took daring risks under a trademark worth protecting.

Like an impresario (or a smart rock-music star) Twain worried about the next step when his vogue started to fade. As the dollars rolled in during the 1870s from several fronts, such as Mark Twain's Self-Pasting Scrapbook, newspaper stories noted his fine head for business. He was gaining status as a self-made tycoon, not just as a self-taught writer or a self-promoting personality. That fellow humorist thought Twain's abilities "might be profitably employed in directing the practical every-day affairs of life." Reporters who dogged the river trip were impressed by his traveling secretary. He had begun to look like a one-man syndicate. To that interviewer in 1891 he would sigh that the dictaphone had not proved useful so far to a "literary or business man." Ironically, he must have decided that a businessman operates on firmer ground than an author, especially a humorist with a fickle public. By 1889 Twain believed that *A Connecticut Yankee in King Arthur's Court* was his "swan song," that he would not have to write for money anymore. Huck, in his first paragraph, calls his creator "Mr. Mark Twain." Mr. Twain had already come to feel entitled to let himself go at his own best gait.

Huck would have goggled at both Mr. Twain's luxurious home and the family's expensive travels. Their style of life took a lot more cash than rafting. In spite of the surefire coups ahead like the mechanical typesetter, Twain's books and lecturing still covered most of the bills and investments. Some of the final touches on *Huckleberry Finn* may reflect the fact that he was mounting a tour with Cable, which carried its own conflicts of imagemaking. As the tour's financial backer, Twain went in for brash advertising and colorful interviews; as the costar he fretted that Cable showed greater dignity with audiences. Eventually Cable produced an anecdote that seems to mark a crisis in 1885. But the problem, which festered long ago, had the clarity of a syndrome by the time *Huckleberry Finn* was projected. A persona—really a nimble troupe of personae—had grown famous as Mark Twain. With the public watching always more intently, that persona had to narrow his erratic swings and move up from buffo capers while increasing his appeal, had to—we now see—keep adjusting a synthesis of his strengths and improved opportunities. Privately, as Justin Kaplan suggests, Twain hobnobbed with the gentry but understood that his pass listed the trade of entertainer as the reason for admission. Would they keep inviting him to banquets if he no longer gave a hilarious speech? In the marrow of his character did he want to join their clubs if that required taming his humor into polite banter? He knew he could not suppress its wild side if he tried, yet he realized that some of them would find Huck too gamey.

Though a few biographers make him close to paranoiac, his tactical problems were treacherous. He had to feel wary that Huck's attitudes might irritate not just the gentry but also the lions of respectability. The reaction from the directors of the Concord (Massachusetts) Public Library proves that some of the danger was real. They had allies not only in New England but also across the country, not merely in Sunday schools but also throughout a society hoping for enough discipline to give capitalism a smooth

Frontispiece for the first American edition of Adventures of Huckleberry Finn *(Mark Twain House, Hartford, Connecticut)*

roadbed. The biography packed with Duke's Cigarettes held up at praising Huck as "this young scapegrace of a hero" whose courage and manliness are the "better side of ruffianism, which is the result of American independence of character."[11] Later, Twain himself was no more positive than to describe him as a boy of "sound heart & a deformed conscience." That left plenty of distance between a river-rat and an upper-middle-class ornament of Hartford. Huck has worn well because his creator tempered his own dissenting instincts and comic impetus with shrewd calculation of the risks he was running.

Just as some biographers cannot forgive Twain for showing any caution, others cannot mediate between the outside or psychic pressures and his backbone of glorious autonomy.[12] As yet, after all, nobody has come close to matching *Huckleberry Finn*. But while composing it Twain struggled through a series of cruxes for his public image. As he started he was agonizing over how to support Rutherford B. Hayes for president without stirring up the comic paragraphers. His speech at the Whittier dinner soon gave him a vivid lesson in the handicaps of his persona and the bad bounces of his reputation.[13] However, his triumph with impudent humor at the Grant banquet in 1879 left him giddy as he was completing *A Tramp Abroad* (1880), which vacillated on how to present Mark Twain. Then *The Prince and the Pauper* (1881) puzzled his hardcore readers, who were only partly reassured by *Life on the Mississippi* (1883). Meanwhile, his three daughters now flanked him in hotel lobbies and depots, observed and observing. Thirteen-year-old Susy, around as Gerhardt shaped that bust, started a biography of her father in the spring of 1885 because the press kept underrating him. Of course her devotion imposed a handicap, too. Above all, *Huckleberry Finn* was a bold move, but it pulled against solid forces. We have to follow both strands without stumbling into confusion, without forgetting that humor feeds on psychic release.

Howells had given Twain a prestigious boost through an essay in *Century* magazine for September 1882. That reinforced his confidence but perhaps worried him about reaching a status he could not afford to honor or might disgrace impulsively. In April 1884 a poll for literary "Immortals" still alive left him tied at fourteen with Warner and no doubt torn among smugness, jealousy, surprise, and uncertainty about how he ought to feel. While sitting for Gerhardt and checking the page proofs of his masterpiece, he dashed off an impious sketch for the much despised *New York Sun*.[14] Yet he sent it both free and unsigned; his tactics had wavered again. Once published, *Huckleberry Finn* influenced the shifting images, too. As it slowly gained ground with respectable critics, he paraded his downhome side more publicly. Nevertheless, as late as the 1890s his own praise usually showed less enthusiasm than an interviewer's leading questions. For the right audience he could volunteer some other book as his best, particularly *Personal Recollections of Joan of Arc*.

Why didn't he sign the sketch for the *New York Sun?* Why did he insert the heliotype? Because, realizing that his novel was fundamentally serious, he wanted to post a warning for the public? If so, what about that almost silly "Notice" to readers also added very late? Or did the bust say: Don't confuse me totally with the ragged, naive, barely literate narrator? Many reviewers assumed that *Huckleberry Finn* was aimed at the juvenile audience.[15] That cooking of the witch-pie (chap. 37) is kid stuff, and much of the Evasion anticipates the Our Gang cliché of children outwitting the adults. Too conscious of position and fame to merge into a poor-white "scapegrace," Twain would never again pitch Huck's voice above the firmly boyish level. His next vernacular heroes have at least the maturity of Hank Morgan and Captain Stormfield, waiting long in the wings. But they fascinate posterity much less than Huck. The man behind him had also aged. While not drooping emotionally before his bankruptcy anyway, he had built the new dimensions of his image that left less room for surrender to comic élan.

— *One Hundred Years of Huckleberry Finn: The Boy, His Book, and American Culture,* edited by Robert Sattelmeyer and J. Donald Crowley (Columbia: University of Missouri Press, 1985), pp. 26–40

1. Jacob Blanck, *Bibliography of American Literature* (New Haven: Yale University Press, 1957), describes three distinct states but praises Merle Johnson, whose *A Bibliography of Mark Twain* (New York: Harper, 1935) discusses the "literally dozens of states" in "almost as many colors" and gives the "last-minute addition" of the heliotype as a main cause for the exceptional tangle of minor textual points. For convenience I later use *frontispiece* more loosely than experts might like.
2. Samuel C. Webster, *Mark Twain, Business Man* (Boston: Little, Brown, 1946), pp. 273–77; this volume is the source for any further letters from Twain to Charles L. Webster. See also Henry Nash Smith and William M. Gibson, eds., *Mark Twain-Howells Letters* (Cambridge: Harvard University Press, 1960), 2:500–502.
3. *Literary World* 16 (7 February 1885): 49. For Warner see *Critic* 2 (18 October 1884): 185; reprinted from *Hartford* (Conn.) *Courant,* 9 October, p. 1. For front photographs of the bust see *Harper's Monthly* 71 (October 1885): 721 and *Harper's Weekly* 31 (1 April 1887): 248; the side view used can be seen in Hamlin Hill and Walter Blair, eds., *The Art of Huckleberry Finn* (San Francisco: Chandler, 1962 [1st ed.] or 1969 [2d ed.]). Twainians have wondered over a stripped-to-the-waist photograph, reproduced in Milton Meltzer, *Mark Twain Himself* (New York: Crowell, 1960), p. 182. Perhaps it was posed for the use of Gerhardt, who wanted photographs of his subject; see the anecdote in *Mark Twain-Howells Letters,* 2:498. The *Hartford Courant* reported (28 November 1884, p. 2) that the bust "has been more recently shown in New York" and "will be taken to the New Orleans exposition." It now rests in the entrance hall of Twain's restored Hartford house.
4. For Twain's comment on Kemble's *Life* cartoon, see *Mark Twain, Business Man,* p. 246. Meltzer reproduces many cartoons of Twain, and I have been locating others.
5. *Mark Twain, Business Man,* pp. 388–89; see also Robert Pack Browning et al., eds., *Mark Twain's Notebooks and Journals: Vol. III (1883–1891)* (Berkeley: University of California Press, 1979), p. 348.
6. 10 November 1896, p. 5. Dating of the first Sarony photograph (reproduced often, as in Meltzer, *Mark Twain Himself,* p. 182) is still unsure; it could have been made as early as 1883. Interestingly, the 1895 photograph was highly similar in pose and clothing, including the over-

coat. Twain went back to the firm in 1900. Around 1886–1887 Twain went also to the studio of Benjamin J. Falk, the "prominent New York Photographic artist and innovator"–*Notebooks and Journals*, 3:275. The comment in 1905 comes from a longer passage in a letter to Samuel H. Row, printed in Marlen E. Pew, "Samuel L. Clemens Interviews the Famous Humorist, Mark Twain," *Seattle* (Wash.) *Star*, 30 November 1905, p. 8.

7. From the interview just cited.

8. Hamlin Hill, ed., *Mark Twain's Letters to His Publishers, 1867–1894* (Berkeley: University of California Press, 1967), pp. 106–7.

9. Raymond Blathwayt, "Mark Twain on Humor . . ." *New York World*, 31 May 1891, p. 26; *New York Times*, 27 March 1901, p. 6.

10. John Henton Carter (Commodore Rollingpin), "A Day with Mark Twain," reprinted in my *Critical Essays on Mark Twain, 1867–1910* (Boston: G. K. Hall, 1982), pp. 61–64.

11. Among other places, no doubt, this booklet can be found at the Manuscripts Department of the Duke University Library and the Meine Collection at the University of Illinois (Urbana). Its opinion of *Huck Finn* was a close paraphrase from the review by Thomas Sergeant Perry in *Century* 30 (May 1885): 171. From the shelter of Twain's Oxford degree, the sedate critic Hamilton Mabie could defend *Tom Sawyer* only obliquely: "there was a grave question in the minds of some people whether such a stage of society was a proper subject for literary presentation; whether it was not too rudimentary for art"–*Outlook* 87 (23 November 1907): 652.

12. Of course Twain encouraged the overreading of his character. Henry Nash Smith has done most to move beyond the Brooks-DeVoto debate by exploring Twain's changing attitudes toward his writing. Though rightly acclaimed, Justin Kaplan finds too much inner melodrama in Twain's career. A fresh wave of biographical analysis is proceeding more dispassionately; for example, see Leland Krauth, "The Proper Pilot: A New Look at 'Old Times on the Mississippi,'" *Western Illinois Regional Studies* 2 (1979): 52–69. More specifically, Krauth argues that in shaping the cub-pilot essays for an *Atlantic Monthly* audience Twain took care to imply the solidity and seriousness of his own character in 1875.

13. Critics have yet to analyze exactly how the persona of the narrating miner failed to work. Anybody who sees the sketch as hidden aggression ought to ponder "The Nature of Deference and Demeanor" in Erving Goffman, *Interaction Ritual: Essays in Face-to-Face Behavior* (Chicago: Aldine, 1967).

14. I make the case for ascription in "Who Wants To Go To Hell? An Unsigned Mark Twain Sketch?" *Studies in American Humor*, n.s. 1 (1982): 6–16. On reading my essay, Robert H. Hirst, general editor of the Mark Twain Project, Bancroft Library, University of California, Berkeley, sent me a copy of the galleys for "Hunting for H––" that evidently were mailed to Twain by W. M. Laffan of the *Sun*.

15. See Victor Fischer's beautifully thorough "Huck Finn Reviewed: The Reception of *Huckleberry Finn* in the United States, 1885–1897," *American Literary Realism* 16 (1983): 1–57.

The Further Adventures of Huck Finn

Mark Twain made several attempts to revive Huck Finn in other narratives–the earliest of which he began working on before Adventures of Huckleberry Finn *was even published–but none of his efforts produced works that added to his literary reputation.*

Huck Finn after *Huck Finn*
Claude M. Simpson Jr.

Given the general acclaim accorded *The Adventures of Tom Sawyer* and, more profoundly, *Adventures of Huckleberry Finn,* how are we to account for a certain disappointment we feel with the sequels? Sequels are seldom as successful as the original works they follow, but Mark Twain showed in *Huckleberry Finn* that he could plumb greater depths and achieve a more incisive social criticism than he had attempted in the earlier work. If his own powers had matured between 1876 and 1884, why did he not succeed in his numerous attempts to recapture the magic of his best work by reintroducing what Henry Nash Smith has called the Matter of Hannibal? The familiar stories are *Tom Sawyer Abroad* (1894) and *Tom Sawyer, Detective* (1896), both written during troublous times when Twain was facing bankruptcy or was trying to regain solvency after the crash; writing these novellas was as important for solacing the author's anxieties as for the cash they produced. Other pieces lay unpublished until they appeared in Walter Blair's volume in the Mark Twain Papers series, *Hannibal, Huck & Tom.*[1] They include a slight anecdote which Blair has entitled "Doughface," and three uncompleted manuscripts: "Huck Finn and Tom Sawyer among the Indians," "Tom Sawyer's Conspiracy," and "Tom Sawyer's Gang Plans a Naval Battle." To these should be added the "Schoolhouse Hill" fragment of *The Mysterious Stranger,* in which Tom and Huck are among the characters; and a no-longer extant manuscript of 1902 bringing back Tom and Huck as old men.

Many commentators have noted that the dangers in *Tom Sawyer* are largely make-believe, whereas in *Huckleberry Finn* they become genuine. The cave scene in *Tom Sawyer* perhaps belies this limitation, but in most other contexts the mischief-making, even when accompanied by serious consequences, is treated as healthy boyish fun once we have been made fearful for a time. In *Tom Sawyer Abroad* we and the boys are never more than spectators, literally viewing the world from a safe distance in a balloon; and our detachment is such that we feel few pangs when the professor falls out and is lost over the ocean. Jim's plight is serious in "Tom Sawyer's Conspiracy" when he is arrested for a murder he didn't commit, but Tom's very bravura in compound-

Huck Out West

This 6 July 1884 letter to Webster shows Mark Twain considering a new Huck Finn adventure while Adventures of Huckleberry Finn *was still being prepared for publication.*

Dear Charley–

Send to me, right away, a book by *Lieut. Col. Dodge, USA,* called "25 Years on the Frontier"–or some such title–I don't remember just what. Maybe it is "25 Years Among the Indians," or maybe "25 Years in the Rocky Mountains." But the name of the *author* will guide you. I think he has written only the one book; & so any librarian can tell you the title of it.

I want several other *personal narratives* of life & adventures out yonder on the Plains & in the Mountains, if you can run across them—especially life *among the Indians.* Send what you can find. I mean to take Huck out there.

Yrs truly
S L Clemens

–Mark Twain, Business Man, p. 265

ing difficulties by deliberately manufacturing a motive to implicate Jim makes us feel that we are re-enacting the "Evasion" chapters of *Huckleberry Finn.* Twain is operating the oldest of suspense plots—making the victim's case as hopeless as possible before rescuing him—and in "Tom Sawyer's Conspiracy" it is more effective than in *Huckleberry Finn* chiefly because it isn't played out as long and Twain foregoes the Phelps plantation grotesque prisoner routines.

"Huck Finn and Tom Sawyer among the Indians" is a promising cousin to *Huckleberry Finn* in the seriousness of the major plotline. But the Indian murders and kidnappings are deliberate anti-romantic responses to the noble savagism often present in Cooper, and when evidence points to the likely rape of Peggy Mills we are in the presence of a motif which Twain could scarcely pursue very far even if he intended to sidestep it eventually. Thus here too Twain fails to exploit the potentialities realized in *Huckleberry Finn.*

One key to the effectiveness of all these pieces is Huck's role in them. Twain must have recognized how much he gained in colloquial vigor, directness of impression, and unconscious irony by replacing the omniscience of *Tom Sawyer* with Huck's first-person narration, for the point of view established in *Huckleberry Finn* persists in all the continuations except "Schoolhouse Hill." Although the play of humor varies from piece to piece, Huck's "voice" remains relatively constant and his outsider's view of the world continues to be a recognizable mixture of innocence and shrewd-

ness. Huck's eyes, however, are fixed on Tom's world, and the sequels repeat the patterns of *Tom Sawyer* and the framing chapters of *Huckleberry Finn,* in which Tom dominates and Huck is generally passive.

What we miss, what we are prepared to respond to, is Huck without Tom; for only in Tom's absence can Huck's qualities emerge naturally, freed from the powerful aggressiveness of Tom's managerial instincts. Now and then this opportunity arises. The one occasion in *Tom Sawyer* when Huck is free from Tom comes when he stalks Injun Joe and partner to the Widow Douglas' house, a rather minor link in the sequence with no particular value in foreshadowing the possibilities which Twain would realize in the central chapters of *Huckleberry Finn.* In "Tom Sawyer's Conspiracy" Huck's one scene without Tom occurs on a steamboat when he encounters the King and the Duke. Here Huck's innocence rather than his wariness and skepticism is uppermost as the scruffy pair pump him for information without his becoming aware that they are the murderers of the slave-trader. And in "Huck and Tom among the Indians" Huck has one opportunity to show his quick-wittedness when threatened by a pair of horse-thieves. But these scenes are exceptional.

Nonetheless, all the continuations give lively evidence of Twain's improvisational talent and are carefully enough conceived to merit our attention. It need not surprise us that Twain only occasionally approached the sustained freshness of *Huckleberry Finn;* he tried repeatedly to do so and the very persistence with which he cast Huck and Tom in commanding roles invites us to see what he made of their return appearances.

"Huck and Tom among the Indians" is a longish fragment written most probably in the summer of 1884, within a few months after Twain had finished *Huckleberry Finn.* Invoking the end of that novel (as do most of the other continuations) it takes up Tom's suggestion that they "go for howling adventures amongst the Injuns, over in the Territory." The tale moves more or less along the Oregon Trail from western Missouri to Wyoming and allows Twain to portray a group of plains Indians in action. Initially Tom is in charge, developing plans for them to slip away from a relative's hemp farm near the Kansas border, outfitted and provisioned for several weeks in the open; he has harangued Huck and Jim on the nobility of the Indian race and has overcome their natural doubts. When the three join up with a family of Oregon-bound emigrants, they soon encounter a most amiable and friendly Indian band, and Tom is ecstatic. Before long, however, the Indians make their move, murdering Mr. and Mrs. Mills and their three sons, kidnapping their two daughters and Nigger Jim, and stealing horses and mules. The rest of the unfinished story traces the search for the captives under the leadership of young Peggy Mills's fiancé, Brace Johnson, who arrives after the massacre and hopes that Peggy, rather than suffer rape at the hands of the Indians, will have killed herself with a dirk he had given her.[2]

Beyond being the narrator, Huck plays a more active role here than in any of the other continuations and in this respect the story texture is closest of all to that of *Huckleberry Finn*. For one thing, Tom is relatively subdued. He takes the lead in preparing for the trek and he reads signs that foreshadow Indian duplicity, but he does not indulge his fancy for theatrics. And he subsides into passivity in the presence of Brace Johnson, an experienced plainsman and Indian fighter modeled after Wild Bill Hickok. On several occasions Tom is off-stage and Huck can concentrate on what he himself is doing and thinking. When confronted by a pair of horse-thieves he escapes by a trick which includes his old defensive strategy of inventing a plaintive family history to disarm suspicion. And in a piece of routine melodrama he finds Peggy's dirk after he has mercifully lied to Brace, for he had insisted that it was in her possession when she was kidnapped. Huck is almost caught with the dirk and decides that if he buries it, Brace will be sure to find it; instead he hides it in the lining of his jacket. Though his shrewdness here is relatively slight, it is motivated by his characteristic reluctance to hurt others. In this compassionate spirit he contrives a second lie to relieve Brace's mind, telling him that he and Tom have found Peggy's body at the Indian camp and have buried it. Twain is firmly enough in control of tone to resist letting Tom embroider the scheme. Later Tom is uncommonly gentle and considerate when he devises a means of explaining away the lie if they have to.

Despite its central purpose of debunking a romanticized view of Indian behavior, "Huck and Tom among the Indians" remains a rambling picaresque sketch, enlivened by several episodes which instruct us in life on the plains but do not advance the plot. Tom is lost in the fog and Huck experiences a waterspout (we would call it a flash flood); a man rescued from the wilds is crazed with hunger and dies from gorging himself when Huck's back is turned. These bits of lore show us Brace's expertise: he knows how to find Tom in the fog, how to trail the Indian band, how to size up the party of horse-thieves, how to anticipate and avoid the waterspout, how to infer the Indians' treatment of their white captives. As Blair has shown, Twain got much of this from Col. Richard I. Dodge's *The Plains of the Great West* (1877). He acquired the book as he was preparing to write the story which, he told his nephew, would "take Huck Finn out there" to the Indian country, and though

the working-out of the tale allows only occasional importance to Huck, it is suggestive that he should have seemed central to Twain.[3] Doubtless the recently finished novel influenced Twain's impulse to think of the projected yarn as another "Huck" story. But Huck cannot transfer the knowledge of his milieu from the Mississippi River to the western plains, and in effect it is Brace Johnson who usurps the position of authority which Twain had partially granted Tom (and in Tom's absence, Huck) in the earlier books. A similar shift away from Huck would take place when next Twain brought back the boys.

Tom Sawyer Abroad began in August 1892 as "Huck Finn in Africa," and during the month of writing it Twain recorded other tentative titles, including "New Adventures of Huckleberry Finn," "Huckleberry Finn and Tom Sawyer Abroad," and "Huckleberry Finn Abroad," before he settled on the final wording. He wrote his publishing partner Fred Hall, "I have started Huck Finn and Tom Sawyer (still 15 years old) and their friend the freed slave Jim around the world in a stray balloon"; elsewhere in the letter he said that "Huck writes it and Tom is along."[4] But the tale gives no such incidental role to Tom, despite the apparent emphasis on Huck implied in all the tentative titles. Tom is the central figure throughout, and Huck and Jim are his straight-men, providing the necessary ignorance or pragmatic literalness to generate a familiar sort of debate. Tom is the same old romantic, exploiting his love of ritualism in proposing at the outset that they play crusade à la Walter Scott to rescue "the Holy Land from the paynim."[5] Huck, with some logic, can't see the sense of driving people off their own land, even if the victims are heathen and the conquerors are Christian; Jim thinks the three of them would need practice before they could kill innocent people.

This pattern is relatively standard through the tale, and though sometimes interesting, is too predictable to offer much fresh amusement. Perhaps the most successful of these dialogues is an argument over the color of Indiana, which from the balloon is green but on the map is pink, and Huck is not easily reconciled to the difference. A few moments of liveliness accompany a discussion of longitude and time zones, which pose for Jim the incomprehensible idea that the world could come to an end in some regions but with no last day in others, "en de dead wouldn't be called" (p. 46). In a touch of what we might term double-deadpan technique, Tom explains to Huck that a Moslem is "a person that [isn't] a Presbyterian. So," says Huck, "there is plenty of them in Missouri, though I didn't know it before" (p. 196).

Of all the continuations, only *Tom Sawyer Abroad* exploits humor of situation, as when Jim is stranded atop the head of the Sphinx or they experience the deception of mirages. Now and then, too, some of Huck's healthy skepticism glints through, as when he lets us see ironically that he accepts Tom's claim to have located the very treasure hill of an Arabian Nights tale, or when he substitutes a plain Cairo brick for Tom's historic relic and Tom is none the wiser. And Huck is scornful of the mud-hut that Tom identifies as Joseph's granary, commenting that Tom "made more fuss over it than I would make if I stuck a nail in my foot" (p. 196).

In a few asides Huck reveals his old capacity for compassion. He sympathizes when the balloonist professor is ragged by a merciless St. Louis rabble—he "was just a genius, as the papers said, which wasn't his fault" (p. 22). His soliloquy on "ornithologers" who kill birds to study them is indeed sentimentalized and homiletic, but his musings on the joys of ballooning and the defects of civilization come straight from the pages that celebrate raft-life in *Huckleberry Finn*. And Huck's language still retains some of the exuberance rarely seen in his later narrations: not merely malapropisms like "the solar sister" or "rich as Creosote," but virtuoso effects of the sort that describe Jim's snoring: "soft and blubbery, at first [,] then a long rasp, then a stronger one, then a half-a-dozen horrible ones like the last water sucking down the plug-hole of a bath-tub, then the same with more power to it, and some big coughs and snorts flung in, the way a cow does that is choking to death" (pp. 147–48).

Jules Verne's *Five Weeks in a Balloon* (1869, transl. of *Cinq semaines en ballon*, 1862) anticipated Twain's story in several interesting respects. It took three adult aeronauts across Africa, though from east to west, and included Sahara sequences in which the balloonists encounter lions, puzzle out the phenomenon of a mirage, witness one caravan buried in a sandstorm before their eyes, and see the bleached remains of another strewn across the desert floor. Each of these motifs appears also in *Tom Sawyer Abroad*. But where Verne was content to accept contemporary balloon technology with relatively few innovations, Twain has moved far beyond the state of the art in the 1890's to employ what could have only been considered visionary: operation without ballast or valves, speeds of 100–300 m.p.h., and a revolutionary (perhaps nuclear?) fuel source "a thousand times the strongest in the earth . . . there's power aboard to last five years" (p. 25).[6]

Lacking a central purpose such as the search for sources of the Nile which gave timely focus to Verne's narrative, *Tom Sawyer Abroad* resorts to various diversions to relieve the essential featurelessness of travel over the Atlantic Ocean and the north Afri-

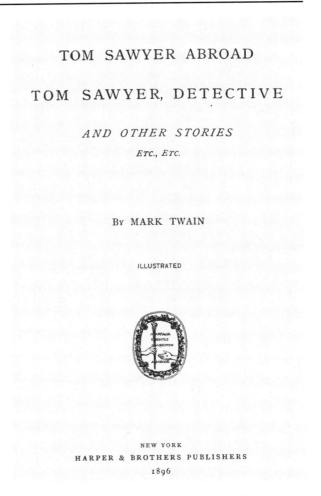

Title page for the only sequels to The Adventures of Tom Sawyer *and* Adventures of Huckleberry Finn *that were published in Twain's lifetime (Mark Twain House, Hartford, Connecticut)*

can desert. Tom tells two stories from the Arabian Nights and alludes to three others, usually provoking a discussion in which Jim and perhaps Huck can challenge the point of the tale or worry over interpreting it. A topical digression explores the illogic of contemporary American customs duties (suggestive of the debate in *A Connecticut Yankee* over the merits of free trade vs. protective tariff as understood by Cleveland democrats), and a comment on railroad ownership reflects the age of the robber baron, not the ostensible 1850 setting of *Tom Sawyer Abroad*. Still another sequence, and a tedious one, could be called "swearing as a fine art" and begins with Tom's discussion of "scientific cussing" by medieval popes. As filler these passages and others like them are moderately successful, but they lack the fresh crispness, the natural inventiveness of their counterparts in *Huckleberry Finn*, and one feels that Twain is working his effects as a good journeyman, yet without the touches of genius that flash in his most effective pages.

The ending of *Tom Sawyer Abroad* is surprisingly weak but is not to be excused merely because Twain intended to leave the way open for continuing the travel narrative. The final plot shift is neither humorous nor burlesque; it is trivial and unmotivated. On Mount Sinai Tom breaks his corncob pipe and sends Jim ballooning back to Missouri for a spare, with letters from "Tom Sawyer the Errornort." Jim makes the round trip successfully but brings orders from Aunt Polly for Tom to return, and the story shuts down as the three "shoved for home, and not feeling very gay, neither" (p. 208). Twain's inspiration tank had once more run dry.

Before *Tom Sawyer Abroad* was published Twain was at work on "Tom Sawyer's Mystery," ultimately titled *Tom Sawyer, Detective* and published late in 1896 after serialization in *Harper's Magazine*. In tone and content it is perhaps the least slanted toward a young audience of all the Tom and Huck series. Aside from fearsome talk of ghosts and their habits, the principal concession to a nostalgic view of a child's world occurs at the beginning, when Twain depicts Tom's skill in manipulating his Aunt Polly. She has told him that the Phelpses are in trouble down in Arkansas and need him to cheer them up. Spring fever has hit him and he's delighted for an excuse to leave school, but he's afraid that if he shows much enthusiasm his aunt will change her mind, so he feigns indifference until she insists. From this point the mood darkens as Tom and Huck take a steamboat down the Mississippi and on the trip encounter three robbers in a Pardoner's Tale aftermath of intrigue and melodramatic treachery. The groundwork is thus laid for a murder and subsequent trial. The locale and the people were familiar ground for Twain, though the physical setting is of virtually no importance. Plot is uppermost here, with emphasis on the mysterious murder circumstantially linked to Uncle Silas Phelps but ultimately solved by Tom through shrewd deduction. In "Tom Sawyer's Conspiracy" he would make a similar spectacular courtroom appearance, but with nothing like the intricate psychological elements he confronts in the Phelps trial.

Once again Huck is the narrator, armed with an effective vernacular, conscious of Tom's flair for dramatic effects, but seldom playing an active part himself. On occasion his misgivings register, as when Tom describes the glory they would enjoy if they are the ones to tell about the murder and, as he says, "paint it up fine." Huck replies, "I reckon it ain't going to suffer none for lack of paint . . . when you start in to scollop the facts."[7] Later Tom spins an elaborate fantasy in

which he imagines finding the corpse, tracking the murderer, and so on. Huck brings him up short, saying, "Well, . . . you better find the corpse first; I reckon that's a-plenty for to-day. For all we know, there ain't any corpse" (p. 162).

The one ludicrous moment comes when Huck tries to persuade Aunt Sally that it is normal to hunt blackberries at night with dog and lantern. Otherwise the Huck touches are largely linguistic, continuing the idiomatic habits of earlier books, with malapropisms at the level of "remainders" of the "diseased" and "lawyer for the prostitution." Some of his descriptions are vivid but just escape fine-writing: "The moon come a-swelling up out of the ground, now, powerful big and round and bright, behind a comb of trees, like a face looking through prison bars, and the black shadders and white places begun to creep around, and it was miserable quiet and still and night-breezy and graveyardy and scary" (pp. 139–40). A more natural piece of colloquial inspiration occurs as he and Tom arrive at the Phelps house and, says Huck, "here come the dogs piling around us to say howdy" (p. 143).

Although Twain keeps a tight rein on his temptation to improvise and controls his narrative with unusual skill, he must be pardoned for at least two lapses that he failed to mend. One of these is his pointed dating of Tom and Huck's arrival at the Phelps plantation on September 2d, although it had been early spring when they left Missouri a few days before. Neither season is crucial for the story; either would have served. Twain's other oversight may be attributable to his tinkering plot detail without proper attention to motivation. On the steamboat when the swindler Jake Dunlap tells Tom and Huck of his plans to give his two confederates the slip and return to his Arkansas village in disguise, Tom observes that Jake's voice is enough like his twin's to stir up the neighbors' memories. Jake resolves to "play deef and dumb" to get around the problem. Subsequently when Jake is killed by the other robbers his twin Jubiter assumes not only Jake's disguise but by unexplained coincidence his deaf-mute role as well. This shift of identities, clothing, and props parallels an important motif in Twain's play of 1877, "Cap'n Simon Wheeler, the Amateur Detective," where the desperado is also named Jake and the supposed victim of the killing resorts to the deaf-mute stratagem to keep his voice from being recognized.[8]

The story moves along briskly, helped by Jake's account of the diamond theft and the friction among the three robbers which prepares us for violent action of a rather hackneyed cast. This is only a preliminary sequence, however, and is invented by

Twain to provide a corpse on which the major plot depends. Thereafter the central figure is the old sleepwalking Silas Phelps, a striking example of emotional pathos who confesses the murder in all sincerity and does his best to convict himself, although the blow he struck Jubiter was by no means fatal. The shift in Silas' character from simpleminded ineffectuality to the semi-grandeur of pathological anxiety and guilt is well handled, though not original with Twain, since this motif was in the source he alludes to (vaguely and inaccurately) in a footnote.[9]

The fact that Twain was retelling a story may account for the tightness of the central plot. But it did not keep him from domesticating the Danish original or from devising a happy ending, which turns on Tom's recognizing Jubiter by a nervous habit of drawing a cross on his cheek (Tom had seen him do this when he had visited the Phelpses the year before and had been involved with the rescue of Nigger Jim).[10] Once he has cleared Phelps of murdering Jubiter, Tom is able to reconstruct the chain of events, some of which he and Huck had witnessed without understanding them at the time. And although the fellow-swindlers who killed Jake are lost sight of, the Dunlap brothers who had plotted against Phelps are brought to justice, the diamonds are recovered, and Tom generously shares the reward with Huck.

Huck has practically nothing to do in *Tom Sawyer, Detective* except for his role as reporter and occasional foil for Tom, whose superior wisdom is much less undercut here than in *Huckleberry Finn.* "When Tom Sawyer seen a thing," says Huck, "it just got up on its hind legs and *talked* to him—told him everything it knowed. *I* never see such a head" (p. 144).

I pass over "Doughface," a brief anecdote in which a young girl in a false face literally frightens the wits out of an old lady. Although told by Huck, it offers no insight into his character after the opening sentences, which relate a succession of boyish trades climaxing in the mask the girl borrows. Likewise, "Tom Sawyer's Gang Plans a Naval Battle" gives Huck only a bystander's view; the sketch peters out after a few pages of impresario Tom managing his pawns—less effectively than in the famous whitewashing enterprise. These two pieces, probably from the late 1890's, cannot be dated precisely and their interest is limited to vernacular narration, which does not of itself guarantee life to trifling story ideas.

But Twain's powers of invention had not failed, as he showed in "Tom Sawyer's Conspiracy." This novella, the most nearly completed of his Huck and Tom manuscripts, occupied Twain off and on from 1897 to 1900, along with a spate of other pieces, mostly unfinished, some invoking the Hannibal scene and stirring early memories, others spinning the fantasies associated with his obsessive problems of dream and reality, guilt and exorcism. Thanks to his mercurial moods Twain was able in the midst of gloom and despair to recapture the ebullient mood of earlier years. "Tom Sawyer's Conspiracy" is an ingenious extravaganza, especially in the early chapters which evolve from Tom's plan "to get the people in a sweat about the ablitionists." The town is already worried lest strangers "run off some of our niggers to freedom" (Blair, p. 171) and Tom devises ways of fanning rumor until virtual hysteria grips the citizens. He invents a mythical "Sons of Freedom" organization whose cryptic handbills are the more effective because his amateurish woodblock carving prints backwards. And when martial law is declared, he gets himself and Huck appointed as spies, with passes to move freely through the town, and Nigger Jim is certified too, to spy among his race. Tom prints a "protection-paper" to post on many townspeople's doors, causing consternation among those not so favored.

To make his conspiracy convincing, however, requires an incident, and Tom plans an elaborate scheme in which Huck will offer to lead the slave-trader Bradish to a runaway in exchange for part of the reward. Tom will black up for the role, and will unlock his chains and escape in the night. When Bradish discovers his loss the town will be sure that abolitionists are at work. This is the plan. But when Huck makes his offer Bradish says he already has a runaway in custody and can't manage another. Tom wants to take the runaway's place but Huck sobers him by saying, "That's a five-hundred-dollar nigger; you ain't a five-hundred-dollar nigger, I don't care *how* you dress up" (p. 202). That night Tom looks in on Bradish's sleeping runaway, discovering that he is white (he mistakenly blackened his palms) and that a key to the chains is hidden in a shoe. Tom discovers something else he won't divulge to Huck, but it's clear that other people are playing out Tom's scheme, with a fake runaway and probably a confederate to collect the reward. Huck is all for telling the sheriff, but such direct methods are not Tom's style.

Thus the drift of "Tom Sawyer's Conspiracy" through the first of its two major sequences. Tom is the undoubted mastermind who allows few contributions from either Huck or Jim. When time hangs heavy he steers them through the possible alternatives of starting a civil war, a revolution, or an insurrection, before they finally settle on a conspiracy. He supervises their ritual—in the mood of the opening *Huckleberry Finn* chapters—and he copes with the priggish tattletale Sid Sawyer, though at the cost of delib-

"HE SAID HE WOULD SAIL HIS BALLOON AROUND THE WORLD."

"'RUN! RUN FO' YO' LIFE!'"

Illustrations from Tom Sawyer Abroad, *one of several stories featuring Tom and Huck that Mark Twain worked on after*
Adventures of Huckleberry Finn *(drawing by Daniel Beard; Mark Twain House, Hartford, Connecticut)*

erately exposing himself to scarlet fever to get Sid sent away. These childish touches recede once the conspiracy gets under way. In their place Twain develops a fairly serious social critique as he shows community values being tested by the stirring up of fears and prejudice. He is, however, surprisingly sympathetic with the townspeople's foibles, at a time when he was also evolving the "damned human race" determinism of *What Is Man?*. The citizenry, for all their gullibility, are not satirized as pointedly as is Hacker, an unimaginative detective whom Twain had ridiculed farcically under other names in the Simon Wheeler play and novel (where there are three of him) and in "The Stolen White Elephant" (where he becomes a whole Pinkerton force).

In the second half of "Tom Sawyer's Conspiracy" the issues suddenly change when Bradish is found murdered and circumstantial evidence implicates Nigger Jim. Jim had come upon Bradish's body and was on his way to give the alarm when he was waylaid and accused of the brutal slaying. Tom, always adept at make-believe, is delighted with the opportunity for heroics, and though the boys visit Jim in jail, Tom is not much preoccupied with sympathy for him. His mind is on the murderers and the excitement of tracking them. When the trail leads to the Mississippi River Huck and Tom take to a steamboat where Huck encounters the two old confidence men from *Huckleberry Finn*. The King and the Duke pump him about Jim, and Huck realizes that if the pair of frauds can claim that they have a prior right to Jim for a crime committed down river Jim could escape the present murder charge and he and Tom could buy Jim back from the King and the Duke. They fall in with the plan and Huck believes it is working, but the pair do not appear until Jim is found guilty and they suddenly turn up in the courtroom to claim him. Tom recognizes a voice he had overheard at the slave-shed and proves that they are the murderers by producing a print of the King's left foot and the something that he had not shown Huck—the Duke's false teeth.

The story stops here, as well it might. If a final windup were required it would be no great matter—in *Tom Sawyer, Detective* a page sufficed for a coda following the courtroom climax. The psychological impact of that story, however, is lacking in the second half of "Tom Sawyer's Conspiracy." Instead we are treated to a frenetic series of pursuit scenes which scarcely follow a straight line but resemble the path of a dog on the beach. Fundamentally Tom's Tyl Eulenspiegel mischievousness in setting the town on its ear gives way to a callous exploitation of a helpless human being. In the closing chapters of *Huckleberry Finn*

when Jim is being held captive in the Phelpses' slave-cabin, the needless complications which Tom invents are gross indignities heaped on Jim's head, though they pass as burlesque of a romantic chivalric tradition and Jim's life is not in the balance. There Huck can at least protest with a small voice of common sense. In the "Conspiracy" story, however, he seldom disagrees, for, he says, Tom "had so much confidence it was catching" (p. 214); and when Tom occasionally suffers a moment of contrition and blames himself for Jim's danger, Huck cheers him up and only occasionally allows himself an unspoken critical comment. In both fictions Jim is eventually freed, but the spotlight is on Tom and his stage-management and Huck is a forgotten onlooker. He has become used to that role but he's capable of much more.

This is almost the end of Huck. He does return once more, in an early draft of the story we know as *The Mysterious Stranger*. The "Schoolhouse Hill" fragment (1898)[11] introduces the Satan Jr. figure, a fifteen-year-older named "44," as a new boy in the Petersburg school which Tom, Sid, Becky Thatcher and others attend. Huck joins them on the grounds before school takes up but after a moment disappears from the sketch entirely. Other manuscripts of the story shift the locale to a European setting of long ago which nonetheless bears distinct resemblances to Hannibal, and one can see familiar Missouri types among the boys in the foreground. Even a young first-person narrator takes over the story, but Theodor Fischer is no Huck nor does he attempt a vernacular voice.

Finally, letters and notes show that in 1902 Twain worked on a manuscript in which Huck and Tom are old men looking back over their lives and exaggerating a good deal.[12] This was an idea he had entertained through the years—one of his plans for the *Tom Sawyer* story had called for him to carry Tom's career to the age of 37 or 40,[13] and another would have described a reunion after fifty years, featuring General Sawyer, Bishop Finn, Detective Inspector Sid Sawyer, and Rear-Admiral Joe Harper (Blair, p. 245). A note of 1891 sketched a scene with Huck as an old man now crazy, attended by Tom as they try to talk of old times: "both are desolate, life has been a failure, all that was lovable, all that was beautiful is under the mold. They die together."[14] It is not clear whether the 1902 piece would have dwelt on the triumphs or the tragedies of existence. Perhaps Twain could not have been comfortable with either. In any case he abandoned the sketch after writing some thirty-eight thousand words and apparently destroyed the manuscript, "for fear I might some day finish it" (Blair, p. 20).

The repeated linkages to *Huckleberry Finn* in the sequels suggest that Twain was trying to recapture qualities of that novel whenever he returned to the Hannibal scene and his youthful memories. The evidence of these continuations, however, suggests that although he never ceased to see the value of Huck as an outsider and foil, he was primarily concerned with Huck's narrative voice rather than the full range of the youth's personality. By not creating opportunities for Huck to continue to reveal himself in all his ironic depths, Twain misjudged the essence of his greatest book and sacrificed opportunities he may never have been aware of.

—*American Humor: Essays Presented to John C. Gerber,* edited by O. M. Brack, Jr. (Scottsdale, Ariz.: Arete Publications, 1977), pp. 59–72

1. (Berkeley and Los Angeles: University of California Press, 1969).

2. In his excellent commentary on the fragment Walter Blair, perhaps following Bernard DeVoto's unpublished notes, sees prudishness as one reason for Twain's abandoning the story. It is true that in the early chapters Peggy doesn't know why Brace had asked her to promise that she would kill herself if captured, but the reader can hardly miss the implications filtered through Huck's deadpan report. Later, says Huck, again noncommittally, Brace "explained it to me, and then it was all clear" (p. 113). In the last chapter Huck finds a bloody scrap of Peggy's dress and Brace discovers four stakes in the ground strongly suggesting that a captive has been spread-eagled for rape or torture. Given this much evidence of a central plot motif, one suspects that Twain recoiled from the whole idea not because of difficulties with an ending, for a happy resolution would have been simple for an author so skilled in confounding circumstantial evidence. If, on the other hand, he wished to underline Indian savagery, he had already generated most of the shock value of a tragic conclusion, and he could properly have felt that a happy ending would undermine the one serious reason for writing the story.

3. S. L. Clemens to Charles L. Webster, July 6, 1884, *Mark Twain, Business Man* (Boston: Little, Brown, 1946), p. 265.

4. August 10, 1892, *Mark Twain's Letters to His Publishers,* ed. Hamlin Hill (Berkeley and Los Angeles: University of California Press, 1967), pp. 314–15. The earliest form of the title appears in a notebook entry which Hill quotes, p. 315: "Began 'Huck Finn in Africa' August 5, 1892." On September 4 he wrote Hall, p. 318, that the 40,000-word manuscript was finished and announced the title in its final form, with a subtitle "Part I—In the Great Sahara" which reflects Twain's hope to extend the travel narrative indefinitely. Earlier, pp. 313–14, he had thought of hitching onto the story a draft of "Those Extraordinary Twins" rewritten with Huck as narrator.

5. *Tom Sawyer Abroad* (London, 1894), p. 13. The Chatto & Windus text is preferred as being based directly on a copy of Twain's typescript. The American edition, published by Charles L. Webster & Co., is a hybrid inasmuch as the first two-thirds derive from the *St. Nicholas* magazine version, considerably scrubbed up by its editor Mrs. Mary Mapes Dodge; only the last third of the Webster text reproduces Twain's typescript. See O. M. Brack, Jr., "Mark Twain in Knee Pants: The Expurgation of *Tom Sawyer Abroad*," *Proof,* 2 (1972): 145–51.

6. The free fantasies of Dan Beard's illustrations reflect a very primitive state of aeronautics: the balloon is a horizontal sausage with bat-like wings, and the underslung car is an open boat with figurehead and its own pair of wings.

7. *Tom Sawyer Abroad, Tom Sawyer, Detective, and Other Stories* (New York: Harper & Brothers, 1896), p. 43.

8. *Mark Twain's Satires & Burlesques,* ed. Franklin R. Rogers (Berkeley and Los Angeles: University of California Press, 1967), pp. 220–89.

9. 'That is, he speaks of being indebted to "an old-time Swedish criminal trial," a slip for Danish. Actual events in the life of a minister Sören Qvist in the early seventeenth century were the basis of "The Minister of Veilby" (1829) by Steen Steensen Blicher, and it is this version which was told to Twain, presumably by Anna Lillie Greenough who after the death of her husband Charles Moulton married Johan Henrik Hegermann-Lindencrone, Danish ambassador to the United States, 1872–80. All this is set out in J. Christian Bay, "*Tom Sawyer, Detective:* The Origin of the Plot," *Essays Offered to Herbert Putnam . . .* (New Haven: Yale University Press, 1929), pp. 80–88. The Blicher version contains the motif of the sleepwalking minister who ultimately confesses the murder; he is convicted and executed. Years later a beggar turns up and relates how the minister struck him during a quarrel, whereupon he exchanged clothes with a dead man and he and his brother buried the body so it could be found, and he himself fled the country. The story has more recently been told by Janet Lewis, whose novel *The Trial of Sören Qvist* (1947) generally follows Blicher but concludes with the parson's execution.

10. Chapter I planted other evidence for identifying Jubiter: long ago his schoolboy friends at the swimming hole had noted a cluster of moles on his left thigh which suggested the planet Jupiter and created his nickname. Twain improved on this hoary motif but did not bother to write it out of the story.

11. *Mark Twain's Mysterious Stranger Manuscripts,* ed. William M. Gibson (Berkeley and Los Angeles: University of California Press, 1969), pp. 175–220.

12. Blair, pp. 15–20. On October 20, 1902, W. D. Howells wrote Twain, "what I shall enjoy most will be the return of the old fellows to the scene, and their tall lying." *Mark Twain-Howells Letters,* ed. H. N. Smith and W. M. Gibson (Cambridge: Harvard University Press, 1960), 2: 747.

13. Hamlin Hill, *Mark Twain and Elisha Bliss* (Columbia, Mo.: University of Missouri Press, 1964), p. 102.

14. *Mark Twain's Notebook,* ed. A. B. Paine (New York: Harper & Brothers, 1935), p. 212.

Marketing and Reception

After he had written four hundred pages of "Huck Finn's Autobiography," Mark Twain wrote William Dean Howells in August 1876 that he might "possibly pigeonhole or burn the MS when it is done." Nearly seven years later, he commented on his nearly completed novel in a July 1883 letter to his friend: "I shall like it, whether anybody else does or not." These two statements, taken together, indicate Twain's longstanding uncertainty about Adventures of Huckleberry Finn, both about what he was doing when he was writing it and what he had achieved when it was finished. Whether or not he was ever serious about abandoning his story or burning the manuscript, he eventually committed himself to the project and decided the novel should be published. But he remained anxious about how his work would be received. In presenting Adventures of Huckleberry Finn to the public Twain was sometimes open to the ideas of others—from going along with Charles Webster's suggestion that he leave out the raft episode in preparing the novel for the press to allowing Richard W. Gilder to freely edit selections from the novel for The Century Illustrated Monthly Magazine—but he could also be fiercely and defiantly protective of his work. When Joel Chandler Harris defended the novel in a May 1885 review, he wrote a note of thanks "for the good word about Huck, that abused child of mine who has had so much unfair mud flung at him."

Mark Twain also had a reason beyond authorship for wanting Adventures of Huckleberry Finn to succeed, for it was to be the first book published by his own publishing house. Although the Charles L. Webster Publishing Company was named after his business agent and nephew by marriage, it belonged to Sam Clemens, who supplied the capital to underwrite the company. As businessman as well as artist, Twain took an eager interest in the promotion and marketing of Adventures of Huckleberry Finn.

Mark Twain with George Washington Cable during their "Twins of Genius" lecture tour, which preceded the American publication of Adventures of Huckleberry Finn *(Clifton Waller Barrett Collection, University of Virginia)*

Selling *Huck Finn* by Subscription

Mark Twain evidently signed a contract to establish the Charles L. Webster Publishing Company in May 1884, but by then the author had already been relying on Webster to attend to his multifarious business dealings (investments, patents, and of course publishing) as well as to his personal affairs (such as later seeing that the furnace in the Clemenses' Hartford house was in good working order). Though Clemens was disappointed in his previous publishers, most notably Elisha Bliss and James R.

Osgood, he remained convinced that subscription sale was the most lucrative method of publication. Subscription publishing required a large sales force prowling the countryside selling "subscriptions" to a forthcoming book. The agents carried with them a prospectus, which featured the table of contents, samples of illustrations, and a specimen of the text, and because they worked entirely on commission, their sales techniques were typically aggressive. This marketing approach bypassed the ordinary routes of trade publishers and retail stores and did not rely so heavily on reviews in newspapers and magazines.

Whatever imaginative and emotional investment Twain had in Adventures of Huckleberry Finn *while he was writing it, in his letters to Webster, the book was treated as a commercial property that needed to be "pushed," as these excerpts show.*

In this first excerpt–from a letter that, as was typical, began with the greeting "Dear Charley" and was signed "SLC"–Mark Twain suggests a marketing plan that was later rejected by his previous publisher, the American Publishing Company.

Mark Twain to Charles L. Webster, 29 February 1884

Let us canvass Huck Finn and Tom Sawyer both at once, selling both books for $4.50 where a man orders both, and arranging with the Pub Co that I shall have half the profit on all Sawyers so sold, and also upon all that *they* sell while our canvass lasts.

Also, canvass Finn, Sawyer, and Prince all at once–a reduced price where a man orders the three.

It's a good idea–*don't forget to arrange for it.*

–*Mark Twain's Letters to His Publishers, 1867–1894*
(Berkeley & Los Angeles: University of
California Press, 1962), p. 172

* * *

This excerpt is from a letter written after the two men discussed Adventures of Huckleberry Finn *while traveling together on a train.*

Mark Twain to Webster, 12 April 1884

Here is a question which has been settled not less than 30 times, & *always* in the same way–& yet you asked me about it once more in the cars. This is the answer–& it has never received any other: *The book is to be issued when a big edition has been sold–& not before.*

Now write it up somewhere, & keep it in mind; & let us consider that question settled, & answered, and done with.

There is *no date* for the book. It can issue the 1st of December if 40,000 have been sold. It must wait till they *are* sold, if it is seven years.

Write it up, & don't forget it any more. . . .

I sent the MS. To-day. Let Kemble rush–time is already growing short. As fast as he gets through with the chapters, take them & read & select your matter for your canvassing book. . . .

Remember, Osgood fooled away no end of time on his canvassing book, & *then* got out one that was eminently calculated to destroy the sale.

–*Mark Twain, Business Man* (Boston: Little, Brown, 1946), p. 248

* * *

Charles L. Webster, circa 1884, Twain's nephew by marriage, business agent, and publishing partner. The two men corresponded often during the middle 1880s, but in 1887 an assistant replaced Webster as Twain's main contact in regard to publishing matters (from Mark Twain, Business Man, *Thomas Cooper Library, University of South Carolina).*

Mark Twain wanted to be sure that the canvassing book did not include the episode in which Huck observes raftsmen because he had already published it in Life on the Mississippi; *he later decided not to include the raft episode in the novel.*

Mark Twain to Webster, 14 April 1884

Keep it diligently in mind that we don't issue till we have made a *big sale.* Bliss never issued with less than 43,000 orders on hand, except in one instance–& it usually took him 5 or 6 months' canvassing to get them.

Get at your canvassing early and drive it with all your might, with an intent and purpose of issuing on the 10th or 15th of next December (the best time in the year to tumble a big pile into the trade); but if we haven't 40,000 subscriptions then, we simply postpone publication till we've *got* them. It is a plain, simple policy, and would have saved both of my last books if it had been followed. There is not going to be any reason whatever, why this book should not succeed–& it shall & *must.*

(Form 3.)

CONFIDENTIAL TERMS TO AGENTS.

MARK TWAIN'S NEW BOOK:

"ADVENTURES OF HUCKLEBERRY FINN."

TOM SAWYER'S COMPANION.

MAGNIFICENT AND UNPARALLELED OFFER TO CANVASSERS.

A CHANCE TO MAKE MONEY FOR ALL.

To every Canvasser selling *fifty* copies of the book, we will send *five* additional copies *free.*
To every Canvasser selling *one hundred* copies of the book, we will send *Ten* additional copies *free.*
To every Canvasser selling *one hundred and fifty* copies of the book, we will send *fifteen* additional copies *free.*
To every Canvasser selling *Two Hundred* copies of the book, we will send *twenty* additional copies *free.*
For all sales above two hundred copies, agents will receive *five copies free* for every *fifty* copies sold.
To take advantage of the above unprecedented offer, the books must all be sold to bona fide subscribers, at the full retail price.
The above Premiums are entirely in addition to the liberal discounts offered below.

HARD FACTS!

Five Hundred and Twenty-five Thousand (over Half a Million) Copies Mark Twain's Books

Have been sold in *this country alone; to say nothing of the immense* sales in England and Germany.

MARK TWAIN'S BOOKS ARE THE QUICKEST SELLING IN THE WORLD.

AGENTS! SECURE EASY WORK AND SURE PAY BY GETTING A MARK TWAIN AGENCY.

HOW TO GET AN AGENCY.

Among the circulars sent, you will notice one in blank, headed "APPLICATION FOR AGENCY." You will fill this out, naming the amount enclosed and the book and territory wanted. To each agent is given a certain field, and he must not canvass outside the prescribed limits. His first choice of territory is given him if it is not already assigned; if it is, his second or third choice is given: provided he gives us satisfactory evidence of his ability and experience to work the territory, and conduct the agency successfully—we reserving the right to cancel the agency if not so conducted. Upon the receipt of this "APPLICATION FOR AGENCY," properly filled out, with proper amount inclosed for outfit, the territory asked for is assigned, the outfit forwarded, and the applicant informed that he has an agency and the sole and the exclusive sale of the book in the territory assigned. If he is a new agent, advice is given him how to get to work and such other instructions as will guarantee success.

OUTFIT FOR CANVASSING.

This consists of a Bound Prospectus book, fully representing the work. Showing the Style of Binding, Paper, Size of Page, Type, Engravings, etc., etc., also Circulars, Blanks, Notices, and a Private Instruction-Book, teaching the agent how to proceed with the business.

THESE ARE SENT POST-PAID FOR 75 CENTS,

Which must invariably accompany all orders for Canvassing books.

☞ POSITIVELY NO PROSPECTUSES GIVEN AWAY. ☜

The amount paid for outfit deducted on first order of ten or more copies.

WE FURNISH BOOKS TO AGENTS AS FOLLOWS:

		Retail Prices.	To Agents.	Agents' Profit.
In Fine English Cloth Binding, Plain Edges,		$2.75 style,	$1.65	$1.10
Leather Library	" Sprinkled "	3.25 "	1.95	1.30
Half Morocco	" Marbled "	4.25 "	2.55	1.70

Although this is a companion book to "Adventures of Tom Sawyer," yet *each* book is *complete* in itself.
Some parties however wish both books. In order to accommodate all such, we offer to supply them in *blue* cloth bindings *only*, at the greatly reduced price of $4.75 per set retail; furnishing them to the agent at $2.80 per set: agent's profit, $1.95. We also furnish "The Prince and The Pauper," and "Adventure of Huckleberry Finn," in *green* cloth *only*, at $5.00 per set retail; furnishing them to the agent at $3.00; agents profit, $2.00.

☞ SPECIAL ADDITIONAL INDUCEMENTS ☜

We will charge you nothing for *packing boxes.*
We will pay exchange on drafts when amount is over $20.00.
We will pay charges on money sent us by Express when amount is over $20.00.
We will furnish all books given to editors for notices at one-half Agents' prices. but in every instance a copy of the paper containing the notice, for which a book is wanted, must be received by us.
We allot Agents certain specified territory to canvass. No other Agent is allowed to go into that territory, so long as the Agent to whom it is assigned canvasses satisfactorily and abides by our rules and regulations.
We sell the book exclusively by subscription, and every Agent pledges to do the same.
Finally, we give you a book the people want, by the greatest living humorist in the world.
If you can act as Agent for us, please signify your willingness at your earliest possible convenience. If unable to do so, *please oblige us* by handing this to some *intelligent person* of your acquaintance, whom you think might be willing to act for us in your stead. The *very reasonable price* of this work brings it within the reach of all classes. Those applying immediately, with remittances, will secure a choice territory.
When you write us, please give your POST OFFICE address in full, naming the TOWNSHIP as well as the COUNTY in which you live. Please name the territory you prefer to canvass; also say where or in what paper you saw the advertisement that induced you to send for this circular.
Hoping that you will at once engage with us in the sale of this most valuable and popular work, we remain very respectfully yours,

CHAS. L. WEBSTER & CO., Publishers,

658 Broadway, New York.

(OVER.)

Advertisement for sales agents (from Walter Blair, Mark Twain and Huck Finn *[Berkeley: University of California Press, 1960], Thomas Cooper Library, University of South Carolina)*

If we make any change, it must be simply a change from 40,000 to 50,000 before issuing. The Tramp issued with 48,000. . . .

Be particular & don't get any of that *old* matter into your canvassing book–(the *raft* episode.)

–*Mark Twain, Business Man*, pp. 248–249

* * *

Circumstances, including the problem of a defaced illustration, prevented Webster from publishing the novel in December.

Mark Twain to Webster, 23 May 1884

Order 30,000 copies of Huck Finn to be printed & bound. The same to be paid for in cash on delivery. . . .

Begin your canvass early, & *drive* it; for if, by the 5th of December, we have 40,000 orders, we will publish on the 15th, & "dump" books the same day & catch the holiday trade. Otherwise we will continue the canvass till we strike the full figure of 40,000 orders.

Now let's never allow ourselves to *think* of issuing with any *less* than 40,000 while there's a ghost of a show to get them.

–*Mark Twain, Business Man*, p. 255

* * *

Mark Twain was constantly involving himself in one potentially profitable project or another. In this excerpt he refers to board games designed to teach children important historial events or the reigns of English monarchs.

Mark Twain to Webster, 1 July 1884

Bear in mind that as soon as Huck Finn is published, you will go to work & publish one or two of the historical games–so be governed accordingly. There's bushels of dividends in those games. . . .

You want to look out for the Canadian pirates. Bliss used to swear that they laid in with pressmen & printing-office boys & bought advance sheets of one of my books & got the book out before we did.

–*Mark Twain, Business Man*, p. 263

Readings for the Platform

This excerpt from a 20 September 1884 letter to Webster shows Mark Twain's first step in preparing for his upcoming lecture tour.

I would like to find an *unbound* copy of Huck Finn in Hartford when I reach there–I want to select readings from it for the platform, immediately.

–*Mark Twain, Business Man*, p. 277

Huckleberry Finn on a Lecture Tour

Beginning on 5 November 1884, Mark Twain and the Southern novelist George Washington Cable embarked on a reading and lecture tour throughout the East and Midwest. Except for a brief respite for the Christmas season, the tour lasted four months and included more than sixty cities. James B. Pond, the promoter for the tour, billed the two speakers as the "Twins of Genius." Clemens's interest in the lecture tour was to raise capital for his publishing concern, but he also used the opportunity to advertise Adventures of Huckleberry Finn. *One of his most frequent readings was a selection from chapter 14, which he had originally intended to call "Learning a Nigger to Argue," but Cable advised him that the title was needlessly offensive, and he changed the title to "King Sollermun." Toward the end of the tour, his selection from* Adventures of Huckleberry Finn *was more often from the "evasion" episode on the Phelps farm, which was labeled "Tom's Extraordinary Adventure." These excerpts from reviews and news articles provide an indication of how Twain and his work were being perceived in the months preceding publication.*

Canada was an early stop on the grueling lecture tour because Mark Twain needed to arrange for British copyright protection for his forthcoming novel, which was published in England on 10 December 1884.

The Genial Mark
Toronto Globe, 9 December 1884

. . . Following Mr. Cable came

MARK TWAIN

He was, of course, received with great applause and for some moments could not proceed. When he did speak it was evident from the first word that the audience would enjoy his reading. After listening to him for five minutes one would be quite ready to accept as solemn truth the story he tells about his preparations for his first lecture, when he found a man who was led

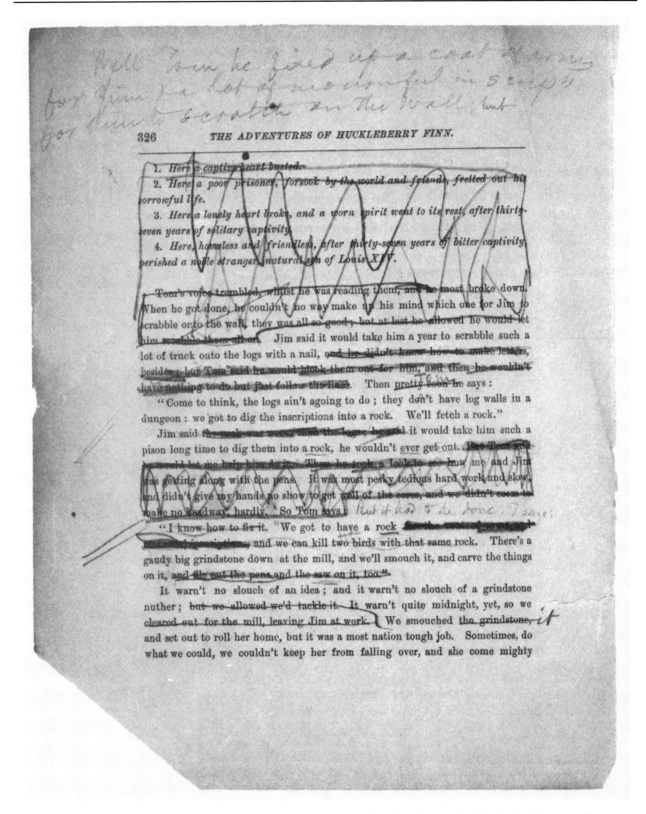

Proof sheet from Adventures of Huckleberry Finn *revised by Mark Twain for oral presentation. His "readings" were actually memorized recitations (Mark Twain Papers, The Bancroft Library, University of California, Berkeley).*

"I Never Enjoyed You More"

This excerpt is from a 14 November 1884 from William Dean Howells.

My Dear Clemens:

Three of us went to hear you read last night and I think I never enjoyed you more. You were as much yourself before those thousands as if you stood by my chimney-corner grinding away to the household your absence bereaves here. You are a great artist, and you do this public thing so wonderfully that I don't see how you could ever bear to give it up.

—I thought that the bits from Huck Finn told the best—at least I enjoyed them the most. That is a mighty good book, and I should like to hear you read it all. But everything of yours is good for platform reading. . . .

—Mark Twain Papers, The Bancroft Library, University of California, Berkeley

to laugh so heartily because of his (Mark's) "drawling infirmity of speech," as he calls it. It is not an infirmity but a peculiarity. His deep voice and his pronunciations of many words are of Missouri, where he was brought up, his nasal twang is of New England where he has spent a good many years, and his drawl is of Mark Twain. Now and again he jerks a short sentence out with wonderful rapidity, but that over, he relapses into his regular gait. He reads, however, with more care than is at first noticeable, and when he is imitating Huck Finn or the old negro telling a ghost story, his utterance changes enough to produce the impression he wishes to produce, but it is always a Huck Finn or a negro who talks like Mark Twain. He is most at home when relating his personal adventures. When he is personating Mark Twain he does it to the life and is an immense success. Every word almost is a joke, every modulation of his voice shows new and unsuspected fun in writings that may have been read over a dozen times. During his readings the house was convulsed with laughter. There were times when all laughed together. There were times when one would see a joke before the others grasped it, and would guffaw aloud, then stop short, till half the crowd laughing at him and the other half at the joke would start off, and the pioneer laugher, reassured, would lead the laugh and keep it up some seconds after the rest were quiet. When his audience laughed Mark Twain stopped with the air of a man who wished only to do his duty, and when they were quiet he resumed "with countenance grave as a horse's," as Will Carleton says. Mark Twain's first reading was prefaced with a few remarks. The remarks are given verbatim, and a

portion of the selection is given also, as nearly as it could be heard and written. The reader said:–

"Ladies and gentlemen,–You find me appointed to read something entitled 'King Solermunn,' if it may strictly be called reading where you don't use any book, but it is from a book, an unpublished story of mine called

'THE ADVENTURES OF HUCKLEBERRY FINN.'

It is a sort of continuation, or sequel, if you please, of a former story of mine, 'Tom Sawyer.' Huck Finn is an outcast, an uneducated, ragged boy, son of the town drunkard in a Mississippi River village, and he is running away from the brutalities of his father, and with him is a negro man, Jim, who is fleeing from slavery, and these two are in concealment in a wood on an island in the Mississippi River. They can't venture to travel in the day time, so they hide during the day and travel at night, and they entertain each other with conversations sometimes useful and sometimes otherwise. The story is written from the mouth of Huck Finn. Jim is telling Huck about all manner of occult things, all manner of signs which show that bad luck will come to them. After he has exhausted a good many of them, Huck says:–

"Ain't they any good-luck signs?"

"No; ain't no use in 'em. W'at you want to know when good luck coming? Want to try to keep it off? Only signs of any 'count is bad-luck signs. But dar's one good-luck sign. When a man's got hairy arms like a animal, dat's a sign he's goin' to be rich. Dat's a good sign."

"Well, you got hairy arms. You ever been rich?"

"Yes, sir; I been rich once, an' I'll be rich agin. I had fourteen dollars, once, all at one time. Yes, seh. Any 'o de boys 'll tell you so."

"What did you do with it?"

"Well, I speck'lated wid it and got busted up. Yes, sir. I tuck an' put dat money inter live stock. I put ten dollars inter a cow and she died on my hands. Live stock is pow'rful resky."

"Well, you lost ten dollars."

"No, I didn't lose it all, for I sole de hide and taller for a dollar and ten cents."

"Well then what did you do? Did you speckilate again?"

"Well you might call it so."

(Here followed a reference to some person evidently a friend of Jim, whose name the reporter did not catch.) He tuck in and started a bank, an' he sed—anybody put in a dollar he pay him four more at de end o' de year. Well, all de niggers went in. But dey didn't hab much. I was de only one dat had much, an' so I stuck out for more'n four dollars, an' I sed if he didn't gib it I'd take an' start a bank myself. Well, de fac' is dey warn't enough bisness for two banks. He knew dat, an' he knew he could clean me out.

A Thomas Nast cartoon, published in the January 1882 issue of Harper's Weekly, *mocking the requirement that Mark Twain had to travel to Canada to obtain British copyright protection for* The Prince and the Pauper. *To secure British copyright for* Adventures of Huckleberry Finn, *Twain arranged his lecture tour to be in Canada on the proper day (Thomas Cooper Library, University of South Carolina).*

He sed I could put five dollars in, an' at de end o' de year he'd pay me thirty-five dollars. An' so I done it. Den I think I doan want dat thirty dollars lyin' still de whole year; I better take an' invest it, keep it moving. Dar was a nigger catched a wood flat floating down de river, an' I bought it from him and sed he could go an' get de thirty dollars at de end o' de year. Well, dat night somebody stole de wood flat, an' next day de bank busted, so we didn't any o' us get no money."

"What did you do with the ten cents?"

"Well, first I thought I'd spend it, but den I had a dream, an' de dream said to take and give de ten cents to dat nigger——(here occurred a name which sounded like Baalam) let him invest it an' make a rise for me, for he's mighty lucky. I gave de ten cents to Baalam, an' he was in church, an' while he was in church he heard de preacher say whoever gave to de poo' lent to de Lord, an' was bound to get his money back a hundred times. Well, dat looked pretty good, an' Baalam thought it looked pretty safe, an' he gave de ten cents to de poo', an' he laid low ter see what was gwyne to cum of it."

"What did come of it, Jim?"

"Nothin' ever cum of it. Nothin' ever cum of it, Huck. I cou'd never collect it no way."

"Didn't you get the ten cents?" (The words of the answer were not distinctly caught, but they were in effect a negative.)

"How do you put faith in the sign, how do you know you're going to be rich?"

"Well, you take a look at it—I'se rich now. I'se rich already. I run away. I ain't a slave no more, and I'se worth eight hundred dollars. In any market I'se worth eight hundred dollars. You knows dat, Huck said. I'se rich now, just de same as if I had eight hundred dollars exactly. Still, betwixt you an' me, I don't like it invested in dat way. My experience in live stock is resky; makes no difference if its in cows or niggers, its resky, an' I would feel much more easy if I had de eight hundred dollars an' somebody else had de nigger."

The selection of which the above is a part, was received with loud applause.

*   *   *

The subheadings for this article proclaimed the reviewer's dissatisfaction with the performance: "IT IS AN ADVERTISING HIPPODROME / Neither of Them Reads Well—'Mark Twain' Losing His Ground."

"Twain" and Cable
The Pittsburg Dispatch, 30 December 1884

S.L. Clemens, better known as "Mark Twain," and Mr. George W. Cable recited selections from their own writings last night at the Cumberland Presbyterian church. The congregation was large, and there was an air of intellectuality about the people that betokened keen appreciation and accurate comprehension. One thing was noticeable among the listeners: Nearly everyone had a long nose. If those who were there will glance at each other's companion, this exceptional gathering of long and well-shaped noses will be easily discerned. The occasion was supposed to be a humorous one. Long noses indicate serious intelligence. It may be because the entertainment was a church performance, the true character of it was not suspected.

Mr. Cable, who has become known to the public as the writer of "Old Creole Days," "The Grandissimes" and "Dr. Sevier," was the first to appear. When he mounted the pulpit, he looked like an elf, save his big head, long pointed brown beard and Vandyke moustache. He was dressed in conventional black, with clawhammer coat. The forehead is fairly broad, and medium high; it has an blunt appearance. His sloping, narrow shoulders and diminutive height, set off by his big head and full face, give him a pompous air, which is increased by an assumed dignity of speech and put-on deepness of voice that tends to make the irreverent laugh.

ADVERTISING THEIR BOOKS.
He introduced himself to the audience in a labored humorous way, which he had evidently caught by association with his leading man and comedian,

"Mark Twain"—caught by inoculation from an imperfect virus quill. He began by doing a silly thing, which was followed by his co-partner in this enterprise of advertising each other's books. The silly thing was to announce that he would not read the piece announced on the programme but another, viz. "Narcisse's Visit to Widow Riley," a selection from "Dr. Sevier." The choice was not excellent, but it really could make little difference, for Mr. Cable soon proved himself not only a poor reader, but a positively bad reader, or reciter. He has no mimic power. When he attempted to interpret "Widow Riley's" part, which is given in the brogue of a simpering, coquettish widow, he failed dismally. His voice, utterly untrained and with but little compass, got to a pitch where it became simply ridiculous.

Mark Twain and Mr. Cable recited alternately. As Mr. Cable began the show, it is well to finish with him before speaking of the author of "Tom Sawyer." Mr.

THE ADVENTURES
OF

HUCKLEBERRY FINN

(TOM SAWYER'S COMRADE)

SCENE : THE MISSISSIPPI VALLEY
TIME : FORTY TO FIFTY YEARS AGO

BY

MARK TWAIN
(SAMUEL L. CLEMENS)

WITH 174 ILLUSTRATIONS

London
CHATTO & WINDUS, PICCADILLY
1884

[All rights reserved]

Title page for the first English edition, which was received at the British Museum on 10 December 1884, the date the first Canadian edition was given copyright protection (Special Collections, Thomas Cooper Library, University of South Carolina)

Cable's next effort was a visit from "Ristofalo" to the "Widow Riley." "Ristofalo" is a placid, unexcitable, unemotional being, whom Mr. Cable fairly represented in his courtship of the widow. His recital of the widow's lines were ludicrous–not the lines, but Mr. Cable's recital. His want of elocutionary powers was woefully displayed here, and the thought could not be kept back that so far as Mr. Cable was concerned this scheme of his and Mr. Clemens's was an unwarranted hippodrome.

At Mr. Cable's next call he, instead of following out the programme, substituted two Creole songs which he said retained African barbarity, and he asserted that the latter part was all he retained of the songs. Mr. Cable spoke better than he knew in that. It was barbarous. Even though he rendered them true to life, there was no excuse for producing them, for they were neither instructive nor amusing. While he was chanting them the audience was craning their necks and looking in the direction of the "stage entrance," as if they expected every moment to see Mr. Clemens come out clad in a blanket with face painted and hair bedecked with feathers, waving a tomahawk, and dance a savage war dance. Mr. Clemens missed his opportunity.

The final appearance of Mr. Cable was when he recited "Mary's Night Ride," from "Dr. Sevier." This describes the race for life of a woman on horseback carrying her babe in her arms, as she tries to escape the "lines" of the Confederate soldiers. There is all possible opportunity for realistic declamation. Mr. Cable made many of his audience laugh by his shouting and ranting. He declaimed in a reckless manner, that showed he had no idea of either elocution or declamation. Whilst he points to Mary flying at a mile a minute out of danger, instead of following his pointed finger with his eye, he looks at the audience, who in turn glance from his eyes to his finger, and mentally ask "where is Mary?"

"MARK TWAIN"

When the six-foot, raw-boned "Mark Twain," with his swallow-tail coat and white tie, stepped out, he looked 30 years older than he did when he appeared in this city 17 years ago. His kinky, bushy hair and his heavy moustache have grown gray. The face has become thin. The eyes are somewhat sunken. The square jaw bones cut a sharper line than ever. The humorist now appears a sad victim of his own jokes. Although he said he would not be introduced, "because he had been 17 years ago," many of his hearers who had heard him before, at that introduction, would have required another, to have known him.

His preliminary remarks were devoted to his change of programme. He then related or recited

his adventures with a young lady in Switzerland, who made believe she knew him, and asked him all sorts of questions about imaginary beings, to all of which he had answered as though he knew the people. It was funny; and, although Mr. Clemens's drawling manner of speech, which of itself is quaint and laughter-provoking, has grown more marked and his words are not always heard, he succeeded in delighting his listeners. He recited most of the evening with his eyes closed, and in a manner of fact sort of way that was comical. Still he did not make his own writings half so laughable as they are made every day by elocutionists all over the land.

The next selection was from "Huckleberry Finn," a kind of sequel to "Tom Sawyer," and which is not yet published. It related the troubles of two prankish boys who freed a slave imprisoned in an old cabin. There were a hundred ludicrous incidents in it, which could but stir the risibilities of a very appreciative audience. In his second call he continued the story of the boys' comical tricks and perplexities, which in spite of his inanimate recital, kept the hearers in a smile all the while he spoke.

The last was a commonplace humorosity, built up, carpenter-like, out of the grammatical idiosyncrasies of the German language, a source of fun for alleged funnymen as general and as common as robbing the chicken coop and stealing watermelons. It was a painful production that must have cost its author much labor but gave little mental satisfaction. There is nothing very funny about it. It lacks that spontaneousness that is the real sign of pure mirth and humor. Besides, it was heavy and execrably read. In this recitation he seems to have taken lessons from Mr. Cable.

The whole performance was a hippodrome. Either's works shine better in books than when read by them. The unbecomingness and the charlatanism of an author's going around the country reading from the proofs of a book he is about to publish are degrading to literature. How Mr. Clemens could allow himself to do it is past comprehension. Still, viewed in the light of the miserable performance of Mr. Cable, he may feel that he is a benefactor, for his recitals are so much superior to those from "Dr. Sevier." At best it is very sad to see men who have done clever literary work, "barn-storming" the country with their own works. If the works are good, it is a lowering of the dignity of the authors that is anything but commendable, and if they are not good, to read them in public is almost a crime. It is true Dickens read his works on the platform, but it never added to his fame, and it did lower him in that he became general, common.

* * *

Mark Twain and George W. Cable
St. Louis Daily Globe Democrat, 10 January 1885

Mark Twain and George W. Cable entertained about 700 of their admirers in Mercantile Library Hall last night. They gave recitals of selections from their respective work, Mark Twain having four pieces on the programme and Mr. Cable the same number. Cable chose passages from his novel *Dr. Sevier,* in which he aimed to illustrate the characters of Narcisse, the Creole, Kate Riley and Mary Richley. All his recitals were successful in pleasing the audience, and before the evening was at an end the author of Creole Days was a strong favorite with all present. Mark Twain did not fail, however, to hold his own. He kept the assemblage in excellent humor with his literary surprises, and in the "King Sollermun" passage from *Huckleberry Finn,* the "Tragic Tale of a Fishwife," he which he illustrated the reckless distribution of genders among the nouns of the German language, and in the other selections he tickled the risibles of the audience to an extent that satisfactorily established the popular quality of his humor at least. Mr. Cable is quietly dramatic in his manner, and has a pleasant, pliable voice. His dialectic efforts, too, are very fair. Twain's voice has the resonance of a cracked steamboat whistle. He enunciates slowly, gesticulates with his head, and keeps either hand in a pants pocket during his stay on the stage. Last night's programme will be repeated this afternoon, and tonight new selections will be given.

* * *

This review is from a newspaper in Keokuk, Iowa.

Twain-Cable
The Daily Gate City, 15 January 1885

Mark Twain's characteristic introduction of himself last night at its close shaped itself into an apology for his having been the cause of bringing from pleasant homes and cheerful firesides the large audience that assembled at the opera house last night. We venture the assertion, however, that every one present felt fully repaid for the discomfort experienced in fighting their way through the fiercest snow storm of the season by the excellence of the entertainment furnished them by Mark Twain who certainly is entitled to rank as our foremost humorist and George W. Cable, the distinguished southern novelist. Mr. Cable was first upon the program and gave a reading from Dr. Sevier, but unfortunately the greatest portion of it was lost to the audience by

reason of the interruptions caused by the late comers. Mark Twain came next and the appearance of the ungainly body and the shaggy head was the signal for applause. He remarked after the performance that he had grown handsomer of late. If this is the fact, and it is generally understood that Twain is truthful, we feel grateful that he didn't appear before us in his previous condition. As far as looks are concerned Twain would never capture a premium at a beauty show, but when it comes to story telling the best judges would pronounce him chief. He called the audience friends and fellow townsmen, told them he was glad to resume an intercourse that had been broken off years ago, said he was sorry to have been the cause of bringing them out upon such a night, but that they were no worse off than the people of some seventy-five cities already visited by them this season, that a storm generally preceded their coming, and that if feeling well they always left a famine behind them. After this, as a sort of introduction and preliminary, he waded into an extract from his new book and caused many a laugh by his funny description of the discussion of the merits of and demerits of "King Sollermun" between the darkey Jim and Huckleberry Finn.

Mr. Cable's next reading was from Dr. Sevier also and dealt with Kate Riley, Richling and Ristofalo, the latter part of it being devoted to the wooing of the widow by the Italian and was given in a decid-

---

Angelic and Diabolic Spirits

The original heading for this news item was "The Author and the Humorist Arrive in the City To-Day."

While Mr. J. B. Pond was this morning standing in the rotunda of the Southern Hotel with Samuel C. Clemens (Mark Twain) standing upon one side of him and George W. Cable upon the other, the POST-DISPATCH reporter present was struck by the touching likeness which the group bore to that beautiful legend which provides a human being with two attendant spirits, one of them of diabolical mien always urging them on to commit felonies and misdemeanors, the other, of angelic aspect, constantly coaxing him to give up his criminal ways. Mark Twain's features, familiarized to the public by several brands of chewing tobacco, cigars and cigarettes, are so well known that it only becomes necessary to describe the appearance of his less Mephistophelian companion. Mr. Cable is, or rather, if he were to be a woman, he would be what the society editors describe as a petite brunette.

—The St. Louis Post-Dispatch, 9 January 1885

edly clever manner. Mark Twain then convulsed the audience with a side-splitting history of his tussle with the German language and his lamentable failure to properly declare their adjectives or master the intricacies of the gender of their nouns. Being recalled he told his very funny stuttering story and another being demanded he spun a sailor yarn to the entire satisfaction of the audience.

For the regular number on the program Mr. Cable at this point substituted several pleasing Creole songs which were well received. Twain then gave "a Trying Situation" which was followed by Mr. Cable in a descriptive reading. He had kept his best for the last and his dramatic rendition of "Mary's Night Ride" won for him most heart applause. The performance was closed with a personal reminiscence by Mark Twain detailing his experience with the duello in his days of roughing it in the rowdy west.

* * *

The Twain-Cable Combination
Indianapolis Journal, 8 February 1885

A very fine audience greeted Mr. George W. Cable and Mr. Samuel L. Clemens, at the Plymouth Church, last night, but not so large as the one they faced when here less than a month ago. This is to be accounted for, probably, because of the matinee in the afternoon, when the programme was the same as that given at night, and also because it is easy to have the taste palled with the peculiar entertainment they give. Mr. Cable's principle selections were from the Grandissimes, introducing the character of Ravel Innerarity, with his wonderful picture of "Louisiana Refusing to Enter the Union," and the announcement of his marriage as he changes boats on the beautiful waters of Lake Catharine. The preamble to this latter appearance of the Creole artist was a splendid bit of landscape painting, soft and sensuous with the beauty of that Southern sky, air and water in and about the chain of lakes forming the back water-way between New Orleans and the gulf. He again interpolated three of the creole love songs, and closed his part of the programme with "Mary's Night Ride," from Dr. Sevier, a bit of artistic work, eager and intense both in the writing and the reading. It is much the best thing Mr. Cable gave. Mark Twain was as funny as ever. His encounter with the newspaper interviewer, in which he broke down that redoubtable personage with his atrocious burlesques upon fact, put the audience in a mood to be tickled

THE
"Mark Twain"-Cable Readings.

PROGRAMME.

1. FROM DR. SEVIER.—NARCISSE AND JOHN AND MARY RICHLING
   " Mistoo 'Ichlin', in fact, I can baw that fifty dolla' f'om you myself."
   GEO. W. CABLE.

2. ADVANCE SHEETS FROM "THE ADVENTURES OF HUCKLEBERRY FINN.—"KING SOLLERMUNN."
   MARK TWAIN.

3. FROM DR. SEVIER.—KATE RILEY, RICHLING AND RISTOFALO.
   GEO. W. CABLE.

4. TRAGIC TALE OF THE FISHWIFE.
   MARK TWAIN.

5. FROM DR. SEVIER.—NARCISSE PUTS ON MOURNING FOR "LADY BYRON."
   GEO. W. CABLE.

6. A TRYING SITUATION.
   MARK TWAIN.

7. FROM DR. SEVIER.—MARY'S NIGHT RIDE.
   GEO. W. CABLE.

8. A GHOST STORY.
   MARK TWAIN.

J. B. POND, MANAGER, EVERETT HOUSE, NEW YORK.

CARRIAGES AT 10.

A program for a performance of the "Twins of Genius"
(Berg Collection, New York Public Library)

to death with the story of Huck Finn and Tom Sawyer in their arrangement of "Jim's" escape from the cabin in accordance with the dramatic unities of history and romance; with the mistake of the Blue Jay, who attempted to fill up the dismantled cabin with acorns dropped through a knot-hole in the roof; and the story of his duel in Nevada, in which he was converted from a blood-thirsty hunter of men into a mild and cooing dove, who, having a controversy with a person now, would take him out quietly and talk with him, and reason with him—and kill him. In answer to a furious encore, Twain gave the adventure of the miner's cat, which was blown up in a blast, and ever afterward exhibited an unconquerable aversion to quartz mining. As an entirety the evening was most enjoyable, and if it seemed less full of zest than the previous one, it was because the novelty had somewhat worn away, and not that the performance was below standard. The general verdict was expressed by a fair auditor in the gallery, who, while Mr. Twain was telling of his duel, gave a long-protracted half-musical shriek, dying away in a hysteria and a rupture of whalebone.

Prepublication in *The Century*

More than a quarter of Adventures of Huckleberry Finn *appeared in* The Century Illustrated Monthly Magazine *in the three months prior to the publication of the novel in the United States. Mark Twain evidently thought of* The Century *excerpts as a form of promotion for his novel. That the editor, Richard Watson Gilder, made significant changes to his text— in some instances amounting to bowdlerization—apparently did not trouble the author. Always a bit uncertain about genteel taste and how to defer to it, Twain sometimes left such editorial decisions to others. He did not, however, carry over Gilder's alterations into the printed novel.*

In this essay Arthur Scott mistakenly assumed that The Century *excerpts were set from the manuscript instead of galley sheets, but he is generally right about Twain's deference to Gilder's editorial judgment.*

The *Century Magazine*
Edits *Huckleberry Finn,* 1884–1885
Arthur L. Scott

At the first appearance of Mark Twain's *Huckleberry Finn* a superintendent of public schools in the West wrote an angry letter to Richard Watson Gilder, who had printed portions of the novel in the *Century*.[1] The gentlemanly editor replied in part as follows:

Dear Sir: We thank you sincerely for your kind and frank letter. We understand the points to which you object in Mark Twain's writings, but we cannot agree with you that they are "destitute of a single redeeming quality." . . . Mr. Clemens has great faults; at times he is inartistically and indefensibly coarse, but we do not think anything of his that has been printed in the *Century* is without very decided value, literary and otherwise. . . .

Mark Twain is not a giber at religion or morality. He is a good citizen and believes in the best things. Nevertheless there is much of his writing that we would not print for a miscellaneous audience. If you should ever carefully compare the chapters of *Huckleberry Finn* as we printed them, with the same as they appear in his book, you will see the most decided difference. These extracts were carefully edited for a magazine audience with his full consent.[2]

Since Gilder had printed more than one-fourth of the novel, it is doubtful that the superintendent ever did "carefully compare" the two texts. Today, however, such a comparison provides us with a ready insight into the genteel culture of an era which ignored *Tom Sawyer* and abused *Huckleberry Finn,* while taking *The Prince and the Pauper* to its heart.[3] But even this popular medieval romance was not wholly acceptable to the conservative Gilder, who complained: ". . . some of the fun sprinkled through the story grates on the ear."[4] Obviously, therefore, Gilder was hardly the man to buy rights to *Huckle-berry Finn* without the privilege of editing, even though the original manuscript had already been carefully pruned by both Mrs. Clemens and William Dean Howells.[5] As a New York civic and cultural leader, moreover, Gilder may have felt duty-bound to reject certain parts of this extraordinary new book. He also had to consider his *Century* readers who, during that winter of 1884–1885, were peacefully enjoying the more bland fare of Henry James's *The Bostonians* and of Howells's *The Rise of Silas Lapham.* Gilder's problem, then, was to select fitting episodes from Mark Twain's manuscript and (with the author's "full consent") to sieve them of that which he believed "indefensibly coarse."

Which of the fascinating episodes of *Huckleberry Finn* did Gilder select? In December, 1884, he opened with Chapters XVII and XVIII–the full account of the Grangerford-Shepherdson feud.[7] He began the adventure with two paragraphs from Chapter XIX describing the idyllic life of Huck and Jim on the river. These paragraphs serve as an artistic introduction to the cruel episode. In January, 1885, Gilder followed with brief extracts from Chapters VIII and XIV. The *Century* calls this installment "Jim's Investments, and King Sollermun." It is merely comic dialogue between Huck and Jim on these two diverse topics. The February selection is much the longest of the three printed by Gilder. It runs from Chapter XIX through Chapter XXVIII, with the significant omission of the two powerful scenes revolving about Colonel Sherburn, who coolly murders old Boggs and then tongue-lashes the craven mob which comes to lynch him. In this section, the King and Duke make their appearance, work their newspaper and camp-meeting frauds, play Shakespeare and *The Royal Nonesuch,* and finally pose as the Wilks heirs from England. The selection concludes with the arrival of the true heirs.

Statistically, the *Century* episodes span about 34 per cent of the novel, but actually print only about 28 per cent of it. In other words, approximately 18 per cent of the material has been omitted. Of these omissions, about two dozen are trivial in length (3 lines or less), another two dozen are minor (4–10 lines) and nine are major (15 lines or more). In addition, there are four brief alterations of wording.

Even the smallest of these deletions and changes may give a significant clue to the polite literary fashion of the eighties. For example, the expression "to be in a sweat" about something was apparently taboo, because it is deleted once, and twice it is euphemized to "worrying about" and "in such a hurry." Nor was it permitted to mention nakedness. Gone are the lines, therefore, where Huck speaks of himself and Jim on the raft as being "always naked day and night," because they hated

"AT THE COURT-HOUSE!

FOR THREE NIGHTS ONLY!

The World-Renowned Tragedians,

DAVID GARRICK THE YOUNGER!

AND

EDMUND KEAN THE ELDER!

Of the London and Continental Theaters,

In their Thrilling Tragedy of

THE KING'S CAMELOPARD;

OR,

THE ROYAL NONESUCH!!!

Admission 50 cents."

Well, all day him and the king was hard at
it, rigging up a stage, and a curtain, and a
row of candles for foot-lights; and that night
the house was jam full of men in no time

AT THE COURT HOUSE!

FOR 3 NIGHTS ONLY!

The World-Renowned Tragedians

DAVID GARRICK THE YOUNGER!

AND

EDMUND KEAN THE ELDER!

Of the London and Continental Theatres,

In their Thrilling Tragedy of

THE KING'S CAMELOPARD

OR

THE ROYAL NONESUCH!!!

Admission 50 cents.

Then at the bottom was the biggest line of all—which said:

LADIES AND CHILDREN NOT ADMITTED.

"There," says he, "if that line don't fetch them, I dont know Arkansaw!"

The Bricksville poster as edited by Richard Gilder for The Century *(top) and as it appeared in the novel, at the end of chapter 22
(left, Thomas Cooper Library, University of South Carolina; right, Mark Twain House, Hartford, Connecticut)*

clothes. The word "naked" is also left out of the description of the King's appearance in *The Royal Nonesuch;* and Gilder even omits the next sentence in which Huck says he had better not describe the king's get-up in greater detail. Such a deletion, of course, weakens the implications of the bawdy scene. It does not damage the narrative, however, as badly as does the omission of all reference to the famous last line on the poster advertising this show: "Then at the bottom was the biggest line of all, which said: LADIES AND CHILDREN NOT ADMITTED." And excised is the Duke's shrewd comment, "'There,' says he, 'if that line don't fetch them, I don't know Arkansaw!'" This is needed not only for the satire, but also to explain the capacity turn-out for a show in a small town where the rascals' Shakespearean performance has flopped just the night before. The words "mush" and "hogwash" did not

get by Gilder, either. No longer does the undertaker slide the coffin lid along "as soft as mush," and the King's funeral oration no longer has its "soul-butter" mixed with "hogwash." And poor Huck is not even permitted to say "by jings"—appropriate though it seems in the situation.

If Mark Twain's style often got too slangy, his mood at times must also have been thought irreverent. Gilder cut off the punch-ending to Chapter XXIV, where the two dead beats feign grief on learning of Peter Wilks's death: "and both of them took on about that dead tanner like they'd lost the twelve disciples. Well, if I ever struck anything like it, I'm a nigger." Again, as the King joyously lets the Wilks gold-pieces flow through his fingers, he is no longer allowed to chortle: "'Thish yer comes of trust'n to Providence. It's the best way, in the long run. I've tried 'em all, and ther' ain't no better way.'" And finally, in Chapter XX,

201

"Dramatic and Powerful"

This excerpt, from a 7 January 1885 letter by Clemens's friend, poet and critic E. C. Stedman, concerns the first installment from the novel published in The Century, *the Grangerford-Shepherdson feud (see pages 51–56 in "Backgrounds and Sources" of this volume).*

My Dear Clemens,

Of course it is aggravating <u>not</u> to be able to quote from your <u>Vendetta</u> in the Dec. Century, which, to my mind, is not only the most finished and condensed thing you have done but as dramatic and powerful an episode as I know in literature. . . .

–Mark Twain Papers, The Bancroft Library,
University of California, Berkeley

Glider completely eliminates the preacher's arm-waving sermon at the camp meeting.

It may be that Gilder was also afraid lest people misinterpret Huck's observation about how natural it is to hide under a bed, "when you are up to anything private." Five lines are deleted here. Gone, too is the memorable picture of the King passing his hat at the camp meeting, when "every little while the prettiest kind of girls, with tears running down their cheeks, would up and ask him would he let them kiss him for to remember him by; and he always done it; and some of them he hugged and kissed as many as five or six times."

On three occasions, moreover, Gilder deletes specific descriptions of the corpse of Peter Wilks, how it was arranged in the coffin, and precisely where the bag of money was placed upon it. The realism may have been too real. The *Century* likewise omits all mention of the dead cats brought in by the third-night audience at *The Royal Nonesuch,* and in general minimizes the stench which was "too various" even for Huck. Also expurgated is the mention of shooting stars, together with Jim's homely comparison of them to eggs that "got spoiled and was hove out of the nest." In this spirit of good taste, Gilder likewise killed characteristic punch lines of the following nature: The Duke wonders what the third-night crowd at *Nonesuch* is doing now that its intended victims have fled. Thinking of the "sickly eggs by the barrel, and rotten cabbages, and such things," he makes the purged comment, "'They can turn it into a picnic if they want to—they brought plenty provisions.'"

Last among these shorter deletions are some descriptive passages which the modern reader might prefer to include. For instance, cut from Chapter XXVII is the gently comic description (half a page) of the undertaker seating the funeral guests. This description—useful for establishing the personality of this dignitary—closes with the comment: "He was the softest, glidingest, stealthiest man I ever see; and there warn't no more smile to him than there is to a ham."

About the longest deletions it is hard to generalize, since they may be due partly to space limitation. There are five omissions of two to twelve pages in length. Consider, for instance, the powerful Boggs-Sherburn scenes—twelve pages in Chapters XXI and XXII. Before we jump to the conclusion that these scenes were too strong for *Century* readers, we must remember that the same readers had already survived the Grangerford-Shepherdson feud. Moreover, not only does this long omission save space, but it also lends unity to the two histrionic scenes by making the regal farce now follow close on the heels of the Shakespeare. This would explain also the omission of the "bully circus" which Huck attended after the lynch mob broke up. Surely, there was nothing offensive in this happy circus episode!

It is interesting that in the entire first installment concerning the feud there is only one deletion. This is the "Ode to Stephen Dowling Bots, Dec'd"—that six-verse obituary lampoon about the boy whose "soul did from this cold world fly/By falling down a well." Gilder, it seems, did not appreciate this sort of literary clowning, for he also excised those two well-known pages in Chapter XXI where the Duke—from imperfect memory—teaches the King to recite Hamlet's soliloquy.

The other three excisions of length are quite diverse in nature. The first is the graphic description in Chapter XXI of the muddy, hog-ridden village of Bricksville, Arkansas, whose gaping, ornery, tobacker-chawing citizens enjoyed nothing so much as "putting turpentine on a stray dog and setting fire to him, or tying a tin pan to his tail and see him run himself to death." Could this memorable description have been purged as "inartistically and indefensibly coarse?" The next major cut is the last three and one-half pages of Chapter XXIII. Half of this is sheer farce, as Huck scrambles history in order to explain to Jim about British kings and dukes. The other half contains perhaps the most sentimental passage in the novel: Jim's touching account of how he discovered that scarlet fever had left his little daughter both deaf and dumb. In addition to its emotional impact, this latter passage is psychologically important in the education of Huck. Why Gilder—in an era of sentiment—left it out of the *Century* is a mystery. The last big cut is five pages of comic dialogue in Chapter XXVI between Huck and Joanna Wilks, the suspicious harelip, who pumps the poor boy completely dry of fabrications about his life in England. Although good clean fun in itself, this dialogue does interrupt the main action and is dispensable.

In addition to these excisions, there are approximately twenty more (ranging in length from a brief clause up to half a page) which simply eliminate redundant material of a descriptive or expository nature. In every case the deletion serves to tighten the narrative line, as well as to conserve space. Since even the proudest author could hardly cavil at this kind of editing, it would be pointless to document it here.

Except for finding euphemisms for being "in a sweat," the only editing discussed so far has been that which was accomplished with strokes of the blue pencil. As a matter of fact, this is about the only kind of editing done to *Huck* for the *Century*. Such was not the case, for example, when *The Innocents Abroad* was revised for publication in England.[8] We may deduce, therefore, that Gilder or one of his associates prepared the text of *Huckleberry Finn* for magazine publication and that Mark Twain only read the proofs. Twain himself probably changed the first words of Chapter XVII from "In about a minute" to "In about half a minute," because it is doubtful that any editor would quibble about so small a detail.

The only other *alteration* (as distinct from deletions) is most certainly the work of the author himself. In the book, Chapter VIII ends with Jim joking about being rich, because he owns himself and he is worth $800.00; but he moans, "'I wisht I had de money, I wouldn' want no mo'.'" For the *Century*, this final comment is strengthened to read: "'But live stock's too resky, Huck;—I wisht I had de eight hund'd dollars en somebody else had de nigger.'" This has the hallmark. This also represents the most important of the three textual changes or deletions made in the first two *Century* installments. Oddly, of the more than fifty instances of editorial tampering, only three occur in the first two installments, which comprise more than one-third of the excerpts. (The other two are the "a minute" change and the deletion of the "Ode to Stephen Dowling Bots, Dec'd.") For some reason, the editor's pencil slashed severely only at the final installment.

Just twenty years after publishing these portions of *Huckleberry Finn* in his magazine, Gilder asserted: "[Twain's writings] have, through practice and through a determined search for the exact word, gradually increased in verbal felicity. . . . there is a general advance in artistic qualities. . . ."[9] To state in 1904 that there is "a general advance in artistic qualities" implies that there must have been plenty of room for improvement in 1884. That Gilder did not slash *Huck* more savagely than he did, therefore, is a

tribute either to his own self-restraint or to Mark Twain's stubbornness. Doubtless to the former, since it is well known that the two men remained good friends to the end.

That winter, moreover, Mark Twain was too busy to be stubborn about so small a matter. He was giving readings with George Washington Cable; he was negotiating with General Grant to publish his memoirs; and he was himself publishing *Huckleberry Finn* in a book form which he knew would outlive mere magazine excerpts. A quick glance could show him that Gilder was not completely emasculating his novel. Beyond that he probably did not much care. Careful examination today, however, does prove that by means of judicious selection and deletion, Richard Watson Gilder did try to cram Mark Twain's sprawling narrative into something more or less resembling the chaste, urbane, conventional mold of its two bedfellows—*The Bostonians* and *The Rise of Silas Lapham.*

—American Literature, 27 (1955), 356–362

1. Mark Twain's bibliographer merely says of *Huck:* "An advance chapter appeared also in *Century,* February, 1885, with the title 'Royalty on the Mississippi'" (Merle Johnson, *A Bibliography of the Writings of Mark Twain,* revised edition, New York 1935, p. 50). Actually almost a dozen chapters of the novel were printed in the *Century Magazine,* Dec., 1884, Jan. and Feb., 1885.

2. Rosamond Gilder, ed. *Letters of Richard Watson Gilder* (Boston, 1916), pp. 398–399. Gilder also sent a copy of this letter to Mark Twain.

3. For the receptions of these novels, see Arthur L. Vogelback, "The Publication and Reception of *Huckleberry Finn* in America," *American Literature,* XI, 260–272 (Nov., 1939), and "*The Prince and the Pauper:* A Study in Critical Standards," *ibid.,* XIV, 48–54 (March, 1942).

4. Gilder cited an instance: "In speaking of the king's 'taster,' whose duty it was to make sure that poison had not been put in the royal food, the author wonders "why they did not use a dog or a plumber'" ("Mark Twain's *The Prince and the Pauper*" [review] *Century,* N.S. I, 784, March, 1882).

5. For analyses of this original editing, see DeLancey Ferguson, "Huck Finn Aborning," *Colophon,* N.S. III, 171–180 (Spring, 1938) and Bernard DeVoto, *Mark Twain at Work* (Cambridge, Mass., 1942).

6. Paine is in error when he states that *Silas Lapham* appeared as a *Century* serial in the summer of 1882. He confuses it with Howells's *A Modern Instance.* See Albert Bigelow Paine, ed., *Letters of Mark Twain* (Definitive Edition, New York, 1933), XXXIV, 420–421.

7. All references to chapters are to The Author's National Edition of Mark Twain's Writings.

8. See Arthur L. Scott, "Mark Twain's Revisions of *The Innocents Abroad* for the British Edition of 1872," *American Literature,* XXV, 43–61 (March, 1953).

9. "Mark Twain: A Glance at His Spoken and Written Art," *Outlook,* LXXVIII, 844 (Dec. 3, 1904).

456   *JIM'S INVESTMENTS, AND KING SOLLERMUN.*

Just down the slope a slender aspen stood,
And, in its leafy hammocks, noon by noon,
We watched the clover crimson to the wood,
And sweet glade-roses blush to welcome June.

Beside the door-stone, in those days of old,
Great mountain lilies grew, and I have read
Upon their scrolls of onyx, sprayed with gold,
The records of the words our Saviour said.

We were God's small interpreters; we knew
What the tall corn leaves talked of in their sleep;
We caught the secrets of the rain and dew,
And love them now for what we know they keep.

Ah, well! I sought the school-house yesterday,
And found amid the ferny wilderness,
A pile of fallen timbers, warped and gray,
A heap of chimney bricks in mossy dress.

We children have grown old; we hear the rush
Of a new generation close behind,
Yon clustering yew-trees hide the sunset's flush;
Our locks are toying with the evening wind.

Within my soul, where, many years, have met
Pride and self-love, to-day this past of mine—
A tearful Mary—brings a sweet regret
Folded in perfume to the Saviour's shrine.

Mary A. Leonard.

JIM'S INVESTMENTS, AND KING SOLLERMUN.*

BY MARK TWAIN.

Jim knowed all kinds of signs. He said he knowed 'most everything. I said it looked to me like all the signs was about bad luck, and so I asked him if there warn't any good-luck signs. He says:

"Mighty few — an' *dey* ain' no use to a body. What you want to know when good luck's a-comin' for? want to keep it off?" And he said: "Ef you's got hairy arms en a hairy breas', it's a sign dat you's agwyne to be rich. Well, dey's some use in a sign like dat, 'kase it's so fur ahead. You see, may be you's got to be po' a long time fust, en so you might git discourage' en kill yo'sef 'f you didn' know by de sign dat you gwyne to be rich bymeby."

"Have you got hairy arms and a hairy breast, Jim?"

"What's de use to ax dat question? don' you see I has?"

"Well, are you rich?"

"No; but I ben rich wunst, and gwyne to be rich agin. Wunst I had fo'teen dollars, but I tuck to speculat'n', en got busted out."

"What did you speculate in, Jim?"

"Well, fust I tackled stock."

"What kind of stock?"

"Why, live stock. Cattle, you know. I put ten dollars in a cow. But I ain' gwyne to resk no mo' money in stock. De cow up 'n died on my han's."

"So you lost the ten dollars."

"No; I didn' lose it all. I on'y los' 'bout nine of it. I sole de hide en taller for a dollar en ten cents."

"You had five dollars and ten cents left. Did you speculate any more?"

"Yes. You know dat one-laigged nigger dat b'longs to ole Misto Bradish? Well, he sot up a bank, en say anybody dat put in a dollar would git fo' dollars mo' at de en' er de year. Well, all de niggers went in, but dey didn' have much. I wuz de on'y one dat had much. So I stuck out for mo' dan fo' dollars, en I said 'f I didn' git it I'd start a bank mysef. Well, o' course dat nigger want' to keep me out er de business, bekase he say dey warn't business 'nough for two banks, so he say I could put in my five dollars en he pay me thirty-five at de en' er de year.

"So I done it. Den I reck'n'd I'd inves' de thirty-five dollars right off en keep things

* See "An Adventure of Huckleberry Finn: with an Account of the Famous Grangerford-Shepherdson Feud," by Mark Twain, in THE CENTURY for December.

Pages from the January 1885 issue of The Century, *the second installment from the novel published in the magazine; illustrations are by E. W. Kemble (Thomas Cooper Library, University of South Carolina)*

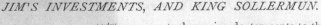

tuck en give de ten cents to the po', en laid low to see what wuz gwyne to come of it."

"Well, what did come of it, Jim?"

"Nuffn' never come of it. I couldn' manage to k'leck dat money no way; en Balum he couldn'. I ain' gwyne to len' no mo' money 'dout I see de security. Boun' to git yo' money back a hund'd times, de preacher says! Ef I could git de ten *cents* back, I'd call it squah, en be glad er de chanst."

"Well, it's all right, anyway, Jim, long as you're going to be rich again some time or other."

"Yes — en I's rich now, come to look at it. I owns myse'f, en I's wuth eight hund'd dollars. But live stock's too resky, Huck; — I wisht I had de eight hund'd dollars en somebody else had de nigger."

I read considerable to Jim about kings, and dukes, and earls, and such, and how gaudy they dressed, and how much style they put on, and called each other your majesty, and your grace, and your lordship, and so on, 'stead of mister; and Jim's eyes bugged out, and he was interested. He says:

"I didn't know dey was so many un um. I haint hearn 'bout none un um, skasely, but ole King Sollermun, onless you counts dem kings dat's in a pack er k'yards. How much do a king git?"

"Get?" I says; "why, they get a thousand dollars a month, if they want it; they can have just as much as they want; everything belongs to them."

"*Ain*' dat gay? En what dey got to do, Huck?"

THE PRESIDENT OF THE BANK.

a-movin'. Dey wuz a nigger name' Bob, dat had ketched a wood-flat, en his marster didn' know it; en I bought it off'n him, en told him to take de thirty-five dollars when de en' er de year come; but somebody stole de wood-flat dat night, en nex' day de one-laigged nigger say de bank's busted. So dey didn' none uv us git no money."

"What did you do with the ten cents, Jim?"

"Well, I 'uz gwyne to spen' it, but I had a dream, en de dream tole me to give it to a nigger name' Balum — Balum's Ass dey call him, for short; he's one er dem chuckle-heads, you know. But he's lucky, dey say, en I see I warn't lucky. De dream say let Balum inves' de ten cents en he'd make a raise for me. Well, Balum he tuck de money, en when he wuz in church he hear de preacher say dat whoever give to de po' len' to de Lord, en boun' to git his money back a hund'd times. So Balum he

SOLLERMUN AND HIS WIVES.

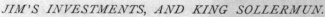

458   *JIM'S INVESTMENTS, AND KING SOLLERMUN.*

THE STORY OF SOLLERMUN.

"*They* don't do nothing! Why, how you talk! They just set around."

"No — is dat so?"

"Of course it is. They just set around, except maybe when there's a war; then they go to the war. But other times they just lazy around; or go hawking — just hawking and sp— Sh! — d' you hear a noise?"

We skipped out and looked; but it warn't nothing but the flutter of a steam-boat's wheel, away down coming around the point; so we come back.

"Yes," says I, "and other times, when things is dull, they fuss with the parlyment; and if everybody don't go just so, he whacks their heads off. But mostly they hang round the harem."

"Roun' de which?"

"Harem."

"What's de harem?"

"The place where he keep his wives. Don't you know about the harem? Solomon had one; he had about a million wives."

"Why, yes, dat's so; I — I'd done forgot it. A harem's a bo'd'n-house, I reck'n. Mos' likely dey has rackety times in de nussery. En I reck'n de wives quarrels considable; en dat 'crease de racket. Yit dey say Sollermun de wises' man dat ever live'. I doan' take no stock in dat. Becase why? Would a wise man want to live in de mids' er such a blimblammin' all de time? No — 'deed he wouldn't. A wise man 'ud take en buil' a biler-factry; en den he could shet *down* de biler-factry when he want to res'."

"Well, but he *was* the wisest man, anyway; because the widow she told me so, her own self."

"I doan k'yer what de widder say, he warn't no wise man, nuther. He had some er de dad-fetchedes' ways I ever see. Does you know 'bout dat chile dat he 'uz gwine to chop in two?"

"Yes, the widow told me all about it."

"*Well*, den! Warn' dat de beatenes' notion in de worl'? You jes' take en look at it a minute. Dah's de stump, dah — dat's one er de women; heah's you — dat's de yuther one; I's Sollermun; en dish-yer dollar bill's de chile. Bofe un you claims it. What does I do? Does I shin aroun' 'mongs' de neighbors en fine out which un you de bill *do* b'long to, en han' it over to de right one, all safe en soun', de way dat anybody dat had any gumption would? No — I take en whack de bill in *two*, en give haf un it to you, en de yuther half to de yuther woman. Dat's de way Sollermun was gwine to do wid de chile. Now, I want to ast you: what's de use er dat half a bill? — can't buy nuth'n wid it. En what use is a half a chile? I wouldn't give a dern for a million un um."

"But hang it, Jim, you've clean missed the point — blame it, you've missed it a thousand mile."

"Who? Me? Go 'long. Doan' talk to *me* 'bout yo' pints. I reck'n I knows sense when I sees it; en dey ain' no sense in sich doin's as dat. De 'spute warn't 'bout half a chile; de 'spute was 'bout a whole chile; en de man dat think he kin settle a 'spute 'bout a whole chile wid a half a chile, doan' know enough to come in out'n de rain. Doan' talk to me 'bout Sollermun, Huck, I knows him by de back."

"But I tell you, you don't get the point."

"Blame de pint! I reck'n I knows what I knows. En mine you, de *real* pint is down furder — it's down deeper. It lays in de way Sollermun was raised. You take a man dat's got on'y one er two chillen; is dat man gwyne to be waseful o' chillen? No, he aint; he can't 'ford it. *He* knows how to value 'em. But you take a man dat's got 'bout five million chillen runnin' roun' de house, en it's diffunt. *He* as soon chop a chile in two as a cat. Dey's plenty mo'. A chile er two, mo' er less, warn't no consekens to Sollermun, dad fetch him!"

ROYALTY ON THE MISSISSIPPI:

AS CHRONICLED BY HUCKLEBERRY FINN.*

BY MARK TWAIN.

Soon as it was night, out we shoved; when we got her out to about the middle, we let her alone, and let her float wherever the current wanted her to. Then we lit the pipes, and dangled our legs in the water and talked about all kinds of things.

Sometimes we'd have that whole river all to ourselves for the longest time. Yonder was the banks and the islands, across the water; and may be a spark,— which was a candle in a cabin window,— and sometimes on the water you could see a spark or two, on a raft or a scow, you know ; and may be you could hear a fiddle or a song coming over from one of them crafts. It's lovely to live on a raft. We had the sky up there all speckled with stars, and we used to lay on our backs and look up

so many. Jim said the moon could 'a' *laid* them; well, that looked kind of reasonable, so I didn't say nothing against it, because I've seen a frog lay most as many, so of course it could be done.

Once or twice of a night we would see a steamboat slipping along in the dark, and now and then she would belch a whole world of sparks up out of her chimbleys, and they would rain down in the river and look awful pretty; then she would turn a corner, and her lights would wink out and her pow-wow shut off and leave the river still again; and by and by her waves would get to us, a long time after she was gone, and joggle the raft a bit, and after that you wouldn't hear nothing for you couldn't tell how long, except may be frogs or something.

After midnight the people on shore went to bed, and then for two or three hours the shores was black — no more sparks in the cabin windows. These sparks was our clock — the first one that showed again meant morning was coming, so we hunted a place to hide and tie up right away.

One morning, about daybreak, I found a canoe and crossed over a chute to the main shore,— it was only two hundred yards,— and paddled about a mile up a crick amongst the cypress woods to see if I couldn't get some berries. Just as I was passing a place where a kind of a cow-path crossed the crick, here comes a couple of men tearing up the path as tight as they could foot it. I thought I was a goner, for whenever anybody was after anybody I judged it was *me* — or may be Jim. I was about to dig out from there in a hurry, but they was pretty close to me then, and sung out and begged me to save their lives; said they hadn't been doing nothing, and was being chased for it; said there was men and dogs a-coming. They wanted to jump right

"AND DOGS A-COMING."

at them, and discuss about whether they was made, or only just happened. Jim he allowed they was made, but I allowed they happened. I judged it would have took too long to *make*

in, but I says:

"Don't you do it. I don't hear the dogs and horses yet. You've got time to crowd through the brush and get up the crick a lit-

*See THE CENTURY for December and January. The negro Jim is escaping on a raft from slavery in Missouri, and Huck Finn is running away from a drunken and cruel father.— ED.

First and last pages of the twenty-four-page third installment from the novel published in the February 1885 issue of The Century *(Thomas Cooper Library, University of South Carolina)*

ROYALTY ON THE MISSISSIPPI. 567

as to get them to let Miss Mary Jane go aboard? Now *you* know he ain't. What *will* he do, then? Why, he'll say, 'It's a great pity, but my church matters has got to get along the best way they can; for my niece has been exposed to the dreadful pluribus-unum mumps, and so it's my bounden duty to set down here and wait the three months it takes to show on her if she's got it.' But never mind, if you think it's best to tell your uncle Harvey ——"

"Shucks, and stay fooling around here, when we could all be having good times in England, whilst we was waiting to find out whether Mary Jane's got it or not? Why, you talk like a muggins."

"Well, anyway, may be you better tell some of the neighbors."

"Listen at that, now. You do beat all for natural stupidness. Can't you *see* that *they'd* go and tell? Ther' ain't no way but just to not tell anybody at *all*."

"Well, may be you're right — yes, I judge you *are* right."

"But I reckon we ought to tell Uncle Harvey she's gone out awhile, anyway, so he won't be uneasy about her?"

"Yes, Miss Mary Jane she wanted you to do that. She says, 'Tell them to give Uncle Harvey and William my love and a kiss, and say I've run over the river to see Mr. — Mr. — what *is* the name of that rich family your uncle Peter used to think so much of? — I mean the one that ——"

"Why, you must mean the Apthorps, ain't it?"

"Of course. Bother them kind of names! a body can't ever seem to remember them, half the time, somehow. Yes, she said, say she has run over for to ask the Apthorps to be sure and come to the auction and buy this house, because she allowed her uncle Peter would ruther they had it than anybody else; and she's going to stick to them till they say they'll come, and then, if she ain't too tired, she's coming home; and if she is, she'll be home in the morning, anyway. She said, don't say nothing about the Proctors, but only about the Apthorps — which'll be perfectly true, because she *is* going there to speak about their buying the house; I know it, because she told me so herself."

"All right," they said, and cleared out to lay for their uncles, and give them the love and the kisses, and tell them the message.

Everything was all right now. The girls wouldn't say nothing because they wanted to go to England; and the king and the duke would ruther Mary Jane was off working for the auction than around in reach of Dr. Rob-

inson. I felt very good. I judged I had done it pretty neat; I reckoned Tom Sawyer couldn't 'a' done it no neater himself. Of course he would 'a' throwed more style into it; but I can't do that very handy, not being brung up to it.

Well, they held the auction in the public square, along towards the end of the afternoon, and it strung along, and strung along; and the old man he was on hand and looking his level pisonest, up there alongside of the auctioneer, and chipping in a little Scripture now and then, or a little goody-goody saying of some kind; and the duke he was around goo-gooing for sympathy all he knowed how, and just spreading himself generly.

But by and by the thing dragged through, and everything was sold — everything but a little old trifling lot in the graveyard; so they'd got to work *that* off. I never see such a giraft as the king was for wanting to swallow *everything*. Well, whilst they was at it, a steamboat landed, and in about two minutes up comes a crowd a-whooping and yelling and laughing and carrying on.

THE TRUE BROTHERS.

They was fetching a very nice-looking old gentleman along, and a nice-looking younger one, with his right arm in a sling. And my souls, how the people yelled, and laughed, and kept it up!

Mark Twain.

The Contemporary Reception

The contemporary reception of Mark Twain's greatest novel comprises epistolary reactions of readers as well as professional reviews, a selection of which appear in this section.

The response to the novel was complicated by several factors, three of which are addressed in this excerpt from Victor Fischer's important essay "Huck Finn Reviewed: The Reception of Huckleberry Finn *in the United States, 1885–1897." Fischer refers here to the work of Arthur Lawrence Vogelback, a critic who had earlier examined the publication and reception of the novel.*

"Thoroughly Publicized"
Victor Fischer

Huckleberry Finn was one of the most thoroughly publicized of Mark Twain books, and some account of this publicity—much of it adventitious—forms a necessary background to the contemporary reaction. On the three-month speaking tour that immediately preceded publication (November 1884–early February 1885), Mark Twain often read excerpts from it that were reviewed, quoted, and paraphrased by reporters. During this same period, he frequently gave interviews that were in part about his book.[1] Excerpts from it were syndicated in newspapers independently of the *Century*'s selections.[2] And just before (and after) publication, several much publicized crises involving the manufacture and sale of the book kept it in the news, not always favorably: (1) The obscene engraving. In late November 1884, Charles L. Webster . . . was alerted to an engraving in the book that had been surreptitiously altered to make it obscene; the defective illustration had already been distributed in copies of the salesmen's prospectus, but not in copies of the book. On 27 November 1884 the New York *World* told the story of this embarrassment, and its account was reprinted and rehashed by other newspapers, particularly in New York City. (2) The Estes & Lauriat lawsuit. In December 1884, even before Mark Twain's agents had copies of the book in hand, the Boston booksellers Estes & Lauriat published a catalog that advertised the book at a price below the standard agents' price. By 3 January 1885 Mark Twain had instituted a lawsuit, the progress of which was carefully followed in the press, with the Boston papers printing especially full accounts.[3] (3) The Concord Library ban. As Vogelback pointed out, the banning of *Huckleberry Finn* by the Concord Public Library in mid-March 1885, together with Mark Twain's subsequent letter to the Concord Free Trade Club published on 2 April, stimulated newspaper comment because editors took the opportunity to reflect on the book itself. . . .

–*American Literary Realism, 1870–1910,*
16 (Spring 1983): 3

1. For accounts of the readings, see Paul Fatout, *Mark Twain on the Lecture Circuit* (Bloomington: Indiana Univ. Press, 1960), pp. 214-229, and Guy A. Cardwell, *Twins of Genius* (Michigan State College Press, 1953). In addition, Paul Fatout has generously left on deposit in the Mark Twain Papers a large collection of photocopies of contemporary newspaper accounts of the tour. For a list of contemporary interviews, see Louis J. Budd, "A Listing of and Selection from Newspaper and Magazine Interviews with Samuel L. Clemens, 1874–1910," *American Literary Realism,* 10 (Winter 1977), 3–5.

2. An account of the syndication will be given in the forthcoming *Adventures of Huckleberry Finn,* ed. Walter Blair and Victor Fischer (Berkeley, Los Angeles, London: Univ. of California Press, 1984).

3. See Arthur Lawrence Vogelback, "The Publication and Reception of *Huckleberry Finn* in America," *American Literature,* 11 (November 1939), pp. 262-263, for quotations from the *World* story and citations to others. Merle Johnson, *A Bibliography of the Works of Mark Twain,* rev. ed. (New York: Harper and Brothers, 1935), pp. 47–49, and Walter Blair *Mark Twain and Huck Finn,* pp. 364–367, give accounts of the discovery and subsequent flurry when the publisher demanded the return of the mutilated page from the distributed prospectuses, and the printer was forced to replace the page in "thousands" of already printed volumes. See the bibliography to this article for a list of newspaper stories dealing with the obscene engraving and the Estes & Lauriat lawsuit.

* * *

In this excerpt Fischer discusses the general results of Mark Twain's attempt to "stage manage" the reception of his novel, focusing on the effect the author's role as a businessman had on the perception of his achievement as a writer. Twain's lawsuit against Estes & Lauriat as well as his pursuit of a publishing contract with former president Ulysses S. Grant for his memoirs are considered.

"Two Rough Categories"
The Reviewers and *Adventures of Huckleberry Finn*
Victor Fischer

Mark Twain's efforts to stage-manage the reception of his book in the United States through a favorable review by "an authority" that would influence the succeeding reviews failed. He did limit the initial critical arena by sending out a relatively small number of review copies, but this strategy yielded both good and bad reviews. By inadvertence he

ADVENTURES

OF

HUCKLEBERRY FINN

(TOM SAWYER'S COMRADE).

SCENE: THE MISSISSIPPI VALLEY.
TIME: FORTY TO FIFTY YEARS AGO.

BY

MARK TWAIN.

WITH ONE HUNDRED AND SEVENTY-FOUR ILLUSTRATIONS.

NEW YORK:
CHARLES L. WEBSTER AND COMPANY.
1885.

Title page for the first American edition (Mark Twain House,
Hartford, Connecticut)

failed to get the early, influential *Atlantic* and *Century* reviews he thought necessary, although both magazines later reviewed the book favorably. He did elicit four strong, favorable reviews in New York and Hartford newspapers within a month of sending out the first review copies and during the same period he received three more favorable reviews in San Francisco. He evidently dropped his original plan to extend the arena by sending out three hundred more copies, however, partly because: (1) the book was selling well anyway; (2) the widespread reaction to the Concord Library ban may have convinced him that the newspapers would not now consider the book on its own merits, and in any case he could no longer hope to influence reception by sending out copies of good reviews along with the books; and (3) his time was increasingly taken up with other business matters, in particular the Grant memoirs.

Although Mark Twain's plan failed, his theory of how a book is treated by reviewers—that the earliest review was sure to influence the latest—is partly confirmed by the reception accorded *Huck Finn*. An analysis of the reviews and opinions in the newspapers that wrote about *Huck* makes it clear that certain newspapers did indeed have such influence. The reviews in the Springfield *Daily Republican,* the *Boston Daily Advertiser,* the New York *World* and *Sun,* among others, were all widely reprinted or quoted, particularly those of the *Advertiser* and the *World*. While these newspapers may not have served as outright arbiters of taste, their attitudes were disseminated by the papers that chose to quote and reprint their stories, although outside of Boston, the *Advertiser* was often quoted to oppose it as well as to agree with it.

Contemporary critics of *Huck Finn* can be placed in two rough categories: those who took the book seriously and reviewed it, favorably or unfavorably, as a work; and those who wrote about it as a "scandale," an event, or an episode in Mark Twain's life.

It is clear that *Huck Finn* challenged the most basic assumptions that the former critics had about novels. Critics schooled in the "genteel tradition" looked for refined language, an elevating, exemplary hero, and a clear moral—such critics praised *The Prince and the Pauper* as Mark Twain's best book. For them, the mockery of Miss Watson's Providence, the depiction of Pap's delirium tremens, Huck's facility as a liar, not to mention the violence and corruption of the society along the river, inevitably seemed "coarse," "grotesque," in "bad taste," and not very funny. The most extreme of these welcomed the Concord Library committeeman's characterization of the book as "trash of the veriest sort." On the other side were the critics who prized the "Western" side of Mark Twain, who saw truthfulness in his characterizations and his picture of vanished life along the river, praised his use of the vernacular, and recognized the book as a "tour de force," "a work of literary art" far superior to anything he had yet written. Many reviewers fell somewhere between these two extremes, evidently torn between their expectations about ideal literature (especially for children) and their recognition of the book's extraordinary qualities.

Although it is tempting to associate critical bias with region—viewing Boston as the defender of the genteel tradition, New York and Hartford as more liberal centers, San Francisco as representative of the frontier, for example—such association would clearly be an oversimplification. The Boston papers differed among themselves, and were clearly at odds with the *Atlantic Monthly*. The New York *Sun* and New York *World* were obviously in different camps. Although one might expect the San Francisco papers to share a unique Western perspective, and for the most part they did share it, they too were divided about Mark Twain's book. Moreover, attitudes traveled. Thus the New York *World*'s charge of "irreverence which makes parents, guardians and people who are at all good and proper ridiculous," sounds very much like the later charges of the Concord Library Committee and the Springfield *Republican*. Similarly, the San Francisco *Alta California,* which commended Mark Twain's picture of river life as written in his "best style and full of genuine humor," repeated the Boston *Advertiser*'s regret that he should have laid himself open to charges of "coarseness" and "bad taste."

But it is the second group of stories about *Huck Finn*—those that were not so much reviews of the book as editorial responses to the Concord ban, or to Mark Twain's alleged character or conduct—that show how difficult Mark Twain's literary situation was. In Massachusetts, the unfavorable opinions of the book increased in intensity from the initial reviews of the *Century* episodes through the response to the Free Trade Club letter. By the end, seemingly every newspaper and magazine published in Boston (other than the *Atlantic*) had come out against the book and the tone and content of many of the stories make clear that they saw not only Mark Twain's book, but the author himself as a challenge to genteel values. It is instructive to note which events brought about disapproving stories, and to note also how those stories about the author affected the reception of his book. Two events—the lawsuit against Estes & Lauriat, and the contract negotiations to publish Grant's memoirs—are useful examples.

Mark Twain's attempt to get an injunction against Estes & Lauriat to stop their offering *Huck Finn* at a cut price for trade sales before it was published in the United States, was viewed unfavorably by a number of Massachusetts papers, and the reaction spilled over onto *Huck Finn*. On 15 January, a month before *Huck*'s U. S. publication date, the Springfield *Republican* wrote in defense of Estes & Lauriat, "Mr. Clemens's book, though not yet published here, was published in England several weeks ago, as appears by the fact that it is reviewed in the literary papers, and if the subscribers of the *Century* magazine do not protest they will get it all in advertising extracts."[1] The following day, the Boston *Morning Journal* wrote: "If the extracts from Huckleberry Finn, already published are fair samples of the whole book, we cannot see why Estes & Lauriat want to sell it less than the subscription price. A man ought to pay $2 75 for the privilege of reading the book. It will teach him a lesson."[2]

Two ideas are implicit in the *Republican* story: that because the book had already been published in England, Mark Twain's claim that it had not been published (in the United States) was illegitimate; and that the episodes in the *Century* magazine had no intrinsic value, having been put there only as "advertising extracts." Mark Twain was represented as making false claims for the purpose of increasing his profit, and as publishing extracts from his book for the same purpose. Implicit in the *Journal* story is the idea that anybody who pays the absurdly high price that Mark Twain charges for his book will have been defrauded and will deserve what he gets. In short, Mark Twain was a liar, whose books were inherently worthless but made fraudulent by the way he sold them, a mercenary fellow who was not above taking advantage of the public for his own profit. . . . [T]hese charges were explicitly stated in a number of reviews and newspaper stories after the Concord Library ban. Some of them were repeated in the stories about the Grant contract.

In early March, when the progress of Grant's final illness was front-page news across the country, the newspapers gave a great deal of attention to the story

" WHO DO YOU RECKON IT IS ? "

The drawing of Uncle Silas by E. W. Kemble as it appeared in the prospectus and the corrected version that was published in the novel (left, Library of Congress; right, from Adventures of Huckleberry Finn, *Mark Twain House, Hartford, Connecticut)*

that the Webster company, rather than the *Century* company, would be publishing Grant's memoirs. Although several papers wrote about the contract in a neutral way, or simply as a news story, for many it was the occasion for further negative comment on Mark Twain or his new book. In stories about how the Webster company had prevailed over the *Century,* Mark Twain was depicted as a "spoiler," prompted by mercenary self-interest. Even some of the more sympathetic stories hinted he was a little too sharp, or clever, at business. The Detroit *Post* printed a dispatch that was evidently syndicated in several papers, saying that Mark Twain "has not been so reckless a humorist as to share the profits of his fun with anybody."[3] The Springfield *Republican* called the negotiations a "disagreeable episode." Noting that arrangements with the Century company were nearly settled, "when in stepped Mark Twain and spoiled it all." The *Republican* added that "it is intimated that Mark Twain cannot have any more of his 'Huckleberry Finn' literature published hereafter in those offended pages. The readers of the magazine may well hope the last item of this news is true."[4]

Stories like these, influenced by attitudes toward Mark Twain as a businessman, clearly rebounded on his new book, worsening the effect of other stories

about the obscene cut, the Concord Library ban, and the Free Trade Club letter. The Springfield *Republican* and the San Francisco *Examiner* even linked their memory of "notorious" episodes in his past–his speech at the Whittier dinner in Boston and his *Territorial Enterprise* newspaper hoaxes–with their low opinion of *Huck Finn.*

Despite the evident distaste in some quarters for Mark Twain's commercial success, and despite his failure to secure an early favorable review "by an authority," *Huck Finn* was reviewed favorably and intelligently in a number of newspapers–in particular, the New York *Sun,* the Hartford *Courant, Post,* and *Times,* and the San Francisco *Chronicle.* It was also well defended by these and others in the discussion of the Concord Library ban.

–*American Literary Realism, 1870–1910,*
16 (Spring 1983): 34–37

1. Springfield *Daily Republican,* 15 January 1885, p. 4.
2. Boston *Morning Journal,* 16 January 1885, p. 2.
3. Detroit *Post,* 8 March 1885, p. 1.
4. Springfield *Daily Republican,* 9 March 1885, p. 4.

* * *

"A Stroke of Misfortune"
An Obscene Engraving in *Huckleberry Finn*

This newspaper story, in which the offending image is erroneously described, was originally titled "Mark Twain in a Dilemma." The subtitle for the story read: "A Victim of a Joke He Thinks the Most Unkindest Cut of All. A Prospectus of "Huckleberry Finn" that was Apt to Bring the Author of the Bantling into Trouble–A Stroke of Misfortune from an Engraver's Stylus."

Hartford, Conn., Nov. 28–"Huckleberry Finn," Mark Twain's new book, was complete last March, but owing to complications and differences with his publishers, it has not yet appeared, although it has been extensively announced–a prospectus of the story sent out and the opening chapters recently published in the Century. When the book was finished last month Mark Twain made a proposition in regard to its publication to the American Publishing Company of this city, which published his "Innocents Abroad" and his later works. From them the company, which heretofore had been but a small concern, achieved a reputation and standing equal to any of the older established publishing houses of the country. Mark Twain on his side obtained royalties amounting in all to over $400,000. When "Huckleberry Finn," the sequel to "Tom Sawyer," was completed, Twain again made a proposition to his publishers to produce this new work. Negotiations were commenced, but never completed. The parties could not agree to terms. Evidently Mark Twain considered that he had built up the American Publishing Company, while they seemed to think themselves the founders of his fame and fortune. Liberal royalties were offered Twain by the publishing company, but he refused to accept them. The final offer was that the profits should be divided, each of the parties to receive 50 per cent, of the proceeds from the sale of the new work. This proposition was not satisfactory to the author, who wanted 60 per cent of the profits. This offer the company refused to accept, and he determined on entering a new business–combining that of the publisher with that of author.

Mark Twain had a nephew residing in New York in whose business ability he had great confidence. This man, whose name is Charles L. Webster, is engaged in the book-publishing business at No. 658 Broadway. He entered into a partnership with his nephew to produce his new work and to supervise all the mechanical details of its production. The copy was all sent to him and by him given to the printers. In order to properly embellish the book the services of a leading metropolitan engraver were secured, and from this comes all the trouble into which Hartford's popular author is now plunged. The engravings, after having been cut on the plates, were sent to the electrotyper. One of the plates represented a man with a downcast head, standing in the foreground of a particularly striking illustration. In front of him was a ragged urchin with a look of dismay overspreading his countenance. In the background, and standing behind the boy, was an attractive-looking young girl, whose face was enlivened by a broad grin. Something which the boy or man had said or done evidently amused her highly. The title of the cut was "In a Dilemma; What Shall I do?"

When the plate was sent to the electrotyper a wicked spirit must have possessed him. The title was suggestive. A mere stroke of the awl would suffice to give to the cut an indecent character never intended by the author or engraver. It would make no difference in the surface of the plate that would be visible to the naked eye, but when printed would add to the engraving a characteristic which would be repudiated not only by the author, but by all the respectable people of the country into whose hands the volume should fall. The work of the engraver was successful. It passed the eye of the inspector and was approved. A proof was taken and submitted. If the alteration of the plate was manifested in the proof it was evidently attributed to a defect in the press and paper, which would be remedied when the volume was sent to the press. Now the work was ready for printing.

In issuing books to be sold by "subscription only" the publishers first strike off a large number of prospectuses, which are to be used by the agents when soliciting subscribers to the work. Some 3,000 of these prospectuses, with the defective cut, were presented and distributed to the different agents throughout the country. The entire work had passed the eyes of the various readers and inspectors and the glaring indecency of the cut had not been discovered. Throughout the country were hundreds of agents displaying the merits of the work and elaborating on the artistic work of the engravings. It was remarkable that while the defect was so palpable, none of the agents noticed it, or if he did, he failed to report it to the publishers. Possibly they might have considered the alteration intentional, as the title to the illustration was now doubly suggestive.

At last came a letter from the Chicago agent calling attention to the cut. Then there was consternation in the office of the publishers. Copies of the prospectus were hauled from the shelf and critically examined. Then for the first time it dawned on the publishers that such an illustration would condemn the work. Immediately all the agents were telegraphed to and the prospectuses were called in. The page containing the cut was torn from the book, a new and perfect illustration being substituted. Agents were supplied with the improved volumes and are now happy in canvassing for a work to which there can be no objection, while they smile at the prospects of heavy commissions. But the story leaked out. Several opposition publishers got hold of the cut, however, and these now adorn their respective offices.

–New York World (semi-weekly version), 28 November 1884, p. 8

Mark Twain's Lawsuit against Estes & Lauriat

In this excerpt from his 15 December 1884 letter to Webster, Mark Twain reacts to having seen an advertisement for Adventures of Huckleberry Finn, *published in England but not in America, at a reduced rate in the catalogue of the publisher and bookseller Estes & Lauriat.*

Charley, if this is a lie, let Alexander & Green sue them for damages instantly. And if we have no chance at them in law, tell me at once & I will publish them as thieves and swindlers. S L CLEMENS Hadn't you better send 6 witnesses to try to buy 3 copies each? Use their testimony. . . .

I think you better print the enclosed in *fac simile* of my handwriting, & put a copy in every canvasser's hands. S L C

"Huckleberry Finn."

My new book is not out of the press; no man has a copy of it; yet Estes & Lauriat, of Boston announce it as "now ready," & for sale by them—& at a reduced price. These people deliberately lied when they made that statement. Since it was a lie which could in no possible way advantage them, it was necessarily a purely malicious lie, whose only purpose was to injure me, who have in no way harmed them.

They will have an immediate opportunity to explain, in court, & pay for the opportunity of explaining.

Mark Twain

—*Mark Twain, Business Man,* p. 284–285

The case against the bookseller brought Twain publicity but no satisfaction as this account from a Boston newspaper shows.

An interesting lawsuit has just been decided in Boston. It was brought by Mark Twain against the well-known publishing house of Estes & Lauriat, and was decided in favor of the defendants, the court refusing the injunction asked for by the plaintiff. The main points of the case are thus given in the *Advertiser:*

Estes & Lauriat are a firm of booksellers and publishers located in Boston. In their last holiday catalogue appeared an advertisement in which a new work entitled *Huckleberry Finn,* written by the plaintiff under the name of Mark Twain, was offered for sale at a price reduced from $2.75 to $2.25. The book is sold on what is known as the subscription plan, and the regular subscription price is $2.75. The canvass for the book has been in progress for some months. The advertisement to sell the work for less than the subscription price is working great injury to the regular sales by subscription. The book is not yet published, and will not be before February. On December 3, 1884, the title of the work was deposited with the librarian of Congress to secure a copyright. Charles L. Webster & Co. of New York, are the general managers and authorized agents of the plaintiff in the publication and sale of the book. Numerous canvassing agents are appointed in different parts of the country. These agents purchase the books, but bind themselves by contract to sell only to subscribers, and not to the trade, and for the full retail price. Prior to the time the catalogue was issued, several persons called at the place of business of Estes & Lauriat, and offered them the book at such prices that they could afford to sell it at $2.25, and still make a fair profit. Dummies of the book were left for examination. Two of the persons who called had previously sold Estes & Lauriat other works of the author. Estes & Lauriat contracted with these persons to take one hundred or more copies of the book, and then inserted in their holiday catalogue about to be published, the advertisement referred to. Up to this time, about thirty orders for the book have been received by them. They had no knowledge of the terms of the contract between the plaintiff, or his publishers and their canvassing agents. They say the prior works of the author published by subscription, have been freely offered to them at large discounts. As soon as suit was brought, they cut out the page from the catalogue containing the advertisement, and they have not since, and do not propose to distribute any more catalogues containing the advertisement.

—*The Literary World,* 21 February 1885, p. 66

William Ernest Henley, British poet and critic, is believed to have reviewed Adventures of Huckleberry Finn *for the* Athenaeum. *He was best known for his poem "Invictus" (National Portrait Gallery).*

As Adventures of Huckleberry Finn *was first published in London in December 1884, three months before it was released in the United States, the earliest reviews appeared in England. The author of this unsigned review may have been William Ernest Henley.* The Athenaeum, *an influential "journal of Literature, Science, the Fine Arts, Music and the Drama," was published in London.*

"Mark Twain at His Best"
Review of *Adventures of Huckleberry Finn*
The Athenaeum, 2983 (27 December 1884): 855

For some time past Mr. Clemens has been carried away by the ambition of seriousness and fine writing. In *Huckleberry Finn* he returns to his right mind, and is again the Mark Twain of old time. It is such a book as he, and he only, could have written. It is meant for boys; but there are few men (we should hope) who, once they take it up, will not delight in it. It forms a companion or sequel, to *Tom Sawyer.* Huckleberry Finn, as everybody knows, is one of Tom's closest friends; and the present volume is a record of the adventures which befell him soon after the event which made him a person of property and brought Tom Sawyer's story to a becoming conclusion. They are of the most surprising and delightful kind imaginable, and in the course of them we fall in with a number of types of character of singular freshness and novelty, besides being schooled in half a dozen extraordinary dialects—the Pike County dialect in all its forms, the dialect of the Missouri negro, and "the extremest form of the backwoods South-Western dialect," to wit. Huckleberry, it may be noted, is stolen by his disreputable father, to escape from whom he contrives an appearance of robbery and murder in the paternal hut, goes off in a canoe, watches from afar the townsfolk hunting for his dead body, and encounters a runaway negro—Miss Watson's Jim—an old particular friend of Tom Sawyer and himself. With Jim he goes south down the river, and is the hero of such scrapes and experiences as make your mouth water (if you have ever been a boy) to read of them. We do not purpose to tell a single one; it would be unfair to author and reader alike. We shall content ourselves with repeating that the book is Mark Twain at his best, and remarking that Jim and Huckleberry are real creations, and the worthy peers of the illustrious Tom Sawyer.

* * *

These excerpts are from an early unsigned American review that appeared a month before the novel was officially published in the United States.

"Intensely Humorous"
Review of *Adventures of Huckleberry Finn*
Detroit Free Press, 10 January 1885, p. 8

"Good wine needs no bush;" and a book by Mark Twain needs no beating about the bush. One takes it as the children do sweetmeats, with trusting confidence. Mark's newest new book is so new that it is not fairly out yet and will not be until the 18th of February; but those who have seen it describe it as the brightest and most humorous work he has ever written, and the advance sheets, as far as they go, corroborate that statement fully.

Readers of *Tom Sawyer* do not need to be told who "Huckleberry Finn" is. He is Tom's comrade and Tom has very accommodatingly consented to act now as *his* comrade. Their adventures and those of a negro with no name to speak of but "Jim," fill forty-three bright and intensely humorous chapters, making a volume considerably larger than Tom Sawyer.

"A *Positive* Order"
Sending Out Review Copies

While on his lecture tour, Mark Twain wrote to advise Webster. These excerpts are from his letters, all sent within three weeks, regarding the strategy of sending out copies of Adventures of Huckleberry Finn *to reviewers. This first excerpt is from a 23 January 1885 letter.*

A day or two after the book issues, you want to send a cloth copy to the prominent journals & magazines of the country.–Perhaps you better send to the prominent *magazines* NOW (with unbound copies to make extracts from.)

–*Mark Twain, Business Man,* p. 294

This instruction is from a 27 January letter.

The following is a *positive* order: Send no copy of the book to *any* newspaper until after the Century or the Atlantic shall have reviewed it.

What we want is a favorable review, by an authority–then immediately distribute the book among the press.

–*Mark Twain, Business Man,* p. 298

This excerpt is from an 8 February letter.

In 3 more weeks this platform-campaign will be over, & then I shall hope to get in a good humor and stay so. . . .

And we must talk over the propriety of sending out 300 press copies *early*–say Feb. 23d–without waiting for the magazines–Heavens & earth! the book ought to have been reviewed in the *March* Century & Atlantic!–how have we been dull enough to go &

overlook that? It is an irreparable blunder. It should have been attended to, weeks ago, when we named the day of publication. If we had but done *that,* we could flood the country with press copies the 25th of Feb., for then the Magazines would already have given the key-note to the reviews.

–*Mark Twain, Business Man,* p. 299

Although this last excerpt, from a letter sent on 10 February, sounds a marked note of despair, Twain in a little more than a month would learn that the novel was a commercial success.

I am not able to see that anything can save Huck Finn from being another defeat, unless you are expecting to do it by tumbling books into the trade, & I suppose you are not calculating upon any sale there worth speaking of, since you are not binding much of an edition of the book.

As to notices, I suggest this plan: Send immediately, copies (bound & unbound) to the Evening Post, Sun, World, & the Nation; the Hartford Courant, Post & Times; the principal Boston dailies; Baltimore American. (*Never* send any to N. Y. Graphic.)

Keep a sharp lookout, & if the general tone of the resulting notices is *favorable,* then send out your 300 press copies over the land, for that may *possibly* float a further canvass & at least create a bookstore demand. No use to wait for the magazines–how in *hell* we overlooked that unspeakably important detail, utterly beats my time. We have not even arranged to get English notices from Chatto & shove *them* into the papers ahead of our publication.

–*Mark Twain, Business Man,* p. 300

The opening chapter is eminently Twainesque and brings the reader right into the heart of things at the start. . . .

Thereupon Huckleberry starts off from the point where Tom and he found the money hidden by the robbers, and the music begins at once with the entire orchestra on duty.

We were just about to state what the motive and moral of the book are, and dimly outline the plot, when we caught sight on the title page of the following "notice:" "Persons attempting to find a motive in this narrative will be prosecuted; persons

attempting to find a moral in it will be banished; persons attempting to find a plot in it will be shot."

We have decided therefore, that it will be far more pleasant for the reader to find motive, moral and plot for himself. The illustrations, of which there are nearly 200, are singularly good. Among them is a fine full-page heliotype of the author's bust (the reader will be kind enough to make no pun here) by Karl Gerhardt.

* * *

Brander Mathews, literature professor at Columbia University circa 1890. Speaking on the occasion of Mark Twain's seventieth birthday in 1905, he described Adventures of Huckleberry Finn *as "the* Odyssey *of the Mississippi" (portrait by E. E. Simmons, Columbia University).*

The author of this unsigned review, originally titled "Huckleberry Finn," was the American critic Brander Matthews. The Saturday Review was an influential English periodical. Excerpts.

"The Region of Art"
Review of *Adventures of Huckleberry Finn*
The Saturday Review, 59 (31 January 1885): 153–154

The boy of to-day is fortunate indeed, and, of a truth, he is to be congratulated. While the boy of yesterday had to stay his stomach with the unconscious humour of *Sanford and Merton,* the boy of to-day may get his fill of fun and of romance and of adventure in *Treasure Island* and in *Tom Brown* and in *Tom Sawyer,* and now in a sequel to *Tom Sawyer,* wherein Tom himself appears in the very nick of time, like a young god from the machine. Sequels of stories which have been widely popular are not a little risky. *Huckleberry Finn* is a sharp exception to this general rule. Although it is a sequel, it is quite as worthy of wide popularity as *Tom Sawyer.* An American critic once neatly declared that the late

G. P. R. James hit the bull's-eye of success with his first shot, and that for ever thereafter he went on firing through the same hole. Now this is just what Mark Twain has not done. *Huckleberry Finn* is not an attempt to do *Tom Sawyer* over again. It is a story quite as unlike its predecessor as it is like. Although Huck Finn appeared first in the earlier book, and although Tom Sawyer reappears in the later, the scenes and the characters are otherwise wholly different. Above all, the atmosphere of the story is different. *Tom Sawyer* was a tale of boyish adventure in a village in Missouri, on the Mississippi river, and it was told by the author. *Huckleberry Finn* is autobiographical; it is a tale of boyish adventure along the Mississippi river told as it appeared to Huck Finn. There is not in Huckleberry Finn any one scene quite as funny as those in which Tom Sawyer gets his friends to whitewash the fence for him, and then uses the spoils thereby acquired to attain the highest situation of the Sunday school the next morning. Nor is there any distinction quite as thrilling as that awful moment in the cave when the boy and the girl are lost in the darkness, and when Tom Sawyer suddenly sees a human hand bearing a light, and then finds that the hand is the hand of Indian Joe, his one mortal enemy; we have always thought that the vision of the hand in the cave in *Tom Sawyer* is one of the very finest things in the literature of adventure since Robinson Crusoe first saw a single footprint in the sand of the seashore. But though *Huckleberry Finn* may not quite reach these two highest points of *Tom Sawyer,* we incline to the opinion that the general level of the later story is perhaps higher than that of the earlier. For one thing, the skill with which the character of Huck Finn is maintained is marvelous. We see everything through his eyes—and they are his eyes and not a pair of Mark Twain's spectacles. And the comments on what he sees are his comments—the comments of an ignorant, superstitious, sharp, healthy boy, brought up as Huck Finn had been brought up; they are not speeches put into his mouth by the author. One of the most artistic things in the book—and that Mark Twain is a literary artist of a very high order all who have considered his later writings critically cannot but confess—one of the most artistic things in *Huckleberry Finn* is the sober self-restraint with which Mr. Clemens lets Huck Finn set down, without any comment at all, scenes which would have afforded the ordinary writer matter for endless moral and political and sociological disquisition. We refer particularly to the account of the Grangerford-Shepherdson feud, and of the shooting of Boggs by Colonel Sherburn. Here are two incidents of the rough old life of the South-Western States, and of the Mississippi Valley forty or fifty years ago, of the old life which is now rapidly passing away under the influence of advancing civ-

---

"Incredibly Well Done"

This excerpt is from a February 1885 letter from Robert Louis Stevenson to J. A. Symonds.

Have you read <u>Huckleberry Finn?</u> It contains many excellent things; above all the whole story of a healthy boy's dealings with his conscience, incredibly well done.

—*Letters and Miscellany of Robert Louis Stevenson,*
edited by Sidney Colvin (New York: Scribners, 1911)

At some unspecified time years later, Stevenson told Twain's biographer Albert Bigelow Paine, "It is a book I have read four times, and am quite ready to begin again to-morrow."

---

ilization and increasing commercial prosperity, but which has not wholly disappeared even yet, although a slow revolution in public sentiment is taking place. The Grangerford-Shepherdson feud is a vendetta as deadly as any Corsican could wish, yet the parties to it were honest, brave, sincere, good Christian people, probably people of deep religious sentiment. Not the less we see them taking their guns to church, and, when occasion serves, joining in what is little better than a general massacre. The killing of Boggs by Colonel Sherburn is told with equal sobriety and truth; and the later scene in which Colonel Sherburn cows and lashes the mob which has set out to lynch him is one of the most vigorous bits of writing Mark Twain has done.

In *Tom Sawyer* we saw Huckleberry Finn from the outside; in the present volume we see him from the inside. He is almost as much a delight to any one who has been a boy as was Tom Sawyer. But only he or she who has been a boy can truly enjoy this record of his adventure, and of his sentiments and of his sayings. Old maids of either sex will wholly fail to understand him or to like him, or to see his significance and his value. Like Tom Sawyer, Huck Finn is a genuine boy; he is neither a girl in boy's clothes like many of the modern heroes of juvenile fiction, nor is he a "little man," a full-grown man cut down; he is a boy, just a boy, only a boy. And his ways and modes of thought are boyish. As Mr. F. Anstey understands the English boy, and especially the English boy of the middle classes, so Mark Twain understands the American boy, and especially the American boy of the Mississippi Valley of forty or fifty years ago. The contrast between Tom Sawyer who is the child of respectable parents, decently brought up, and Huckleberry Finn, who is the child of the town

drunkard, not brought up at all, is made distinct by a hundred artistic touches, not the least natural of which is Huck's constant reference to Tom as his ideal of what a boy should be. When Huck escapes from the cabin where his drunken and worthless father had confined him, carefully manufacturing a mass of very circumstantial evidence to prove his own murder by robbers, he cannot help saying, "I did wish Tom Sawyer was there. I knowed he would take an interest in this kind of business, and thrown in the fancy touches. Nobody could spread himself like Tom Sawyer in such a thing as that." Both boys have their full share of boyish imagination; and Tom Sawyer, being given to books, lets his imagination run on robbers and pirates and genies, with a perfect understanding with himself that, if you want to get fun out of this life, you must never hesitate to make believe very hard; and, with Tom's youth and health, he never finds it hard to believe and to be a pirate at will, or to summon an attendant spirit, or to rescue a prisoner from the deepest dungeon 'neath the castle moat. But in Huck his imagination has turned to superstition; he is a walking repository of the juvenile folklore of the Mississippi Valley—a folklore partly traditional among the white settlers, but largely influenced by intimate association with the negroes. When Huck was in his room at night all by himself waiting for the signal Tom Sawyer was to give him at midnight, he felt so lonesome he wished he was dead. . . . And, again, later in the story, not at night this time, but in broad day-light, Huck walks along a road:

> When I got there it was all still and Sunday-like, and hot and sunshiny—the hands was gone to the fields; and there was them kind of faint dronings of bugs and flies in the air that makes it seem so lonesome and like everybody's dead and gone; and if a breeze fans along and quivers the leaves, it makes you feel mournful, because you feel like it's spirits whispering—spirits that's been dead ever so many years—and you always think they're talking about *you*. As a general thing it makes a boy wish *he* was dead, too, and done with it all.

Now, none of these sentiments are appropriate to Tom Sawyer, who had none of the feeling for nature which Huck Finn had caught during his numberless days and nights in the open air. Nor could Tom Sawyer either have seen or set down this instantaneous photograph of a summer storm. . . .

The romantic side of Tom Sawyer is shown in most delightfully humorous fashion in the account of his difficult devices to aid in the easy escape of Jim, a runaway negro. Jim is an admirably drawn character. There have been not a few fine and firm portraits of negroes in recent American fiction, of which Mr. Cable's Bras-Coupé in

The Grandissimes is perhaps the most vigorous, and Mr. Harris's Mingo and Uncle Remus and Blue Dave are the most gentle. Jim is worthy to rank with these; and the essential simplicity and kindliness and generosity of the Southern negro have never been better shown than here by Mark Twain. Nor are Tom Sawyer and Huck Finn and Jim the only fresh and original figures in Mr. Clemens's new book; on the contrary, there is scarcely a character of the many introduced who does not impress the reader at once as true to life—and therefore as new, for life is so varied that a portrait from life is sure to be as good as new. That Mr. Clemens draws from life, and yet lifts his work from the domain of the photograph to the region of art, is evident to any one who will give his work the honest attention which it deserves. Mr. John T. Raymond, the American comedian, who performs the character of Colonel Sellers to perfection, is wont to say that there is scarcely a town in the West and South-West where some man did not claim to be the original of the character. And as Mark Twain made Colonel Sellers, so has he made the chief players in the present drama of boyish adventure; they are taken from life, no doubt, but they are so aptly chosen and so broadly drawn that they are quite as typical as they are actual. They have one great charm, all of them—they are not written about and about; they are not described and dissected and analysed; they appear and play their parts and disappear; and yet they leave a sharp impression of indubitable vitality and individuality. No one, we venture to say, who reads this book will readily forget the Duke and the King, a pair of as pleasant "confidence operators" as one may meet in a day's journey, who leave the story in the most appropriate fashion, being clothed in tar and feathers and ridden on a rail. Of the more broadly humorous passages—and they abound—we have not left ourselves space to speak; they are to the full as funny as in any of Mark Twain's other books; and, perhaps, in no other book has the humourist shown so much artistic restraint, for there is in Huckleberry Finn no mere "comic copy," no straining after effect; one might almost say that there is no waste word in it. Nor have we left ourselves room to do more than say a good word for the illustrations, which, although slight and unpretending, are far better than those to be found in most of Mark Twain's books. For one thing, they actually illustrate—and this is a rare quality in illustrations nowadays. They give the reader a distinct idea of the Duke and the King, of Jim and of Colonel Sherburn, of the Shepherdsons and the Grangerfords. They are all by one artist, Mr. E. W. Kemble, hitherto known to us only as the illustrator of the Thompson Street Poker Club, as an amusing romance of highly-coloured life in New York.

* * *

These excerpts are from a review that was subtitled "Some Interesting Skeletons from Life on the Mississippi River Forty Years Ago."

Mark Twain's New Story
Review of Adventures of Huckleberry Finn
New York Sun, 15 February 1885, p. 3

The greatest living authority on the Mississippi River and on juvenile cussedness gives notice at the beginning of the book, the "Adventures of Huckleberry Finn," that persona attempting to find a motive, moral, or a plot in the narrative will be prosecuted, banished, or shot, according to the variety of the offence. Yet Mark Twain's last story can brag of both a motive and a fairish plot, while a beautiful moral decorates nearly every one of its shining pages, namely, that it is better and nobler to be simply and directly to the purpose than to put on frills of overelaborate mendacity, or to wander from the main chance into the byways of unnecessary prevarication. That is what is taught by the careers of Huckleberry Finn and Tom Sawyer: and along with the lesson we get no end of stirring incident, river lore, human nature, philology, and fun. . . .

Thus it always was with Huckleberry Finn. His fabrications lay in strata, and if any penetrating person, like this woman, succeeded in getting through one thickness it was only to strike a subjacent layer, which usually proved satisfactory. Huck was never stumped. In the course of the varied and entertaining adventures with which the historian has filled this book the hero frequently indulges in bursts of candor: but it is always a voluntary performance on his part. He is never forced, beguiled, or surprised into telling the truth when from his point of view a fiction is the proper thing for the occasion. His resources are unfailing: and at times, in the more complicated situations into which his fortunes bring him as he makes his way down the Mississippi with Jim, his statements become marvels of ingenious complexity, like a series of carved ivory balls within balls, or a part of Japanese boxes. And yet each individual lie is perfectly simple and generally plausible. For this reason his achievements are really more artistic, although much less elaborate and showy, than those of the better-known Tom Sawyer who possessed a far livelier imagination and a far greater fund of general information on which to draw in an emergency. Tom's school was the ornate. Huckleberry's the practical; and yet the latter perhaps for this very reason persisted in looking up to his comrade as to a superior being, his master in the art. . . .

Who on earth except Mark Twain would ever cotton to a youth like Huckleberry Finn for the hero of what is neither a boys' book nor a grown-up novel? And who else, having elected to record the scrapes of this uncommonly able descendant of Ananias and without mitigating any of his innumerable lies or blinking any of his countless sins against the common decencies of literature could so present his character and misdeeds as to hold the reader through four hundred pages and then dismiss him Huck's friend for life? We want to say something too about Mark Twain's good English. His book, for the most part, is made up of words of one syllable.

* * *

This anonymous review, originally titled "New Publications," was the first of three positive reviews of Mark Twain's novel to appear in Hartford newspapers. It reveals the local origin of the incident in chapter 27 in which the undertaker silences a dog during Peter Wilks's funeral.

"Exceedingly Droll"
Review of *Adventures of Huckleberry Finn*
Hartford Evening Post, 17 February 1885, p. 3

The people are eagerly welcoming Mark Twain's new book; even now Mr. John Bliss is taking subscriptions in Hartford—work contemporary to similar work all over the country—for this latest contribution to the droll. Before the reader hardly gets upon the threshold he is confronted with the humor of the author. Read this notice: "Persons attempting to find a motive in this narrative will be prosecuted, persons attempting to find a moral in it will be banished; persons attempting to find a plot in it will be shot. By order of the author, per G. G., chief of ordnance." On the sheet just previous, the representation of personified humor appears in a fine heliotype of Karl Gerhardt's profile bust of Mr. Clemmens; the frontispiece is the same subject's other ego in part—if a transfusion of literary life may constitute this—to wit: a full length of Huckleberry Finn, himself, smiling, holding up a dead rabbit in one hand while a gun in the other reveals the weapon of slaughter. The author explains, to correct the possible impression that all the characters were trying to talk alike without succeeding—that he has used a number of dialects, to wit, the Missouri negro dialect; the extremest form of the backwards South-Western dialect; the ordinary "Pike county" dialect; and four modified varieties of the last. "The shadings," he says, "have not been done in a hap-hazard fashion, or by guess work; but painstakingly, and with the trustworthy guidance and support of personal familiarity with these several forms of speech."

As a storehouse therefore of dialect, even more than as a book of humor, the volume is valuable. What if the trans-Atlantic critics with their usual keen appreciation should find this the overpowering merit of the book? There are many pleasant episodes, innumerable original characters, situations so exceedingly droll that

THE UNDERTAKER.

"HE HAD A RAT!"

The undertaker at Peter Wilks's funeral (drawings by E. W. Kemble; from Adventures of Huckleberry Finn, *Mark Twain House, Hartford, Connecticut)*

The Undertaker and the Dog

The review of Mark Twain's novel in the 17 February 1885 issue of the Hartford Evening Post *indicated that Huck's story of the popular undertaker, excerpted here, originated in the eastern city, not in a village along the Mississippi.*

When the place was packed full the undertaker he slid around in his black gloves with his softy soothering ways, putting on the last touches, and getting people and things all ship-shape and comfortable, and making no more sound than a cat. He never spoke; he moved people around, he squeezed in late ones, he opened up passageways, and done it with nods, and signs with his hands. Then he took his place over against the wall. He was the softest, glidingest, stealthiest man I ever see; and there warn't no more smile to him than there is to a ham.

They had borrowed a melodeum—a sick one; and when everything was ready a young woman set down and worked it, and it was pretty skreeky and colicky, and everybody joined in and sung, and Peter was the only one that had a good thing, according to my notion. Then the Reverend Hobson opened up, slow and solemn, and begun to talk; and straight off the most outrageous row busted out in the cellar a body ever heard; it was only one dog, but he made a most powerful racket, and he kept it up right along; the parson he had to stand there, over the coffin, and wait—you couldn't hear yourself think. It was right down awkward, and nobody didn't seem to know what to do. But pretty soon they see that long-legged undertaker make a sign to the preacher as much as to say, "Don't you worry—just depend on me." Then he stooped down and begun to glide along the wall, just his shoulders showing over the people's heads. So he glided along, and the powwow and racket getting more and more outrageous all the time; and at last, when he had gone around two sides of the room, he disappears down cellar. Then in about two seconds we heard a whack, and the dog he finished up with a most amazing howl or two, and then everything was dead still, and the parson begun his solemn talk where he left off. In a minute or two here comes this undertaker's back and shoulders gliding along the wall again; and so he glided and glided around three sides of the room, and then rose up, and shaded his mouth with his hands, and stretched his neck out towards the preacher, over the people's heads, and says, in a kind of a coarse whisper, *"He had a rat!"* Then he drooped down and glided along the wall again to his place. You could see it was a great satisfaction to the people, because naturally they wanted to know. A little thing like that don't cost nothing, and it's just the little things that makes a man to be looked up to and liked. There warn't no more popular man in town than what that undertaker was.

—Adventures of Huckleberry Finn, pp. 232–233

one denounces over again with added emphasis as absurdly false the pessimistic idea that the best things have already been said; here is a garden replete with new varieties. It would not be fair to the expectant reader (to be numbered by the thousand) to give any outline of the narrative, save in the briefest manner. "Huckleberry" is a bad boy and a sharp one, who makes many acquaintances in his island retreats and river wanderings and finally assists in stealing an antebellum "nigger"–a philanthropic act that will long keep his memory green. The "He had a rat" story put into a funeral scene, where it actually occurred in this city, will be recognized by a number of Hartford people, who have had many hearty laughs at it in its chrysalis period. Translated into Mr. Twain's sublimated prose atmosphere, it will be looked for with eagerness.

There are 174 illustrations in the book. Most of them are well designed and executed. They are on the average very expressive and calculated to explain the text to a nicety. We have to find fault here with only one thing about *Huckleberry Finn*–Mr. Clemmens leads us to presume by a drawing or two to be found on the closing pages that somebody is going to die, and then he grossly disappoints us by letting him live. Of course we know the "good die young," but that has been shown to be an exploded fallacy–as a generalization that is; the "bad die young" is an apothegm more in accordance with scientific and biblical truth. The hero of these 366 pages would have lived not less altogether in vain than is now the fact had he been killed by indignant citizens.

* * *

Fischer suggests that this unsigned review "was probably written by one of Clemens's friends who were connected with the paper: Charles Dudley Warner, one of the owners and editors, or Charles Hopkins Clark, the assistant editor."

"As Serious as it is Amusing"
Review of *Adventures of Huckleberry Finn*
The Hartford Courant, 20 February 1885, p. 2

In his latest story, *Huckleberry Finn* (Tom Sawyer's Comrade), by Mark Twain, Mr. Clemens has made a very distinct literary advance over Tom Sawyer, as an interpreter of human nature and a contributor to our stock of original pictures of American life. Still adhering to his plan of narrating the adventures of boys, with a primeval and Robin Hood freshness, he has broadened his canvas and given us a picture of a people, of a geographical region, of a life that is new in the world. The scene of his romance is the Mississippi river. Mr. Clemens has written of this river before specifically, but he has not before presented it to the imagination so distinctly nor so powerfully. Huck Finn's voyage down the Mississippi with the run away nigger Jim, and with occasionally other companions, is an adventure fascinating in itself as any of the classic outlaw stories, but in order that the reader may know what the author has done for him, let him notice the impression left on his mind of this lawless, mysterious, wonderful Mississippi, when he has closed the book. But it is not alone the river that is indelibly impressed upon the mind, the life that went up and down it and went on along its banks are projected with extraordinary power. Incidentally, and with a true artistic instinct, the villages, the cabins, the people of this river become startlingly real. The beauty of this is that it is apparently done without effort. Huck floating down the river happens to see these things and to encounter the people and the characters that made the river famous forty years ago—that is all. They do not have the air of being invented, but of being found. And the dialects of the people, white and black—what a study are they; and yet nobody talks for the sake of exhibiting a dialect. It is not necessary to believe the surprising adventures that Huck engages in, but no one will have a moment's doubt of the reality of the country and the people he meets.

Another thing to be marked in the story is its dramatic power. Take the story of the Southern Vendetta—a marvelous piece of work in a purely literary point of view—and the episode of the duke and the king, with its pictures of Mississippi communities, both of which our readers probably saw in the *Century* magazine. They are equaled in dramatic force by nothing recently in literature.

We are not in this notice telling the story or quoting from a book that nearly everybody is sure to read, but it is proper to say that Mr. Clemens strikes in a very amusing way certain psychological problems. What, for instance, in the case of Huck, the son of the town drunkard, perverted from the time of his birth, is conscience, and how does it work? Most amusing is the struggle Huck has with his conscience in regard to slavery. His conscience tells him, the way it has been instructed, that to help the runaway, nigger Jim to escape—to aid in stealing the property of Miss Watson, who has never injured him, is an enormous offense that will no doubt carry him to the bad place; but his affection for Jim finally induces him to violate his conscience and risk eternal punishment in helping Jim to escape. The whole study of Huck's moral nature is as serious as it is amusing, his confusion of wrong as right and his abnormal mendacity, traceable to his training from infancy, is a singular contribution to the investigation of human nature.

Taking Issue with Mark Twain's Diction

This item appeared in an unsigned column titled "Slings and Arrows."

Mark Twain makes the hero of his new book tell the story in what is supposed to be a boy's dialect. On the very second page this "low down," uneducated urchin is made to say "commence," where any boy, especially if he hadn't ben to school would have said "begin." The less education the more Anglo-Saxon, and, generally, the better grammar. Mark ought to know this.

—The Boston Globe, 20 February 1885, p. 4

These contradictions, however, do not interfere with the fun of the story, which has all the comicality, all the odd way of looking at life, all the whimsical turns of thought and expression that have given the author his wide fame and made him *sui generis.* The story is so interesting so full of life and dramatic force, that the reader will be carried along irresistibly, and the time he loses in laughing he will make up in diligence to hurry along and find out how things come out.

The book is a small quarto, handsomely printed and bound, and illustrated by 174 drawings which enter fully into the spirit of the book, and really help to set forth the characters. (Published by Charles L. Webster & Co.: New York. Sold by subscription only.)

* * *

"Thoroughly Interesting and Mirth-Provoking"
Review of *Adventures of Huckleberry Finn*
Montreal Star, 21 February 1885, p. 3

Some acute American critics have discovered that Mark Twain's humor—so much of it as is contained in this volume at any rate—has lost its savor. Strangely enough the ordinary reader does not arrive at the same conclusion, for to his untrained perception the book seems to overflow with comic incident and humorous expression. All, or nearly all, who have laughed over *Tom Sawyer,* will not fail to heartily enjoy the predicaments of vagabond "Huck," and marvel at the address with which he lies himself out of the most difficult straits. Their sympathies too will be claimed for runaway Jim, whose colored skin only served to disguise his "white inside." They will wax merry over the poetic justice meted out to the King and Duke, and hold their sides over Tom Sawyer's expedients for making the escape of Jim difficult,

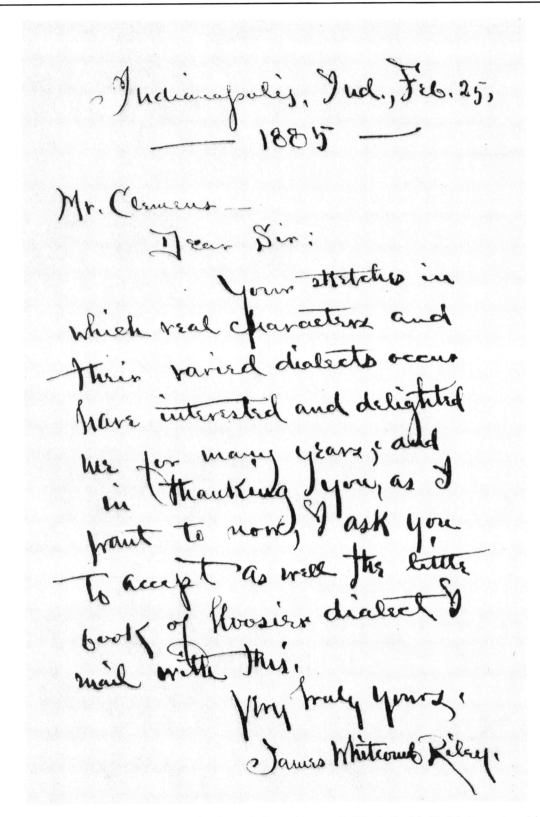

Indianapolis, Ind., Feb. 25,
— 1885 —

Mr. Clemens —
            Dear Sir:
                    Your sketches in
which real characters and
their varied dialects occur
have interested and delighted
me for many years; and
in thanking you, as I
want to now, I ask you
to accept as well the little
book of Hoosier dialect I
mail with this.
                    Very truly yours,
                            James Whitcomb Riley.

The response of James Whitcomb Riley, a book reviewer who became known as the "Hoosier Poet" for his dialect poems, to receiving a copy of Adventures of Huckleberry Finn *(Mark Twain Papers, The Bancroft Library, University of California, Berkeley)*

after the manner of "the most approved authorities." They will even reflect deeply over the state of society portrayed by the author and admire the ingenuity with which the different dialects are sustained by the various characters to whom they are proper. Finally they will conclude that rarely have they read a more thoroughly interesting and mirth-provoking book, or one that so entirely satisfied their anticipations. As to the many illustrations that accompany the letter-press, we can give them no higher praise than by saying that the artist has thoroughly understood the conceptions of the author, and has embodied them in forms which appeal to the reader's eyes as strongly as the pictures presented by Mark Twain possess the mind.

* * *

This review was unsigned but is believed to have been written by Robert Bridges, an editor for the start-up magazine Life *and later an editor for* Scribners.

Mark Twain's Blood-Curdling Humor
Review of *Adventures of Huckleberry Finn*
Robert Bridges
Life, 5 (26 February 1885): 119

Mark Twain is a humorist or nothing. He is well aware of this fact himself, for he prefaces the *Adventures of Huckleberry Finn* with a brief notice, warning persons in search of a moral, motive or plot that they are liable to be prosecuted, banished or shot. This is a nice little artifice to scare off the critics—a kind of "trespassers on these grounds will be dealt with according to law."

However, as there is no penalty attached, we organized a search expedition for the humorous qualities of this book with the following hilarious results:

A very refined and delicate piece of narration by Huck Finn, describing his venerable and dilapidated "pap" as afflicted with delirium tremens, rolling over and over, "kicking things every which way," and "saying there was devils ahold of him," This chapter is especially suited to amuse the children on long, rainy afternoons.

An elevating and laughable description of how Huck killed a pig, smeared its blood on an axe and mixed in a little of his own hair, and then ran off, setting up a job on the old man and the community, and leading them to believe him murdered. This little joke can be repeated by any smart boy for the amusement of his fond parents.

A graphic and romantic tale of a Southern family feud, which resulted in an elopement and from six to eight choice corpses.

A polite version of the "Giascutus" story, in which a nude man, striped with the colors of the rainbow, is exhibited as "The King's Camelopard; or, The Royal Nonesuch," This is a good chapter for Lenten parlor entertainments and church festivals.

A side-splitting account of a funeral, enlivened by a "sick melodeum," a "long-legged undertaker," and a rat episode in the cellar.

* * *

"A Little Gratitude"

The author of this 28 February 1885 letter was a contributor to Mark Twain's Library of Humor. *The headnote to his contribution there reads: "William Livingstone Alden made his reputation as the humorous editor of the New York Times. . . . He has published some eight volumes, mostly of a humorous character."*

Dear Mr. Clemens

I took up an alleged critical paper the other day & found a column pitching in to Huckleberry Finn.

Now I dont suppose you care a [shaw] either for that opinion, or for any other opinion of a book that can't help selling, but I want to relieve my mind.

I have read the extracts from the book in the <u>Century</u> & enjoyed them more than I ever enjoyed any magazine articles anywhere. I want to tell you that the Grangerford feud lays over anything you ever wrote. The deceased painter of pathetic pictures:—the boy who was always ready to bet that he'd "get one of them"—and that exhaustive criticism of the Pilgrim's Progress—"the statements were interesting but tough"—are simply heavenly.

If any body tells you that you are not as funny as you used to be or that you are written out—cheerful and helpful remarks that idiots usually make concerning successful men, please tell them they lie. Webb published the Jumping Frog, & you have never surpassed that Grangerford feud. I don't believe you ever approached it.

You neednt read this, but it is soothing to me to write it, for I have a little gratitude in my composition.

Alden followed up his first response with a note dated 15 March.

I have just read Huck through in course. It is the best book ever written.

—Mark Twain Papers, The Bancroft Library,
University of California, Berkeley

This excerpt is from a notice in the Current Literature section of a London publication.

"Serious Thought . . . Merry Laughter"
Review of *Adventures of Huckleberry Finn*
Congregationalist, 14 (March 1885): 251

A new book from the pen of Mark Twain hardly needs an introduction from any reviewer. It carries it own recommendation with it in the name of its author, who never writes without furnishing us with as abundant material for serious thought as for merry laughter. Huckleberry Finn has all the characteristic qualities of its author: his quaint humour, his abundant common sense, his genial sympathy, his felicitous skill in hitting off the peculiarities both of classes and of individuals.

* * *

The anonymous author of this influential review compares Mark Twain's novel to George Wilbur Peck's newspaper sketches about a mischievous boy who plays practical jokes on his father, which were collected and published as Peck's Bad Boy and His Pa *in 1883. The review was subtitled, "'Humor' of a Very Low Order—Wit and Literary Ability Wasted on a Pitiable Exhibition of Irreverence and Vulgarity."*

Mark Twain's Bad Boy
Review of *Adventures of Huckleberry Finn*
New York World, 2 March 1885, p. 7

Were Mark Twain's reputation as a humorist less well founded and established, we might say that this cheap and pernicious stuff is conclusive evidence that its author has no claim to be ranked with Artemus Ward, Sydney Smith, Dean Swift, John Hay, or any other recognized humorist above the grade of the author of that outrageous fiction, *Peck's Bad Boy.* *Huckleberry Finn* is the story (told by himself) of a wretchedly low, vulgar, sneaking and lying Southern country boy of forty years ago. He runs away from a drunken father in company with a runaway negro. They are joined by a couple of rascally imposters, and the Munchausenlike "adventures" that fill the work are encountered in the course of a raft voyage down the Mississippi. The humor of the work, if it can be called such, depends almost wholly on the scrapes into which the quartet are led by the rascality of the impostors, "Huck's" lying, the negro's superstition and fear and on the irreverence which makes parents, guardians and people who are at all good and proper ridiculous. That such stuff should be considered humor is more than a pity. Even the author objects to it being considered literature. But what can be said of a man of Mr. Clemens's wit, ability

and position deliberately imposing upon an unoffending public a piece of careless hackwork in which a few good things are dropped amid a mass of rubbish, and concerning which he finds it necessary to give notice that "persons attempting to find a motive in this narrative will be prosecuted; persons attempting to find a moral in it will be banished; persons attempting to find a plot in it will be shot." The story is entirely on the free-and-easy style, or, as the hero himself would express it, "it just sloshes along anyhow." There is an abundance of moving accidents by fire and flood, a number of situations more or less unpleasant in which he involves his dramatis personae and then leaves them to lie themselves out of it, a series of episodes and digressions apparently introduced to give Mr. Twain's peculiar sense of humor a breathing spell, and finally two or three unusually atrocious murders in cold blood, thrown in by way of incidental diversion.

The action of the story is laid in the Mississippi Valley and the time, very thoughtfully, from forty to fifty years back. Huck Finn, the quondam comrade of Tom Sawyer, after being put through a course of "sprouts and civilization" at the hands of the Widow Douglas, is reclaimed by his disreputable old father and carried off to the woods. The various doings and sayings of the pair were told with infinite grace and fancy and an excrutiating [*sic*] funny account of an attack of delirium tremens with which the old man is seized is introduced with thrilling effect. Finally Huck, to escape the frequent corrections with which parental authority sees fit to favor him, determines to run away and to avoid possible pursuit ingeniously contrives to make it appear that he has been murdered. The details are interesting and boys intending to leave their childhood's home to kill Indians will probably profit by them. After enjoying from a safe hiding place the moral sensation of seeing the village turn out in force to discover the secret of his untimely taking off he is unexpectedly joined by Jim, Miss Watson's nigger, who is running away to avoid being sold down South, and the two set off down the river on a raft. They meet, of course, with numerous misadventures from which they are extricated by Huck's remarkable ability to lie straight out from the shoulder. In fact, the reader will soon discover for himself that Huck's spiritual perceptions are confined to an unwavering belief in signs of bad luck. He prays for fish-hooks on one occasion and don't get them and accordingly "takes no stock in Providence."

The entertainment which the two frauds, who are known as the "King" and the "Duke," give at one of the river towns is also extremely elevated in character, and the "Royal Nonesuch" should find a favored place in the list of parlor exhibitions. The villainous attempt to defraud the orphans out of their inheritance, the cream of which was cleverly skimmed off for the *Century,* is however, their grand coup for a fortune. The two rascals pass themselves off as the two brothers from England and claim the property. The impostors succeed in deceiving everybody, though at times they run pretty close to the wind, notably on the occasion of their first meeting with the friends of him who, as the King expresses it, now lies "cold but joyful." . . .

Of course the real heirs turn up, and the pretended relatives are obliged to leave in a hurry. The remainder of the book is taken up in telling how Huck, with the assistance of Tom Sawyer, who comes up smiling in the thirty-third chapter, contrive the release of Jim, who has been captured and is being held by Silas Phelps, Tom Sawyer's uncle, until he can be claimed. Jim is in much the same position as the celebrated pirate of the Spanish Main, who lay in a loathsome dungeon for nineteen years, and then, struck by a happy thought, opened the window and got out. There is no difficulty at all about contriving his escape, so the two friends are forced to supply the difficulty. Tom has read about famous prisoners in history, and insists on Jim's adopting all their customs. Accordingly he is kept hard at work scratching inscriptions on the walls of his dungeon cell, fabricating rope ladders and the like. Finally they fill his cabin full of garter snakes and rats for him to cheer his loneliness by taming. It works to a charm. . . .

Then the escape takes place in which Tom Sawyer gets a bullet in his leg and they are all ignominiously brought back and Tom confesses that Miss Watson had died three months back, freeing Jim in her will.

The author informs us in an explanatory note that he uses no less than seven dialects, to wit: "The Missouri negro dialect, the extremest form of the backwoods Southwestern dialect, the ordinary Pike County dialect and four modified varieties of this last." Discriminating which is which in this extraordinary assortment will be found a pleasant literary amusement for people who are fond of puzzles.

* * *

This anonymous review refers to Mark Twain's lawsuit against Estes & Lauriat.

"Flat, Stale and Unprofitable"
Review of *Adventures of Huckleberry Finn*
Boston Evening Traveller, 5 March 1885, p. 1

It is little wonder that Mr. Samuel Clemens, otherwise Mark Twain, resorted to real or mock law-

suits, as may be, to restrain some real or imaginary selling of *The Adventures of Huckleberry Finn* as a means of advertising that extraordinary senseless publication. Before the work is disposed of, Mr. Mark Twain will probably have to resort to law to compel some to sell it by any sort of bribery or corruption. It is doubtful if the edition could be disposed of to people of average intellect at anything short of the point of the bayonet. This publication rejoices in two frontispieces, of which the one is supposed to be a faithful portrait of Huckleberry Finn, and the other an engraving of the classic features of Mr. Mark Twain as seen in the bust made by Karl Gerhardt. The taste of this gratuitous presentation is as bad as is the book itself, which is an extreme statement. Mr. Clemens has contributed some humorous literature that is excellent and will hold its place, but his *Huckleberry Finn* appears to be singularly flat, stale and unprofitable. . . .

* * *

These excerpts are from an anonymous review originally titled "Huckleberry Finn—*Mark Twain's New Story.*"

"Good and Lively"
Review of *Adventures of Huckleberry Finn*
Hartford Times, 9 March 1885, p. 4

Everybody will want to see *Huckleberry Finn,* Mr. Clemens's story—a sort of continuation of his *Tom Sawyer.* It is a tale of the Mississippi River, as that mighty stream and its commerce and travel presented themselves to the observer away back in Clay and Polk times, or thereabout. It is a good book, and it does teach a certain moral, notwithstanding the author's disclaimer; it teaches, without seeming to do it, the virtue of honest simplicity, directness, truth. As to stirring incidents, the story is full of them. It will hugely please the boys, and also interest people of more mature years.

Mr. Clemens describes things as they really were, in Missouri—and as they still are, to a somewhat modified extent; and this book is as good as a trip through all the regions of which it treats. The author is a good observer, as well as a humorist.

It is in one of those scrawny, ragged Missouri towns, that abounded a few years ago even more than now, that the boy "Huck Finn," lived. How boylike the touches are—painted by a master hand, as every part of every picture shows—may be judged by Huck's account of his studies with the Widow Douglas, and the annoying supervision to which he was subjected in addition by her sister, Miss Watson, a prim old maid, in goggles. . . .

"In Stepped Mark Twain and Spoiled It All"

Another factor that doubtless affected Mark Twain's image during the period when Adventures of Huckleberry Finn *was being reviewed was his efforts to secure the publishing rights to the memoirs of Ulysses S. Grant. As is clear in this excerpt from a news report titled "Changed Publishers," Grant was an enormously sympathetic figure and Mark Twain's venture was viewed with suspicion.*

GRANT'S PLUCK
THE GREAT GENERAL BOUND TO FINISH HIS REMINISCENCES

Special to the Detroit Post.

New York, March 7–Gen. Grant is exerting himself to get his reminiscences written out before death stops his pen. He has had more ease from pain during the week than was anticipated, and has been able to work several hours every day. In order to hasten the composition, an amanuensis was employed–a woman who could use a typewriter as rapidly as he would be likely to dictate: but his constitutional lack of fluency was aggravated by the unusual process, and it was soon found also that the use of his voice, even in a whisper, brought on inflation and swelling to his diseased throat. Therefore he returned to pen and ink. He writes slowly, his average rate being only about one hundred words an hour, and that is lowered by frequent meditation. He has never practiced at composition for publication, and it comes awkwardly. The first volume of the proposed work has been edited thoroughly by an expert, whose duty however, was limited to a verbal and grammatical revision. He was warned not to alter the meanings except on consultation. The second volume is about half done, but Grant has made copious notes for the remainder so that they could be written out after his death if necessary.

NO MORE "CENTURY" ARTICLES

There has been a falling out between Grant and Roswell Smith, the manager of the *Century* company. It was all but concluded that the autobiography should be published by that concern. The general was paid $1,000 for his war article in the February number of the *Century,* and it was decided that further passage from his forthcoming book should be first published in the magazine. Arrangements for the making of the pictures and printing of the volumes were made and terms were nearly settled on the basis of a royalty. The negotiations did not result in a contract, however, and for the failure Mark Twain is understood to be responsible. Mark has not been so reckless a humorist as to share the profits of his fun

with anybody. He has mastered the subscription book business. He is his own publisher and wholesaler, being the principal though unmentioned partner in the firm of Charles L. Webster & Co., the Webster being a relative, who marshals and directs the soliciting agents with which the whole country is made to swarm. Grant received an offer from Mark, through Webster, to take his son Jesse into the enterprise of publishing and circulating the reminiscences. The fact was shown to him that the mechanical cost of producing each $3 volume would not exceed 30 cents, provided large editions were sold, and that a clear profit treble the royalty offered by Smith could be realized. As this scheme promised to yield a considerable fortune for his family, and make a business for a son, Grant went into it.

"There was no completed bargain to break, as between us and the general," said Smith today, "but we supposed it to be settled that the *Century* imprint would go on the title page of the book. He came to our office almost daily to consult about the matter and our advice as to the material and makeup of the work was generally sought and followed. Understand, though, that we have no grievance. He had the right to go elsewhere, and his object was principally to create a place for one of his sons–a thing which we were hardly prepared to do."

There is a great deal more bitterness than Smith intimates, and it is certain that no more papers by Grant will appear in the *Century.* Some say that Mark Twain has incidentally closed the pages of the magazine to say further transcripts from his forthcoming books, which will be a loss of advertising. He is in town to help Webster in the new project. The terms of the partnership between them and the Grants are not divulged, further than that Mark advances the considerable capital required to put the books on the market.

–Detroit Post, 8 March 1885, p. 1

Stories about Grant and his decision to change publishers ran in newspapers across the country, with some papers commenting sharply on Mark Twain and his role. In a story titled "Gen Grant, Mark Twain, and The Century" in the 9 March issue of the Springfield Republican, *the reporter wrote that Grant's deal with* The Century *was "all but concluded . . . when in stepped Mark Twain and spoiled it all." Later, he wrote, "it is intimated that Mark Twain cannot have any more of his "Huckleberry Finn" literature published hereafter in those offended pages. The readers of the magazine may well hope the last item of this news is true."*

The book is good and lively, all the way through. Not the least of its merits is the fidelity with which it paints the characters and the scenes with which the story deals. Mark Twain's art is of the pre-Raphaelite kind. He paints living pictures, and he makes his fibbing young hero a character that the reader is bound to like, in spite of himself. Engravings are seen on almost every page; very fair pictures, that really help, not mar, the story.

* * *

This unsigned review was by a critic who evidently had long followed Mark Twain's career and celebrity.

"A Pot-Boiler in its Baldest Form"
Review of *Adventures of Huckleberry Finn*
San Francisco Daily Examiner, 9 March 1885

The San Francisco agents of this book give notice that, though some unavoidable delays have occurred, this volume is now ready for delivery to subscribers. As to the work itself, it is well described by the author, as being without a motive, a moral, or a plot. The only reason to be, as the French say, is probably that the author thought he could make some money by publishing a book of some kind, and here it is—such as it is. It is apparently, as the art critics say, a pot-boiler in its baldest form. As a picture of life in the Southwest, however, there is little to be said in the book's favor, though there are several passages which are drawn with much ability, with occasionally a touch of a sort of grotesque pathos which greatly interests the reader. As to the rest, it is very much of the same character as many of the author's Pacific Coast sketches, in the utter absence of truth and being unlike anything that ever existed in the earth, above the earth, or in the waters under the earth. Some twenty-two years since, when Mr. Clemens was working as a reporter on the *Territorial Enterprise,* published in Virginia City, Nevada, he signalized his career by getting up a series of startling stories, the most prominent feature of which was the lack of a grain of fact. One of Clemens' most notorious lucubrations in this line was the report of the massacre of a whole family at Van Sickles or Empire City, which caused much horror and also great annoyance. Mark Twain contended that this was a good joke, and the parties who were inconvenienced should not have got angry. When, however, it was his ox that was gored, there were no such feelings of equanimity exhibited on his side of the house. For instance, afterward, when he paid a visit to his old haunts on the Comstock, a party of his former inti-

---

> ### "Take a Tumble"
>
> *Not all of the responses sent to Mark Twain about his novel were laudatory, as is shown by this 10 March 1885 letter.*
>
> Dear Sir
> For God's sake give a suffering public a rest on your labored wit–Shoot your trash & quit it–You are only an <u>imitator of Artemus Ward</u> & a sickening one at that & <u>we are sick of you,</u> For God's sake take a tumble & give U.S. a rest.–U. S.–
>
> –Mark Twain Papers, The Bancroft Library, University of California, Berkeley

mates played a practical joke on him, he was one of the maddest mortals who could be seen in a day's march. Something, however, should be said in praise of the style in which the book has been published. It is plentifully illustrated with engravings of no mean skill, and is well printed in fine, clear type.

* * *

This anonymous review was originally titled "Mark Twain's New Book."

"Wearisome and Labored"
Review of *Adventures of Huckleberry Finn*
Boston Advertiser, 12 March 1885, p. 2

Mark Twain's *Adventures of Huckleberry Finn* had a certain relishable flavor when mixed up with the miscellaneous assortment of magazine literature; but in a book form, and covering more than 350 pages, they are wearisome and labored. It would be about as easy to read through a jest book, as to keep up one's interest in the monotonous humor and the dialectic variations of "Huck Finn's" narrative. Here and there are snatches of Mark Twain's best work, which could be read over and over again, and yet bring each time an outburst of laughter; but one cannot have the book long in his hands without being tempted to regret that the author should so often have laid himself open to the charge of coarseness and bad taste. The illustrations are admirable in their way. As to the general character of the book, it may be sufficient to remind the reader of the author's notice, that "all persons attempting to find a motive in this narrative will be prosecuted; persons attempting to find a moral in it will be banished; persons attempting to find a plot in it will be shot."

* * *

"A Handsome Success"

In mid March, Mark Twain received news that Adventures of Huckleberry Finn was selling well. The Webster Company was then preparing to publish Ulysses S. Grant's memoirs and Twain was anxious about both projects. This excerpt is from his 16 March 1885 letter to Webster.

Your news is splendid. Huck certainly *is* a success, & from the standpoint of my own requirement. This result sets my fears about at rest as regards the General's book. . . .

Every time you sell a thousand Huck's let me know. It's a handsome success.

—Mark Twain, Business Man, p. 307

This anonymous review appeared in the Current Literature section.

"Writing for the Market"
Review of *Adventures of Huckleberry Finn*
San Francisco Bulletin, 14 March 1885, p. 1

Mark Twain long since learned the art of writing for the market. His recent books have the character of commercial ventures. He probably estimates in advance his profits. His books are not sold to any great extent over the counters of booksellers, but are circulated by subscription agents. Lately Mark Twain, it is reported, has become the silent partner in a publishing house, the imprint of which is on the present volume. Those who read *Tom Sawyer* and like it will probably read *Huckleberry Finn,* and like it in a less degree. No book has been put on the market with more advertising. When Mark Twain represented "Tom Sawyer" as getting a job of free whitewashing done by his cronies, because there was fun in it, and only just enough to go around, he disclosed his own tactics in the matter of free advertising. When it was given out that some one had tampered with the engravings in the printing office, in a mysterious way, that accounted for the delay in bringing out the book, it secured at the same time many thousand dollars' worth of free advertising. Then the *Century* gave the enterprise a lift by publishing a chapter of the book in advance, which, while an advertisement, was still a readable article. *Huckleberry Finn* has been introduced to the world as it were, with the blare of trumpets. It comes also with the warning: "Persons attempting to find a motive in

this narrative will be prosecuted; persons attempting to find a moral in it will be banished; persons attempting to find a plot in it will be shot." So then, there is neither motive, moral, nor plot. But there still remain one hundred and seventy-four wood cuts, which, according to the view of the author, ought to be liberally peppered through the volume. Many of the designs are drawn with spirit, and are all executed well enough for the plan of the book.

The tone of the volume is indicated in the opening paragraphs. . . .

The author starts out by telling his juvenile readers that there are some lies in his book—that most people lie, and that it is not very bad after all. Of course the warning is timely that persons attempting to seek a moral in the story should be banished. . . .

It is an amusing story if such scrapwork can be called a story. The author rarely fails when he sets out to tickle the ribs of young or old. There is so little genuine wit in the world, that the little must be

HE SOMETIMES LIFTED A CHICKEN.

Huck borrowing a chicken on one of his nightly visits to villages along the river. Some contemporary critics objected to what they regarded as Mark Twain's countenancing of Huck's fabrications and petty thefts (drawing by E. W. Kemble; from Adventures of Huckleberry Finn, *Mark Twain House, Hartford, Connecticut).*

made to go a great way. Mark Twain has the genuine vein; it nearly pinches out here and there, and in many places it is hardly an inch wide by miners' measurement. The funny book will always be read in this world of dryness and dearth. Many fastidious people hide their scruples, because they want to be amused. Comedy pays better than tragedy. The author contrives to puncture a great many shams. His satire in this respect, even when he declares that it is aimless, is directed with a purpose. Whether young people who read this volume will be the better for it will be an open question. Here is another paragraph where the warning not to seek for a moral might be applicable:

> Every night, now, I used to slip ashore, towards ten o'clock, at some little village, and buy ten or fifteen cents' worth of meal or bacon or other stuff to eat; and sometimes I lifted a chicken that warn't roosting comfortable, and took him along. Pap always said, take a chicken when you get a chance, because if you don't want him yourself you can easy find somebody that does, and a good deed ain't ever forgot. I never see pap when he didn't want the chicken himself, but that is what he used to say, anyway.

The author turns his knowledge of Western dialects to account. Mississippi river scenes and associations are always available. The art of book-making from Twain's point of view is well illustrated. He is alive always to the fact that young people will not read a dull book. He never makes a dull one. There is very little of literary art in the story. It is a string of incidents ingeniously fastened together. The spice of juvenile wickedness and dare-deviltry give a zest to the book. "Huckleberry Finn" is, in a restricted sense, a typical character. Yet the type is not altogether desirable, nor is it one that most parents who want a future of promise for their young folks would select without some hesitation. The trouble with "Tom Sawyer" and "Huckleberry Finn" is not that they are too good for this world; even as the world goes, they are not good enough. Beyond the recognition that there is a great deal of "fun," as boys would put the case, it must also be admitted that not a little of the "assisted wit" is of the more dreary sort, as if the author was subjected to a pretty hard strain at times to work his facetious vein. The book is attractive enough to command commercial success, and that, it may be supposed, was the inspiring motive in its production.

* * *

This reviewer is believed to be George Hamlin Fitch, the regular critic for the newspaper.

Mark Twain's Readable New Story
Review of *Adventures of Huckleberry Finn*
San Francisco Chronicle, 15 March 1885, p. 6

The Adventures of Huckleberry Finn must be pronounced the most amusing book Mark Twain has written for years. It is a more minute and faithful picture of Southwestern manners and customs fifty years ago than was *Life on the Mississippi,* while in regard to the dialect it surpasses any of the author's previous stories in the command of the half-dozen species of patois which passed for the English language in old Missouri. Mark Twain may be called the Edison of our literature. There is no limit to his inventive genius, and the best proof of its range and originality is found in this book, in which the reader's interest is so strongly enlisted in the fortunes of two boys and a runaway negro that he follows their adventures with keen curiosity, although his common sense tells him that the incidents are as absurd and fantastic in many ways as the *Arabian Nights.* Here is where the genius and the human nature of the author come in. Nothing else can explain such a *tour de force* as this, in which the most unlikely materials are transmuted into a work of literary art. The plot is extremely simple. Huckleberry Finn, who appeared incidentally in the veracious adventures of Tom Sawyer, concludes to go down the Mississippi to get rid of his drunken father. He falls in with a runaway negro, and the book is given up to the adventures of this couple on a raft on the river, reenforced by two sharpers known as the Duke and the King, and afterward by Tom Sawyer. In many parts of the book, but especially at the outset, some of the conversations are unnecessarily spun out, on the style of the elder Dumas when he was writing at so much the word, but when the story gets under good headway it is remarkably well proportioned, and the interest is never allowed to flag for a moment. The very best episodes are those which detail the swindling schemes of the two river sharpers, who impose upon Huckleberry and the negro by declaring that they are scions of royalty. These chapters were printed in the *Century* under the title of "Royalty on the Mississippi," but they left the fate of the two heroes in doubt, so that most readers of the performances of the "Royal Nonesuch," and the personation of the two brothers from England will want to know what was the final result of their schemes.

The incidental descriptions of character are always good. Take for instance, this small picture of Huck's father—a typical Pike county drunkard:

First page of letter from Oliver Wendell Holmes acknowledging receipt of a copy of Adventures of Huckleberry Finn. *Holmes went on to thank Clemens for "the inward delight and the outward relaxation of features" his books "never failed to produce. I hope you are well and will keep so, for you have made and will make the world happier so long as it has had your books and can hope for new ones" (Mark Twain Papers, The Bancroft Library, University of California, Berkeley).*

He was most 50, and he looked it. His hair was long and tangled and greasy and hung down, and you could see his eyes shining through it like he was behind vines. It was all black, no gray; so was his long, mixed-up whiskers. There warn't no color in his face, where his face showed—it was white; not like another man's white, but a white to make a body sick, a white to make a body's flesh crawl—a tree-toad white, a fish-belly white. As for his clothes—just rags, that was all.

On the raft, while floating down the Mississippi, Huck has an excellent opportunity to exercise his gift for lying. This is simply phenomenal. The boy enjoys mendacity; he lies for the mere lust of lying, and the ingenuity with which he piles one fiction on top of another will excite the reader's wonder and admiration. Just before the runaways get fairly started, Huck visits a neighboring town to get information and encounters a farmer's wife. He is dressed up in an old calico gown and pretends to be a girl searching for her relations. The woman suspects his sex and tries various devices to ascertain if her suspicions are true. Among these is threading a needle and throwing a bar of lead at the rats which swarm around the house. Finally she makes Huck own up that he is a boy. . . .

Some of the most succulent humor is connected with the swindling exploits of the Duke and the King, who "work" the towns along the bank and make considerable money. Their crowning work was in playing the role of the English heirs of old Peter Wilks, a moneyed resident of one of the river towns, who had just died. In the construction of this plot Mark Twain surpasses himself and the amount of really plausible lies which he manages to dovetail together is something extraordinary. A half-dozen times the adventures are on the eve of exposure, but their fertility and luck save them. Space is lacking here to do more than give one extract from this episode, which is a story in itself, descriptive of the Arkansas undertaker at the funeral of old Peter . . .

There are dozens of descriptive bits as good as this and others in which there is no attempt at caricature, such, for instance, as the picture of the old one-horse cotton plantation of Phelps, which any one who has seen the South will recognize as a type. What Mark Twain can do in short sketches of persons is shown by the portrait of old Mrs. Hotchkiss, which is one of the best things in the book. Anyone who has ever lived in the Southwest, or who has visited that section, will recognize the truth of all these sketches and the art with which they are brought into this story. To all readers we can commend the story as eminently readable. The person who can withstand the abounding humor of this book must be proof against all jokes except of the Joe Miller order. The volume is very well gotten up, the illustrations adding materially to the fun of the story.

* * *

In this excerpt, the anonymous reviewer refers to the soprano Adelina Patti, who was then performing in San Francisco.

Tom Sawyer's Chum
Review of *Adventures of Huckleberry Finn*
San Francisco Morning Call, 17 March 1885, p. 5

When Patti sings the world must applaud, and when Mark Twain writes the world must laugh. The author of *Innocents Abroad, Roughing It, Tom Sawyer,* etc., has taken the gauge of popular appreciation in literature, and directed his course by it. Clemens knows two things well, and he studies only to qualify himself to improve his knowledge. They are: First, that the authorship of "Mark Twain" is enough in itself to create a demand for a book; and second, that shavings will flash up into a flame and make a big, bright fire quicker than solid logs, though they may not burn so long. He weaves a plot out of incidents framed and fastened together with humor, keeping in view always the fact that grotesqueness, even while reaching down into the depths of human nature for a sentiment or passion to present, is more profitable than a staid conformity to the conventional ideals of things. People will give dollars to see a clown when they would not give a farthing to hear a sermon. Therefore, grotesqueness of idea, grotesqueness in pointing a moral, grotesqueness as an abstract thing, is Clemens's capital stock, and his latest issue is in the shape of a book of about 370 pages, illustrated with 174 cuts, each one of which is an exponent of the capital, representing a character or act having some close relationship to the *Adventures of Huckleberry Finn.* While the book has been thoroughly advertised by the usual methods, yet it is fair to say that Clemens needs less advertising than almost any living author. The announcement that Mark Twain is going to write a book is sufficient. The report spreads like an epidemic disease, and from that moment everybody is waiting for it. Huckleberry Finn is a boy—as represented in the picture on the cover of the book—without any of the adjuncts of aggression or action; simply a boy with patched knees, a slouch hat, his pantaloons held up by one suspender, and his hands thrust deep into his pockets. He stands contemplatively in a sort of heroic attitude, and with an expression of countenance that betrays a mind deeply involved in boy's business—plotting mischief. Huckleberry is Tom Sawyer's comrade. Birds of a feather flock together. In the commencement of the book, the lad refers to that companionship and the record of it in *The Adventures of Tom Sawyer,* gives Mr. Twain the credit of having "told the truth, mainly." The author prefaces this work with an admonition that it will be hazardous for anyone to undertake to find a motive, a moral or a plot in it. Yet it will be apparent to the reader that it contains all three of these things. The motive is the author's, a financial consideration; the plot—well, even omnipotence has not yet created a wretch of a boy who was not pregnant with plots; the moral every reader must draw for himself. In the commencement Huckleberry foreshadows the character of his incipient virtues. "The Widow Douglas, she took me for her son and allowed she would civilize me, but it was rough living in the house all the time, considering how dismal, regular and decent the widow was in all her ways, and so when I couldn't stand it no longer I lit out."

Of these praiseworthy efforts on the part of the widow Huckleberry gives a sample, to show how little she understood human nature in its early developments. . . .

The future of such a boy is sadly too apparent. If he escape the gallows it is simply because the gallows doesn't come in his way. In Huckleberry's case it was a chastening providence that wrought such a change of heart.

The book in a word, is a narrative of a boy thoroughly imbued with a boy's depravity and prompted by the instincts of a boy's wild nature. In order that the reader may not suppose that all the diversified characters were trying to talk alike and not succeeding, the author says in an explanatory note that "A number of dialects are used, to wit: The Missouri negro dialect; the extremest form of the backwoods Southwestern dialect; the ordinary Pike County dialect, and four modified varieties of the last." The shadings have not been done in a haphazard fashion, or by guesswork, but painstakingly, and with the trustworthy guidance and support of personal familiarity with these several forms of speech. It is a story that every one may read and at least be entertained. It is at times immensely amusing, and fully sustains Mr. Clemens's well-earned reputation as a humorous writer.

* * *

"Bad Taste"
Review of *Adventures of Huckleberry Finn*
San Francisco Alta California, 24 March 1885, p. 2

Mark Twain's latest addition to so-called humorous literature has been probably the best advertised book of the present age, through publication of extracts in magazines, dissensions among publishers and threatened injunctions from the author against enterprising firms, who have desired to forestall the firm in which Mark Twain is interested, in the publication of the book. As a self-advertiser, Mark Twain has become more of a success than as a humorist, as is shown by the *Adventures of Huckleberry Finn.* The experiences narrated in the book are supposed to have occurred on the Mississippi river some

forty to fifty years ago, and the chief interest attached to the work is found in the descriptions of that river, on which Mark Twain is supposed to have served an apprenticeship on a steamboat. As to the general character of the book, the author's introductory notice will be a hint, as follows: "All persons attempting to find a motive in this narrative will be prosecuted; persons attempting to find a moral in it, will be banished; persons attempting to find a plot in it will be shot." The book contains some clever descriptions of Mississippi river life, that are written in Mark Twain's best style and full of genuine humor, but much of the book shows evidence of great disposition to prolong the agony, or story, while the author often lays himself open to the charge of bad taste, if not coarseness. While the manners and customs of the Mississippi river people at that period may have been crude and peculiar to other sections, there is a manifest tendency to exaggeration, for the sake of ridicule, that satiates the average reader, and when forced humor is prolonged through 350 pages it becomes wearisome and monotonous. The illustrations are cleverly executed, and the book is gotten up in good style.

* * *

The unsigned author of this defense of Adventures of Huckleberry Finn *was doubtless reacting to negative reviews of the novel—specifically the review that appeared in the 5 March 1885 issue of the* Boston Evening Traveller—*as well as to the action of the Concord Public Library. Twain commented on this editorial as well as on the review that had appeared in the 15 March issue of the same paper in a letter to his sister: "The Chronicle understands the book—those idiots in Concord are not a court of last resort, & I am not disturbed by their moral gymnastics."*

Ruling Out Humor
A Response to the Concord Public Library Ban
San Francisco Chronicle, 29 March 1885, p. 4

The action of the Concord Public Library in excluding Mark Twain's new book, *Huckleberry Finn,* on the ground that it is flippant and irreverent, is absurd. The managers of this library evidently look on this book as written for boys, whereas we venture to say that upon nine boys out of ten much of the humor, as well as the pathos, would be lost. The more general knowledge one has the better he is fitted to appreciate this book, which is a remarkably careful sketch of life along the Mississippi river forty years ago. If one has lived in the South he can appreciate the art with which the dialect is managed,

First page of Clemens's draft of a letter to the secretary of the Concord Free Trade Club, with emendations by William Dean Howells
(Mark Twain Papers, The Bancroft Library, University of California, Berkeley)

Becoming the Pet of Massachusetts:
Mark Twain and the Concord Library Ban

The decision by the Concord Free Public Library committee to remove Adventures of Huckleberry Finn *from circulation was national news. The 17 March 1885 issue of* The New York Times *carried a brief item, "Mark Twain's Book Condemned," reporting the news from the Massachusetts city from the day before: "The Concord Public Library Committee has unanimously decided to exclude Mark Twain's new book 'Huckleberry Finn,' from the shelves of that institution, as 'flippant, irreverent, and trashy.'"*

The following excerpt is from a fuller, front-page story.

. . . Said one member of the committee: "While I do not wish to state it as my opinion that the book is absolutely immoral in its tone, still it seems to me that it contains but very little humor, and that little is of a very coarse type. If it were not for the author's reputation the book would undoubtedly meet with severe criticism. I regard it as the veriest trash." Another member says: "I have examined the book and my objections to it are these: It deals with a series of adventures of a very low grade of morality; it is couched in the language of a rough, ignorant dialect, and all through its pages there is a systematic use of bad grammar and an employment of rough, coarse, inelegant expressions. It is also very irreverent. To sum up, the book is flippant and irreverent in its style. It deals with a series of experiences that are certainly not elevating. The whole book is of a class that is more profitable for the slums than it is for respectable people, and it is trash of the veriest sort."

—*St. Louis Globe-Democrat*, 17 March 1885

On 25 March 1885, the Boston Daily Advertiser *reported that the Concord Free Trade Club had made Mark Twain a member, connecting the action to the ban placed on* Adventures of Huckleberry Finn *by the public library.*

Concord has made a sort of amends to Mark Twain, whose "Huckleberry Finn" it lately refused a place on its library shelves, by making him a member of its Free Trade Club. If the school of philosophy will now come forward with an honorary membership in its faculty for Mr. Twain, all, we have no doubt, will be forgiven.

Mark Twain responded to the honor in this 28 March letter sent to Frank A. Nichols, the secretary of the Concord Free Trade Club, that was published a few days later—and republished and quoted many times. The letter was published in the Daily Advertiser *on 2 April.*

Dear Sir,–
I am in receipt of your favor of the 24th instant conveying the gratifying intelligence that I have been made an honorary member of the Free Trade Club of Concord, Massachusetts, and I desire to express to the club, through you, my grateful sense of the high compliment thus paid me. It does look as if Massachusetts were in a fair way to embarrass me with kindnesses this year. In the first place, a Massachusetts judge has just decided in open court that a Boston publisher may sell, not only his own property in a free and unfettered way, but also may as freely sell property which does not belong to him but to me; property which he has not bought and which I have not sold. Under this ruling I am now advertising that judge's homestead for sale, and, if I make as good a sum out of it as I expect, I shall go on and sell out the rest of his property.

In the next place, a committee of the public library of your town have condemned and excommunicated my last book and doubled its sale. This generous action of theirs must necessarily benefit me in one or two additional ways. For instance, it will deter other libraries from buying the book; and you are doubtless aware that one book in a public library prevents the sale of a sure ten and a possible hundred of its mates. And, secondly, it will cause the purchasers of the book to read it, out of curiosity, instead of merely intending to do so, after the usual way of the world and library committees; and then they will discover, to my great advantage and their own indignant disappointment, that there is nothing objectionable in the book after all.

And finally, the Free Trade Club of Concord comes forward and adds to the splendid burden of obligations already conferred upon me by the Commonwealth of Massachusetts, an honorary membership which is worth more than all the rest, just at this juncture, since it indorses me as worthy to associate with certain gentlemen whom even the moral icebergs of the Concord Library committee are bound to respect.

May the great Commonwealth of Massachusetts endure forever, is the heartfelt prayer of one who, long a recipient of her mere general good will, is proud to realize that he is at last become her pet.

Thanking you again, dear sir, and gentlemen,
I remain,
Your obliged servant,
S. L. Clemens
(Known to the Concord Winter School of Philosophy as "Mark Twain.")

—*Boston Daily Advertiser*, 2 April 1885, p. 2

exactly as he can in Joel Chandler Harris' *Uncle Remus,* or in Craddock's Tennessee mountain tales. If he has not he will be forced to take it on trust. So with the characters. They are peculiarly Southern, but only those who have lived south of Mason and Dixon's line can thoroughly appreciate the fidelity to nature with which they have been drawn. When the boy under 16 reads a book he wants adventure and plenty of it. He doesn't want any moral thrown in or even implied; the elaborate jokes worked out with so much art, which are Mark Twain's specialty, are wasted upon him. All the character sketches go for nothing with this eager reader, who demands a story. To be sure, here is a story in the astonishing series of adventures of "Huck" Finn and the runaway negro, but it is so overlaid with this embroidery of jokes, sketches and sarcasm, that the story really forms the least part of it. Take the whole latter part of the book, which is given up to the ludicrous attempt to free the negro, Jim, from his imprisonment on the Arkansas plantation. This is a well-sustained travesty

of the escapes of great criminals, and can only be fully appreciated by one who has read what it ridicules. Running all through the book is the sharpest satire on the ante-bellum estimate of the slave. Huckleberry Finn, the son of a worthless, drunken, poor white, is troubled with many qualms of conscience because of the part he is taking in helping the negro to gain his freedom. This has been called exaggerated by some critics, but there is nothing truer in the book. The same may be said of the ghastly feud between the Shepherdsons and the Grangerfords, which is described with so much dramatic force. The latter depicts a phase of Southern life which the advance in civilization has had no power to alter. The telegraphic reports of periodical affrays in the South and Southwest show that the medieval blood-feud is still in force there and receives the countenance of the best society.

These are only a few instances which go to show that this is not a boy's book and does not fall under the head of flippant and worthless literature. Of its

Cartoon by H. T. Webster that appeared in the New York Herald Tribune *on 7 December 1948 (from* The Best of H. T. Webster *[New York: Simon and Schuster, 1953])*

"The Reality of the Southern *Vendetta*"

In the latter half of March 1885, Mark Twain received a letter from Reginald Cholmondeley, an English friend who was skeptical of the depiction of the Grangerfords and Shepherdsons. Twain wrote back within the month assuring Cholmondeley that feuds such as the one he described had indeed existed in "Kentucky, Tennessee, and Arkansas" within his "time and memory."

The following 10 August 1885 letter mailed from Cincinnati suggests that many of Twain's countrymen were even less inclined to accept the existence of blood feuds in their midst than was Cholmondeley.

My Dear "Mark Twain"

I have been compelled on more than one occasion to listen to objections from readers of "The adventures of Huckleberry Finn" to the sketch of the Grangerford and Shepherdson family feud. The mildest form of criticism concludes usually with the statement that to assume the existence of such a state of things in any part of this county is "unnatural, unreasonable "ridiculous and absurd." When replying, in some heat I must confess, that this scene though sketched in your matchless style is in so far as the facts go but a leaf from the daily record of our day and times, I have been asked with triumphant scorn to produce the data for my assertion which you will readily understand are not always at hand. The enclosed clipping from the Cincinnati Enquirer of Aug. 10th reveals a case in point and is only one of many brought to the notice of the intelligent newspaper reader every year. If it lies in your power either as a writer or publisher to bring this knowledge to the attention of the <u>lunkheads</u> who disbelieve in the reality of the southern <u>vendetta,</u> I pray you do so, and confer an everlasting favor upon

Yours Truly
J. C. Fuller

—Mark Twain Papers, The Bancroft Library,
University of California, Berkeley

humor nothing need be said. There is a large class of people who are impervious to a joke, even when told by as consummate a master of the art of narration as Mark Twain. For all these the book will be dreary, flat, stale and unprofitable. But for the great body of readers it will furnish much hearty, wholesome laughter. In regard to the charge of grossness, there is not a line in it which cannot be read by a pure-minded woman. There are too few books of genuine humor produced nowadays to have one of them stigmatized as unfit for general reading, and it is on this ground only that the absurd attack of these New England library authorities is worth notice.

* * *

This anonymous review appeared in a column titled "Belles Lettres, Poetry, and Fiction."

"Lively and Fresh"
Review of *Adventures of Huckleberry Finn*
British Quarterly Review, 81 (1 April 1885): 465–466

It is but seldom that continuations of popular books succeed. *Huckleberry Finn* is really a continuation of *Tom Sawyer*—a book which did not a little to make a reputation. But Mark Twain, if he is sometimes a little coarse, sometimes a little irreverent, and inclined to poke fun at the Old Testament, is decidedly a humorist, and it must be admitted that in this volume he is full of spirit and wit and drollery. Huckleberry Finn's adventures are told with a prevailing dryness and sense of reality which do much to compensate for offences against taste. Mr. Clemens writes with a keen eye to the young generation, and he knows they can stomach a good deal of that sort of thing, if they only get what they really like. "Huck," after a great many early escapades in the company of Tom Sawyer, is put under the charge of a certain Widow Douglas to be, as he puts it, civilized. He escapes from her, finding the monotony of respectability too much for him; but Tom hunted him up, and said "he was going to start a band of robbers, I might join him if I would go back to the widow, and be respectable." He went back and did his best. The widow tried him with "long graces" and preachings and readings from the Bible. "She learned me," he says, "about Moses and the Bulrushers; and I was in a sweat to find out all about him; but by and by she let it out that Moses had been dead a considerable long time; so then I didn't care no more about him; because I don't take no stock in dead people." Huck's father, of whom we see a great deal, is not a desirable person, but he is cleverly sketched, and the negro Jim, whom Huck finds in Jackson's Island in the Mississippi, to which he made tracks when he had run away, is presented with much cleverness, and made useful. The whole book is lively and fresh, and proves that Mark Twain's vein, if not quite inexhaustible, is abundant. The engravings are very clever and really illustrate the book.

* * *

The Real Huck Finn

Mark Twain was irritated by what he regarded as the hostility of certain newspapers. This is a note from his 4 April 1885 letter to Webster purportedly explaining the "true" origin of Huck Finn. Twain intended to have it published in the New York Sun, *but his wife convinced him not to follow through with the prank.*

He is two persons in one—namely, the author's two uncles, the present editors of the Boston Advertiser and the Springfield Republican. In character, language, clothing, education, instinct, and origin, he is the painstakingly and truthfully drawn photograph and counterpart of these two gentlemen as they were in the time of their boyhood, forty years ago. The work has been most carefully and conscientiously done, but this boy's language has been toned down and softened, here and there, in deference to the taste of a more modern and fastidious day.

—*Mark Twain's Letters to His Publishers,*
pp. 187–188

"A Faithful Record"

This excerpt is from John Hay's 14 April 1885 letter to "My Dear Clemens."

I have taken my time about acknowledging the receipt of your "Huckleberry Finn" because I am a slow reader and much worried by a good many things. But I finished it a day or two ago, and now write to thank you most sincerely for the pleasure you have given me. It is a strange life you have described, one which I imagine must be already pretty nearly obsolete in most respects. I, who grew up in the midst of it, have almost forgotten it, except when I read of it in your writings—the only place, I think, where a faithful record of it survives. To me the great interest of this, and your other like books, independent of their wit and humor and pathos, which everybody can see, is "documentary." Without them I should not know today, the speech and the way of living, with which I was familiar as a child. Huck Finns and Tom Sawyers were my trusted friends—though I had to cultivate them as the early Christians did their religion—in out of the way places. I am glad to meet them again in your luminous pages. . . .

—Mark Twain Papers, The Bancroft Library,
University of California, Berkeley

"Back in Memory"

This excerpt is from a 23 April 1885 letter of Thomas S. Nash, a childhood friend of Sam Clemens. Clemens differed from Nash in his memory of the fate of Jim Finn, the prototype for Pap. As Clemens recalled it, the man who died in a fire at the jail was a tramp passing through town, whereas Jim Finn was found dead in a tan vat.

Dear old friend

I have waited a long time for an opportunity of inflicting on you some more of my poor penmanship and bad grammar, but did not know for certain whether you were out west interviewing the earliest settlers or down South among the Cannibal Islands hence you have been spared the infliction until now and I hope not to tire you with too many words.

In the first place dear Sam I was very grateful for the kind letter you wrote me from Keokuk, and have added allready to my deep gratitude by sending me your new Book Huckleberry Finn, which I received some time since. I have not owing to the press of business had a chance to read much of it. I read several Chapters in the "Century" and was very anxious to find out how the "Duke" & the "<u>Dolphin</u>" <u>were finally checked off.</u> The mere mention of the Book takes me back in memory to "<u>old Jim Finn</u> of <u>Craig's Alley</u>" who if I remember right perished with the burning of the old Calaboose on front St. . . .

Time flies swiftly away and admonishes me to up and doing. So I will bring my somewhat extended letter to a close, but cannot do so without renewing my deep sense of gratitude for the beautiful Book you wrote and which so kindly sent me—I shall value it <u>highly,</u> as I can <u>in memory see you speak as I read</u>—Don't forget me <u>Sam.</u> I cherish the memory of all the friends of my youth, whether they have in the struggle of life gained wealth and fame or merely like myself still possess only a <u>plain but honest name</u>

—Mark Twain Papers, The Bancroft Library,
University of California, Berkeley

This unsigned review in a Massachusetts newspaper is ascribed to Franklin B. Sanborn, a journalist and ardent abolitionist who had helped fund John Brown's ill-fated rebellion. He associates the vices of antebellum Missouri with Thomas Hart Benton, a pro-Western expansionist senator from that state.

Mark Twain and Lord Lytton
Review of *Adventures of Huckleberry Finn*
Franklin B. Sanborn
Springfield Republican, 27 April 1885, pp. 2–3

It would be difficult to make Englishmen believe that the adventures of Huckleberry Finn and Tom Sawyer are as important to the loose-girt muse of fiction as the highbred sentiments of Lord Glenaveril and his German parson-Pylades,—yet such is the fact; and even as a work of dramatic art, the new book of Mark Twain has more merit than Lord Lytton's. I cannot subscribe to the extreme censure passed upon this volume, which is no coarser than Mark Twain's books usually are, while it has a vein of deep morality beneath its exterior of falsehood and vice, that will redeem it in the eyes of mature persons. It is not adapted to Sunday-school libraries, and should perhaps be left unread by growing boys; but the mature in mind may read it, without distinction of age or sex, and without material harm. It is in effect an argument against negro-slavery, lynching, whisky-drinking, family feuds, promiscuous shooting, and nearly all the vices of Missouri in the olden time, when Benton represented that state in the Senate; and before the people of western Missouri undertook to colonize Kansas in the interest of slavery, and then to force that institution upon the freemen who went there from the North. As a picture of Missouri life and manners it is simply invaluable, and goes farther to explain the political history of the United States from 1854 to 1860 than any other work I have seen,—and I have been reading in that direction of late. Huck Finn's father is the drunken poor white of Missouri, upon whom Atchison and his betters relied to fight slavery into Kansas; and the Grangerfords, Shepherdsons and Col. Sherburn are the gentlemen of courage and wealth who sometimes led on and sometimes thwarted the diabolism of the poor whites. I hardly know where one could find a more lively sketch of the fire-eating, affectionate, proud and courteous southern homicide than that given by poor Huck Finn in his account of the Grangerford family. . . .

This is a curious reproduction of the manners that prevailed in the time of Benton and Clay, and farther back, in the days of Andrew Jackson, who used to drink his morning draught as described, and then hand the tumbler to one of his suite, who would pour in water and drink the heeltap, as Huck Finn and Buck Grangerford do in this sketch. In other parts of the book there is exaggeration, and too much that is merely grotesque and coarse,—but in its best portions it is true to the life and very effective. There are needless complications in the plot, and there is more joking than is best for the story,—but on the whole the plot is not a bad one, and the joking is unavoidable and generally harmless, considering what the author's conception of his characters seems to be. Like all professed humorists, he carries the joke too far, and "runs it into the ground," but in its best estate his fun is irresistible, though it is very little helped by the so-called illustrations of his

book. These throw some light on the housing, dress and external circumstances of the personages, but seldom reproduce, as the author does, their internal struggles and entanglements. There is hardly anything so true to human nature in the whole realm of casuistry as the young hero's meditations with himself over his duty regarding the runaway slave, Jim, when it first dawns upon the boy that he is an accomplice in the escape from slavery. . . .

So he deceives the fugitive and sets out for the shore in the canoe, while his grateful companion says: "Jim won't ever forgit you, Huck; you's de bes' fren' Jim's ever had; en you's de *only* fren' ole Jim's got now." Huck then goes on: "I was paddling off, all in a sweat, to tell on him; but when he says this, it seemed to kind of take the tuck all out of me. I went along slow then, and I wasn't right down certain whether I was glad I started or whether I warn't. When I was 50 yards off Jim says: 'Dah you goes, de ole true Huck; de only white genlman dat ever kep' his promise to ole Jim.' Well, I just felt sick. But I says, I *got* to do it—I can't get *out* of it." However, he deceives two white men who are looking for runaways, gets $40 in gold out of them in compassion for his assumed father's sickness with the small-pox, and goes back to Jim without betraying him, "feeling bad and low, because I knowed very well I had done wrong." "Then I thought a minute, and says to myself, hold on—s'pose you'd a done right and give Jim up; would you felt better than what you do now? No, says I, I'd feel bad—I'd feel just the same way I do now. Well, then, says I, what's the use you learning to do right, when it's troublesome to do right, and ain't no trouble to do wrong and the wages is just the same? I was stuck. I couldn't answer that. So I reckoned I wouldn't bother no more about it, but after this always do whichever come handiest at the time."

Good people must make no mistake about the teachings of this book; for although the author declares that "persons attempting to find a moral in it will be banished," and though the Concord library committee have banished the book itself as immoral, I can see nothing worse in it than in the story of Samson, which contains a great deal of deliberate lying, or the story of Noah, which has a good deal about drinking, rafting, and high water. It is indeed a legend of prehistoric times, and for aught I know, may be a sun-myth or a freshet-myth, or the story of a geological period. As a work of art it is an improvement on *Tom Sawyer* and has the air of reality which *The Prince and the Pauper* lacks. Lord Lytton should read it before finishing *Glenaveril*.

***

A Late Notice in the *Atlantic Monthly*

Mark Twain had hoped that early positive reviews of Huckleberry Finn in The Century *and the* Atlantic Monthly *would set the tone for subsequent newspaper reviews. As it turned out* Huckleberry Finn *received late notices in both magazines. This brief notice appeared in the middle of the Books-of-the-Month column.*

Mark Twain's new book for young folks, The Adventures of Huckleberry Finn (C. L. Webster & Co.), is in some sense a sequel to The Adventures of Tom Sawyer, though each of the two stories is complete in itself. Huckleberry Finn, Tom Sawyer's old comrade, is not only the hero but the historian of his adventures, and certainly Mr. Clemens himself could not have related them more amusingly. The work is sold only by subscription.

—*The Atlantic Monthly,* 55 (April 1885): 576

Thomas Sergeant Perry's review, originally appearing in a column titled "Open Letters," came too late to influence newspaper reviewers.

"Capital Reading"
Review of *Adventures of Huckleberry Finn*
T. S. Perry
The Century Illustrated Monthly Magazine,
    30 (May 1885): 171–172

Mark Twain's *Tom Sawyer* is an interesting record of boyish adventure; but, amusing as it is, it may yet be fair to ask whether its most marked fault is not too strong adherence to conventional literary models? A glance at the book certainly does not confirm this opinion, but those who recall the precocious affection of Tom Sawyer, at the age when he is losing his first teeth, for a little girl whom he has seen once or twice, will confess that the modern novel exercises a very great influence. What is best in the book, what one remembers, is the light we get into the boy's heart. The romantic devotion to the little girl, the terrible adventures with murderers and in huge caves, have the air of concessions to jaded readers. But when Tom gives the cat Pain-Killer, is restless in church, and is recklessly and eternally deceiving his aunt, we are on firm ground—the author is doing sincere work.

This later book, *Huckleberry Finn,* has the great advantage of being written in autobiographical form. This secures a unity in the narration that is most valuable; every scene is given, not described; and the result is a vivid picture of Western life forty or fifty years ago. While *Tom Sawyer* is scarcely more than an apparently fortuitous collection of incidents, and its thread is one that has to do with murders, this story has a more intelligible plot. Huckleberry, its immortal hero, runs away from his worthless father, and floats down the Mississippi on a raft, in company with Jim, a runaway negro. This plot gives great opportunity for varying incidents. The travelers spend some time on an island; they outwit every one they meet; they acquire full knowledge of the hideous fringe of civilization that then adorned the valley; and the book is a most valuable record of an important part of our motley American civilization.

What makes it valuable is the evident truthfulness of the narrative, and where this is lacking and its place is taken by ingenious invention, the book suffers. What is inimitable, however, is the reflection of the whole varied series of adventures in the mind of the young scapegrace of a hero. His undying fertility of invention, his courage, his manliness in every trial, are an incarnation of the better side of the ruffianism that is one result of the independence of Americans, just as hypocrisy is one result of the English respect for civilization. The total absence of morbidness in the book—for the *mal du siècle* has not yet reached Arkansas—gives it a genuine charm; and it is interesting to notice the art with which this is brought out. The best instance is perhaps to be found in the account of the feud between the Shepherdsons and the Grangerfords, which is described only as it would appear to a semi-civilized boy of fourteen, without the slightest condemnation or surprise,—either of which would be bad art,—and yet nothing more vivid can be imagined. That is the way that a story is best told, by telling it, and letting it go to the reader unaccompanied by sign-posts or directions how he shall understand it and profit by it. Life teaches its lessons by implication, not by didactic preaching; and literature is at its best when it is an imitation of life and not an excuse for instruction.

As to the humor of Mark Twain, it is scarcely necessary to speak. It lends vividness to every page. The little touch in *Tom Sawyer,* page 105, where, after the murder of which Tom was an eye-witness, it seemed "that his school-mates would never get done holding inquests on dead cats and thus keeping the trouble present to his mind," and that in the account of the spidery six-armed girl of Emmeline's picture in *Huckleberry Finn,* are in the author's happiest vein. Another admirable instance is to be seen in Huckleberry Finn's mixed feelings about rescuing Jim, the negro, from slavery. His perverted views regarding the unholiness of his actions are most instructive and amusing. It is possible to feel, however, that the fun in the long account of Tom Sawyer's artificial imitation of escapes from prison is somewhat forced; everywhere simplicity is a good rule, and while the account of the Southern *vendetta* is a masterpiece, the caricature of books of adventure leaves us cold. In one we have a bit of life; in the other Mark Twain is demolishing something that has no place in the book.

Yet the story is capital reading, and the reason of its great superiority to *Tom Sawyer* is that it is, for the most part, a consistent whole. If Mark Twain would follow his hero through manhood, he would condense a side of American life that, in a few years, will have to be delved out of newspapers, government reports, county histories, and misleading traditions by unsympathetic sociologists.

* * *

Huckleberry Finn and His Critics
Review of *Adventures of Huckleberry Finn*
Joel Chandler Harris
Atlanta Constitution, 26 May 1885, p. 4

A very deplorable fact is that the great body of literary criticism is mainly perfunctory. This is not due to a lack of ability or to a lack of knowledge. It is due to the fact that most of it is from the pens of newspaper writers who have no time to elaborate their ideas. They are in a hurry, and what they write is hurried. Under these circumstances it is not unnatural that they should take their cues from inadequate sources and give to the public opinions that are either conventional or that have no reasonable basis.

All this is the outcome of the conditions and circumstances of American life. There is no demand for sound criticism any more than there is a demand for great poetry. We have a leisure class, but its tastes run toward horses, yachting and athletic sports, in imitation of the English young men who occasionally honor these shores with their presence. The imitation, after all, is a limping one. The young Englishman of leisure is not only fond of outdoor sports, but of books. He has culture and taste, and patronizes literature with as much enthusiasm as he does physical amusements. If our leisure class is to imitate the English, it would be better if the imitation extended somewhat in the direction of culture.

The American leisure class—the class that might be expected to patronize good literature and to

create a demand for sound, conservative criticism—is not only fond of horses, but is decidedly horsey. It is coarse and uncultivated. It has no taste in either literature or art. It reads few books and buys its pictures in Europe by the yard.

We are led to these remarks by the wholly inadequate verdict that has recently been given in some of the most prominent newspapers as to the merits of Mark Twain's new book, *The Adventures of Huckleberry Finn*. The critics seem to have gotten their cue in this instance from the action of the Concord library, the directors of which refused the book a place on their shelves. This action, as was afterwards explained, was based on the fact that the book was a work of fiction, and not because of the humorous characteristics that are popularly supposed to attach to the writings of Mr. Clemens. But the critics had got the cue before the explanation was made, and they straightway proceeded to inform the reading public the book was gratuitously coarse, its humor unnecessarily broad, and its purpose crude and inartistic.

Now, nothing could be more misleading than such a criticism as this. It is difficult to believe that the critics who have condemned the book as coarse, vulgar and inartistic can have read it. Taken in connection with *The Prince and the Pauper,* it marks a clear and distinct advance in Mr. Clemens's literary methods. It presents an almost artistically perfect picture of life and character in the southwest, and it will be equally valuable to the historian and to the student of sociology. Its humor, which is genuine and never-failing, is relieved by little pathetic touches here and there that vouch for its literary value.

It is the story of a half illiterate, high-spirited boy whose adventures are related by himself. The art with which this conception is dealt with is perfect in all its details. The boy's point of view is never for a moment lost sight of, and the moral of the whole is that this half illiterate boy can be made to present, with perfect consistency, not only the characters of the people whom he meets, but an accurate picture of their social life. From the artistic point of view, there is not a coarse nor vulgar suggestion from the beginning to the end of the book. Whatever is coarse and crude is in the life that is pictured, and the picture is perfect. It may be said that the humor is sometimes excessive, but it is genuine humor—and the moral of the book, though it is not scrawled across every page, teaches the necessity of manliness and self-sacrifice.

Atlanta, Ga. 1 June, 1885

My Dear Mr. Clemens:

I enclose you a little notice of Huckleberry Finn contributed to the Editorial columns of The Constitution. It is less a review of the book than of its critics, but it is the best I could find time to do. It fails to express ~~more than~~ half my admiration for the book, for I think that its value as a picture of life and as a study in philology will yet come to be recognized by those whose recognition is worth anything. It is the most original contribution that has yet been made to American literature.

I hope you are well and happy. My regards to Mrs. Clemens and the little girls. I was thinking of sending the little girls copies of the English editions of my books, but I have hesitated for fear of seeming too obtrusive or something. Faithfully yours:

Joel Chandler Harris

Cover letter Joel Chandler Harris sent with his article, "Huckleberry Finn and His Critics." Twain wrote "From 'Uncle Remus'" on its envelope (Mark Twain Papers, The Bancroft Library, University of California, Berkeley).

Recognizing a Masterpiece

As Fischer shows in this excerpt from his essay, the initial mixed reception of Adventures of Huckleberry Finn *in a few years gave way to appreciative recognition.*

After the Reviewers
Victor Fischer

Within six years of publication, *Huck Finn* had left most of its detractors behind. In 1891, the year that the Webster company published the second edition, Andrew Lang pronounced it "nothing less" than a "masterpiece."[1] The following year, Brander Matthews called it a "great book," and quoted Robert Louis Stevenson's opinion that it was "the strongest book which had appeared in our language in its decade."[2] By the time the Harper edition came out in 1896, the personal attacks on Mark Twain that had interfered with the book's initial reception had been dispelled by the author's bankruptcy and subsequent efforts to pay off his debts. *Huck* was by then commonly called his best book.

In 1896, *Punch* published an appreciation of the book that called it "a bit of the most genuine and incisive humour ever printed," "a great book," and a "Homeric book—for Homeric it is in the true sense, as no other English book is, that I know of."[3] Later that year, the Harper edition was the occasion of almost universal approbation among the magazines that reviewed it, the one exception being the *Outlook,* which favorably reviewed the new plates and binding, but said ominously, "Concerning the work of Mark Twain from the standpoint of American literature and humor, *The Outlook* will have more to say at a future day."[4] The *Nation* noted that *Huck*'s "power to interest and amuse has suffered nothing in the dozen years since it first saw the light."[5] The *Critic* called it a "masterpiece" which one read again "with even more zest and appreciation than before," and added:

> Our English cousins consider the book Mr. Clemens's masterpiece, and *The Athenaeum* has declared it to be "one of the six greatest books published in America." It would probably be difficult to find many cultured people who have not read the story, but it would be even more difficult, we opine, to find many cultured people who do not desire to read it again.[6]

The Chicago *Dial* called *Huck* "nearly, if not quite, the best of the books that we owe to Mr. Clemens" (but did not add which of his books was thought better).[7] The *Independent* wrote:

"Full of Fun"

Excerpt from an 8 June 1885 letter from Orion Clemens.

My Dear Brother:–
I just now met John H. Craig, the leading lawyer here, and possessing the chief local reputation as a poet and popular orator.

He says he read Huckleberry Finn through, and then re-read it and studied the points. In his view Huckleberry Finn is as distinctly a created character as Falstaff. The dialogues between him and Jim are inimitable, and the dialect perfect. How you could get down to their ideas, especially Jim's of King Sollerman, and manage so many dialects he does not see[.] His boys lie on the floor and read it, and race over, and laugh. It is full of fun.

Tom Sawyer was read and loaned till it had to be re-covered; and Huckleberry will soon start on the same journey.

He regards Jim as a very clear-cut character, standing out with Huckleberry['s] natural distinctness. He can see them. To him they are real characters.

The feud is a perfect picture. . . .

–Mark Twain Papers, The Bancroft Library,
University of California, Berkeley

A "Wholesome Book"

These excerpts are from a letter Harris sent to the editors of The Critic *on the occasion of what the magazine called "Mark Twain's Semi-Centennial."*

There must be some joke about this matter, or else fifty years are not as burdensome as they were in the days when men were narrow-minded and lacked humor—that is to say, when there was no Mark Twain to add salt to youth and to season old age. . . .

And yet I am glad that he is fifty years old. He has earned the right to grow old and mellow. He has put his youth in his books, and there it is perennial. His last book is better than his first, and there his youth is renewed and revived. I know that some of the professional critics will not agree with me, but there is not in our fictive literature a more wholesome book than 'Huckleberry Finn.' It is history, it is romance, it is life. Here we behold human character stripped of all tiresome details; we see people growing and living; we laugh at their humor, share their griefs; and, in the midst of it all, behold we are taught the lesson of honesty, justice and mercy.

–*The Critic* (28 November 1885): 253

Cover for a French translation published in 1886 (Library of the University of Illinois at Urbana-Champaign)

This is Mr. Clemens's masterpiece. It is a book that will live, not as a great story, but as a truthful, tho somewhat exaggerated sketch, or series of sket[c]hes, of Southern life in the days of slavery. No other writer has equaled Mark Twain in making the absolute impression of what were the salient, distinguishing features of that life.[8]

Harper's Monthly used in its advertising copy the following statement from the Philadelphia *Ledger:*

We are suspicious of the middle-aged person who has not read "Huckleberry Finn"; we envy the young person who has it still in store. . . . After the humor of the book has had its way then the pathos will be apparent, and later still will come the recognition of the value of these sketches as pictures of a civilization now ended.[9]

In the same issue of *Harper's,* Laurence Hutton reviewed the new edition, saying that Huck "is one of the most original and the most delightful juvenile creations of fiction," and concluded:

Happy the boy, of any age, who is to read "Huckleberry Finn" for the first time. It is safe to say that he will run the risk of prosecution in order to discover its motive; that he will take the chances of banishment rather than miss its moral; and, if he is anything of a mildly profane boy, "he'll be shot if he don't find its plot."[10]

In 1897, Brander Matthews compared Mark Twain with Cervantes "in that he makes us laugh first and think afterwards." Noting that three generations had laughed over *Don Quixote* "before anybody suspected that it was more than a merely funny book," he summed up:

It is perhaps rather with the picaroon romances of Spain that "Huckleberry Finn" is to be compared than

Cartoon from the August 1902 issue of the Kansas City Journal *that refers to the banning of* Adventures of Huckleberry Finn *by the
Denver Public Library because of its vulgarity and the bad example it set for youth. The recognition of the novel as a masterpiece
did not prevent it from being controversial. It continued to face fierce critics throughout
the twentieth century (Collection of Louis J. Budd).*

with the masterpiece of Cervantes; but I do not think it
will be a century or take three generations before we
Americans generally discover how great a book
"Huckleberry Finn" really is, how keen its vision of
character, how close its observation of life, how sound
its philosophy.[11]

–*American Literary Realism, 1870–1910,*
16 (Spring 1983): 37–38

1. Andrew Lang, *London Illustrated News,* 98 (14 February
   1891), 222; reprinted in *Critic,* 18 (7 March 1891), *Critic,*
   19 (25 July 1891), and *Mark Twain: The Critical Heritage,*
   ed. Frederick Anderson, with the assistance of Kenneth
   M. Sanderson (New York: Barnes and Noble, 1971), pp.
   131–135.
2. Brander Matthews, *Cosmopolitan,* 12 (March 1892), 636–
   640.
3. *Punch,* 4 January 1896, pp. 4–5.
4. *Outlook,* 53 (13 June 1896), 1115. No later assessment of
   Mark Twain in the *Outlook* has been found.
5. *Nation,* 62 (11 June 1896), 454.
6. *Critic,* 28 (20 June 1896), 446.
7. Chicago *Dial,* 21 (1 July 1896), 24.
8. *Independent,* 48 (23 July 1896), 19.
9. *Harper's Monthly,* 93 (September 1896), *Advertiser,* p. 3.
10. *Harper's Monthly,* 93 (September 1896), *Literary Notes,* p.
    2.
11. Brander Matthews, *Book Buyer,* n.s. 13 (January 1897),
    978–979.

Reputation

Gertrude Stein once remarked, "the creator of a new composition in the arts is an outlaw until he is a classic, there is hardly a moment in between." One of the remarkable things about Adventures of Huckleberry Finn *is that the title character has remained an outlaw at the same time that his book has become a classic. Before his death, Mark Twain knew that this novel had acquired a reputation that would live for a good long time. But he could not have predicted the critical and popular currents that have sustained its reputation. While he may have foreseen the banning of* Adventures of Huckleberry Finn *(by the Concord Public Library and elsewhere) on the grounds that it was the "veriest trash" and set no good example for America's youth, he doubtless would have been mystified by subsequent bannings on the basis of its supposed racism, for his intention was to expose and condemn racial bigotry, not reinforce it.*

When, late in his life, Twain attacked with all the vitriol he could muster the imperialist policies of his country, he was sometimes accused of being un-American. Barely a month after his death in 1910, however, one cartoon featured Uncle Sam reading the novel and thanking its author for the pleasure it had given, and Huck Finn has since become a freckled emblem of the American character. On the other hand, communists have subsequently praised the novel for offering a powerful critique of capitalistic America.

Samuel L. Clemens the businessman had tried to protect his nom de plume by registering it as a trademark, but he overlooked the market value of "Huck Finn." During his lifetime, the name "Mark Twain" was used to market cereal and cigars, but how could Twain have known that "Huck Finn" would become the brand name for a multitude of enterprises, from designating a "cake walk" to furnishing the name for a Japanese nightclub specializing in the "punk scene"? Mark Twain and Adventures of Huckleberry Finn *belong to the world.*

Huckleberry Finn in the Canon

In this 1987 essay Louis J. Budd touches upon all the elements that constitute this section on the reputation of Adventures of Huckleberry Finn—*the ongoing controversy over its depiction of racial themes, its worldwide popularity, its entrance into virtually every level of American culture—at the same time that he examines how the novel has come to be recognized as a "classic."*

The Recomposition of
Adventures of Huckleberry Finn
Louis J. Budd

Ten years ago my title might have been catchy or at least puzzling. These days, anyone who keeps up with the trends in criticism assumes that I will somehow play upon the principle—most commonly associated with Stanley Fish—that the meaning of a text "has no effective existence outside of its realization in the mind of a reader," that each reader creates the text during the process of absorbing the words that an author has strung together. Furthermore, anyone on the cutting edge expects that my own deep content will reveal that a definitive interpretation of *Adventures of Huckleberry Finn* is not defensible, not even for a truly self-analytic critic who constructed it. The recomposition of *Huckleberry Finn* I much more simply propose, however, involves examining some versions held by various constituencies or interpretive communities.

Those constituencies are various indeed. For example, *Reader's Digest* played up the centennial of *Huckleberry Finn*. In turn, its story quoted Charles Kuralt as speaking for "the feelings of millions of the book's admirers" when he declared on TV: "If I had to say as much about America as I possibly could in only two words, I would say these two words: 'Huck Finn.'" Rising beyond provinciality, John Barth recently proclaimed *Huckleberry Finn* one of "the most profound, transcendent literary images the human imagination has ever come up with." A supposedly scientific poll showed that 96% of college faculty now put *Huckleberry Finn* at the very head of the list of reading for entering freshmen, 68% of whom claim to have already done their duty, that is, to have recomposed the novel in their minds—with some large degree of reverence if they had seen, for instance, a feature article in the *Washington Post* of January 1986. After comparing Huck and Elvis Presley as our national "bad boys," it decides that *Huckleberry Finn* is "the greatest work of art by an American, the Sistine Chapel of our civilization." That's a tall

UNCLE SAM: "YOU'VE LEFT ME MANY A PLEASANT HOUR, MARK TWAIN!"

Cartoons that appeared in newspapers following the death of Samuel L. Clemens on 21 April 1910: top, Denver Post, *23 April 1910; bottom,* New York Evening World, *25 April 1910 (Collection of Louis J. Budd)*

order for a story told by a boy who tries to convince the doctor that Tom Sawyer "had a dream and it shot him" in the leg or who thinks that the trick riders in a circus are performing in their "drawers and undershirt."

Obviously there are now many worshipful, sometimes astonishing interpretations of *Huckleberry Finn*.[1] But even with those readers who may take the novel more calmly or humorously, the concept of recomposition can raise a gamut of problems. Least exciting but perhaps the most important in the long run is the problem of a definitively edited text. In 1986 we will get the long awaited, fully documented text of *Huckleberry Finn* from the Mark Twain Project at the University of California in Berkeley. From being able better to follow Twain's revisions, we will then recompose, that is, will read *Huckleberry Finn* more insightfully, in some passages at least. Actually, the more spartan edition that the Mark Twain Library released in 1985 suggests new points for analysis. As a distorted doppelgänger to that text, Charles Neider has persuaded Doubleday to publish his edition that cuts nine thousand words, mainly from the late chapters. Obviously, his constituency—may it never grow into even a lunatic fringe!—will experience a somewhat different novel.

Any complete survey of recomposition must consider the side-effects of the many versions reshaped for movies, television, and the current Broadway musical *Big River*. Presumably the fallout has ended from the comic strip entitled *Tom Sawyer and Huck Finn* that prospered during the 1920s. Far more important, then and now, because they have a kind of official authority are the shortened or simplified editions handed out in some of our secondary schools. I'm too simple-minded to comprehend what needs simplifying in *Huckleberry Finn*. But some folks are quick to decide that they must streamline mental life for the rest of us. If they had got to the Rosetta stone with a chisel and hammer we still might not be able to decipher hieroglyphics. Anybody who looks into the pre-college curriculum will be startled to find out what publishers have done, deliberately as well as carelessly, to the texts of the classic novels.

As a third and still more disturbing kind of recomposition, especially active in recent years, *Huckleberry Finn* has suffered a long though not crowded history of proposed bannings, seldom successful, and of pious bowdlerizing. In 1931, Harper and Brothers published a selective text to serve better the cause of "wholesome happiness for boys and girls." Some members of the PTA's still get uneasy about Huck's contempt for Sunday school, his flair for lying, and his decision to "go to Hell." They can often get their way simply by complaining to the school librarian, who wields more power of censorship through choice of editions than we may realize. Still, we can usually make

Twain's own best weapon—laughter—triumph over such complaints if they make the mistake of fighting in the open.

But the charges of racism, when pressed by PTA-committed moderates in the black community, trouble me deeply. For 1885 *Huckleberry Finn* clearly gave heart to the anti-racists, I would argue anywhere. However, we have marched a good way toward racial equality since then, and the novel now may reinforce, in many touches, attitudes that we would like to overcome completely. But what's to be done? I'm not satisfied by the black publisher whose edition substitutes "slave" for the admittedly overdone use of the word "nigger," which Huck would naturally both hear and write. The crux is really the portrayal of Jim, that is, of his character, emotions, motives, and intelligence, and nobody can fundamentally recompose Jim without pretty much wrecking the novel. In conscience the least that we can do is to resist the idea that because we have enshrined *Huckleberry Finn* as a classic, it just cannot be racist at times. Incidentally, what is the unintended effect of bannings or rewritings? Does such publicity encourage the young to get hold of *Huckleberry Finn* on their own or else to make sure that they get what used to be called the unexpurgated, unabridged version of, say, *Lady Chatterley's Lover*? At least it's clear that all those who hear about a proposed censorship come to the novel with different attitudes than they would have had otherwise.

From a fourth kind of recomposition the problem of Jim will soon get more insistent because the original illustrations by E. W. Kemble will become familiar again. In ten years, I expect, most college editions will carry them. There's a puzzle here for Marshall McLuhan or Father Walter Ong. Why have we ignored the illustrations that were common for later nineteenth-century fiction, especially as serialized in the quality magazines, and that in fact appeared in many a novel up until World War I, when they somewhat bafflingly disappeared? Why are we just as suddenly rediscovering them along with the obvious fact that they conditioned the responses of the readers who saw them? The Kemble illustrations have already made a comeback in the facsimile edition that Harper & Row is tying to its new college anthology of American literature. Likewise, all editions, in boards or paperback, from the Mark Twain Project will reproduce all the original illustrations. As yet, nobody has cared to tangle with the fact that when Twain himself hired Kemble he was actually a broad-stroke cartoonist distant by many degrees of achievement from illustrators like Howard Pyle or Joseph Pennell.

Kemble's drawings will heighten our awareness toward the effect of illustrations by other artists with varying talent and literary taste. Some of the Norman Rockwell set, first published in 1940, have had wide circulation apart from the novel itself; Thomas Hart Benton created another prestigious set in 1942. Recently, a scholar interested in pointing out Rockwell's subtly heavy hand has quoted, in basic agreement, the claim of the Heritage Club that "you will never again think of Mark Twain's book without thinking" of its Rockwell illustrations. Nevertheless, far more influential collectively have been the workaday artists who decorated the scores of editions that have kept multiplying since *Huckleberry Finn* passed out of copyright into the public domain. These drawings, often hired casually by the editor of some reprint house, have had as much influence on the engrossed reader as the movie or television images though—to cloud my argument—one edition of *Huckleberry Finn* used still photographs from the film of 1920. On a different level and in a mood far from Kemble, Barry Moser's woodcuts for the luxurious Pennyroyal edition (1985) will make any reader slow down to ponder them.

A fifth kind of recomposition that mostly baffles me occurs through the translations of *Huckleberry Finn*. As of 1982 a scholar could list translations into at least fifty-three languages of forty-seven countries. Once we get over our national pride we start recognizing that these translations present, to some degree, a different novel. Japanese scholars report that *Huckleberry Finn* was especially hard to recreate before their language was modernized. Even now, we hear that *Huckleberry Finn* carries along three difficult problems on its trans-Pacific flight: 1) how to replicate transculturally a colloquial first-person narration, that is, to give it the correct ease within a literature still not used to such a viewpoint; 2) "how to show the sense of time going slowly like the Mississippi"—a problem I don't even comprehend since I'm more ignorant about Japanese than Twain's Jim is about French; and 3) "how to translate the word 'sivilize' when it starts with an 's'." The dean of Russian translators, using *Huckleberry Finn* as a prime example, argues that it's impossible to transmute the vernacular of one people into that of another and therefore advises against even trying.[2] Startlingly to those of us who treasure Bernard DeVoto's rhapsodies about Huck's language or Henry Nash Smith's analysis of its social thrust, he asserts that Soviet readers are fully enchanted by a version that aims at a colorless style. Foreign-language editions tend toward vivid and domesticated drawings, however, which surely distort how their audiences visualize and therefore react to Twain's characters.

Rather than pursue any of those five kinds of recomposition further I will center on a more fundamental, larger one that has a smaller problem embedded in it. The larger problem is: when, how, and even

why was *Huckleberry Finn* acclaimed as a classic and what effect has this canonization had on the readings of the novel? The smaller problem asks: what was the relationship in 1884–1885 between *The Adventures of Tom Sawyer* and *Adventures of Huckleberry Finn*? This last question primarily concerns not Twain's intentions but the responses of his readership. More specifically, when and how, and to what extent and by whom (that is, holding common readers distinct from professional critics) has *Huckleberry Finn* become separated from the earlier novel and what results has this had for readings of it?

Of course the separation has usually had the purpose of elevating *Huckleberry Finn* above *Tom Sawyer,* and by now most critics imply a hopelessly lower status and even a parasitic future for the earlier novel. But as literary historians we need to understand that *Tom Sawyer* has suffered not only from invidious comparisons by modern critics but from guilt by association now and then, ever since 1885. When the *Springfield Republican* condemned both novels, it really was attacking the new arrival as sweepingly as it could. In 1910 when Arnold Bennett, after praising both novels as "episodically . . . magnificent," then called Twain "always a divine amateur" and thus launched a cliché that would sound intelligent for the next fifty years, he surely had *Huckleberry Finn* more in mind than *Tom Sawyer*.

At the start anyway, in 1885, the pattern was fairly clear.[3] Comparison was natural, inevitable. While reviewers could have groaned, of course, about a falling off, they mostly proclaimed *Huckleberry Finn* better than *Tom Sawyer*. Notice: not of a much brighter magnitude, just better. Twain himself clearly expected his readers to have known about and liked Tom Sawyer. Many reviewers assumed that the new novel was a direct sequel, as signaled by the echoing of titles, the subtitle, and Huck's opening sentence. Consistently, so professional a critic as William Dean Howells, partial both to Twain and to plebeian-democratic values, would discuss the two novels together or else switch between them without quite seeming to notice that he had done so. However, a few critics made the linkage in order to belabor both books, as when the *Springfield Republican* complained that "they are no better in tone than the dime-novels which flood the blood-and-thunder reading population." The verdict of joint "dime-novel sensationalism" was reaffirmed by a textbook as late as 1913. Actually, the point had more substance than we care to learn from today.

Up until Twain's death in 1910, the two books were bracketed much more often than one of them was elevated far beyond the other. The continued linkage had the effect of keeping *Huckleberry Finn* within the genre of the juvenile book, that is, of seeing Huck as an

A display of Mark Twain advertising ephemera, including a box of "Huck Finn" penny caramels (from Sotheby's, The Mark Twain Collection of Nick Karanovich, 19 June 2003)

eternal boy rather than an adolescent who is growing up fast while we watch. Today, most interpretations assume that Huck acquires some adult values beyond Tom's or even crosses over into maturity alone. But I don't mean to segregate the two novels misleadingly. Besides other Twain books, *The Prince and the Pauper* (1882) and *Life on the Mississippi* (1883) arrived between them. Well into the 1920s a few critics perceived some sort of trilogy–based either on the boy's book or the Mississippi Valley. In the latter case these critics encouraged readers to approach *Huckleberry Finn* not as entertainment or palatable didacticism for the young but as genre realism or what we now call social history. After *Pudd'nhead Wilson* arrived, the Mississippi Writings looked still firmer as a unit, and the first Twain volume in the Library of America has lately reinforced that pattern.

Twain's death in 1910, Albert Bigelow Paine's worshipful three-volume biography in 1912, and the diligence of Harper's at pushing its collected editions kept the commentary expanding until it becomes manageable best by a mind that grasps pattern boldly or has a gift for style. Under the charm of eloquent subtlety we can even admire some critic instead of Twain without quite realizing it. Overall, at least through the 1920s, I still perceive more linkage than separation between *Tom Sawyer* and *Huckleberry Finn* though the most sophisticated instances of such criticism did see the later novel as intensifying–not transcending–the finest qualities of its forerunner. Stuart P. Sherman's once-famous chapter in the *Cambridge History of American Literature* (1920) did proclaim an ascent yet still respected the lower range. In his judgment, Twain "wrote his second masterpiece of Mississippi fiction with a desire to express what in *Tom Sawyer* he had hardly attempted." If a different gloss of that passage encourages a charge that I am resisting the facts, let me warn that the contributors to the *Cambridge History* often disagreed as sharply as the football fans at ole state university and the newer "aggie" or "tech" college. The *CHAL* chapter on "Books for Children" bracketed *Tom Sawyer* and *Huckleberry Finn* as "stories of the American boy," equally suspect by some libraries for their "general unimprovingness." Relentlessly the chapter also bracketed Tom and Huck with "the author's third book for young people," *The Prince and the Pauper*.

The future grew clearer throughout the 1920s, especially after Van Wyck Brooks exempted *Huckleberry Finn* from his scathing indictment of Twain's character and writings. But, before turning to the effects on *Huckleberry Finn* of its becoming an adult classic in a category by itself among Twain's books, I should post the warning that the gap between it and *Tom Sawyer* has not grown impassable for everybody. The critics who

address the college-graduate, general readers have continued to mix scenes and ideas from both novels. In 1942 Bernard DeVoto complained about a book "rather violently created" when thirty-seven out of forty-two ballots for the ten leading American novels merged *Tom Sawyer* and *Huckleberry Finn*. Curiously, in a fused analysis the quotations usually dip into Huck's vernacular but the scenes singled out will usually come from *Tom Sawyer*, with the fence-painting episode well in the lead. In fact, it's the only Mark Twain tableau honored with a U.S. postage stamp, in turn modeled on Norman Rockwell's painting.

As a steady, almost unnoticed influence on recomposition, American publishers have continued to find that a joint edition is highly marketable. Any preface or blurb will of course emphasize the reasons for the pairing, and any illustrations will of course use the same boys for both novels. That pattern applies still more firmly to foreign editions.[4] Given the inevitable sequence in any such editions, all but their most independent-minded readers enter *Huckleberry Finn* after *Tom Sawyer* has shaped their sensibilities. Even Norman Mailer, somewhere between the age of eleven and thirteen, followed that sequence and was "disappointed": "The character of Tom Sawyer whom I had liked so much in the first book was altered, and did not seem nice any more." The readers of a combined translation usually prefer *Tom Sawyer*, but such a comparison is unfair because they miss some of Huck's humor, surely. Likewise, the Hollywood versions of *Huckleberry Finn* have usually followed soon after one of *Tom Sawyer* and have continued much of its tone and its aim at a children's audience. The recent, three-part, color film entitled *The Adventures of Tom Sawyer and Huckleberry Finn,* which reportedly scored a big hit on Soviet television, presents Tom and Huck as three or four years younger than American critics would expect. Surprisingly, the four-hour version that ran on PBS stations here in 1986 treats Tom and Huck definitely as boys, not yet clearly adolescent.

Twain himself was glaringly slow to identify *Huckleberry Finn* as his greatest work. Of course, his reasons may be tangential. Writers are reluctant to belittle their other books by identifying one as the isolated summit or a proof that they had peaked early. Furthermore, Twain had notorious conflicts of ambition. Once, confessing to a reporter that his choice wavered, he explained that "it just depends on the mood I'm in." Eventually he groaned at how interviewers kept asking such questions as, "What is your favorite book?" That question was more and more often posed leadingly, with *Huckleberry Finn* expected as the answer, thereby implying that his touch had kept slipping since 1885. One of his neighbors would recall that Twain in 1908 instructed him as a ten-year-old "to be sure to remem-

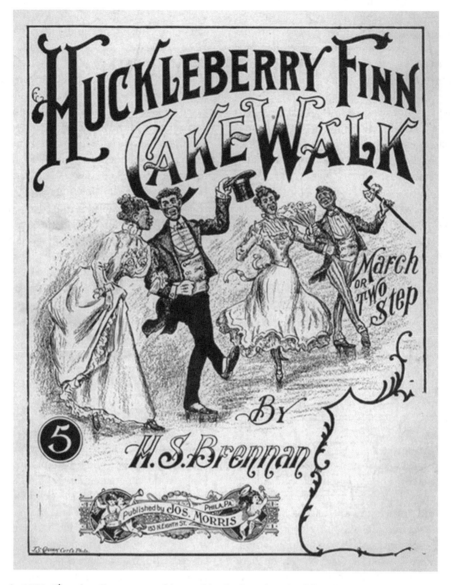

Cover for sheet music, 1900. The cakewalk was a type of dance originating in a plantation-life tradition that sanctioned the slaves' making fun of their masters. In the late nineteenth century the tradition was corrupted by minstrel shows so that the dancers were seen as bumblers (American Sheet Music Archives, Duke University Library).

ber when I was grown up that he had told me himself" that *Personal Recollections of Joan of Arc* was "his best book."

It's easy to imagine a tinge of defeatism in Twain's voice, especially about the candidacy of *Joan of Arc* (1896). For a number of reasons such as the rising tide of immigration and, conversely, the movement of the United States toward world power, the 1890s had brought a new urgency at trying to define the American spirit. Among living writers Twain was soon elevated as its finest exemplar, and among his books *Huckleberry Finn* was increasingly nominated as the long awaited

"great American Novel." Before his death in 1910 he had to recognize that *Huckleberry Finn* was gathering a distinctive aura of acclaim.

In the early 1920s William Lyon Phelps of Yale broke the old praise barrier as the first—so far as I know—to declare that *Huckleberry Finn* "is not only the great American novel. It is America." Perhaps quoting from prefaces for hire is unfair, yet I can't help exhuming Clifton Fadiman's salute in 1940 to Twain as "our Chaucer, our Homer, our Dante, our Virgil" because *Huckleberry Finn* "is the nearest thing we have to a national epic." "Just as the Declaration of Independence

. . . contains in embryo our whole future history as a nation, so the language of *Huckleberry Finn* (another declaration of independence) expresses our popular character, our humor, our slant."

Phelps, conscious of his mission as an apostle of literature, was always more cautious; he had soared to a record altitude only after much encouragement. Still, without polls to back me up, I propose that the decade of full canonization for *Huckleberry Finn* ran from 1932, when Bernard DeVoto published *Mark Twain's America*, to 1942, when he published *Mark Twain at Work*. In 1932 he made a passionate case for its humor, poetry, authenticity, irreverence, and egalitarianism. Then his long essay in *Mark Twain at Work* gave it the dignity both of a complex gestation and of the dark themes needed under emerging criteria to qualify it as a masterpiece.

After World War II, as the American Century finally started according to some, the stature of *Huckleberry Finn* grew self-evident. If a crowning touch was needed, it descended in 1950 from the reigning emperor of taste with T. S. Eliot's introduction for a reprint: "So we come to see Huck himself in the end as one of the permanent symbolic figures of fiction; not unworthy to take a place with Ulysses, Faust, Don Quixote, Hamlet and other great discoveries that man has made about himself." Though Eliot's list of Huck's peers may startle more than it enlightens us, its impact is imposing, even menacing: if you don't grasp *Huckleberry Finn* as a profoundly adult work of literature, then you are a childish, inadequate reader. DeVoto, disdaining such languid phrases as "not unworthy," had boiled with scorn toward dissenters. Also, he threatened them with the suspicion of lacking robustness or else a sense of humor, more grievous sins in his catechism than falling short of high culture. Actually, the very mention of a "classic" or "masterpiece" carries an undertone of intimidation. Fortunately for our self-respect, the most blatant example that I know comes from mainland China. A visiting teacher of American literature describes how her class got "incredibly excited" at a member "for daring to question" Twain's grammar. Persisting, he had to be squelched with; "Comrade! We've been over this! Remember, this is a masterpiece! Mark Twain doesn't make mistakes!"[5]

We now value the novel so keenly as innovative, lyrical, and rebellious that we like to believe that not only the Victorians, early or lingering, failed to appreciate it but so has every generation before our very own. Collectively, we now admire it so much that we take some of the credit for its existence and even feel some reassurance because of it. The lead editorial in the *New York Times* on New Year's day for 1984 tried to exorcise the long-dreaded Age of Orwell by invoking 1884 as "an epochal year for American culture" because it pro-

duced *Huckleberry Finn*. In fact, an impressive range of events celebrated its centennial which, taking advantage of a technicality for dating the first edition, stretched the festivities through both 1984 and 1985.[6]

I had promised to discuss when, how, and why *Huckleberry Finn* attained the status of a classic. Though settling the exact "when" is shaky enough, the "how" is a slippery enterprise because analyzing the levels of audience or the psychology of the marketplace—commercial or academic—has proved rudimentary so far and, in my opinion, will always remain so. Therefore I focus on a single area of the how by arguing that for *Huckleberry Finn* to soar majestically as a classic it first had to be divorced from *Tom Sawyer*. Most crucially, it had to live down its rumored past as a children's book.[7] The most graceful way out that can still honor the facts is to argue that *Huckleberry Finn* belongs to those rare books written for children, like *Alice's Adventures in Wonderland* or *The Hobbit*, that have transcended their genre. That allows a reasonably dignified divorce though we should recognize that *Tom Sawyer*, going strong on the backlist, soon caught up with *Huckleberry Finn* and then stayed ahead during Twain's final years of triumph as an elder statesman, both literary and social. Still, to block any chance of reconciliation, Alfred Kazin, in his much praised *An American Procession* (1984), dishonors the facts in asserting that while "it is impossible to imagine Tom Sawyer as anything but a boy, [a] sassy brat, imagination in America has often indulged itself in the fantasy of Huck Finn grown old."

Another aspect related to or following after "how" reminds me of a get-rich manual entitled "Making Your First Million Is the Hardest." Once a text not only lands within the canon but gets certified as a classic, it plugs into rich sources of energy. It becomes part of a reciprocating process; society uses it for serious rites of passage and also as a marker, a blip on the SAT's, or a shared point of reference and allusion, of images and archetypes. Two summers ago I saw a play of local fame about a counterfeiter who keeps his handcrafted thousand-dollar bills in a copy of *Huckleberry Finn*; we can either explicate that detail or just consider it a touch of what the social psychologists call "bonding conversation." However, an accepted classic also gets woven into the highest culture, into the discourse of the intellectual elite who keep validating their status with each other, and even into the web of intertextuality that modernist writing has increasingly developed. In short, a classic gets institutionalized at all levels of literacy, and its status tends to keep rising, earning those next millions more and more easily.

By now *Huckleberry Finn* has sold about twenty million copies. Of course, a classic can eventually fade away. But, with luck from time and place, it can reach a

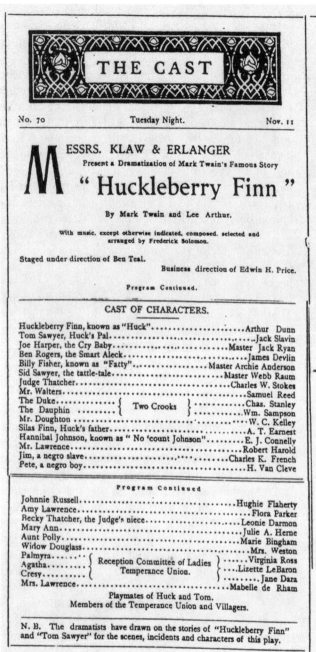

Program for a 1902 musical production loosely based on Twain's novel (Billy Rose Theatre Collection, New York Public Library for the Performing Arts, Astor, Lenox, and Tilden Foundation)

gravity-free orbit above the clinging mass of new attempts to win our attention. Quite simply a classic "has got it made." As for *Huckleberry Finn,* a scholar recently assured the *Los Angeles Times* that it is the "most common American reading experience, except for the Bible." When Twain, heady over his first big triumph, bragged that *The Innocents Abroad* "sells right along just like the Bible," he was almost prophetic. In fact, when

William J. Bennett, as director of the National Endowment for the Humanities, toted up a poll asking which books "all students should read in high school," *Huckleberry Finn* ranked third, right after the Shakespeare tragedies and the founding American documents but ahead of the Bible.[8] These are evidently the four front-runners that change rankings depending on the pollster or else the constituency.

In asking "why" *Huckleberry Finn* did in fact climb toward such company I may sound feeble-minded when the answer is obvious, that is, its merits infused by a genius. But Frank Kermode's brilliant analysis in *The Classic* (1975) demonstrates that, for the typical case, the why is tricky. In discussing the trials that a classic text must pass through, he surprisingly ignores any criteria of profundity and also of formalist perfection. To the contrary, he argues that the text must be loose-jointed enough to allow posterity to slide over the dull or anti-humanistic passages. Few of us find prolonged patches of dullness in *Huckleberry Finn*. But if we dare to run the danger of being called owlish, we start finding holes in Huck's armor as a natural gentleman. To keep the raft supplied he sometimes "lifted a chicken that warn't roosting comfortable, and took him along. Pap always said, take a chicken when you get a chance, because if you don't want him yourself you can easy find somebody that does, and a good deed ain't ever forgot" (chap. 12). "Before daylight," to balance the menu, Huck "borrowed a watermelon, or a mushmelon, or a punkin, or some new corn, or things of that kind." However, Huck and Jim, to ease their consciences, decide not to steal crabapples and persimmons. "We warn't feeling just right, before that, but it was all comfortable now. I was glad the way it come out, too, because crabapples ain't ever good, and the p'simmons wouldn't be ripe for two or three months yet." All that is funny enough, but it won't stand up to serious ethical questioning and it would grate on the owner of those chickens.

If we dare to sound like kneejerk humanitarians, we can likewise find a few breaks in Huck's reputedly endless flow of sympathy. Notice, for instance, how he bullies and even ridicules the younger Wilks girl who has a hare-lip. More important, several social-minded critics have puzzled at how calmly Huck assumes the fact of Jim's death when a steamboat smashes their raft. Huck comes off still worse in the famous passage when he lies to Aunt Sally that his steamboat was delayed by an accident, which "killed a nigger" (chap. 32). We jeer at Aunt Sally, but actually Huck had cast the first stone of racism.

Kermode also argues that the text of a classic must be "naive," that is, it must be generalized enough to allow successive generations to read into it a meaning adapted to their own time or, in effect, to recompose it. Groaning slightly, we can agree that *Huckleberry Finn* meets this criterion. It now holds the position of the most heavily discussed novel in American literature. Among the many hundred articles and the twenty or so entire books or pamphlets devoted to it, the opposing interpretations glare at each other so fiercely that its text starts to look like merely a pretext for our own originality or else pugnaciousness. Justin Kaplan quips that the "lettered classes" have turned it into a "sort of fresh-water *Moby-Dick*."

I don't propose to reserve *Huckleberry Finn* for those who would pay it homage decorously. The quarrels attract still more readers who admire it hugely; for most of them it radiates good spirits, perhaps into a personal or cosmic void. Likewise, its reputation as a classic keeps attracting its share of those mini-Fausts who, like Thomas Wolfe's persona in the stacks of the Harvard Library, choose pell-mell among more books than anybody can find time for. Desperate, some of them become professional students of literature who may get to read *Huckleberry Finn* many times. They then perceive and share among themselves the nuances that no single mind could pick up by itself.

Unfortunately, after absorbing the nuances they may start harping on the flaws, especially because too many critics assume that a classic has somehow laid claim to perfection. I don't mean to sound ungrateful. The intense, quizzical scrutiny sensitizes us to passages that we had overlooked. Several years ago a capable Twainian asked me what Jim means in telling Huck's fortune: "you wants to keep 'way fum de water as much as you kin, en don't run no resk, 'kase it's down in de bills dat you's gwyne to git hung" (chap. 4). Since then I have wondered if that's a portentous touch or a minstrel-show level of joke at Jim's expense. Because I can't decide, I'm tempted, however, to turn querulous toward the text.

To refocus on the point toward which I had started, *Huckleberry Finn* is being read quite differently now than in 1885. More specifically, its achieved status is having enough influence to justify the term "recomposition." In recomposing, however, we may do a much poorer job than Twain. Above all, we may be making *Huckleberry Finn* too solemn. Though Russell Baker proves almost daily that his sense of humor is sharp, he has decided—reacting against the charges that *Huckleberry Finn* can confirm racism in children or adolescents—that readers must reach the age of thirty-five before they are mature enough for it and, besides, must have qualified themselves by a spread of experiences. One learned critic has concluded that it is "certainly a very sad book."

Comedy, to be sure, is more idiosyncratic than tragedy and entails a cruel paradox: the harder we try to explain or just insist on humor, the sillier we look. So I am embarrassed to confess uncertainty whether T. S. Eliot, in his elderly reverence toward *Huckleberry Finn*, misses a joke or else disposes others to do so. Huck, in itemizing the haul from an abandoned shanty, rounds off with: ". . . just as we was leaving I found a tolerable good curry-comb, and Jim he found a ratty old fiddle-bow, and a wooden leg. The straps was broke off of it, but barring that, it was a good enough leg, though it was too long for me and not long enough for Jim, and we couldn't find the other one, though we hunted all around." Eliot judges that the "grim precision" about the contents of the shanty and "especially the wooden leg, and the fruitless search for its mate . . . reminds us at the right moment of the kinship of mind and the sympathy between the boy outcast from society and the negro fugitive from the injustice of society."[9] Eliot reminds me in turn of the anecdote about the man who complained that it had been hard not to laugh right out loud during Twain's lecture in the basement of a church. The thickening dignity of *Huckleberry Finn* has dampened our reactions. We are afraid that by enjoying Jim's prophecy of Huck's fate as a jagged non-sequitur we will overlook a multiple warhead of profundities; we start rummaging for the symbolisms of that matching wooden leg. Underneath such worries hides the assumption that tragedy is far superior to comedy. To the extent that we want to venerate *Huckleberry Finn* as a tragedy, we have to start bending the text to project Huck as a rounded character rather than a chain of often inconsistent though handy attitudes.

Another worrisome way in which prestige as a classic shapes our reading is that we assume that *Huckleberry Finn* needs to be restated abstractly because the "discovery of meaning is the goal of the critical enterprise," because first-rate criticism is "synonymous with interpretation." Furthermore, that interpretation operates from supposedly self-evident principles. "The first requirement of a work of art in the twentieth century is that it should do nothing" and especially that it must avoid serving any social purpose. Some critics now hold that literature must be cut off from common experience in order to save it. Such a surgical strike is deadly to Twain, who interacted with his audiences much more intimately, in fact more physically than the high-culture authors in his time or today; from his apprenticeship onward, he stayed alert to responses as conditioned by and conditioning the daily life of his readers. Any distancing through abstractions does greatest harm of all to the stunningly vivid, concrete world of *Huckleberry Finn.* When we elevate its values above gritty place and time we are trying to "sivilize" Huck as mechanically as Miss Watson did and are muffling its post-bellum topicalities as well as its continuing impact on socio-cultural discourse.

More basically, by making *Huckleberry Finn* an official masterpiece we may have turned the book against its best qualities. It once challenged—and then, by forcing its way in, changed—the canon of American literature. By doing so it undermined the authority of canon-making itself, the designating of a

---

"Questionable Companionship" Mark Twain Responds to Being Banned in Brooklyn

Adventures of Huckleberry Finn and The Adventures of Tom Sawyer were removed from the Children's Department of the Brooklyn Public Library in 1905 by the supervisor of the department, whom fellow librarian Asa Don Dickinson described as "a conscientous and enthusiastic young woman." Dickinson, who did not support the ban, wrote to Mark Twain requesting "a word or two to say in witness" of Huck's good character. He received the following reply, dated 21 November 1905.

Dear Sir:

I am greatly troubled by what you say. I wrote Tom Sawyer and Huck Finn for adults exclusively, and it always distresses me when I find that boys and girls have been allowed access to them. The mind that becomes soiled in youth can never again be washed clean; I know this by my own experience, and to this day I cherish an unappeasable bitterness against the unfaithful guardians of my young life, who not only permitted but compelled me to read an unexpurgated Bible through before I was 15 years old. None can do that and ever draw a clean, sweet breath again this side of the grave. Ask that young lady—she will tell you so.

Most honestly do I wish that I could say a softening word or two in defense of Huck's character, since you wish it, but really in my opinion it is no better than those of Solomon, David, Satan, and the rest of the sacred brotherhood.

If there is an unexpurgated biblein the Children's Department, won't you please help that young woman remove Huck and Tom from that questionable companionship?

Sincerely yours,
S. L. Clemens.

I shall not show your letter to any one—it is safe with me.

—Mark Twain's Autobiography, edited by Albert
Bigelow Paine (New York & London:
Harpers, 1924), v. 2, pp. 335–336

Dickinson read the letter to the head of the Children's Department and it was discussed among the librarians, but the books were not returned to the department, though they remained available in the library's main shelves. News of the limited banning of the books and rumors about Twain's letter reached newspaper reporters in the months that followed.

---

set of classic texts. A decade after *Huckleberry Finn* was published, Thorstein Veblen argued that the academics' insistence on the idea of classics laid out merely another path of wasteful, conspicuous consumption for the leisure class. Within the last decade of our times, analysis of canon-building, which makes the classic its keystone, has grown much grimmer. We now have to consider seriously the argument that the officially sanctioned, elite culture functions as one of the ways by which the economically and politically dominant maintain their power through peaceful assent from the populace rather than naked coercion. Though I cannot read Twain as quasi-Marxist I can insist that *Huckleberry Finn* should stick as a bone in the throat to dull conservatism.

At times anyway, such as in *Huckleberry Finn,* Twain was subversive toward peaceful, unexamined assent. Later he insisted that he had learned long ago to question any consensus: "I tremble and the goose-flesh rises on my skin every time I encounter one . . . ten to one there's a trap under that thing somewhere." A consensus may deny more truth than it affirms. As Barbara Herrnstein Smith warns regarding classics, "when the value of a work is seen as unquestionable," then "humanistic scholars and academic critics" tend to "'save the text' by transferring the locus of its interest to more formal or structural features and/or allegorizing its potentially alienating ideology to some more general ('universal') level where it becomes more tolerable and also more readily interpretable in terms of contemporary ideologies."[10] To state her point bluntly, a classic tends to get co-opted, to get neutered. Furthermore, if we keep insisting that a text is a classic, we encourage this suspicion that it cannot attract readers entirely on its own.

To its peril, *Huckleberry Finn* is now absorbed into the canon, which once again looks solidly fixed to the young or to the instinctively reverential. Ironically, Twain's break-in has made the canon more attractive and therefore more defensible against the new heretics who always prowl outside the temple. Compounding the irony, science fiction is trying to get respect from departments of English these days, and there's an overstated drive to certify Twain as one of its founders. However, that drive could instead lower his standing among those academics who want to keep sci-fi in the outer darkness, which sci-fi reminds us is really out there.

I don't want to end with my eyes fixed on outer space, cosmic or intellectual. Close to home, I am worried about keeping the undergraduate major in literature a vibrant and challenging yet sometimes immediately pleasurable experience. Specifically, I worry that the canonical recomposition of *Huckleberry Finn* will make new readers approach it too cautiously, even timidly, contrary to Twain's predominant mood, which could joke that "I am glad that the

old masters [of painting] are all dead, and I only wish they had died sooner," which could say that "a very good library may be started just by leaving" Jane Austen's novels out of it, which would "rather be damned to John Bunyan's heaven" than read Henry James's *Bostonians,* which could have Huck in a "sweat to find out all about" Moses until he hears that Moses "had been dead a considerable long time; so then I didn't care no more about him; because I don't take no stock in dead people."

Professional insistence that some text is a classic may not be so much intimidating as simply dispiriting. Norman Mailer believes that "secretly we expect less reward" from a classic than from a "good contemporary novel." Maybe that's why he waited almost fifty years before reading *Huckleberry Finn* again, until he was paid to do so. Of course, Mailer is one of a kind and can't be used to prove Frank Kermode's observation that "it is only when we see some intelligent non-professional confronted by a critical essay from our side of the fence that we see how esoteric we are."[11] Since Kermode feels "moderate rejoicing" because criticism has grown into a formidable expertise, he qualifies as a friendly spokesman for the idea that we academics "have to think of ourselves as exponents of various kinds of secondary interpretation—spiritial understandings, as it were, compared with carnal, and available only to those who, in second-century terms, have circumcised ears, that is, are trained by us."

I don't mean to pose an either-or choice or, much less, to fan the anti-intellectualism that has been getting warm again, lately. But I hope that readers will always feel free to approach, to recompose *Huckleberry Finn* for themselves with the freshness and zest promised by a small California newspaper in 1885:

> The adventures of "Huckleberry Finn". . . will amuse and interest you, where other books prove insipid. . . . Mark Twain is certainly in his element; for this book, while intensely interesting as a narrative—holding the reader's attention with a tenacity that admits of no economy in the midnight oil—is also at the top of the list as a humorous work. Interwoven in its text are side-splitting stories, sly hints at different weaknesses of society, and adventures of the most humorous description.[12]

How many critics have done much better since then in less than a hundred words?

Still, with or without their help and whether or not the future will recompose the novel to their satisfaction, *Huckleberry Finn* will continue to contradict Twain's own definition of a classic as a book that everybody praises and nobody reads.

—The Missouri Review, 10, no. 1 (1987): 113–129

1. To document this essay closely would pile up the citations, as can be seen from Thomas A. Tenney's definitive "An Annotated Checklist of Criticism on *Adventures of Huckleberry Finn, 1884–1984*," in *Huck Finn among the Critics: A Centennial Selection,* ed. M. Thomas Inge (Frederick, Md.: University Publications of America, 1985). That volume also contains an excellent sampling of criticism, old and new. The diversity of current approaches appears fully in *One Hundred Years of "Huckleberry Finn": The Boy, His Book and American Culture,* ed. Robert Sattelmeyer and J. Donald Crowley (Columbia: Univ. of Missouri Press, 1985).

2. *The Art of Translation: Kornei Chukovsky's "A High Art,"* trans. and ed. Lauren G. Leighton (Knoxville: Univ. of Tennessee Press, 1984), 126–29. Jan B. Gordon's essay in *One Hundred Years of "Huckleberry Finn"* analyzes the problems not of language but of underlying mores for Japanese readers.

3. See the precise, impressive study by Victor Fischer, "*Huck Finn* Reviewed: The Reception of *Huckleberry Finn* in the United States, 1885–1897," *American Literary Realism, 1870–1910,* 16 (1983), 1–57. My introduction for *New Essays on "Adventures of Huckleberry Finn"* (Cambridge Univ. Press, 1985) tries to survey its critical history up to the present.

4. Alexei Zverev, "Mark Twain / Why We Love Him, Too," *Soviet Life,* No. 11 (350), November 1985, 63, asserts that "these two best-known of Mark Twain's books have merged into one for the contemporary Soviet reader."

5. Marilyn Krysl, "Under the Jade Vault: Lei Feng Salutes Mark Twain," *Journal of Higher Education,* 55 (1984), 556–57. Actually, it's not clear to me which passage in the Tom-Huck novels is being discussed.

6. I try to record the highlights and the most typical comments in "How Old Is Huck Finn?" in *Dictionary of Literary Biography Yearbook 1985,* ed. Jean Ross (Detroit: Gale, 1986).

7. In "*Huck Finn*'s First Century: A Bibliographical Survey," *American Studies International,* 22, ii (1984), 90, Carl Dolmetsch concludes that "before the 1940s, *Huck Finn*'s well-established popularity was principally as a book for children, like *Tom Sawyer,* with the result that most readers came to it too early to see more than its adventure-story surface." In *One Hundred Years of "Huckleberry Finn"* see pp. 166–67 of Alan Gribben's insightful essay on the shared "boy-book elements."

8. See *Washington Post,* 12 August 1984, A12. However, the "church-state issue" evidently handicapped the Bible.

9. "Introduction," *Adventures of Huckleberry Finn* (New York: Cresset, 1950).

10. "Contingencies of Value," *Critical Inquiry,* 10 (1983), 28–30.

11. "Institutional Control of Interpretation," in *The Salmagundi Reader,* eds. Robert Boyers and Peggy Boyers (Bloomington: Indiana Univ. Press, 1983), 364.

12. *Napa Register,* 8 May 1885. I thank Victor Fischer (of the Mark Twain Project) for sharing this item with me. Though plagiarized from a promotional flyer for the novel, it ran as a review.

Literary Legacy

This essay examines the influence of Mark Twain and his most memorable creation upon popular and literary culture.

Huckleberry Finn's Heirs
Tom Quirk

I

When one takes up the question of the legacy of Mark Twain and more particularly that of *Huckleberry Finn,* one takes up a question of American literary and cultural history. As Louis J. Budd has so compellingly shown, "Mark Twain" is a cultural property in whom Samuel Clemens invested much of his creative energy, an image whose manufacture and marketing he carefully monitored. That image has since gone the way of most slickly advertised commodities and has lost much of its aggressive force; if its fire has dimmed, however, its glow remains perhaps too comfortably available to us.[1] Despite the legion of Twain scholars devoted to amassing, interpreting, and consolidating the ever growing store of information about Twain and his work, one senses that he has become a self-perpetuating institution whose interest and vitality depend very little upon scholarly or critical opinion. Even if the American public were suddenly to become as ignorant and illiterate as so many of his fictional creations it has one way or another come to know and embrace, even if a multitude of scholars and critics were to close the shop and go fishing, even if politicians were to cease quoting and misquoting him, the living legacy that is "Mark Twain" (by no means the least interesting of Clemens's imaginative creations) would continue to function in its haphazard but persistent and palpable way.

This is an inquiry into a literary bequest, and I shall at length explore the relations three writers in particular (Ring Lardner, Willa Cather, and Langston Hughes) bear to Twain and especially to the achievement of *Huckleberry Finn.* The examples of these three do not begin to indicate the possibilities or the existing realities of an imaginative inheritance, nor are they the most obvious choices one ought to make if the concern is with being convincing rather than suggestive. But, together, these very different writers do exemplify both the variable richness and, at least in the case of Lardner, the particular burdens of the patrimony of Huckleberry Finn. These same literary relations are separable from the institution that has become "Mark Twain," of course, but the full extent of Twain's literary influence or the larger significance of his place within our culture cannot be fully comprehended without first acknowledging, even in a superficial way, how completely he has entered and helped to define the popular American

Cover for sheet music of a popular novelty song, 1917 (American Sheet Music Archives, Duke University Library)

point of view. For, unlike other American authors, it is simply not the case that Mark Twain is merely an academic specialty. Like it or not, Twain criticism must take into account and to a degree respond to popular reception and understanding. Whether the general public has "got Twain right" is finally beside the point. Because Mark Twain is an American institution, the public will always have a say in how he is to be understood. Scholars or critics who remain indifferent to popular belief about the man or his work will have missed much that is significant in their subject. And if their methods or vocabulary are persistently arcane or obscure, the response of the common reader, sooner or later, will serve as tonic corrective to the indulgence.

Mark Twain is "ours" by virtue of a participation in a social community that forges and forever modifies a consensual view of all its institutions. Mark Twain and Huck Finn are not to be found in archives and libraries alone. I have myself cashed a check at the Mark Twain Bank. I have visited the Tom Sawyer Youth League, on whose field Huck Finn Little League teams sometimes play. I have traveled through the Mark Twain Forest and, in another state, driven on the Clemens Center Parkway. I have passed a real estate company called Mark Twain Properties, and Mark Twain Country Antiques, Mark Twain Travel Agency, Mark Twain Motor Inn, and the Huck Finn Motel. I have declined the opportunity to have a Becky

Thatcher burger, but I have played eighteen holes on the Mark Twain Community Golf Course and know firsthand why Twain thought golf "is a good walk spoiled."

All this is by way of saying that the literary portion of Twain's bequest is something of a codicil, as is appropriate to a man whose life was comprised of a string of apprenticeships and varying occupations but who, to his own surprise, found one day that he had become a "literary person." The strangely independent life of Mark Twain as a cultural icon is nevertheless founded upon his historical profession as an American author. And when one attempts to implicate this same literary person in American literary history, the difficulty is not how to place Mark Twain, but *which* Twain to take up. Twain, as author, personality, and institution, has been divided and subdivided. For all the divisions, however, he mysteriously remains an unfracturable imaginative presence in modern life.

At least since Van Wyck Brooks's *The Ordeal of Mark Twain* it has been fashionable to parcel Twain out, to discover tensions and conflicts in the rich and problematic personality that struck so many contradictory poses: he is a thwarted artist somehow victimized both by his own Western origins and the oppressiveness of Victorian America; he is a man divided against himself, whose dual identity is represented by his given name and his adopted persona; he is both socially constructed and psychically bedeviled. He has been expurgated and emulated, sanitized and bastardized, banned and exalted. And, of course, he has been anthologized. One need only enumerate a few of the titles to indicate how variously available he is to us: *The Family Mark Twain, The Hidden Mark Twain, The Comic Mark Twain Reader, The Birds and Beasts of Mark Twain, Mark Twain: Wit and Wisecracks, A Treasury of Mark Twain, A Pen Warmed Up in Hell.* Doubtless some version of Twain is represented in every American household that keeps books at all. Yet some other portion is likely forbidden entrance.[2]

Scholars and critics have followed him abroad and into his household. They have contemplated his relation to the South, the North, the East, and the West; his relation to his friends and to his relations, to Susy and Orion and Livy and W. D. Howells. They have considered his opinions (and he was a man of inexhaustible opinion) on law, liquor, race, religion, women, history, animals, technology, colonialism, dreams; on the English, the French, the Boers, and, the Germans (and, of course, their dreaded language); on Shelley, Scott, Cooper, and Mary Baker Eddy. And they have "placed" him in the literary tradition. Most notably, of course, there is the Mark Twain who serves as the chief exponent of the southwest humor tradition, whose place within and contribution to that same tradition

have been exhaustively traced by Walter Blair and others.[3] But there are other Mark Twains: the science fiction writer, the fabulist, the moral philosopher, the dramatist, the satirist, the critic, the lecturer, the prophet and the buffoon, the sage and the literary comedian, the fictionist and the metafictionist.

The literary influence of Twain has developed along manifold lines, prompted varying expressions and forms, and naturally led to different conclusions. One strand of this influence is evident in the straightforward continuation of the adventures of Huck and Tom. Clement Wood's *More Adventures of Huckleberry Finn,* John Seelye's critical and fictional rendering of *The True Adventures of Huckleberry Finn,* Greg Matthews's *The Further Adventures of Huckleberry Finn,* not to mention Twain's own disappointing attempts to extend the exploits of Huck and Tom in *Tom Sawyer, Detective, Tom Sawyer Abroad,* and *Huck Finn and Tom Sawyer among the Indians,* all these are deliberate sequels and self-conscious extensions of that inheritance.

The technical virtuosity of *Huckleberry Finn* that has become an available resource for other writers marks out another track of Twain's influence. Moreover, the appropriation of Twain's techniques and the detectable thematic similarities between that book and later American writing have in turn become a means to create and understand a portion of American literary history. For such history is made of linkages and affiliations, and in the case of *Huckleberry Finn,* one has a book that other writers have gone to school on; or, as T. S. Eliot put it, Twain discovered in that novel a "new way of writing," valid not only for himself but also for others.[4] The claim may be extravagant. Still, it is difficult to imagine how *To Kill a Mockingbird, Adventures of Augie March, Winesburg, Ohio* or *One Flew Over the Cuckoo's Nest* could have come to be, or at least to have taken quite the same form, had not their creators had the example of *Huckleberry Finn* to draw upon. One may trace a lineage, various as these texts may be, from *Huckleberry Finn* through, say, Sherwood Anderson's "I Want to Know Why" to Faulkner's "The Bear" to Salinger's *Catcher in the Rye* and, finally, to Robert Gover's *The $100 Misunderstanding.* The result is a thematic and stylistic continuity that may or may not pass as a specimen of literary history.

And of course, one may work backward as well. One of the several ironies of the legacy of *Huckleberry Finn* is that a novel which so amusingly calls into question notions of "style" and reverence for received opinion has itself become an aesthetic criterion that may be applied retroactively. Herman Melville's *Redburn,* though it is sometimes forgotten, is narrated by a mere boy, about fifteen years old. As effective as this young narrator's response to a multitude of evils on board the

Highlander or to the pervasive squalor of Liverpool is, one cannot quite help wondering how Huck might have described them. How wide, one is tempted to ask, might the readership of the *Biglow Papers* be today, had Lowell subtracted from his narrative voices both Hosea Biglow and Homer Wilbur and confined himself to the perspective of Birdofredom Sawin? Nor can one help contemplating the very different effects—the pathos, the moral indictment—Rebecca Harding Davis's "Life in the Iron Mills" might have achieved had the Welsh puddler Hugh Wolfe told his own story. Instead, the raw artistic impulse and half-articulate understanding of the world of the ironworker is symbolized in the crude figure in korl rather than embedded and disclosed in the narrative voice itself.

Since the publication of *Huckleberry Finn,* in some fashion, both figurative and real, modern American writers have often enough recognized a kinship between themselves and the boy who modestly sought to tell his own story plainly and directly but who spoke out of a well of ignorance of literary observance and accepted tradition so profound that it amounts to a form of rebellion. And far from suffering from some anxiety of influence, American writers have been rather more anxious than otherwise to claim some portion of the patrimony. For Mark Twain, whatever else he may have offered them, supplied American authors with an image of the author as American.

That image is kaleidoscopically shifty, of course. Even Twain's representation of himself in his *Autobiography* is problematic, and a spate of biographers has attempted to decipher the enigmatic personality with whom we nevertheless confidently claim some acquaintance and intimacy. The several lives of Mark Twain mapped by biographers, fully documented and painstakingly constructed, may seem queer impersonations compared with the Twain that has entered into the public imagination by largely precritical routes. Twain himself, at any rate, banked on the appreciation of what he called his "submerged clientele" and made his direct appeal to the popular mind.

The appearance of familiarity (the seeming democratic availability of the man), combined with fond recollection of the part his imagination of childhood played in many of our own young lives, has helped along the living institution that goes by the same name. However much Samuel Clemens promoted and protected during his lifetime the "Mark Twain" label (itself a registered trademark), after his death the myth has appeared miraculously immune to correction and revision; or rather, the revisions are absorbed into an inviolable and ever larger image that accepts the rebukes and contradictions without pause or diminishment. Mark Twain

the institution has acquired increasing momentum in part by the sheer attention it has received and in part by those instruments and individuals that have propelled it forward.

II

One of the most remarkable forums for sustaining and to a degree sanitizing the popular image of Mark Twain that Sam Clemens had invented was the publication of the *Mark Twain Journal* (originally the *Mark Twain Quarterly*). First published in 1936, this journal was to serve as the official publication of the International Mark Twain Society and originated from Webster Groves, Missouri. Though the journal was not exclusively devoted to Mark Twain, its editor, Cyril Clemens, frequently solicited and received endorsements, testimonials, and reminiscences about Mark Twain and his work from every quarter of the globe, from presidents, prime ministers, and potentates, along with appreciative remarks from lesser mortals. The statements were often published in the journal, usually on the front cover. Taken together, whatever their substance, the net effect is of a catalog of what Emmeline Grangerford called "tributes."

The *Mark Twain Journal* did much to consolidate and legitimize the idea that Mark Twain is an indispensable part of American culture, and as if to clinch the point, Cyril Clemens obtained statements from every president from FDR to Richard Nixon, each testifying to an immense admiration of him. For our purposes, however, the most interesting and valuable service Cyril Clemens performed was to extract a multitude of testimonials from important professional writers, several of which were published in his journal. Surely, Mark Twain is the American author most commented upon by other writers. It was in a letter to Cyril Clemens that Willa Cather recalled that she had read *Huckleberry Finn* twenty times; George Bernard Shaw admitted that Mark Twain paved the way for his caustic wit; James Barrie, Edwin Markham, W. B. Yeats, Langston Hughes, and T. S. Eliot confessed to their genuine admiration of him, though for rather different reasons.

In a letter to Clemens, F. Scott Fitzgerald wrote his interesting assessment of *Huckleberry Finn:*

> Huckleberry Finn took the first journey *back*. He was the first to look *back* at the republic from the perspective of the west. His eyes were the first eyes that ever looked at us objectively that were not eyes from overseas. There were mountains at the frontier but he wanted more than mountains to look at with his restless eyes. . . . He wanted to find out about men and how they lived together. And because he turned back we have him forever.[5]

Poster for the Russian release of the silent movie produced by Paramount in 1920
(*from* The Annotated Huckleberry Finn [*New York: Norton, 2001,*
Richland County Public Library])

Less familiar is Gertrude Stein's note of appreciation: "Mark Twain, who is as deep and as broad as the Mississippi River and the Mississippi river [sic] is as deep and as broad as a river possibly could be which makes Mark Twain the pleasantest and the most wonderful thing he did and the Mississippi ever might try."[6] Here was a tribute fully in keeping with the populist identity of the journal and worthy of the boast of a Mike Fink—sired by the Missouri hills and dam'd by the Mississippi River, in his turn, Mark Twain created the River itself and made it a common possession.

These and other witnessings for the genius of Twain and, most particularly, for *Adventures of Huckleberry Finn* belong in the company of those testimonials made by American writers but published elsewhere, and, together, they verify a sense of a profound literary inheritance. Yet what, precisely, that inheritance was, and is, remains indefinite. It would have amused Twain himself that he is often considered a locus and a lens through which we may define literary tradition. For T. S. Eliot the novel was a rarity, and its author ranked with those most un-American writers, Dryden and Swift, as

one who had rejuvenated the language, brought it up-to-date and thereby "purified" the dialect of the tribe. For Faulkner and his generation, Anderson and Dreiser were the literary fathers, but Twain was the father of them all, and *Huckleberry Finn* was his best book.[7] As a rule, it seems, American writers were rather anxious to claim a kinship with the orphan boy that the upright citizens from St. Petersburg to Concord had rejected.

Ernest Hemingway's estimate of the novel has become the most memorable and most often cited appraisal, however: "All modern American literature comes from one book by Mark Twain called *Huckleberry Finn*. If you read it you must stop where Nigger Jim is stolen from the boys. That is the real end. The rest is just cheating. But it's the best book we've had. All American writing comes from that. There was nothing before. There has been nothing as good since."[8] Perhaps I am eccentric in detecting something oddly self-serving about the praise. Hemingway's famous remarks are a cluster of unrestrained superlatives grossly exaggerated, excessive to the point of fawning bad taste, so grandiosely authoritative as to be fatuous. They are a curious, even surreal, blend of the traditionary and the ahistorical: "All American literature comes from one book etc."; it is the "best book we've had etc."; "There was nothing before. There has been nothing as good since."

It is not that Hemingway claims too much, but that he claims more than we can comprehend. *Huckleberry Finn,* he would have us believe, is one bright explosive moment in our literary history—before, was blind groping, the American imagination enslaved to inauthentic, because un-American, custom; after, a falling off and inevitable disappointment and diminishment. He restricts the inestimable glory of Mark Twain to one novel, and yet, he also advises that we do not finish the book, that a full quarter of it is "just cheating."

There is something canny about Hemingway's estimation, however sincere the sentiment. For, in effect, he has taken Twain out of the game altogether. Hawthorne and Melville, Emerson and Thoreau, Dickinson and Whitman (and, after all, it is books, not novels, writing, not fiction, that Hemingway is talking about) become naughts; the Mark Twain of *Huckleberry Finn* becomes an infinite. What remains, is . . . well, Hemingway perhaps. Still, there is something profoundly accurate about the remark as well. *Adventures of Huckleberry Finn* is not merely the object of scrutiny and interpretation; it has become the means by which we measure and come to understand much of American writing. Hemingway's appropriation and refinement of the example of that novel is well known, yet it may be that the example he himself supplies blinds us to other features of Twain's legacy.

Such at least was the opinion of Ralph Ellison who, in "Twentieth-Century Fiction and the Black Mask of Humanity," observed that Huck's decision to help Jim to freedom (a decision that marks him as wicked and condemned to hell) represents Twain's full acceptance of his own responsibility in the existing social order and condition. This, says Ellison, is the "tragic face" behind the comic mask of Huckleberry Finn. This is also what, in his estimation, has largely disappeared in the work of modern American writers. In the case of Hemingway, the writer appropriated Twain's technical innovations but missed or declined the moral vision the technique was meant to dramatize.[9] The consequences, not just for Hemingway but for American literature, are significant: "Thus what for Twain was a means to a moral end became for Hemingway an end in itself. And just as the trend toward technique for the sake of technique and production for the sake of the market lead to the neglect of the human need out of which they spring, so do they lead in litera-

ture to a marvelous technical virtuosity won at the expense of a gross insensitivity to fraternal values."[10]

Clearly, the acceptance of this responsibility in the case of a man like Twain, who tended to suffer from guilty feelings over events he could not possibly control and whose imagination often exceeded his deliberate purpose, is a complicated one. Nevertheless, Ellison's insight into the social responsibility of the novelist has its inexact parallels in Twain's inner life, and it points to a significant feature of his imaginative presence in our own time. To appropriate the narrative device of telling a story from the point of view of someone who does not fully comprehend the humor of his expression or the gravity of his experience, but who is nonetheless able to suggest some indefinite dis-ease about that world, opens up innumerable possibilities for the novelist. But, finally, the force of those narratives depends less upon technique than upon the capacity to fully imagine the life and inherent dignity of another. This is but another way of saying what James M. Cox has already said: "If the 'incorrect' vernacular of *Huckleberry Finn* is to be more than decor, it must enact an equally 'incorrect' vision. Otherwise, the style becomes merely a way of saying rather than a way of being."[11]

Fully half the achievement of *Huckleberry Finn* lies, I believe, in Twain's remarkable and quite momentary ability to so completely identify himself with Huck's interior life that he was able to give that figure voice, often at the expense of his own conscious literary intentions. What is submerged beneath the vernacular observations of this outcast boy is not solely an adult satire or the private complaints and disenchantments of the author. Nor is the novel merely imaginative indulgence in the freedoms and freshness of childhood. In addition, there is the fully felt complicity in the social and emotional condition of his created characters.

In modern fiction, often the same narrative technique masks the author's felt presence and achieves what we have come to admire as aesthetic detachment. By contrast, what is remarkable about *Huckleberry Finn* is that Twain so committed himself to the lifeworld of his young outcast and, later, his black companion. It is true that Twain's disguised grievances and yearnings are imbedded in the narrative as well. What is also masked, however, is a sense of his own implication and guilt in the prevailing hurt and tyranny that is the social world of the novel. Twain's creative impulses no doubt began in the simple desire to escape the cares of the adult world, but life along the Mississippi became a recalcitrant world of its own that was not to be displaced by the figures of the imagination or sheer technical skill. Perhaps the severest test of the realist writer lies not so much in looking on life directly but in taking the risk that life as it is imaginatively depicted may return the gaze and make it known that it has formed its own independent measurements and judgments of the author. Eventually, when Twain's creation stood as accusation and plea to the creator, he did not retreat from the responsibility.

My point here is that there is some evidence to suggest not only that Ellison is perhaps right about the course of American fiction and the too easy forfeiture of an acute moral vision, but also that Twain reveals poignantly and by snatches the subconscious costs such responsibility may exact and the pain and courage it may require to disclose, even covertly, a personal stake in the prevailing social ethos of the country.[12] There is a further point implicit in Ellison's observation and one, perhaps, worth developing. It is unimaginable, not to say intolerable, to divorce the literary manner of, say, Dr. Johnson, or Voltaire, from his literary matter. Their style and moral vision are inseparably fused. Not so, it seems, with Mark Twain.

III

Quite apart from the liability that the reader may dismiss the serious intent of comedy, a risk that any humorist runs, Twain's technical achievements and improvisations in *Huckleberry Finn* are also and all too easily detachable from what Howells described as the strong tide of moral earnestness in the man, and from the creative energy that gave birth to this new way of writing. By way of illustration, we might linger over the example of Ring Lardner; for in him we have a figure whose talents invited comparisons with Twain, but whose achievements, though considerable, failed (as Ellison says Hemingway failed) to take full advantage of a rich double legacy.

Ernest Hemingway no doubt detected in Huck's account of his experiences the submerged hurt and confusion of a boy who had witnessed far more than he could articulate or even cared to remember, but who naively disclosed a portion of a sensibility from which the rest could clearly be inferred and felt. It remained for Hemingway in his own work to convey, often brilliantly, a precarious sense of woundedness and conflict that owes something to Twain's example. In Sherwood Anderson, too, one can sense an allegiance to a path marked out by *Huckleberry Finn,* his favorite book by his favorite author. Often Anderson's masterly evocations are of events witnessed or overheard precisely at a time when the narrating mind vaguely realized that they were important, but whose subsequent telling is nagged into existence by the very perplexity they have since engendered. These storyteller's stories are powerful because they render the effort to comprehend something the reader understands all the more forcefully by the pained artlessness of the narration. However, his

narrators' recollections often soften into mere regret (as in "The Triumph of the Egg") or lament (as in "I'm a Fool"). Sometimes they reveal a dark and half-mystical naturalism (as in "A Death in the Woods"). Anderson's absurdities frequently serve not so much as comic correctives as they diagnose pathologies or picture for the reader the disturbingly blighted lives of what Anderson called "grotesques."

Hemingway and Anderson freely acknowledged their debts to Twain, but in the early years of the century it was Ring Lardner who was, in many minds, the heir apparent to the author of *Huckleberry Finn.* In 1924, Edmund Wilson asked, "Will Ring Lardner, then, go on to his *Huckleberry Finn* or has he already told all he knows?" One never knows, he concedes, but Lardner benefits from Twain's same freedom of view and approaches his fictions with a "perceptive interest in human beings instead of with a naturalist's formula." For Sherwood Anderson, in 1919, Lardner was a "word fellow, one who cares about the words of our American speech and who is perhaps doing more than any other American to give new force to the words of our everyday life." But his artistic devotion might also conceal some secret hurt that he carried within him, some "shy hungry child" that did not risk exposure. This covering up is forgivable if "he is really using his talent for sympathetic understanding of life, if in secret he is being another Mark Twain and working in secret on his own *Huckleberry Finn.*" At any rate, for Anderson, not even Twain had a "more sensitive understanding of the fellow in the street, in the hooch joint, the ball-park, and the city suburb." And in 1924, H. L. Mencken also invited comparison with Twain, but he worried that Lardner would be lost to contemporary neglect, that his special vernacular talents would sink beneath the weight of their own particularity of reference. In other words, Mencken feared that Lardner's greatest ally, American speech itself, would move on its own devious course and leave Lardner's vernacular trapped in a linguistic past beyond retrieval by later generations.[13]

In the 1920s the comparisons to Twain were probably justified, but Lardner had already refused them. "I wouldn't consider Mark Twain our greatest humorist," he told an interviewer in 1917. "I guess George Ade is. Certainly he appeals to us more than Mark Twain does because he belongs to our own time." Lardner, as a man of his own time, confessed that he knew of the life and characters Twain described only by "hearsay." He admires Twain's fiction, but he prefers Tarkington's Penrod stories. "I've known Booth Tarkington's boys and I've not known those of Mark Twain. Mark Twain's boys are tough and poverty stricken and they belong to a period very different from that of our own boys. But we all know Penrod and his boys."[14] It is common to turn Lardner's words against

Poster for a 1924 play (Redpath Chautauqua Special Collections, University of Iowa, Iowa City)

him, to argue that his privileged upbringing in Niles, Michigan, deprived him of the larger democratic sympathies that animated Twain's creations. There is something to this, of course, but the relative social distance between Lardner and his created characters (his nurses, boxers, barbers, and baseball players) is no greater than the distance between Twain and Pap Finn, Aunt Rachel, or the king and the duke.

Nor can it be convincingly maintained that Lardner did not enjoy the same literary opportunities provided by his own historical moment. His literary career as journalist, fiction writer, and dramatist spanned an era as rich in material ripe for exploitation and satire as the 1880s and 1890s. The Progressive era and the aftermath of the Great War manifested their enthusiasms, disappointments, and sentimental excesses in different ways, but Lardner was alert to the thickening complications and intricacies that were so rapidly changing the direction of American life—the abandonment of rural and pastoral prerogatives in favor of urban excitements; the nervous entrance into the community of nations on equal terms; and the rhetoric of confidence and opportunity uttered in the face of debilitat-

ing poverty and prejudice, irresistible social stratification, and the incomprehensible reticulations of social existence.

There was a richness of literary possibility available to such an intelligence as his—outrageous ironies and absurdities, American originals in the speakeasy and the dugout, and a multitude of American languages and dialects that he might faithfully transcribe. Lardner's Alibi Ike, for example, in his own way, belongs in the company of Scotty Briggs and Jim Blaine as someone comically unaware of his hilarious effects upon both his companions and his readers. The difference is that Twain catches his figures at a precise moment (Scotty in the unaccustomed presence of the parson and Jim Blaine in a state of perfect and "symmetrical" drunkenness); one can imagine them functioning profitably and comfortably on other occasions. However, Alibi Ike's proliferating and inexhaustible fund of excuses marks him as someone whose own considerable gifts and modest affections not only will always be cause for begrudging amusement, but also will likewise keep him outside the community whose admiration and acceptance he so urgently desires.

In his most famous story, "Haircut," Lardner reveals, through the barber narrator's recitation and headshaking and amused assent to the cruel adventures of Jim Kendall, a survival of the Bricksville crew in modern American life. The violence, laziness, coarseness, and vast indifference of the community are confided to the patron by a vernacular narrator who discloses more about himself and his town than he knows. Kendall gets his come-uppance at last–a literal-minded, half-wit boy, Paul Dickson, shoots and kills him. However it is idiocy, not innocence, that corrects the mischief and rights the moral imbalance, and one can hardly find consoling affirmations in this fact.

The life of Midge Kelly in "Champion" is a very unfunny restatement of Twain's "Story of the Bad Little Boy." Like Twain's bad boy, Midge abuses his mother, strikes his siblings, cheats his friends, and yet prospers–he becomes a champion prizefighter. Kelly's self-absorbed callousness and cruelty are more active and pernicious and therefore more sinister, however. The reason lies, I think, not in the character's violent profession but in the author's tone and narrative detachment, in the easy acceptance of the Midge Kellys of the world as brutal and incontestable facts of social existence.

At the other end of the scale are Lardner's non-sense plays, hilariously unactable and unproducible absurdist dramas. (One of his stage directions reads: *The curtain is lowered for seven days to denote the lapse of a week.*) At times, as in "Gaspiri (The Upholsterers)," they are reminiscent of Twain's "Encounter with an Interviewer":

> *First Stranger* Where was you born?
> *Second Stranger* Out of wedlock.
> *First Stranger* That's a mighty pretty country around there.
> *Second Stranger* Are you married?
> *First Stranger* I don't know. There's a woman living with me, but I can't place her.[15]

In Lardner, too, there is an originality of experimentation and imaginative conception that rivals Twain's. His humor owed more to "literary humorists" such as Artemus Ward and Petroleum Nasby, however, than it did to the coarser and more ribald tradition of Thorpe's Jim Doggett or Hooper's Simon Suggs. Nevertheless, like Twain, he extended the range of the vernacular comedy when he applied it to the epistolary form inherited from Richardson instead of to the picaresque tradition that Twain had adopted in *Huck Finn*. This occurred in 1916 when he collected his Jack Keefe stories and published the first of his Busher novels, *You Know Me Al*.

Bold as the experiment was, however, it shifted the vernacular away from the sources of oral tradition in a way that committed the author to a different kind of humor, one that might enlist our pity but was not likely to enlarge our sympathies. For, as James Cox has so elegantly shown, Jack's ungrammaticality reveals in the narrative consciousness an "unassimilated correctness" and an "abortive formality";[16] Jack strains for acceptability, but we his readers are first aware of his awkwardness and self-consciousness at the level of language. The predictable result of this shift is a certain enforced condescension established in the reader. Huck is fleeing social usage; thus, the apt lack of restraint in his language. Huck's readers, because we like his company, follow him in wish and imagination. Jack Keefe, by contrast, so desires admittance into a social order and community (whose terms are implicitly defined by the linguistic correctness he continually violates) that his constantly renewed efforts only further defeat his purposes. More to the point, because Lardner's comedy cannot function in the absence of an unstated but thoroughly understood social and linguistic propriety, to laugh at all means that we must laugh at the narrator, not through him.

What in Huck Finn is innocence becomes in Jack Keefe debilitating ignorance. Huck's self-deprecation is transformed in Jack to exasperating self-deception. Interestingly, because Huck is a child who has never had a childhood, we have access to a laughable and contemptible world in which his youthful point of view supplies a perspective that is more mature than the adult world Huck cannot fully understand. Jack Keefe, by contrast, is a man-child who does not know how to grow up. His fears are translated into "manly" boasts and threats followed hard and fast by accommodation, chop logic, and extenuation, comic gestures of self-protection and self-exposure. Keefe's misspellings and malapropisms are the verbal equivalent to his social maladjustments, and far from supplying his narrative with vernacular lyricism they mark him as a yokel and easy amusement to all around him.

At times, one almost feels that if Jack could correct his grammar, he could correct his life. But Jack Keefe is immersed in and controlled by a world of contracts, waivers, and lawsuits (for "none support"), a world of language so far beyond him that his own vernacular projections of self only announce his failure and acquiescence. His letters home to Bedford, to the Al who knows him so well, are letters of confused desperation. They come from Chicago and Philadelphia and New York, cities that are eating him alive, but it is clear he will never get to that little yellow house back in Bedford. He wants, by way of compensation for his real losses, to contrive imaginary gains, to be the hero of his own life, if only for his pal back home. What prevents even so momentary a satisfaction, one senses, is his inability to displace the real world with a vividly imagined one. His powers of self-absorption and self-deception are great, but there is no commensurate imaginative faculty or confident verbal facility that might displace the real world that presses in on him. Like Tom Sawyer, Jack has romantic illusions, but, unlike him, he has no joyful sense of playing a part. Like Huck, Jack has a vernacular perspective on events, but, unlike him, his language limits his world and insures his victimage. Even in his preconcerted boasts, his words recoil upon him: "Some man stopped me and asked me did I want to go to a show. He said he had a ticket. I asked him what show and he said the Follies. I never heard of it but I told him I would go if he had a ticket to spare. He says I will spare you this one for three dollars. I says You must take me for some boob. He says No I wouldn't insult no boob. So I walks on but if he had of insulted me I would of busted him."[17] His sentiments and attempts to cope are annihilated by the same language that serves to communicate his hurt and pride:

> It is all off between Violet and I. She wasn't the sort of girl I suspected. She is just like them all Al. No heart. I wrote her a letter from Chicago telling her I was sold to San Francisco and she wrote back a postcard saying something about not haveing no time to waste on bushers. What do you know about that Al? Calling me a busher. I will show them. She wasn't no good Al and I figure I am well rid of her. Good riddance is rubbish as they say.[18]

These comic deflations and distortions amuse but they don't provoke. Lardner's vernacular is not mere ornament; it is integral to the fabric of his fiction and his artistic purpose. What is disturbing, however, is that there is a bite and sting without apparent aim or direction, an unmistakable satirical impulse without a comprehensible satirical object. In the absence of a clearly inferable moral norm, the comedy recurs to the purely arbitrary norm of social usage, including the standard English usage Keefe so comically manhandles and mangles. Unlike the typical reaction to Huck, our comic understanding of the Busher does not serve as a link between our sympathies and a larger awareness of the human spectacle. Quite the contrary, our pity and amusement are additional insults to his confused condition.

Simply put, psychologically, morally, and emotionally, Ring Lardner's Jack Keefe is not the descendant of Huckleberry Finn but the country cousin of J. Alfred Prufrock. The Busher is in fact Prufrock in a jersey and cleats. What separates Huck and Jack in the imagination is not so much attributable to differences in artistic perception, genre, or craft as it is the inevitable result of enlisting the vernacular to perform the detached analysis of the interior life instead of to examine the fate of the republic and the moral constitution of its citizens. If the writer is to adopt a vernacular narrator the reader is to take seriously, then sooner or later he or she must also adopt certain democratic sympathies and endorse certain fraternal values implicit in the register of the narrative voice itself.

The same artistic detachment that is likely to be praised in one quarter (in Eliot or Hemingway or Joyce) is cause, in another, for complaint. Clifton Fadiman, for instance, has insisted that Lardner's fiction is motivated by a "triangle of hate," and that the resulting product is a cold-blooded misanthropy. The judgment is no doubt too severe. Ring Lardner was an exquisite craftsman and a great humorist, but the resources of Twain's technique, isolated from a concern with a larger social vision come soon enough to appear as mere cagey evasions or, worse, a string of one-liners. When the writer possesses a vernacular vision but no special gifts for dialect, however, an indebtedness to Twain's example will likely go unnoticed. This is the case with Willa Cather.

IV

At first glance, any comparison of Willa Cather to Mark Twain must seem strained, perhaps farfetched. One of the few people ever to propose a fundamental connection between these two is Eudora Welty. Cather and the Twain of *Huckleberry Finn,* she observed, "stand together in *bigness.*" In their "sense of it, their authority over it" they share only this similarity: "they are totally unlike except in their greatest respects, except in being about something big."[19] Surely it is not vastness of scene or profound purpose Welty detected in them, but some sure artistic commitment to a palpable yet transcendentally authorizing ideal that dignifies their respective heroes. Huckleberry Finn and Ántonia Shimerda or Alexandra Bergson are small people, really, smaller still measured against the extent of the Mississippi River or the breadth of the Nebraska sky. But there is a homey grandeur to them as well, as if the river and the sky deferred to their presence or tended to their needs. In this "greatest respect" Twain and Cather belong together. But there are more tangible links as well.

Cather's admiration of Twain is familiar. For her, there were only three American novels that had the possibility of a long, long life: *The Scarlet Letter, Adventures of Huckleberry Finn,* and *The Country of the Pointed Firs.* "I can think of no others that confront time and change so serenely," she wrote. Later generations, she predicted, will come upon these works and exclaim, a "masterpiece." The thrill of sudden discovery will be as Frost's mower who discovers in the afternoon a tuft of meadow flowers the mower in the morning had spared and will gaze upon it and wonder. The poise and serenity she discerned in these three novels will speak to the future

Cartoon by H. T. Webster from the 24 May 1926 issue of the New York World *(Collection of Louis J. Budd)*

and supply "the one message that even the scythe of Time spares."[20]

In a letter to Cyril Clemens, Cather recalled an encounter with a Russian violinist in Paris. He had grown up along a river too, and he told her that ever since he had read a Russian translation of *Huckleberry Finn* he had wanted to see the Mississippi, a river that must be even more wonderful and romantic than the Volga. Cather questioned the man about the novel, a bit skeptical that it could have had such an effect on him. He remembered it perfectly "But how in the world could the talk of Nigger Jim be translated into Russian?" she wondered.

> And what would become of the seven shadings of Southern dialect which the author in his preface tells the reader must not be confounded one with the other? It seemed to me that the most delightful things in "Huckleberry Finn" must disappear in a translation. One could easily translate Parkman or Emerson, certainly: but how translate Mark Twain? The only answer seems to be that if a book has vitality enough, it can live through even the brutalities of translators.[21]

Cather's recorded reactions to *Huckleberry Finn* are interesting because they identify and value features of the novel that are sometimes missed. First, in her estimation, the best work of Hawthorne, Jewett, and Twain escape the contingencies of time and the modifications of taste. The remark is all the more interesting since *The Scarlet Letter, Adventures of Huckleberry Finn* and, in its own special way, *The Country of the Pointed Firs* are all historical novels, but historical novels with a difference. Cather made the distinction between historical novels (such as Flaubert's *Salammbô*) that regard the past from the privileged vantage point of the present and thereby acquire a certain condescension toward their subjects, and those (such as Thomas Mann's Joseph novels) that explore the material from behind, as it were, as though the characters were not foregone conclusions, whose lives instead were made of choices and whose motives were projections into a future of hope and possibility. Surely, that is a quality that characterizes *Huckleberry Finn* and, perhaps, that is also what Roy Harvey Pearce is getting at when he points out that Huck is trapped in his book, that he forever exists as a possibility, not an actuality.[22] It also happens to be the quality that Cather sought to achieve in her own historical novels, particularly in the best of them, *Death Comes for the Archbishop*.

The second observation, derived from her conversation with the Russian violinist, implies that *Huckleberry Finn* thrives on a quality and vitality of feeling that is not only apart from the density of its dialect but stronger even than the inevitable butcheries of translation. This second point is a correlative of the first. If works of the imagination are to escape history, they must also escape the bondage of language. In her most familiar essay, "The Novel Démeublé," she speaks elegantly on this point: "Whatever is felt upon the page without being specifically named there that, one might say, is created. It is the inexplicable presence of the thing not named, of the overtone divined by the ear but not heard by it, the verbal mood, the emotional aura of the fact or the thing or the deed, that gives high quality to the novel or the drama as well as to poetry itself."[23]

Huckleberry Finn is dense with what Henry James called "the solidity of specification," and especially dense in its attachment to the precise rendering of American speech, but its dialect only solidifies the verbal mood established in the reader. Pap Finn is a living character, not because he speaks a historically conditioned language, but because his bigotry and ranting speech is still poisonous to the ear. Like a figure from Bunyan's *Pilgrim's Progress,* Pap is a deputy for baseness itself; his truest idiom is brute and degrading ignorance. We hear his words, but we divine his presence.

Cather, however, did not possess Twain's gift for dialect, and she seems to have known it. Nevertheless, in 1913, when she accepted her native Nebraska material in her novel *O Pioneers!,* she "hit the home pasture" and discovered, as Twain had discovered in the return to the experience of his youth along the Mississippi, a sudden liberation of the imagination. And, like her narrator Jim Burden in *My Ántonia,* she came to believe that it would be a fine thing to be the first to bring the muse into one's own country. Sooner or later, she remarked, the writer rediscovers the material of one's birth and circumstance, material that, because it is typically taken for granted, produces no special excitement or interest. But when the "inner feeling" of the familiar mysteriously shapes itself on the page and supplants the purely writerly desire to build "external stories," then the writer will have resumed "his one really precious possession."[24]

Cather often observed that a writer's authentic experience, and thus her most valuable literary material, is acquired before the age of fifteen, and she was fond of quoting the advice Sarah Orne Jewett once offered to her: "Of course, one day you will write about your own country. In the meantime, get all you can. One must know the world *so well* before one can know the parish."[25] It was Jewett who provided the example of the writer who wrote about her own country unashamedly and with what Cather once called the "gift of sympathy," but Twain's example must have served her as well. Certainly the dignity and respect with which Twain treats Huck and Jim were qualities she might admire and emulate. At any rate, Cather was especially proud that, in *O Pioneers!,* she had created for the first time in American fiction Swedish characters who were not portrayed as lumpish buffoons.

Cather's admiration of *Huckleberry Finn* is there plainly enough, but the impress of his influence or the mark of his peculiar gifts is difficult to locate in her own work. Her fiction by no means participates in the traditions of American humor. In fact, unless one has inspected her letters (in which she reveals a comic wit and vivacity and, at times, wholesome self-parody), one is apt to conclude that she is much like the undertaker at the Wilks funeral, with no more smile to her than a ham. And unless one is familiar with her early criticism, there is little ground to suspect a barbed, even malicious, satiric wit. Particularly in her early fiction (as in "The Willing Muse" or "The Garden Lodge"), one finds the comedy of situation but no particular inclination to exploit the latent humor of it. In sum, in Willa Cather one has a writer who has a vernacular vision but no extraordinary vernacular capabilities.

Her kinship with Twain is detectable almost entirely in her eventual discovery that the land and people of her youth were worthy of literary treatment. Ántonia Shimerda, Nancy Till, Spanish Johnny, Aunt Tillie, Alexandra Bergson, old Rosicky, and so many others are vernacular characters, but Cather had to find extravernacular means to convey a richness and interest of personality and purpose that might so easily degenerate into mere comedy of language. Her Czechs, Poles, Germans, and Swedes are typically immigrants or first-generation Americans. They, like their spoken English, are rendered awkward by the process of assimilation and accommodation to a new country and a new language. Unlike Twain's characters, however, Cather's immigrants are trying to speak alike and not succeeding. Beneath the hard consonants and hesitant cadences, however, is fierce pride and fluent intelligence. But how to convey these qualities she so much admired in the Nebraska neighbors of her youth? Her usual solution to this problem is brilliantly simple—she avoids the difficulty altogether.

It is true that her characters sometimes speak their own language, but they are seldom if ever capable of speaking their own world. Consider, for example, Frank Shabata, in *O Pioneers!*: "I never mean to do not'ing to dat boy. I ain't had not'ing ag'in dat boy. I always like dat boy fine." Cather's vernacular speech is perfectly adequate, but it is unequal to the quality of feeling the author has for the characters themselves. However, she found other means to convey human personality without sacrificing the felt quality of speech. For example, after Frank's protestation in the passage above, he says, "I forget English. We not talk here [prison], except swear."[26] More often, as in the speech of Spanish Johnny or Wünsch in *The Song of the Lark,* she

inserts into their otherwise standard English dialogue Spanish or German phrases (often song lyrics or proverbs) in order to suggest linguistic as well as rich historical and cultural difference.

Cather is ever alert to the social force of language throughout her fiction. In *The Song of the Lark,* we are told that Mrs. Kronborg spoke Swedish to her sisters and colloquial English to her neighbors. Her daughter Thea, "who had a rather sensitive ear, until she went to school never spoke at all except in monosyllables."[27] More often still, the narrator serves as translator in the manner that Hemingway adopted some time later in *For Whom the Bell Tolls.* In *O Pioneers!* the narrator notes that Ivar, whom the neighbors consider queer, even crazy, "never learned to speak English and his Norwegian was quaint and grave, like the speech of the more old-fashioned people." Following this explanation, Ivar speaks: "Mistress, . . . the folk have been looking coldly at me of late. You know there has been talk."[28] His helpless dignity is registered at the level of cadence and syntax instead of at the level of diction.

Only twice does Cather use a first-person narrator whose youth and limited comprehension bear the marks of Huck Finn, and in both instances it is sensibility, not dialect, that invites the comparison. In *My Mortal Enemy,* she has a young woman named Nellie Birdseye tell the story of the sophisticated and beautiful Myra Henshawe. When they first meet, the young Nellie receives instruction on dress and manner at a time when her interest in the allurements that will make her a woman are paramount. But as the years go by, it becomes apparent that Myra Henshawe's life is utter repudiation of those same things that made her so interesting to the young woman. Myra's husband, Oswald, somehow preserves the original love and vitality of feeling he first felt for his wife throughout the subtractions of age and impoverishment. The distressing result is that Oswald becomes his wife's "mortal enemy," a reminder of her lost youth and beauty and station, and in the end she turns from him to tend her rosary and die by the sea. The novel is a devastating study of marriage as an institution and love as a force that ends in contempt. The narrator understands but little of this, however, and her limitations only make the tale more disturbingly poignant.

Less bitter, if no less effective, is "Two Friends." It begins: "Even in early youth, when the mind is so eager for the new and untried, while it is still a stranger to faltering and fear, we yet like to think that there are certain unalterable realities, somewhere at the bottom of things. These anchors may be ideas; but more often they are merely pictures, vivid memories, which in some unaccountable and very personal way give us courage." For the unnamed narrator, that anchor is the friendship she observes in Mr. Dillon and Mr. Trueman. These men have little in common. The first is an Irish Catholic, a Democrat, and a banker; the second a Protestant, a Republican, and a rancher. But for the thirteen-year-old child who plays jacks on the boardwalk along the brick wall where the two meet to chat every evening, there is something precious and valuable in their casual conversation. It is talk she no longer recalls and at the time did not understand except for the quality of voice that engaged in it. Of Dillon, she remembers, "Every sentence he uttered was alive, never languid, perfunctory, slovenly, unaccented. When he made a remark, it not only meant something, but sounded like something,—sounded like the thing he meant."[29]

She listens to these two men who reveal to her quite accidentally, and more in the quality of the voice than in anything else, "the strong bracing reality of successful, large-minded men who had made their way in the world when business was still a personal adventure."[30] But when Dillon travels to Chicago and becomes enthusiastic by the bloated rhetoric of Bryant's "Cross of Gold" speech, he returns to her small town a changed man. His voice becomes shrill, convinced of its mission. It becomes unnatural. The end of the friendship is at hand: it dissolves in a "quarrel of principle." No degree of self-interest could have damaged this friendship, the narrator believes. Political ideology and rhetoric despise affection and destroy its attachments.

For the child the loss is a permanent regret. Much older, the scar of that ruptured friendship is still tender to the narrator who as a child admired it as a truth in the world. And when at odd moments it is touched by accidental circumstance, "it rouses the old uneasiness; the feeling of something broken that could so easily have been mended; of something delightful that was senselessly wasted, of a truth that was accidentally distorted—one of the truths we want to keep."[31]

"Two Friends" was written in 1931, and perhaps Cather was responding to a multitude of fallen friendships occasioned by the Depression and "quarrels of principle" over the several political strategies advanced to repair the economy. At any rate, by most any reckoning, Willa Cather's own political conservativism must seem quaint, amusing, even touching. She opposed FDR's New Deal, but she sent money and packages back to folks in Webster County, Nebraska, who were having a rough go of it. During World War II, she was more encouraged by the fact that they were still giving concerts in bomb-torn London than by Patton's military triumphs. But her own social vision was grounded in bigness—in the old truths of friendship, desire, and courage, enabling attachments which are prior to political commitment. In that greatest respect, Cather also resembles Mark Twain.

In one of his boldest imaginative experiments, Twain pits the comprehensive and repressive political structures of the Church and a feudal economy against Hank Morgan's technological innovation and progressive social engineering. The result is comic disaster, culminating in the Battle of the Sand Belt. But the novel ends with a delirious Hank reaching out across the centuries for his wife, Sandy, and his daughter, Hello Central. And in *Huckleberry Finn,* it is the sound heart in an ignorant boy that, however briefly, defeats the powerful claims of civilized society. Cather's *Death Comes for the Archbishop* ends with Archbishop Latour facing death with equanimity and poise, but his thoughts are not on eternity but the beginnings of lifelong association and friendship with Joseph Vaillant. Alexandra Bergson's story ends with the prediction of her death: "Fortunate country, that is one day to receive hearts like Alexandra's into its bosom, to give them out again in the yellow wheat, in the rustling corn, in the shining eyes of youth!"[32] For Jim Burden, Ántonia's face and gestures "somehow reveal the meaning in common things"; she lent herself "to immemorial human attitudes which we recognize by instinct as universal and true."[33]

Eudora Welty once observed that there is no "middle distance" in Cather's best work. Instead of the dense complexities of social life and political compromise, there is the broad sweep of time and space and a handful of human figures whose lives are dignified in common things. This is the portion of Huck's legacy Cather claimed for her characters. For Langston Hughes's Jesse B. Semple, such a life is unavailable, the middle distance of the color line crowds in upon him. Simple confronts it not with serenity and poise but with comic wit and intelligent complaint, and the result is a latter day vernacular hero.

V

While it is true that Langston Hughes read and admired *Huckleberry Finn,*[34] the question of a literary inheritance derived from a white writer (whose own racial attitudes are more than a little problematic) is particularly complicated.[35] Still, Hughes was gratified by the critic Ben Lehman's observation that Hughes's Jesse Semple (more familiarly known as "Simple") was a worthy successor to the comic creations of Mark Twain: "I'd not thought of it before myself," Hughes responded. "But [I] am glad if there's something of the same quality there, naturally."[36] The remark is aptly phrased, for Hughes neither denies nor affirms a correspondence between his created character and his humor and those of Mark Twain; if there is the happy accident of broad appeal and analogous humorous effects, so much the better. Though he became a Knight of the Mark Twain Society and later wrote an appreciative introduction to *Pudd'nhead Wilson* in 1959, Langston Hughes left no recorded statement of deliberate emulation of Twain, nor was he subjected to the burden of a reviewer's predictions or appraisals of him in those terms as Lardner had been. Not that he could have ever been pegged by a critic, anyway. His talents were too various and his achievements too diverse to lend themselves to easy identification.

Hughes wrote plays, poems and songs, autobiography and history, translations, travel literature and fiction, children's verse and stories, serious criticism and journalism. He even tried his hand at opera, and at one time contemplated collaborating on a "cantata" or a "composition with orchestra, singers, and perhaps a Narrator, perhaps to be called MISSOURI after my native state. . . . It could have history in it, and Mark Twain, and the rivers, and a bit of folk lore."[37] Like Twain, too, Langston Hughes was an avid student of American humor. As if in answer to the volume *Mark Twain's Library of Humor,* Hughes published an anthology called *The Book of Negro Humor.* The prefatory note to this collection is pointedly unfunny and offhandedly personal and revealing:

> Humor is laughing at what you haven't got when you ought to have it. Of course, you laugh by proxy. You're really laughing at the other guy's lacks, not your own. That's what makes it funny—the fact that you don't know you are laughing at yourself. Humor is when the joke is on you but hits the other fellow first—before it boomerangs. Humor is what you wish in your secret heart were not funny, but it is, and you must laugh. Humor is your own unconscious therapy.[38]

How unconscious the therapy of writing the Jesse Semple sketches was for Hughes is uncertain. He once remarked that Simple "is just myself talking to me. Or else me talking to myself."[39] Arnold Rampersad speculates that through the interplay between Boyd (a thinly veiled version of Hughes himself) and Jesse Semple (the plainspoken figure whose lack of restraint and simple vitality Hughes envied), Hughes's comic sketches continually play about the edges of the author's subterranean fears and desires.[40] Whatever the nature of the author's compelling interest in the figure of Jesse Semple and the dramatic opportunities he provided, it was sufficient stimulus to carry him through two decades and more than 150 Simple sketches published in the Chicago *Defender* and the *New York Post,* ample material for the four book-length collections that eventually would be published.

For our purposes, however, it is enough to say that the origins of the imagined character (his complaints, preoccupations, and enthusiasms) sprang from powerful internal initiatives within the author that ulti-

Title page for a 1926 French translation of Adventures of Huckleberry Finn *(Buffalo and Erie County Public Library)*

mately had little to do with literary tradition or even artistic ambition. But we may recast these same private conflicts in public terms by recurring to Ralph Ellison's contemplation of the abandoned legacy of *Huckleberry Finn.* For Ellison's appraisal of the deficiencies of modern American fiction, when measured against the achievement of *Huck Finn,* is answered in the example of the Simple sketches.

Mark Twain's portrayal of Jim, according to Ellison, avoided the stereotyped characterizations that came all too naturally to later writers. Jim is never idealized but is "drawn in all his ignorance and superstition, with his good traits and his bad. He, like all men, is ambiguous, limited in circumstance but not in possibility." Yet at the same time, and largely through Huck's relation to him, Jim is a potent symbol as well, not merely of the Negro but "as a symbol of Man." Huck's own adolescent and slow-dawning recognition of Jim's humanity simultaneously clarifies for the reader the relation Huck must sooner or later bear toward the existing social order and yet makes tangible and vivid his resistance to that same community.[41]

For Huck, like Jim, serves a double function in the novel. In his relation to the river and to Jim, Huck is a humanist; in his relation to the larger social community, he is an individualist. Thus, Huck "embodies the two major conflicting drives operating in nineteenth-century America. And if humanism is man's basic attitude toward a social order which he accepts, and individualism his basic attitude toward one he rejects, one might say that Twain, by allowing these two attitudes to argue dialectically in his work of art, was as highly moral an artist as he was a believer in democracy, and vice versa."[42] Langston Hughes, however, combined in a single figure the functions Twain had distributed between Jim and Huck, and he named him Jesse B. Semple.

It is a critical commonplace to observe that Simple is an Everyman figure. His originality as a character derives almost entirely from Hughes's confident resistance of freakish literary excess and dramatic effect. Simple is compellingly ordinary, and the achievement is a rarity. "In all of Negro fiction," wrote Blyden Jackson in 1968, "the Negro who is unabashedly and simply an *average man* is as rare as once, in that same fiction, octoroons were disturbingly numerous."[43] There is nothing conciliatory in the averageness of Simple, however. His sometimes fantastic flights of imagination, his concocted dramas of revenge, his hep prayers for reconciliation are underwritten by a seemingly incurable sanity and hope.

Jesse Semple rants, raves, grumbles, and complains, but he invariably lands upon his moral and emotional feet. He imagines a righteous catastrophe, but he settles for a beer. In "Simple Prays a Prayer," Jesse takes as the text for an impromptu sermon Jesus' commandment to love one another. "I know the Bible, too," he insists:

"My Aunt Lucy read it to me. She read how He drove the moneychangers out of the Temple. Also how He changed the loaves and fishes into many and fed the poor—which made the rulers in their high places mad because they didn't want the poor to eat. Well, when Christ comes back this time, I hope He comes back mad His own self. I hope He drives the Jim Crowers out of their high places, every living last one of them from Washington to Texas! I hope he smites white folks down!"

"You don't mean all white folks, do you?"

"No," said Simple. "I hope He lets Mrs. Roosevelt alone."[44]

What begins in frustration and anger ends in comic charity. In the end, Simple does not speak out of personal despair. Momentarily convinced by his own rhetoric, he speaks instead from an invented position of power. His prayer, if only in the imagination, serves as incantation and enacts an angry second coming that has the whole force of Christian dogma behind it. It is Simple's mercy, however, not God's, that spares Mrs. Roosevelt. In that quick double movement, Hughes supplies his vernacular hero with a common humanity, both as the indignant victim of a real society he inhabits and condemns (an individualist, in Ellison's terms) and a full partner in the community he imagines (a humanist).

This is humor in the subjunctive mood, and it is pervasive in the Simple sketches. In "High Bed," Simple imagines the freedom of a rocket ship: "I sure would rock so far away from this color line in the U.S.A., till it wouldn't be funny. I might even build me a garage on Mars and a mansion on Venus."[45] In "Confused" Jesse confides that he loves being black but likewise knows that in racist America he is marked for life. In one of his quick-tempo poetic riffs he defines his condition: "I am a Son of Ham from down in 'Bam and there ain't none other like I am. Solid black from front to back! And one thing sure—it won't fade Jack!"[46] In a single gesture, Simple asserts both his unique individuality and his solidarity with the black community and against the prevailing social oppression of African-Americans.

Unlike the Irishman or the Jew, a change of name will never change his social identity. But if it could and he desired to pass for white, Simple would take the name Patrick McGuire:

"If I was going to pass for white, I might as well pass good. With an Irish name, I could be Mayor of New York."

"A fine Mayor you would make."

"A fine Mayor is right," said Simple proudly. "I would immediately issue a decree right away"

"To what effect?"

"To the effect that any colored man who wants to rent an apartment downtown can rent one and no landlord can tell him, 'We do not rent to colored.'"[47]

Boyd has trapped his friend, however, for he reminds him that as Patrick McGuire, Simple is no longer black. And he confuses Jesse still further by asking, "However, if you were white, sir, listen—would you want your daughter to marry a Negro?" "If my daughter didn't have no better sense," is his reply. But Simple knows that the question of intermarriage is always brought in to confuse the issue and is quick to remind his friend that, in point of fact, he doesn't have a daughter, he is not white, and even if he did have a daughter, she would not be white since he himself would simply be passing for white:

> "We was having a nice simple argument and you had to confuse the issue. Buy me a beer."
> "You drink too much," I said.
> "Please don't confuse another issue," said Simple.[48]

"Radioactive Redcaps" is yet another fantasy of empowerment. Simple imagines an atomic bomb falling in Harlem and that he has become "atomized." Once "charged," he fancies, he will "take charge." He would be able to set off a chain reaction, and "I am getting my chain ready now." By simply calling up his former landlady on the telephone, he will be able to atomize her like a "Japanese tuna." Why, asks Boyd, do you think you will be able to survive an atomic explosion? His answer is to the point: "If Negroes can survive white folks in Mississippi," said Simple, "we can survive anything."[49]

Simple's circumstances are comically curious, but they are unremarkable. Though he typically speaks in or around Paddy's Bar in Harlem, he has traveled up north from Virginia, with a stopover in Baltimore (enough time to make a bad marriage with Isabel, who refuses to pay for their divorce). On Harlem streets, Simple cadges a beer from Boyd and literally talks his life. Sometimes, he reports to Boyd, he cozies up to his "after-hours gal," Zarita; but he actively courts and, once his divorce comes through, eventually marries his fiancee, Joyce. He tries to set a good example for his distant cousin "F. D." (Franklin Delano Roosevelt Brown), who has come up north to be with him. He frets over his homely cousin Minnie, complains about his heartless landlady, and pokes fun at Joyce's social-climbing friend, Mrs. Sadie Maxwell-Reeves.

These are the ingredients of Simple's everyday life. They humanize his fictional existence, but they never eclipse the external pressures of the color line that threaten to crush or distort that same humanity. Boyd believes his friend reduces everything to the race issue. "Your semantics makes things too simple," he says. Jesse's reply is as direct as it is comically outrageous:

> "Whatever you are talking about with your *see-antics*, Jack, at my age a man gets tired of the same kind of eggs each and every day—just like you get tired of the race problem. I would like to have an egg some morning that tastes like a pork chop."
> "In that case, why don't you have pork chops for breakfast instead of eggs?"
> "Because there is never no pork chops in my icebox in the morning."
> "There would be if you would put them there the night before."

> "No," said Simple, "I would eat them up the night before—which is always the trouble with the morning after—you have practically nothing left from the night before except the race problem."[50]

By turns, Simple is cantankerous, magnanimous, shrewd, discouraged, gentle, ferocious, and generous, which is to say he is an unevenly average man. By turns, too, he is Huck Finn and Jim. Like Huck, people are constantly pecking on him, intent on improving and civilizing him. (Joyce one time tells him to hush and listen to an Italian libretto; Simple complains to his friend Boyd the next day, "I don't see why culture can't be in English.") And his resistance is sometimes as innocently evasive as Huck's; he too steps out at night (until the "A. M.," as Jesse is apt to say) to seek relief from custom and restraint. But, like Jim and unlike Huck, Simple desires admittance into and full partnership in the social order, not as it is, but as it ought to be.

It is both understandable and curious that Jesse Semple (and his creator) are so often regarded as out-of-date. Even in his own day, Hughes was accused of "backing into the future looking at the past."[51] But if there were ever a literary character who knows that politics is personal, it is Jesse Semple. Freedom means, among other, much more serious things, being able to gnaw a pork bone at your own front window. Joyce reports that this is simply not done and that Emily Post says "DON'T": "'Baby,' I says, 'Emily Post were white. Also, I expect, rich. That woman had plenty of time to gnaw her bones at the table. Me, I work.'"[52] Lack of freedom, on the other hand, means feeling the pain of restraint as acutely as the bunions on his feet. ("If anybody was to write the history of my life, they should start with my feet," he says in "Feet Live Their Own Life.")[53]

These sudden verbal incongruities and dislocations are the common stuff of humor, but Hughes has appropriated conventional comic devices and made them serve not only the uses of satire and comedy but also the purpose of advancing a mature social vision. "With one exception," remarks Roger Rosenblatt in his elegant essay on Simple, "black literature has produced no full, self-sustaining humorous hero, either out of the desire to avoid reproducing end men, or because end men seem out of place in the depictions of a nightmare." And as he rightly observes, Jesse, like Huck, is a regionalist comic character, but, in a sense deeper and larger than geography, Simple's "region" is his blackness. Jesse Semple's dialect is the fundamental condition of his being, and he is eloquent. In structure, subject, and effect, Simple's casual talk has the quality of a streetwise, secular sermon. His vernacular speech is, to

E. W. Kemble's drawing of Huck, Jim, and Tom for a 1932
Limited Editions Club publication of Adventures of
Huckleberry Finn *(from* The Annotated
Huckleberry Finn, *Richland County*
Public Library)

reemphasize Cox's distinction, a way of being, not a way of saying. And Rosenblatt makes explicit the connection between Twain and Hughes we have been contemplating in a general way: "Twain said he was always preaching when he wrote, that if humor emerged as part of the sermons, fine, but that he would have written the sermons in any case. . . . [Simple's] sermons are part of himself and so they are humorous naturally, but because like Twain he is first a moral man, then a humorist, we realize that amusement is not the most important reaction intended."[54]

What Hughes did intend, I believe, was to supply an image of an Everyman, who also happens to be black. Not that his blackness is incidental to the effect. Quite the contrary. Simple's personal experience—his deprivations, aggravations, and anger, as well as his hope, optimism, and resilience—mirror the condition and the welfare of the republic. Jesse Semple will never belong to Dubois's "talented tenth"; nor does he even begin to qualify as one of Harriet Beecher Stowe's "moral miracles." Still, in his own minor and ordinary way he is a miracle nonetheless. A democratic society can survive, even prosper, without a talented tenth (black or white), but it can never rise above the condition of the least of its well-meaning citizens, its Everyman or Everywoman. The final literary and moral effect of Jesse Semple is not that he is a potential enemy too dangerous to be ignored, but that he is a potential ally, too valuable to be neglected.

VI

By now it should be clear that the neglected legacy of *Huckleberry Finn* I have been attempting to identify as a vernacular vision is, in fact, a hopelessly old-fashioned liberal humanism, available equally to common readers, gifted writers, and, perhaps, even to literary critics. Twain banked on the approval of his "submerged clientele" (banked on them in a commercial as well as a moral sense), and the result was an image of the American author as a public man. He was, and is, the nation's funny fellow, but I doubt that even the most casually amused reader doesn't truly wish that Twain's humor were not funny.

Huckleberry Finn, Ántonia Shimerda, and Jesse B. Simple are vernacular moral heroes. They have suffered (though quite unequally) abuse, rejection, assault, and disenfranchisement, and they have survived. But that is not the foundation of their strength or the origin of our important interest in them. They are, it is true, wounded characters, but they are neither stronger for the hurt nor debilitated by the recollection of it. They are, we like to think, better than the conditions of their existence.

If modern American literature began with *Huckleberry Finn,* Huck (as a character and not a literary device) bears faint and uneven resemblance to so many of those figures of the imagination who claim a kinship with him. Huck Finn is often lonely, but he is never alienated. He is frequently petty, but seldom trivial. He is guilt ridden and self-deprecating, but he is never paralyzed by those feelings. Huckleberry Finn is nothing more than a fictional creation; and as decent a man as Mark Twain seems to have been, he was never so good as his created character. And as good as Huck is, he is not so very good; he is only better than he ought to be.

"Moral reform," says Thoreau, "is the effort to throw off sleep. To be awake is to be alive. I have never yet met a man who was quite awake. How could I have looked him in the eye?" But, when Huck plays a trick on Jim, Jim not only looks Huck in the eye but scolds and humbles him, too. It is precisely in this dramatized moment that one feels that the moral inheritance which is a part of the legacy of *Huckleberry Finn* will never degenerate into the sanctimonious or obscure. The example of Mark Twain involves writing about something, on behalf of some half-realized and dimly felt obligation not to the social order or to ideological prescription, but to the nagging impulsions of the imagination. The social responsibility of the novelist is always there, perhaps most importantly there when the author writes about something he or she cannot quite understand.

Perhaps it is fitting that a writer of our own day, who not so coincidentally wears his own white suit like a badge, should reintroduce in rather different terms the substance of Ellison's criticism of modern fiction. Tom Wolfe, in "Stalking the Billion-Footed Beast: A Literary Manifesto for the New Social Novel," argued for a reinvigorated social realism in American fiction. Judging from the number of responses and the degree of lively and angry interest this manifesto received, he touched a nerve in a way that Ellison's critique never did. Quite apart from the soundness of Wolfe's argument that contemporary writers have shied away from the provocative and inexhaustible literary opportunities that the "real" world throws in their way on an almost daily basis, Wolfe's reply to his several detractors is worth citing: "With very few exceptions, the towering achievements [in the novel] have taken the form of a detailed realism of the sort I am referring to. And why? Because a perfectly sound and natural instinct told them that it is impossible to portray characters vividly, powerfully, convincingly, except as part of the society in which they find themselves."[55]

I am not at all certain that these same instincts prescribe a definite literary manner, the manner of Zola, Tolstoy, or Flaubert, for example. But they implicate the reader and the writer in contemplating the world not only as it is but as it might be. In "Prologues To What Is Possible," Wallace Stevens imagines an ordinary man on an extraordinary voyage:

What self, for example, did he contain that had not yet been loosed,
Snarling in him for discovery as his attentions spread,
As if all his hereditary lights were suddenly increased
By an access of color, a new and unobserved, slight dithering,
The smallest lamp, which added its puissant flick, to which he gave
A name and privilege over the ordinary of his commonplace—
A flick which added to what was real and its vocabulary.[56]

This is a fragile and temporary hope, this puissant flick added to the "ordinary of his commonplace." It may give rise to grand vernacular dreams and to the vocabulary of human possibility, but like all dreams it may be dismissed with a flick of the wrist. In "Jazz, Jive, and Jam," Jesse Semple relates his own plans for improving "interracial meetings": "In my opinion, jazz, jive, and jam would be better for race relations than all this high-flown gab, gaff, and gas orators put out." If he had his way, he would liven things up with the music of Duke Ellington or Count Basie. And he would offer to the meeting his own resolution:

"*Resolved:* that we solve the race problem! Strike up the band! Hit it men! Aw, play that thing! 'How High the Moon!' How high! Wheee-ee-e!."

"What did Joyce say to that?" I demanded.

"Joyce just thought I was high," said Simple.[57]

—*Coming to Grips with Huckleberry Finn: Essays on a Book, a Boy, and a Man* (Columbia: University of Missouri Press, 1993), pp. 106–146

1. *Our Mark Twain: The Making of His Public Personality*, (Philadelphia: University of Pennsylvania Press, 1983). In our own time, Budd writes, Mark Twain's public personality "stands in danger of functioning as Everybody's Mark Twain in a much less fundamental or provocative way than during his prime" (230). In part, this essay means to explore and speculate about the loss of power of Mark Twain as a literary benefactor rather than as a public commodity. Still, these two elements of Twain's legacy are inevitably intertwined.

2. His *1601,* for example, (originally titled *Conversation, as It Was by the Social Fireside, in the Time of the Tudors*) has run through probably one hundred editions, and many of those have been printed by and have changed hands in men's lodges and clubs, as though flatulence in the Queen's Court is really more funny than the blue jay yarn.

3. A succinct but comprehensive view of a feature of the American humor tradition particularly germane to this essay is provided by Blair in "'A Man's Voice, Speaking': A Continuum in American Humor," in *Veins of Humor,* ed. Harry Levin, Harvard English Studies 3 (Cambridge: Harvard University Press, 1972), 185–204.

4. "American Literature and the American Language," *Washington University Studies in Language and Literature* (St. Louis, 1953), 16.

5. The observation was made in a letter in 1935, but it was first published on the cover of the Summer 1965 issue of the *Mark Twain Journal.*

6. The note was given to the Mark Twain Society when Stein was in St. Louis. It was first published on the cover of the Summer 1971 issue of the *Mark Twain Journal.* Alice B. Toklas signed the letter in the margin, apparently as a way of seconding the remarks.

7. See respectively Eliot's "American Literature and the American Language," 16–17, and an interview with William Faulkner by Jean Stein, *Paris Review* (Spring 1956): 46–47.

8. *The Green Hills of Africa* (New York: Charles Scribner's Sons, 1935), 22.

9. In *Mark Twain: An American Prophet* (Boston: Houghton Mifflin Co., 1970) Maxwell Geismar makes the same point as Ellison, less charitably perhaps, but far more succinctly: "It is curious incidentally that Hemingway, who derived so much from Mark Twain's prose, learned so little from his spirit" (372–73).

10. "Twentieth-Century Fiction and the Black Mask of Humanity," *in Shadow and Act* (New York: New American Library, 1966), 52. When Ellison's essay was first published in *Confluence* (December 1953), he asked that an editorial note be included that indicated that it was written just after the war and reflected the "bias and shortsightedness" he felt at the time. Such bias is certainly understandable when an African-American observes, as so many had after

that and other wars, that the patriotism of minorities, upon which the republic depended during a national emergency, was a negligible consideration when white America went back to business as usual.

11. *Mark Twain: The Fate of Humor* (Princeton: Princeton University Press, 1966), 176.

12. Needless to say, Twain is not exempt from the charge of retreat from contaminations of the political and social fabric of the republic. In letters, he sometimes insisted that the first responsibility of citizenship was to keep "clean"; in *A Connecticut Yankee* he averred that the primary obligation of the individual was to preserve some "atom" of self and let the rest land in "Sheol"; in my essay "Life Imitating Art" . . . I have argued that in "The Private History of a Campaign That Failed," Twain sought to justify his own "desertion" not only from the Confederate Army but also from an active involvement in the fate of the nation. In *Huckleberry Finn,* however, and mostly through an exploration of the character of Jim and Huck's complex relation to him, Twain divested himself of the role of comic satirist safely above the objects of his contempt and began to develop themes that were bound to recoil upon him, not only as an individual but also as a citizen.

13. See respectively, Wilson, "Mr. Lardner's American Characters," *Dial* (July 1924): 69–72; Anderson, "Four American Impressions: Gertrude Stein, Paul Rosenfeld, Ring Lardner, Sinclair Lewis," in *The Portable Sherwood Anderson,* ed. Horace Gregory, revised edition (New York: Viking Penguin, 1972), 430–31; and Mencken, "Lardner," in *Prejudices: A Selection,* ed. James T. Farrell (New York: Vintage Books, 1958), 197–201. Mencken's fears point to another aspect of Twain's legacy. Despite his own appreciative remarks about Lardner in *The American Language,* it is quite true that much of Lardner is lost to the contemporary reader. Mencken worried that the shifting historical course of the American language might trap Lardner in his own time and later generations would serve him up, if at all, "as a sandwich between introduction and notes." This last remark is insightful, but not so much because Mencken's disdain of the "perfesser" is warranted. Instead, the American speech that Twain transcribed was also broadcast throughout the world from the lecture platform, and a host of Twain imitators have since sustained our familiarity with a language that has long since passed from the scene. In addition, Lardner has not enjoyed the special labors of scholars (particularly Robert Ramsay and Frances Emerson) to preserve that speech. In a word, there is no *Ring Lardner Lexicon* as there is a *Mark Twain Lexicon.*

14. "Three Stories a Year Are Enough for a Writer," *New York Times Magazine,* March 25, 1917, 44.

15. *The Ring Lardner Reader,* ed. Maxwell Geismar (New York: Charles Scribner's Sons, 1963), 602.

16. See "Toward Vernacular Humor," *Virginia Quarterly Review* 46 (Spring 1970), especially 321–25.

17. *You Know Me Al: A Busher's Letters* (1916) (New York: Vintage Books, 1984), 66.

18. Ibid., 53.

19. "The House of Willa Cather," reprinted in *Critical Essays on Willa Cather,* ed. John J. Murphy (Boston: G. K. Hall and Co., 1984), 73.

20. See *Willa Cather on Writing: Critical Studies on Writing as an Art* (New York: Alfred A. Knopf, 1949), 58.

21. A facsimile of the undated letter with the author's corrections and deletions (which are not reproduced in the above quotation) is printed on the back cover of the *Mark Twain Journal* 15 (Winter 1973–1974).

22. See "Yours Truly, Huck Finn," in *One Hundred Years of "Huckleberry Finn": The Boy, His Book, and American Culture; Centennial Essays,* ed. Robert Sattelmeyer and J. Donald Crowley (Columbia: University of Missouri Press, 1985), 313–24. Pearce's essay, along with Cather's observations about the historical novel and her own example of the genre, might prove instructive to New Historicists, who typically regard texts as socially and linguistically constructed artifacts. Some texts, and *Huckleberry Finn* is one, drive beyond historical contingency precisely because their impulsions and art drive beyond the condition of language itself.

23. *Willa Cather on Writing,* 41.

24. See the "Preface" to *Alexander's Bridge,* new edition, (Boston: Houghton Mifflin, 1922), v–ix.

25. Ibid., vii.

26. *O Pioneers!* (Boston: Houghton Mifflin Co., 1913), 293–94.

27. *The Song of the Lark,* revised edition (Boston: Houghton Mifflin Co., 1932), 20.

28. *O Pioneers!,* 90–91.

29. In *Obscure Destinies* (1932) (New York: Vintage Books, 1974), 193, 206.

30. In ibid., 218.

31. In ibid., 230.

32. *O Pioneers!,* 309.

33. *My Ántonia* (1918) (Boston: Houghton Mifflin Co., 1954), 353.

34. According to Arnold Rampersad, in *The Life of Langston Hughes,* vol. 1, *1902–1941: I, Too, Sing America* (New York: Oxford University Press, 1986), 19, Hughes was so "thrilled" by a reading of *Adventures of Huckleberry Finn* that he became a lifelong admirer of Twain.

35. Given the general tendency of the argument of this essay, I hope it goes without saying that I do not mean to examine the intricate and controversial response of African-American readers and writers to *Huckleberry Finn.* It should be apparent that I am more interested here in the broadly humanistic vernacular vision embodied in Hughes's Simple sketches than in whether or not *Huck Finn* is a racist book. Those interested in this latter question will find instructive James S. Leonard, Thomas A. Tenney, and Thadious M. Davis, eds., *Satire or Evasion? Black Perspectives on "Huckleberry Finn"* (Durham: Duke University Press, 1992). Arnold Rampersad's "*Adventures of Huckleberry Finn* and Afro-American Literature" particularly deals with Twain and his influence upon African-American writers.

36. Quoted in Arnold Rampersad, *The Life of Langston Hughes,* vol. 2, *1941–1967: I Dream a World* (New York: Oxford University Press, 1988), 223.

37. Quoted in Rampersad, *Life of Langston Hughes* 2: 253.

38. *The Book of Negro Humor* (New York: Dodd, Mead, and Co., 1966), vii.

39. Quoted in Rampersad, *Life of Langston Hughes* 2: 64–65.

40. See ibid., 2: 64–65.

41. "Twentieth-Century Fiction and the Black Mask of Humanity," 48–49. Ellison never says so explicitly, but the whole thrust of his essay clearly implies that the terms of Huck's conflict are to be abstracted from the ingredients of a child's experience and in no way depend

on the boy's self-conscious comprehension of his situation. The whole artistic and historical justification of Huck's "adolescence," Ellison observes, is that Twain was "depicting a transitional period" in American life, and that, correspondingly, adolescence is "the time of the 'great confusion' during which both individuals and nations flounder between accepting and rejecting the responsibilities of adulthood" (50). If Huck actively and knowingly chose to perform a noble moral act, as some critics never tire of insisting he does do, the moral "message" of the book would be unmistakable, and readers would never have been able to consign the novel to the interests of a "boy's book." By the same token, however, the novel would have lost all its moral and humanizing force, since Huck would have embraced generalized and idealized fraternal values instead of responding to a felt attachment to Jim as an individual. If this were so, and since no "civilization" ever really denies its support of these values in the abstract, one might say that Huck's "problem" was solved, socially and politically, with the Emancipation Proclamation. But Twain knew, and Ellison knows, that the full and continuing interest of Huck's decision to go to hell and to help Jim has nothing to do with helping a race or advancing a political agenda but with preferring a known reality (Jim) over an abstract penalty (hell). Or, as Willa Cather said of Thomas Mann's historical novels, *Huckleberry Finn* deals with a figure who "chooses," not with one who, rightly or wrongly, "chose." Huck's decision is revitalized with every reading precisely because, in its dramatic essentials, it is pre-ideological and pre-political.

42. Ibid., 50–51.
43. "A Word about Simple," reprinted in *Langston Hughes, Black Genius: A Critical Evaluation,* ed. Therman B. O'Daniel (New York: William Morrow and Co., 1971), 116.
44. In *The Best of Simple* (1961) (New York: Hill and Wang, 1988), 10.
45. In ibid., 57.
46. In *Simple Speaks His Mind* (New York: Simon and Schuster, 1950), 173–74.
47. "Confused," in ibid., 174.
48. Ibid., 175.
49. In *Best of Simple,* 212, 213.
50. "Two Sides Not Enough," in ibid., 214–16.
51. Owen Dodson, quoted in Richard Barksdale, *Langston Hughes: The Poet and His Critics* (Chicago: American Library Association, 1977), 87.
52. "Bones, Bombs, Chicken Necks," in *Best of Simple,* 200.
53. In ibid., 3.
54. "The Negro Everyman, and His Humor," in *Veins of Humor,* ed. Harry Levin, 225–41, 235.
55. Wolfe's essay appeared in *Harper's Magazine* (November 1989). The editors solicited responses from several novelists to the piece, and selections from those reactions appeared in the "Letters" section of the magazine in the February 1990 issue. Wolfe's response to his critics, from which the above quotation is taken, appeared in the March 1990 issue.
56. *The Collected Poems of Wallace Stevens* (New York: Alfred A. Knopf, 1968), 516–17.
57. *Best of Simple,* 242–43, 244–45.

* * *

Scores of novelists and critics have commented directly or indirectly on Adventures of Huckleberry Finn. *Even those who have disparaged Twain's achievement have done so with the tacit understanding that his novel is central to the literary history of the United States.*

A Sampling of Writers on *Huckleberry Finn*

. . . it was not until he had written *Tom Sawyer* that [Mark Twain] could be called a novelist. Even now I think he should rather be called a romancer, though such a book as *Huckleberry Finn* takes itself out of the order of romance and places itself with the great things in picaresque fiction. Still, it is more poetic than picaresque, and of deeper psychology. The probable and credible soul that the author divines in the son of the town-drunkard is one which we might each own brother, and the art which portrays this nature at first hand in the person and language of the hero, without pose or affectation, is fine art.

–William Dean Howells, "Mark Twain: An Inquiry," *The North American Review,* February 1901

. . . Once when I was in [William] Morris's house, a superior anti-Dickens sort of man (sort of man that thinks Dickens is no gentleman) was annoyed by Morris disparaging Thackeray. With studied gentleness he asked whether Morris could name a greater master of English. Morris promptly said "Mark Twain." This delighted me extremely, as it was my own opinion; and I then found that Morris was an incurable Huckfinomaniac. This was the more remarkable, as Morris would have regarded the Yankee at the Court of King Arthur as blasphemy, and would have blown your head off for implying that the contemporaries of Joan of Arc could touch your own contemporaries in villainy.

–George Bernard Shaw to Samuel L. Clemens, 3 July 1907

"Bunner has told me what he thinks," he said when Trent referred to the American's theory. "I don't find myself convinced by it, because it doesn't really explain some of the oddest facts. But I have lived long enough in the United States to know that such a stroke of revenge, done in a secret, melodramatic way, is not an unlikely thing. It is quite a characteristic feature of certain sections of the labour movement there. Americans have a taste and a talent for that sort of business. Do you know *Huckleberry Finn?*"

"Do I know my own name?" exclaimed Trent.

"Well, I think the most American thing in that great American epic is Tom Sawyer's elaboration of an extremely difficult and romantic scheme, taking days to carry out, for securing the escape of the nigger Jim, which could have been managed quite easily in twenty minutes. You know how fond they are of lodges and brotherhoods. Every college club has its secret signs and handgrips. You've heard of the Know-Nothing movement in politics, I dare say, and the Ku Klux Klan. Then look at Brigham Young's penny-dreadful tyranny in Utah, with real blood. The founders of the Mormon State were of the purest Yankee stock in America; and you know what they did. It's all part of the same mental tendency. Americans make fun of it among themselves. For my part, I take it very seriously."

–E. C. Bentley, *Trent's Last Case* (1913)

I believe that "Huckleberry Finn" is one of the great masterpieces of the world, that it is the full equal of "Don Quixote" and "Robinson Crusoe," that it is vastly better than "Gil Blas," "Tristram Shandy," "Nicholas Nickleby" or "Tom Jones." I believe that it will be read by human beings of all ages, not as a solemn duty but for the honest love of it, and over and over again, long after every book written in America between the years 1800 and 1860, with perhaps three exceptions, has disappeared entirely save as a classroom fossil. I believe that Mark Twain had a clearer vision of life, that he came nearer to its elementals and was less deceived by its false appearances, than any other American who has ever presumed to manufacture generalizations, not excepting Emerson. I believe that, admitting all his defects, he wrote better English, in the sense of cleaner, straighter, vivider, saner English, than either Irving or Hawthorne. I believe that four of his books–"Huck," "Life on the Mississippi," "Captain Stormfield's Visit to Heaven," and "A Connecticut Yankee"–are alone worth more, as works of art and as criticisms of life, than the whole output of Cooper, Irving, Holmes, Mitchell, Stedman, Whittier and Bryant. I believe that he ranks well above Whitman and certainly not below Poe. I believe that he was the true father of our national literature, the first genuinely American artist of the blood royal.

By comparison with that copiousness and energy and originality, "faults" cease to count. To say that some of the plotting of "Huckleberry Finn" is imperfect or that some of the episodes are unconvincing is as irrelevant as it would be to complain, as one critic did, that Coleridge's "Ancient Mariner" was "improbable."

–H. L. Mencken, *The Smart Set,* February 1913

I wouldn't consider Mark Twain our greatest humorist. I guess George Ade is. Certainly he speaks to us more than Mark Twain does because he belongs to our own time. . . . Mark Twain's boys are tough and poverty stricken and they belong to a period very different from that of our own boys.

–Ring Lardner, *New York Times Magazine,* 25 March 1917

When the brook chatters or at night when the moon comes up and the winds plays in the corn, a man hears the whispering of the gods.

Mark got to that once–when he wrote *Huck Finn.* He forgot Howells and the good wife and everyone. Again he was the half savage, tender, god-worshipping, believing boy. He had a proud conscious innocence.

–Sherwood Anderson to Van Wyck Brooks, 1918

Huckleberry Finn is the American epic hero. Greece had Ulysses. America must be content with an illiterate lad. He expresses our germinal past. He expresses the movement of the American soul through all the sultry climaxes of the Nineteenth Century.

–Waldo Frank, *Our America* (1919)

"I am a poet [says Jurgen], and I make literature."

"But in Philistia to make literature and to make trouble for yourself are synonyms," the tumblebug explained. "I know, for already we of Philistia have been pestered by three of these makers of literature. Yes, there was Edgar, whom I starved and hunted until I got tired of it. . . . And there was Walt, whom I chivvied and battered from place to place. . . . Then later there was Mark, whom I frightened into disguising himself in a clown's suit, so that nobody might suspect him to be a maker of literature. . . ."

"Now, but these three," cried Jurgen, "are the glory of Philistia: and of all that Philistia has produced, it is these three alone, whom living ye made least of, that to-day are honored wherever art is honored."

–James Branch Cabell, *Jurgen* (1919)

[Mark Twain's] whole unconscious life, the pent-up river of his own soul, had burst its bonds and rushed forth, a joyous torrent! Do we need any other explanation of the abandon, the beauty, the eternal freshness of *Huckleberry Finn?*

–Van Wyck Brooks, *The Ordeal of Mark Twain* (1924)

If I were asked to name three American books which have the possibility of a long, long, life, I would say at once: *The Scarlet Letter, Huckleberry Finn,* and *The Country of the Pointed Firs.*

–Willa Cather, preface to *The Best Stories of Sarah Orne Jewett* (1925)

Huckleberry Finn took the first journey back. He
was the first to look back at the republic from the perspective of
the west. His eyes were the first eyes that ever looked at us
objectively that were not eyes from overseas. There were mountains
at the frontier but he wanted more than ~~that~~ mountains to look at with his rest -
less eyes--he wanted to find out about men and how they lived together.
And because he turned back we have him forever.

F. Scott Fitzgerald.

*Statement Fitzgerald provided for a banquet celebrating the centennial of Mark Twain's birth (Arlyn and Matthew J. Bruccoli Collection of
F. Scott Fitzgerald, Thomas Cooper Library, University of South Carolina)*

Mark Twain, who is as deep and as broad as the Mississippi River and the Mississippi river *[sic]* is as deep and as broad as a river possibly could be which makes Mark Twain the pleasantest and the most wonderful thing he did and the Mississippi ever might try.

—Gertrude Stein, note given to the Mark Twain Society in St. Louis, 1934

All modern American literature comes from one book by Mark Twain called *Huckleberry Finn.* If you read it you must stop where Nigger Jim is stolen from the boys. That is the real end. The rest is just cheating. But it's the best book we've had. All American writing comes from that. There was nothing before. There has been nothing as good since.

—Ernest Hemingway, *The Green Hills of Africa* (1935)

Jim is the best example in nineteenth century fiction of the average Negro slave (not the tragic mulatto or the noble savage), illiterate, superstitious, yet clinging to his hope for freedom, to his love for his own. And he is completely believable.

—Sterling Brown, *The Negro in American Fiction* (1935)

Though a white American, a mocker of religion, he too, perhaps, must have caught some inkling in his life of that tendency so widepread in the vast Mississippi Valley that made men and women stand aside and gaze with wistful and baffled eyes upon their own lives. . . . In my reading of Twain the experience of my childhood would return and reinforce what I was reading and make it *strangely familiar.*"

—Richard Wright, "Memories of My Grandmother"

My favorite was *Huckleberry Finn;* probably, I realize now, because of its richness in sense impressions of the type that made my own boyhood so vivid.

—Grant Wood, *Mark Twain Quarterly,* Fall 1937

He [Mark Twain] was surrounded by such an aura of wonder, and so beloved for *Tom Sawyer* and *The Adventures of Huckleberry Finn [sic]* that most contemporary eyes could not see that he had no historical insight, no philosophical genius. . . . he was a clown, with a clown's reward in money, and in popularity that needed his sensational interviews and articles, his white suits and princely ways of life to continue him as a figure.

—Edgar Lee Masters, *Mark Twain: A Portrait* (1938)

[In *Huckleberry Finn,* Mark Twain] produced a model of the vernacular style which has served as a foundation for some of the best and most characteristic writers of the present day. He showed them that

Cover for a 1935 Russian edition for Adventures of Huckleberry Finn *(Buffalo and Erie County Public Library)*

a living manner of writing is not to be sought in the seventeenth and eighteenth century writers of England, but in the literary language of their own people.

—W. Somerset Maugham, *The Saturday Evening Post*, 6 January 1940

Take out Tom Sawyer and [*Huckleberry Finn* is] the greatest book ever written.

—Sinclair Lewis, circa 1941, quoted in Mark Shorer, *Sinclair Lewis: An American Life*

The damned human race is displayed with derision and abhorrence, yet this is on the ground that it has fallen short of its own decencies. Moreover at least *Huckleberry Finn* has a hero, the only heroic character (apart from Joan of Arc . . .) he ever drew, and it is the essence of what Mark Twain had to say that the hero is a Negro slave.

—Bernard DeVoto, introduction, *The Portable Mark Twain* (1946)

Huck Finn is alone: there is no more solitary character in fiction. The fact that he has a father only emphasizes his loneliness; and he views his father with a terrifying detachment. So we come to see Huck himself in the end as one of the permanent symbolic figures of fiction; not unworthy to take a place with Ulysses, Faust, Don Quixote, Don Juan, Hamlet and other great discoveries that man has made about himself.

—T. S. Eliot, introduction, *Adventures of Huckleberry Finn* (1950)

About six months ago I re-read *Huckleberry Finn*, by Mark Twain, for the first time since I was a boy, and I was trying when I read it to put myself back in the position of what it would seem like to re-read the book without knowing the United States very well. Because *Huckleberry Finn* is one of those books which is a key book for understanding the United States; just as I think one could take other books, English books—shall I say *Oliver Twist?*—as corresponding pictures of a British attitude.

—W. H. Auden, "Huck and Oliver," *The Listener*, October 1953

After Twain's compelling image of black and white fraternity the Negro generally disappears from fiction as a rounded human being. And if already in Twain's time a novel which was optimistic concerning a democracy which would include all men could not escape being banned from public libraries, by our day his great drama of interracial fraternity has become, for most Americans at least, an amusing boy's story and nothing more.

—Ralph Ellison, "Twentieth-Century Fiction and the Black Mask of Humanity," *Confluence*, December 1953

Interviewer: You must feel indebted to Sherwood Anderson, but how do you regard him as a writer?

Faulkner: He was the father of my generation of American writers and the tradition of American writing which our successors will carry on. He has never received his proper evaluation. Dreiser is his older brother and Mark Twain the father of them both. . . .

Interviewer: What about your favorite characters?

Faulkner: . . . . Huck Finn, of course, and Jim. Tom Sawyer I never liked much—an awful prig.

—William Faulkner, interview, *Paris Review*, 1956

Some eight years ago I met, in Paris, a Russian violinist who had

heard that I was "from the West", ~~and who~~ after a few moments of conversation,

he
eagerly asked me whether I was from "the Mississippi".   I asked him whether

he meant from the State of Mississippi.   He looked perplexed and put his hand

to his forehead and said eagerly - "But the river, the river?"   Oh yes, I

told him, I had crossed the Mississippi river many times.   He said at once

that this river was the thing in America that he most wished to see!   He,

himself, was born and grew up on another great river, in a little town on the

            when
Volga, ~~but while~~ he was ~~still~~ a little boy he had read a Russian translation of

"Huckleberry Finn", and had always thought that the Mississippi must be much

more wonderful and romantic than the Volga.   I questioned him a little about

the book - he seemed to remember it perfectly.   But how in the world could

        Talk   nigger
the ~~negro speech~~ of Jim be translated into Russian, and what would become of

          severn shadings of Southern dialect
the ~~seven shadings of Southern~~   which the author in his preface

tells the reader must not be confounded one with the other?   It seemed to me

that the most delightful things in "Huckleberry Finn" must disappear in a

translation.   One could ~~easily~~ translate Parkman or Emerson, certainly; but how

translate Mark Twain?   The only answer seems to be that if a book has vitality

enough, it can live through even the brutalities of translators.

Willa Cather

Willa Cather's revised typescript of an undated letter in which she recalls a Russian violinist's love for a translation of
Adventures of Huckleberry Finn *(back cover,* Mark Twain Journal, *Winter 1973–1974)*

[Huckleberry Finn] is a jerky, uneven, patchwork tale. . . . yet it is the crown of our literature.
—Herman Wouk, *San Francisco Chronicle,* August 1956

No more beautiful or instructive example of the artist's dilemma, of the source of his passions, and how, if ever, he must lovingly resolve them, is available to us than this passion of Mark Twain, resolved in *Huckleberry Finn.*
—Wright Morris, *The Territory Ahead* (1957)

Decidedly Twain does not belong with the Flauberts and the Henry Jameses who fussed and labored to remove every slight flaw. He belongs instead with Balzac and Dickens, the great restless creators who never strove for one kind of perfection because perhaps they had something better to do. They had energy and originality and gusto. Our first impulse is to say of them what Dryden said of Shakespeare: "Here is God's plenty."
—Joseph Wood Krutch, *The New York Times,*
March 1960

[Huckleberry Finn is] the first Southern novel in which the action is generated inside the characters. It is not perhaps the masterpiece that the academic Mark Twain "industry" has made it out to be; yet for the reason I have indicated, it is a work of great originality and historical importance.
—Allen Tate, *The Virginia Quarterly Review,*
Summer 1968

I think I must have read *Huck Finn* just before I entered high school, when I was about thirteen. That's the only book I've read almost perennially. I've read it every two or three years since then.
—William Styron, interview, *Chicago Tribune
Book World,* October 1968

I guess the only American writer that influenced me at all would be Mark Twain—*Huck Finn.*
—Walker Percy, interview, "An Afternoon with Walker Percy," *Notes on Mississippi Writers* (1971)

There are, indeed, incoherences in Huckleberry Finn. But the book survives everything. It survives not merely because it is a seminal invention of a language for American fiction, nor because Huck's search for a freedom of "consciousness" dramatizes the new philosophical spirit which was to find formulation with William James; nor because it is a veracious and compelling picture of life in a time and place, or because Huck is vividly alive as of that time and place; nor because, in the shadow of the Civil War and the bitter aftermath, it embodies a deep skepticism about the millennial dream of America, or because it hymns youthful hope and gallantry in the face of the old desperate odds of the world. All these things, and more, are there, but the book survives ultimately because all is absorbed into a powerful, mythic image.
—Robert Penn Warren, *The Southern Review* (1972)

There are images in fiction that haunt my imagination, so much so that I even keep a little list of them. Foremost of them are: Odysseus trying to get home; Scheherazade telling her stories; Don Quixote riding with Sancho across LaMancha; and Huckleberry Finn floating down the river. I would love one day, without aspiring to include myself in that biggest of leagues, to come up with a similar image, one that was as much larger than the book in which it appeared as those images are larger than those stories in which they appear. I love language, and I really believe that Huck's language, Huck's voice, is as much a substance in that novel as the image of Huck and Jim drifting down the Mississippi.
—John Barth, interview, *Contemporary Literature,*
Winter 1981

The mark of how good "Huckleberry Finn" has to be is that one can compare it to a number of our best modern American novels and it stands up page for page, awkward here, sensational there—absolutely the equal of one of those rare, incredible first novels that come along once or twice in a decade.
—Norman Mailer, *The New York Times Book Review,*
December 1984

I can't honestly say that I consciously changed my precious writing style because of *Huck* . . . but I'm quite certain that it and Twain seeped into the well and in later years I dropped the bucket into that well and came up with a respect for and concern with the colloquial and the everyday bric-a-brac of life as the backbone of "literature."
—Irvin Faust, *DLB Yearbook,* 1985

Among so many other constant illuminations in the book, the dawning in Huck of what it is to be truly grownup on the inside—that is, what it is to be Jim—is one of the ceaselessly satisfying experiences in all of literature.
—Nat Hentoff, *DLB Yearbook,* 1985

Reading Mark Twain's stories as a child, I came across the word *nigger* and put the book down.
—Margaret Walker, *Richard Wright:
Daemonic Genius* (1988)

I don't know if you can write at all, seriously, without invoking race, especially Southerners. Of

*Cover for the DVD of the 1939 movie starring Mickey Rooney as
Huck and Rex Ingram as Jim (Richland County Public Library)*

course, people like Melville did look into that subject as well. But it's almost impossible for us to write seriously without bringing in race. From Twain's *Huckleberry Finn* to all of Faulkner's stuff, the best of that stuff, the best of, I would say, Southern literature would have race involved.

–Ernest Gaines, interview, March 1993

I [Easy Rawlins] . . . took up the empty time with a book. I'd picked up *Huckleberry Finn* at a used book store in Santa Monica. A few liberal libraries and the school system had wanted to ban the book because of the racist content. Liberal-minded whites and blacks wanted to erase racism from the world. I applauded the idea but my memory of Huckleberry wasn't one of racism. I remember Jim and Huck as friends out on the river. I could have been either one of them.

–Walter Mosley, *Black Betty* (1994)

The Adventures of Huckleberry Finn [sic] has little to offer in the way of greatness. There is more to be learned about the American character *from* its canonization than *through* its canonization.

–Jane Smiley, *Harper's Magazine,* December 1995

The source of my unease reading this amazing, troubling book now seems clear: an imperfect coming to terms with three matters Twain addresses–Huck Finn's estrangement, soleness and morbidity as an outcast child; the disproportionate sadness at the center of Jim's and his relationship; and the secrecy in which Huck's engagement with (rather than escape from) a racist society is necessarily conducted. It is also clear that the rewards of my efforts to come to terms have been abundant.

–Toni Morrison, introduction,
Adventures of Huckleberry Finn (1996)

African American Critics on
Huckleberry Finn

In his 1948 introduction to Adventures of Huckleberry Finn *the influential critic Lionel Trilling declared that Mark Twain's novel was a central document in American culture and one of the great books of the world. Two years later, T. S. Eliot affirmed Trilling's judgment. After the Supreme Court's ruling in* Brown v. Board of Education *in 1954, Twain's so-called masterpiece was often studied in the now-desegregated classroom, and an inevitable reaction followed. In 1957 the New York City Board of Education removed* Adventures of Huckleberry Finn *from the list of approved texts for elementary and junior-high schools. In subsequent decades school boards, concerned teachers, parents, and literary critics have struggled with the question of racism in the novel.*

The main objections to the novel are threefold: Twain's use of the word nigger *(a word that appears more than two hundred times in the book) is demeaning and offensive to African American children who are forced to read the book; Jim is a minstrel-show figure, a caricature of an African American man presented as a degrading stereotype; and finally, that though Twain at times addresses serious moral questions, the last chapters of the book are pure burlesque and indicate that the author had abandoned satire for farce. Critics and educators have debated the issue of race from strongly held positions: "The book is not racist because . . . ." "The book is racist because . . . ". "*Adventures of Huckleberry Finn *is not racist, but the literary sophistication required to discern Mark Twain's true intent is quite above the capacities of junior high school, or even high school students, white or black." "The solution to the problem is not to ban the book but to learn how to teach it better."*

Ever since its American publication in 1885, Adventures of Huckleberry Finn *has been controversial—and on occasion has been banned in certain libraries and localities. From its initial condemnation on narrow grounds by the Concord Public Library committee, the debate about the novel has evolved and become more consequential. The contemporary debate involves a host of long-standing issues and includes questions of free speech and matters of interpretation and aesthetic judgment. Critics argue over the accuracy of Twain's representation of chattel slavery and Jim's dialect, and the degree of the novel's moral seriousness. It would perhaps be too much to say that a critical consensus has been achieved on any of the important issues raised by Twain's novel.*

What follows is a sampling of opinion by African American teachers, literary scholars, and historians—two full-length essays and excerpts from other critics. It should come as no surprise that there is no standard view among African American scholars any more than there is among Anglo-American scholars.

Cover for a 1950 Hebrew edition of Adventures of Huckleberry Finn *(Buffalo and Erie County Public Library)*

The Case Against *Huck Finn*
John H. Wallace

The Issue

The *Adventures of Huckleberry Finn,* by Mark Twain, is the most grotesque example of racist trash ever written. During the 1981–82 school year, the media carried reports that it was challenged in Davenport, Iowa; Houston, Texas; Bucks County, Pennsylvania; and, of all places, Mark Twain Intermediate School in Fairfax County, Virginia. Parents in Waukegan, Illinois, in 1983 and in Springfield, Illinois, in 1984 asked that the book be removed from the classroom—and there are many challenges to this book that go unnoticed by the press. All of these are coming from black parents and teachers after complaints from their children or students, and frequently they are supported by white teachers, as in the case of Mark Twain Intermediate School.

For the past forty years, black families have trekked to schools in numerous districts throughout the country to say, "This book is not good for our children," only to be turned away by insensitive and often unwittingly racist teachers and administrators who respond, "This book is a classic." Classic or not, it should not be allowed to continue to cause our children embarrassment about their heritage.

Louisa May Alcott, the Concord Public Library, and others condemned the book as trash when it was published in 1885. The NAACP and the National Urban League successfully collaborated to have *Huckleberry Finn* removed from the classrooms of the public schools of New York City in 1957 because it uses the term "nigger." In 1969 Miami-Dade Junior College removed the book from its classrooms because the administration believed that the book creates an emotional block for black students which inhibits learning. It was excluded from the classrooms of the New Trier High School in Winnetka, Illinois, and removed from the required reading list in the state of Illinois in 1976.

My own research indicates that the assignment and reading aloud of *Huckleberry Finn* in our classrooms is humiliating and insulting to black students. It contributes to their feelings of low self-esteem and to the white students' disrespect for black people. It constitutes mental cruelty, harassment, and outright racial intimidation to force black students to sit in the classroom with their white peers and read *Huckleberry Finn*. The attitudes developed by the reading of such literature can lead to tensions, discontent, and even fighting. If this book is removed from the required reading lists of our schools, there should be improved student-to-student, student-to-teacher, and teacher-to-teacher relationships.

"Nigger"

According to *Webster's Dictionary*, the word "nigger" means a Negro or a member of any dark-skinned race of people and is *offensive*. Black people have never accepted "nigger"as a proper term–not in George Washington's time, Mark Twain's time, or William Faulkner's time. A few white authors, thriving on making blacks objects of ridicule and scorn by having blacks use this word as they, the white authors, were writing and speaking for blacks in a dialect they perceived to be peculiar to black people, may have given the impression that blacks accepted the term. Nothing could be further from the truth.

Some black authors have used "nigger," but not in literature to be consumed by children in the classroom. Black authors know as well as whites that there is money to be made selling books that ridicule black people. As a matter of fact, the white child learns early in life that his or her black peer makes a good butt for a joke. Much of what goes on in the classroom reinforces

'Gee, Huck — Teacher Says I Shouldn't Play With You'

Cartoon by Jacob Burck that appeared in the 15 September 1957 issue of the Chicago Sun Times, *after the board of education for New York City dropped* Adventures of Huckleberry Finn *from the approved textbook lists for elementary and junior-high-school students (Collection of Louis J. Budd)*

this behavior. Often the last word uttered before a fight is "nigger." Educators must discourage the ridicule of "different" children.

In the Classroom

Russell Baker, of the *New York Times* (14 April 1982), has said (and Jonathan Yardley, of the *Washington Post* [10 May 1982], concurred),

Kids are often exposed to books long before they are ready for them or exposed to them in a manner that seems almost calculated to evaporate whatever enthusiasm the students may bring to them. . . . Very few youngsters of high school age are ready for *Huckleberry Finn*. Leaving aside its subtle depiction of racial attitudes and its complex view of American society, the book is written in a language that will seem baroque, obscure and antiquated to many young people today. The vastly sunnier *Tom Sawyer* is a book for kids, but *Huckleberry Finn most emphatically is not.*

The milieu of the classroom is highly charged with emotions. There are twenty to thirty unique personalities with hundreds of needs to be met simultaneously. Each student wants to be accepted and to be like the white, mid-

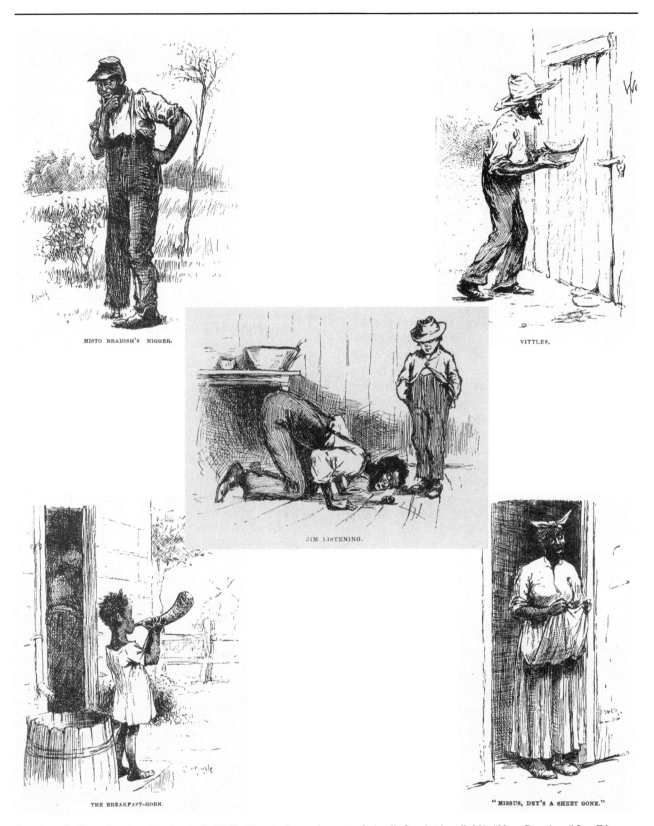

MISTO BRADISH'S NIGGER.

VITTLES.

JIM LISTENING.

THE BREAKFAST-HORN.

"MISSUS, DEY'S A SHEET GONE."

Drawings of African American characters by E. W. Kemble, who became known professionally for what he called his "Negro Drawings." In a February 1930 essay for The Colophon, *Kemble recalled how he used a young boy as his single model "for every character in the story—man, woman and child. Jim the Negro seemed to please him the most. He would jam his little black wool cap over his head, shoot out his lips and mumble coon talk all the while he was posing." Mark Twain's approval of Kemble's depictions has been cited by critics of the novel as evidence of the author's racism (from* Adventures of Huckleberry Finn, *Mark Twain House, Hartford, Connecticut).*

dle-class child whom he perceives to be favored by the teacher. Since students do not want their differences highlighted, it is best to accentuate their similarities; but the reading of *Huck Finn* in class accentuates the one difference that is always apparent—color.

My research suggests that the black child is offended by the use of the word "nigger" anywhere, no matter what rationale the teacher may use to justify it. If the teacher permits its use, the black child tends to reject the teacher because the student is confident that the teacher is prejudiced. Communications are effectively severed, thwarting the child's education. Pejorative terms should not be granted any legitimacy by their use in the classroom under the guise of teaching books of great literary merit, nor for any other reason.

Equal Protection and Opportunity
in the Classroom

To paraphrase Irwin Katz,[1] the use of the word "nigger" by a prestigious adult like a teacher poses a strong social threat to the black child. Any expression by a white or black teacher of dislike or devaluation, whether through harsh, indifferent, or patronizing behavior, would tend to have an unfavorable effect on the performance of black children in their school work. This is so because *various psychological theories suggest that the black students' covert reactions to the social threat would constitute an important source of intellectual impairment.*

Dorothy Gilliam, writing in the *Washington Post* of 12 April 1982, said, "First Amendment rights are crucial to a healthy society. No less crucial is the Fourteenth Amendment and its guarantee of equal protection under the law." *The use of the word "nigger" in the classroom does not provide black students with equal protection and is in violation of their constitutional rights. Without equal protection, they have neither equal access nor equal opportunity for an education.*

One group of citizens deeply committed to effecting change and to retaining certain religious beliefs sacred to themselves are members of the Jewish religion. In a publication issued by the Jewish Community Council (November 1981), the following guidelines were enunciated regarding the role of religious practices in public schools: "In no event should any student, teacher, or public school staff member feel that his or her own beliefs or practices are being questioned, infringed upon, or compromised by programs taking place in or sponsored by the public school." Further, "schools should avoid practices which operate to single out and isolate 'different' pupils and thereby [cause] embarrassment."[2]

I endorse these statements without reservation, for I believe the rationale of the Jewish Community Council is consistent with my position. I find it incongruent to contend that it is fitting and proper to shelter

"The Pith of the American Literature Curriculum"

Peaches Henry contends that Mark Twain had an "equivocal attitude" toward blacks in his life and his fiction.

The factor of racial uncertainty on the part of Twain, its manifestation in his best-loved piece, and its existence in American society should not be a barrier to *Huckleberry Finn*'s admittance to the classroom. Instead, this should make it the pith of the American literature curriculum. The insolubility of the race question as regards *Huckleberry Finn* functions as a model of the fundamental racial ambiguity of the American mind-set. Active engagement with Twain's novel provides one method for students to confront their own deepest racial feelings and insecurities. Though the problems of racial perspective present in *Huckleberry Finn* may never be satisfactorily explained for censors or scholars, the consideration of them may have a practical, positive bearing on the manner in which America approaches race in he coming century.

—from Peaches Henry, "The Struggle for Tolerance: Race and Censorship in *Huckleberry Finn*," in *Satire or Evasion? Black Perspectives on* Huckleberry Finn, p. 44

children from isolation, embarrassment, and ridicule due to their religious beliefs and then deny the same protection to other children because of the color of their skin. The basic issue is the same. It is our purpose to spare children from scorn, to increase personal pride, and to foster the American belief of acceptance on merit, not color, sex, religion, or origin.

The Teacher

Many "authorities" say *Huckleberry Finn* can be used in our intermediate and high school classrooms. They consistently put stipulations on its use like the following: It must be used with appropriate planning. It is the responsibility of the teacher to assist students in the understanding of the historical setting of the novel, the characters being depicted, the social context, including prejudice, which existed at the time depicted in the book. Balanced judgment on the part of the classroom teacher must be used prior to making a decision to utilize this book in an intermediate or high school program. Such judgment would include taking into account the age and maturity of the students, their ability to comprehend abstract concepts, and the methodology of presentation.

Any material that requires such conditions could be dangerous racist propaganda in the hands of even

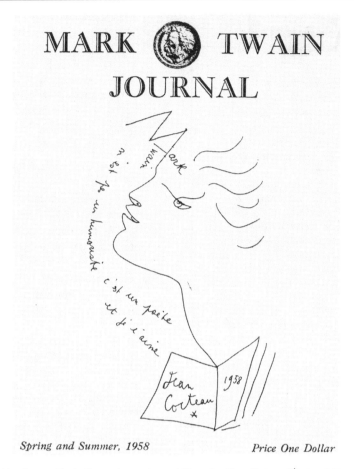

MARK TWAIN JOURNAL

Spring and Summer, 1958

Price One Dollar

Cover for journal with tribute to Twain from writer, artist, and filmmaker Jean Cocteau. The inscription reads "Mark Twain is not a humorist, he is a poet, and I love him" (Collection of Tom Quirk).

our best teachers. And "some, not all, teachers are hostile, racist, vindictive, inept, or even neurotic," though "many are compassionate and skillful."[3] Teacher attitudes are important to students. Some teachers are marginal at best, yet many school administrators are willing to trust them with a book that maligns blacks. *Huckleberry Finn* would have been out of the classroom ages ago if it used "dago," "wop," or "spic."

When "authorities" mention the "historical setting" of *Huckleberry Finn,* they suggest that it is an accurate, factual portrayal of the way things were in slavery days. In fact, the book is the outgrowth of Mark Twain's memory and imagination, written twenty years after the end of slavery. Of the two main characters depicted, one is a thief, a liar, a sacrilegious corn-cob-pipe-smoking truant; the other is a self-deprecating slave. No one would want his children to emulate this pair. Yet some "authorities" speak of Huck as a boyhood hero. Twain warns us in the beginning of *Huckleberry Finn,* "Persons attempting to find a motive in this narrative will be prosecuted; persons attempting to find a moral in it will be banished; persons attempting to find a plot in it will be shot." I think we ought to listen to

Twain and stop feeding this trash to our children. It does absolutely nothing to enhance racial harmony. The prejudice that existed then is still very much apparent today. Racism against blacks is deeply rooted in the American culture and is continually reinforced by the schools, by concern for socioeconomic gain, and by the vicarious ego enhancement it brings to those who manifest it.

Huckleberry Finn is racist, whether its author intended it to be or not. The book implies that black people are not honest. For example, Huck says about Jim: "It most froze me to hear such talk. He wouldn't ever dared to talk such talk in his life before. Just see what a difference it made in him the minute he judged he was about free. It was according to the old saying, 'give a nigger an inch and hell take an ell.' Thinks I, this is what comes of my not thinking"(chap. 16). And in another section of the book, the Duke, in reply to a question from the King, says: "Mary Jane'll be in mourning from this out; and the first you know the nigger that does up the rooms will get an order to box these duds up and put 'em away; and do you reckon a nigger can run across money and not borrow some of it?"(chap. 26).

One of America's Best Pieces of Ironic Fiction

Richard Barksdale acknowledges that "ironic fiction, whether from the past or the present, is difficult to teach, especially to young teenagers, who usually founder on deliberately oversubtle misstatements."

So, although Jim's roots lie deep in the soil of slavery and American racism, although his is an honest and forthright portrayal of a slave runaway, and although young black teenagers are traumatized by reading about the Jims of slavery time, the great difficulty with *Adventures of Huckleberry Finn* is that it is one of America's best pieces of ironic fiction. To a nation that was and is sharply divided on matters of race, Twain's novel suggests that friendships between black and white can best be forged by the least of us, and then only under the worst of circumstances. Undoubtedly, only a reading audience of some maturity and perceptive insight—an audience that can probe for lurking truths under surface facts and figures and events—can grasp the far-reaching implications of the adventures of a white Huck and a black Jim floating down the river of American life. As Francis Bacon once wrote, "Reading maketh the full man"; but not all and sundry in our error-ridden society can sit and sup at fiction's table without occasionally feeling the pain and anguish generated by that error-ridden society.

—from Richard Barksdale, "History, Slavery, and Thematic Irony in *Huckleberry Finn*," in *Satire or Evasion? Black Perspectives on* Huckleberry Finn, p. 55

Huckleberry Finn also insinuates that black people are less intelligent than whites. In a passage where Huck and Tom are trying to get the chains off Jim, Tom says: "They couldn't get the chain off, so they just cut their hand off and shoved. And a leg would be better still. But we got to let that go. There ain't necessity enough in this case; and, besides, Jim's a nigger, and wouldn't understand the reason for it"(chap. 35). On another occasion, when Tom and Huck are making plans to get Jim out of the barn where he is held captive, Huck says: "He told him everything. Jim, he couldn't see no sense in most of it, but he allowed we was white folks and knowed better than him; so he was satisfied, and said he would do it all just as Tom said"(chap. 36).

Twain said in *Huckleberry Finn,* more than one hundred years ago, what Dr. W. B. Shockley and A. R. Jensen are trying to prove through empirical study today.[4] This tells us something about the power of the printed word when it is taught to children by a formidable institution such as the school.

Huckleberry Finn even suggests that blacks are not human beings. When Huck arrives at Aunt Sally's house, she asks him why he is late:

"We blowed a cylinder head."
"Good gracious! anybody hurt?"
"No'm. Killed a nigger."
"Well, it's lucky; because sometimes people do get hurt." (Chap. 32)

There are indications that the racist views and attitudes implicit in the preceding quotations are as prevalent in America today as they were over one hundred years ago. *Huckleberry Finn* has not been successful in fighting race hate and prejudice, as its proponents maintain, but has helped to retain the status quo.

The Black Student
In 1963 John Fisher, former president of Columbia Teachers College, stated:

The black American youngster happens to be a member of a large and distinctive group that for a very long time has been the object of special political, legal, and social action. . . . To act as though any child is separable from his history is indefensible. In terms of educational planning, it is *irresponsible*.
Every black child is the victim of the history of his race in this country. On the day he enters kindergarten, he carries a burden *no white child* can ever know, no matter what other handicaps or disabilities he may suffer.[5]

The primary school child learns, almost the minute he enters school, that black is associated with dirtiness, ugliness, and wickedness. Much of what teachers and students think of the black child is color based. As a result, the black pupil knows his pigmentation is an impediment to his progress.

As early as the fifth grade, the black student studies American history and must accept his ancestors in the role of slaves. This frustrating and painful experience leaves scars that very few educators, writers, and especially English teachers can understand. We compound these problems for black children when we force them to read aloud the message of *Huckleberry Finn*. It is so devastatingly traumatic that the student may never recover. How much pain must a black child endure to secure an education? No other child is asked to suffer so much embarrassment, humiliation, and racial intimidation at the hands of so powerful an institution as the school. The vast majority of black students have no tolerance for either "ironic" or "satirical" reminders of the insults and degradation heaped upon their ancestors in slavery and postslavery times.

Dorothy Gilliam (*Washington Post,* 12 April 1982) makes a good case for protecting the rights of students when she says, "Where rights conflict, one must sometimes supersede the other. Freedom of speech does not, for example, allow words to be deliberately used in a way that would cause someone to suffer a heart attack. By the same token, the use of words in ways that cause psychological and emotional damage is an unacceptable exercise of free speech."

Racism

If indeed, as *Huckleberry Finn*'s proponents claim, the book gives a positive view of blacks and has an antislavery, antiracist message, then the Nazi party, the Ku Klux Klan, and the White Citizens Council must see something different. Most of the hate mail received when a school in northern Virginia restricted the use of the book was from these groups.

It is difficult to believe that Samuel Clemens would write a book against the institution of slavery; he did, after all, join a Confederate army bent on preserving that peculiar institution. Also, he could not allow Huck to help Jim to his freedom. It seems he was a hodgepodge of contradictions.

Huckleberry Finn is an American classic for no other reason than that it ridicules blacks to a greater extent than any other book given our children to read. The book and racism feed on each other and have withstood the test of time because many Americans insist on preserving our racist heritage.

Marguerite Barnett (1982) points out:

By ridiculing blacks, exaggerating their facial features, and denying their humanity, the popular art of the Post-Civil-War period represented the political culture's attempt to deny blacks the equal status and rights awarded them in the Emancipation Proclamation. By making blacks inhuman, American whites could destroy their claim to equal treatment. Blacks as slaves posed no problem because they were under complete domination, but blacks as free men created political problems. The popular culture of the day supplied the answer by dehumanizing blacks and picturing them as childlike and inferior.[6]

In this day of enlightenment, teachers should not rely on a book that teaches the subtle sickness of racism to our young and causes so much psychological damage to a large segment of our population. We are a multicultural, pluralistic nation. We must teach our young to respect all races, ethnic groups, and religious groups in the most positive terms conceivable.

Recommendations

This book should not be used with children. It is permissible to use the original *Huckleberry Finn* with students in graduate courses of history, English, and social

science if one wants to study the perpetration and perpetuation of racism. The caustic, abrasive language is less likely to offend students of that age group because they tend to be mature enough to understand and discuss issues without feeling intimidated by the instructor, fellow students, or racism.

My research relating to *Huckleberry Finn* indicates that black parents and teachers, and their children, and students, have complained about books that use the word "nigger" being read aloud in class. Therefore, I recommend that books such as *Huckleberry Finn, The Slave Dancer,* and *To Kill a Mockingbird* be listed as racist and excluded from the classroom.

If an educator feels he or she must use *Huckleberry Finn* in the classroom, I would suggest my revised version, *The Adventures of Huckleberry Finn Adapted,* by John H. Wallace. The story is the same, but the words "nigger"and "hell" are eradicated. It no longer depicts blacks as inhuman, dishonest, or unintelligent, and it contains a glossary of Twainisms. Most adolescents will enjoy laughing at Jim and Huck in this adaptation.[7]

—Satire or Evasion? Black Perspectives on Huckleberry Finn, edited by James S. Leonard and Thomas A. Tenney (Durham, N.C.: Duke University Press, 1992), pp. 16–24

1. Martin Deutsch, Irwin Katz, and Arthur R. Jensen, *Social Class, Race, and Psychological Development* (New York: Holt, Rinehart, and Winston, 1968) 256–57.
2. Jewish Community Council of Greater Washington, *Guidelines on Religion and the Public School* (Washington, D.C., 1981).
3. Robert D. Strom, *The Innercity Classroom* (Columbus, Ohio: Charles E. Merrill, 1966) 104.
4. [Wallace's reference here is to doctrines of biological determinism, especially to the notion that some racial groups are genetically superior, in certain ways, to other groups–ED.]
5. Harry A. Passow, *Education in Depressed Areas* (New York: Teachers College P [Columbia U], 1963) 265.
6. Documentation on this statement by Marguerite Barnett (possibly from a dissertation) is not currently available.
7. For additional reading on the subject of racial considerations in education, see James A. Banks and Jean D. Grambs, *Black Self-Concept: Implications for Education and Social Science* (New York: McGraw-Hill, 1972); Robert F. Biehler, *Psychology Applied to Teaching* (Boston: Houghton Mifflin, 1971); Gary A. Davis and Thomas F. Warren, *Psychology of Education: New Looks* (Lexington, Mass.: Heath, 1974); Marcel L. Goldschmid, *Black Americans and White Racism* (New York: Holt, Rinehart, and Winston, 1970); Donnarae MacCann and Gloria Woodard, *The Black American in Children's Books* (Metuchen, N.J.: Scarecrow, 1972).

* * *

"Sells Jim's Soul Down the River for Laughs"

Taking issue with Ralph Ellison's positive reading of Adventures of Huckleberry Finn, *Bernard Bell argues that Twain shows a "failure of moral courage in reducing the complexity of Jim's assumption of manhood to a minstrel mask in the closing chapters."*

It is sad but true for many black readers that Twain's "Nigger" Jim is the best example of the humanity of black American slaves in nineteenth-century white American fiction. It is ironic, finally, as Ellison observed more than twenty-five years ago, that "down at the deep dark bottom of the melting pot, where the private is public and the public is private, where black is white and white is black, where the immoral becomes moral and the moral is anything that makes one feel good (or that one has the power to sustain), the white man's relish is apt to be the black man's gall." Having boasted to Andrew Lang of writing for the belly rather than the head of the white post-Reconstruction masses, Twain—nostalgically and metaphorically—sells Jim's soul down the river for laughs at the end of *Adventures of Huckleberry Finn.*

—from Bernard Bell, "Twain's 'Nigger' Jim: The Tragic Face behind the Minstrel Mask," in *Satire or Evasion? Black Perspectives on* Huckleberry Finn, p. 138

A version of this article served as the basis for the keynote speech Professor Smith delivered at the Huckleberry Finn Centenary Conference at the University of Missouri in April 1884.

Huck, Jim and American Racial Discourse
David L. Smith

They [blacks] are at least as brave, and more adventuresome [compared to whites]. But this may perhaps proceed from a want of fore-thought, which prevents their seeing a danger till it be present. . . . They are more ardent after their female: but love seems with them to be more an eager desire, than a tender delicate mixture of sentiment and sensation. Their griefs are transient. Those numberless afflictions, which render it doubtful whether heaven has given life to us in mercy or in wrath, are less felt, and sooner forgotten with them. In general, their existence appears to participate more of sensation than reflection. To this must be ascribed their disposition to sleep when abstracted from their diversions, and unemployed in labor.

—Thomas Jefferson, *Notes on the State of Virginia*[1]

Almost any Euro-American intellectual of the nineteenth century could have written the preceding words. The notion of Negro inferiority was so deeply pervasive among those heirs of "The Enlightenment" that the categories and even the vocabulary of Negro inferiority were formalized into a tedious, unmodulated litany. This uniformity increased rather than diminished during the course of the century. As Leon Litwack and others have shown, even the Abolitionists, who actively opposed slavery, frequently regarded blacks as inherently inferior. This helps to explain the widespread popularity of colonization schemes among Abolitionists and other liberals.[2] As for Jefferson, it is not surprising that he held such ideas, but it is impressive that he formulated so clearly at the end of the eighteenth century what would become the dominant view of the Negro in the nineteenth century. In many ways, this Father of American Democracy—and quite possibly of five mulatto children—was a man of his time and ahead of his time.[3]

In July of 1876, exactly one century after the American Declaration of Independence, Mark Twain began writing *Adventures of Huckleberry Finn,* a novel which illustrates trenchantly the social limitations which American "civilization" imposes on individual freedom.[4] The book takes special note of ways in which racism impinges upon the lives of Afro-Americans, even when they are legally "free." It is therefore ironic that *Huckleberry Finn* has often been attacked and even censored as a racist work. I would argue, on the contrary, that except for Melville's work, *Huckleberry Finn* is without peers among major Euro-American novels for its explicitly anti-racist stance.[5] Those who brand the book "racist" generally do so without having considered the specific form of racial discourse to which the novel responds. Furthermore, *Huckleberry Finn* offers much more than the typical liberal defenses of "human dignity" and protests against cruelty. Though it contains some such elements, it is more fundamentally a critique of those socially constituted fictions—most notably romanticism, religion, and the concept of "the Negro"—which serve to justify and to disguise selfish, cruel, and exploitative behavior.

When I speak of "racial discourse," I mean more than simply attitudes about "race" or conventions of talking about "race." Most importantly, I mean that "race" itself is a discursive formation, which delimits social relations on the basis of alleged physical differences.[6] "Race" is a strategy for relegating a segment of the population to a permanent inferior status. It functions by insisting that each "race" has specific, definitive, inherent behavioral tendencies and capacities, which distinguish it from other "races." Though scientifically specious, "race" has been powerfully effective as an ideology and as a form of social definition, which serves the interests of Euro-American hegemony. In America, race has been deployed against numerous groups, including Native Americans, Jews, Asians, and even—for brief periods—an assortment of European immigrants.

For obvious reasons, however, the primary emphasis historically has been on defining "the Negro" as a deviant from Euro-American norms. "Race" in America means white supremacy and black inferiority,[7] and "the Negro," a socially constituted fiction, is a generalized, one-dimensional surrogate for the historical reality of Afro-American people. It is this reified fiction which Mark Twain attacks in *Huckleberry Finn.*

Twain adopts a strategy of subversion in his attack on race. That is, he focuses on a number of commonplaces associated with "the Negro," and then he systematically dramatizes their inadequacy. He uses the term "nigger," and he shows Jim engaging in superstitious behavior. Yet he portrays Jim as a compassionate, shrewd, thoughtful, self-sacrificing and even wise man. Indeed, his portrayal of Jim contradicts every claim presented in Jefferson's description of "the Negro." Jim is cautious, he gives excellent advice, he suffers persistent anguish over separation from his wife and child, and he even sacrifices his own sleep in order that Huck may rest. Jim, in short, exhibits all the qualities that "the Negro" supposedly lacks. Mark Twain's conclusions do more than merely subvert the justifications of slavery, which was already long since abolished. Mark Twain began this book during the final disintegration of Reconstruction, and his satire on antebellum Southern bigotry is also an implicit response to the Negrophobic climate of the post-Reconstruction era.[8] It is troubling, therefore, that so many readers have completely misunderstood Mark Twain's subtle attack on racism.

Twain's use of the word "nigger" has provoked some readers to reject the novel.[9] As one of the most offensive words in our vocabulary, "nigger" remains heavily shrouded in taboo. A careful assessment of this term within the context of American racial discourse, however, will allow us to understand the particular way in which the author uses it. If we attend closely to Twain's use of the word, we may find in it not just a trigger to outrage, but more importantly, a means of understanding the precise nature of American racism and Mark Twain's attack on it.

Most obviously, Mark Twain uses "nigger" throughout the book as a synonym for "slave." There is ample evidence from other sources that this corresponds to one usage common during the Antebellum period. We first encounter it in reference to "Miss Watson's big nigger, named Jim" (Ch. 2). This usage, like the term "nigger stealer," clearly designates the "nigger"

as a piece of property: a commodity, a slave. This passage also provides the only apparent textual justification for the common critical practice of labeling Jim, "Nigger Jim," as if "nigger" were a part of his proper name. This loathsome habit goes back at least as far as Albert Bigelow Paine's biography of Mark Twain (1912).[10] In any case, "nigger" in this sense connotes an inferior, even subhuman, creature, who is properly owned by and subservient to Euro-Americans.

Both Huck and Jim use the word in this sense. For example, when Huck fabricates his tale about the riverboat accident, the following exchange occurs between him and Aunt Sally:

> "Good gracious! anybody hurt?"
> "No,m. Killed a nigger."
> "Well, it's lucky, because sometimes people do get hurt." (Ch. 32).

Huck has never met Aunt Sally prior to this scene, and in spinning a lie which this stranger will find unobjectionable, he correctly assumes that the common notion of Negro subhumanity will be appropriate. Huck's off-hand remark is intended to exploit Aunt Sally's attitudes, not to express Huck's own. A nigger, Aunt Sally confirms, is not a person. Yet this exchange is hilarious, precisely because we know that Huck is playing upon her glib and conventional bigotry. We know that Huck's relationship to Jim has already invalidated for him such obtuse racial notions. The conception of the "nigger" is a socially constituted and sanctioned fiction, and it is just as false and as absurd as Huck's explicit fabrication, which Aunt Sally also swallows whole.

In fact, the exchange between Huck and Aunt Sally reveals a great deal about how racial discourse operates. Its function is to promulgate a conception of "the Negro" as a subhuman and expendable creature, who is by definition feebleminded, immoral, lazy, and superstitious. One crucial purpose of this social fiction is to justify the abuse and exploitation of Afro-American people by substituting the essentialist fiction of "Negro-ism" for the actual character of individual Afro-Americans. Hence, in racial discourse every Afro-American becomes just another instance of "the Negro"—just another "nigger." Mark Twain recognizes this invidious tendency of race-thinking, however, and he takes every opportunity to expose the mismatch between racial abstractions and real human beings.

For example, when Pap drunkenly inveighs against the free mulatto from Ohio, he is outraged by what appears to him as a crime against natural laws (Ch. 6). In the first place, a "free nigger" is, for Pap, a contradiction in terms. Indeed, the man's clothes, his demeanor, his education, his profession, and even his silver-headed cane bespeak a social status normally achieved by only a small elite of white men. He is, in other words, a "nigger" who refuses to behave like a "nigger." Pap's ludicrous protestations discredit both himself and other believers in "the Negro," as many critics have noted. But it has not been sufficiently stressed that Pap's racial views correspond very closely to those of most of his white Southern contemporaries, in substance if not in manner of expression. Such views were held not only by poor whites but by all "right-thinking" Southerners, regardless of their social class. Indeed, not even the traumas of the Civil War would cure Southerners of this folly. Furthermore, Pap's indignation at the Negro's right to vote is precisely analogous to the Southern backlash against the enfranchisement of Afro-Americans during Reconstruction. Finally, Pap's comments are rather mild compared to the anti-Negro diatribes which were beginning to emerge among politicians even as Mark Twain was writing *Huckleberry Finn*. He began writing this novel during the final days of Reconstruction, and it seems more than reasonable to assume that the shameful white supremacist bluster of that epoch–exemplified by Pap's tirade–informed Mark Twain's critique of racism in *Huckleberry Finn*.[11]

Pap's final description of this Ohio gentleman as "a prowling, thieving, infernal, white-shirted free-nigger" (Ch. 6) almost totally contradicts his previous description of the man as a proud, elegant, dignified figure. Yet this contradiction is perfectly consistent with Pap's need to reassert "the Negro" in lieu of social reality. Despite the vulgarity of Pap's personal character, his thinking about race is highly conventional and, therefore, respectable. But most of us cannot respect Pap's views, and when we reject them, we reject the standard racial discourse of both 1840 and 1880.

A reader who objects to the word "nigger" might still insist that Mark Twain could have avoided using it. But it is difficult to imagine how Mark Twain could have debunked a discourse without using the specific terms of that discourse. Even when Mark Twain was writing his book, "nigger" was universally recognized as an insulting, demeaning word. According to Stuart Berg Flexner, "Negro" was generally pronounced as "nigger" until about 1825, at which time Abolitionists began objecting to that term.[12] They preferred "colored person" or "person of color." Hence, W. E. B. Du Bois reports that some black Abolitionists of the early 1830s declared themselves united "as men, . . . not as slaves; as 'people of color,' not as 'Negroes,'"[13] Writing a generation later in *Army Life in a Black Regiment* (1869), Thomas Wentworth Higginson deplored the common use of "nigger" among freedmen, which he regarded as evidence of low self-esteem.[14] The objections to "nigger,"

"Twain Challenges America to Be Better"

Huck's story springs from Mark Twain's anguished but loving look at his country. As Huck lights out for the Territory, he goes to inhabit a physical space that is but a parallel to his own new and expanded consciousness. The long sojourn on the river with Jim has allowed Huck to move beyond the empty abstraction of the word "nigger" to the recognition of a black man's humanity. Huck's transformation from boy to man, from one who accepts the dictates of a flawed social code to one who triumphantly aligns himself with the values of the natural world, represents Twain's best hope for a country that must give up its prolonged innocence and acknowledge the claims of history. In *Huckleberry Finn*, Twain challenges America to be better, to live up to its shining promise.

–from Betty H. Jones, "Huck and Jim: A Reconsideration," in *Satire or Evasion? Black Perspectives on* Huckleberry Finn, p. 172

---

then, are not a consequence of the modern sensibility but had been common for a half century before *Huckleberry Finn* was published. The specific function of this term in the book, however, is neither to offend nor merely to provide linguistic authenticity. Much more importantly, it establishes a context against which Jim's specific virtues may emerge as explicit refutations of racist presuppositions.

Of course, the concept of the "nigger" entails far more than just the deployment of certain vocabulary. Most of the attacks on the book focus on its alleged perpetuation of racial stereotypes. Mark Twain does indeed use racial stereotypes here. That practice could be excused as characteristic of the genre of humor within which Mark Twain works. Frontier humor relies upon the use of stock types, and consequently, racial stereotypes are just one of many types present in *Huckleberry Finn*. Yet while valid, such an appeal to generic convention would be unsatisfactory, because it would deny Mark Twain the credit which he deserves for the sophistication of his perceptions.[15]

As a serious critic of American society, Mark Twain recognized that racial discourse depends upon the deployment of a system of stereotypes which constitute "the Negro" as fundamentally different from and inferior to Euro-Americans. As with his handling of "nigger," Mark Twain's strategy with racial stereotypes is to elaborate them in order to undermine them. To be sure, those critics are correct who have argued that

Mark Twain uses this narrative to reveal Jim's humanity. Jim, however, is just one individual. Much more importantly, Mark Twain uses the narrative to expose the cruelty and hollowness of that racial discourse which exists only to obscure the humanity of *all* Afro-American people.

One aspect of *Huckleberry Finn* which has elicited copious critical commentary is Mark Twain's use of superstition.[16] In nineteenth-century racial discourse, "the Negro" was always defined as inherently superstitious.[17] Many critics, therefore, have cited Jim's superstitious behavior as an instance of negative stereotyping. One cannot deny that in this respect Jim closely resembles the entire tradition of comic darkies,[18] but to observe this similarity is a negligible feat. The issue is: does Twain merely reiterate clichés, or does he use these conventional patterns to make an unconventional point? A close examination will show that in virtually every instance, Mark Twain uses Jim's superstition to make points which undermine rather than revalidate the dominant racial discourse.

The first incident of this superstitious behavior occurs in Chapter 2, as a result of one of Tom Sawyer's pranks. When Jim falls asleep under a tree, Tom hangs Jim's hat on a branch. Subsequently, Jim concocts an elaborate tale about having been hexed and ridden by witches. The tale grows more grandiose with each repetition, and eventually Jim becomes a local celebrity, sporting a five-cent piece on a string around his neck as a talisman. "Niggers would come miles to hear Jim tell about it, and he was more looked up to than any nigger in that country," the narrator reports. Jim's celebrity finally reaches the point that "Jim was most ruined, for a servant, because he got so stuck up on account of having seen the devil and been rode by witches." This is, no doubt, amusing. Yet whether Jim believes his own tale or not—and the "superstitious Negro" thesis requires us to assume that he does—the fact remains that Jim clearly benefits from becoming more a celebrity and less a "servant." It is his owner, not Jim, who suffers when Jim reduces the amount of his uncompensated labor.[19]

This incident has often been interpreted as an example of risible Negro gullibility and ignorance, as exemplified by blackface minstrelsy. Such a reading has more than a little validity, but can only partially account for the implications of this scene. If not for the final sentence, such an account might seem wholly satisfactory, but the information that Jim becomes, through his own storytelling, unsuited for life as a slave, introduces unexpected complications. Is it likely that Jim has been deceived by his own creative prevarications especially given what we learn about his character subsequently? Or has he cleverly exploited the

Cover for a comic book that was published in September 1967
(Collection of Tom Quirk)

conventions of "Negro superstition" in order to turn a silly boy's prank to his own advantage?

Regardless of whether we credit Jim with forethought in this matter, it is undeniable that he turns Tom's attempt to humiliate him into a major personal triumph. In other words, Tom gives him an inch, and he takes an ell. It is also obvious that he does so by exercising remarkable skills as a rhetorician. By constructing a fictitious narrative of his own experience, Jim elevates himself above his prescribed station in life. By becoming, in effect, an author, Jim writes himself a new destiny. Jim's triumph may appear to be dependent upon the gullibility of other "superstitious" Negroes, but since we have no direct encounter with them, we cannot know whether they are unwitting victims of Jim's ruse or not. A willing audience need not be a totally credulous one. In any case, it is intelligence, not stupidity, which facilitates Jim's triumph. Tom may have had his chuckle, but the last laugh, clearly, belongs to Jim.

In assessing Jim's character, we should keep in mind that forethought, creativity and shrewdness are qualities that racial discourse—as in the passage from Thomas Jefferson—denies to "the Negro." In that sense, Jim's darky performance here subverts the fundamental definition of the darky. For "the Negro" is defined to be an object, not a subject. Yet does an object construct its own narrative? Viewed in this way, the fact of superstition, which traditionally connotes ignorance and unsophistication, becomes far less important than the ends to which superstition is put. This inference exposes, once again, the inadequacy of a positivist epistemology, which holds, for example, that "a rose is a rose is a rose." No one will deny the self-evidence of a tautology; but a rose derives whatever meaning it has from the context within which it is placed (including the context of traditional symbolism.) It is the contextualizing activity, not *das Ding-an-sich,* which generates meaning. Again and again, Twain attacks racial essentialism by directing our attention, instead, to the particularity of individual action. We find that Jim is not "the Negro." Jim is Jim, and we, like Huck, come to understand what Jim is by attending to what he does in specific situations.

In another instance of explicitly superstitious behavior, Jim uses a hairball to tell Huck's fortune. One may regard this scene as a comical example of Negro ignorance and credulity, acting in concert with the ignorance and credulity of a fourteen-year-old white boy. That reading would allow one an unambiguous laugh at Jim's expense. If one examines the scene carefully, however, the inadequacy of such a reductive reading becomes apparent. Even if Jim does believe in the supernatural powers of this hair ball, the fact remains that most of the transaction depends upon Jim's quick wits. The soothsaying aside, much of the exchange

between Huck and Jim is an exercise in wily and understated economic bartering. In essence, Jim wants to be paid for his services, while Huck wants free advice. Jim insists that the hair ball will not speak without being paid. Huck, who has a dollar, will only admit to having a counterfeit quarter. Jim responds by pretending to be in collusion with Huck. He explains how to doctor the "quarter" so that "anybody in town would take it in a minute, let alone a hair ball" (Ch. 4). But obviously it is not the hair ball who will benefit from acquiring and spending this counterfeit coin.[20]

In this transaction, Jim serves his own interests while appearing to serve Huck's interests. He takes a slug which is worthless to Huck, and through the alchemy of his own cleverness, he contrives to make it worth twenty-five cents to himself. That, in antebellum America, is not a bad price for telling a fortune. But more importantly, Mark Twain shows Jim self-consciously subverting the prescribed definition of "the Negro," even as he performs within the limitations of that role. He remains the conventional "Negro" by giving the white boy what he wants, at no real cost, and by consistently appearing to be passive and subservient to the desires of Huck and the hair ball. But in fact, he serves his own interests all along. Such resourcefulness is hardly consistent with the familiar, one-dimensional concept of "the superstitious Negro."

And while Jim's reading is formulaic, it is hardly simple-minded. He sees the world as a kind of Manichean universe, in which forces of light and darkness—white and black—vie for dominance. Pap, he says, is uncertain what to do, torn between his white and black angels. Jim's advice, "to res' easy en let de ole man take his own way" (Ch. 4), turns out to be good advice, because Huck greatly enjoys life in the cabin, despite Pap's fits of drunken excess. This mixture of pleasure and pain is precisely what Jim predicts. Admittedly, Jim's conceptual framework is not original. Nonetheless, his reading carries considerable force, because it corresponds so neatly to the dominant thematic patterns in this book, and more broadly, to the sort of dualistic thinking which informs much of Mark Twain's work. (To take an obvious example, consider the role reversals and character contrasts in *Pudd'nhead Wilson* or *The Prince and the Pauper*). And most immediately, Jim's comments here reflect tellingly upon his situation as a black slave in racist America. The slave's fate is always torn between his master's will and his own.

In this reading and other incidents, Jim emerges as an astute and sensitive observer of human behavior, both in his comments regarding Pap and in his subtle remarks to Huck. Jim clearly possesses a subtlety and intelligence which "the Negro" allegedly lacks. Mark

Covers for translations of Adventures of Huckleberry Finn: *top, Turkey, 1960; bottom left, Sweden, 1965; bottom right, Germany, 1968 (Buffalo and Erie County Public Library)*

"Well-Meant, Noble Sounding Error"

I am grateful that among the many indignities inflicted on me in childhood, I escaped *Huckleberry Finn.* As a black parent, however, I sympathize with those who want the book banned, or at least removed from required reading lists in schools. While I am opposed to book banning, I know that my children's education will be enhanced by not reading *Huckleberry Finn.* It is, in John Gardner's phrase, a "well-meant, noble sounding error" that "devalue[s] the world."

–from Julius Lester, "Morality and *Adventurers of Huckleberry Finn,*" in *Satire or Evasion? Black Perspectives on* Huckleberry Finn, p. 200

Twain makes this point more clearly in the debate scene in chapter 14. True enough, most of this debate is, as several critics have noted, conventional minstrel-show banter. Nevertheless, Jim demonstrates impressive reasoning abilities, despite his factual ignorance. For example, in their argument over "Poly-voo-franzy," Huck makes a category error by implying that the difference between languages is analogous to the difference between human language and cat language. While Jim's response–that man should talk like a man–betrays his ignorance of cultural diversity, his argument is perceptive and structurally sound. The humor in Huck's conclusion, "you can't learn a nigger how to argue," arises precisely from our recognition that Jim's argument is better than Huck's.

Throughout the novel, Mark Twain presents Jim in ways which render ludicrous the conventional wisdom about "Negro character." As an intelligent, sensitive, wily and considerate individual, Jim demonstrates that one's race provides no useful index of one's character. While that point may seem obvious to many contemporary readers, it is a point rarely made by nineteenth-century Euro-American novelists. Indeed, except for Melville, J. W. DeForest, Albion Tourgee, and George Washington Cable, white novelists virtually always portrayed Afro-American characters as exemplifications of "Negroness." In this regard, the twentieth century has been little better. By presenting us a series of glimpses which penetrate the "Negro" exterior and reveal the person beneath it, Twain debunks American racial discourse. For racial discourse maintains that the "Negro" exterior is all that a "Negro" really has.

This insight in itself is a notable accomplishment. Twain, however, did not view racism as an isolated phenomenon, and it was his effort to place racism within the context of other cultural traditions which produced the most problematic aspect of his novel. For it is in the final chapters–the Tom Sawyer section–which most critics consider the weakest part of the book, that Twain links his criticisms of slavery and Southern romanticism, condemning the cruelties which both of these traditions entail.[21] Critics have objected to these chapters on various grounds. Some of the most common are that Jim becomes reduced to a comic darky,[22] that Tom's antics undermine the seriousness of the novel, and that these burlesque narrative developments destroy the structural integrity of the novel. Most critics see this conclusion as an evasion of the difficult issues which the novel has raised. There is no space here for a discussion of the structural issues, but it seems to me that as a critique of American racial discourse, these concluding chapters offer a harsh, coherent, and uncompromising indictment.

Tom Sawyer's absurd scheme to "rescue" Jim offends, because the section begins with Huck's justly celebrated crisis of conscience, which culminates in his resolve to free Jim, even if doing so condemns him to hell. The passage which leads to Huck's decision, as familiar as it is, merits reexamination:

I'd see him standing my watch on top of his'n, stead of calling me, so I could go on sleeping; and see him how glad he was when I come back out of the fog; and when I come to him again in the swamp, up there where the feud was; and such like times; and would always call me honey, and pet me, and do everything he could think of for me, and how good he always was; and at last I struck the time I saved him by telling the men we had small-pox aboard, and he was so grateful, and said I was the best friend old Jim ever had in the world, and the *only* one he's got now; and then I happened to look around, and see that paper. . . . I studied a minute, sort of holding my breath, and then says to myself: 'All right, then, I'll *go* to hell'–and tore it up. (Ch. 31)

The issue here is not just whether or not Huck should return a fugitive slave to its proper owner. More fundamentally, Huck must decide whether to accept the conventional wisdom, which defines "Negroes" as subhuman commodities, or the evidence of his own experience, which has shown Jim to be a good and kind man and a true friend.

Huck makes the obvious decision, but his doing so represents more than simply a liberal choice of conscience over social convention. Mark Twain explicitly makes Huck's choice a sharp attack on the Southern church. Huck scolds himself: "There was the Sunday school, you could a gone to it; and if you'd done it they'da learnt you, there, that people that acts as I'd been acting about that nigger goes to everlasting fire"

Welcome to HUCK FINN'S HOME PAGE!

Japanese Version

■What's HUCK FINN?■

"HUCK FINN" has been operating since 1981 in IMAIKE the most exciting district of Japan's central city, NAGOYA..

We have dynamic live gigs almost every day featuring the best indy bands from Japan and over seas.

As you enter the club, you desend the stairs into a completely matt black room, full of people excitedly anticl pating what will happen tonight. Recently the "NAGOYA punk scene" has been the focus of national and international attention.

This began and continues to be centralized at "HUCK FINN".

Web-page advertisement for a Japanese nightclub <http: www2.nicnet.jp/imaike_t/huckfinn/index_e.html>

(Ch. 31). Yet despite Huck's anxiety, he transcends the moral limitations of his time and place. By the time Twain wrote these words, more than twenty years of national strife, including the Civil War and Reconstruction, had established Huck's conclusion regarding slavery as a dominant national consensus; not even reactionary Southerners advocated a reinstitution of slavery. But since the pre–Civil War southern church taught that slavery was God's will, Huck's decision flatly repudiates the church's teachings regarding slavery. And implicitly, it also repudiates the church as an institution by suggesting that the church functions to undermine, not to encourage, a reliance on one's conscience. To define "Negroes" as subhuman removes them from moral consideration and therefore justifies their callous exploitation. This view of religion is consistent with the cynical iconoclasm that Twain expressed in *Letters from the Earth* and other "dark" works.[23]

In this context, Tom Sawyer appears to us as a superficially charming but fundamentally distasteful interloper. His actions are governed not by conscience but rather by romantic conventions and literary "authorities." Indeed, while Tom may appear to be a kind of renegade, he is in essence thoroughly conventional in his values and proclivities. Despite all his boyish pranks, Tom represents a kind of solid respectability–a younger version of the

Southern gentleman, as exemplified by the Grangerfords and the Shepherdsons.[24] Hence, when Tom proposes to help Huck steal Jim, Huck laments that "Tom Sawyer fell, considerable, in my estimation. Only I couldn't believe it. Tom Sawyer a *nigger stealer!*" (Ch. 33). Such liberating

---

"Our Enduring Sense of What America Means"

Huckleberry Finn brings alive our enduring sense of what America means to all the struggling and suffering peoples of the earth. In the character of the slave Jim, Twain embodied natural goodness and a love of liberty. . . . In the relationship between Huck and Jim, Twain dramatized our persistent hope of brotherhood. We do well in studying Mark Twain to bear in mind William Dean Howells's advice: "I warn the reader that if he leaves out of the account an indignant sense or fight and wrong, a scorn of all affectation and pretense, an ardent hate of meanness and injustice, he will come infinitely short of knowing Mark Twain."

–from Charles H. Nichols. "'A True Book– With Some Stretchers': *Huck Finn* Today," in *Satire or Evasion? Black Perspectives on* Huckleberry Finn, p. 214

activity is proper for Huck, who is not respectable, but not for Tom, who is. As with the previous example, however, this one implies a deep criticism of the status quo. Huck's act of conscience, which most of us now (and in Twain's own time) would endorse, is possible only for an outsider. This hardly speaks well for the moral integrity of southern (or American) "civilization."

To examine Tom's role in the novel, let us begin at the end. Upon learning of the failed escape attempt and Jim's recapture, Tom cries out, self-righteously: "Turn him loose! he ain't no slave; he's as free as any cretur that walks this earth!" (Ch. 42). Tom has known all along that his cruel and ludicrous scheme to rescue the captured "prisoner" was being enacted upon a free man; and indeed, only his silence regarding Jim's status allowed the scheme to proceed with Jim's cooperation. Certainly, neither Huck nor Jim would otherwise have indulged Tom's foolishness. Tom's gratuitous cruelty here in the pursuit of his own amusement corresponds to his less vicious prank against Jim in Chapter 2. And just as before, Twain converts Tom's callous mischief into a personal triumph for Jim.

Not only has Jim suffered patiently, which would, in truth, represent a doubtful virtue (Jim is not Uncle Tom); he demonstrates his moral superiority by surrendering himself in order to assist the doctor in treating his wounded tormentor. This is hardly the behavior which one would expect from a commodity, and it is *precisely* Jim's status—man or chattel—which has been fundamentally at issue throughout the novel. It may be true that Tom's lengthy juvenile antics subvert the tone of the novel, but they also provide the necessary backdrop for Jim's noble act. Up to this point we have been able to admire Jim's good sense and to respond sentimentally to

his good character. This, however, is the first time that we see him making a significant (and wholly admirable) moral decision. His act sets him apart from everyone else in the novel except Huck. And modestly (if not disingenuously), he claims to be behaving just as Tom Sawyer would. Always conscious of his role as a "Negro," Jim knows better than to claim personal credit for his good deed. Yet the contrast between Jim's behavior and Tom's is unmistakable. Huck declares that Jim is "white inside" (Ch. 40). He apparently intends this as a compliment, but Tom is fortunate that Jim does not behave like most of the whites in the novel.

Twain also contrasts Jim's self-sacrificing compassion with the cruel and mean-spirited behavior of his captors, emphasizing that white skin does not justify claims of superior virtue. They abuse Jim, verbally and physically, and some want to lynch him as an example to other slaves. The moderates among them, however, resist, pointing out that they could be made to pay for the destruction of private property. As Huck observes: "the people that's always the most anxious for to hang a nigger that hain't done just right, is always the very ones that ain't the most anxious to pay for him when they've got their satisfaction out of him" (Ch. 42). As if these enforcers of white supremacy did not appear contemptible enough already, Mark Twain then has the doctor describe Jim as the best and most faithful nurse he has ever seen, despite Jim's "resking his freedom" and his obvious fatigue. These vigilantes do admit that Jim deserves to be rewarded, but their idea of a reward is to cease punching and cursing him. They are not even generous enough to remove Jim's heavy shackles.

NAT HENTOFF: *Huck Finn Better Get Out of Town by Sundown*

NAT HENTOFF: *'Is Any Book Worth the Humiliation of Our Kids?'*

NAT HENTOFF: *Huck Finn and the Shortchanging of Black Kids*

NAT HENTOFF: *'These Are Little Battles Fought in Remote Places'*

Headlines for a series of articles that appeared in The Village Voice *in May 1982 in which Nat Hentoff examined the ongoing censorship debate about Twain's novel: "Although* Catcher in the Rye *and the works of Kurt Vonnegut and Judy Blume are currently the most frequently censored books in school libraries, no novel has been on the firing line so long and so continuously as* Huckleberry Finn. *What is there about this book that manages to infuriate, differently, each generation of Americans? What does it tell us that we don't want to hear?" (Thomas Cooper Library, University of South Carolina).*

A wood engraving by Barry Moser for The Centenary Edition of Huckleberry Finn *(from Sotheby's,*
The Mark Twain Collection of Nick Karanovich, 19 June 2003)

Ultimately, *Huckleberry Finn* renders a harsh judgment on American society. Freedom from slavery, the novel implies, is not freedom from gratuitous cruelty; and racism, like romanticism, is finally just an elaborate justification which the adult counterparts of Tom Sawyer use to facilitate their exploitation and abuse of other human beings. Tom feels guilty, with good reason, for having exploited Jim, but his final gesture of paying Jim off is less an insult to Jim than it is Mark Twain's commentary on Tom himself. Just as slaveholders believe that economic relations (ownership) can justify their privilege of mistreating other human beings, Tom apparently believes that an economic exchange can suffice as atonement for his misdeeds. Perhaps he finds a forty-dollar token more affordable than an apology.

But then, just as Tom could only "set a free nigger free," considering, as Huck says, "his bringing-up" (Ch. 42), he similarly could hardly be expected to apologize for his pranks. Huck, by contrast, is equally rich, but he *has* apologized to Jim earlier in the novel. And this is the point of Huck's final remark, rejecting the prospect of civilization. To become civilized is not just to become like Aunt Sally. More immediately, it is to become like Tom Sawyer.

Jim is indeed "as free as any cretur that walks this earth." In other words, he is a man, like all men, at the mercy of other men's arbitrary cruelties. In a sense, given Twain's view of freedom, to allow Jim to escape to the North or to have Tom announce Jim's manumission earlier would be an evasion of the

Twain Classic Bounced From Class Again

Prestigious Girls School Joins Debate Over 'Huckleberry Finn'

Headline in the 4 March 1995 issue of The Washington Post. *The story begins: "National Cathedral School, one of the most prestigious private schools for girls in the Washington area, has become the latest area school to pull Mark Twain's "'Adventures of Huckleberry Finn'" from its curriculum amid a national debate over how the American classic should be presented" (Thomas Cooper Library, University of South Carolina).*

novel's ethical insights. While one may escape from legal bondage, there is no escape from the cruelties of this "civilization." There is no promised land where one may enjoy absolute personal freedom. An individual's freedom is always constrained by one's social relations to other people. Being legally free does not spare Jim from gratuitous humiliation and physical suffering in the final chapters, precisely because Jim is still regarded as a "nigger." Even if he were as accomplished as the mulatto from Ohio, he would not he exempt from mistreatment. Furthermore, since Tom represents the hegemonic values of his society, Jim's "freedom" amounts to little more than an obligation to live by his wits and to make the best of a bad situation, just as he has always done.

Slavery and racism, then, are social evils that take their places alongside various others which the novel documents, such as the insane romanticism that inspires the Grangerfords and Shepherdsons blithely to murder each other, generation after generation. Mark Twain rejects entirely the mystification of race and demonstrates that Jim is in most ways a better man than the men who regard him as their inferior. But he also shows how little correlation there may be between the treatment one deserves and the treatment one receives.

If this conclusion sounds uncontroversial from the perspective of the 1980s, we would do well to remember that it contradicts entirely the overwhelming and optimistic consensus of the 1880s. No other nineteenth-century novel so effectively locates racial discourse within the context of a general critique of American institutions and traditions. Indeed, the novel suggests that real individual freedom, in this land of the free, cannot be found. "American civilization" enslaves and exploits rather than liberates. It is hardly an appealing message.

Given the subtlety of Mark Twain's approach, it is not surprising that most of his contemporaries misunderstood or simply ignored the novel's demystification of race. Despite their patriotic rhetoric, they, like Pap, were unprepared to take seriously the

implications of "freedom, justice, and equality." They, after all, espoused an ideology and an explicit language of race that was virtually identical to Thomas Jefferson's. Yet racial discourse flatly contradicts and ultimately renders hypocritical the egalitarian claims of liberal democracy. The heart of Mark Twain's message to us is that an honest person must reject one or the other. But hypocrisy, not honesty, is our norm. Many of us continue to assert both racial distinction and liberal values simultaneously. If we, a century later, continue to be confused about *Adventures of Huckleberry Finn,* perhaps it is because we remain more deeply committed to both racial discourse and a self-deluding optimism than we care to admit.[25]

—Satire or Evasion? Black Perspectives on Huckleberry Finn, *pp. 103–120*

---

1. *The Portable Thomas Jefferson,* ed. Merrill D. Peterson (New York: Viking, 1975) 187–88.
2. The literature on the abolition movement and on antebellum debates regarding the Negro is, of course, voluminous. George M. Fredrickson's excellent *The Black Image in the White Mind* (New York: Harper Torchbooks, 1971) is perhaps the best general work of its kind. Fredrickson's *The Inner Civil War* (New York: Harper Torchbooks, 1971) is also valuable, especially pp. 53–64. Leon Litwack, in *North of Slavery* (Chicago: U of Chicago P, 1961) 214–46, closely examines the ambivalence of abolitionists regarding racial intermingling. Benjamin Quarles presents the most detailed examination of black abolitionists in *Black Abolitionists* (New York: Oxford UP, 1969), although Vincent Harding offers a more vivid (and overtly polemical) account of their relationships to white Abolitionists; see *There Is a River* (New York: Harcourt, Brace, Jovanovich, 1981).
3. The debate over Jefferson's relationship to Sally Hemings has raged for two centuries. The most thorough scholarly accounts are by Fawn Brodie, who suggests that Jefferson did have a prolonged involvement with Hemings (*Thomas Jefferson, an Intimate History* [New York: Norton, 1974]), and by Virginius Dabney, who endeavors to exonerate Jefferson of such charges (*The Jefferson Scandals* [New York: Dodd, Mead, 1981]). Barbara Chase-Riboud presents a fictionalized version of this rela-

tionship in *Sally Hemings* (New York: Viking, 1979). The first Afro-American novel, *Clotel; Or the President's Daughter* (1853; New York: Arno, 1969) by William Wells Brown, was also based on this alleged affair.

4. For dates of composition, see Walter Blair, "When Was *Huckleberry Finn* Written?" *American Literature,* 30 (Mar. 1958): 1–25.

5. For a discussion of Melville's treatment of race, Carolyn Karchner's *Shadow Over the Promised Land* (Baton Rouge: Louisiana State UP, 1980) is especially valuable. Also noteworthy are two articles on "Benito Cereno": Joyce Adler, "Melville's *Benito Cereno:* Slavery and Violence in the Americas," *Science and Society* 38 (1974), 19–48; and Jean Fagan Yellin, "Black Masks: Melville's *Benito Cereno,*" *American Quarterly* 22 (Fall 1970): 678–89. Rayford Logan, *The Negro in American Life and Thought: The Nadir, 1877–1901* (New York: Dial, 1954), and Lawrence J. Friedman, *The White Savage: Racial Fantasies in the Postbellum South* (Englewood Cliffs, NJ: Prentice-Hall, 1970), provide detailed accounts of the racist climate in post-Reconstruction America, emphasizing the literary manifestations of such attitudes. Friedman's discussion of George Washington Cable, the outspoken southern liberal (99–118), is very informative. For a general historical overview of the period, C. Vann Woodward's *Origins of the New South* (Baton Rouge: Louisiana State UP, 1971) and *The Strange Career of Jim Crow,* 3rd ed. (New York: Oxford UP, 1974) remain unsurpassed. John W. Cell, in *The Highest Stage of White Supremacy* (New York: Cambridge UP, 1982), offers a provocative reconsideration of Woodward's arguments. Finally, Joel Williamson's *The Crucible of Race* (New York: Oxford UP, 1984) documents the excessively violent tendencies of southern racism at the end of the century.

6. My use of "racial discourse" has some affinities to Foucault's conception of "discourse." This is not, however, a strictly Foucaultian reading. While Foucault's definition of discursive practices provides one of the most sophisticated tools presently available for cultural analysis, his conception of power seems to me problematic. I prefer an account of power which allows for a consideration of interest and hegemony. Theorists such as Marshall Berman, *All That Is Solid Melts into Air* (New York: Simon & Schuster, 1982) 34–35, and Catherine A. MacKinnon, "Feminism, Marxism, Method, and the State: An Agenda for Theory," *Signs,* 7.3 (1982): 526, have indicated similar reservations. However, Frank Lentricchia ("Reading Foucault [Punishment, Labor, Resistance]," *Raritan* 1.4 [1981]: 5–32; 2.1 [1982]: 41–70) has made a provocative attempt to modify Foucaultian analysis, drawing upon Antonio Gramsci's analysis of hegemony in *Selections from the Prison Notebooks* (New York: International Publishers, 1971). See Foucault, *The Archaeology of Knowledge, Power/ Knowledge,* ed. Colin Gordon (New York: Pantheon, 1980), esp. 92–108, and *The History of Sexuality,* vol. 1 (New York: Vintage, 1980), esp. 92–102.

7. This is not to discount the sufferings of other groups. But historically, the philosophical basis of Western racial discourse–which existed even before the European "discovery" of America–has been the equation of "good" and "evil" with light and darkness (or white and black.) See Jacques Derrida, "White Mythology," *New Literary History* 6 (1974), 5–74; Winthrop Jordan, *White Over Black* (New York: Norton, 1968) 1–40; and Cornel West, *Prophesy Deliverance* (Philadelphia: Westminster P, 1982) 47–65.

German stamp celebrating Twain's most famous characters (Collection of Thomas Quirk)

Economically, the slave trade, chattel slavery, agricultural peonage, and color-coded wage differentials have made the exploitation of African Americans the most profitable form of racism. Finally, Afro-Americans have long been the largest American "minority" group. Consequently, the primacy of "the Negro" in American racial discourse is "overdetermined," to use Louis Althusser's term (*For Marx* [London: Verso, 1979] 87–126). The acknowledgment of primary status, however, is hardly a claim of privilege.

8. See Lawrence I. Berkove, "The Free Man of Color in *The Grandissimes* and Works by Harris and Mark Twain," *Southern Quarterly* 18.4 (1981): 60–73; Richard Gollin and Rita Gollin, "*Huckleberry Finn* and the Time of the Evasion," *Modern Language Studies* 9 (Spring 1979) 5–15; Michael Egan, *Mark Twain's Huckleberry Finn: Race, Class and Society* (Atlantic Highlands, NJ: Humanities P, 1977) esp. 66–102.

9. Nat Hentoff's series of four columns in the *Village Voice* 27 (1982): "Huck Finn Better Get Out of Town by Sundown" (May 4); "Is Any Book Worth the Humiliation of Our Kids?" (May 11); "Huck Finn and the Shortchanging of Black Kids" (May 18); and "These Are Little Battles Fought in Remote Places" (May 25).

10. *Mark Twain, A Biography* (New York: Harper, 1912).

11. See Arthur G. Pettit, *Mark Twain and the South* (Lexington: U of Kentucky P, 1974).

12. *I Hear America Talking* (New York: Van Nostrand Reinhold, 1976) 57.

13. *The Souls of Black Folk,* in *Three Negro Classics,* ed. John Hope Franklin (New York: Avon, 1965) 245.

14. (Boston: Beacon, 1962) 28.

15. See Ralph Ellison, "Change the Joke and Slip the Yoke," in *Shadow and Act* (New York: Random House, 1964) 45–59; Chadwick Hansen, "The Character of Jim and the Ending of *Huckleberry Finn,*" *Massachusetts Review* 5

Dust jacket for the most authoritative edition of Mark Twain's novel, which was edited after the discovery of the first half of the manuscript and published by the University of California Press (Collection of Tom Quirk)

"The True Visionary Center"

This is an excerpt from Jocelyn Chadwick-Joshua's introduction for her critical study of Twain's novel.

Tom's conscious deception and equally conscious disregard for Jim's visibility and humanity both reveal the dilemma of indifference, ethnic intolerance, and continual denial of basic human rights, basic rights afforded even the lowliest white. But more profound than the dark and foreboding canopy of apathy and inhumanity in the conclusion is Twain's final rendering of Jim. Functioning as parallel and substantive themes, with equal strength, Jim's heroism, his self-reliance, his tenacity, and his assertion of choice emerge clearly and indisputably. So, with this duality framing the final chapters, the question becomes whether Tom's deception and his uninhibited revelation symbolize the final, resonant theme in this novel, as many opponents assert. I think not.

Although Jim does go back in chains and does suffer terribly not only at the hands of the Phelpses but at the hands of Tom Sawyer himself, his sacrifice, his deliberate decision to be quiet when brought back, and his sentiments, as expressed in the last chapter, all combine to reinforce not Tom and the ruse but Jim and his humanity and resourcefulness. It is this rethinking of the southern slave that is the true visionary center of this novel. Once a student listening to a lecture asked me, "Is Huck still a racist at the end of the novel?" The more significant question raised by the conclusion is one that Twain posed to his nineteenth-century audience as well as to us: In the face of the cancerous cruelty of the peculiar institution, what will it take to move humanity from passive complacency to active, even risky, opposition in order to effect significant change?

–*The Jim Dilemma: Reading Race in 'Huckleberry Finn'* (Jackson: University of Mississippi Press, 1998): xx–xxi

(Autumn 1963): 45–66; Kenneth S. Lynn, *Mark Twain and Southwestern Humor* (Boston: Little, Brown, 1959).

16. See especially Daniel Hoffman, "Jim's Magic: Black or White?" *American Literature* 32 (Mar. 1960), 47–54.

17. Even the allegedly scientific works on the Negro focused on superstition as a definitive trait. See, for example, W. D. Weatherford, *Negro Life in the South* (New York: Young Men's Christian Association P, 1910); and Jerome Dowd, *Negro Races* (New York: Macmillan, 1907). No one has commented more scathingly on Negro superstition than William Hannibal Thomas in *The American Negro* (1901; New York: Negro Universities P, 1969); by American definitions he was a Negro himself.

18. See Fredrick Woodard and Donnarae MacCann, "*Huckleberry Finn* and the Traditions of Blackface Minstrelsy," *Interracial Books for Children Bulletin* 15.1–2 (1984): 4–13.

19. Daniel Hoffman, in *Form and Fable in American Fiction* (New York: Oxford UP, 1961), reveals an implicit understanding of Jim's creativity, but he does not pursue the point in detail (331).

20. See Thomas Weaver and Merline Williams, "Mark Twain's Jim: Identity As An Index to Cultural Attitudes," *American Literary Realism* 13 (Spring 1980): 19–30.

21. See Lynn Altenbernd, "Huck Finn, Emancipator," *Criticism* 1 (1959): 298–307.

22. See, for example, Leo Marx, "Mr. Eliot, Mr. Trilling and *Huckleberry Finn*," *American Scholar* 22 (Autumn 1953): 423–40; and Neil Schmitz, "Twain, *Huckleberry Finn,* and the Reconstruction," *American Studies* 12 (Spring 1971): 59–67.

23. A number of works comment on Twain's religious views and the relation between his critiques of religion and of racism. See Allison Ensor, *Mark Twain and the Bible* (Lexington: U of Kentucky P, 1969); Arthur G. Pettit, "Mark Twain and the Negro, 1867–1869," *Journal of Negro History* 56 (Apr. 1971), 88–96; and Gollin and Gollin 5–15.

24. See Hoffman, *Form and Fable* 327–28.

25. I would like to thank my colleagues, David Langston and Michael Bell, for the helpful suggestions they offered me regarding this essay.

Works by Mark Twain

BOOKS: *The Celebrated Jumping Frog of Calaveras County, and Other Sketches* (New York: C. H. Webb, 1867; London: Routledge, 1867).

The Innocents Abroad, or the New Pilgrims' Progress (Hartford, Conn.: American Publishing, 1869); republished in 2 volumes as *The Innocents Abroad and The New Pilgrims' Progress* (London: Hotten, 1870).

Mark Twain's (Burlesque) Autobiography and First Romance (New York: Sheldon, 1871; London: Hotten, 1871).

Roughing It (London: Routledge, 1872).

The Innocents at Home (London: Routledge, 1872).

Roughing It, augmented edition (Hartford, Conn.: American Publishing, 1872)—comprises *Roughing It* and *The Innocents at Home.*

A Curious Dream; and Other Sketches (London: Routledge, 1872).

The Gilded Age: A Tale of Today, by Twain and Charles Dudley Warner (Hartford, Conn.: American Publishing, 1873; 3 volumes, London: Routledge, 1874).

Mark Twain's Sketches, New and Old (Hartford, Conn.: American Publishing, 1875).

Old Times on the Mississippi, pirated edition (Toronto: Belford, 1876); republished as *The Mississippi Pilot* (London: Ward, Lock, 1877).

The Adventures of Tom Sawyer (London: Chatto & Windus, 1876; Hartford, Conn.: American Publishing, 1876).

A True Story, and The Recent Carnival of Crime (Boston: Osgood, 1877).

An Idle Excursion (Toronto: Rose-Belford, 1878); expanded as *Punch, Brothers Punch! And Other Sketches* (New York: Slote, Woodman, 1878).

A Tramp Abroad (London: Chatto & Windus / Hartford, Conn.: American Publishing, 1880).

"1601" Conversation, As It Was by the Social Fireside, in the Time of the Tudors (Cleveland, 1880).

The Prince and the Pauper (London: Chatto & Windus, 1881; Boston: Osgood, 1882).

The Stolen White Elephant (London: Chatto & Windus, 1882); republished as *The Stolen White Elephant, Etc.* (Boston: Osgood, 1882).

Life on the Mississippi (London: Chatto & Windus, 1883; Hartford, Conn.: Osgood, 1883)—includes *Old Times on the Mississippi.*

The Adventures of Huckleberry Finn (London: Chatto & Windus, 1884); republished as *Adventures of Huckleberry Finn* (New York: Webster, 1885).

A Connecticut Yankee in King Arthur's Court (New York: Webster, 1889); republished as *A Yankee at the Court of King Arthur* (London: Chatto & Windus, 1889).

The American Claimant (New York: Webster, 1892; London: Chatto & Windus, 1892).

Merry Tales (New York: Webster, 1892).

The £1,000,000 Bank-Note and Other New Stories (New York: Webster, 1893; London: Chatto & Windus, 1893).

Tom Sawyer Abroad by Huck Finn (New York: Webster, 1894; London: Chatto & Windus, 1894).

Pudd'nhead Wilson, A Tale (London: Chatto & Windus, 1894); augmented as *The Tragedy of Pudd'nhead Wilson and the Comedy of Those Extraordinary Twins* (Hartford, Conn.: American Publishing, 1894).

Personal Recollections of Joan of Arc by the Sieur Louis de Conte (New York: Harper, 1896; London: Chatto & Windus, 1896).

Tom Sawyer Abroad, Tom Sawyer, Detective, and Other Tales (New York: Harper, 1896).

Tom Sawyer, Detective, as Told by Huck Finn, and Other Stories (London: Chatto & Windus, 1896).

How to Tell a Story and Other Essays (New York: Harper, 1897).

Following the Equator (Hartford, Conn.: American Publishing, 1897); republished as *More Tramps Abroad* (London: Chatto & Windus, 1897).

The Man That Corrupted Hadleyburg and Other Stories and Essays (New York & London: Harper, 1900); enlarged as *The Man That Corrupted Hadleyburg and Other Stories and Sketches* (London: Chatto & Windus, 1900).

A Double Barreled Detective Story (New York & London: Harper, 1902).

My Début as a Literary Person, with Other Essays and Stories, volume 23 of *The Writings of Mark Twain,* Autograph Edition (Hartford, Conn.: American Publishing, 1903).

A Dog's Tale (New York & London: Harper, 1904).

Extracts from Adam's Diary Translated from the Original MS. (New York & London: Harper, 1904).

King Leopold's Soliloquy: A Defense of His Congo Rule (Boston: P. R. Warren, 1905).

Eve's Diary Translated from the Original MS. (London & New York: Harper, 1906).

What Is Man? (New York: De Vinne Press, 1906); enlarged as *What Is Man? And Other Essays* (New York & London: Harper, 1917).

The $30,000 Bequest and Other Stories (New York & London: Harper, 1906).

Christian Science with Notes Containing Corrections to Date (New York & London: Harper, 1907).

A Horse's Tale (New York & London: Harper, 1907).

Is Shakespeare Dead? (New York & London: Harper, 1909).

Extract from Captain Stormfield's Visit to Heaven (New York & London: Harper, 1909).

Mark Twain's Speeches, compiled by F. A. Nast (New York & London: Harper, 1910).

The Mysterious Stranger, a Romance, edited by Albert Bigelow Paine and Frederick A. Duneka (New York & London: Harper, 1916); enlarged as *The Mysterious Stranger and Other Stories,* edited by Paine (New York & London: Harper, 1922).

The Curious Republic of Gondour and Other Whimsical Sketches (New York: Boni & Liveright, 1919).

Mark Twain's Speeches, edited by Paine (New York & London: Harper, 1923).

Europe and Elsewhere, edited by Paine (New York & London: Harper, 1923).

Mark Twain's Autobiography, 2 volumes, edited by Paine (New York & London: Harper, 1924).

Sketches of the Sixties, by Twain and Bret Harte (San Francisco: Howell, 1926).

The Adventures of Thomas Jefferson Snodgrass, edited by Charles Honce (Chicago: Pascal Covici, 1928).

Mark Twain's Notebook, edited by Paine (New York & London: Harper, 1935).

Letters from the Sandwich Islands Written for the Sacramento Union, edited by G. Ezra Dane (San Francisco: Grabhorn Press, 1937).

The Washoe Giant in San Francisco, edited by Franklin Walker (San Francisco: Fields, 1938).

Mark Twain's Travels with Mr. Brown, edited by Walker and Dane (New York: Knopf, 1940).

Mark Twain in Eruption, edited by Bernard DeVoto (New York & London: Harper, 1940).

Mark Twain at Work, edited by DeVoto (Cambridge, Mass.: Harvard University Press, 1942).

Mark Twain, Business Man, edited by Samuel Charles Webster (Boston: Little, Brown, 1946).

Mark Twain of the ENTERPRISE, edited by Henry Nash Smith (Berkeley: University of California Press, 1957).

Traveling with the Innocents Abroad: Mark Twain's Original Reports from Europe and the Holy Land, edited by Daniel Morley McKeithan (Norman: University of Oklahoma Press, 1958).

Contributions to the Galaxy, 1868–1871, by Mark Twain, edited by Bruce R. McElderry Jr. (Gainesville, Fla.: Scholars' Facsimiles and Reprints, 1961).

Letters from the Earth, edited by DeVoto (New York: Harper & Row, 1962).

Mark Twain's "Which was the Dream" and Other Symbolic Writings of the Later Years, edited by John S. Tuckey (Berkeley: University of California Press, 1966).

Mark Twain's Satires and Burlesques, edited by Franklin R. Rogers (Berkeley: University of California Press, 1967).

Clemens of the "Call": Mark Twain in San Francisco, edited by Edgar M. Branch (Berkeley: University of California Press, 1969).

Mark Twain's "Mysterious Stranger" Manuscripts, edited by William M. Gibson (Berkeley: University of California Press, 1969).

Mark Twain's Hannibal, Huck, & Tom, edited by Walter Blair (Berkeley: University of California Press, 1972).

Mark Twain's Fables of Man, edited by Tuckey (Berkeley: University of California Press, 1972).

Mark Twain's Notebooks & Journals, volume 1, 1855–1873, edited by Frederick Anderson, Michael B. Frank, and Kenneth M. Sanderson; volume 2, 1877–1883, edited by Anderson, Lin Salamo, and Bernard L. Stein; volume 3, 1883–1891, edited by Robert Pack Browning, Frank, and Salamo (Berkeley: University of California Press, 1975, 1979).

Mark Twain Speaking, edited by Paul Fatout (Iowa City: University of Iowa Press, 1976).

Mark Twain Speaks for Himself, edited by Fatout (West Lafayette, Ind.: Purdue University Press, 1978).

The Devil's Race-Track: Mark Twain's "Great Dark" Writings, edited by Tuckey (Berkeley: University of California Press, 1980).

Wapping Alice, Printed for the First Time, edited by Hamlin Hill (Berkeley: Bancroft Library, University of California, 1981).

The Adventures of Tom Sawyer by Mark Twain: A Facsimile of the Author's Holograph Manuscript, 2 volumes (Frederick, Md.: University Publications of America / Washington, D.C.: Georgetown University Library, 1982).

Adventures of Huckleberry Finn (Tom Sawyer's Comrade) by Mark Twain: A Facsimile of the Manuscript, 2 volumes (Detroit: Gale Research, 1983).

Huck Finn: the Complete Buffalo Manuscript–Teaching and Research Digital Edition, CD-ROM (Buffalo & Erie County Public Library, 2002).

Edition: *The Annotated Huckleberry Finn,* edited by Michael Patrick Hearn (New York & London: Norton, 2001).

Collections: *The Writings of Mark Twain,* Autograph Edition, 25 volumes (Hartford, Conn.: American Publishing, 1899–1907).

The Writings of Mark Twain, Author's National Edition, 25 volumes (New York & London: Harper, 1899–1917).

The Writings of Mark Twain, Definitive Edition, 37 volumes, edited by Albert Bigelow Paine (New York: Wells, 1922–1925).

The Oxford Mark Twain, 29 volumes (New York: Oxford University Press, 1996).

Editions prepared by the University of California Press by the members of the Mark Twain Project: *Roughing It,* edited by Franklin R. Rogers and Paul Baender (Berkeley: University of California Press, 1972). Revised edition, edited by Harriet Elinor Smith and Edgar Marquess Branch, with Lin Salamo and Robert Pack Browning (Berkeley: University of California Press, 1993).

What Is Man? And Other Philosophical Writings, edited by Baender (Berkeley: University of California Press, 1973).

A Connecticut Yankee in King Arthur's Court, edited by Bernard L. Stein (Berkeley: University of California Press, 1979).

The Prince and the Pauper, edited by Victor Fischer and Salamo, with the assistance of Mary Jane Jones (Berkeley: University of California Press, 1979).

Early Tales & Sketches, Volume 1 (1851–1864), edited by Branch and Robert H. Hirst, with the assistance of Harriet Elinor Smith (Berkeley: University of California Press, 1979).

The Adventures of Tom Sawyer; Tom Sawyer Abroad; Tom Sawyer, Detective, edited by John C. Gerber, Baender, and Terry Firkins (Berkeley: University of California Press, 1980).

Early Tales & Sketches, Volume 2 (1864–1865), edited by Branch and Hirst, with the assistance of Smith (Berkeley: University of California Press, 1981).

Adventures of Huckleberry Finn, edited by Walter Blair and Fischer, with the assistance of Dahlia Armon and Smith (Berkeley: University of California Press, 1988). Revised edition, edited by Fischer and Salamo with the late Walter Blair (Berkeley: University of California Press, 2003).

LETTERS: *Mark Twain's Letters,* 2 volumes, edited by Albert Bigelow Paine (New York: Harper, 1917).

Mark Twain's Letters to Will Bowen, edited by Theodore Hornberger (Austin: University of Texas Press, 1941).

The Love Letters of Mark Twain, edited by Dixon Wecter (New York: Harper, 1949).

Mark Twain to Mrs. Fairbanks, edited by Wecter (San Marino, Cal.: Huntington Library, 1949).

Mark Twain–Howells Letters, 2 volumes, edited by Henry Nash Smith and William M. Gibson (Cambridge, Mass.: Harvard University Press, 1960).

Mark Twain's Letters to Mary, edited by Lewis Leary (New York: Columbia University Press, 1961).

The Pattern for Mark Twain's Roughing It: Letters from Nevada by Samuel and Orion Clemens, 1861–1862, edited by Franklin R. Rogers (Berkeley & Los Angeles: University of California Press, 1961).

Mark Twain's Letters from Hawaii, edited by A. Grove Day (New York: Appleton-Century, 1966).

Mark Twain's Letters to His Publishers, edited by Hamlin Hill (Berkeley: University of California Press, 1967).

Mark Twain's Correspondence with Henry Huttleston Rogers, 1893–1909, edited by Leary (Berkeley: University of California Press, 1969).

Mark Twain's Letters, volume 1, 1853–1866, edited by Edgar M. Branch, Michael B. Frank, and Kenneth M. Sanderson; volume 2, 1867–1868, edited by Harriet Elinor Smith and Richard Bucci; volume 3, 1869, edited by Victor Fischer and Frank; volume 4, 1870–1871, edited by Fischer, Frank, and Lin Salamo (Berkeley: University of California Press, 1988–1995).

PAPERS:

The major collections of Samuel Clemens's papers are at the Bancroft Library, University of California, Berkeley; the Beinecke Library, Yale University; the New York Public Library; the Mark Twain Memorial and Stowe-Day Foundation, Hartford, Connecticut; the Library of Congress; the Houghton Library, Harvard University; the Buffalo and Erie County Public Library; the Harry Ransom Humanities Research Center, University of Texas, Austin; the Mark Twain Museum, Hannibal, Missouri; the Vassar College Library; the Alderman Library, University of Virginia; and the Center for Mark Twain Studies at Quarry Farm, Elmira College, New York.

Works about Mark Twain
and *Adventures of Huckleberry Finn*

See also the Twain entries in *DLB 11: American Humorists, 1800–1950; DLB 12: American Realists and Naturalists; DLB 23: American Newspaper Journalists, 1873–1900; DLB 64: American Literary Critics and Scholars, 1850–1880; DLB 74: American Short-Story Writers Before 1880; DLB 186: Nineteenth-Century American Western Writers;* and *DLB 189: American Travel Writers, 1850–1915.* Also see the entries on *Adventures of Huckleberry Finn* in *DLB Yearbook 1985.*

Bibliographies

Adams, Lucille, and Buffalo Public Library. *Huckleberry Finn: A of the Huckleberry Finn Collection at the Buffalo Public Library.* Buffalo: Buffalo Public Library, 1950.

Gribben, Alan. "Removing Mark Twain's Mask: A Decade of Criticism and Scholarship," *ESQ: Journal of the American Renaissance,* 26 (1980): 100–108, 149–171.

Johnson, Merle. *A Bibliography of the Works of Mark Twain, Samuel Langhorne Clemens: A List of First Editions in Book Form and of First Printings in Periodicals and Occasional Publications of His Varied Literary Activities.* Revised and enlarged edition. New York & London: Harper, 1935.

McBride, William M. *Mark Twain: A Bibliography of the Collections of the Mark Twain Memorial and the Stowe-Day Foundation.* Hartford, Conn.: McBride, 1984.

Tenney, Thomas A. *Mark Twain: A Reference Guide.* Boston: G. K. Hall, 1977.

Union Catalog of Clemens' Letters, edited by Paul Machlis. Berkeley: University of California Press, 1986.

Union Catalog of Letters to Clemens, edited by Machlis. Berkeley: University of California Press, 1992.

Biographies

Andrews, Kenneth. *Nook Farm: Mark Twain's Hartford Circle.* Cambridge, Mass.: Harvard University Press, 1950.

Brashear, Minnie M. *Mark Twain, Son of Missouri.* Chapel Hill: University of North Carolina Press, 1934.

Caron, James E. *Mark Twain, Unsanctified Newspaper Reporter.* Columbia: University of Missouri Press, 2008.

DeVoto, Bernard. *Mark Twain's America.* Boston: Little, Brown, 1932.

Duckett, Margaret. *Mark Twain and Bret Harte.* Norman: University of Oklahoma Press, 1964.

Emerson, Everett. *The Authentic Mark Twain: A Literary Biography of Samuel L. Clemens.* Philadelphia: University of Pennsylvania Press, 1984.

Fatout, Paul. *Mark Twain in Virginia City.* Bloomington: Indiana University Press, 1964.

Ferguson, DeLancey. *Mark Twain: Man and Legend.* Indianapolis & New York: Bobbs-Merrill, 1943.

Hill, Hamlin. *Mark Twain: God's Fool.* New York: Harper & Row, 1973.

Hoffman, Andrew. *Inventing Mark Twain: The Lives of Samuel Langhorne Clemens.* New York: Morrow, 1997.

Hoffman, Andrew. *Inventing Mark Twain: The Lives of Samuel Langhorne Clemens.* New York: Morrow, 1997.

Kaplan, Fred. *The Singular Mark Twain: A Biography.* New York: Doubleday, 2003.

Kaplan, Justin. *Mr. Clemens and Mark Twain.* New York: Simon & Schuster, 1966.

Messent, Peter. *The Cambridge Introduction to Mark Twain.* Cambridge, U.K., & New York: Cambridge University Press, 2007.

Paine, Albert Bigelow. *Mark Twain, A Biography,* 3 volumes. New York & London: Harper, 1912.

Powers, Ron. *Mark Twain: A Life.* New York : Free Press, 2005.

Sanborn, Margaret. *Mark Twain: The Bachelor Years.* New York: Doubleday, 1990.

Webster, Mark, and Samuel Charles. *Mark Twain, Business Man.* Boston: Little, Brown, 1946.

Wecter, Dixon. *Sam Clemens of Hannibal.* Boston: Houghton Mifflin, 1952.

Journals

The Mark Twain Annual: The Journal of the Mark Twain Circle of America. 2001– .

Mark Twain Circular. Published in association with the Mark Twain Circle. Charleston, S.C., 1987.

Mark Twain Journal. Kirkwood, Mo. 1954–1983, Charleston, S,C. 1984– . Continues *Mark Twain Quarterly.*

Mark Twain Quarterly. International Mark Twain Society. 1936–1953.

Books, Book Sections, and Articles

Allingham, Philip V. "Patterns of Deception in *Huckleberry Finn* and *Great Expectations*," *Nineteenth-Century Literature,* 46 (March 1992): 447–472.

Alter, Robert. "Heirs of the Tradition," in his *Rogue's Progress: Studies in the Picaresque Novel.* Cambridge, Mass.: Harvard University Press, 1964, pp. 106–132.

Altschuler, Mark. "Motherless Child: Huck Finn and a Theory of Moral Development," *American Literary Realism, 1870–1910,* 22 (Fall 1989): 31–42.

Anderson, Douglas. "*Huckleberry Finn* and Emerson's 'Concord Hymn,'" *Nineteenth-Century Fiction,* 40 (June 1985): 43–60.

Anderson. "Reading the Pictures in *Huckleberry Finn*," *Arizona Quarterly,* 42 (Summer 1986): 100–120.

Andrews, William L. "Mark Twain and James W. C. Pennington: Huckleberry Finn's Smallpox Lie," *Studies in American Fiction,* 9 (Spring 1981): 103–112.

Anspaugh, Kelly. "The Innocent Eye? E. W. Kemble's Illustrations to *Adventures of Huckleberry Finn*," *American Literary Realism, 1870–1910,* 25 (Winter 1993): 16–30.

Arac, Jonathan. *Huckleberry Finn as Idol and Target: The Functions of Criticism in Our Time.* Madison: University of Wisconsin Press, 1997.

Asselineau, Roger. "A Transcendentalist Poet Named Huckleberry Finn," *Studies in American Fiction,* 13 (Autumn 1985): 217–226.

Banta, Martha. "Escape and Entry in *Huckleberry Finn*," *Modern Fiction Studies,* 14 (Spring 1968): 79–91.

Barclay, Donald A. "Interpreted Well Enough: Two Illustrators' Visions of *Adventures of Huckleberry Finn*," *Horn Book Magazine,* 68 (May–June 1992): 311–319.

Bassett, John Earl. "*Huckleberry Finn:* The End Lies in the Beginning," *American Literary Realism, 1870–1910,* 17 (Spring 1984): 89–98.

Beaver, Harold. *Huckleberry Finn.* London & Boston: Unwin Hyman, 1988.

Beidler, Gretchen M. "Huck Finn as Tourist: Mark Twain's Parody Travelogue," *Studies in American Fiction,* 20 (Autumn 1992): 155–167.

Beidler, Peter G. "Fawkes' Identified: A New Source for *Huckleberry Finn?*" *English Language Notes,* 29 (March 1992): 54–60.

Beidler. "The Raft Episode in *Huckleberry Finn*," *Modern Fiction Studies,* 14 (Spring 1968): 11–20.

Bercovitch, Sacvan. "What's Funny About Huckleberry Finn," *New England Review-Middlebury Series,* 20, no. 1 (1999): 8–28.

Berkove, Lawrence I. "The Free Man of Color in *The Grandissimes* and Works by Harris and Mark Twain," *Southern Quarterly: A Journal of the Arts in the South,* 18 (Summer 1980): 60–73.

Berkove. "The 'Poor Players' of *Huckleberry Finn*," *Papers of the Michigan Academy of Science, Arts, and Letters,* 53 (1968): 291–310.

Berret, Anthony J. "Huckleberry Finn and the Minstrel Show," *American Studies,* 27, no. 2 (1986): 37–49

Berret. "The Influence of *Hamlet* on *Huckleberry Finn*," *American Literary Realism, 1870–1910,* 18 (Spring–Autumn 1985): 196–207.

Birchfield, James. "Jim's Coat of Arms," *Mark Twain Journal,* 14 (Summer 1969): 15–16.

Bird, John. "The Chains of Time: Temporality in *Huckleberry Finn*," *Texas Studies in Literature and Language,* 32 (Summer 1990): 262–276.

Bird. "'These Leather-Face People': Huck and the Moral Art of Lying," *Studies in American Fiction,* 15 (Spring 1987): 71–80.

Black, Ronald J. "The Psychological Necessity of the Evasion Sequence in *Huckleberry Finn*," *CEA Critic,* 52 (Summer 1990): 35–44.

Blackburn, Alexander. "Confidence Men in *Huckleberry Finn*," in his *The Myth of the Picaro: Continuity and Transformation of the Picaresque Novel, 1554–1954.* Chapel Hill, N.C.: The University of North Carolina Press, 1979, pp. 177–187.

Blair, Walter. "Mark Twain, Hank, and Huck," in his *Horse Sense in American Humor: From Benjamin Franklin to Ogden Nash.* 1942. New York: Russell & Russell, 1962, pp. 195–217.

Blair. *Mark Twain and Huck Finn.* Berkeley & Los Angeles: University of California Press, 1960.

Blair. "When Was *Huckleberry Finn* Written?" *American Literature,* 30 (March 1958): 1–25.

Blakemore, Steven. "Huck Finn's Written World," *American Literary Realism, 1870–1910,* 20 (Winter 1988): 21–29.

Bluefarb, Sam. "Huckleberry Finn: Escape from Conscience and the Discovery of the Heart," in his *The Escape Motif in the American Novel: Mark Twain to Richard Wright.* Columbus: Ohio State University Press, 1972, pp. 12–24.

Boland, Sally. "The Seven Dialects in *Huckleberry Finn*," *North Dakota Quarterly,* 36 (Summer 1968): 30–40.

Boughn, Michael. "Rethinking Mark Twain's Skepticism: Ways of Knowing and Forms of Freedom in the *Adventures of Huckleberry Finn*," *Arizona Quarterly,* 52 (Winter 1996): 31–48.

Branch, Edgar M. "Mark Twain: Newspaper Reading and the Writer's Creativity," *Nineteenth-Century Fiction,* 37 (March 1983): 576–603.

Brenner, Gerry. "More than a Reader's Response: A Letter to 'De Ole True Huck,'" *Journal of Narrative Technique,* 20 (Spring 1990): 221–234.

Briden, Earl F. "Huck's Great Escape: Magic and Ritual," *Mark Twain Journal,* 21 (Spring 1983): 17–18.

Briden. "Huck's Island Adventure and the Selkirk Legend," *Mark Twain Journal,* 18 (Winter 1976–1977): 12–14.

Briden. "Kemble's 'Specialty' and the Pictorial Countertext of *Huckleberry Finn*," *Mark Twain Journal,* 26 (Fall 1988): 2–14.

Budd, Louis J. "*Adventures of Huckleberry Finn*," in *American History through Literature, 1870–1920,* edited by Tom Quirk and Gary Scharnhorst. Detroit: Scribners/ Thomsom Gale, 2006, pp. 13–23.

Budd. "Another Source for the Small-Pox Lie in *Huckleberry Finn?*" *Mark Twain Circular,* 12 (April–June 1998): 2–3.

Budd. "Huck at 100: How Old Is *Huckleberry Finn?*" in *Dictionary of Literary Biography Yearbook: 1985,* edited by Jean W. Ross. Detroit: Gale Research, 1986, pp. 12–19.

Budd. Introduction. *Adventures of Huckleberry Finn (Tom Sawyer's Comrade): A Facsimile of the Manuscript.* Volume 1. Detroit: Gale Research, 1983, pp. ix–xx.

Budd. "The Recomposition of *Adventures of Huckleberry Finn*," *Missouri Review,* 10, no. 1 (1987): 113–129.

Budd. "The Southward Currents under Huck Finn's Raft," *Mississippi Valley Historical Review,* 46 (September 1959): 222–237.

Burgess, Anthony. "Mark Twain and James Joyce," *Mark Twain Journal,* 13 (Winter 1966–1967): 1–2.

Camfield, Gregg. "'I Wouldn't Be as Ignorant as You for Wages': Huck Talks Back to His Conscience," *Studies in American Fiction,* 20 (Autumn 1992): 169–175.

Camfield. "Sentimental Liberalism and the Problem of Race in Huckleberry Finn," *Nineteenth-Century Literature,* 46 (June 1991): 96–113.

Cardwell, Guy A. "The Bowdlerizing of Mark Twain," *ESQ: A Journal of the American Renaissance,* 21, no. 3 (1975): 179–193.

Carey-Webb, Allen. "Racism and *Huckleberry Finn:* Censorship, Dialogue, and Change," *English Journal,* 82 (November 1993): 22–34.

Carkeet, David. "The Dialects in Huckleberry Finn," *American Literature: A Journal of Literary History, Criticism, and Bibliography,* 51 (November 1979): 315–332.

Carkeet. "The Source for the Arkansas Gossips in *Huckleberry Finn*," *American Literary Realism, 1870–1910,* 14 (Spring 1981): 90–92.

Carrington, George C., Jr. *The Dramatic Unity of Huckleberry Finn.* Columbus: Ohio State University Press, 1976.

Carter, Everett. "The Modernist Ordeal of Huckleberry Finn," *Studies in American Fiction,* 13 (Autumn 1985): 169–183.

Cecil, L. Moffitt. "The Historical Ending of *Adventures of Huckleberry Finn:* How Nigger Jim Was Set Free," *American Literary Realism, 1870–1910,* 13 (Autumn 1980): 280–283.

Chadwick-Joshua, Jocelyn. *The Jim Dilemma: Reading Race in* Huckleberry Finn. Jackson: University Press of Mississippi, 1998.

Chase, Richard. "Mark Twain and the Novel," in his *The American Novel and Its Tradition.* Garden City, N.Y.: Doubleday, 1957, pp. 139–149.

Colwell, James L. "Huckleberries and Humans: On the Naming of Huckleberry Finn," *PMLA,* 86 (January 1971): 70–76.

Covici, Pascal, Jr. "Fooling Poor Old Huck," in his *Mark Twain's Humor: The Image of a World.* Dallas, Tex.: Southern Methodist University Press, 1962, pp. 159–185.

Cox, James M. *Mark Twain: The Fate of Humor.* Princeton: Princeton University Press, 1966.

Cox. "Mark Twain: The Height of Humor," in his *The Comic Imagination in American Literature,* edited by Louis D. Rubin Jr. New Brunswick, N.J.: Rutgers University Press, 1973, pp. 139–148.

Cox. "Toward Vernacular Humor," *Virginia Quarterly Review,* 46 (Spring 1970): 311–330.

Cummings, Sherwood. "Crisis: *Huckleberry Finn*," in his *Mark Twain and Science: Adventures of a Mind.* Baton Rouge: Louisiana State University Press, 1988, pp. 123–158.

Cummings. "Mark Twain's Moveable Farm and the Evasion," *American Literature: A Journal of Literary History, Criticism, and Bibliography,* 63 (September 1991): 440–458.

David, Beverly R. "Mark Twain and the Legends for *Huckleberry Finn*," *American Literary Realism, 1870–1910,* 15 (Autumn 1982): 155–165.

David. "The Pictorial *Huck Finn:* Mark Twain and His Illustrator, E. W. Kemble," *American Quarterly,* 26 (October 1974): 331–351.

Derwin, Susan. "Impossible Commands: Reading *Adventures of Huckleberry Finn*," *Nineteenth-Century Literature,* 47 (March 1993): 437–454.

DeVoto, Bernard. *Mark Twain at Work*. Cambridge: Harvard University Press, 1942.

Doyno. "Textual Addendum," in *Adventures of Huckleberry Finn*. New York: Random House, 1996, pp. 365–388.

Dyson, A. E. "Huckleberry Finn and the Whole Truth," *Critical Quarterly* (London), 3 (Spring 1961): 29–40.

Egan, Michael. *Mark Twain's* Huckleberry Finn: *Race, Class and Society*. London: Chatto & Windus for Sussex University Press, 1977.

Eliot, T. S. "Introduction," in *Adventures of Huckleberry Finn*. New York: Chanticleer Press, 1950, pp. vii–xvi.

Ellis, James. "The Bawdy Humor of THE KING'S CAMELOPARD or THE ROYAL NONESUCH," *American Literature: A Journal of Literary History, Criticism, and Bibliography*, 63 (December 1991): 729–735.

Ellison, Ralph. "Change the Joke and Slip the Yoke," *Partisan Review*, 25 (Spring 1958): 212–222.

Ellison. "Twentieth-Century Fiction and the Black Mask of Humanity," *Confluence: An International Forum*, 2, no. 4 (1953): 3–21.

Emerson, Everett. "A New Voice," in his *Mark Twain: A Literary Life*. Philadelphia: University of Pennsylvania Press, 2000, pp. 140–163.

Ensor, Allison. "The Contribution of Charles Webster and Albert Bigelow Paine to *Huckleberry Finn*," *American Literature: A Journal of Literary History, Criticism, and Bibliography*, 40 (May 1968): 222–227.

Ensor. "The Location of the Phelps Farm in 'Huckleberry Finn,'" *South Atlantic Bulletin: A Quarterly Journal Devoted to Research and Teaching in the Modern Languages and Literatures*, 34 (May 1969): 7.

Ensor. "The 'Opposition Line' to The King and The Duke in *Huckleberry Finn*," *Mark Twain Journal*, 14 (Winter 1968–1969): 6–7.

Fertel, R. J. "'Free and Easy'? Spontaneity and the Quest for Maturity in the *Adventures of Huckleberry Finn*," *Modern Language Quarterly*, 44 (June 1983): 157–177.

Fetterley, Judith. "Disenchantment: Tom Sawyer in *Huckleberry Finn*," *PMLA*, 87 (January 1972): 69–74.

Fiedler, Leslie A. "A Backward Glance O'er Travelled Roads," in *What Was Literature? Class Culture and Mass Society*. New York: Simon & Schuster, 1982, pp. 232–245.

Fiedler. "Come Back to the Raft Ag'in, Huck Honey!" *Partisan Review*, 15 (June 1948): 664–671.

Fiedler. "*Huckleberry Finn*: The Book We Love to Hate," *Proteus: A Journal of Ideas*, 1 (Fall 1984): 1–8.

Fields, Wayne. "When the Fences Are Down; Language and Order in *The Adventures of Tom Sawyer* and *Huckleberry Finn*," *Journal of American Studies* (Cambridge, England), 24, no. 3 (1990): 369–386.

Fischer, Victor. "Huck Finn Reviewed: The Reception of *Huckleberry Finn* in the United States, 1885–1897," *American Literary Realism, 1870–1910*, 16 (Spring 1983): 1–57.

Fishkin, Shelley Fisher. *Was Huck Black?: Mark Twain and African-American Voices*. New York: Oxford University Press, 1993.

Frank, Waldo. "The Land of the Pioneer," in his *Our America*. 1919. New York: AMS Press, 1972, pp. 37–44.

Freedman, Samuel N. "The First Edition of *Huckleberry Finn*: An Overview," *Proteus: A Journal of Ideas*, 1 (Fall 1984): 36–40.

French, William C. "Character and Cruelty in Huckleberry Finn: Why the Ending Works," *Soundings: an Interdisciplinary Journal*, 81, 11–2 (1998): 157–79.

Fulton, Joe B. "'Playing Double': The Ethics of Realism in *Adventures of Huckleberry Finn*," in his *Mark Twain's Ethical Realism: The Aesthetics of Race, Class, and Gender*. Columbia: University of Missouri Press, 1997, pp. 53–87.

Furnas, J. C. "The Crowded Raft: *Huckleberry Finn* and Its Critics," *American Scholar*, 54 (1985): 517–524.

Gabler-Hover, Janet A. "Sympathy Not Empathy: The Intent of Narration in *Huckleberry Finn*," *Journal of Narrative Technique*, 17 (Winter 1987): 67–75.

Gardner, Richard M. "*Huck Finn's* Ending: The Intimacy and Disappointment of Tourism," *Journal of Narrative Technique*, 24 (Winter 1994): 55–68.

Gerber, John C. "Adventures of Huckleberry Finn," *Mark Twain*, Boston, Mass.: Twayne, 1988, pp. 95–114.

Gerber. "Practical Editions: Mark Twain's *The Adventures of Tom Sawyer* and *Adventures of Huckleberry Finn*," *Proof. The Yearbook of American Bibliographical and Textual Studies*, 2 (1972): 285–292.

Gibson, William M. "The 'Boy Books,'" in his *The Art of Mark Twain*. New York: Oxford University Press, 1976, pp. 97–125.

Godden, Richard, and Mary A. McCay. "Say It Again, Sam[bo]: Race and Speech in *Huckleberry Finn* and *Casablanca*," in his *Mississippi Quarterly: The Journal of Southern Culture*, 49 (Fall 1996): 657–682.

Gollin, Richard, and Rita Gollin. "*Huckleberry Finn* and the Time of the Evasion." *Modern Language Studies*, 9 (Spring 1979): 5–15.

Gribben, Alan. "'Good Books and a Sleepy Conscience': Mark Twain's Reading Habits," *American Literary Realism, 1870–1910*, 9 (Autumn 1976): 295–306.

Gribben. "'I Detest Novels, Poetry and Theology': Origin of a Fiction Concerning Mark Twain's Reading," *Tennessee Studies in Literature*, 22 (1977): 154–161.

Gribben. "Manipulating a Genre: *Huckleberry Finn* as Boy Book," *South Central Review: The Journal of the South Central Modern Language Association*, 5 (Winter 1988): 15–21.

Gribben. "Removing Mark Twain's Mask: A Decade of Criticism and Scholarship (Part II)," *ESQ: A Journal of the American Renaissance*, 26 (1980): 149–171.

Gribben. "'Stolen from Books, Tho' Credit Given': Mark Twain's Use of Literary Sources," *Mosaic: A Journal for the Comparative Study of Literature and Ideas* (Winnipeg, Canada), 12 (Summer 1979): 149–155.

Gribben. "Those Other Thematic Patterns in Mark Twain's Writings," *Studies in American Fiction*, 13 (Autumn 1985): 185–200.

Hansen, Chadwick. "The Character of Jim and the Ending of *Huckleberry Finn*," *Massachusetts Review*, 5 (Autumn 1963): 45–66.

Harris, Susan K. "*Adventures of Huckleberry Finn*: Huck Finn," in her *Mark Twain's Escape From Time: A Study of Patterns and Images* (Columbia: University of Missouri Press, 1982), pp. 60–71.

Haslam, Gerald W. "*Huckleberry Finn*: Why Read the Phelps Farm Episode?" *Research Studies: A Quarterly Publication of Washington State University*, 35 (September 1967): 189–197.

Haupt, Clyde V. Huckleberry Finn *on Film: Film and Television Adaptations of Mark Twain's Novel, 1920–1993*. Jefferson, N.C.: McFarland, 1994.

Hearn, Michael Patrick. "Mark Twain, E .W. Kemble, and *Huckleberry Finn*," *American Book Collector*, new series 2 (November–December 1981): 14–19.

Hengstebeck, Marylee. "*Huck Finn*, Slavery, and Me," *English Journal*, 82 (November 1993): 32.

Henrickson, Gary P. "Biographers' Twain, Critics' Twain, Which of the Twain Wrote the 'Evasion'?" *Southern Literary Journal*, 26 (Fall 1993): 14–29.

Hentoff, Nat. "The University of Mark Twain," *Washington Post*, 16 January 1993, p. A23.

Hill, Hamlin. "Mark Twain: Audience and Artistry," *American Quarterly*, 15 (Spring 1963): 25–40.

Hill, Richard. "Overreaching: Critical Agenda and the Ending of *Adventures of Huckleberry Finn*," *Texas Studies in Literature and Language*, 33 (Winter 1991): 492–513.

Hiscoe, David W. "The 'Abbreviated Ejaculation' in *Huckleberry Finn*," *Studies in American Humor*, new series 1 (1983): 191–197.

Hoag, Gerald. "The Delicate Art of Geography: The Whereabouts of the Phelps Plantation in *Huckleberry Finn*," *English Language Notes*, 26 (June 1989): 63–66.

Holland, Laurence B. "A 'Raft of Trouble': Word and Deed in *Huckleberry Finn*," *Glyph: Johns Hopkins Textual Studies*, 5 (1979): 69–87.

Horwitz, Howard. "'Ours by the Law of Nature': Reading, Romance, and Independents on Mark Twain's River," in his *By the Law of Nature: Form and Value in Nineteenth-Century America*. New York: Oxford University Press, 1991, pp. 87–119.

Howell, Elmo. "Mark Twain and the Phelps Farm Episode: Another Look at *Huckleberry Finn*," *Interpretations: A Journal of Ideas, Analysis, and Criticism*, 5 (1973): 1–8.

Howell. "Uncle Silas Phelps: A Note on Mark Twain's Characterization," *Mark Twain Journal*, 14 (Summer 1968): 8–12.

Howells, William Dean. *My Mark Twain*. New York & London: Harper, 1910.

Hunt, Alan, and Carol Hunt. "The Practical Joke in *Huckleberry Finn*," *Western Folklore*, 51 (April 1992): 197–202.

Hunter, Jim. "Mark Twain and the Boy-Book in 19th-Century America," *College English*, 24 (March 1963): 430–438.

Jacobson, Marcia. "Mark Twain," in *Being a Boy Again: Autobiography and the American Boy Book*. Tuscaloosa: University of Alabama Press, 1994, pp. 44–70.

Kaufmann, David. "Satiric Deceit in the Ending of *Adventures of Huckleberry Finn*," *Studies in the Novel*, 19 (Spring 1987): 66–78.

Kelley, Karol. "*Huckleberry Finn* as a Popular Novel," *Proteus: A Journal of Ideas*, 1 (Fall 1984): 19–26.

Kelley. "Rhetorical Engagement with Racism: Harriet Beecher Stowe's *Uncle Tom's Cabin* and Mark Twain's *Adventures of Huckleberry Finn*." *Literator: Journal of Literary Criticism and Linguistics* (Potchefstroom, South Africa), 19 (April 1998): 65–78.

Kiskis, Michael J. "*Huckleberry Finn* and Family Values," *This Is Just to Say: NCTE Assembly on American Literature*, 12 (Winter 2001): 1–7.

Kiskis. "Of Huck and Marlow: The Compelled Storyteller in Mark Twain and Joseph Conrad," in *Selected Essays From the Fiftieth Anniversary International Congress of the Polish Institute of Arts and Sciences of America*, edited by M. B. Biskupski and James S. Pula. Volume III. Boulder, Colo.: East European Monographs, 1993, pp. 143–153.

Knoenagel, Axel. "Mark Twain's Further Use of Huck and Tom," *International Fiction Review* (Fredericton, Canada) 19, no. 2 (1992): 96–102.

Kokernot, Walter. "'The Burning Shame' Broadside," *Mark Twain Journal,* 29 (Fall 1991): 33–35.

Kolb, Harold H., Jr. "Mark Twain, Huck Finn, and Jacob Blivens: Gilt-Edged, Tree-Calf Morality in *The Adventures of Huckleberry Finn,*" *Virginia Quarterly Review,* 55 (Autumn 1979): 653–669.

Kraus, W. Keith. "'Huckleberry Finn': A Final Irony," *Mark Twain Journal,* 14 (Winter 1967–1968): 18–19.

Krause, Sydney. "Twain's Method and Theory of Composition," *Modern Philology,* 56 (February 1959): 167–177.

Krauth, Leland. *Proper Mark Twain.* Athens: University of Georgia Press, 1999, pp. 166–188.

Kruse, Horst H. "Annie and Huck: A Note on *The Adventures of Huckleberry Finn,*" *American Literature: A Journal of Literary History, Criticism, and Bibliography,* 39 (May 1967): 207–214.

Kruse. "Gerstaecker's *The Pirates of the Mississippi* and Mark Twain's *Adventures of Huckleberry Finn,*" *American Literary Realism, 1870–1910,* 31 (Winter 1999): 1–14.

Lindberg, John. "*The Adventures of Huckleberry Finn* as Moral Monologue," *Proteus: A Journal of Ideas,* 1 (Fall 1984): 41–49.

Lowenherz, Robert J. "The Beginning of 'Huckleberry Finn,'" *American Speech,* 38 (October 1963): 196–201.

Lowery, Robert E. "The Grangerford-Shepherdson Episode: Another of Mark Twain's Indictments of the Damned Human Race," *Mark Twain Journal,* 15 (Winter 1970): 19–21.

Lynn, Kenneth S. "Welcome Back from the Raft, Huck Honey!" *American Scholar,* 46 (Summer 1977): 338–347.

Lynn. "You Can't Go Home Again," in his *Mark Twain and Southwestern Humor.* Boston: Little, Brown, 1959, pp. 198–245.

Macdonald, Dwight. "Mark Twain: An Unsentimental Journey," *New Yorker,* 9 April 1960: 174–185.

Machan, Tim William. "The Symbolic Narrative of *Huckleberry Finn.*" *Arizona Quarterly,* 42 (Summer 1986): 131–140.

MacKethan, Lucinda H. "Huck Finn and the Slave Narratives: Lighting Out as Design," *Southern Review,* 20 (April 1984): 247–264.

Mailloux, Steven. "Rhetorical Hermeneutics as Reception Study: Huckleberry Finn and 'The Bad Boy Boom,'" in *Reconceptualizing American Literary Cultural Studies: Rhetoric, History, and Politics in the Humanities,* edited by William E. Cain. New York: Garland, 1996, pp. 35–56.

Mailloux. "The Rhetorical Use and Abuse of Fiction: Eating Books in Late Nineteenth-Century America," *Boundary 2: An International Journal of Literature and Culture,* 17 (Spring 1990): 133–157.

Manierre, William R. "Huck Finn, Empiricist Member of Society," *Modern Fiction Studies,* 14 (Spring 1968): 57–66.

Manierre. "'No Money for to Buy the Outfit': *Huckleberry Finn* Again," *Modern Fiction Studies,* 10 (Winter 1964–1965): 341–348.

Manierre. "On Keeping the Raftsmen's Passage in *Huckleberry Finn,*" *English Language Notes,* 6 (December 1968): 118–122.

Marks, Barry A. "The Making of a Humorist: The Narrative Strategy *of Huckleberry Finn,*" *Journal of Narrative Technique,* 12 (Spring 1982): 139–145.

Marshall, Gregory. "Blood Ties as Structural Motif in *Huckleberry Finn,*" *Mark Twain Journal,* 21 (Spring 1983): 44–46.

Marudanayagam, P. "The Theme of Interethnic Male Bonding: Twain and Fiedler," in *Mark Twain and Nineteenth Century American Literature,* edited by E. Nageswara Rao. Hyderbad, India: American Studies Research Centre, 1993, pp. 72–78.

Marx, Leo. "Mr. Eliot, Mr. Trilling, and *Huckleberry Finn,*" *American Scholar,* 22 (1953): 423–440.

Marx. "The Pilot and the Passenger: Landscape Conventions and the Style of *Huckleberry Finn,*" *American Literature,* 28 (January 1957): 129–146.

Mason, Ernest D. "Attraction and Repulsion: Huck Finn, 'Nigger' Jim, and Black Americans Revisited," *CLA Journal,* 33 (September 1989): 36–48.

McCullough, Joseph B. "Uses of the Bible in *Huckleberry Finn,*" *Mark Twain Journal,* 19 (Winter 1978–1979): 2–3.

McKay, Janet Holmgren. "Going to Hell: Style in Huck Finn's Great Debate," *Interpretations: A Journal of Ideas, Analysis, and Criticism,* 13 (Fall 1981): 24–30.

McKay. "'Tears and Flapdoodle': Point of View and Style in *The Adventures of Huckleberry Finn,*" *Style,* 10 (Winter 1976): 41–50.

McMahan, Elizabeth E. "The Money Motif: Economic Implications in *Huckleberry Finn,*" *Mark Twain Journal,* 15 (Summer 1971): 5–10.

Mensh, Elaine, and Harry Mensh. *Black, White, and Huckleberry Finn: Re-Imagining the American Dream.* Tuscaloosa: University of Alabama Press, 2000.

Michelson, Bruce. "Huck and the Games of the World," *American Literary Realism, 1870–1910,* 13 (Spring 1980): 108–121.

Michelson. "The Quarrel with Romance," in his *Mark Twain on the Loose: A Comic Writer and the American Self.* Amherst: University of Massachusetts Press, 1995, pp. 95–158.

Miller, Bruce E. "*Huckleberry Finn:* The Kierkegaardian Dimension," *Illinois Quarterly,* 34 (September 1971): 55–64.

Miller, J. Hillis. "Three Problems of Fictional Form: First-Person Narration in *David Copperfield* and *Huckleberry Finn,*" in *Experience in the Novel: Selected Papers from the English Institute,* edited by Roy Harvey Pearce. New York: Columbia University Press, 1968, pp. 21–48.

Miller, Leo. "Huckleberries and Humans," *PMLA,* 87 (March 1972): 314.

Monteiro, George. "Narrative Laws and Narrative Lies in *Adventures of Huckleberry Finn,*" *Studies in American Fiction,* 13 (Autumn 1985): 227–237.

Morris, Linda A. *Gender Play in Mark Twain: Cross-Dressing and Transgression.* Columbia: University of Missouri Press, 2007, pp. 31–57.

Morrison, Toni. Introduction. *Adventures of Huckleberry Finn.* New York: Oxford University Press, 1996, pp. xxxi–xli.

Murphy, Kevin. "Illiterate's Progress: The Descent into Literacy in *Huckleberry Finn,*" *Texas Studies in Literature and Language,* 26 (Winter 1984): 363–387.

Nagel, James. "*Huck Finn* and *The Bear:* The Wilderness and Moral Freedom." *English Studies in Africa,* (Johannesburg, South Africa), 12 (1969): 59–63.

Nigro, August J. "The Undiscovered Country in *Huckleberry Finn,*" in his *The Diagonal Line: Separation and Reparation in American Literature.* Selinsgrove, Pa.: Susquehanna University Press, 1984, pp. 88–97.

Oehlschlaeger, Fritz H. "Huck Finn and the Meaning of Shame," *Mark Twain Journal,* 20 (Summer 1981): 13–14.

Opdahl, Keith. "'The Rest Is Just Cheating': When Feelings Go Bad in *Adventures of Huckleberry Finn,*" *Texas Studies in Literature and Language,* 32 (Summer 1990): 277–293.

Opdahl. "'You'll Be Sorry When I'm Dead': Child-Adult Relations in *Huck Finn,*" *Modern Fiction Studies,* 25 (Winter 1979–1980): 613–624.

Papp, James. "How Huck Finn Was Red: The Communist and Post-Communist Condition of Mark Twain," *Essays in Arts and Sciences,* 27 (October 1998): 83–93.

Pauly, Thomas H. "Directed Readings: The Contents Tables in *Adventures of Huckleberry Finn,*" *Proof. The Yearbook of American Bibliographical and Textual Studies,* 3 (1973): 63–68.

Pearce, Roy Harvey. "'The End. Yours Truly, Huck Finn' Postscript," *Modern Language Quarterly,* 24 (September 1963): 253–256.

Pearce. "Huck Finn in His History," *Etudes Anglaises,* (Paris, France), 24 (July–September 1971): 283–291.

Peck, Richard E. "The Campaign That . . . Succeeded," *American Literary Realism, 1870–1910,* 21 (Spring 1989): 3–12.

Piacentino, Edward J. "The Significance of Pap's Drunken Diatribe against the Government in *Huckleberry Finn,*" *Mark Twain Journal,* 19 (Summer 1979): 19–21.

Pinsker, Sanford. "Huckleberry Finn, Modernist Poet," *Midwest Quarterly,* 24, no. 3 (1983): 261–273.

Portelli, Alessandro. "Mark Twain's Tower of Babel," in his *The Text and the Voice: Writing, Speaking, and Democracy in American Literature.* New York: Columbia University Press, 1994, pp. 173–177.

Powell, Jon. "Trouble and Joy from 'A True Story' to *Adventures of Huckleberry Finn:* Mark Twain and the Book of Jeremiah," *Studies in American Fiction,* 20 (Autumn 1992): 145–154.

Pribek, Thomas. "Huckleberry Finn: His Masquerade and His Lessons for Lying," *American Literary Realism, 1870–1910,* 19 (Spring 1987): 68–79.

Prioleau, Elizabeth. "'That Abused Child of Mine': Huck Finn as a Child of an Alcoholic," *Essays in Arts and Sciences,* 22 (October 1993): 85–98.

Quirk, Tom. *Coming to Grips with Huckleberry Finn: Essays on a Book, a Boy, and a Man.* Columbia: University of Missouri Press, 1993.

Quirk. *Mark Twain and Human Nature.* Columbia: University of Missouri Press, 2007, pp. 104–113, 141–163.

Railton, Stephen. "Jim and Mark Twain: What Do Dey Stan' For?" *Virginia Quarterly Review,* 63 (Summer 1987): 393–408.

Robinson, Forrest G. "The Characterization of Jim in *Huckleberry Finn,*" *Nineteenth-Century Literature,* 43 (December 1988): 361–391.

Robinson. "The Silences in *Huckleberry Finn,*" *Nineteenth-Century Fiction,* 37 (June 1982): 50–74.

Rosenthal, M. L. "Alice, Huck, Pinocchio, and the Blue Fairy: Bodies Real and Imagined," *Southern Review,* 29 (July 1993): 486–490.

Rowe, Joyce A. "Mark Twain's Great Evasion: *Adventures of Huckleberry Finn,*" in her *Equivocal Endings in Classic American Novels: The Scarlet Letter; Adventures of Huckleberry Finn; The Ambassadors; The Great Gatsby.* Cambridge: Cambridge University Press, 1988, pp. 46–74.

Rubin, Louis D., Jr. "Mark Twain's South: Tom and Huck," in *The American South: Portrait of a Culture,* edited by Rubin. Baton Rouge: Louisiana State University Press, 1980, pp. 190–205.

Rule, Henry B. "A Brief History of the Censorship of *The Adventures of Huckleberry Finn,*" *Lamar Journal of the Humanities,* 12 (Spring 1986): 9–18.

Sawicki, Joseph. "Authority/Author-ity: Representation and Fictionality in *Huckleberry Finn*," *Modern Fiction Studies,* 31 (Winter 1985): 691–702.

Schacht, Paul. "The Lonesomeness of Huckleberry Finn," in *On Mark Twain: The Best from* American Literature, edited by Louis J. Budd and Edwin H. Cady. Durham, N.C.: Duke University Press, 1987, pp. 209–221.

Scheick, William J. "The Spunk of a Rabbit: An Allusion in *The Adventures of Huckleberry Finn*," *Mark Twain Journal,* 15 (Summer 1971): 14–16.

Schmitz, Neil. "Huckspeech," in his *Of Huck and Alice: Humorous Writing in American Literature.* Minneapolis: University of Minnesota Press, 1983, pp. 96–125.

Schmitz. "On American Humor," *Partisan Review,* 47, no. 4 (1980): 559–577.

Schmitz. "The Paradox of Liberation in *Huckleberry Finn*," *Texas Studies in Literature and Language,* 13 (Spring 1971): 125–136.

Seelye, John. "The Craft of Laughter: Abominable Showmanship and *Huckleberry Finn*," *Thalia: Studies in Literary Humor* (Ottawa, Canada), 4 (Spring–Summer 1981): 19–25.

Segal, Harry G. "Life Without Father: The Role of the Paternal in the Opening Chapters of *Huckleberry Finn*," *Journal of American Studies* (Cambridge, England), 27 (April 1993): 19–33.

Sewell, David R. "Not All Trying to Talk Alike: Varieties of Language in *Huckleberry Finn*," in his *Mark Twain's Languages: Discourse, Dialogue, and Linguistic Variety.* Berkeley: University of California Press, 1987, pp. 85–109.

Shafer, Aileen Chris. "Jim's Discourses in Huckleberry Finn," *Southern Studies: An Interdisciplinary Journal of the South,* new series 1 (Summer 1990): 149–163.

Shaw, Peter. "The Genteel Fate *of Huckleberry Finn*," *Partisan Review,* 60, no. 3 (1993): 434–449.

Shear, Walter. "Twain's Early Writing and Theories of Realism," *Midwest Quarterly: A Journal of Contemporary Thought,* 30 (Autumn 1988): 93–103.

Simpson, Claude M., Jr. "Huck Finn after *Huck Finn*," in *American Humor: Essays Presented to John C. Gerber,* edited by O. M. Brack Jr. Scottsdale, Ariz.: Arete Publications, 1977, pp. 59–72.

Skandera-Trombley, Laura. "Mark Twain's Cross-Dressing Oeuvre," *College Literature,* 24 (June 1997): 82–96.

Skandera-Trombley. "Mark Twain's Mother of Invention," *Mark Twain Journal,* 31 (Fall 1993): 2–10.

Sloane, David E. E. *Adventures of Huckleberry Finn: American Comic Vision.* Boston: Twayne, 1988.

Sloane. "Mark Twain and Race." *Journal of English Language and Literature* (Seoul, Korea), 44 (Winter 1998): 869–885.

Sloane and Sherri Farley. "'My Uncle B.C.M. Farthing, the ORIGINAL Huckleberry Finn': The Sherri Farley and David L. Ritterhouse Documents," *Mark Twain Journal,* 32 (Fall 1994): 31–40.

Smith, Henry Nash. "Mark Twain: *The Adventures of Huckleberry Finn*," in *The American Novel: From James Fenimore Cooper to William Faulkner,* edited by Wallace Stegner. New York: Basic Books, 1965, pp. 61–72.

Smith. *Mark Twain: The Development of a Writer.* New York: Atheneum, 1967.

Southard, Bruce, and Al Muller. "Blame It on Twain: Reading American Dialects in *The Adventures of Huckleberry Finn*," *Journal of Reading,* 36 (May 1993): 630–634.

Stein, Allen F. "Return to Phelps Farm: *Huckleberry Finn* and the Old Southwestern Framing Device," *Mississippi Quarterly: The Journal of Southern Culture,* 24 (Winter 1970–1971): 111–116.

Strout, Cushing. "'Working on the Circumstances': Twain's Huck, Faulkner's Chick, and the Negro," in his *Making American Tradition: Visions and Revisions From Ben Franklin to Alice Walker.* New Brunswick, N.J.: Rutgers University Press, 1990, pp. 152–163.

Thomas, Brook. "Language and Identity in the *Adventures of Huckleberry Finn*," *Mark Twain Journal,* 20 (Winter 1980–1981): 17–21.

Tracy, Robert. "Prisoners of Style: Dickens and Mark Twain, Fiction and Evasion," *Dickens Studies Annual: Essays on Victorian Fiction,* 16 (1987): 221–246.

Trilling, Lionel. "Introduction." *Adventures of Huckleberry Finn.* New York: Rinehart, 1948, pp. v–xviii.

von Frank, Albert J. "Huck Finn and the Flight From Maturity," *Studies in American Fiction,* 7 (Spring 1979): 1–15.

Warren, Robert Penn. "Mark Twain," *Southern Review,* new series 8 (July 1972): 459–492.

Wells, David M. "More on the Geography of 'Huckleberry Finn,'" *South Atlantic Bulletin: A Quarterly Journal Devoted to Research and Teaching in the Modern Languages and Literatures,* 38 (November 1973): 82–86.

Welsh, J. M. "Disney Does Huck Finn: Never the Twain Shall Meet," *Literature Film Quarterly,* 21, no. 3 (1993): 170, 237.

Werge, Thomas. "Huck, Jim and Forty Dollars," *Mark Twain Journal,* 13 (Winter 1965–1966): 15–16.

Wexman, Virginia. "The Role of Structure in *Tom Sawyer* and *Huckleberry Finn*," *American Literary Realism, 1870–1910,* 6 (Winter 1973): 1–11.

Wieck, Carl F. *Refiguring* Huckleberry Finn. Athens: University of Georgia Press, 2000.

Wiggins, Robert A. "The Craft of *Huckleberry Finn*," in his *Mark Twain: Jackleg Novelist.* Seattle: University of Washington Press, 1964, pp. 55–71.

Wilson, James D. "*Adventures of Huckleberry Finn:* From Abstraction to Humanity." *Southern Review,* new series 10 (January 1974): 80–94.

Wilson. "History as Palimpsest: The Layers of Time in *Life on the Mississippi,*" *Journal of the American Studies Association of Texas,* 25 (1994): 32–39.

Wonham, Henry B. "The Disembodied Yarnspinner and the Reader of *Adventures of Huckleberry Finn*," *American Literary Realism, 1870–1910,* 24 (Fall 1991): 2–22.

Woodward, Robert H. "Teaching *Huckleberry Finn* to Foreign Students," *Mark Twain Journal,* 13 (Winter 1966–1967): 5–7.

Zuckert, Catherine H. "Law and Nature in The Adventures of Huckleberry Finn," *Proteus: A Journal of Ideas,* 1 (Fall 1984): 27–35.

Collections of Essays

Bloom, Harold, ed. with intro. *Huck Finn.* New York & Philadelphia: Chelsea House, 1990.

Budd. Louis J., ed. *New Essays on* Adventures of Huckleberry Finn. Cambridge, U.K.: Cambridge University Press 1985.

Inge, Thomas M., ed. *Huck Finn among the Critics: A Centennial Selection.* Frederick, Md.: University Publications of America, 1985.

Leonard, James S., Thomas A. Tenney, and Thadious M. Davis, eds. *Satire or Evasion?: Black Perspectives on* Huckleberry Finn. Durham: Duke University Press, 1992.

Sattelmeyer, Robert, and J. Donald Crowley, eds. *One Hundred Years of Huckleberry Finn: The Boy, his Book, and American Culture: Centennial Essays.* Columbia: University of Missouri Press, 1985.

Simpson, Claude M., ed. *Twentieth Century Interpretations of* Adventures of Huckleberry Finn. Englewood Cliffs, N.J.: Prentice-Hall, 1968.

Audiorecordings

Adventures of Huckleberry Finn, read by Norman Dietz. Prince Frederick, Md.: Recorded Books, 1991.

The Adventures of Huckleberry Finn, read by Dick Hill. Grand Haven, Mich.: Brilliance Corp., 1992.

Videorecordings

Burns, Ken, et al. *Mark Twain.* PBS; distributed by Warner Home Video, 2001.

C-Span. "Mark Twain: *Adventures of Huckleberry Finn.*" *American Writers.* <http://www.americanwriters.org>.

Holbrook, Hal, and Mark Twain. *Hal Holbrook in Mark Twain Tonight!* Columbia Records, 1972.

Hossick, Malcolm. *Mark Twain: A Concise Biography.* Famous Authors Series. West Long Branch, N.J.: Kultur International Films, 1996.

Recommended Websites

Center for Mark Twain Studies. <http://www.elmira.edu/academics/ar_marktwain.shtml>.

Mark Twain. Jim Zwick.<http://www.boondocks-net.com/twainwww/ 2002>.

Mark Twain Circle. <http://www.citadel.edu/faculty/leonard/mtcircular.htm >.

Mark Twain Forum. <http://www.yorku.ca/twainweb/ Forum>.

Mark Twain in His Times. Stephen Railton. <http://etext.virginia.edu/railton/index2.html>.

Mark Twain Papers and Project. Bancroft Library. <http://bancroft.berkeley.edu/MTP/>.

Cumulative Index

Dictionary of Literary Biography, Volumes 1-343
Dictionary of Literary Biography Yearbook, 1980-2002
Dictionary of Literary Biography Documentary Series, Volumes 1-19
Concise Dictionary of American Literary Biography, Volumes 1-7
Concise Dictionary of British Literary Biography, Volumes 1-8
Concise Dictionary of World Literary Biography, Volumes 1-4

Cumulative Index

DLB before number: *Dictionary of Literary Biography,* Volumes 1-343
Y before number: *Dictionary of Literary Biography Yearbook,* 1980-2002
DS before number: *Dictionary of Literary Biography Documentary Series,* Volumes 1-19
CDALB before number: *Concise Dictionary of American Literary Biography,* Volumes 1-7
CDBLB before number: *Concise Dictionary of British Literary Biography,* Volumes 1-8
CDWLB before number: *Concise Dictionary of World Literary Biography,* Volumes 1-4

Erdrich, Louise
1954- DLB-152, 175, 206; CDALB-7

Erenburg, Il'ia Grigor'evich 1891-1967 . . .DLB-272

Erichsen-Brown, Gwethalyn Graham
(see Graham, Gwethalyn)

Eriugena, John Scottus circa 810-877 . . . . .DLB-115

Ernst, Paul 1866-1933 . . . . .DLB-66, 118

Erofeev, Venedikt Vasil'evich
1938-1990 . . . . .DLB-285

Erofeev, Viktor Vladimirovich
1947-   .DLB-285

Ershov, Petr Pavlovich 1815-1869 . . . . . . .DLB-205

Erskine, Albert 1911-1993 . . . . .Y-93

At Home with Albert Erskine Y-00

Erskine, John 1879-1951 . . . . .DLB-9, 102

Erskine, Mrs. Steuart ?-1948 . . . . .DLB-195

Ertel', Aleksandr Ivanovich
1855-1908 . . . . .DLB-238

Ervine, St. John Greer 1883-1971. . . . . . . .DLB-10

Eschenburg, Johann Joachim
1743-1820 . . . . .DLB-97

Escofet, Cristina 1945- DLB-305

Escoto, Julio 1944- DLB-145

Esdaile, Arundell 1880-1956 . . . . .DLB-201

Esenin, Sergei Aleksandrovich
1895-1925 . . . . .DLB-295

Eshleman, Clayton 1935- DLB-5

Espaillat, Rhina P. 1932- DLB-282

Espanca, Florbela 1894-1930 . . . . .DLB-287

Espriu, Salvador 1913-1985 . . . . .DLB-134

Ess Ess Publishing Company DLB-49

Essex House Press DLB-112

Esson, Louis 1878-1943 . . . . .DLB-260

Essop, Ahmed 1931- DLB-225

Esterházy, Péter 1950- DLB-232; CDWLB-4

Estes, Eleanor 1906-1988. . . . . .DLB-22

Estes and Lauriat DLB-49

Estienne, Henri II (Henricus Stephanus)
1531-1597 . . . . .DLB-327

Estleman, Loren D. 1952- DLB-226

Eszterhas, Joe 1944- DLB-185

Etherege, George 1636-circa 1692 . . . . . . .DLB-80

Ethridge, Mark, Sr. 1896-1981. . . . . .DLB-127

Ets, Marie Hall 1893-1984. . . . . .DLB-22

Etter, David 1928- DLB-105

Ettner, Johann Christoph 1654-1724 . . . . .DLB-168

Eucken, Rudolf 1846-1926 . . . . .DLB-329

Eudora Welty Remembered in
Two Exhibits .Y-02

Eugene Gant's Projected Works. Y-01

Eupolemius fl. circa 1095. . . . . .DLB-148

Euripides circa 484 B.C.-407/406 B.C.
. . . . .DLB-176; CDWLB-1

Evans, Augusta Jane 1835-1909. . . . . .DLB-239

Evans, Caradoc 1878-1945. . . . . .DLB-162

Evans, Charles 1850-1935 . . . . .DLB-187

Evans, Donald 1884-1921 . . . . .DLB-54

Evans, George Henry 1805-1856. . . . . .DLB-43

Evans, Hubert 1892-1986 . . . . .DLB-92

Evans, Mari 1923- DLB-41

Evans, Mary Ann (see Eliot, George)

Evans, Nathaniel 1742-1767 . . . . .DLB-31

Evans, Sebastian 1830-1909 . . . . .DLB-35

Evans, Ray 1915-2007 . . . . .DLB-265

M. Evans and Company DLB-46

Evaristi, Marcella 1953- DLB-233

Evenson, Brian 1966- DLB-335

Everett, Alexander Hill 1790-1847 . . . . . . .DLB-59

Everett, Edward 1794-1865 . . . . . . .DLB-1, 59, 235

Everson, R. G. 1903- DLB-88

Everson, William 1912-1994 . . . . . .DLB-5, 16, 212

Evreinov, Nikolai 1879-1953 . . . . .DLB-317

Ewald, Johannes 1743-1781 . . . . .DLB-300

Ewart, Gavin 1916-1995 . . . . .DLB-40

Ewing, Juliana Horatia 1841-1885. . . .DLB-21, 163

The Examiner 1808-1881 . . . . .DLB-110

Exley, Frederick 1929-1992 . . . . . . .DLB-143; Y-81

Editorial: The Extension of Copyright Y-02

von Eyb, Albrecht 1420-1475. . . . . .DLB-179

Eyre and Spottiswoode DLB-106

Ezekiel, Nissim 1924-2004. . . . . .DLB-323

Ezera, Regīna 1930- DLB-232

Ezzo ?-after 1065 . . . . .DLB-148

F

Faber, Frederick William 1814-1863 . . . . . .DLB-32

Faber and Faber Limited DLB-112

Faccio, Rena (see Aleramo, Sibilla)

Facsimiles
The Uses of Facsimile: A Symposium. Y-90

Fadeev, Aleksandr Aleksandrovich
1901-1956 . . . . .DLB-272

Fagundo, Ana María 1938- DLB-134

Fainzil'berg, Il'ia Arnol'dovich
(see Il'f, Il'ia and Petrov, Evgenii)

Fair, Ronald L. 1932- DLB-33

Fairfax, Beatrice (see Manning, Marie)

Fairlie, Gerard 1899-1983 . . . . .DLB-77

Faldbakken, Knut 1941- DLB-297

Falkberget, Johan (Johan Petter Lillebakken)
1879-1967 . . . . .DLB-297

Fallada, Hans 1893-1947 . . . . .DLB-56

The Famished Road, 1991 Booker Prize winner,
Ben Okri DLB-326

Fancher, Betsy 1928- Y-83

Fane, Violet 1843-1905 . . . . .DLB-35

Fanfrolico Press DLB-112

Fanning, Katherine 1927-2000 . . . . .DLB-127

Fanon, Frantz 1925-1961 . . . . .DLB-296

Fanshawe, Sir Richard 1608-1666 . . . . . . .DLB-126

Fantasy Press Publishers DLB-46

Fante, John 1909-1983. . . . . DLB-130; Y-83

Al-Farabi circa 870-950. . . . . .DLB-115

Farabough, Laura 1949- DLB-228

Farah, Nuruddin 1945-   . . .DLB-125; CDWLB-3

Farber, Norma 1909-1984 . . . . .DLB-61

A Farewell to Arms (Documentary). DLB-308

Fargue, Léon-Paul 1876-1947 . . . . .DLB-258

Farigoule, Louis (see Romains, Jules)

Farjeon, Eleanor 1881-1965. . . . . .DLB-160

Farley, Harriet 1812-1907 . . . . .DLB-239

Farley, Walter 1920-1989 . . . . .DLB-22

Farmborough, Florence 1887-1978 . . . . . . .DLB-204

Farmer, Beverley 1941- DLB-325

Farmer, Penelope 1939- DLB-161

Farmer, Philip José 1918- DLB-8

Farnaby, Thomas 1575?-1647 . . . . .DLB-236

Farnese, Isabella (Suor Francesca di Gesù Maria)
1593-1651 . . . . .DLB-339

Farningham, Marianne (see Hearn, Mary Anne)

Farquhar, George circa 1677-1707 . . . . .DLB-84

Farquharson, Martha (see Finley, Martha)

Farrar, Frederic William 1831-1903 . . . . . .DLB-163

Farrar, Straus and Giroux DLB-46

Farrar and Rinehart. DLB-46

Farrell, J. G. 1935-1979 . . . . .DLB-14, 271, 326

Farrell, James T. 1904-1979 . . . .DLB-4, 9, 86; DS-2

Fast, Howard 1914-2003 . . . . .DLB-9

Faulkner, William 1897-1962
. . . . . .DLB-9, 11, 44, 102, 316, 330; DS-2; Y-86;
CDALB-5

Faulkner and Yoknapatawpha
Conference, Oxford, Mississippi Y-97

Faulkner Centennial Addresses. Y-97

"Faulkner 100–Celebrating the Work,"
University of South Carolina,
Columbia .Y-97

Impressions of William Faulkner Y-97

William Faulkner and the People-to-People
Program Y-86

William Faulkner Centenary
Celebrations Y-97

The William Faulkner Society. Y-99

George Faulkner [publishing house] DLB-154

Faulks, Sebastian 1953- DLB-207

Fauset, Jessie Redmon 1882-1961 . . . . .DLB-51

Faust, Frederick Schiller (Max Brand)
1892-1944 . . . . .DLB-256

Faust, Irvin
1924- DLB-2, 28, 218, 278; Y-80, 00

Cumulative Index

G

J

F. Tennyson Neely [publishing house] DLB-49

Negoițescu, Ion 1921-1993 .... DLB-220

Negri, Ada 1870-1945 .... DLB-114

Nehru, Pandit Jawaharlal 1889-1964 .... DLB-323

Neihardt, John G. 1881-1973 ..... DLB-9, 54, 256

Neidhart von Reuental
circa 1185-circa 1240 .... DLB-138

Neilson, John Shaw 1872-1942 .... DLB-230

Nekrasov, Nikolai Alekseevich
1821-1877 .... DLB-277

Nekrasov, Viktor Platonovich
1911-1987 .... DLB-302

Neledinsky-Meletsky, Iurii Aleksandrovich
1752-1828 .... DLB-150

Nelligan, Emile 1879-1941 .... DLB-92

Nelson, Alice Moore Dunbar 1875-1935 .. DLB-50

Nelson, Antonya 1961- DLB-244

Nelson, Kent 1943- DLB-234

Nelson, Richard 1950- DLB-341

Nelson, Richard K. 1941- DLB-275

Nelson, Thomas, and Sons [U.K.] DLB-106

Nelson, Thomas, and Sons [U.S.] DLB-49

Nelson, William 1908-1978 .... DLB-103

Nelson, William Rockhill 1841-1915 ..... DLB-23

Nemerov, Howard 1920-1991 ..... DLB-5, 6; Y-83

Németh, László 1901-1975 .... DLB-215

Nepos circa 100 B.C.-post 27 B.C. DLB-211

Nêris, Salomêja 1904-1945 .. DLB-220; CDWLB-4

Neruda, Pablo 1904-1973 .... DLB-283, 331

Nerval, Gérard de 1808-1855 .... DLB-217

Nervo, Amado 1870-1919 .... DLB-290

Nesbit, E. 1858-1924 .... DLB-141, 153, 178

Ness, Evaline 1911-1986 .... DLB-61

Nestroy, Johann 1801-1862 .... DLB-133

Nettleship, R. L. 1846-1892 .... DLB-262

Neugeboren, Jay 1938- DLB-28, 335

Neukirch, Benjamin 1655-1729 .... DLB-168

Neumann, Alfred 1895-1952 .... DLB-56

Neumann, Ferenc (see Molnár, Ferenc)

Neumark, Georg 1621-1681 .... DLB-164

Neumeister, Erdmann 1671-1756 .... DLB-168

Nevins, Allan 1890-1971 .... DLB-17; DS-17

Nevinson, Henry Woodd 1856-1941 .... DLB-135

The New American Library DLB-46

New Directions Publishing Corporation... DLB-46

The New Monthly Magazine 1814-1884 ..... DLB-110

New York Times Book Review Y-82

John Newbery [publishing house] DLB-154

Newbolt, Henry 1862-1938 .... DLB-19

Newbound, Bernard Slade (see Slade, Bernard)

Newby, Eric 1919-2006 .... DLB-204

Newby, P. H. 1918-1997 .... DLB-15, 326

Thomas Cautley Newby
[publishing house] DLB-106

Newcomb, Charles King 1820-1894... DLB-1, 223

Newell, Peter 1862-1924 .... DLB-42

Newell, Robert Henry 1836-1901 .... DLB-11

Newhouse, Edward 1911-2002 .... DLB-335

Newhouse, Samuel I. 1895-1979 .... DLB-127

Newman, Cecil Earl 1903-1976 .... DLB-127

Newman, David 1937- DLB-44

Newman, Frances 1883-1928 .... Y-80

Newman, Francis William 1805-1897.... DLB-190

Newman, G. F. 1946- DLB-310

Newman, John Henry
1801-1890 .... DLB-18, 32, 55

Mark Newman [publishing house] DLB-49

Newmarch, Rosa Harriet 1857-1940.... DLB-240

George Newnes Limited DLB-112

Newsome, Effie Lee 1885-1979 .... DLB-76

Newton, A. Edward 1864-1940 .... DLB-140

Newton, Sir Isaac 1642-1727 .... DLB-252

Nexø, Martin Andersen 1869-1954 ..... DLB-214

Nezval, Vítěslav
1900-1958 .... DLB-215; CDWLB-4

Ngugi wa Thiong'o
1938- DLB-125; CDWLB-3

Niatum, Duane 1938- DLB-175

The Nibelungenlied and the *Klage*
circa 1200 .... DLB-138

Nichol, B. P. 1944-1988 .... DLB-53

Nicholas of Cusa 1401-1464 .... DLB-115

Nichols, Ann 1891?-1966 .... DLB-249

Nichols, Beverly 1898-1983 .... DLB-191

Nichols, Dudley 1895-1960 .... DLB-26

Nichols, Grace 1950- DLB-157

Nichols, John 1940- Y-82

Nichols, Mary Sargeant (Neal) Gove
1810-1884 .... DLB-1, 243

Nichols, Peter 1927- DLB-13, 245

Nichols, Roy F. 1896-1973 .... DLB-17

Nichols, Ruth 1948- DLB-60

Nicholson, Edward Williams Byron
1849-1912 .... DLB-184

Nicholson, Geoff 1953- DLB-271

Nicholson, Norman 1914-1987 .... DLB-27

Nicholson, William 1872-1949 .... DLB-141

Ní Chuilleanáin, Eiléan 1942- DLB-40

Nicol, Eric 1919- DLB-68

Nicolai, Friedrich 1733-1811 .... DLB-97

Nicolas de Clamanges circa 1363-1437... DLB-208

Nicolay, John G. 1832-1901 and
Hay, John 1838-1905 .... DLB-47

Nicole, Pierre 1625-1695 .... DLB-268

Nicolson, Adela Florence Cory (see Hope, Laurence)

Nicolson, Harold 1886-1968 ....DLB-100, 149

"The Practice of Biography," in
*The English Sense of Humour and
Other Essays* DLB-149

Nicolson, Nigel 1917-2004 .... DLB-155

Ní Dhuibhne, Éilís 1954- DLB-319

Niebuhr, Reinhold 1892-1971 ......DLB-17; DS-17

Niedecker, Lorine 1903-1970 .... DLB-48

Nieman, Lucius W. 1857-1935 .... DLB-25

Nietzsche, Friedrich
1844-1900 ....DLB-129; CDWLB-2

Mencken and Nietzsche: An Unpublished
Excerpt from H. L. Mencken's *My Life
as Author and Editor* Y-93

Nievo, Stanislao 1928- DLB-196

Niggli, Josefina 1910-1983 .... Y-80

Nightingale, Florence 1820-1910 .... DLB-166

Nijō, Lady (Nakano-in Masatada no Musume)
1258-after 1306 .... DLB-203

Nijō Yoshimoto 1320-1388 .... DLB-203

Nikitin, Ivan Savvich 1824-1861 ....DLB-277

Nikitin, Nikolai Nikolaevich 1895-1963 ...DLB-272

Nikolev, Nikolai Petrovich 1758-1815.... DLB-150

Niles, Hezekiah 1777-1839 .... DLB-43

Nims, John Frederick 1913-1999 .... DLB-5

Tribute to Nancy Hale Y-88

Nin, Anaïs 1903-1977 .... DLB-2, 4, 152

Nína Björk Árnadóttir 1941-2000 .... DLB-293

Niño, Raúl 1961- DLB-209

Nissenson, Hugh 1933- DLB-28, 335

Der Nister (Pinchas Kahanovitch [Pinkhes
Kahanovitsh]) 1884-1950 .... DLB-333

Niven, Frederick John 1878-1944 .... DLB-92

Niven, Larry 1938- DLB-8

Nixon, Howard M. 1909-1983 .... DLB-201

Nizan, Paul 1905-1940 .... DLB-72

Njegoš, Petar II Petrović
1813-1851 ....DLB-147; CDWLB-4

Nkosi, Lewis 1936- DLB-157, 225

Noah, Mordecai M. 1785-1851 .... DLB-250

Noailles, Anna de 1876-1933 .... DLB-258

Nobel Peace Prize
The Nobel Prize and Literary Politics Y-88

Elie Wiesel Y-86

Nobel Prize in Literature
Shmuel Yosef Agnon DLB-329

Vicente Aleixandre DLB-108, 329

Ivo Andrić DLB-147, 329; CDWLB-4

Miguel Ángel Asturias DLB-113, 290,
329; CDWLB-3

Samuel Beckett DLB-13, 15, 233, 319,
321, 329; Y-90; CDBLB-7

Saul Bellow DLB-2, 28, 299, 329;
Y-82; DS-3; CDALB-1

Jacinto Benavente DLB-329

Cumulative Index

ISBN-13: 978-0-7876-8161-6
ISBN-10: 0-7876-8161-X

90000

9 780787 681616